Lecture Notes in Computer Science 4636

Commenced Publication in 1973
Founding and Former Series Editors:
Gerhard Goos, Juris Hartmanis, and Jan van Leeuwen

Grigoris Antoniou   Uwe Aßmann
Cristina Baroglio   Stefan Decker
Nicola Henze   Paula-Lavinia Patranjan
Robert Tolksdorf (Eds.)

Reasoning Web

Third International Summer School 2007
Dresden, Germany, September 3-7, 2007
Tutorial Lectures

 Springer

Volume Editors

Grigoris Antoniou
FORTH, Heraklion, Greece
E-mail: antoniou@ics.forth.gr

Uwe Aßmann
Technische Universität Dresden, Germany
E-mail: uwe.assmann@inf.tu-dresden.de

Cristina Baroglio
Università degli Studi di Torino, Italy
E-mail: baroglio@di.unito.it

Stefan Decker
DERI and National University of Ireland, Galway
E-mail: stefan.decker@deri.org

Nicola Henze
Universität Hannover, Germany
E-mail: henze@kbs.uni-hannover.de

Paula-Lavinia Patranjan
Ludwig-Maximilians-Universität München, Germany
E-mail: paula.patranjan@ifi.lmu.de

Robert Tolksdorf
Freie Universität Berlin, Germany
E-mail: tolk@inf.fu-berlin.de

Library of Congress Control Number: 2007933835

CR Subject Classification (1998): H.4, H.3, C.2, H.5, J.1, K.4, K.6, I.2.11

LNCS Sublibrary: SL 3 – Information Systems and Application, incl. Internet/Web
and HCI

ISSN   0302-9743
ISBN-10   3-540-74613-7 Springer Berlin Heidelberg New York
ISBN-13   978-3-540-74613-3 Springer Berlin Heidelberg New York

Springer is a part of Springer Science+Business Media

springer.com

© Springer-Verlag Berlin Heidelberg 2007
Printed in Germany

Typesetting: Camera-ready by author, data conversion by Scientific Publishing Services, Chennai, India
Printed on acid-free paper   SPIN: 12115853   06/3180   5 4 3 2 1 0

Preface

The summer school series Reasoning Web focuses on theoretical foundations, current approaches, and practical solutions for reasoning in a Web of Semantics. It has established itself as a meeting point for experts from research and industry, and students undertaking their PhDs in related fields. This volume contains the tutorial notes of the Reasoning Web summer school 2007, which was held in Dresden, Germany, in September 2007. This summer school was the third school of the Reasoning Web series, following the very successful predecessors held in Malta and Lisbon.

The first part of the 2007 edition is devoted to "Fundamentals of Reasoning and Reasoning Languages" and surveys concepts and methods for rule-based query languages. Further, it gives a comprehensive introduction to description logics and its usage.

Reactive rules and rule-based policy representation are covered in the second part on "Rules and Policies." A thorough discussion on the importance of rule interchange in the Web and promising solution strategies is given together with an overview on current W3C initiatives.

Finally, the third part is devoted to "Applications of Semantic Web Reasoning," and demonstrates practical uses of Semantic Web reasoning. The academics viewpoint is presented by a contribution on reasoning in Semantic Wikis. The industry's viewpoint is presented by contributions that discuss the importance of semantic technologies for search solutions for enterprises, for creating an enterprise knowledge base with Semantic Wiki representations, and Semantic Web Service discovery and selection in B2B scenarios.

We would like to thank all lecturers of the Reasoning Web summer school 2007 for giving interesting and inspiring tutorials. Further, we thank the local organizers in Dresden for their efficient and great work, and Norbert Eisinger from the Ludwig-Maximilians-Universität München and Jan Małuszyński from the University of Linköping, they made our job as Program Committee members very enjoyable and smooth.

September 2007

Grigoris Antoniou
Uwe Aßmann
Cristina Baroglio
Stefan Decker
Nicola Henze
Paula-Lavinia Pătrânjan
Robert Tolksdorf

Organization

Program Committee

Grigoris Antoniou, Information Systems Laboratory – FORTH, Greece
Uwe Aßmann, Technische Universität Dresden, Germany
Cristina Baroglio, Università degli Studi di Torino, Italy
Stefan Decker, DERI and National University of Ireland, Galway, Ireland
Nicola Henze, Leibniz Universität Hannover, Germany (Chair)
Paula-Lavinia Pătrânjan, Ludwig-Maximilians-Universität München, Germany
Robert Tolksdorf, Freie Universität Berlin, Germany

Local Organization

Michael Schroeder, Transinsight and Technische Universität Dresden, Germany

Applications Chair

Cristina Baroglio, Università degli Studi di Torino, Italy

Proceedings Chair

Paula-Lavinia Pătrânjan, Ludwig-Maximilians-Universität München, Germany

Sponsoring Institutions

Technische Universität Dresden

Network of Excellence REWERSE

Transinsight

Table of Contents

Foundations of Rule-Based Query Answering

François Bry[1], Norbert Eisinger[1], Thomas Eiter[2],
Tim Furche[1], Georg Gottlob[2,3], Clemens Ley[1],
Benedikt Linse[1], Reinhard Pichler[2], and Fang Wei[2]

[1] Institute for Informatics, University of Munich,
Oettingenstraße 67, D-80538 München, Germany
http://www.pms.ifi.lmu.de/
[2] Institute of Information Systems, Vienna University of Technology,
Favoritenstraße 11/184-3, A-1040 Vienna, Austria
http://www.kr.tuwien.ac.at/, http://www.dbai.tuwien.ac.at/
[3] Oxford University Computing Laboratory,
Wolfson Building, Parks Road, Oxford, OX1 3QD, England
http://web.comlab.ox.ac.uk/oucl/people/georg.gottlob.html

Abstract. This survey article introduces into the essential concepts and
methods underlying rule-based query languages. It covers four complementary areas: declarative semantics based on adaptations of mathematical logic, operational semantics, complexity and expressive power, and
optimisation of query evaluation.

The treatment of these areas is foundation-oriented, the foundations
having resulted from over four decades of research in the logic programming and database communities on combinations of query languages and
rules. These results have later formed the basis for conceiving, improving, and implementing several Web and Semantic Web technologies, in
particular query languages such as XQuery or SPARQL for querying
relational, XML, and RDF data, and rule languages like the "Rule Interchange Framework (RIF)" currently being developed in a working group
of the W3C.

Coverage of the article is deliberately limited to declarative languages
in a classical setting: issues such as query answering in F-Logic or in
description logics, or the relationship of query answering to reactive rules
and events, are not addressed.

1 Introduction

The foundations of query languages mostly stem from logic and complexity theory. The research on query languages has enriched these two fields with novel
issues, original approaches, and a respectable body of specific results. Thus, the
foundations of query languages are arguably more than applications of these
two fields. They can be seen as a research field in its own right with interesting
results and, possibly, even more interesting perspectives. In this field, basic and
applied research often are so tightly connected that distinguishing between the
two would be rather arbitrary. Furthermore, this field has been very lively since

G. Antoniou et al. (Eds.): Reasoning Web 2007, LNCS 4636, pp. 1–153, 2007.

the late 1970s and is currently undergoing a renaissance, the Web motivating query and rule languages with novel capabilities. This article aims at introducing into this active field of research.

Query languages have emerged with database systems, greatly contributing to their success, in the late 1970s. First approaches to query languages were inspired by mathematical logic. As time went by, query languages offering syntactical constructs and concepts that depart from classical logic were being developed, but still, query languages kept an undeniably logical flavour. The main strengths of this flavour are: compound queries constructed using connectives such as "and" and "or"; rules expressed as implications; declarative semantics of queries and query programs reminiscent of Tarski's model-theoretic truth definition; query optimisation techniques modelled on equivalences of logical formulas; and query evaluators based on methods and heuristics similar to, even though in some cases simpler than, those of theorem provers.

With the advent of the Web in the early 1990s things have changed. Query languages are undergoing a renaissance motivated by new objectives: Web query languages have to access structured data that are subject to structural irregularities – so-called "semi-structured data" – to take into account rich textual contents while retrieving data, to deliver structured answers that may require very significant reorganisations of the data retrieved, and to perform more or less sophisticated forms of automated reasoning while accessing or delivering meta-data. All these issues have been investigated since the mid 1990s and still are. Further issues of considerable relevance, which, up till now, have received limited attention, include: query processing in a distributed and decentralised environment, query languages for search engines, search as a query primitive, and semantical data alignment.

The current query language renaissance both, takes distance from the logical setting of query languages, and builds upon it. On the one hand, recent Web query languages such as XPath and XQuery seem to be much less related to logic than former relational query languages such as SQL and former object-oriented query languages such as OQL. On the other hand, expressly logic-based Web query languages such as the experimental language Xcerpt [28,141,30,29] have been proposed, and Semantic Web query languages such as RQL, RDQL, and SPARQL clearly have logical roots (see [14,73] for surveys on Web and Semantic Web query languages). Furthermore, language optimisers and evaluators of XPath and XQuery exploit techniques formerly developed, thus bringing these languages back to the logical roots of query languages. At the beginning of this ongoing query language renaissance, a principled and summarised presentation of query language foundations surely makes sense.

1.1   What Are Query Languages? Tentative Definitions

A first definition of what query languages are considers what they are used for: they can be defined as specialised programming languages for selecting and retrieving data from "information systems". These are (possibly very large) data repositories such as file systems, databases, and (all or part of) the World Wide

Web. Query languages are specialised inasmuch as they are simpler to use or offer only limited programming functionalities that aim at easing the selection and retrieval of data from information systems.

A second attempt at defining what query languages are is to consider their programming paradigms, i.e., the brand of programming languages they belong to: query languages are declarative languages, i.e., languages abstracting out how (query) programs are to be evaluated. This makes query languages both easier to use – an advantage for the human user – and easier to optimise – an advantage for the computer. The declarativity of query languages is the reason for their close relationship to logic: declarative languages are all in some way or other based on logic.

A third approach to define what query languages are considers their major representatives: SQL for relational databases, OQL for object-oriented databases, XPath and XQuery for HTML and XML data, and RQL, RDQL, and SPARQL for RDF data. Forthcoming are query languages for OWL ontologies. Viewed from this angle, what have query languages in common? First, a separation between query programs and accessed data, requiring to compile query programs without any knowledge at all or with only limited knowledge of the data the compiled query programs are to access. Second, a dedication to data models, many, if not all, of which are strongly rooted in logic.

Query languages, as a research field, can also be defined by the issues being investigated. Central issues in query languages research include:
- query paradigms (e.g., visual, relational, object-oriented, and navigational query languages),
- declarative semantics,
- complexity and expressive power,
- procedural semantics,
- implementations of query evaluators,
- query optimisation (e.g., equivalence of queries).

Further query language issues include: integrity constraints (languages, expressive power, complexity, evaluation, satisfiability, maintenance); incremental or distributed evaluation of queries; evaluation of queries against data streams; storage of large collections of queries (e.g., for publish-subscribe systems); approximate answers; query answering in presence of uncertain information; query answering in presence of inconsistent information; querying special data (e.g., constraints, spatial data, graphic data); algorithms and data structures for efficient data storage and retrieval.

1.2   Coverage of This Survey

This survey article on the foundations of query languages is focused on logic, complexity and expressive power, and query optimisation. The reasons for such an admittedly limited focus are manifold. First, this focus arguably provides with a corner stone for most of the past and current research on query languages. Second, this focus covers a rather large field that could hardly be enlarged in a survey and introductory article. Third, such a focus provides with a unity of concerns and methods.

1.3 Structure of This Survey

This survey article is organised as follows. Section 1 is this introduction. Section 2 introduces a few general mathematical notions that are used in later sections. Section 3 is devoted to syntax. It introduces the syntax of classical first-order predicate logic,[1] then of fragments of first-order predicate logic that characterise classes of query languages. This section shows how the syntax of the various practical query languages can be conveyed by the syntax of first-order predicate logic. Section 4 introduces into classical first-order model theory, starting with Tarski model theory, the notion of entailment, Herbrand interpretations, and similar standard notions, explaining the relevance of these notions to query languages. After this main part, the section covers Herbrand model theory and finite model theory, which have a number of interesting and rather surprising properties that are relevant to query languages. Section 5 then treats the adaptations of classical model theory to query and rule languages, covering minimal model semantics and fixpoint semantics and discussing approaches to the declarative semantics of rule sets with negation. A subsection on RDF model theory rounds out this section. Sections 6 and 7 introduce into the operational semantics of query programs, considering positive rule sets and rule sets with non-monotonic negation, respectively. These two sections present (terminating) algorithms for the (efficient) evaluation of query programs of various types. Section 8 is devoted to complexity and expressive power of query language fragments. Section 9 introduces into query optimisation, successively considering query containment, query rewriting, and query algebras.

The purpose of Sections 3 and 4 is to make the article self-contained. Therefore these sections are entirely expository. They should make it possible for readers with limited knowledge of mathematical logic – especially of classical first-order predicate logic – to understand the foundations of query languages. For those readers who already have some of that knowledge and mathematical practice, the sections should help recall notions and state terminologies and notations.

2 Preliminaries

2.1 General Mathematical Notions

By a *function* we mean, unless otherwise stated, a *total function*.

We consider zero to be the smallest *natural number*. The set of natural numbers is $\mathbb{N} = \{0, 1, 2, 3, \ldots\}$.

Definition 1 (Enumerable). *A set S is called* enumerable, *if there is a surjection $\mathbb{N} \to S$. A set S is called* computably enumerable *(or recursively enumerable), if it is enumerable with a surjection that is computable by some algorithm.*

---

[1] Sometimes called simply "first-order logic", a short form avoided in this article.

Note that any finite set is enumerable and computably enumerable. The infinite set of all syntactically correct C programs is computably enumerable and thus enumerable. Its subset consisting of all syntactically correct C programs that do not terminate for each input is enumerable, but not computably enumerable.

2.2 Logic vs. Logics

The development of logic started in antiquity and continued through mediaeval times as an activity of philosophy aimed at analysing rational reasoning. In the late 19th century parts of logic were mathematically formalised, and in the early 20th century logic turned into a tool used in a (not fully successful) attempt to overcome a foundational crisis of mathematics. The fact that logic is not restricted to analysing reasoning in mathematics became somewhat eclipsed during those decades of extensive mathematisation, but came to the fore again when computer science discovered its close ties to logic. Today, logic provides the foundations in many areas of computer science, such as knowledge representation, database theory, programming languages, and query languages.

Logic is concerned with statements, which are utterances that may be true or false. The key features of logic are the use of formal languages for representing statements (so as to avoid ambiguities inherent to natural languages) and the quest for computable reasoning about those statements. *"Logic"* is the name of the scientific discipline investigating such formal languages for statements, but any of those languages is also called *"a logic"* – logic investigates logics.

3 Syntax: From First-Order Predicate Logic to Query Language Fragments of First-Order Predicate Logic

This section introduces the syntax of *first-order predicate logic*, which is the most prominent of logics (formal languages) and occupies a central position in logic (the scientific discipline) for several reasons: it is the most widely used and most thoroughly studied logic; it is the basis for the definition of most other logics; its expressive power is adequate for many essential issues in mathematics and computer science; its reasoning is computable in a sense to be made precise in Section 4; it is the most expressive logic featuring this kind of computability [110].

Practical query and rule languages depart from first-order predicate logic in many respects, but nonetheless they have their roots in and can conveniently be described and investigated in first-order predicate logic.

Subsection 3.1 below contains the standard definitions of first-order predicate logic syntax. The second subsection 3.2 discusses fragments (or sublanguages) of first-order predicate logic that correspond to common query or rule languages. The last subsection 3.3 discusses several modifications of the standard syntax that are used in some areas of computer science.

3.1 Syntax of First-Order Predicate Logic

First-order predicate logic is not just a single formal language, because some of its symbols may depend on the intended applications. The symbols common to all languages of first-order predicate logic are called *logical symbols*, the symbols that have to be specified in order to determine a specific language are called the *signature* (or *vocabulary*) of that language.

Definition 2 (Logical symbol). *The* logical symbols *of first-order predicate logic are:*

symbol class		symbols	pronounced
punctuation symbols		,) (	
connectives	0-ary	$\perp$	*bottom, falsity symbol*
		$\top$	*top, truth symbol*
	1-ary	$\neg$	*not, negation symbol*
	2-ary	$\wedge$	*and, conjunction symbol*
		$\vee$	*or, disjunction symbol*
		$\Rightarrow$	*implies, implication symbol*
quantifiers		$\forall$	*for all, universal quantifier*
		$\exists$	*exists, existential quantifier*
variables		$u\ v\ w\ x\ y\ z\ \dots$ possibly subscripted	

The set of variables is infinite and computably enumerable.

Definition 3 (Signature). *A* signature *or* vocabulary *for first-order predicate logic is a pair* $\mathcal{L} = \left(\{Fun_{\mathcal{L}}^n\}_{n \in \mathbb{N}}, \{Rel_{\mathcal{L}}^n\}_{n \in \mathbb{N}} \right)$ *of two families of computably enumerable symbol sets, called* n-ary function symbols *of* $\mathcal{L}$ *and* n-ary relation symbols *or* predicate symbols *of* $\mathcal{L}$*. The 0-ary function symbols are called* constants *of* $\mathcal{L}$*. The 0-ary relation symbols are called* propositional relation symbols *of* $\mathcal{L}$*.*

Note that any of the symbol sets constituting a signature may be empty. Moreover, they need not be disjoint. If they are not, the signature is called *overloaded*. Overloading is usually uncritical, moreover it can be undone by annotating each signature symbol with its symbol class (*Fun* or *Rel*) and arity whenever required.

First-order predicate logic comes in two versions: *equality* may or may not be built-in. The version with built-in equality defines a special 2-ary relation symbol for equality, written $=$ by some authors and written $\doteq$ or differently by authors who want to avoid confusion with the same symbol at the meta level. In this article we assume first-order predicate logic without equality, unless built-in equality is explicitly mentioned.

Definition 4 ($\mathcal{L}$-term). *Let* $\mathcal{L}$ *be a signature. We define inductively:*

1. *Each variable* x *is an* $\mathcal{L}$*-term.*
2. *Each constant* c *of* $\mathcal{L}$ *is an* $\mathcal{L}$*-term.*
3. *For each* $n \geq 1$*, if* f *is an* n-ary *function symbol of* $\mathcal{L}$ *and* $t_1, \dots, t_n$ *are* $\mathcal{L}$*-terms, then* $f(t_1, \dots, t_n)$ *is an* $\mathcal{L}$*-term.*

Definition 5 ($\mathcal{L}$-atom). *Let* $\mathcal{L}$ *be a signature. For* $n \in \mathbb{N}$*, if* p *is an* n-ary *relation symbol of* $\mathcal{L}$ *and* $t_1, \dots, t_n$ *are* $\mathcal{L}$*-terms, then* $p(t_1, \dots, t_n)$ *is an* $\mathcal{L}$*-atom or atomic* $\mathcal{L}$*-formula. For* $n = 0$ *the atom may be written* $p()$ *or* p *and is called a propositional* $\mathcal{L}$*-atom.*

Definition 6 ($\mathcal{L}$-formula). *Let $\mathcal{L}$ be a signature. We define inductively:*

1. *Each $\mathcal{L}$-atom is an $\mathcal{L}$-formula.*   *(atoms)*
2. *$\bot$ and $\top$ are $\mathcal{L}$-formulas.*   *(0-ary connectives)*
3. *If φ is an $\mathcal{L}$-formula, then*
   $\neg\varphi$ is an $\mathcal{L}$-formula.   *(1-ary connectives)*
4. *If φ and ψ are $\mathcal{L}$-formulas, then*
   $(\varphi \wedge \psi)$ and $(\varphi \vee \psi)$ and $(\varphi \Rightarrow \psi)$ are $\mathcal{L}$-formulas.   *(2-ary connectives)*
5. *If x is a variable and φ is an $\mathcal{L}$-formula, then*
   $\forall x\varphi$ and $\exists x\varphi$ are $\mathcal{L}$-formulas.   *(quantifiers)*

In most cases the signature $\mathcal{L}$ is clear from context, and we simply speak of terms, atoms, and formulas without the prefix "$\mathcal{L}$-". If no signature is specified, one usually assumes the conventions:

> $p, q, r, \ldots$ are relation symbols with appropriate arities.
>
> $f, g, h, \ldots$ are function symbols with appropriate arities $\neq 0$.
>
> $a, b, c, \ldots$ are constants, i.e., function symbols with arity 0.

The set of terms is a formal language for representing individuals about which statements can be made. The set of formulas is the formal language for representing such statements. For example, constants a and b might represent numbers, function symbol f an arithmetic operation, and relation symbol p an arithmetic comparison relation. Then the term $f(a, f(a, b))$ would also represent a number, whereas the atomic formula $p(a, f(a, b))$ would represent a statement about two numbers.

Unique Parsing of Terms and Formulas. The definitions above, in particular the fact that parentheses enclose formulas constructed with a binary connective, ensure an unambiguous syntactical structure of any term or formula. For the sake of readability this strict syntax definition can be relaxed by the convention that $\wedge$ takes precedence over $\vee$ and both of them take precedence over $\Rightarrow$. Thus, $q(a) \vee q(b) \wedge r(b) \Rightarrow p(a, f(a, b))$ is a shorthand for the fully parenthesised form $((q(a) \vee (q(b) \wedge r(b))) \Rightarrow p(a, f(a, b)))$. Likewise, one usually assumes that $\wedge$ and $\vee$ associate to the left and $\Rightarrow$ associates to the right. As a further means to improve readability, some of the parentheses may be written as square brackets or curly braces.

Definition 7 (Subformula). *The subformulas of a formula φ are φ itself and all subformulas of immediate subformulas of φ.*

- *Atomic formulas and $\bot$ and $\top$ have no immediate subformulas.*
- *The only immediate subformula of $\neg\psi$ is ψ.*
- *The immediate subformulas of $(\psi_1 \wedge \psi_2)$ or $(\psi_1 \vee \psi_2)$ or $(\psi_1 \Rightarrow \psi_2)$ are ψ_1 and ψ_2.*
- *The only immediate subformula of $\forall x\psi$ or $\exists x\psi$ is ψ.*

Definition 8 (Scope). *Let φ be a formula, Q a quantifier, and $Qx\psi$ a subformula of φ. Then Qx is called a quantifier for x. Its scope in φ is the subformula ψ except subformulas of ψ that begin with a quantifier for the same variable x.*

Each occurrence of x in the scope of Qx is bound in φ by Qx. Each occurrence of x that is not in the scope of any quantifier for x is a free occurrence of x in φ.

Example 9 (Bound/free variable). Let φ be $\big(\forall x[\exists x p(x) \wedge q(x)] \Rightarrow [r(x) \vee \forall x s(x)]\big)$. The x in $p(x)$ is bound in φ by $\exists x$. The x in $q(x)$ is bound in φ by the first $\forall x$. The x in $r(x)$ is free in φ. The x in $s(x)$ is bound in φ by the last $\forall x$.

Let φ' be $\forall x\big([\exists x p(x) \wedge q(x)] \Rightarrow [r(x) \vee \forall x s(x)]\big)$. Here both the x in $p(x)$ and the x in $r(x)$ are bound in φ' by the first $\forall x$.

Note that being bound or free is not a property of just a variable occurrence, but of a variable occurrence relative to a formula. For instance, x is bound in the formula $\forall x\, p(x)$, but free in its subformula $p(x)$.

Definition 10 (Rectified formula). *A formula φ is* rectified, *if for each occurrence Qx of a quantifier for a variable x, there is neither any free occurrence of x in φ nor any other occurrence of a quantifier for the same variable x.*

Any formula can be rectified by consistently renaming its quantified variables. The formula $(\forall x[\exists x p(x) \wedge q(x)] \Rightarrow [r(x) \vee \forall x s(x)])$ from the example above can be rectified to $(\forall u[\exists v p(v) \wedge q(u)] \Rightarrow [r(x) \vee \forall w s(w)])$. Note that rectification leaves any free variables free and unrenamed. Another name for rectification, mainly used in special cases with implicit quantification, is *standardisation apart*.

Definition 11 (Ground term or formula, closed formula). *A* ground term *is a term containing no variable. A* ground formula *is a formula containing no variable. A* closed formula *or* sentence *is a formula containing no free variable.*

For example, $p(a)$ is a ground atom and therefore closed. The formula $\forall x\, p(x)$ is not ground, but closed. The atom $p(x)$ is neither ground nor closed. In Example 9 above, the formula φ is not closed and the formula φ' is closed.

Definition 12 (Propositional formula). *A* propositional formula *is a formula containing no quantifier and no relation symbol of arity > 0.*

Propositional vs. Ground. Propositional formulas are composed of connectives and 0-ary relation symbols only. Obviously, each propositional formula is ground. The converse is not correct in the strict formal sense, but ground formulas can be regarded as propositional in a broader sense:

If $\mathcal{L}$ is a signature for first-order predicate logic, the set of ground $\mathcal{L}$-atoms is computably enumerable. Let $\mathcal{L}'$ be a new signature defining each ground $\mathcal{L}$-atom as a 0-ary relation "symbol" of $\mathcal{L}'$. Now each ground $\mathcal{L}$-formula can also be read as a propositional $\mathcal{L}'$-formula.

Note that this simple switch of viewpoints works only for ground formulas, because it cannot capture the dependencies between quantifiers and variables.

Definition 13 (Polarity). *Let φ be a formula. The* polarities *of occurrences of its subformulas are* positive *or* negative *as follows:*

– *The polarity of φ in φ is positive.*
– *If ψ is $\neg\psi_1$ or $(\psi_1 \Rightarrow \psi_2)$ and occurs in φ,*
  the polarity of ψ_1 in φ is the opposite of the polarity of ψ in φ.

– *In all other cases, if ψ is an occurrence in φ of a subformula with immediate subformula ψ', the polarity of ψ' in φ is the same as the polarity of ψ in φ.*

The polarity counts whether an occurrence of a subformula is within the scope of an even or odd number of negations. The left-hand immediate subformula of an implication counts as an implicitly negated subformula.

Definition 14 (Universal formula). *A formula φ is* universal, *iff each occurrence of $\forall$ has positive and each occurrence of $\exists$ has negative polarity in φ.*

For instance, $\forall x\,([\neg\forall y\,p(x,y)] \Rightarrow [\neg\exists z\,p(x,z)])$ is a universal closed formula, whereas $\forall x\,([\neg\forall y\,p(x,y)] \Rightarrow [\neg\forall z\,p(x,z)])$ is not universal.

Definition 15 (Prenex form). *A formula φ is in* prenex form, *iff it has the form $Q_1x_1\ldots Q_nx_n\,\psi$ where $n \geq 0$ and the Q_i are quantifiers and ψ contains no quantifier. The quantifier-free subformula ψ is called the* matrix *of φ.*

Obviously, a formula in prenex form is universal iff it does not contain $\exists$. Each formula can be transformed into an equivalent formula in prenex form (equivalent in the sense of $\models\!\mid$ from Section 4).

Notation 16 (Term list notation). *Let $\boldsymbol{u} = t_1,\ldots,t_k$ be a list of terms, let f and p be a k-ary function and relation symbol. Then $f(\boldsymbol{u})$ is a short notation for the term $f(t_1,\ldots,t_k)$ and $p(\boldsymbol{u})$ for the atom $p(t_1,\ldots,t_k)$.*

Let $\boldsymbol{x} = x_1,\ldots,x_n$ be a list of variables and φ a formula. Then $\forall\boldsymbol{x}\varphi$ is a short notation for $\forall x_1\ldots\forall x_n\,\varphi$ and $\exists\boldsymbol{x}\varphi$ for $\exists x_1\ldots\exists x_n\,\varphi$. In the case $n = 0$ both $\forall\boldsymbol{x}\varphi$ and $\exists\boldsymbol{x}\varphi$ stand for φ.

Definition 17 (Universal/existential closure). *Let φ be a formula. Let $\boldsymbol{x}$ be the list of all variables having a free occurrence in φ. The* universal closure $\forall^*\varphi$ *is defined as $\forall\boldsymbol{x}\varphi$ and the* existential closure $\exists^*\varphi$ *as $\exists\boldsymbol{x}\varphi$.*

Technically, a quantifier-free formula such as $((p(x,y) \wedge p(y,z)) \Rightarrow p(x,z))$ contains free variables. It is fairly common to use quantifier-free notations as shorthand for their universal closure, which is a closed universal formula in prenex form, in this case $\forall x\forall y\forall z((p(x,y) \wedge p(y,z)) \Rightarrow p(x,z))$.

3.2   Query and Rule Language Fragments of First-Order Predicate Logic

Notation 18 (Rule). *A* rule $\psi \leftarrow \varphi$ *is a notation for a not necessarily closed formula $(\varphi \Rightarrow \psi)$. The subformula φ is called the* antecedent *or* body *and ψ the* consequent *or* head *of the rule. A rule $\psi \leftarrow \top$ may be written $\psi \leftarrow$ with empty antecedent. A rule $\bot \leftarrow \varphi$ may be written $\leftarrow \varphi$ with empty consequent.*

Implicit Quantification. Typically, a rule is a shorthand notation for its universal closure. The set of free variables in a rule $\psi \leftarrow \varphi$ can be partitioned into the variables $\boldsymbol{x}$ that occur in ψ and the variables $\boldsymbol{y}$ that occur in φ but not in ψ.

Then the universal closure $\forall \boldsymbol{x} \forall \boldsymbol{y}(\psi \leftarrow \varphi)$ is equivalent to $\forall \boldsymbol{x}(\psi \leftarrow \exists \boldsymbol{y}\varphi)$ in the sense of $\models$ (Section 4). Thus, the free variables occurring only in the rule antecedent can be described as implicitly *universally* quantified *in the entire rule* or implicitly *existentially* quantified *in the rule antecedent*. The two alternative descriptions mean the same, but they can be confusing, especially for rules with empty consequent.

Definition 19 (Literal, complement). *If A is an atom, both A and $\neg A$ are literals. The literal A is* positive, *the literal $\neg A$ is* negative, *and the two are a pair of* complementary *literals. The complement of A, written $\overline{A}$, is $\neg A$, the complement of $\neg A$, written $\overline{\neg A}$, is A.*

Definition 20 (Clause). *A clause is a disjunction of finitely many literals. A clause is written $A_1 \vee \ldots \vee A_k \leftarrow L_1 \wedge \ldots \wedge L_n$ in rule notation, which stands for the disjunction $A_1 \vee \ldots \vee A_k \vee \overline{L_1} \vee \ldots \vee \overline{L_n}$ with atoms A_i and literals L_j, $k \geq 0$, $n \geq 0$. A clause represents its universal closure.*

Any formula of first-order predicate logic can be transformed into a finite set of clauses with essentially the same meaning (see Section 4).

3.2.1 Logic Programming

Logic programming considers clauses with non-empty consequent as *programs* and clauses with empty consequent as *goals* used for program invocation. The operational and declarative semantics of logic programs depend on whether the antecedent is a conjunction of atoms or of arbitrary literals and whether the consequent is just a single atom or a disjunction of several atoms.

Definition 21 (Clause classification). *Let $k, n \in \mathbb{N}$, let A, A_j, B_i be atoms and L_i be literals. The following names are defined for special forms of clauses.*

	Name		*Form*	
Horn clause	definite clause		$A \leftarrow B_1 \wedge \ldots \wedge B_n$	$k = 1, n \geq 0$
		unit clause[2]	$A \leftarrow$	$k = 1, n = 0$
	definite goal		$\leftarrow B_1 \wedge \ldots \wedge B_n$	$k = 0, n \geq 0$
		empty clause[3]	$\leftarrow$	$k = 0, n = 0$
	normal clause		$A \leftarrow L_1 \wedge \ldots \wedge L_n$	$k = 1, n \geq 0$
	normal goal		$\leftarrow L_1 \wedge \ldots \wedge L_n$	$k = 0, n \geq 0$
	disjunctive clause		$A_1 \vee \ldots \vee A_k \leftarrow B_1 \wedge \ldots \wedge B_n$	$k \geq 0, n \geq 0$
	general clause		$A_1 \vee \ldots \vee A_k \leftarrow L_1 \wedge \ldots \wedge L_n$	$k \geq 0, n \geq 0$

A finite set of definite clauses is called a *definite program*. Definite programs invoked by definite queries represent a fragment of first-order predicate logic with especially nice semantic properties. In the context of the programming language

---

[2] Unit clauses are also called *facts*, which is meant in a purely syntactic sense although the word suggests a semantic sense.

[3] The empty clause is usually denoted $\square$ in the literature on automated deduction.

Prolog this fragment is sometimes called "pure Prolog". The generalisation to normal clauses and normal queries allows to use negation in antecedents, which may be handled as in Prolog by negation as failure. Programs with disjunctive clauses are investigated in the field of disjunctive logic programming.

Definite programs do not have the full expressive power of first-order predicate logic. For example, given relation symbols *person, male, female*, it is not possible to express with definite clauses that each person is male or female. This requires a disjunctive clause $male(x) \lor female(x) \leftarrow person(x)$ or a normal clause $male(x) \leftarrow person(x) \land \neg female(x)$. The two are equivalent in the classical sense of $\models$ (see Section 4), but their operational treatment might be different.

3.2.2 Datalog

Logic-based formalisations of query languages can be based on concepts of logic programming, but with a number of specifics:

- Function symbols other than constants are excluded. Thus, the only terms are variables and constants.
- Relation symbols are partitioned into those that may occur in the data to be queried, called *extensional*, and those that may not, called *intensional*.
- Clauses are assumed to be *range restricted*, which essentially requires that all variables in the consequent of a clause also occur in its antecedent.

Definition 22 (Database schema and instance, extensional, intensional). *Let $\mathcal{L} = \left(\{Fun_{\mathcal{L}}^n\}_{n\in\mathbb{N}}, \{Rel_{\mathcal{L}}^n\}_{n\in\mathbb{N}} \right)$ be a signature with $Fun_{\mathcal{L}}^n = \emptyset$ for $n > 0$.*

A database schema over $\mathcal{L}$ is a nonempty, finite subset $\mathcal{D} \subseteq \bigcup_{n\in\mathbb{N}} Rel_{\mathcal{L}}^n$. The relation symbols in $\mathcal{D}$ and any atoms constructed with them are called extensional. *The other relation symbols and atoms are called* intensional.

A database instance for $\mathcal{D}$ is a finite set of extensional ground atoms.

Definition 23 (Range restricted). *A general clause is* range restricted *if each variable occurring anywhere in it occurs in a positive literal of its antecedent.*

Specialised to definite clauses, range restriction means that each variable occurring in the consequent also occurs in the antecedent of the clause.

Definition 24 (Datalog). *A datalog clause is a range restricted definite clause*[4] *whose consequent is an intensional atom.*

A datalog program is a finite set of datalog clauses.

In a database instance, the set of all extensional atoms sharing the same n-ary relation symbol amounts to an extensional specification of an n-ary relation. These relations are also referred to as the *extensional database (EDB)*. In a datalog program, the set of all datalog clauses whose consequent atoms share the same n-ary relation symbol amounts to an intensional specification of an n-ary relation. These relations are also referred to as the *intensional database (IDB)*.

---

[4] Some authors define datalog clauses without requiring that they are range restricted.

The antecedent of a datalog clause may contain both extensional and intensional atoms, thus accessing both kinds of relations.

Note that range restriction implies that datalog unit clauses are ground. Such clauses are typically needed as base cases for recursive definitions.

The distinction between extensional and intensional is a pragmatic one. It is useful in processing datalog programs written for querying: clauses whose consequents contain only intensional atoms can be pre-processed, e.g., rewritten or compiled, without knowledge of the database instance to be queried.

On the other hand the distinction is no point of principle. Any pair of a datalog program and a database instance can be fused into an exclusively intensional form by writing each extensional atom from the database instance as a datalog unit clause and redeclaring all relation symbols as intensional. Conversely, any such "fused" datalog program can be separated into an intensional and a (new) extensional part: provided that a relation symbol r occurs in the consequents of unit clauses only, each of these unit clauses $r(c_1, \ldots, c_k) \leftarrow$ is written as an extensional atom $r'(c_1, \ldots, c_k)$ with an additional interfacing datalog clause $r(x_1, \ldots, x_k) \leftarrow r'(x_1, \ldots, x_k)$ for a new relation symbol r'. The new relation symbols are then declared to be extensional.

Many variants of datalog have been defined by modifying the plain version introduced here. Such restricted or extended versions of datalog are motivated by their interesting expressive power and/or complexity or by their correspondence to classes of queries defined by other formalisation approaches. See Section 8 for more details and [46] for a survey. Here we list just some of these versions of datalog.

- *Monadic datalog* is datalog where all intensional relation symbols are unary.
- *Nonrecursive datalog* is datalog without direct or indirect recursion.
- *Linear datalog* is datalog where each clause antecedent contains at most one intensional atom (thus restricting the form of recursion).
- *Disjunctive datalog* is datalog with disjunctive instead of definite clauses.
- *Datalog$^\neg$* is datalog with normal instead of definite clauses.
- *Nonrecursive datalog$^\neg$* is datalog$^\neg$ without direct or indirect recursion.
- *Disjunctive datalog$^\neg$* is datalog$^\neg$ with general instead of normal clauses.

3.2.3   Conjunctive Queries

The most trivial form of nonrecursive datalog is obtained by disallowing intensional relation symbols in rule antecedents. If in addition the datalog program is restricted to just one clause, the consequent of this clause contains the only occurrence of an intensional relation symbol. By a wide-spread convention this unique intensional relation symbol is called the answer relation symbol and the rule is called a conjunctive query.

Definition 25 (Conjunctive query). *A conjunctive query is a datalog rule* $ans(\boldsymbol{u}) \leftarrow r_1(\boldsymbol{u}_1) \wedge \ldots \wedge r_n(\boldsymbol{u}_n)$ *where* $n \geq 0$, *the* r_i *are extensional and ans is an intensional relation symbol,* $\boldsymbol{u}, \boldsymbol{u}_1, \ldots, \boldsymbol{u}_n$ *are lists of terms of appropriate length, and the rule is range restricted, i.e., each variable in* $\boldsymbol{u}$ *also occurs in at least one of* $\boldsymbol{u}_1, \ldots, \boldsymbol{u}_n$.

A boolean conjunctive query *is a conjunctive query where **u** is the empty list, i.e., the answer relation symbol ans is propositional.*

The following examples of conjunctive queries assume that *parent* is a 2-ary and *male* and *female* are 1-ary extensional relation symbols. The first two are examples of boolean conjunctive queries.

$ans() \leftarrow parent(mary, tom)$	*is Mary a parent of Tom?*
$ans() \leftarrow parent(mary, y)$	*does Mary have children?*
$ans(x) \leftarrow parent(x, tom)$	*who are Tom's parents?*
$ans(x) \leftarrow female(x) \wedge parent(x, y) \wedge parent(y, tom)$	*who are Tom's grandmothers?*
$ans(x, z) \leftarrow male(x) \wedge parent(x, y) \wedge parent(y, z)$	*who are grandfathers and their grandchildren?*

The class of conjunctive queries enjoys interesting complexity properties (see Section 8), but its expressive power is limited. Given only the extensional relation symbols above, the following query types cannot be expressed as conjunctive queries:

1. *who are parents of Tom or Mary?*
   requires disjunction in rule antecedents or more than a single rule.
2. *who are parents, but not of Tom?*
   requires negation in rule antecedents.
3. *who are women all of whose children are sons?*
   requires universal quantification in rule antecedents. Note that variables occurring only in the antecedent of a conjunctive query (such as y in the examples above) are interpreted as if existentially quantified in the antecedent.
4. *who are ancestors of Tom?*
   requires recursion, i.e., intensional relation symbols in rule antecedents.

Conjunctive queries have been extended to make some of these query types expressible and to allow comparisons with classes of relational algebra queries.

Basic conjunctive queries as defined above correspond to the *SPC subclass* of relational algebra queries constructed with selection, projection, cartesian product (or, alternatively, join).

Conjunctive queries extended with disjunction in rule antecedents correspond to the *SPCU subclass* of relational algebra queries, which incorporates union.

Conjunctive queries extended with negation, disjunction, and quantification in rule antecedents (but no recursion) are known as *first-order queries* and correspond to the full class of relational algebra queries.

However, for an exact correspondence first-order queries have to be restricted to *domain independent* queries. This is a semantic characterisation that excludes queries for which the answers depend on information that may not be completely available. For instance, the set of answers to $ans(x) \leftarrow \neg parent(x, x)$ comprises all of humanity – or, depending on the domain of individuals under consideration, all mammals or all vertebrates. This problem does not arise iff the query is domain independent. Unfortunately, domain independence is undecidable.[5] But there are several syntactic, i.e., decidable, criteria that are sufficient for domain independence. Range restricted general clauses (Definition 21), for example, are domain independent.

Another subclass of first-order queries restricts rule antecedents to formulas from the so-called *guarded fragment* of first-order predicate logic, where quantifiers have to be "guarded" by atoms containing the quantified variables (see the subsection on range restricted quantification on page 18). The guarded fragment corresponds to the *semijoin algebra*, the variant of the full relational algebra obtained by replacing the join operator by the semijoin operator [105]. See Section 9 for more details.

In summary, the various extensions to conjunctive queries cover all of the query types above except the last one, which requires recursion. Some of the extensions are obviously not datalog, but only from a syntactic point of view. They can be expressed with nonrecursive datalog¬ provided that more than one rule is allowed. In other words, the expressive power of datalog is strictly greater than that of relational algebra, and the add-on is due to recursion.

3.2.4   Single-Rule Programs (sirups)

Datalog programs containing a single non-unit clause and possibly some unit clauses have been introduced in order to study various "degrees" of recursion. They are called *single-rule programs*, sirups for short.

Pure sirups are datalog programs consisting of a single rule and no unit-clause. In particular, conjunctive queries are pure sirups. *Single ground fact sirups* are datalog programs consisting of a single rule and at most one ground unit clause. *General sirups* are datalog programs consisting of a single rule and some unit clauses. For each of these classes its linear subclass is also of interest.

It turns out that even such strongly restricted classes of sirups have essentially the same complexity and expressive power as general datalog programs [79].

3.3   Syntactic Variations of First-Order Predicate Logic Relevant to Query Languages

Programming and modelling languages from various areas of computer science often provide constructs that resemble terms or formulas of first-order predicate logic. Such constructs sometimes deviate from their logical counterparts in certain aspects, which in most cases are more a matter of convenience than of fundamental principles. By considering such constructs as syntactic variants – typically, more convenient ones – of logical terms or formulas, logic's semantic apparatus becomes applicable and can be used to define the meaning of such constructs.

---

[5] Basically, because if φ is not domain independent, then $(\varphi \wedge \psi)$ is domain independent iff ψ is unsatisfiable, an undecidable property.

3.3.1   Variations from Object-Oriented and Knowledge Representation Formalisms

Record-like Structures. Language constructs resembling records or structures of imperative programming languages are meant for collecting all data about some real object in a single syntactic unit:

```
Person
    firstName: Mary
    lastName:  Miller
    bornIn:    1984
```

Regardless of its concrete syntax, such a construct can be seen as syntactic sugar for the ground atom $person(Mary, Miller, 1984)$ or for the ground formula $person(c) \land firstName(c) \doteq Mary \land lastName(c) \doteq Miller \land bornIn(c) \doteq 1984$. The former translation is sufficient for simple structures, the latter, assuming built-in equality, can represent more complex ones.

Cyclic Structures. Some object-oriented programming or modelling languages allow self-references such as:

```
Employee
    firstName: Mary
    lastName:  Miller
    bornIn:    1984
    superior:  SELF
```

Here the keyword SELF refers to the very syntactic unit in which it occurs. First-order predicate logic does not support "cyclic terms" or "cyclic formulas", thus there is no direct translation to logic.

Constructs like SELF represent *implicit references*, in contrast to *explicit references* such as unique identifiers or keys. Implicit references have the purpose to restrict the user's possibilities for manipulating references, but they are implemented using explicit references. Roughly speaking, implicit references are explicit references with information hiding. Translating explicit references to logic is straightforward, and it is just the information hiding aspect that has no counterpart in logic. Logic – like the relational and other data models – can represent information, but is not concerned with information hiding.

Object Identity. Another feature of object-oriented programming or modelling languages is a so-called "object identity", which allows to distinguish between objects that are syntactically equal, such as two objects representing two people whose personal data happens to coincide:

```
Person                      Person
    firstName: Mary             firstName: Mary
    lastName:  Miller           lastName:  Miller
    bornIn:    1984             bornIn:    1984
```

Logic is referentially transparent, meaning that it does not distinguish between syntactically equal "copies". Thus, there is no direct translation to logic of objects with object identity.

As in the case of cyclic structures, object identity is a concept for implicit reference, which is based on explicit references but hides some information. Again, it is only the information hiding aspect that cannot be translated to logic.

Positions vs. Roles. The position of arguments in a term or atom such as *person*(*Mary, Miller*, 1984) is significant. Exchanging the first two arguments would result in the representation of a different person.

Some languages allow to associate an identifier, a so-called *role*, with each argument position. An argument is then written as a pair *role* $\dashrightarrow$ *term*, such as *person*(*firstName* $\dashrightarrow$ *Mary*, *lastName* $\dashrightarrow$ *Miller*, *bornIn* $\dashrightarrow$ 1984), alternatively *person*(*lastName* $\dashrightarrow$ *Miller*, *firstName* $\dashrightarrow$ *Mary*, *bornIn* $\dashrightarrow$ 1984), which are considered to be the same. The record-like constructs above correspond most naturally to such a notation using roles.

A syntax with roles has several advantages. It admits arbitrary orderings of arguments and is therefore more flexible. It improves readability, especially with high numbers of arguments. Moreover, it can handle "don't care" arguments more conveniently by simply omitting them rather than representing them by wildcard variables. Such arguments are frequent in queries,

Nevertheless, it does not change the expressive power. The standard syntax *person*(*Mary, Miller*, 1984) can be seen as an abbreviated form of a role-based notation *person*(*1* $\dashrightarrow$ *Mary*, *2* $\dashrightarrow$ *Miller*, *3* $\dashrightarrow$ 1984) using positions as roles. Conversely, the role identifiers can simply be numbered consecutively, thus transforming the role-based notation into the notation using positions as roles, of which the standard syntax is just an abbreviated form.

3.3.2   Variations from Relational Databases

Atoms vs. Tuples. In logic, an atom *person*(*Mary, Miller*, 1984) formalises a statement about two names and a number. Logic is concerned with statements that may be true or false. Relational databases, on the other hand, are concerned with relations or tables, which are sets of tuples. Under this perspective the point of the example above is that the tuple of the two names and the number belongs to the relation, formalised (*Mary, Miller*, 1984) $\in$ *person*. Obviously, the two formalisations are directly interchangeable.

The different concerns of the two fields also result in different notions of variables. In logic, variables are used as placeholders for the things about which statements are made, as in *person*(*Mary, Miller*, x). In relational databases, variables are used as placeholders for tuples, as in $x \in person$, with notations like x_3 or $x.3$ for accessing a single coordinate of a tuple x, here the third one.

Positions vs. Roles, continued. The alternative to base the notation on positions or on roles also exists for the tuple notation. A standard tuple is a member of a cartesian product of sets and therefore ordered. Another possibility is to regard a tuple as an unordered collection of pairs *role* $\dashrightarrow$ *value*. In the latter case the notation for accessing a single coordinate of a tuple x is x_{bornIn} or $x.bornIn$ using the role instead of the position.

Combined, those alternatives result in four notational variants, which are interchangeable:

Atom

| positions | $person(Mary, Miller, 1984)$ |
| roles | $person(firstName \dashrightarrow Mary,\ lastName \dashrightarrow Miller,\ bornIn \dashrightarrow 1984)$ |

Tuple

| positions | $(Mary, Miller, 1984) \in person$ |
| roles | $(firstName \dashrightarrow Mary,\ lastName \dashrightarrow Miller,\ bornIn \dashrightarrow 1984) \in person$ |

Relational Calculus. Relational calculus was the first logic-based formalisation of query languages. Early versions of the relational calculus were called "tuple calculus" and "domain calculus". The difference was mainly which of the notational variants above they used.

A relational calculus query has the form $\{u \mid \varphi\}$ where u is a list of terms, i.e., variables or constants, φ is a formula, and the variables in u are exactly the free variables in φ.

Recall conjunctive queries (Definition 25) and their extensions. The relational calculus query above can be seen as simply another notation for $ans(u) \leftarrow \varphi$. The discussion about the correspondence to relational algebra depending on the syntactic form of φ is therefore as in the subsection on conjunctive queries.

Relational Algebra. Relational algebra is not a logic-based approach and does not really belong in this subsection, but it was the first formalisation of query languages and usually the frame of reference for later ones.

Relational algebra considers relations in the mathematical sense and a small number of operators with which relational expressions can be constructed. Typical operators are selection, projection, cartesian product, union, intersection, set difference, division, join. Some of these operators can be defined in terms of others. Various classes of relational algebra queries are characterised by the subset of operators they may use.

3.3.3   Logical Variations

Range Restricted Quantification. Both natural language and mathematics tend to exercise some control over the range of quantified variables.

Rather than saying *"for everything there is something that is the first one's parent"*, formalised as $\forall x \exists y\, parent(y, x)$, it would seem more natural to say *"for every person there is a person who is the first one's parent"*, formalised as $\forall x(person(x) \Rightarrow \exists y(person(y) \land parent(y, x)))$. Similar examples abound in mathematics, where theorems rarely start with *"for everything there is something such that ... "*, but more typically with *"for every polynomial P there is an integer n such that ... "*

The characteristic of formulas resulting from such statements is that each quantifier for a variable is combined with an atom that restricts the range of the quantified variable. This intuition can be formalised as follows.

Definition 26 (Formula with range restricted quantification). *Let $\mathcal{L}$ be a signature. $\mathcal{L}$-formulas with range restricted quantification, here abbreviated RR-formulas, are defined inductively:*

1. *Each quantifier-free $\mathcal{L}$-formula is an RR-formula.*
2. *Each $\mathcal{L}$-formula constructed from a connective and an appropriate number of RR-formulas is an RR-formula.*
3. *If φ is an RR-formula and A is an atom and $\boldsymbol{x}$ is a subset of the free variables in A, then $\forall \boldsymbol{x}(A \Rightarrow \varphi)$ and $\exists \boldsymbol{x}(A \wedge \varphi)$ are RR-formulas. The atom A is called the* range *for the variables in $\boldsymbol{x}$.*

The atom A combined with a quantifier is also called a *guard*. The guarded fragment discussed earlier in connection with conjunctive queries is a further restriction of this class of formulas, with the additional requirement that all variables that are free in φ also occur in A. This enforces a kind of layering: all variables that are free in a subformula occur in the atom guarding the innermost quantifier in whose scope the subformula is.

[26] gives a generalisation of Definition 26 allowing for non-atomic ranges.

Many-Sorted First-Order Predicate Logic. In the field of programming languages it is advantageous to associate types with expressions. The same idea for first-order predicate logic is to associate *sorts*[6] with terms.

This requires a new symbol class called *sort symbols*. A signature then specifies for each relation symbol p not just an arity n, but an n-tuple of sort symbols written $(s_1 \times \ldots \times s_n)$, and for each function symbol f not just an arity n, but an $(n+1)$-tuple of sort symbols written $(s_1 \times \ldots \times s_n \rightarrow s_{n+1})$, where $s_1, \ldots, s_n$ are the argument sorts and s_{n+1} is the result sort of the symbol. Moreover, each variable is associated with a sort symbol.

With these modifications it is straightforward to extend the definitions of terms and atoms by the obvious compatibility requirements between argument sorts and result sorts of subterms.

Example 27 (Many-sorted first-order predicate logic)

Sort symbols	$\{person, company\}$	
Signature		
2-ary relation symbol	*married : person × person*	
	employs : company × person	
constant	*Tom : person*	*Web5.0 : company*
	Mary : person	
1-ary function symbol	*founder : company → person*	
Formulas	*married(Tom, Mary) ∧ employs(Web5.0, Tom)*	
	$\exists x{:}company\ employs(x, founder(Web5.0))$	
	$\forall x{:}company\ \exists y{:}person\ employs(x, y)$	

In this example, *founder(Tom)* is not a term because of the clash between the subterm's result sort *person* and the required argument sort *company*. Likewise, *married(Tom, Web5.0)* is not a formula.

---

[6] The word *type* would clash with historically established terminology.

Classical first-order predicate logic is the special case of the many-sorted version with exactly one sort symbol, which is not explicitly written.

Many-sorted first-order predicate logic can be translated into the classical version. Each sort symbol s is translated into a unary relation symbol $\widehat{s}$. Part of the signature information from the example above translates as $\widehat{person}(Tom)$ and $\forall x(\widehat{company}(x) \Rightarrow \widehat{person}(founder(x)))$. The last of the formulas from the example translates as $\forall x(\widehat{company}(x) \Rightarrow \exists y(\widehat{person}(y) \wedge employs(x,y)))$. Note that the translation results in a formula with range restricted quantification, the fragment discussed earlier.

Thus, introducing sorts does not affect the expressive power. But it allows static sort checking and thus improves error detection. Moreover, a many-sorted formalisation of a problem needs fewer and smaller formulas than the corresponding classical formalisation.

The idea of introducing sorts can be extended to hierarchies or networks of sorts without losing these advantages.

4   Declarative Semantics: Fundamentals of Classical Model Theory

The classical semantics of first-order predicate logic, i.e., the attribution of meaning to formulas of first-order predicate logic, follows an approach proposed by Alfred Tarski in the 1930s. This approach has a salient characteristic: The interpretation of a compound term and the truth value of a compound formula are defined recursively over the structure of the term or formula, respectively. As a consequence, to know the truth value in an interpretation $\mathcal{I}$ of a compound formula φ, it suffices to know the values in $\mathcal{I}$ of the immediate constituents of φ. This is clearly advantageous for computing, as it provides with a well-defined, finite, and restricted computation scope. However, this approach to semantics has a considerable drawback: its allowing for any kind of sets for interpreting terms makes it apparently incomputable.

A theorem due to Jacques Herbrand shows that this drawback is overcome if only *universal formulas* are considered: If such formulas are true in some interpretation, whose domain may well not be computably enumerable, then they are also true in a so-called *Herbrand interpretation*, whose domain is the computably enumerable set of all variable-free terms of the given signature. Furthermore, a technique known as *Skolemization*[7] transforms every formula into a universal formula while preserving satisfiability, i.e., the interpretability of a formula as true in some interpretation. Herbrand's theorem and Skolemization make entailment, and thus query answering, semi-decidable and thus amenable to computing.

The first and main subsection below introduces more precisely the notions, techniques, and results mentioned above as well as the treatment of equality in

---

[7] Named after Thoralf Skolem, one of its inventors. Moses Schönfinkel independently proposed it as well.

first-order predicate logic. The subsection is concluded by remarks on inadequacies of classical semantics for query languages. The shorter subsections following the main one show how some, if not all, of these inadequacies can be overcome. Alas, these solutions bear new problems.

4.1 Classical Tarski Model Theory

In the following, a signature $\mathcal{L}$ for first-order predicate logic is assumed.

4.1.1 Interpretations, Models, and Entailment

Definition 28 (Variable assignment). *Let D be a nonempty set. A variable assignment in D is a function V mapping each variable to an element of D. We denote the image of a variable x under an assignment V by x^V.*

Definition 29 ($\mathcal{L}$-Interpretation). *Let $\mathcal{L}$ be a signature. An $\mathcal{L}$-interpretation is a triple $\mathcal{I} = (D, I, V)$ where*

- *D is a nonempty set called the* domain *or* universe *(of discourse) of $\mathcal{I}$.*
  ***Notation:** $dom(\mathcal{I}) := D$.*
- *I is a function defined on the symbols of $\mathcal{L}$ mapping*
  - *each n-ary function symbol f to an n-ary function $f^I : D^n \to D$. For $n = 0$ this means $f^I \in D$.*
  - *each n-ary relation symbol p to an n-ary relation $p^I \subseteq D^n$. For $n = 0$ this means either $p^I = \emptyset$ or $p^I = \{()\}$.*
  ***Notation:** $f^{\mathcal{I}} := f^I$ and $p^{\mathcal{I}} := p^I$.*
- *V is a variable assignment in D.*
  ***Notation:** $x^{\mathcal{I}} := x^V$.*

The domain is required to be nonempty because otherwise neither I nor V would be definable. Moreover, an empty domain would cause anomalies in the truth values of quantified formulas. As before, when the signature $\mathcal{L}$ is clear from context, we drop the prefix "$\mathcal{L}$-" and simply speak of interpretations.

Definition 30. *The value of a term t in an interpretation $\mathcal{I}$, denoted $t^{\mathcal{I}}$, is an element of $dom(\mathcal{I})$ and inductively defined:*

1. *If t is a variable or a constant, then $t^{\mathcal{I}}$ is defined as above.*
2. *If t is a compound term $f(t_1, \ldots, t_n)$, then $t^{\mathcal{I}}$ is defined as $f^{\mathcal{I}}(t_1^{\mathcal{I}}, \ldots, t_n^{\mathcal{I}})$*

Notation 31. *Let V be a variable assignment in D, let V' be a partial function mapping variables to elements of D, which may or may not be a total function. Then $V[V']$ is the variable assignment with*

$$x^{V[V']} = \begin{cases} x^{V'} & \text{if } x^{V'} \text{ is defined} \\ x^V & \text{if } x^{V'} \text{ is undefined} \end{cases}$$

Let $\mathcal{I} = (D, I, V)$ be an interpretation. Then $\mathcal{I}[V'] := (D, I, V[V'])$.
By $\{x_1 \mapsto d_1, \ldots, x_k \mapsto d_k\}$ we denote the partial function that maps x_i to d_i and is undefined on other variables. In combination with the notation above, we omit the set braces and write $V[x_1 \mapsto d_1, \ldots, x_k \mapsto d_k]$ and $\mathcal{I}[x_1 \mapsto d_1, \ldots, x_k \mapsto d_k]$.

Definition 32 (Tarksi, model relationship). *Let $\mathcal{I}$ be an interpretation and φ a formula. The* relationship *$\mathcal{I} \models \varphi$, pronounced "$\mathcal{I}$ is a* model *of φ" or "$\mathcal{I}$ satisfies φ" or "φ is true in $\mathcal{I}$", and its negation $\mathcal{I} \not\models \varphi$, pronounced "$\mathcal{I}$ falsifies φ" or "φ is false in $\mathcal{I}$", are defined inductively:*

$$
\begin{array}{lll}
\mathcal{I} \models p(t_1, \ldots, t_n) & \text{iff} \quad (t_1^{\mathcal{I}}, \ldots, t_n^{\mathcal{I}}) \in p^{\mathcal{I}} & \text{(n-ary } p, \ n \geq 1) \\
\mathcal{I} \models p & \text{iff} \quad () \in p^{\mathcal{I}} & \text{(0-ary } p) \\
\mathcal{I} \not\models \bot & & \\
\mathcal{I} \models \top & & \\[4pt]
\mathcal{I} \models \neg\psi & \text{iff} \quad \mathcal{I} \not\models \psi & \\
\mathcal{I} \models (\psi_1 \wedge \psi_2) & \text{iff} \quad \mathcal{I} \models \psi_1 \text{ and } \mathcal{I} \models \psi_2 & \\
\mathcal{I} \models (\psi_1 \vee \psi_2) & \text{iff} \quad \mathcal{I} \models \psi_1 \text{ or } \mathcal{I} \models \psi_2 & \\
\mathcal{I} \models (\psi_1 \Rightarrow \psi_2) & \text{iff} \quad \mathcal{I} \not\models \psi_1 \text{ or } \mathcal{I} \models \psi_2 & \\[4pt]
\mathcal{I} \models \forall x \, \psi & \text{iff} \quad \mathcal{I}[x \mapsto d] \models \psi \text{ for each } d \in D & \\
\mathcal{I} \models \exists x \, \psi & \text{iff} \quad \mathcal{I}[x \mapsto d] \models \psi \text{ for at least one } d \in D &
\end{array}
$$

For a set S of formulas, $\mathcal{I} \models S$ iff $\mathcal{I} \models \varphi$ for each $\varphi \in S$.

Definition 33 (Semantic properties). *A formula, or a set of formulas, is*

valid *or a* tautology	*iff it is satisfied in each interpretation*
satisfiable	*iff it is satisfied in at least one interpretation*
falsifiable	*iff it is falsified in at least one interpretation*
unsatisfiable *or* inconsistent	*iff it is falsified in each interpretation*

Note that a formula or a set of formulas can be both satisfiable and falsifiable, for instance, any propositional atom p is. The formulas $(p \vee \neg p)$ and $\top$ are valid. The formulas $(p \wedge \neg p)$ and $\bot$ are unsatisfiable.

Definition 34 (Entailment and logical equivalence). *Let φ and ψ be formulas or sets of formulas.*

$\varphi \models \psi$, *pronounced: "φ entails ψ" or "ψ is a (logical) consequence of φ",*
    iff for each interpretation $\mathcal{I}$: if $\mathcal{I} \models \varphi$ then $\mathcal{I} \models \psi$.
$\varphi \,\vDash\!\dashv\, \psi$, *pronounced: "$\varphi$ is (logically) equivalent to ψ",*
    iff $\varphi \models \psi$ and $\psi \models \varphi$.

The following result is immediate. It shows that the semantic properties and entailment can be translated into each other. Being able to determine one of validity, unsatisfiability, or entailment, is sufficient to determine all of them.

Theorem 35 (Translatability between semantic properties and entailment). *Let φ and ψ be formulas.*

φ *is valid*	*iff $\neg\varphi$ is unsatisfiable*	*iff $\top \models \varphi$.*
φ *is unsatisfiable*	*iff $\neg\varphi$ is valid*	*iff $\varphi \models \bot$.*
$\varphi \models \psi$	*iff $(\varphi \Rightarrow \psi)$ is valid*	*iff $(\varphi \wedge \neg\psi)$ is unsatisfiable.*

Being able to determine validity or unsatisfiability is also sufficient to determine logical equivalence, which is just mutual entailment. The definition of $\varphi \,\vDash\!\dashv\, \psi$ means that φ and ψ have the same models. Either of them may be replaced by the other without affecting any truth values. This is often exploited for transformations in proofs or in optimising queries or rule sets.

Proposition 36 (Model-preserving transformations). *Let* φ, φ', ψ, ψ', χ *be formulas. The following equivalences hold:*

- $\varphi \mathrel{\vDash\dashv} \varphi'$ *if* φ' *is a rectified form of* φ
- $\varphi \mathrel{\vDash\dashv} \varphi'$ *if* $\psi \mathrel{\vDash\dashv} \psi'$ *and* φ' *is obtained from* φ *by replacing an occurrence of the subformula* ψ *by* ψ'

- $(\varphi \vee \psi) \mathrel{\vDash\dashv} (\psi \vee \varphi)$ $\qquad\qquad$ $(\varphi \wedge \psi) \mathrel{\vDash\dashv} (\psi \wedge \varphi)$
- $((\varphi \vee \psi) \vee \chi) \mathrel{\vDash\dashv} (\varphi \vee (\psi \vee \chi))$ $\qquad$ $((\varphi \wedge \psi) \wedge \chi) \mathrel{\vDash\dashv} ((\varphi \wedge (\psi \wedge \chi))$
- $((\varphi \vee \psi) \wedge \chi) \mathrel{\vDash\dashv} ((\varphi \wedge \chi) \vee (\psi \wedge \chi))$ $\quad$ $((\varphi \wedge \psi) \vee \chi) \mathrel{\vDash\dashv} ((\varphi \vee \chi) \wedge (\psi \vee \chi))$
- $(\bot \vee \varphi) \mathrel{\vDash\dashv} \varphi$ $\qquad\qquad\qquad\qquad$ $(\top \wedge \varphi) \mathrel{\vDash\dashv} \varphi$
- $(\varphi \vee \neg\varphi) \mathrel{\vDash\dashv} \top$ $\qquad\qquad\qquad\qquad$ $(\varphi \wedge \neg\varphi) \mathrel{\vDash\dashv} \bot$
- $(\varphi \vee \varphi) \mathrel{\vDash\dashv} \varphi$ $\qquad\qquad\qquad\qquad$ $(\varphi \wedge \varphi) \mathrel{\vDash\dashv} \varphi$
- $(\varphi \vee (\varphi \wedge \psi)) \mathrel{\vDash\dashv} \varphi$ $\qquad\qquad\quad$ $(\varphi \wedge (\varphi \vee \psi)) \mathrel{\vDash\dashv} \varphi$

- $\qquad\qquad\qquad\qquad\quad$ $\neg\neg\varphi \mathrel{\vDash\dashv} \varphi$

- $\neg(\varphi \vee \psi) \mathrel{\vDash\dashv} (\neg\varphi \wedge \neg\psi)$ $\qquad\qquad$ $\neg(\varphi \wedge \psi) \mathrel{\vDash\dashv} (\neg\varphi \vee \neg\psi)$
- $(\varphi \Rightarrow \psi) \mathrel{\vDash\dashv} (\neg\varphi \vee \psi)$ $\qquad\qquad$ $\neg(\varphi \Rightarrow \psi) \mathrel{\vDash\dashv} (\varphi \wedge \neg\psi)$
- $((\varphi \vee \varphi') \Rightarrow \psi) \mathrel{\vDash\dashv} ((\varphi \Rightarrow \psi) \wedge (\varphi' \Rightarrow \psi))$ $\quad$ $(\varphi \Rightarrow (\psi \wedge \psi')) \mathrel{\vDash\dashv} ((\varphi \Rightarrow \psi) \wedge (\varphi \Rightarrow \psi'))$
- $(\varphi \Rightarrow \bot) \mathrel{\vDash\dashv} \neg\varphi$ $\qquad\qquad\qquad\qquad$ $(\top \Rightarrow \varphi) \mathrel{\vDash\dashv} \varphi$

- $\qquad\qquad\qquad$ *in general* $\forall x \exists y \varphi \mathrel{\nvDash\dashv} \exists y \forall x \varphi$

- $\forall x \forall y \varphi \mathrel{\vDash\dashv} \forall y \forall x \varphi$ $\qquad\qquad\qquad$ $\exists x \exists y \varphi \mathrel{\vDash\dashv} \exists y \exists x \varphi$
- $\neg\forall x \varphi \mathrel{\vDash\dashv} \exists x \neg\varphi$ $\qquad\qquad\qquad\quad$ $\neg\exists x \varphi \mathrel{\vDash\dashv} \forall x \neg\varphi$
- $\forall x (\varphi \wedge \psi) \mathrel{\vDash\dashv} (\forall x \varphi \wedge \forall x \psi)$ $\qquad$ $\exists x (\varphi \vee \psi) \mathrel{\vDash\dashv} (\exists x \varphi \vee \exists x \psi)$
- $\exists x (\varphi \wedge \psi) \mathrel{\nvDash\dashv} (\exists x \varphi \wedge \exists x \psi)$ $\quad$ *in general* $\quad$ $\forall x (\varphi \vee \psi) \mathrel{\nvDash\dashv} (\forall x \varphi \vee \forall x \psi)$
- $\exists x (\varphi \wedge \psi) \mathrel{\vDash\dashv} (\varphi \wedge \exists x \psi)$ $\quad$ *if x is not free in φ* $\quad$ $\forall x (\varphi \vee \psi) \mathrel{\vDash\dashv} (\varphi \vee \forall x \psi)$
- $\forall x \varphi \mathrel{\vDash\dashv} \varphi$ $\qquad\qquad\qquad$ *if x is not free in φ* $\qquad\qquad$ $\exists x \varphi \mathrel{\vDash\dashv} \varphi$

By exploiting these equivalences, one can take any formula and, without affecting truth values, rectify it, translate $\Rightarrow$ into the other connectives, move quantifiers to the front and $\neg$ into subformulas.

Theorem 37. *Every formula is equivalent to a formula in prenex form. Moreover, every formula is equivalent to a formula in prenex form whose matrix is a conjunction of disjunctions of literals.*

Every universal *formula is equivalent to a conjunction of clauses and equivalent to a finite set of clauses (each clause representing its universal closure).*

The entailment relationship $\varphi \models \psi$ formalises the concept of *logical consequence*. From premises φ follows a conclusion ψ iff every model of the premises is a model of the conclusion.

A major concern in logic used to be the development of *calculi*, also called *proof systems*, which formalise the notion of deductive inference. A calculus defines derivation rules, with which formulas can be derived from formulas by purely syntactic operations. For example, a typical derivation rule might say "from $\neg\neg\varphi$ derive φ". The derivability relationship $\varphi \vdash \psi$ for a calculus holds iff there is a finite sequence of applications of derivation rules of the calculus, which applied to φ result in ψ.

Ideally, derivability should mirror entailment: a calculus is called *sound* iff whenever $\varphi \vdash \psi$ then $\varphi \models \psi$ and *complete* iff whenever $\varphi \models \psi$ then $\varphi \vdash \psi$.

Theorem 38 (Gödel, completeness theorem). *There exist calculi for first-order predicate logic such that $S \vdash \varphi$ iff $S \models \varphi$ for any set S of closed formulas and any closed formula φ.*

Thus, the semantic notion of entailment coincides with the syntactic notion of derivability. This correspondence opens up the prospects to obtain logical consequences by computation, but there are limits to these prospects.

Theorem 39 (Church-Turing, undecidability theorem). *Derivability in a correct and complete calculus is not decidable for signatures with at least one non-propositional relation symbol and a relation or function symbol of arity ≥ 2.*

A corollary of Gödel's completeness theorem is the following famous result.

Theorem 40 (Gödel-Malcev, finiteness or compactness theorem). *Let S be an infinite set of closed formulas. If every finite subset of S is satisfiable, then S is satisfiable.*

The contrapositive of the finiteness/compactness theorem, combined with its trivial converse, is often useful: a set S of closed formulas is unsatisfiable iff some finite subset of S is unsatisfiable.

Corollary 41. *For signatures with at least one non-propositional relation symbol and a relation or function symbol of arity ≥ 2, entailment, unsatisfiability, and validity are semi-decidable but not decidable, and non-entailment, satisfiability, and falsifiability are not semi-decidable.*

4.1.2 Theories

Definition 42 (Model class). *Let $\mathcal{L}$ be a signature and S a set of $\mathcal{L}$-formulas. $Mod_{\mathcal{L}}(S)$ is the class of all $\mathcal{L}$-interpretations $\mathcal{I}$ with $\mathcal{I} \models S$, i.e., the class of all $\mathcal{L}$-models of S.*

We simply write $Mod(S)$ without "$\mathcal{L}$" when we leave the signature $\mathcal{L}$ implicit. Note that in general the class $Mod(S)$ is not a set. For satisfiable S it is nonempty. If it were a set, $Mod(S)$ could be the domain of another model of S, which would be a member of $Mod(S)$ – a similarly ill-defined notion as "the set of all sets".

Definition 43 (Theory). *A theory is a set T of $\mathcal{L}$-formulas that is closed under entailment, i.e., for each $\mathcal{L}$-formula φ, if $T \models \varphi$ then $\varphi \in T$.*

The theory of a class $\mathcal{K}$ of $\mathcal{L}$-interpretations, denoted by $Th(\mathcal{K})$, is the set of all $\mathcal{L}$-formulas φ with $\mathcal{I} \models \varphi$ for each $\mathcal{I} \in \mathcal{K}$, i.e., the set of formulas satisfied by all interpretations in $\mathcal{K}$.

The theory of a set S of $\mathcal{L}$-formulas, denoted by $Th(S)$, is $Th(Mod_{\mathcal{L}}(S))$.

Proposition 44. *$Th(\mathcal{K})$ and $Th(S)$ as defined above are indeed theories, i.e., closed under entailment. In particular, $Th(S) = \{\varphi \mid S \models \varphi\}$.*

Thus, Th can also be regarded as a *closure operator* for the closure under entailment of a set of formulas.

Proposition 45. *Th is a closure operator, i.e., for all sets S, S' of formulas:*

- $S \subseteq Th(S)$ *(Th is* extensive*)*
- *if* $S \subseteq S'$ *then* $Th(S) \subseteq Th(S')$ *(Th is* monotonic*)*
- $Th(Th(S)) = Th(S)$ *(Th is* idempotent*)*

Definition 46 (Axiomatisation). *An* axiomatisation *of a theory T is a set S of formulas with $Th(S) = T$.*

A theory is finitely axiomatisable *if it has an axiomatisation that is finite.*

Finite axiomatisability is important in practice because proofs have finite length and are built up from axioms. If there are finitely many axioms, then the set of all possible proofs is computably enumerable.

Theorem 47. *There are theories that are finitely axiomatisable and theories that are not.*

The theory of equivalence relations is finitely axiomatisable by the three formulas for reflexivity, symmetry, and transitivity. The theory of the natural numbers with addition, multiplication, and the less-than relation is, by Gödel's famous incompleteness theorem, not finitely axiomatisable.

Two trivial theories are finitely axiomatisable. $Th(\emptyset)$ is the set of all valid $\mathcal{L}$-formulas because $Mod_{\mathcal{L}}(\emptyset)$ consists of all $\mathcal{L}$-interpretations. If $S = \{\bot\}$ or any other unsatisfiable set of $\mathcal{L}$-formulas, $Th(S)$ is the set of all $\mathcal{L}$-formulas because $Mod_{\mathcal{L}}(S)$ is empty. In the literature this case is sometimes excluded by adding the requirement of satisfiability to the definition of a theory.

4.1.3   Substitutions and Unification

Definition 48 (Substitution). *A* substitution *is a function σ, written in postfix notation, that maps terms to terms and is*

- *homomorphous, i.e., $f(t_1, \ldots, t_n)\sigma = f(t_1\sigma, \ldots, t_n\sigma)$ for compound terms and $c\sigma = c$ for constants.*
- *identical almost everywhere, i.e., $\{x \mid x$ is a variable and $x\sigma \neq x\}$ is finite.*

The domain of a substitution σ is the finite set of variables on which it is not identical. Its codomain is the set of terms to which it maps its domain.

A substitution σ is represented by the finite set $\{x_1 \mapsto x_1\sigma, \ldots, x_k \mapsto x_k\sigma\}$ where $\{x_1, \ldots, x_k\}$ is its domain and $\{x_1\sigma, \ldots, x_k\sigma\}$ is its codomain.

Mind the difference between Notation 31 and Definition 48: With variable assignments, the notation $\{x_1 \mapsto d_1, \ldots, x_k \mapsto d_k\}$ represents a *partial* function, which for variables other than $x_1, \ldots, x_k$ is undefined. With substitutions, the notation $\{x_1 \mapsto t_1, \ldots, x_k \mapsto t_k\}$ represents a *total* function, which for variables other than $x_1, \ldots, x_k$ is the identity.

For example, the substitution mapping x to a and y to $f(y)$ and any other variable to itself is represented by $\{x \mapsto a,\ y \mapsto f(y)\}$. The shortened notation $\{x/a,\ y/f(y)\}$ will also be used in later sections of this survey.[8]

---

[8] In the literature several notational conventions coexist, including the ones used here and the reverse form $\{a/x,\ f(y)/y\}$. This can be confusing in cases like $\{u/v\}$.

Substitutions can be combined by functional composition, $t(\sigma\tau) = (t\sigma)\tau$. The identity substitution ε, which maps every term to itself, is the neutral element for functional composition.

Definition 49 (Subsumption ordering). *A term s subsumes a term t, denoted $s \leq t$, iff there exists a substitution ϑ with $s\vartheta = t$. One also says that t is an instance of s, or t is more specific than s, or s is more general than t.*

A substitution σ subsumes a substitution τ, denoted $\sigma \leq \tau$, iff there exists a substitution ϑ with $\sigma\vartheta = \tau$. One also says that τ is an instance of σ, or τ is more specific than σ, or σ is more general than τ.

Two terms mutually subsume each other iff they are equal up to variable renaming. Mutual subsumption is an equivalence relation, on whose equivalence classes $\leq$ is a well-founded partial ordering. Its minimum is the equivalence class of all variables. Its maximal elements are the singleton classes of ground terms. If there are function symbols with arity > 0, there are infinite strictly increasing chains: $x \leq f(x) \leq f(f(x)) \leq f(f(f(x))) \leq \ldots$

In the case of substitutions, the ordering is also well-founded. The equivalence class of variable permutations, which includes the identity substitution ε, is the minimum. There are no maximal elements: $\sigma \leq \sigma\{x \mapsto y\}$ for any x, y not in the domain of σ.

Definition 50 (Unification). *Two terms s and t are unifiable, if there exists a substitution σ with $s\sigma = t\sigma$. In this case σ is called a unifier of s and t.*

A most general unifier or mgu is a minimal element w.r.t. the subsumption ordering among the set of all unifiers of s and t. If σ is a most general unifier of s and t, the term $s\sigma$ is called a most general common instance of s and t.

Theorem 51 (Robinson [138], unification theorem). *Any most general unifier of two terms subsumes all their unifiers.*

Thus, any two most general unifiers of two terms mutually subsume each other. This implies that any two most general common instances of two terms are equal up to variable renaming. Furthermore, among the unifiers of two terms there is always an *idempotent* most general unifier σ, that is, $\sigma\sigma = \sigma$. This is the case iff none of the variables from its domain occurs in its codomain.

Definition 52 (Ground substitution, ground instance). *A ground substitution is a substitution whose codomain consists of ground terms only. A grounding substitution for a term t is a ground substitution σ whose domain includes all variables in t, such that $t\sigma$ is ground. A ground instance of t is an instance of t that is ground.*

The application of a substitution σ to a set or tuple of terms, to a quantifier-free formula or set of quantifier-free formulas, or to other mathematical objects having terms as constituents, is defined by canonical extension. Thus, the notion of an instance or a ground instance or a grounding substitution for such an object is also defined canonically. For example, let φ be $p(x) \land q(y, z) \Rightarrow r(x, f(y), z)$

and $\sigma = \{x \mapsto f(v), y \mapsto a\}$. Then $\varphi\sigma$ is $p(f(v)) \wedge q(a, z) \Rightarrow r(f(v), f(a), z)$. One grounding substitution for φ is $\{x \mapsto a, y \mapsto f(a), z \mapsto a, v \mapsto a\}$.

For formulas containing quantifiers, however, it is technically more intricate to define the corresponding notions. We define only special cases involving ground substitutions.

Definition 53 (Instance of a formula). *Let φ be a formula and σ a ground substitution. Then $\varphi\sigma$ is the formula obtained from φ by replacing each free variable occurrence x in φ by $x\sigma$.*

For example, let φ be the formula $(\forall x[\exists x p(x) \wedge q(x)] \Rightarrow [r(x, y) \vee \forall x s(x)])$ and $\sigma = \{x \mapsto a\}$. Then $\varphi\sigma$ is $(\forall x[\exists x p(x) \wedge q(x)] \Rightarrow [r(a, y) \vee \forall x s(x)])$. Note that there may be three kinds of variable occurrences in φ. Those that are free and in the domain of σ, such as x in $r(x, y)$, become ground terms in $\varphi\sigma$. Those that are free and not in the domain of σ, such as y in $r(x, y)$, remain free in $\varphi\sigma$. Those that are bound in φ, such as x in $p(x)$, remain bound in $\varphi\sigma$. Because of the latter case it does not make sense to define grounding substitutions for formulas with quantifiers.

Definition 54 (Ground instance of a formula). *Let φ be a formula. Let φ' be a rectified form of φ. Let φ'' be obtained from φ' by removing each occurrence of a quantifier for a variable. A ground instance of φ is a ground instance of φ''.*

For example, let φ be $(\forall x[\exists x p(x) \wedge q(x)] \Rightarrow [r(x, y) \vee \forall x s(x)])$. A rectified form with quantifiers removed is $([p(v) \wedge q(u)] \Rightarrow [r(x, y) \vee s(w)])$. Assuming a signature with constants a, b, c, d and unary function symbol f, two ground instances of φ are $([p(a) \wedge q(a)] \Rightarrow [r(a, a) \vee s(a)])$ and $([p(a) \wedge q(f(b))] \Rightarrow [r(f(f(c)), c) \vee s(d)])$.

In general the set of ground instances of a non-ground term or formula is infinite, but it is always computably enumerable.

Typically, one is only interested in ground instances of formulas in which all variables are of the same kind: free or universally quantified or existentially quantified.

4.1.4   Herbrand Interpretations

An interpretation according to Tarski's model theory may use any nonempty set as its domain. Herbrand interpretations are interpretations whose domain is the so-called Herbrand universe, the set of all ground terms constructible with the signature considered. This is a syntactic domain, and under the common assumption that all symbol sets of the signature are computably enumerable, so is the Herbrand universe. In an Herbrand interpretation quantification reduces to ground instantiation.

A fundamental result is that Herbrand interpretations can imitate interpretations with arbitrary domains provided that the formulas under consideration are universal. A set of universal formulas has an arbitrary model iff it has an Herbrand model. As a consequence, it is satisfiable iff the set of its ground instances is, which is essentially a propositional problem. These results are the key to algorithmic treatment of the semi-decidable semantic notions: validity, unsatisfiability, entailment.

Definition 55 (Herbrand universe and base). *Let $\mathcal{L}$ be a signature for first-order predicate logic. The* Herbrand universe *$HU_{\mathcal{L}}$ is the set of all ground $\mathcal{L}$-terms. The* Herbrand base *$HB_{\mathcal{L}}$ is the set of all ground $\mathcal{L}$-atoms.*

If $\mathcal{L}$ does not specify any constant, $HU_{\mathcal{L}}$ is empty. From now on we assume that $\mathcal{L}$ specifies at least one constant. As usual, we leave the signature $\mathcal{L}$ implicit when it is clear from context, and write simply HU and HB without "$\mathcal{L}$".

Definition 56 (Herbrand interpretation). *An interpretation $\mathcal{I}$ is an* Herbrand interpretation *if $dom(\mathcal{I}) = HU$ and $f^{\mathcal{I}}(t_1, \ldots, t_n) = f(t_1, \ldots, t_n)$ for each n-ary function symbol f and all $t_1, \ldots, t_n \in HU$.*

Thus, the value of a ground term t in an Herbrand interpretation is the term t itself. Furthermore, it turns out that the truth values of quantified formulas depend on the truth values of their ground instances.

Theorem 57. *Let $\mathcal{I}$ be an Herbrand interpretation and φ a formula that may or may not contain a free occurrence of the variable x.*

- *$\mathcal{I} \models \forall x \varphi$ iff $\mathcal{I} \models \varphi\{x \mapsto t\}$ for each $t \in HU$.*
- *$\mathcal{I} \models \exists x \varphi$ iff $\mathcal{I} \models \varphi\{x \mapsto t\}$ for at least one $t \in HU$.*

According to Definition 32, the right hand sides should be $\mathcal{I}[x \mapsto t] \models \varphi$. The theorem states that the effect of modifying the interpretation's variable assignment can be achieved by applying the ground substitution $\{x \mapsto t\}$ to φ. This result crucially depends on the interpretation's being an Herbrand interpretation. Here are two counter-examples for non-Herbrand interpretations:

Example 58. Consider a signature containing a unary relation symbol p and a constant a and no other symbols. Then the only member of HU is a. Let $\mathcal{I}$ be the non-Herbrand interpretation with $dom(\mathcal{I}) = \{1, 2\}$ and $a^{\mathcal{I}} = 1$ and $p^{\mathcal{I}} = \{1\}$. Then $\mathcal{I} \models p(a)$ and $\mathcal{I}[x \mapsto 1] \models p(x)$ and $\mathcal{I}[x \mapsto 2] \not\models p(x)$.

- $\mathcal{I} \not\models \forall x \, p(x)$, but $\mathcal{I} \models p(x)\{x \mapsto t\}$ for each $t \in HU = \{a\}$.
- $\mathcal{I} \models \exists x \, \neg p(x)$, but $\mathcal{I} \not\models \neg p(x)\{x \mapsto t\}$ for each $t \in HU = \{a\}$.

Example 59. Consider a signature containing a unary relation symbol p and for each arity an infinite and enumerable set of function symbols of that arity. Then the set HU is enumerable. Let $\mathcal{I}$ be a non-Herbrand interpretation with $dom(\mathcal{I}) = \mathbb{R}$, the set of real numbers, with arbitrary definitions for the constants and function symbols, and $p^{\mathcal{I}} = \{t^{\mathcal{I}} \mid t \in HU\} \subseteq \mathbb{R}$.

Since HU is enumerable, there are $r \in \mathbb{R}$ with $r \notin p^{\mathcal{I}}$, thus $\mathcal{I}[x \mapsto r] \not\models p(x)$.

- $\mathcal{I} \not\models \forall x \, p(x)$, but $\mathcal{I} \models p(x)\{x \mapsto t\}$ for each $t \in HU$.
- $\mathcal{I} \models \exists x \, \neg p(x)$, but $\mathcal{I} \not\models \neg p(x)\{x \mapsto t\}$ for each $t \in HU$.

In both examples the reason why the theorem does not hold is that the interpretation uses a domain with more elements than there are ground terms. The latter example shows that this is not only a phenomenon of finite signatures.

Corollary 60. *Let S be a set of universal closed formulas and S_{ground} the set of all ground instances of members of S. For each Herbrand interpretation $\mathcal{I}$ holds $\mathcal{I} \models S$ iff $\mathcal{I} \models S_{ground}$.*

Terms have a fixed value in all Herbrand interpretations. Only the interpretation of relation symbols is up to each particular Herbrand interpretation. This information can conveniently be represented by a set of ground atoms.

Definition 61 (Herbrand interpretation represented by ground atoms). *Let V be some fixed variable assignment in HU. Let $B \subseteq HB$ be a set of ground atoms. Then $HI(B)$ is the Herbrand interpretation with variable assignment V and $p^{HI(B)} = \{(t_1, \ldots, t_n) \mid p(t_1, \ldots, t_n) \in B\}$ for each n-ary relation symbol p.*

Thus, a set B of ground atoms represents the Herbrand interpretation $HI(B)$ that satisfies all ground atoms in B and falsifies all ground atoms not in B. Except for the variable assignment, $HI(B)$ is uniquely determined by B. The notation introduced earlier, $HI(B)[V]$, can be used to specify a particular variable assignment.

Definition 62 (Herbrand interpretation induced by an interpretation). *Let $\mathcal{I}$ be an arbitrary interpretation. The Herbrand interpretation induced by $\mathcal{I}$, denoted $HI(\mathcal{I})$, is $HI(\{A \in HB \mid \mathcal{I} \models A\})$.*

Proposition 63. *For each signature and up to the fixed variable assignment:*
   $HI(\mathcal{I}) = \mathcal{I}$ *iff* $\mathcal{I}$ *is an Herbrand interpretation.*
   There is a bijection between the set of all Herbrand interpretations and the set of all subsets of HB.

Theorem 64 (Herbrand model induced by a model). *Let φ be a universal closed formula. Each model of φ induces an Herbrand model of φ, that is, for each interpretation $\mathcal{I}$, if $\mathcal{I} \models \varphi$ then $HI(\mathcal{I}) \models \varphi$.*

The converse holds for ground formulas, but not in general. Reconsider Examples 58 and 59 above. In both of them $HI(\mathcal{I}) \models \forall x\, p(x)$, but $\mathcal{I} \not\models \forall x\, p(x)$. The examples also show that the correct direction does not hold for non-universal formulas. In both of them $\mathcal{I} \models \exists x\, \neg p(x)$, but $HI(\mathcal{I}) \not\models \exists x\, \neg p(x)$.

At first glance the result may seem weak, but it establishes that if there is a model, there is an Herbrand model. The converse is trivial. Taking into account the finiteness/compactness theorem, we get:

Corollary 65 ("Herbrand Theorem"). *Let S be a set of universal closed formulas and let S_{ground} be the set of all ground instances of members of S. S is unsatisfiable iff S has no Herbrand model iff S_{ground} has no Herbrand model iff there is a finite subset of S_{ground} that has no Herbrand model.*

The latter is essentially a propositional problem, see the discussion on propositional vs. ground on page 8. In the literature, the name *Herbrand theorem* usually refers to this reduction of semantic notions from the first-order level to the propositional level.

4.1.5 Skolemization

The results on Herbrand interpretations cover only universal formulas. Skolemization is a technique to transform a non-universal formula φ into a universal formula φ_{sko}. The transformation is not model-preserving, in general $\varphi \not\models \varphi_{sko}$. But it preserves the existence of models, φ is satisfiable iff φ_{sko} is satisfiable.

Here is an example of the transformation:

φ is the $\mathcal{L}$-formula $\forall y \forall z (married(y, z) \Rightarrow \exists x \, parent(y, x))$

φ_{sko} is the $\mathcal{L}_{sko}$-formula $\forall y \forall z (married(y, z) \Rightarrow parent(y, f(y)))$

where $\mathcal{L}$ is a signature with 2-ary relation symbols *married* and *parent*, in which the 1-ary function symbol f does not occur, and $\mathcal{L}_{sko}$ is $\mathcal{L}$ extended with f. Both formulas are satisfiable and falsifiable.

Let $\mathcal{I}$ be an $\mathcal{L}_{sko}$-interpretation with $\mathcal{I} \models \varphi_{sko}$. Intuitively, for each y for which $parent(y, f(y))$ is true in $\mathcal{I}$, there exists at least one x for which $parent(y, x)$ is true in $\mathcal{I}$, namely $f(y)$. This intuition can be used to show formally that $\mathcal{I} \models \varphi$. Thus, $\varphi_{sko} \models \varphi$.

The converse does not hold. Let $\mathcal{I}$ be the $\mathcal{L}_{sko}$-interpretation with a domain of people for whom it is indeed the case that every married person has a child, and with the "natural" interpretation of the relation symbols and $f^{\mathcal{I}}$ the identity function on the domain. Now $\mathcal{I} \models \varphi$, but $\mathcal{I} \not\models \varphi_{sko}$ because no-one from the domain is their own parent. Thus, $\varphi \not\models \varphi_{sko}$.

However, the fact that $\mathcal{I} \models \varphi$, does not depend on the interpretation of f. We construct another interpretation $\mathcal{I}'$ that differs from $\mathcal{I}$ just in that $f^{\mathcal{I}'}$ maps only childless people to themselves but maps people with children to their firstborn. Still $\mathcal{I}' \models \varphi$, but also $\mathcal{I}' \models \varphi_{sko}$. From a model of φ we have constructed another model of φ, which is also a model of φ_{sko}.

The principles illustrated with this example apply in general.

Definition 66 (Skolemization step). *Let φ be a rectified closed formula containing an occurrence of a subformula $Qx\psi$ where Q is an existential quantifier with positive or a universal quantifier with negative polarity in φ. Let the variables with free occurrences in ψ be $\{x, y_1, \ldots, y_k\}$, $k \geq 0$. Let f be a k-ary function symbol that does not occur in φ.*

Let φ_s be φ with the occurrence of $Qx\psi$ replaced by $\psi\{x \mapsto f(y_1, \ldots, y_k)\}$. Then the transformation from φ to φ_s is called a Skolemization step with Skolem function symbol f and Skolem term $f(y_1, \ldots, y_k)$.

Proposition 67. *If a Skolemization step transforms φ to φ_s, then $\varphi_s \models \varphi$, and for each interpretation $\mathcal{I}$ with $\mathcal{I} \models \varphi$ there exists an interpretation $\mathcal{I}'$ with $\mathcal{I}' \models \varphi$ and $\mathcal{I}' \models \varphi_s$. Moreover, $\mathcal{I}'$ coincides with $\mathcal{I}$ except possibly $f^{\mathcal{I}'} \neq f^{\mathcal{I}}$.*

Corollary 68 (Skolemization). *Let $\mathcal{L}$ be a signature for first-order predicate logic and S a computably enumerable set of closed $\mathcal{L}$-formulas. There is an extension $\mathcal{L}_{sko}$ of $\mathcal{L}$ by new function symbols and a computably enumerable set S_{sko} of universal closed $\mathcal{L}$-formulas, such that S is unsatisfiable iff S_{sko} is unsatisfiable.*

4.1.6 Equality

So far we have considered results for the version of first-order predicate logic without equality. Let us now assume a signature $\mathcal{L}$ containing a special 2-ary relation symbol $\doteq$ for equality.

Definition 69 (Normal interpretation). *An interpretation $\mathcal{I}$ is normal, iff it interprets the relation symbol $\doteq$ with the equality relation on its domain, i.e., iff $\doteq^{\mathcal{I}}$ is the relation $\{(d,d) \mid d \in dom(\mathcal{I})\}$. For formulas or sets of formulas φ and ψ:*

$\mathcal{I} \models_= \varphi$ *iff $\mathcal{I}$ is normal and $\mathcal{I} \models \varphi$.*
$\varphi \models_= \psi$ *iff for each normal interpretation $\mathcal{I}$: if $\mathcal{I} \models_= \varphi$ then $\mathcal{I} \models_= \psi$.*

The version of first-order predicate logic with built-in equality simply makes the normality requirement part of the definition of an interpretation. Let us now investigate the relationship between the two versions.

Definition 70 (Equality axioms). *Given a signature $\mathcal{L}$ with 2-ary relation symbol $\doteq$, the set $EQ_{\mathcal{L}}$ of equality axioms for $\mathcal{L}$ consists of the formulas:*

- $\forall x\ x \doteq x$ *(reflexivity of $\doteq$)*
- $\forall x \forall y (x \doteq y \Rightarrow y \doteq x)$ *(symmetry of $\doteq$)*
- $\forall x \forall y \forall z ((x \doteq y \wedge y \doteq z) \Rightarrow x \doteq z)$ *(transitivity of $\doteq$)*
- *for each n-ary function symbol f, $n > 0$*   *(substitution axiom for f)*
  $\forall x_1 \ldots x_n \forall x_1' \ldots x_n' ((x_1 \doteq x_1' \wedge \ldots \wedge x_n \doteq x_n') \Rightarrow f(x_1, \ldots, x_n) \doteq f(x_1', \ldots, x_n'))$
- *for each n-ary relation symbol p, $n > 0$*   *(substitution axiom for p)*
  $\forall x_1 \ldots x_n \forall x_1' \ldots x_n' ((x_1 \doteq x_1' \wedge \ldots \wedge x_n \doteq x_n' \wedge p(x_1, \ldots, x_n)) \Rightarrow p(x_1', \ldots, x_n'))$

Note that $EQ_{\mathcal{L}}$ may be infinite, depending on $\mathcal{L}$. Actually, symmetry and transitivity of $\doteq$ follow from reflexivity of $\doteq$ and the substitution axiom for $\doteq$ and could be omitted.

Theorem 71 (Equality axioms)

- *For each interpretation $\mathcal{I}$, if $\mathcal{I}$ is normal then $\mathcal{I} \models_= EQ_{\mathcal{L}}$.*
- *For each interpretation $\mathcal{I}$ with $\mathcal{I} \models EQ_{\mathcal{L}}$ there is a normal interpretation $\mathcal{I}_=$ such that for each formula φ: $\mathcal{I} \models \varphi$ iff $\mathcal{I}_= \models_= \varphi$.*
- *For each set S of formulas and formula φ: $EQ_{\mathcal{L}} \cup S \models \varphi$ iff $S \models_= \varphi$.*

Corollary 72 (Finiteness or compactness theorem with equality). *Let S be an infinite set of closed formulas with equality. If every finite subset of S has a normal model, then S has a normal model.*

The results of Theorem 71 indicate that the equality axioms seem to define pretty much of the intended meaning of $\doteq$. However, they do not define it fully, nor does any other set of formulas.

Theorem 73 (Model extension theorem). *For each interpretation $\mathcal{I}$ and each set $D' \supseteq dom(\mathcal{I})$ there is an interpretation $\mathcal{I}'$ with $dom(\mathcal{I}') = D'$ such that for each formula φ: $\mathcal{I} \models \varphi$ iff $\mathcal{I}' \models \varphi$.*

Proof. (sketch) Fix an arbitrary element $d \in dom(\mathcal{I})$. The idea is to let all "new" elements behave exactly like d. Define an auxiliary function π mapping each "new" element to d and each "old" element to itself:

$$\pi : D' \rightarrow dom(\mathcal{I}), \quad \pi(d') := d \text{ if } d' \notin dom(\mathcal{I}), \quad \pi(d') := d' \text{ if } d' \in dom(\mathcal{I}).$$

Define $f^{\mathcal{I}'} : D'^{\,n} \rightarrow D'$, $\quad f^{\mathcal{I}'}(d_1, \ldots, d_n) := f^{\mathcal{I}}(\pi(d_1), \ldots, \pi(d_n))$ and $p^{\mathcal{I}'} \subseteq D'^{\,n}$, $\quad p^{\mathcal{I}'} := \{ (d_1, \ldots, d_n) \in D'^{\,n} \mid (\pi(d_1), \ldots, \pi(d_n)) \in p^{\mathcal{I}} \}$ for all signature symbols and arities. □

By this construction, if $(d, d) \in \doteq^{\mathcal{I}}$ then $(d, d') \in \doteq^{\mathcal{I}'}$ for each $d' \in D'$ and the fixed element $d \in dom(\mathcal{I})$. Hence, any proper extension $\mathcal{I}'$ of a normal interpretation $\mathcal{I}$ does not interpret $\doteq$ with the equality relation on D'.

Corollary 74. *Every satisfiable set of formulas has non-normal models.*

Every model of $EQ_{\mathcal{L}}$ interprets $\doteq$ with a congruence relation on the domain. The equality relation is the special case with singleton congruence classes. Because of the model extension theorem, there is no way to prevent models with larger congruence classes, unless equality is treated as built-in by making interpretations normal by definition.

4.1.7 Model Cardinalities

Theorem 75. *Lower bounds of model cardinalities can be expressed in first-order predicate logic without equality.*

Example: all models of the following satisfiable set of formulas have domains with cardinality ≥ 3:

$$\{ \exists x_1 (\; p_1(x_1) \wedge \neg p_2(x_1) \wedge \neg p_3(x_1)),$$
$$\exists x_2 (\neg p_1(x_2) \wedge \; p_2(x_2) \wedge \neg p_3(x_2)),$$
$$\exists x_3 (\neg p_1(x_3) \wedge \neg p_2(x_3) \wedge \; p_3(x_3)) \; \}$$

Example: all models of the following satisfiable set of formulas have infinite domains: $\quad \{ \forall x \, \neg(x < x), \quad \forall x \forall y \forall z (x < y \wedge y < z \Rightarrow x < z), \quad \forall x \exists y \, x < y \}$.

Theorem 76. *Upper bounds of model cardinalities cannot be expressed in first-order predicate logic without equality.*

Theorem 77. *Each satisfiable set of formulas without equality has models with infinite domain.*

Corollary 78. *Finiteness cannot be expressed in first-order predicate logic without equality.*

The above are immediate consequences of the model extension theorem 73. The remaining results are about the version of first-order predicate logic with built-in equality.

Theorem 79. *Bounded finiteness can be expressed in first-order predicate logic with equality. That is, for any given natural number $k \geq 1$, the upper bound k of model cardinalities can be expressed.*

Example: all normal models of the following satisfiable formula have domains with cardinality ≤ 3: $\qquad \exists x_1 \exists x_2 \exists x_3 \forall y(y \dot= x_1 \vee y \dot= x_2 \vee y \dot= x_3)$.

Theorem 80. *If a set of formulas with equality has arbitrarily large finite normal models, then it has an infinite normal model.*

Proof. Let S be such that for each $k \in \mathbb{N}$ there is a normal model of S whose domain has finite cardinality $> k$. For each $n \in \mathbb{N}$ let φ_n be the formula $\forall x_0 \ldots x_n \exists y(\neg(y \dot= x_0) \wedge \ldots \wedge \neg(y \dot= x_n))$ expressing "more than $n+1$ elements". Then every finite subset of $S \cup \{\varphi_n \mid n \in \mathbb{N}\}$ has a normal model. By the finiteness/compactness theorem with equality, $S \cup \{\varphi_n \mid n \in \mathbb{N}\}$ has a normal model, which obviously cannot be finite, but is also a normal model of S. $\qquad \square$

Corollary 81. *A satisfiable set of formulas with equality has either only finite normal models of a bounded cardinality, or infinite normal models.*

Corollary 82. *Unbounded finiteness cannot be expressed in first-order predicate logic with equality.*

Theorem 83 (Löwenheim-Skolem). *Every satisfiable enumerable set of closed formulas has a model with a finite or infinite enumerable domain.*

Theorem 84 (Löwenheim-Skolem-Tarski). *If a set of closed formulas has a model of some infinite cardinality, it has a model of every infinite cardinality.*

4.1.8 Inadequacy of Tarski Model Theory for Query Languages

The domain of an interpretation according to Tarski may be any nonempty set. On the one hand, this has a tremendous advantage: first-order predicate logic can be used to model statements about any arbitrary application domain. On the other hand, it has effects that may be undesirable in the context of query languages.

For query languages, it is desirable that the following can be expressed:

1. By default, different constants are differently interpreted. The *unique name assumption* is such a frequent requirement in applications that a mechanism making it available by default would come in handy.

Tarski model theory does not provide such a mechanism. Interpretations may well interpret different constants identically, unless formulas explicitly prevent that. An explicit formalisation is cumbersome, albeit possible.

2. Function symbols are to be interpreted as term constructors. In many applications it makes sense to group pieces of data that belong together. For instance, a function symbol *person* might be used to construct a term such as *person(Mary, Miller, 1984)*, which simply serves as a compound data structure. In such cases it does not make sense to interpret the symbol *person* with arbitrary functions. It should be interpreted as just a term constructor.

This is not expressible in first-order predicate logic with Tarski model theory.

3. No more should hold than what is explicitly specified. A *closed world assumption* makes sense in query answering applications such as transportation timetables, which are based on the tacit understanding that no other than the explicitly listed connections are actually available.

Such a minimality restriction corresponds to an induction principle, which does not necessarily hold in Tarski interpretations. In fact, it is well-known that the induction principle cannot be expressed in first-order predicate logic with Tarski model theory.

4. Disregard infinite models. Real-world query answering applications are often finite by their nature and need to consider only interpretations with finite domains. In this case, infinite domains are not only superfluous, but they bring along phenomena that may be "strange" from the viewpoint of the application and would not be found in finite domains.

Consider an application about the hierarchy in enterprises, where a boss's boss is also a boss, but nobody is their own boss. The obvious conclusion is that there must be someone at the top of the hierarchy who does not have a boss. However, this conclusion is not justified for interpretations with infinite domains. The "strange" phenomenon that such a hierarchy may have no top at all has to be taken into account because of interpretations with infinitely many employees, although such interpretations are irrelevant for this application.

For a somewhat more contrived example, consider a group of married couples, where each husband has exactly one sister among the group and no wife has more than one brother among the group. The obvious conclusion[9] is that every wife must have a brother, because otherwise there would be more brothers than sisters in the group, contradicting the assumptions about the numbers of siblings. However, this conclusion is not justified for interpretations with infinite domains. If there are as many couples as there are natural numbers, each husband number n can be the brother of wife number $n + 1$, leaving wife number 0 without a brother, while everyone else has exactly one sibling in the group. The "strange" phenomenon that there may be a bijection between a set and a proper subset can only occur in infinite domains, but for the example such domains are irrelevant.

In order to avoid such "strange" phenomena, it would be necessary to restrict interpretations to finite ones. However, finiteness is not expressible in first-order predicate logic with Tarski model theory.

5. Definability of the transitive closure of a binary relation. The transitive closure of a binary relation is relevant in many query answering applications. Consider a traffic application, where a binary relation symbol r is used to represent direct connections between junctions, e.g., direct flights between airports. Another binary relation symbol t is used to represent direct or indirect connections of any *finite* length, i.e., with finitely many stopovers. Connections of infinite length do not make sense in this application.

---

[9] Excluding polygamy, same-sex marriage, etc.

The mathematical concept for "all connections of any finite length" is called the "transitive closure" of a binary relation. Thus, the intention is that t be interpreted as the relation that is the transitive closure of the relation with which r is being interpreted. An attempt to express this intention in first-order predicate logic could be the following closed formula:

$$\forall x \forall z \Big(t(x,z) \Leftrightarrow \big(r(x,z) \vee \exists y \, [t(x,y) \wedge t(y,z)] \big) \Big) \qquad (\star)$$

Here $\varphi \Leftrightarrow \psi$ abbreviates $(\varphi \Rightarrow \psi) \wedge (\psi \Rightarrow \varphi)$. The $\Leftarrow$ direction makes sure that in every model $\mathcal{I}$ of $(\star)$ the relation $t^{\mathcal{I}}$ is transitive and includes the relation $r^{\mathcal{I}}$. The $\Rightarrow$ direction has the purpose to add an only-if part to the definition of $t^{\mathcal{I}}$.

Each interpretation interpreting t as the transitive closure of the interpretation of r, is indeed a model of $(\star)$. However, the intended converse, that every model of $(\star)$ interprets t as the transitive closure of the interpretation of r, does not hold:

Proof. Let $D = \{1 - 2^{-n} \mid n \in \mathbb{N}\} = \{0, \frac{1}{2}, \frac{3}{4}, \frac{7}{8}, \frac{15}{16}, \ldots\}$.

Let $dom(\mathcal{I}) = D$, let $r^{\mathcal{I}} = \{(1 - 2^{-n}, 1 - 2^{-(n+1)}) \mid n \in \mathbb{N}\}$, the "immediate successor" relation on D, and let $t^{\mathcal{I}}$ be the arithmetic $<$-relation on D. Then $t^{\mathcal{I}}$ is the transitive closure of $r^{\mathcal{I}}$ and $\mathcal{I}$ is a model of $(\star)$.

Let $dom(\mathcal{I}') = D \cup \{1\}$, let $r^{\mathcal{I}'} = r^{\mathcal{I}}$, and let $t^{\mathcal{I}'}$ be the arithmetic $<$-relation on $D \cup \{1\}$. Then $t^{\mathcal{I}'}$ is not the transitive closure of $r^{\mathcal{I}'}$, it contains the additional pairs $(d, 1)$ for all $d \in D$, but there is no connection of finite length via the "immediate successor" relation on D between any $d \in D$ and 1. Yet, $\mathcal{I}'$ is also a model of $(\star)$. $\qquad\square$

This may appear like another instance of point 4. But there are also counterexamples with finite domain:

Proof. Let $D = \{0, 1\}$, let $dom(\mathcal{I}) = D$, let $r^{\mathcal{I}} = \{(0,0), (1,1)\}$, the equality relation on D, and let $t^{\mathcal{I}} = \{(0,0), (0,1), (1,1)\}$, the $\leq$-relation on D. The transitive closure of $r^{\mathcal{I}}$ is $r^{\mathcal{I}}$ itself. Thus, $t^{\mathcal{I}}$ is not the transitive closure of $r^{\mathcal{I}}$. Yet, $\mathcal{I}$ is a model of $(\star)$. $\qquad\square$

If an interpretation interprets t as intended, then it is a model of $(\star)$, but the converse does not hold. Would some fine-tuning of $(\star)$ guarantee that the converse holds, too? In fact, no set of formulas can guarantee that.

Proof. Assume there is a satisfiable set S of closed formulas such that for each interpretation $\mathcal{I}$, $\mathcal{I} \models S$ iff $t^{\mathcal{I}}$ is the transitive closure of $r^{\mathcal{I}}$. That is, for each $(d_0, d) \in t^{\mathcal{I}}$ there are finitely many "stopover" elements $d_1, \ldots, d_k$ with $k \geq 0$, and $\{(d_0, d_1), \ldots, (d_k, d)\} \subseteq r^{\mathcal{I}}$.

Let a and b be constants not occurring in S. For each $n \in \mathbb{N}$ let φ_n be the closed formula as follows:

φ_0 is $t(a,b) \wedge \neg r(a,b)$
φ_1 is $\varphi_0 \wedge \neg \exists x_1 (r(a, x_1) \wedge r(x_1, b))$
φ_2 is $\varphi_1 \wedge \neg \exists x_1 \exists x_2 (r(a, x_1) \wedge r(x_1, x_2) \wedge r(x_2, b))$
φ_3 is $\varphi_2 \wedge \neg \exists x_1 \exists x_2 \exists x_3 (r(a, x_1) \wedge r(x_1, x_2) \wedge r(x_2, x_3) \wedge r(x_3, b))$

$\vdots$

In the traffic scenario, each formula φ_n expresses that there is a connection between (the interpretations of) a and b, but not with n or less stopovers.

For each $n \in \mathbb{N}$ the set $S \cup \{\varphi_n\}$ is satisfied by interpreting t as the transitive closure of r, and a and b as the endpoints of an r-chain with $n + 1$ "stopover" elements in between. Thus, every finite subset of $S \cup \{\varphi_n \mid n \in \mathbb{N}\}$ has a model. By the finiteness/compactness theorem, $S \cup \{\varphi_n \mid n \in \mathbb{N}\}$ has a model $\mathcal{I}$, which is thus also a model of S. In this model, $(a^{\mathcal{I}}, b^{\mathcal{I}}) \in t^{\mathcal{I}}$, because $\mathcal{I}$ satisfies φ_0, but there is no finite set of "stopover" elements with $\{(a^{\mathcal{I}}, d_1), (d_1, d_2), \ldots, (d_k, b^{\mathcal{I}})\} \subseteq r^{\mathcal{I}}$, because $\mathcal{I}$ also satisfies φ_k.

Thus, S has a model $\mathcal{I}$ in which $t^{\mathcal{I}}$ is not the transitive closure of $r^{\mathcal{I}}$, which contradicts the assumption.   □

The transitive closure of a base relation is the *smallest* transitive relation that includes the base relation. This inductive characterisation shows that the phenomenon is in fact an instance of point 3. In first-order predicate logic with Tarski model theory one can enforce that t is interpreted with a transitive relation that includes the transitive closure of the interpretation of r, but one cannot prevent that t is interpreted with a larger transitive relation.

Another instance of the same phenomenon is that the connectedness of a finite directed graph, i.e., the existence of a path of any possible finite length between two nodes, cannot be expressed.

6. Restrictions to specific classes of domains or to specific classes of interpretations. In general, applications are not concerned with all imaginable domains and interpretations, but with limited classes of domains and interpretations. Such restrictions have to be expressed by appropriate formulas – if such formulas exist.

As discussed earlier, the restriction to domains with a given cardinality cannot be expressed in first-order predicate logic without equality. Nor can interpretations be restricted to normal ones. In these cases a way out is to use the version of first-order predicate logic with built-in equality.

But the same kind of problems may arise with application-specific concepts that cannot be expressed. For instance, an application about boards of trustees might require that they consist of an odd number of members in order to avoid inconclusive votes. In first-order predicate logic with or without built-in equality one cannot express the restriction to domains with odd cardinality. In this case there is no way out, a version with suitable built-ins is not available.

Several approaches aim at overcoming some of these problems 1 to 6. For example, considering only *Herbrand interpretations* and *Herbrand models* instead of general interpretations [88], addresses points 1 and 2. Considering only *minimal Herbrand models* addresses point 3. Considering only *finite* interpretations and models, the realm of *finite model theory* [61], addresses point 4. Unfortunately, all such approaches raise new problems themselves. Such approaches and problems are discussed below.

4.2   Herbrand Model Theory

Most of the information in this subsection is based on a technical report by Hinrichs and Genesereth [88]. Herbrand model theory restricts interpretations to Herbrand interpretations (without equality, except if otherwise stated).

Definition 85. *For formulas or sets of formulas φ and ψ:*
   φ is Herbrand valid iff it is satisfied in each Herbrand interpretation.
   φ is Herbrand satisfiable iff it is satisfied in some Herbrand interpretation.
   φ is Herbrand unsatisfiable iff it is falsified in each Herbrand interpretation.
   $\mathcal{I} \models_{Hb} \varphi$ iff $\mathcal{I}$ is an Herbrand interpretation and $\mathcal{I} \models \varphi$.
   $\varphi \models_{Hb} \psi$ iff for each Herbrand interpretation $\mathcal{I}$: if $\mathcal{I} \models_{Hb} \varphi$ then $\mathcal{I} \models_{Hb} \psi$.

4.2.1   Herbrand Model Theory vs. Tarski Model Theory

Obviously, each Herbrand satisfiable formula or set of formulas is Tarski satisfiable. The converse does not hold. Assume a signature with a unary relation symbol p and a constant a and no other symbol, such that the Herbrand universe is $HU = \{a\}$. The set $S = \{p(a), \exists x \neg p(x)\}$ is Tarski satisfiable, but Herbrand unsatisfiable. However, S is Herbrand satisfiable with respect to a larger signature containing an additional constant b. Thus, Herbrand satisfiability depends on the signature, whereas Tarski satisfiability does not.

There are two conventions for establishing the signature of a set of formulas: (1) *explicitly* by an *a priori* specification; (2) *implicitly* by gathering the symbols from the formulas considered. Convention (1) is common in mathematical logic and also underlies the definitions in this survey. Convention (2) is widespread in computational logic. With Tarski model theory, either convention is fine. With Herbrand model theory, convention (2) would not be reasonable: the Herbrand satisfiable set $\{p(a), \neg p(b), \exists x \neg p(x)\}$ would have an Herbrand unsatisfiable subset $\{p(a), \exists x \neg p(x)\}$. In contrast, convention (1) ensures that Herbrand (un)satisfiability translates to subsets/supersets like Tarski (un)satisfiability.

With Tarski model theory, there is no strong correspondence between individuals in the semantic domain and names, i.e., terms as syntactic representations of semantic individuals. Semantic individuals need not have a name (see Examples 58 and 59), and different names may refer to the same semantic individual. With Herbrand model theory, every semantic individual has a name. Moreover, with normal Herbrand interpretations different ground terms represent different individuals, thus incorporating the unique name assumption.

Some momentous results do not copy from Tarski to Herbrand model theory.

Theorem 86. *The following results do not hold for Herbrand model theory: The model extension theorem 73. The Löwenheim-Skolem-Tarski theorem 84. The finiteness/compactness theorem 40.*

Proof. The first two are rather immediate. For the last one assume a signature with a unary relation symbol p, a unary function symbol f, a constant a, and no other symbol. Then the Herbrand base is $HB = \{p(a), p(f(a)), p(f(f(a))), \ldots\}$. Although each finite subset of $S = \{\exists x \neg p(x)\} \cup HB$ is Herbrand satisfiable, S is Herbrand unsatisfiable. $\square$

Note that many of the properties of Tarski model theory that appear to be undesirable for query and rule languages depend on one of the results that do not hold for Herbrand model theory. Another property of Tarski model theory is that some theories are not finitely axiomatisable (see Theorem 47). This is so for Herbrand model theory as well.

Proposition 87. *There are Herbrand interpretations $\mathcal{I}$ for which the theory $Th(\{\mathcal{I}\}) = \{\varphi \mid \mathcal{I} \models_{Hb} \varphi\}$ is not finitely axiomatisable.*

Proof. Assume a signature $\mathcal{L}$ with at least one constant, one function symbol of arity > 0, and one relation symbol of arity > 0. Then the Herbrand base $HB_{\mathcal{L}}$ is infinite, thus its powerset is not enumerable. There is a bijection between this set and the set of all Herbrand interpretations for $\mathcal{L}$ (Proposition 63), which is therefore not enumerable either. On the other hand, the set of $\mathcal{L}$-formulas is enumerable, hence the set of its finite subsets is enumerable. There are more Herbrand interpretations than potential finite axiomatisations.   □

The price for the simplicity of Herbrand model theory is a loss of semi-decidability of semantic properties. Let us start with an immediate consequence of the "Herbrand Theorem" (Corollary 65).

Proposition 88. *Let S be a set of universal closed formulas. Let φ be a closed formula such that $\neg\varphi$ is universal. Then S is Herbrand satisfiable iff S is Tarski satisfiable and $S \models_{Hb} \varphi$ iff $S \models \varphi$.*

Corollary 89. *Herbrand unsatisfiability and Herbrand entailment are not decidable, but they are semi-decidable for formulas meeting the conditions above.*

Theorem 90 ([88]). *For formulas that do not meet the conditions above, Herbrand unsatisfiability and Herbrand entailment are not semi-decidable.*

Herbrand Model Theory for Finite Herbrand Base. A rather natural restriction for applications is to consider only signatures with a finite number of relation symbols and of constants and without function symbols of arity ≥ 1, as in datalog. This restriction ensures that the Herbrand universe HU and the Herbrand base HB are finite, hence there are only finitely many Herbrand interpretations.

The following results are immediate [88]. See also Theorem 57 and the discussion on propositional vs. ground on page 8.

Proposition 91. *If the Herbrand base HB is finite*

- *Quantification can be transformed into conjunction and disjunction.*
- *The expressive power of the logic is the same as for propositional logic with finitely many propositional relation symbols.*
- *Herbrand satisfiability and Herbrand entailment are decidable.*
- *Every theory is finitely axiomatisable.*

Remark 92. Sets that are Tarski satisfiable with infinite domains only, such as $S = \{ \forall x \neg(x < x), \ \forall x \forall y \forall z(x < y \wedge y < z \Rightarrow x < z), \ \forall x \exists y \, x < y \}$, are Herbrand unsatisfiable if the Herbrand universe HU is finite.

4.3   Finite Model Theory

Model theory investigates how syntactic properties of formulas and structural properties of their models relate to each other. Finiteness of the domain is certainly an interesting structural property of interpretations, but it does not have a syntactic counterpart, because finiteness is not expressible in first-order predicate logic (Corollaries 78 and 82). Because of that, finite models were for a long time not a major concern in model theory.

Since the late 1970s, this has changed. Finite model theory gained interest in computer science because of its connections to discrete mathematics, complexity theory, database theory, and to computation in general. Finite interpretations can be encoded as words, i.e., finite sequences of symbols, making computation applicable to model theory. Finite interpretations can describe terminating computations. Databases can be formalised as finite interpretations, such that queries correspond to formulas evaluated against finite interpretations. Complexity classes can be represented as queries (in some logic) that are evaluated against finite interpretations. Because of all these connections, many issues in finite model theory are motivated by computer science.

The purpose of this subsection is to outline salient elementary aspects of "entailment in the finite" and to list results in finite model theory that may be useful for query languages or query evaluation and optimisation methods.

Definition 93. *A finite interpretation is an interpretation with finite domain. For formulas or sets of formulas φ and ψ:*

φ is finitely valid *iff it is satisfied in each finite interpretation.*
φ is finitely satisfiable *iff it is satisfied in some finite interpretation.*
φ is finitely unsatisfiable *iff it is falsified in each finite interpretation.*
$\mathcal{I} \models_{fin} \varphi$ iff $\mathcal{I}$ is a finite interpretation and $\mathcal{I} \models \varphi$.
$\varphi \models_{fin} \psi$ iff for each finite interpretation $\mathcal{I}$: if $\mathcal{I} \models_{fin} \varphi$ then $\mathcal{I} \models_{fin} \psi$.

Finite interpretations are special Tarski interpretations, hence there are obvious inclusions between corresponding notions: each valid formula is finitely valid, each finitely satisfiable formula is satisfiable, etc. These inclusions are proper.

For example, $\{ \forall x \neg(x < x), \quad \forall x \forall y \forall z(x < y \land y < z \Rightarrow x < z), \quad \forall x \exists y \, x < y \}$ is a satisfiable, but finitely unsatisfiable set of formulas, and the single formula $[\forall x \neg(x < x) \land \forall x \forall y \forall z(x < y \land y < z \Rightarrow x < z)] \Rightarrow \exists x \forall y \neg(x < y)$ is finitely valid, but not valid. Strict orderings in finite domains necessarily have maximal elements, but in infinite domains may not have maximal elements.

An example with equality is that any injection of a domain in itself is necessarily surjective in finite domains, but may not be surjective in infinite domains. The formula $\forall x \forall x'(f(x) \doteq f(x') \Rightarrow x \doteq x') \land \neg \forall y \exists x \, y \doteq f(x)$ has normal models, but no finite normal models.

The model relationship (Definition 32) is defined by a recursive algorithm for evaluating a formula in an interpretation. There are several reasons why this algorithm may not terminate for infinite interpretations, such as the quantifier cases or potentially undecidable relations and incomputable functions over the domain. None of these reasons applies to finite domains. Thus we have

Theorem 94. *The theory $Th(\{\mathcal{I}\}) = \{\varphi \mid \mathcal{I} \models_{fin} \varphi\}$ is decidable for each finite interpretation $\mathcal{I}$.*

Definition 95 (Isomorphic interpretations). *Let $\mathcal{L}$ be a signature for first-order predicate logic and let $\mathcal{I}$ and $\mathcal{J}$ be $\mathcal{L}$-interpretations. An isomorphism of $\mathcal{I}$ into $\mathcal{J}$ is a function $\pi : dom(\mathcal{I}) \to dom(\mathcal{J})$ such that*

- $\pi : dom(\mathcal{I}) \to dom(\mathcal{J})$ *is a bijection.*
- $\pi(c^{\mathcal{I}}) = c^{\mathcal{J}}$ *for each constant c of $\mathcal{L}$.*
- $\pi(f^{\mathcal{I}}(d_1, \dots, d_n)) = f^{\mathcal{J}}(\pi(d_1), \dots, \pi(d_n))$
  for each n-ary $(n \geq 1)$ function symbol f of $\mathcal{L}$ and all $d_1, \dots, d_n \in dom(\mathcal{I})$.
- $p^{\mathcal{I}} = p^{\mathcal{J}}$ *for each propositional relation symbol of $\mathcal{L}$*
- $(d_1, \dots, d_n) \in p^{\mathcal{I}}$ *iff* $(\pi(d_1), \dots, \pi(d_n)) \in p^{\mathcal{J}}$
  for each n-ary $(n \geq 1)$ relation symbol p of $\mathcal{L}$ and all $d_1, \dots, d_n \in dom(\mathcal{I})$.

$\mathcal{I} \cong \mathcal{J}$, *pronounced $\mathcal{I}$ and $\mathcal{J}$ are isomorphic, iff such an isomorphism exists.*

Note that the variable assignments of isomorphic interpretations need not be compatible.

Proposition 96. *If $\mathcal{I} \cong \mathcal{J}$, then for each closed formula φ: $\mathcal{I} \models \varphi$ iff $\mathcal{J} \models \varphi$.*
    If π is an isomorphism of $\mathcal{I}$ into $\mathcal{J}$ and V is a variable assignment in $dom(\mathcal{I})$, then $\pi \circ V$ is a variable assignment in $dom(\mathcal{J})$ and for each formula φ:
$\mathcal{I}[V] \models \varphi$ iff $\mathcal{J}[\pi \circ V] \models \varphi$.

Definition 97. *For $k \in \mathbb{N}$ let $\mathbb{N}_k = \{0, \dots, k\}$ denote the initial segment of $\mathbb{N}$ with cardinality $k + 1$. Let V_0 be the variable assignment in $\mathbb{N}_k$ for arbitrary k with $x^{V_0} = 0$ for each variable x.*

Proposition 98. *Each finite interpretation is isomorphic to an interpretation with domain $\mathbb{N}_k$ for some $k \in \mathbb{N}$.*

Proposition 99. *For finite signatures there are for each $k \in \mathbb{N}$ only finitely many interpretations with domain $\mathbb{N}_k$ and variable assignment V_0.*

Proof. For each $k \in \mathbb{N}$ and each $n \in \mathbb{N}$ the set $\mathbb{N}_k^n$ contains $(k + 1)^n$ tuples. Thus there are $2^{((k+1)^n)}$ possible relations and $(k + 1)^{((k+1)^n)}$ possible functions of arity n, to which the finitely many signature symbols can be mapped by an interpretation. $\qquad\square$

Corollary 100. *For finite signatures, the problem whether a finite set of closed formulas has a model with a given finite cardinality, is decidable.*

This makes possible a simple semi-decision procedure for finite satisfiability: iterating k from 1 upwards, check whether the given formulas have a model with cardinality k.

Corollary 101. *For finite signatures, finite satisfiability, finite falsifiability, and finite non-entailment of finite sets of closed formulas are semi-decidable.*

Theorem 102 (Trakhtenbrot). *For signatures with a non-propositional rela-tion symbol and a relation or function symbol of arity ≥ 2, finite validity is not semi-decidable.*

Corollary 103. *For finite signatures with a non-propositional relation symbol and a relation or function symbol of arity ≥ 2, finite satisfiability, finite fal-sifiability, and finite non-entailment of finite sets of closed formulas are semi-decidable, but not decidable. Finite unsatisfiability, finite validity, and finite en-tailment are not semi-decidable,*

This is a remarkable reversal of results in the two model theories: (classical) Tarksi unsatisfiability is semi-decidable and Tarski satisfiability is not, whereas finite satisfiability is semi-decidable and finite unsatisfiability is not.

Corollary 104. *There is no complete calculus for finite entailment.*

Theorem 105. *The finiteness/compactness theorem does not hold for finite model theory.*

Proof. For each $n \in \mathbb{N}$ let φ_n be a finitely satisfiable formula all of whose models have domains with cardinality $\geq n + 1$. Such formulas exist, see the examples to Theorem 75. Then each finite subset of $S = \{\varphi_n \mid n \in \mathbb{N}\}$ is finitely satisfiable, but S is not finitely satisfiable. $\square$

Another difference to Tarski model theory is that finite interpretations can be characterised up to isomorphism by formulas.

Theorem 106. *For each finite interpretation $\mathcal{I}$ there exists a set $S_{\mathcal{I}}$ of closed formulas such that for each interpretation $\mathcal{J}$: $\mathcal{J} \cong \mathcal{I}$ iff $\mathcal{J} \models S_{\mathcal{I}}$.*
  If the signature is finite, there is a single closed formula rather than a set of closed formulas with this property.

This does not extend to infinite interpretations, among other reasons, because there are "not enough" formulas. An example for an interpretation that cannot be characterised up to isomorphism is the standard model of arithmetic, whose domain is the set of natural numbers. If any would-be axiomatisation is satisfied by the standard model, it also has non-standard models that are not isomor-phic to the standard model. In order to characterise the standard model up to isomorphism, an axiomatisation would have to include the induction axiom (or equivalent), which is not expressible in first-order predicate logic.

4.3.1   Finitely Controllable Formulas

Definition 107. *A closed formula is* finitely controllable, *if it is either unsat-isfiable or finitely satisfiable. A fragment of first-order predicate logic is* finitely controllable, *if each closed formula belonging to that fragment is.*

For finitely controllable formulas, satisfiability coincides with finite satisfiability. Note that a satisfiable finitely controllable formula may well have infinite models, but it is guaranteed to have also a finite model.

Theorem 108. *For finite signatures, satisfiability of a finitely controllable closed formula is decidable.*

Proof. By intertwining a semi-decision procedure for Tarski unsatisfiability with a semi-decision procedure for finite satisfiability. □

Because of this, finite controllability is one of the major techniques for proving that satisfiability in some fragment of first-order predicate logic is decidable. If one can show for that fragment that the existence of a model implies the existence of a finite model, decidability follows from the theorem above.

Theorem 109. *The fragments of first-order predicate logic consisting of closed formulas in prenex form with a quantifier prefix of one of the following forms are finitely controllable. The notation Q^* means that there may be zero or more consecutive occurrences of this quantifier.*
- $\exists^*\forall^*$ *possibly with equality*   *(Bernays-Schönfinkel prefix class)*
- $\exists^*\forall\exists^*$ *possibly with equality*   *(Ackermann prefix class)*
- $\exists^*\forall\forall\exists^*$ *without equality*   *(Gödel prefix class)*

As can be seen from their names, these decidable fragments were identified long before computer science existed. A more recent fragment, which is highly relevant to query languages, is the following.

Definition 110 (FO^2). *The fragment of first-order predicate logic with equality whose formulas contain no variables other than x and y (free or bound) is called two-variable first-order predicate logic or FO^2.*

Theorem 111. *FO^2 is finitely controllable.*

As an illustration of the expressive power of this fragment, consider a directed graph. It is possible to express in FO^2 queries such as "does a given node a have an ingoing edge?" or "is every node with property p reachable from a via at most two edges?" More generally, FO^2 can express queries for properties that can be checked by a successive analysis of pairs of elements in the domain. It cannot express queries for global properties that require a simultaneous analysis of larger parts of the domain, such as "is there a cycle in the graph?" In particular, transitivity of a binary relation cannot be expressed.

Many logics that are of interest to knowledge representation, for instance several modal and description logics, can be seen as two-variable logics embedded in suitable extensions of FO^2. See [81] for an overview.

4.3.2   0-1 Laws
The following information is taken from an article by Ronald Fagin entitled "Finite-Model Theory – a Personal Perspective" [66].

As a motivating example, let us assume a signature with 2-ary function symbols $+$ and $\times$ and the set of formulas axiomatising a field.[10] Let φ be the conjunction of these (finitely many) axioms. The negation $\neg\varphi$ of this formula would

---

[10] A field is an algebraic structure where both operations have an inverse. The set of rational numbers $\mathbb{Q}$ with addition and multiplication and the set of real numbers $\mathbb{R}$ with addition and multiplication are examples of fields.

seem to be very uninteresting, because, intuitively, if we consider arbitrary theories, it is highly unlikely that the theory happens to be a field, which means that $\neg\varphi$ is "almost surely true" in such theories.

In order to make this intuition more precise, imagine that a finite interpretation with cardinality n is randomly generated, such that the probability for a ground atom to be true in this interpretation is $\frac{1}{2}$ for each ground atom independently of the truth values of other ground atoms. For formulas φ let $P_n(\varphi)$ denote the probability that such a randomly generated interpretation satisfies φ.

Definition 112. *A formula φ is* almost surely true *iff* $\lim_{n\to\infty} P_n(\varphi) = 1$, *i.e., with increasing cardinality of interpretations the asymptotic probability for φ to be true is 1.*

Theorem 113 (0-1 law). *For each closed formula φ, either φ or $\neg\varphi$ is almost surely true.*

Quoting Fagin [66], who cites Vardi:

> There are three possibilities for a closed formula: it can be surely true (valid), it can be surely false (unsatisfiable), or it can be neither. The third possibility (where a closed formula is neither valid nor unsatisfiable) is the common case. When we consider asymptotic probabilities, there are *a priori* three possibilities: it can be almost surely true (asymptotic probability 1), it can be almost surely false (asymptotic probability 0), or it can be neither (either because there is no limit, or because the limit exists and is not 0 or 1). Again, we might expect the third possibility to be the common case. The 0-1 law says that the third possibility is not only not the common case, but it is, in fact, impossible!

This result may seem like an amusing oddity, but it is a significant tool for proving that certain properties of finite interpretations cannot be expressed in first-order predicate logic.

For instance if there were a closed formula φ_{even} that is satisfied by a finite interpretation iff the domain of this interpretation has even cardinality, then $P_n(\varphi_{even})$ would be 1 for even n and 0 for odd n, hence there would be no limit. By the 0-1 law, this is impossible, therefore such a formula φ_{even} does not exist. Hence, evenness is not expressible in first-order predicate logic.

The same kind of argument based on the 0-1 law can be used to show for many properties of finite interpretations that they are not expressible in first-order predicate logic. Often, such properties involve some form of "counting". It is part of the folklore knowledge about first-order predicate logic that it "cannot count".

There are several theorems similar to the 0-1 law. A research issue in this area is to determine (fragments of) other logics that admit the 0-1 law. For example, see [104].

5   Declarative Semantics: Adapting Classical Model Theory to Rule Languages

The declarative semantics of definite programs can be defined in model-theoretic terms using specific properties of syntactical classes of formulas that are more general than definite clauses.

Definite clauses (Definition 21) are also called *definite rules*. Some authors call them *positive definite rules* when they want to emphasise that they exclude normal clauses, i.e., clauses with negative literals in their antecedent. In line with this terminology, a definite program is also called a set of positive definite rules or simply a *positive rule set*. This terminology will also be used below.

In this section, a signature $\mathcal{L}$ for first-order predicate logic is assumed. Unless otherwise stated, semantic notions such as (un)satisfiability or logical equivalence refer to unrestricted interpretations, i.e., interpretations with domains of any kind, especially of any cardinality.

5.1   Minimal Model Semantics of Definite Rules

This subsection is inspired by [144].

As discussed in Subsection 3.2, a rule is a shorthand notation for its universal closure. Thus, a positive definite rule is on the one hand a special *universal* formula (defined in Subsection 3.1). On the other hand, it is also a special *inductive* formula (defined below).

Both classes of formulas have interesting model-theoretic properties. If a set of universal formulas is satisfiable, then it is Herbrand satisfiable, i.e., it has an Herbrand model. If a set of inductive formulas is satisfiable, then the intersection of its models is also a model, provided that the models intersected are compatible. Moreover, each set of definite inductive formulas is satisfiable.

Together this means that each set of positive definite rules has a unique minimal Herbrand model, which is the intersection of all Herbrand models of the set. This minimal model can be taken as "the meaning" of the set of positive definite rules in a model-theoretic sense.

5.1.1   Compatibility and Intersection of Interpretations

Definition 114 (Compatible set of interpretations). *A set $\{\mathcal{I}_i \mid i \in I\}$ of interpretations with index set I is called* compatible, *iff*

- $I \neq \emptyset$.
- $D = \bigcap \{dom(\mathcal{I}_i) \mid i \in I\} \neq \emptyset$.
- *all interpretations of a function symbol coincide on the common domain:*
  $f^{\mathcal{I}_i}(d_1, \ldots, d_n) = f^{\mathcal{I}_j}(d_1, \ldots, d_n)$ *for each n-ary (n $\geq$ 0) function symbol f, for all $i, j \in I$, and for all $d_1, \ldots, d_n \in D$.*
- *a variable is identically interpreted in all interpretations:*
  $x^{\mathcal{I}_i} = x^{\mathcal{I}_j}$ *for each variable x and all $i, j \in I$.*

Definition 115 (Intersection of a compatible set of interpretations).
Let $\{\mathcal{I}_i \mid i \in I\}$ be a compatible set of interpretations. Then $\bigcap\{\mathcal{I}_i \mid i \in I\}$ is defined as the interpretation $\mathcal{I}$ with

- $dom(\mathcal{I}) = D = \bigcap\{dom(\mathcal{I}_i) \mid i \in I\}$.
- a function symbol is interpreted as the intersection of its interpretations: $f^{\mathcal{I}}(d_1, \ldots, d_n) = f^{\mathcal{I}_i}(d_1, \ldots, d_n)$ for each n-ary $(n \geq 0)$ function symbol f, for an arbitrary $i \in I$, and for all $d_1, \ldots, d_n \in D$.
- a relation symbol is interpreted as the intersection of its interpretations: $p^{\mathcal{I}} = \bigcap_{i \in I} p^{\mathcal{I}_i}$ for each relation symbol p.
- a variable is interpreted like in all given interpretations: $x^{\mathcal{I}} = x^{\mathcal{I}_i}$ for each variable x and an arbitrary $i \in I$.

5.1.2 Universal Formulas and Theories

Let us recall some notions and results from previous sections.

The *polarity* of a subformula within a formula (Definition 13) is positive, if the subformula occurs within the scope of an even number of explicit or implicit negations, and negative, if this number is odd. A formula is *universal* (Definition 14), if all its occurrences of $\forall$ have positive and of $\exists$ have negative polarity. This is the case iff the formula is equivalent to a formula in prenex form containing no existential quantifier (Theorem 37). A *universal theory* is a theory axiomatised by a set of universal formulas.

The Herbrand universe HU is the set of ground terms, and the Herbrand base HB is the set of ground atoms of the given signature (Definition 55). An Herbrand interpretation interprets each ground term with itself (Definition 56). There is a bijection between the set of all Herbrand interpretations and the set of all subsets of HB (Proposition 63). Each subset $B \subseteq HB$ of ground atoms induces the Herbrand interpretation $HI(B)$ that satisfies all ground atoms in B and falsifies all ground atoms not in B.

If a set S of universal formulas has a model $\mathcal{I}$, then the Herbrand interpretation $HI(\mathcal{I})$ induced by $\mathcal{I}$ is also a model of S (Theorem 64). Thus, S is satisfiable iff it has an Herbrand model.

Note that this is easily disproved for non-universal formulas. For example, if the signature consists of a unary relation symbol p and a constant a and no other symbols, then $HB = \{p(a)\}$ and there are exactly two Herbrand interpretations: $HI(\emptyset)$ and $HI(\{p(a)\})$. The formula $p(a) \wedge \exists x \neg p(x)$ is satisfiable, but neither of the two Herbrand interpretations is a model of it. See also Examples 58 and 59 in Section 4.1.

For sets of universal formulas in general, and for sets of positive definite rules in particular, satisfiability coincides with Herbrand satisfiability. This is interesting for two reasons. First, the domain of Herbrand interpretations is (computably) enumerable. Second, Herbrand interpretations are syntactically defined. Being enumerable and syntactically defined, Herbrand interpretations are amenable to computing.

Returning to the notions introduced above, the following result is obtained by straightforward application of the definitions:

Lemma 116. *Let $\{B_i \mid i \in I\}$ be a set of sets of ground atoms, i.e., $B_i \subseteq HB$ for each $i \in I$. If this set is nonempty, then*

- *$\{HI(B_i) \mid i \in I\}$ is a compatible set of interpretations, i.e., its intersection is defined.*
- *$\bigcap\{HI(B_i) \mid i \in I\} = HI\big(\bigcap\{B_i \mid i \in I\}\big)$ i.e., its intersection is the Herbrand interpretation induced by the intersection of the sets of ground atoms.*

Definition 117 (Set of inducers of Herbrand models of a set of formulas). *For a set S of formulas, the set of inducers of its Herbrand models is $Mod_{HB}(S) = \{B \subseteq HB \mid HI(B) \models S\}$.*

Note that although the class $Mod(S)$ of all models of S is not in general a set (Definition 42), the class $Mod_{HB}(S)$ of all inducers of Herbrand models of S is a set: a subset of the powerset of the Herbrand base HB.

Obviously, $Mod_{HB}(S) = \emptyset$ for unsatisfiable S. If S is satisfiable and non-universal, $Mod_{HB}(S)$ may or may not be empty. If S is satisfiable and universal, $Mod_{HB}(S) \neq \emptyset$ and the intersection of the set of its Herbrand models is defined. We introduce a notation for the intersection that is always defined:

Notation 118. *For a set S of formulas:*

$$Mod_{\cap}(S) = \begin{cases} \bigcap Mod_{HB}(S) & \text{if } Mod_{HB}(S) \neq \emptyset \\ HB & \text{if } Mod_{HB}(S) = \emptyset \end{cases}$$

Theorem 119. *If S is universal, then $Mod_{\cap}(S) = \{A \in HB \mid S \models A\}$.*

Proof. If S is unsatisfiable, both sides are equal to HB. If S is satisfiable:

"$\subseteq$": Let $A \in Mod_{\cap}(S)$, thus $A \in B$ for each $B \subseteq HB$ with $HI(B) \models S$. To be shown: $S \models A$. Let $\mathcal{I}$ be an arbitrary model of S. By Theorem 64, $HI(B') \models S$ where $B' = \{A' \in HB \mid \mathcal{I} \models A'\}$. Hence by the first sentence, $A \in B'$, therefore $\mathcal{I} \models A$. Since $\mathcal{I}$ was arbitrary, we have shown $S \models A$.

"$\supseteq$": Let $A \in HB$ with $S \models A$, i.e., each model of S satisfies A. Then for each $B \subseteq HB$ with $HI(B) \models S$ holds $HI(B) \models A$ and therefore $A \in B$. Hence $A \in Mod_{\cap}(S)$. □

The definition guarantees that $HI(Mod_{\cap}(S))$ is always an Herbrand interpretation. If S is universal and unsatisfiable, then $HI(Mod_{\cap}(S))$ satisfies all ground atoms, but is obviously not a model of S. If S is universal and satisfiable, then $HI(Mod_{\cap}(S))$ is the intersection of all Herbrand models of S. It is worth noting that in this case $HI(Mod_{\cap}(S))$ is not necessarily a model of S. The reason is that some formulas in S may be "indefinite":

Example 120. Assume a signature consisting of a unary relation symbol p and constants a and b and no other symbols. Let $S = \{p(a) \vee p(b)\}$. Then $Mod_{HB}(S) = \{ \{p(a)\}, \{p(b)\}, \{p(a), p(b)\} \}$. But $HI(Mod_{\cap}(S)) = HI(\emptyset)$ is not a model of S.

Non-closedness of Herbrand models under intersection is possible for sets of general universal formulas, but, as we shall see, not for sets of positive definite rules. Before coming to that, let us take a look at another property of sets of universal formulas, which is one if their most significant characteristics.

Definition 121 (Subinterpretation). *An interpretation $\mathcal{I}_1$ is a subinterpretation of an interpretation $\mathcal{I}_2$, denoted $\mathcal{I}_1 \subseteq \mathcal{I}_2$, if*

- *$dom(\mathcal{I}_1) \subseteq dom(\mathcal{I}_2)$.*
- *the interpretations of a function symbol coincide on the common domain:*
  $f^{\mathcal{I}_1}(d_1, \ldots, d_n) = f^{\mathcal{I}_2}(d_1, \ldots, d_n)$ for each n-ary (n $\geq$ 0) function symbol f
  and all $d_1, \ldots, d_n \in dom(\mathcal{I}_1)$.
- *the interpretations of a relation symbol coincide on the common domain:*
  $p^{\mathcal{I}_1} = p^{\mathcal{I}_2} \cap dom(\mathcal{I}_1)^n$ for each n-ary (n $\geq$ 0) relation symbol p.
- *a variable is identically interpreted in the interpretations:*
  $x^{\mathcal{I}_1} = x^{\mathcal{I}_2}$ for each variable x.

If in addition $dom(\mathcal{I}_1) \neq dom(\mathcal{I}_2)$, then $\mathcal{I}_1$ is a proper subinterpretation *of $\mathcal{I}_2$.*

The subinterpretation relationship is a partial ordering on interpretations. Given a set of compatible interpretations where all interpretations of a relation symbol coincide on the common domain, its intersection is a subinterpretation of each interpretation in the set.

Lemma 122. *Let $\mathcal{I}_1$ and $\mathcal{I}_2$ be interpretations with $\mathcal{I}_1 \subseteq \mathcal{I}_2$. Let V be an arbitrary variable assignment in $dom(\mathcal{I}_1)$. Let φ be a quantifier-free formula. Then $\mathcal{I}_1[V] \models \varphi$ iff $\mathcal{I}_2[V] \models \varphi$.*

Proof. By structural induction on φ. $\qquad\square$

Theorem 123 (Subinterpretation property of universal formulas). *Let $\mathcal{I}_1$ and $\mathcal{I}_2$ be interpretations with $\mathcal{I}_1 \subseteq \mathcal{I}_2$. For each universal closed formula φ, if $\mathcal{I}_2 \models \varphi$ then $\mathcal{I}_1 \models \varphi$.*

Proof. By considering a prenex form of φ and applying the previous lemma. $\qquad\square$

As an illustration, consider a signature with 2-ary function symbols $+$ and $\times$ and the equality relation symbol $\doteq$. Let $dom(\mathcal{I}_1) = \mathbb{Q}$, the set of rational numbers, and $dom(\mathcal{I}_2) = \mathbb{R}$, the set of real numbers, and let $+$ and $\times$ be interpreted as addition and multiplication on the respective domain. Then $\mathcal{I}_1 \subseteq \mathcal{I}_2$. The formula $\forall x \forall y \ (x+x) \times y \doteq x \times (y+y)$ is true in $\mathcal{I}_2$ (the reals) and, being universal, it is also true in $\mathcal{I}_1$ (the rationals). The non-universal formula $\forall y \exists x \ y \doteq x \times x \times x$ is true in $\mathcal{I}_2$ (the reals), but not true in $\mathcal{I}_1$ (the rationals).

An immediate consequence of the theorem is that if a set of closed formulas is universal, then all subinterpretations of its models are models. A famous result by Łos and Tarski establishes the converse: If a set of closed formulas is satisfied by all subinterpretations of its models, then it is equivalent to a set of universal closed formulas. Thus, the subinterpretation property is a semantic characterisation of the syntactic class of universal formulas.

5.1.3   Inductive Formulas and Theories

Definition 124 (Positive and negative formulas). *A formula φ is called* positive *(or* negative, *respectively) iff every atom occurring in φ has positive (or negative, respectively) polarity in φ.*

Definition 125 (Inductive formula). *A generalised definite rule is a formula of the form* $\forall^*((A_1 \wedge \ldots \wedge A_n) \leftarrow \varphi)$ *where* φ *is positive and the* A_i *are atoms for* $1 \leq i \leq n$. *It is also called a* definite inductive formula.

A generalised definite goal is a formula of the form $\forall^* \varphi$ *where* φ *is negative. It is also called an* integrity constraint.

An inductive formula *is either a generalised definite rule or a generalised definite goal. A* (definite) inductive theory *is a theory axiomatised by a set of (definite) inductive formulas.*

Recall that $\forall^*$ denotes the universal closure. The point of a generalised definite rule is that its only positive atoms are conjunctively connected and that all variables occurring in this conjunction are universally quantified. A generalised definite goal is logically equivalent to a formula $\forall^* \neg \varphi$ and thus to $\forall^*(\bot \leftarrow \varphi)$ with positive φ, which shows the similarity to a generalised definite rule.

Each inductive formula is equivalent to a formula in prenex form whose matrix is a conjunction of Horn clauses (Definition 21) and whose quantifier prefix starts with universal quantifiers for all variables in the consequents followed by arbitrary quantifiers for the remaining variables. For a generalised definite rule, all Horn clauses in the matrix are definite clauses. For a generalised definite goal, all Horn clauses in the matrix are definite goals. It would make sense to call inductive formulas "generalised Horn clauses" (compare Definition 21).

Let us now introduce a partial ordering on interpretations that differs slightly from the subinterpretation relationship:

Definition 126. $\mathcal{I}_1 \leq \mathcal{I}_2$ *for interpretations* $\mathcal{I}_1$ *and* $\mathcal{I}_2$ *if*

- $dom(\mathcal{I}_1) = dom(\mathcal{I}_2)$.
- *the interpretations of a function symbol coincide on the common domain:* $f^{\mathcal{I}_1}(d_1, \ldots, d_n) = f^{\mathcal{I}_2}(d_1, \ldots, d_n)$ *for each* n-*ary* $(n \geq 0)$ *function symbol* f *and all* $d_1, \ldots, d_n \in dom(\mathcal{I}_1)$.
- *the "smaller" interpretation of a relation symbol is a restriction of the other:* $p^{\mathcal{I}_1} \subseteq p^{\mathcal{I}_2}$ *for each* n-*ary* $(n \geq 0)$ *relation symbol* p.
- *a variable is identically interpreted in the interpretations:* $x^{\mathcal{I}_1} = x^{\mathcal{I}_2}$ *for each variable* x

If in addition $p^{\mathcal{I}_1} \neq p^{\mathcal{I}_2}$ *for at least one* p, *then* $\mathcal{I}_1 < \mathcal{I}_2$.

In contrast to the subinterpretation relationship, here the domains of the interpretations are the same. For subinterpretations this would imply that the interpretations of a relation symbol coincide, here the "smaller" one may be a restriction of the other. Given a set of compatible interpretations with the same domain, its intersection is $\leq$ each interpretation in the set.

Lemma 127. *Let* $\mathcal{I}_1$ *and* $\mathcal{I}_2$ *be interpretations with* $\mathcal{I}_1 \leq \mathcal{I}_2$. *Let* V *be an arbitrary variable assignment in* $dom(\mathcal{I}_1)$.

If φ *is a positive formula: if* $\mathcal{I}_1[V] \models \varphi$ *then* $\mathcal{I}_2[V] \models \varphi$
If φ *is a negative formula: if* $\mathcal{I}_2[V] \models \varphi$ *then* $\mathcal{I}_1[V] \models \varphi$

Proof. By structural induction on the matrix of a prenex form of φ. □

An interesting property of sets of generalised definite rules is that they are satisfiable. In particular, the $\leq$-largest Herbrand interpretation, which satisfies all ground atoms, is always a model.

Theorem 128. *For each set S of generalised definite rules, $HI(HB) \models S$.*

Proof. Let S be a set of generalised definite rules, thus its members have the form $\forall^*[(A_1 \wedge \ldots \wedge A_n) \leftarrow \varphi]$ where φ is positive and the A_i are atoms.

Each member of S is logically equivalent to $\forall \boldsymbol{x}[(A_1 \wedge \ldots \wedge A_n) \leftarrow \exists \boldsymbol{y}\varphi]$ where $\boldsymbol{x}$ are the variables occurring in $A_1 \ldots A_n$ and $\boldsymbol{y}$ are the other free variables of φ. It suffices to show that $HI(HB)$ satisfies each instance $[(A_1 \wedge \ldots \wedge A_n) \leftarrow \exists \boldsymbol{y}\varphi]\sigma$ where σ is a ground substitution with domain $\boldsymbol{x}$ (Theorem 57). Each of these instances is $[(A_1\sigma \wedge \ldots \wedge A_n\sigma) \leftarrow (\exists \boldsymbol{y}\varphi)\sigma]$ where the $A_i\sigma$ are ground atoms.

Since $HI(HB)$ satisfies all ground atoms, it satisfies each of these instances and thus each member of S. □

The main result about inductive formulas is that their (compatible) models are closed under intersection.

Theorem 129. *Let S be a set of inductive formulas. If $\{\mathcal{I}_i \mid i \in I\}$ is a set of compatible models of S with the same domain D, then $\mathcal{I} = \bigcap\{\mathcal{I}_i \mid i \in I\}$ is also a model of S.*

Proof. Let V be an arbitrary variable assignment in D. By definition of the partial ordering $\leq$ on interpretations, $\mathcal{I}[V] \leq \mathcal{I}_i[V]$ for each $i \in I$.

Let $\forall^*((A_1 \wedge \ldots \wedge A_n) \leftarrow \varphi)$ with positive φ be a generalised definite rule in S. If $\mathcal{I}[V] \not\models \varphi$, then $\mathcal{I}[V] \models ((A_1 \wedge \ldots \wedge A_n) \leftarrow \varphi)$. If $\mathcal{I}[V] \models \varphi$, then $\mathcal{I}_i[V] \models \varphi$ for each $i \in I$ by Lemma 127. Therefore, since each $\mathcal{I}_i$ satisfies each member of S, $\mathcal{I}_i[V] \models A_j$ for each $i \in I$ and $1 \leq j \leq n$. By Definition 115, $\mathcal{I}[V] \models A_j$ for each j with $1 \leq j \leq n$. Thus $\mathcal{I}[V] \models (A_1 \wedge \ldots \wedge A_n)$ and $\mathcal{I}[V] \models ((A_1 \wedge \ldots \wedge A_n) \leftarrow \varphi)$. In both cases, since V is arbitrary, $\mathcal{I}$ satisfies the considered member of S.

Let $\forall^*\varphi$ with negative φ be a generalised definite goal in S. Then $\mathcal{I}_i[V] \models \varphi$ for each $i \in I$, because each $\mathcal{I}_i$ satisfies each member of S. By Lemma 127, $\mathcal{I}[V] \models \varphi$. Since V is arbitrary, $\mathcal{I}$ satisfies the considered member of S. □

Corollary 130. *If S is a set of inductive formulas and $\{B_i \subseteq HB \mid i \in I\}$ is a nonempty set with $HI(B_i) \models S$ for each $i \in I$, then $HI\big(\bigcap\{B_i \mid i \in I\}\big) \models S$.*

5.1.4   Minimal Models

Definition 131 (Minimal model). *A minimal model of a set of formulas is a $\leq$-minimal member $\mathcal{I}$ of the set of all its models with domain $dom(\mathcal{I})$.*

The partial ordering $\leq$ on interpretations corresponds to the subset relationship $\subseteq$ on sets of n-tuples of the domain with which relation symbols are interpreted. A model is minimal, if there is no other model with the same domain that interprets some relation symbol with a proper subset of n-tuples of the domain. Note that the subset relationship refers to sets that are not syntactic.

For Herbrand interpretations the partial ordering $\leq$ on interpretations corresponds to the subset relationship on their inducers, which are syntactic sets.

Lemma 132. *Let S be a set of formulas.*

- *An Herbrand model of S is minimal iff it is induced by a $\subseteq$-minimal member of $Mod_{HB}(S)$.*
- *If $HI(Mod_\cap(S))$ is a model of S, it is a minimal Herbrand model of S and it is the only minimal Herbrand model of S.*

An Herbrand model $HI(B)$ of S is minimal iff there is no proper subset $B' \subset B$ such that $HI(B')$ is also a model of S. Reconsidering $S = \{p(a) \lor p(b)\}$ from Example 120 above: both $HI(\{p(a)\})$ and $HI(\{p(b)\})$ are minimal Herbrand models of S, and $HI(\{p(a), p(b)\})$ is a non-minimal Herbrand model of S.

Theorem 133. *Let S be a set of inductive formulas. If either each member of S is definite, or S is satisfiable and each member of S is universal, then $HI(Mod_\cap(S))$ is the unique minimal Herbrand model of S.*

Proof. $Mod_{HB}(S) \neq \emptyset$ in the first case by Theorem 128, in the second case by Theorem 64. By Corollary 130, $HI(Mod_\cap(S))$ is a model of S, and by the previous lemma it is the unique minimal Herbrand model of S. □

Noting that positive definite rules (i.e., definite clauses) are both universal and definite inductive formulas, and taking into account Theorem 119, we obtain:

Corollary 134 (Minimal Herbrand Model of a Definite Program). *Each set S of positive definite rules (i.e., each definite program) has a unique minimal Herbrand model. This model is the intersection of all Herbrand models of S. It satisfies precisely those ground atoms that are logical consequences of S.*

This unique minimal model of a set of positive definite rules can be regarded as its natural "meaning".

The notion of minimal model is also defined for non-Herbrand interpretations and therefore also applies to more general classes of formulas than inductive formulas. Typically, for such more general classes of formulas both the uniqueness and the closedness under intersection of minimal models are lost.

Let us now consider a generalisation of inductive formulas for which the notion of minimal models nevertheless retains a useful characterisation.

Definition 135 (Generalised rule). *A generalised rule is a formula of the form $\forall^*(\psi \leftarrow \varphi)$ where φ is positive and ψ is positive and quantifier-free.*

Among others, disjunctive clauses (Definition 21) are generalised rules. The generalised rule $(p(a) \lor p(b) \leftarrow \top)$ is equivalent to the formula from Example 120, which has two minimal Herbrand models.

Note that generalised rules, like generalised definite rules, are not necessarily universal, because their antecedent may contain quantifiers of both kinds.

Definition 136 (Implicant of a positive quantifier-free formula). *Let ψ be a positive quantifier-free formula. The set $primps(\psi)$ of pre-implicants of ψ is defined as follows depending on the form of ψ:*

- $primps(\psi) = \{\,\{\psi\}\,\}$ *if* ψ *is an atom or* $\top$ *or* $\bot$.
- $primps(\neg\psi_1) = primps(\psi_1)$.
- $primps(\psi_1 \wedge \psi_2) = \{\, C_1 \cup C_2 \mid C_1 \in primps(\psi_1),\ C_2 \in primps(\psi_2)\,\}$.
- $primps(\psi_1 \vee \psi_2) = primps(\psi_1 \Rightarrow \psi_2) = primps(\psi_1) \cup primps(\psi_2)$.

The set of implicants *of* ψ *is obtained from* $primps(\psi)$ *by removing all sets containing* $\bot$ *and by removing* $\top$ *from the remaining sets.*

Note that each implicant of a positive quantifier-free formula is a finite set of atoms and that the set of implicants is finite. Forming a conjunction of the atoms in an implicant and a disjunction of all of these conjunctions, results in a *disjunctive normal form*, which is equivalent to the original formula. If ψ is a conjunction of atoms (like the consequent of a generalised definite rule), then it has exactly one implicant, which consists of all of these atoms. If ψ is a disjunction of atoms, then each of its implicants is a singleton set consisting of one of these atoms. Taking into account that the definition of implicants applies to positive and quantifier-free formulas only, the following result is straightforward.

Lemma 137

1. *If C is an implicant of ψ, then $C \models \psi$.*
2. *For any interpretation $\mathcal{I}$, if $\mathcal{I} \models \psi$ then there exists an implicant C of ψ with $\mathcal{I} \models C$.*

Definition 138 (Supported atom). *Let $\mathcal{I}$ be an interpretation, V a variable assignment in $dom(\mathcal{I})$ and $A = p(t_1, \ldots, t_n)$ an atom, $n \geq 0$.*

- *an atom B supports A in $I[V]$ iff*
  $I[V] \models B$ and $B = p(s_1, \ldots, s_n)$ and $s_i^{I[V]} = t_i^{I[V]}$ for $1 \leq i \leq n$.
- *a set C of atoms supports A in $I[V]$ iff*
  $I[V] \models C$ and there is an atom in C that supports A in $I[V]$.
- *a generalised rule $\forall^*(\psi \leftarrow \varphi)$ supports A in I iff for each variable assignment V with $I[V] \models \varphi$ there is an implicant C of ψ that supports A in $I[V]$.*

The idea of an atom being supported is that some atom with the same relation symbol and identically interpreted term list occurs in one of the parts of the consequent of the generalised rule that have to be true when the antecedent is true. It turns out that in minimal models only those atoms are true that have to be true in this sense.

Theorem 139 (Minimal models satisfy only supported ground atoms).
Let S be a set of generalised rules. Let $\mathcal{I}$ be an interpretation with domain D. If $\mathcal{I}$ is a minimal model of S, then: For each ground atom A with $\mathcal{I} \models A$ there is a generalised rule in S that supports A in $\mathcal{I}$.

Proof. Assume that $\mathcal{I}$ is a minimal model of S and there is a ground atom A with $\mathcal{I} \models A$, such that A is not supported in $\mathcal{I}$ by any generalised rule in S.

Let $\mathcal{I}'$ be identical to $\mathcal{I}$ except that $\mathcal{I}' \not\models A$ (by removing just one tuple from the relation $p^{\mathcal{I}}$ for the relation symbol p of A). Then $\mathcal{I}' < \mathcal{I}$.

Consider an arbitrary member $\forall^*(\psi \leftarrow \varphi)$ of S. By assumption it does not support A. Let V be an arbitrary variable assignment in D. We show that $\mathcal{I}'[V] \models (\psi \leftarrow \varphi)$.

If $\mathcal{I}[V] \not\models \varphi$, by Lemma 127 also $\mathcal{I}'[V] \not\models \varphi$, hence $\mathcal{I}'[V] \models (\psi \leftarrow \varphi)$.

If $\mathcal{I}[V] \models \varphi$, then $\mathcal{I}[V] \models \psi$ because $\mathcal{I}$ is a model of S. Furthermore, by assumption for each implicant C of ψ either $\mathcal{I}[V] \not\models C$ or A is not supported in $\mathcal{I}[V]$ by any atom in C.

- If for each implicant C of ψ holds $\mathcal{I}[V] \not\models C$, then $\mathcal{I}[V] \not\models \psi$ by part (2) of Lemma 137, making this case impossible by contradiction.
- If there exists an implicant C of ψ with $\mathcal{I}[V] \models C$, then by assumption A is not supported in $\mathcal{I}[V]$ by any atom in C. By construction $\mathcal{I}'[V]$ agrees with $\mathcal{I}[V]$ on all atoms except those supporting A in $\mathcal{I}[V]$, thus $\mathcal{I}'[V] \models C$. By Lemma 137 (1), $\mathcal{I}'[V] \models \psi$. Hence $\mathcal{I}'[V] \models (\psi \leftarrow \varphi)$.

In all possible cases $\mathcal{I}'$ satisfies the generalised rule under consideration, thus $\mathcal{I}'$ is a model of S, contradicting the minimality of $\mathcal{I}$. $\square$

This result means that minimal models satisfy only such ground atoms as are supported by appropriate atoms in the consequents of the generalised rules. But the relationship between the supporting atom and the supported ground atom is of a semantic nature. The only guaranteed syntactic relationship between the two is that they share the same relation symbol.

Example 140. Consider a signature containing a unary relation symbol p and constants a and b. Let $S = \{ (p(b) \leftarrow \top) \}$.

The interpretation $\mathcal{I}$ with $dom(\mathcal{I}) = \{1\}$ and $a^{\mathcal{I}} = b^{\mathcal{I}} = 1$ and $p^{\mathcal{I}} = \{(1)\}$ is a minimal model of S. (Note that the only smaller interpretation interprets p with the empty relation and does not satisfy the rule.)

Moreover, $\mathcal{I} \models p(a)$. By the theorem, $p(a)$ is supported in $\mathcal{I}$ by $p(b)$, which can be confirmed by applying the definition.

Definition 141. *An interpretation $\mathcal{I}$ has the* unique name property, *if for each term s, ground term t, and variable assignment V in $dom(\mathcal{I})$ with $s^{\mathcal{I}[V]} = t^{\mathcal{I}[V]}$ there exists a substitution σ with $s\sigma = t$.*

Obviously, Herbrand interpretations have the unique name property. For minimal interpretations with the unique name property the relationship between the supporting atom and the supported ground atom specialises to the ground instance relationship, which is syntactic and decidable.

The converse of Theorem 139 does not hold for sets with indefinite rules such as $\{ (p(a) \vee p(b) \leftarrow \top) \}$, because the definition of *supported* cannot distinguish between implicants of rule consequent. Both atoms are supported in the Herbrand model $HI(\{p(a), p(b)\})$ of this set, although the model is not minimal.

Regarding definite rules, there was for some time a tacit conviction that satisfying only supported ground atoms was a sufficient criterion for the minimality of models. In the case of Herbrand interpretations the criterion would even be syntactic. But in fact, the converse of Theorem 139 is refuted by rather trivial counter-examples with definite rules.

Example 142. Consider $S = \{(p \leftarrow p)\}$ and its Herbrand model $HI(\{p\})$. The only ground atom satisfied by $HI(\{p\})$ is p, which is supported in $HI(\{p\})$ by the rule. But $HI(\{p\})$ is not minimal because $HI(\emptyset)$ is also a model of S.

5.2 Fixpoint Semantics of Positive Definite Rules

This subsection first summarises some general results on operators on an arbitrary set and fixpoints of such operators. The arbitrary set will afterwards be specialised to the Herbrand base.

5.2.1 Operators

Definition 143 (Operator). *Let X be a set. Let $\mathcal{P}(X)$ denote its powerset, the set of subsets of X. An* operator *on X is a mapping $\Gamma : \mathcal{P}(X) \to \mathcal{P}(X)$.*

Definition 144 (Monotonic operator). *Let X be a set. An operator Γ on X is* monotonic, *iff for all subset $M \subseteq M' \subseteq X$ holds: $\Gamma(M) \subseteq \Gamma(M')$.*

Definition 145 (Continuous operator). *Let X be a nonempty set.*
   A set $Y \subseteq \mathcal{P}(X)$ of subsets of X is directed, *if every finite subset of Y has an upper bound in Y, i.e., for each finite $Y_{fin} \subseteq Y$, there is a set $M \in Y$ such that $\bigcup Y_{fin} \subseteq M$.*
   An operator Γ on X is continuous, *iff for each directed set $Y \subseteq \mathcal{P}(X)$ of subsets of X holds: $\Gamma(\bigcup Y) = \bigcup \{\Gamma(M) \mid M \in Y\}$.*

Lemma 146. *Each continuous operator on a nonempty set is monotonic.*

Proof. Let Γ be a continuous operator on $X \neq \emptyset$. Let $M \subseteq M' \subseteq X$. Since Γ is continuous, $\Gamma(M') = \Gamma(M \cup M') = \Gamma(M) \cup \Gamma(M')$, thus $\Gamma(M) \subseteq \Gamma(M')$.   □

The converse of this lemma does not hold. Being continuous is a stronger property of operators than being monotonic.
   Note that the main purpose of the definition of continuous is to ensure that the operator commutes with set union. But there is no need to require this for all unions of sets, it suffices for unions of directed sets.

5.2.2 Fixpoints of Monotonic and Continuous Operators

Definition 147 (Fixpoint). *Let Γ be an operator on a set X. A subset $M \subseteq X$ is a* fixpoint *of Γ iff $\Gamma(M) = M$.*

Theorem 148 (Knaster-Tarski, existence of least and greatest fixpoint).
Let Γ be a monotonic operator on a nonempty set X. Then Γ has a least fixpoint $lfp(\Gamma)$ and a greatest fixpoint $gfp(\Gamma)$ with
$$lfp(\Gamma) = \bigcap\{M \subseteq X \mid \Gamma(M) = M\} = \bigcap\{M \subseteq X \mid \Gamma(M) \subseteq M\}.$$
$$gfp(\Gamma) = \bigcup\{M \subseteq X \mid \Gamma(M) = M\} = \bigcup\{M \subseteq X \mid \Gamma(M) \subseteq M\}.$$

Proof. For the least fixpoint let $L = \bigcap\{M \subseteq X \mid \Gamma(M) \subseteq M\}$.

Consider an arbitrary $M \subseteq X$ with $\Gamma(M) \subseteq M$. By definition of L we have $L \subseteq M$. Since Γ is monotonic, $\Gamma(L) \subseteq \Gamma(M)$. With the assumption $\Gamma(M) \subseteq M$ follows $\Gamma(L) \subseteq M$. Therefore (1) $\Gamma(L) \subseteq \bigcap \{M \subseteq X \mid \Gamma(M) \subseteq M\} = L$.

For the opposite inclusion, from (1) and since Γ is monotonic it follows that $\Gamma(\Gamma(L)) \subseteq \Gamma(L)$. By definition of L therefore (2) $L \subseteq \Gamma(L)$. From (1) and (2) follows that L is a fixpoint of Γ.

Now let $L' = \bigcap \{M \subseteq X \mid \Gamma(M) = M\}$. Then $L' \subseteq L$. because L is a fixpoint of Γ. The opposite inclusion $L \subseteq L'$ holds, since all sets involved in the intersection defining L', are also involved in the intersection defining L.

The proof for the greatest fixpoint is similar.   □

Definition 149 (Ordinal powers of a monotonic operator). *Let Γ be a monotonic operator on a nonempty set X. For each finite or transfinite ordinal the* upward *and* downward power *of Γ is defined as*

$$\Gamma \uparrow 0 \quad = \emptyset \qquad\qquad (base\ case) \quad \Gamma \downarrow 0 \quad = X$$
$$\Gamma \uparrow \alpha + 1 = \Gamma(\Gamma \uparrow \alpha) \qquad (successor\ case) \quad \Gamma \downarrow \alpha + 1 = \Gamma(\Gamma \downarrow \alpha)$$
$$\Gamma \uparrow \lambda \quad = \bigcup \{\Gamma \uparrow \beta \mid \beta < \lambda\} \quad (limit\ case) \quad \Gamma \downarrow \lambda \quad = \bigcap \{\Gamma \downarrow \beta \mid \beta < \lambda\}$$

Lemma 150. *Let Γ be a monotonic operator on a nonempty set X. For each ordinal α holds:*

1. $\Gamma \uparrow \alpha \;\subseteq\; \Gamma \uparrow \alpha + 1$
2. $\Gamma \uparrow \alpha \;\subseteq\; lfp(\Gamma)$.
3. *If $\Gamma \uparrow \alpha = \Gamma \uparrow \alpha + 1$, then $lfp(\Gamma) = \Gamma \uparrow \alpha$.*

Proof. 1. and 2. are shown by transfinite induction on α and 3. as follows:

If $\Gamma \uparrow \alpha = \Gamma \uparrow \alpha + 1$, then $\Gamma \uparrow \alpha = \Gamma(\Gamma \uparrow \alpha)$, i.e., $\Gamma \uparrow \alpha$ is a fixpoint of Γ, therefore $\Gamma \uparrow \alpha \subseteq lfp(\Gamma)$ by 2., and $lfp(\Gamma) \subseteq \Gamma \uparrow \alpha$ by definition.   □

Theorem 151. *Let Γ be a monotonic operator on a nonempty set X. There exists an ordinal α such that $\Gamma \uparrow \alpha = lfp(\Gamma)$.*

Proof. Otherwise, for all ordinals α by the previous lemma $\Gamma \uparrow \alpha \subseteq \Gamma \uparrow \alpha + 1$ and $\Gamma \uparrow \alpha \neq \Gamma \uparrow \alpha + 1$. Thus $\Gamma \uparrow$ injectively maps the ordinals onto $\mathcal{P}(X)$, a contradiction as there are "more" ordinals than any set can have elements.   □

Theorem 152 (Kleene). *Let Γ be a continuous operator on a nonempty set X. Then $lfp(\Gamma) = \Gamma \uparrow \omega$. ($\omega$ is the first limit ordinal, the one corresponding to $\mathbb{N}$)*

Proof. By 1. from the previous lemma, it suffices to show that $\Gamma \uparrow \omega + 1 = \Gamma \uparrow \omega$.

$$
\begin{aligned}
\Gamma \uparrow \omega + 1 &= \Gamma(\Gamma \uparrow \omega) &&\text{by definition, successor case}\\
&= \Gamma\big(\bigcup \{\Gamma \uparrow n \mid n \in \mathbb{N}\}\big) &&\text{by definition, limit case}\\
&= \bigcup \{\Gamma(\Gamma \uparrow n) \mid n \in \mathbb{N}\} &&\text{because } \Gamma \text{ is continuous}\\
&= \bigcup \{\Gamma \uparrow n + 1 \mid n \in \mathbb{N}\} &&\text{by definition, successor case}\\
&= \Gamma \uparrow \omega &&\text{by definition, base case} \qquad □
\end{aligned}
$$

An analogous result for the greatest fixpoint does not hold: it may well be that $gfp(\Gamma) \neq \Gamma \downarrow \omega$. Note that the decisive step in the proof depends on the operator being continuous. Being monotonic would not be sufficient. The theory of well-founded semantics uses operators that are monotonic, but not necessarily continuous, and therefore not covered by this theorem.

5.2.3   Immediate Consequence Operator for a Set of Positive Definite Rules

Generalised definite rules according to Definition 125 need not be universal, because so far the results on this class of formulas did not depend on universality. In this subsection, however, we consider only universal formulas.

Recall that an Herbrand interpretation satisfies a set of universal closed formulas iff it satisfies the set of its ground instances (Corollary 60). Assuming a signature with at least one constant, the Herbrand base HB is nonempty.

Let us now apply the results on operators to the case where $X = HB$ and a subset M is a set $B \subseteq HB$ of ground atoms, which induces an Herbrand interpretation. The following generalises a definition first given in [153].

Definition 153 (Immediate consequence operator). *Let S be a set of universal generalised definite rules. Let $B \subseteq HB$ be a set of ground atoms. The immediate consequence operator $\mathbf{T}_S$ for S is:*

$$\mathbf{T}_S : \mathcal{P}(HB) \rightarrow \mathcal{P}(HB)$$
$$B \quad \mapsto \{A \in HB \mid \text{ there is a ground instance } ((A_1 \wedge \ldots \wedge A_n) \leftarrow \varphi)$$
$$\text{of a member of } S \text{ with } HI(B) \models \varphi \text{ and } A = A_i$$
$$\text{for some } i \text{ with } 1 \leq i \leq n \quad \}$$

Lemma 154 ($\mathbf{T}_S$ is continuous). *Let S be a set of universal generalised definite rules. The immediate consequence operator $\mathbf{T}_S$ is continuous.*

Lemma 155 ($\mathbf{T}_S$ is monotonic). *Let S be a set of universal generalised definite rules. The immediate consequence operator $\mathbf{T}_S$ is monotonic, that is, if $B \subseteq B' \subseteq HB$ then $\mathbf{T}_S(B) \subseteq \mathbf{T}_S(B')$.*

Recall that for Herbrand interpretations $HI(B) \leq HI(B')$ iff $B \subseteq B'$. Thus, the immediate consequence operator $\mathbf{T}_S$ is also monotonic with respect to $\leq$ on Herbrand interpretations.

Theorem 156. *Let S be a set of universal generalised definite rules. Let $B \subseteq HB$ be a set of ground atoms. Then $HI(B) \models S$ iff $\mathbf{T}_S(B) \subseteq B$.*

Proof. "only if:" Assume $HI(B) \models S$. Let $A \in \mathbf{T}_S(B)$, i.e., $A = A_i$ for some ground instance $((A_1 \wedge \ldots \wedge A_n) \leftarrow \varphi)$ of a member of S with $HI(B) \models \varphi$. By assumption $HI(B) \models (A_1 \wedge \ldots \wedge A_n)$, hence $HI(B) \models A$, hence $A \in B$ because A is a ground atom.

"if:" Assume $\mathbf{T}_S(B) \subseteq B$. Let $((A_1 \wedge \ldots \wedge A_n) \leftarrow \varphi)$ be a ground instance of a member of S. It suffices to show that $HI(B)$ satisfies this ground instance. If $HI(B) \not\models \varphi$, it does. If $HI(B) \models \varphi$, then $A_1 \in \mathbf{T}_S(B), \ldots, A_n \in \mathbf{T}_S(B)$ by definition of $\mathbf{T}_S$. By assumption $A_1 \in B, \ldots, A_n \in B$. As these are ground atoms, $HI(B) \models A_1, \ldots, HI(B) \models A_n$. Thus $HI(B)$ satisfies the ground instance.   □

5.2.4   Least Fixpoint of a Set of Positive Definite Rules

Corollary 157. *Let S be a set of universal generalised definite rules. Then $lfp(\mathbf{T}_S) = \mathbf{T}_S \uparrow \omega = Mod_\cap(S) = \{A \in HB \mid S \models A\}$ and $HI(lfp(\mathbf{T}_S))$ is the unique minimal Herbrand model of S.*

Proof. By Lemma 155, $\mathbf{T}_S$ is a monotonic operator on HB, and by Theorem 152, $lfp(\mathbf{T}_S) = \mathbf{T}_S \uparrow \omega$.

Note that $Mod_{HB}(S) \neq \emptyset$ by Theorem 128. Now,

$$
\begin{aligned}
lfp(\mathbf{T}_S) &= \bigcap \{B \subseteq HB \mid \mathbf{T}_S(B) \subseteq B\} && \text{by the Knaster-Tarski Theorem 148} \\
&= \bigcap \{B \subseteq HB \mid HI(B) \models S\} && \text{by Theorem 156} \\
&= \bigcap Mod_{HB}(S) && \text{by Definition 117} \\
&= Mod_\cap(S) && \text{by Definition 118} \\
&= \{A \in HB \mid S \models A\} && \text{by Theorem 119}
\end{aligned}
$$

By Theorem 133, $HI(lfp(\mathbf{T}_S))$ is the unique minimal Herbrand model of S.   □

The immediate consequence operator for a set of universal generalised definite rules also has a *greatest fixpoint* (Knaster-Tarski Theorem 148). Using similar proof techniques as above one can show [111] that this greatest fixpoint is $gfp(\mathbf{T}_S) = \mathbf{T}_S \downarrow \omega + 1$, but in general $gfp(\mathbf{T}_S) \neq \mathbf{T}_S \downarrow \omega$. As an example, let $S = \{\forall x(q \leftarrow p(x)), \forall x(p(f(x)) \leftarrow p(x))\}$. Then $\mathbf{T}_S \downarrow \omega = \{q\}$ and $\mathbf{T}_S \downarrow \omega + 1 = \emptyset = gfp(\mathbf{T}_S)$, which in this example is the only fixpoint.

A fixpoint requiring more than ω steps is not in general computably enumerable. The result on the least fixpoint means that $lfp(\mathbf{T}_S)$ is computably enumerable.

The "natural meaning" of a set S of universal generalised definite rules, the unique minimal Herbrand model of S, has several equivalent characterisations. It is the intersection of all Herbrand models of S and satisfies precisely the ground atoms entailed by S. These characterisations allow a declarative understanding of S: each of its rules represents a statement about the application at hand, and a query asks whether something is a logical consequence of these statements, or, equivalently, whether it is true in all their Herbrand models.

The corollary above allows in addition an operational understanding of S based on forward chaining, even though forward chaining is not necessarily the intended operational semantics (backward chaining is in many cases preferable, see Section 6). The unique minimal Herbrand model of S is induced by the smallest fixpoint of $\mathbf{T}_S$. This operator models one step in a forward chaining process: applied to a set of ground atoms, it adds the atoms from the consequents of those ground instances of rules whose antecedent is satisfied in the current set. Being satisfied here means satisfied by the induced Herbrand interpretation, but this can by checked algorithmically using unification. The iteration starts from the empty set. Reaching a fixpoint means that the operator does not generate any new atom. The result guarantees that this happens after finitely many steps or at most as many steps as there are natural numbers.

By the corollary the declarative and this operational semantics coincide: a ground atom is a logical consequence of S if and only if it can be derived by this forward chaining process.

Another procedural semantics based on a backward chaining process called SLD resolution (Subsection 6.4) is also equivalent to the ones above. Backward chaining with SLD resolution succeeds on S with some ground atom as a query if and only if the ground atom is a logical consequence of S.

Authors of rules may thus freely switch between different understandings of their rules, because all of these understandings amount to the same.

Notation 158 (Least fixpoint of a definite program). *For a set S of universal generalised definite rules, the* least fixpoint of S *is* $lfp(S) = lfp(\mathbf{T}_S)$.

5.3   Declarative Semantics of Rules with Negation

The nice results above heavily depend on the rules being positive: their antecedents have to be positive formulas. If the antecedents may contain atoms with negative polarity, as in normal clauses and normal goals (Definition 21), things turn out to be much more difficult. The starting point is to clarify what negative antecedents of rules are supposed to mean.

When working with a set of positive definite rules, more generally, a set of universal generalised definite rules, it is often intuitive to consider everything to be false that does not follow from the set.

This is the common understanding of inductive definitions in mathematics (the inductive definitions of terms and formulas in Section 3 are examples of that). This understanding of inductive definitions is sometimes stressed by concluding the definition, say, of a formula, with "nothing else is a formula".

This is also the common understanding of many specifications one encounters in real life. The time table of a railway company can be seen as a set of ground atoms, each specifying a direct railway connection. The common understanding of such a time table is that any direct connection not explicitly mentioned does not exist. This understanding is naturally extended to connections with changes as follows: if no connections with changes between two places and under certain time constraints can be derived from a time table, then it may be concluded that there are no such connections.

In databases, the common understanding is similar. If a database of students does not list "Mary", then it may be concluded that "Mary" is not a student.

The principle underlying this common understanding has been formalised under the name of "closed world assumption" [137].

It might seem obvious to formalise the closed world assumption by adding additional axioms to the set of formulas so as, so to speak, to complete – or "close" – it. But this is undesirable for two reasons. First, it would blow up the axiomatisation and as a consequence make deduction more time and space consuming. Second, it is in many, if not most, practical cases infeasible – how could one list, or otherwise specify, non-existing train connections or non-students? Note that, in contrast to such applications, mathematics, except in a few cases like inductive definitions, does not rely on closed world assumptions of any kind.

One approach to handling negation was to find deduction methods that employ the closed world assumption without relying on additional, application-dependent, axioms. This approach has two sides: one is to find convenient declarative semantics, i.e., declarative semantics that are both easy to understand and convenient to use in establishing properties; the other is to find efficient automated deduction methods that take the closed world assumption into account.

Another, related approach was to find application independent rewritings of a rule set, which, possibly together with additional application independent axioms, would correspond to the common understanding under the closed world assumption of the original set. This led to the so-called "completion semantics".

Both approaches have yielded unsatisfactory results and are therefore not addressed in the following. Indeed, the intended semantics could not be expressed with Tarski model theory, but required drastic changes to the notion of a model.

The "common understanding" or "intuitive meaning" of a set of rules with negation is what people reading or writing the rules are likely to think they mean. Good candidates for making this common sense notion more precise are the minimal Herbrand models defined earlier. However, not all of them convey the intuitive meaning under the closed world assumption.

Example 159. $S_1 = \{\,(q \leftarrow r \wedge \neg p),\ (r \leftarrow s \wedge \neg t),\ (s \leftarrow \top)\,\}$ has the following three minimal Herbrand models: $HI(\{s, r, q\})$, $HI(\{s, r, p\})$, and $HI(\{s, t\})$.

Intuitively, neither p nor t are "justified" by the rules in S_1. Under the closed world assumption only the first of the minimal models above should be seen as conveying the intuitive meaning of S_1.

The example illustrates that some minimal Herbrand models do not convey the intuitive meaning of rules with negation, because classical model theory treats negated atoms in rule antecedents like (positive) atoms in rule consequents. Indeed, for minimal or non-minimal Herbrand or other models, the rule $(r \leftarrow s \wedge \neg t)$ is equivalent to $(r \vee t \leftarrow s)$ and to $(t \leftarrow s \wedge \neg r)$, hence no interpretation can distinguish these formulas.

Example 160. $S_2 = \{\,(p \leftarrow \neg q),\ (q \leftarrow \neg p)\,\}$ has the following two minimal Herbrand models: $HI(\{p\})$, $HI(\{q\})$.

In this example both minimal Herbrand models of S_2 well convey the intuitive meaning of S_2 under the closed world assumption. Intuitively, the example specifies that exactly one of p and q is true, but it does not specify which.

Example 161. $S_3 = \{\,(p \leftarrow \neg p)\,\}$ has only one minimal Herbrand model: $HI(\{p\})$.

In examples like these, intuition turns out to be somewhat indeterminate and subject to personal preference.

People tending towards a "justification postulate" request dependable justifications for derived truths. The only rule of S_3 does not in this sense "justify" p, because it requires $\neg p$ to hold as a condition for p to hold, thus its outcome violates its own precondition. The "justification postulate" arrives at the conclusion that no model at all conveys the intuitive meaning of S_3, that S_3 should be regarded as inconsistent.

Adherents of a "consistency postulate", on the other hand, insist that every syntactically correct set of normal clauses *is* consistent and must therefore have a model. As there is only one candidate model of S_3, this has to be it, like it or not. Note that the "consistency postulate" is closer to classical model theory, which, for minimal or non-minimal Herbrand or other models, treats the rule in S_3 like the formula p, to which it is logically equivalent.

Example 162. $S_4 = \{(p \leftarrow \neg p),\ (p \leftarrow \top)\}$ has only one minimal Herbrand model: $HI(\{p\})$.

S_4 extends S_3 with a rule enforcing p. Its only minimal Herbrand model, in which p is true, is perfectly intuitive under the closed world assumption – even with the "justification postulate" that considers S_3 to be inconsistent. The new rule in S_4 clearly "justifies" p. Since intuitively p follows from S_4, the antecedent of the rule $(p \leftarrow \neg p)$ is not satisfied, i.e., the rule is satisfied.

As these examples suggest, only some of the minimal Herbrand models of a set of rules with negation should be retained in order to specify the declarative semantics of the set under the closed world assumption. In the literature the retained minimal Herbrand models are often called *canonical models* or *preferred models*. With the "justification postulate" the set of retained minimal Herbrand models may be empty, with the "consistency postulate" it always contains at least one model. Some of the formal approaches to the declarative semantics support the "justification postulate" some the "consistency postulate".

Once the notion of canonical models has been formalised, the notion of entailment (Definition 34) and of a theory (Definition 43) can be adapted such that they consider only canonical models. In contrast to the operator Th for closure under classical entailment, which is monotonic (Proposition 45), the appropriately adapted operator $Th_{canonical}$ is not.

Example 163 (Non-monotonicity). $S_5 = \{(q \leftarrow \neg p)\}$ has two minimal Herbrand models: $HI(\{p\})$ and $HI(\{q\})$. Only the latter conveys the intuitive meaning under the closed world assumption and should be retained as (the only) canonical model. Therefore, $q \in Th_{canonical}(S_5)$.

$S_5' = S_5 \cup \{(p \leftarrow \top)\}$ has only one minimal Herbrand model: $HI(\{p\})$, which also conveys the intuitive meaning under the closed world assumption and should be retained as a canonical model. Therefore, $q \notin Th_{canonical}(S_5')$.

Thus, $S_5 \subseteq S_5'$, but $Th_{canonical}(S_5) \not\subseteq Th_{canonical}(S_5')$.

Note that non-monotonicity is independent of the choice between the two "postulates". However, any semantics *not* complying with the "consistency postulate" (i.e., all or most semantics complying with the "justification postulate"), is non-monotonic in an even stronger sense. With such a semantics, consistency – defined as usual as the existence of models – is not inherited by subsets: S_4 above is consistent, but S_3 is not, although $S_3 \subseteq S_4$.

As the non-monotonicity of the operator is caused by the non-classical treatment of negation, this kind of negation is also called *non-monotonic negation*.

5.3.1 Stratifiable Rule Sets
Some approaches to formalise the semantics of rules with negation make use of a weak syntactic property of sets of rules that ensures stronger results. The idea is to avoid cases like $(p \leftarrow \neg p)$ and more generally recursion through negative literals. For that purpose the set of rules is partitioned into "strata", and negative literals in the antecedents are required to belong to a lower "stratum".

Definition 164 (Stratification). *Let S be a set of normal clauses (Definition 21). A stratification of S is a partition $S_0, \ldots, S_k$ of S such that*

- *For each relation symbol p there is a stratum S_i, such that all clauses of S containing p in their consequent are members of S_i.*
  In this case one says that the relation symbol p is defined in stratum S_i.
- *For each stratum S_j and for each positive literal A in the antecedents of members of S_j, the relation symbol of A is defined in a stratum S_i with $i \leq j$.*
- *For each stratum S_j and for each negative literal $\neg A$ in the antecedents of members of S_j, the relation symbol of A is defined in a stratum S_i with $i < j$.*

A set of normal clauses is called stratifiable, *if there exists a stratification of it.*

Obviously, each definite program is stratifiable by making it its only stratum. The set of normal clauses $S = \{ (r \leftarrow \top), (q \leftarrow r), (p \leftarrow q \wedge \neg r) \}$ is stratifiable in different ways: the stratum S_0 contains the first clause and the stratum S_1 the last one, while the middle clause may belong to either of the strata. If the middle clause is replaced by $(q \leftarrow p \wedge r)$, the set remains stratifiable, but now there is only one stratification, the middle clause belonging to S_1. The set $S = \{ (p \leftarrow \neg p) \}$ is not stratifiable. More generally, any set of normal clauses with a "cycle of recursion through negation" [9] is not stratifiable.

By definition the stratum S_0 always consists of definite clauses (positive definite rules). Hence the truth values of all atoms of stratum S_0 can be determined without negation being involved. After that the clauses of stratum S_1 refer only to such negative literals whose truth values have already been determined. And so on. The principle simply is to work stratum by stratum, see Subsection 7.1.

All results about stratifiable rule sets depend only on the existence of some stratification and are independent of the concrete specification of the strata.

Note that stratifiability evades any commitment as to the "justification" or "consistency postulate", because rule sets where the postulates make a difference are not stratifiable. Even though stratifiable sets of normal clauses seem to be sufficient for many, if not all, practical programming examples, a semantics is desirable that covers all syntactically correct programs. Indeed, one of the purposes of a semantics of programs is to uncover the "meaning" of unintended, syntactically correct programs. The next three subsections describe attempts to define such semantics, which, alas, do not perfectly meet the objective.

5.3.2 Stable Model Semantics

The stable model semantics [77] is defined in terms of a criterion for retaining a minimal Herbrand model of a set of normal clauses. This criterion is expressed in terms of the following transformation named after the authors of [77].

Definition 165 (Gelfond-Lifschitz transformation). *Let S be a (possibly infinite) set of ground normal clauses, i.e., of formulas of the form*

$$A \leftarrow L_1 \wedge \ldots \wedge L_n$$

where $n \geq 0$ and A is a ground atom and the L_i for $1 \leq i \leq n$ are ground literals. Let $B \subseteq HB$. The Gelfond-Lifschitz transform $GL_B(S)$ of S with respect to B is obtained from S as follows:

1. *remove each clause whose antecedent contains a literal $\neg A$ with $A \in B$.*
2. *remove from the antecedents of the remaining clauses all negative literals.*

The transformation corresponds to a partial evaluation of S in the interpretation $HI(B)$. The clauses removed in the first step are true in $HI(B)$ because their antecedent is false in $HI(B)$. The literals removed from the antecedents of the remaining clauses in the second step, are also true in $HI(B)$.

Note that the Gelfond-Lifschitz transform $GL_B(S)$ of a set S of ground normal clauses is a (possibly infinite) set of definite clauses, i.e., a set of universal generalised definite rules. Therefore $GL_B(S)$ has a unique minimal Herbrand model with all characterisations according to Corollary 157.

Definition 166 (Stable Model). *Let S be a (possibly infinite) set of ground normal clauses. An Herbrand interpretation $HI(B)$ is a stable model of S, iff it is the unique minimal Herbrand model of $GL_B(S)$.*

A stable model of a set S of normal clauses is a stable model of the (possibly infinite) set of ground instances of S.

For this notion to be well-defined, we have to ensure that the unique minimal Herbrand model of $GL_B(S)$ is indeed also a model of S.

Lemma 167. *Let S be a set of ground normal clauses and $HI(B)$ an Herbrand interpretation. $HI(B) \models S$ iff $HI(B) \models GL_B(S)$.*

Proof. Let S_1 be the set of clauses obtained from S by applying the first step of the transformation. Each clause in $S \setminus S_1$ is satisfied by $HI(B)$, because its antecedent is falsified by $HI(B)$. Thus, $HI(B) \models S$ iff $HI(B) \models S_1$.

Let S_2 be the set of clauses obtained from S_1 by applying the second step of the transformation. For each clause $C_2 \in S_2$ there is a clause $C_1 \in S_1$ such that C_2 is obtained from C_1 by removing the negative literals from its antecedent. Since $C_1 \in S_1$, for any such negative literal $\neg A$ in its antecedent, $A \notin B$, i.e., $HI(B) \models \neg A$. Therefore, $HI(B) \models C_1$ iff $HI(B) \models C_2$.   □

Theorem 168. *Let S be a set of normal clauses. Each stable model of S is a minimal Herbrand model of S.*

Proof. By definition of a stable model, it suffices to show the result for a set S of *ground* normal clauses.

Let $B' \subseteq B \subseteq HB$ such that $HI(B)$ is a stable model of S and $HI(B')$ is also a model of S, i.e., $HI(B') \models S$. If we establish that $HI(B') \models GL_B(S)$, then $B' = B$ because, by definition of a stable model, $HI(B)$ is the unique minimal Herbrand model of $GL_B(S)$.

Let $C \in GL_B(S)$. By definition of $GL_B(S)$ there exists a clause $D \in S$, such that C is obtained from D by removing the negative literals from its antecedent. If $\neg A$ is such a literal, then $A \notin B$, and, since $B' \subseteq B$, also $A \notin B'$. Therefore, $C \in GL_{B'}(S)$, and by the previous lemma $HI(B') \models C$.   □

It is easy to verify that the stable models of the examples above are as follows:

Example 169
$S_1 = \{ (q \leftarrow r \wedge \neg p),\ (r \leftarrow s \wedge \neg t),\ (s \leftarrow \top) \}$ has one stable model: $HI(\{s, r, q\})$.
$S_2 = \{ (p \leftarrow \neg q),\ (q \leftarrow \neg p) \}$ has two stable models: $HI(\{p\})$ and $HI(\{q\})$.
$S_3 = \{ (p \leftarrow \neg p) \}$ has no stable model.
$S_4 = \{ (p \leftarrow \neg p),\ (p \leftarrow \top) \}$ has one stable model: $HI(\{p\})$.

Thus, the stable model semantics coincides with the intuitive understanding based on the "justification postulate". The unintuitive minimal models of the examples turn out not to be stable, and the stability criterion retains only those minimal models that are intuitive. A set may have several stable models or exactly one or none. Each stratifiable set has exactly one stable model.

The remarks about non-monotonicity on page 58 apply also to stable models, including non-inheritance of consistency by subsets. To give up such a fundamental principle can be seen as a serious drawback of the stable model semantics.

5.3.3   Well-Founded Semantics
The well-founded semantics [155] of a set of normal clauses is defined as the least fixpoint of a monotonic operator that explicitly specifies derivations both of positive and of negative ground literals. Recall that the immediate consequence operator (Definition 153) for a set of definite clauses explicitly specifies derivations only of positive ground literals.

In contrast to the stable model semantics, the well-founded semantics specifies for each set of normal clauses a *single* model, a so-called *well-founded model*.

A well-founded model can be either *total*, in which case it makes each ground atom true or false like a standard model, or *partial*, in which case it makes some ground atoms neither true nor false, but undefined.

Recall that $\overline{L}$ denotes the complement of a literal L with $\overline{A} = \neg A$ and $\overline{\neg A} = A$ for an atom A (Definition 19). HB denotes the Herbrand base, the set of all ground atoms for the given signature.

Notation 170. *For a set I of ground literals:*
$\overline{I} = \{ \overline{L} \mid L \in I \}$ *and* $pos(I) = I \cap HB$ *and* $neg(I) = \overline{I} \cap HB$.
Thus, $I = pos(I) \cup \overline{neg(I)}$.

Definition 171. *A set I of ground literals is* consistent, *iff $pos(I) \cap neg(I) = \emptyset$. Otherwise, I is* inconsistent.
Two sets I_1 and I_2 of ground literals are (in)consistent *iff $I_1 \cup I_2$ is.*
A literal L and a set I of ground literals are (in)consistent *iff $\{L\} \cup I$ is.*

Definition 172 (Partial interpretation). *A partial interpretation is a consistent set of ground literals.*
A partial interpretation I is called total, *iff $pos(I) \cup neg(I) = HB$, that is, for each ground atom A either $A \in I$ or $\neg A \in I$.*
For a total interpretation I, the Herbrand interpretation induced by I is defined as $HI(I) = HI(pos(I))$.

Definition 173 (Model relationship for partial interpretations). *Let I be a partial interpretation. Then $\top$ is satisfied in I and $\bot$ is falsified in I.*

A ground literal L is
  satisfied *or true in I iff $L \in I$.*
  falsified *or false in I iff $\overline{L} \in I$.*
  undefined *in I iff $L \notin I$ and $\overline{L} \notin I$.*
A conjunction $L_1 \wedge \ldots \wedge L_n$ of ground literals, $n \geq 0$, is
  satisfied *or true in I iff each L_i for $1 \leq i \leq n$ is satisfied in I.*
  falsified *or false in I iff at least one L_i for $1 \leq i \leq n$ is falsified in I.*
  undefined *in I iff each L_i for $1 \leq i \leq n$ is satisfied or undefined in I
                              and at least one of them is undefined in I.*
A ground normal clause $A \leftarrow \varphi$ is
  satisfied *or true in I iff A is satisfied in I or φ is falsified in I.*
  falsified *or false in I iff A is falsified in I and φ is satisfied in I.*
  weakly falsified *in I iff A is falsified in I and φ is satisfied or undefined in I.*
A normal clause is
  satisfied *or true in I iff each of its ground instances is.*
  falsified *or false in I iff at least one of its ground instances is.*
  weakly falsified *in I iff at least one of its ground instances is.*
A set of normal clauses is
  satisfied *or true in I iff each of its members is.*
  falsified *or false in I iff at least one of its members is.*
  weakly falsified *in I iff at least one of its members is.*

For a total interpretation I the cases "undefined" and "weakly falsified" are impossible, and obviously the notion of satisfied (or falsified, respectively) in I in the sense above coincides with the notion of satisfied (or falsified, respectively) in $HI(I)$ in the classical sense.

Definition 174 (Total and partial model). *Let S be a set of normal clauses.*
  A total interpretation I is a total model of S, iff S is satisfied in I.
  A partial interpretation I is a partial model of S, iff there exists a total model I' of S with $I \subseteq I'$.

Note that if a ground normal clause is weakly falsified, but not falsified in a partial interpretation I, then its consequent *is* falsified in I and some literals in its antecedent are undefined in I. No extension of I with additional literals can satisfy the consequent. The only way to satisfy the normal clause is to extend I by the complement of one of the undefined antecedent literals, thus falsifying the clause's antecedent. Any extension of I that satisfies all of those antecedent literals, falsifies the normal clause.

Lemma 175. *Let S be a set of normal clauses and I a partial interpretation. If no clause in S is weakly falsified in I, then I is a partial model of S.*

Proof. Let no clause in S be weakly falsified in I. Let $I' = I \cup (HB \setminus neg(I))$, that is, I extended by all ground atoms consistent with I. Then I' is total.
  Consider an arbitrary ground instance $A \leftarrow \varphi$ of a member of S. Since it is not weakly falsified in I, it is by definition not falsified in I either and therefore

satisfied in I, i.e., $A \in I$ or $\overline{L} \in I$ for some literal L in the antecedent φ. This membership cannot be affected by adding literals to I that preserve its consistency. Thus, $A \in I'$ or $\overline{L} \in I'$, and $A \leftarrow \varphi$ is satisfied also in I'.

Hence I' is a total model of S and I is a partial model of S. □

The basis for drawing negative conclusions and the notion most central to the well-founded semantics is that of an *unfounded set* of ground atoms. Given a partial interpretation I, i.e., a set of ground literals that are already known (or assumed) to be true, a set U of ground atoms is unfounded, if the normal clauses at hand give no reason to consider any member of U to be true. More precisely, each atom $A \in U$ occurs in the consequent only of such ground instances of clauses that do not justify A. This can happen for two reasons: because the antecedent of the ground instance is falsified in I or because the antecedent of the ground instance contains an unfounded atom, i.e., a member of U.

Definition 176 (Unfounded set of ground atoms). *Let S be a set of normal clauses, I a partial interpretation, and $U \subseteq HB$ a set of ground atoms.*

U is an unfounded set *with respect to S and I, if for each $A \in U$ and for each ground instance $A \leftarrow L_1 \wedge \ldots \wedge L_n$, $n \geq 1$, of a member of S having A as its consequent, at least one of the following holds:*

1. *$L_i \in \overline{I}$ for some positive or negative L_i with $1 \leq i \leq n$. (L_i is falsified in I)*
2. *$L_i \in U$ for some positive L_i with $1 \leq i \leq n$. (L_i is unfounded)*

A literal fulfilling one of these conditions is called a witness of unusability *for the ground instance of a clause.*

U is a maximal unfounded set *with respect to S and I, iff U is an* unfounded set *with respect to S and I and no proper superset of U is.*

Example 177. Let $S = \{ (q \leftarrow p), (r \leftarrow s), (s \leftarrow r) \}$ and $I = \{\neg p, \neg q\}$. The set $U = \{q, r, s\}$ is unfounded with respect to S and I. The atom q is unfounded by condition 1, the atoms r and s by condition 2.

U is not maximal, because $U' = \{p, q, r, s\}$ is also unfounded w.r.t. S and I. Note that p is unfounded because there is no rule with consequent p. Furthermore, p would even be unfounded if it were satisfied in I.

Note that the empty set is unfounded with respect to every set of normal clauses and every partial interpretation. Note also that the union of sets that are unfounded with respect to the same S and I is also unfounded with respect to the same S and I. As a consequence, the following lemma holds:

Lemma 178. *Let S be a set of normal clauses and I a partial interpretation. There exists a unique maximal unfounded set with respect to S and I, which is the union of all unfounded sets with respect to S and I.*

Starting from "knowing" I in the example above, the atoms r and s depend on each other, but none of them has to be true for other reasons. Thus, if we choose to consider them or one of them to be false, we will not be forced to undo this decision. Making one of them false preserves the other's being unfounded. Generalising this observation, we get:

Lemma 179. *Let S be a set of normal clauses, I a partial interpretation, and U' an unfounded set with respect to S and I, such that $pos(I) \cap U' = \emptyset$.*
For each $U \subseteq U'$, its remainder $U' \setminus U$ is unfounded w.r.t. S and $I \cup \overline{U}$.

Proof. The condition $pos(I) \cap U' = \emptyset$ ensures that $I \cup \overline{U}$ is consistent.

Any atom falsified in I remains falsified in $I \cup \overline{U}$, thus any witness of unusability w.r.t. S and I by condition 1, is also a witness of unusability w.r.t. S and $I \cup \overline{U}$ by condition 1.

Any $A \in U$ that is a witness in U' of unusability w.r.t. S and I by condition 2, is not in $U' \setminus U$ and can no longer satisfy condition 2. But $\overline{A} \in \overline{U} \subseteq I \cup \overline{U}$. Hence, A is a witness of unusability w.r.t. S and $I \cup \overline{U}$ by condition 1.   □

In a sense the lemma allows to make unfounded atoms false without affecting the unfoundedness of others. The next lemma is a kind of opposite direction, in a sense it allows to make falsified atoms unfounded. Recall that $I = pos(I) \cup neg(I)$.

Lemma 180. *Let S be a set of normal clauses and I a partial interpretation. If no clause in S is weakly falsified in I, then $neg(I)$ is unfounded with respect to S and $pos(I)$.*

Proof. Let $A \in neg(I)$ and $A \leftarrow \varphi$ an arbitrary ground instance of a member of S. Since A is falsified in I and $A \leftarrow \varphi$ is not weakly falsified in I, some literal L in φ is falsified in I. If L is positive, then $L \in neg(I)$ and L is a witness of unusability for $A \leftarrow \varphi$ by condition 2. If L is negative, then $L \in \overline{pos(I)}$ and L is a witness of unusability for $A \leftarrow \varphi$ by condition 1.   □

Definition 181. *Let $\mathcal{PI} = \{ I \subseteq HB \cup \overline{HB} \mid I \text{ is consistent} \}$, and note that $\mathcal{P}(HB) \subseteq \mathcal{PI}$. Let S be a set of normal clauses. We define three operators:*

$\mathbf{T}_S : \mathcal{PI} \rightarrow \mathcal{P}(HB)$
$\qquad I \mapsto \{ A \in HB \mid \text{ there is a ground instance } (A \leftarrow \varphi)$
$\qquad\qquad\qquad\qquad \text{of a member of } S \text{ such that } \varphi \text{ is satisfied in } I \}$

$\mathbf{U}_S : \mathcal{PI} \rightarrow \mathcal{P}(HB)$
$\qquad I \mapsto \text{the maximal subset of } HB \text{ that is unfounded with respect to } S \text{ and } I$

$\mathbf{W}_S : \mathcal{PI} \rightarrow \mathcal{PI}$
$\qquad I \mapsto \mathbf{T}_S(I) \cup \overline{\mathbf{U}_S(I)}$

If S is a set of definite clauses, that is, if all antecedents are positive, the operator $\mathbf{T}_S$ coincides with the immediate consequence operator $\mathbf{T}_S$ from Definition 153. Whether or not S is definite, $\mathbf{T}_S(I)$ is a set of ground atoms. The operator $\mathbf{U}_S$ is well-defined by Lemma 178 and also produces a set of ground atoms. Starting from "knowing" I, the ground atoms in $\mathbf{T}_S(I)$ are those that have to be true, whereas those in $\mathbf{U}_S(I)$ are unfounded. Note that the definition of unfounded implies $\mathbf{T}_S(I) \cap \mathbf{U}_S(I) = \emptyset$. This ensures the consistency of $\mathbf{W}_S(I)$, which satisfies what has to be true and falsifies all unfounded ground atoms.

Example 182. Assume a signature with $HB = \{p, q, r, s, t\}$, and let $I_0 = \emptyset$ and $S = \{ (q \leftarrow r \wedge \neg p), (r \leftarrow s \wedge \neg t), (s \leftarrow \top) \}$.

$\mathbf{T}_S(I_0) = \{s\}$	$\mathbf{T}_S(I_1) = \{s, r\}$	$\mathbf{T}_S(I_2) = \{s, r, q\}$
$\mathbf{U}_S(I_0) = \{p, t\}$	$\mathbf{U}_S(I_1) = \{p, t\}$	$\mathbf{U}_S(I_2) = \{p, t\}$
$\mathbf{W}_S(I_0) = \{s, \neg p, \neg t\} = I_1$	$\mathbf{W}_S(I_1) = \{s, r, \neg p, \neg t\} = I_2$	$\mathbf{W}_S(I_2) = \{s, r, q, \neg p, \neg t\}$

$\mathbf{T}_S(\emptyset)$ is nonempty only if S contains a clause with antecedent $\top$ or empty.

Atoms such as p and t, which do not appear in any consequents, are always unfounded. $\mathbf{U}_S(I)$ can never contain the consequent of a satisfied clause instance whose antecedent is satisfied, too. This explains why $\mathbf{U}_S(I_2)$ is maximal. For the maximality of $\mathbf{U}_S(I_1)$ note that for q to be unfounded either r would have to be unfounded, which is impossible by $r \in \mathbf{T}_S(I_1)$, or one of the antecedent literals r and $\neg p$ would have to be falsified in I_1, but r is undefined and $\neg p$ is satisfied in I_1. The maximality of $\mathbf{U}_S(I_0)$ can be confirmed by similar arguments.

Lemma 183. $\mathbf{T}_S$, $\mathbf{U}_S$, and $\mathbf{W}_S$ are monotonic.[11]

Proof. Immediate from the definition of the operators. □

Theorem 184 (Existence of least fixpoint). *Let S be a set of normal clauses. The operator $\mathbf{W}_S$ has a least fixpoint $lfp(\mathbf{W}_S)$ with*
$$lfp(\mathbf{W}_S) = \bigcap\{I \in \mathcal{PI} \mid \mathbf{W}_S(I) = I\} = \bigcap\{I \in \mathcal{PI} \mid \mathbf{W}_S(I) \subseteq I\}.$$
Moreover, $lfp(\mathbf{W}_S)$ is a partial interpretation and a partial model of S.

Proof. The first part follows from the Knaster-Tarski Theorem 148. For the second part, both consistency and that no clause in S is weakly falsified, are shown by transfinite induction. Lemma 175 ensures the model property. □

Definition 185 (Well-founded model). *Let S be a set of normal clauses. The well-founded model of S is its partial model $lfp(\mathbf{W}_S)$.*

The well-founded model may be total, in which case it specifies a truth value for each ground atom, or partial, in which case it leaves some atoms undefined.

The examples considered earlier for the stable model semantics have the following well-founded models. Note that S_1 is the set used for illustrating the operators in the previous example. One more step will reproduce the fixpoint.

Example 186

$S_1 = \{(q \leftarrow r \wedge \neg p), (r \leftarrow s \wedge \neg t), (s \leftarrow \top)\}$ has the well-founded model $\{s, r, q, \neg p, \neg t\}$. It is total.

$S_2 = \{(p \leftarrow \neg q), (q \leftarrow \neg p)\}$ has the well-founded model $\emptyset$. It is partial and leaves the truth values of p and of q undefined.

$S_3 = \{(p \leftarrow \neg p)\}$ has the well-founded model $\emptyset$. It is partial and leaves the truth value of p undefined.

$S_4 = \{(p \leftarrow \neg p), (p \leftarrow \top)\}$ has the well-founded model $\{p\}$. It is total.

Thus, the well-founded semantics coincides with the intuitive understanding based on the "consistency postulate". Each set of normal clauses has a unique

---

[11] But not in general continuous!

model, but this model does not necessarily commit to truth values for all atoms. Each stratifiable set of normal clauses has a total well-founded model.

Note that the operators are monotonic, but not necessarily continuous, thus the Kleene Theorem 152 ensuring that a fixpoint is reached with at most ω steps, is not applicable. Indeed there are examples for which $lfp(\mathbf{W}_S) \neq \mathbf{W}_S \uparrow \omega$.

Example 187. By definition $\mathbf{W}_S \uparrow 0 = \emptyset$. Assume a signature containing no other symbols than those occurring in the following set of normal clauses. Let $S =$
$$\{\, p(a) \leftarrow \top, \quad p(f(x)) \leftarrow p(x), \quad q(y) \leftarrow p(y), \quad s \leftarrow p(z) \land \neg q(z), \quad r \leftarrow \neg s \,\}$$

$\mathbf{T}_S \uparrow 1$	$= \{\, p(a) \,\}$			
$\mathbf{U}_S \uparrow 1$	$= \emptyset$			
$\mathbf{W}_S \uparrow 1$	$= \{\, p(a) \,\}$			
$\mathbf{T}_S \uparrow 2$	$= \{\, p(a),\, p(f(a)) \,\}$	$\cup \{\, q(a) \,\}$		
$\mathbf{U}_S \uparrow 2$	$= \emptyset$			
$\mathbf{W}_S \uparrow 2$	$= \{\, p(a),\, p(f(a)) \,\}$	$\cup \{\, q(a) \,\}$		
$\mathbf{T}_S \uparrow n+1$	$= \{\, p(a), \ldots, p(f^n(a)) \,\}$	$\cup \{\, q(a), \ldots, q(f^{n-1}(a)) \,\}$		
$\mathbf{U}_S \uparrow n+1$	$= \emptyset$			
$\mathbf{W}_S \uparrow n+1$	$= \{\, p(a), \ldots, p(f^n(a)) \,\}$	$\cup \{\, q(a), \ldots, q(f^{n-1}(a)) \,\}$		
$\mathbf{T}_S \uparrow \omega$	$= \{\, p(a), \ldots, p(f^n(a)), \ldots \,\}$	$\cup \{\, q(a), \ldots, q(f^n(a)), \ldots \,\}$		
$\mathbf{U}_S \uparrow \omega$	$= \emptyset$			
$\mathbf{W}_S \uparrow \omega$	$= \{\, p(a), \ldots, p(f^n(a)), \ldots \,\}$	$\cup \{\, q(a), \ldots, q(f^n(a)), \ldots \,\}$		
$\mathbf{T}_S \uparrow \omega+1$	$= \{\, p(a), \ldots, p(f^n(a)), \ldots \,\}$	$\cup \{\, q(a), \ldots, q(f^n(a)), \ldots \,\}$		
$\mathbf{U}_S \uparrow \omega+1$	$= \{\, s \,\}$			
$\mathbf{W}_S \uparrow \omega+1$	$= \{\, p(a), \ldots, p(f^n(a)), \ldots \,\}$	$\cup \{\, q(a), \ldots, q(f^n(a)), \ldots \,\}$	$\cup \{\, \neg s \,\}$	
$\mathbf{T}_S \uparrow \omega+2$	$= \{\, p(a), \ldots, p(f^n(a)), \ldots \,\}$	$\cup \{\, q(a), \ldots, q(f^n(a)), \ldots \,\}$	$\cup \{\, r \,\}$	
$\mathbf{U}_S \uparrow \omega+2$	$= \{\, s \,\}$			
$\mathbf{W}_S \uparrow \omega+2$	$= \{\, p(a), \ldots, p(f^n(a)), \ldots \,\}$	$\cup \{\, q(a), \ldots, q(f^n(a)), \ldots \,\}$	$\cup \{\, \neg s,\, r \,\}$	

It is debatable whether sets of normal clauses like that are likely to be needed in practice. In [155] doubts are expressed that such cases are common. But this position is questionable in view of the fact that the set S above is the (standard) translation into normal clauses of the following set of generalised rules:
$$\{\, p(a) \leftarrow \top, \quad p(f(x)) \leftarrow p(x), \quad q(y) \leftarrow p(y), \quad r \leftarrow \forall z \big(p(z) \Rightarrow q(z) \big) \,\}$$

Admittedly, range restricted universal quantification with ranges returning infinitely many bindings for the quantified variables will, in general, hardly be evaluable in finite time.

However, more advanced evaluation methods might well be devised that could recognise, like in the example above, the necessary truth of a universally quantified formula. Furthermore, computable semantics are needed not only for those programs considered acceptable, but also for those considered buggy – as long as they are syntactically correct. From this point of view it is a serious drawback of the well-founded semantics that it is not always computable.

5.3.4   Stable and Well-Founded Semantics Compared

The well-founded semantics and the stable model semantics relate to each other as follows. For space reasons, the proofs are not included in this survey (they can be found in [155], for instance).

If a rule set is stratifiable (which holds in particular if it is definite), then it has a unique minimal model, which is its only stable model and is also its well-founded model and total.

If a rule set S has a total well-founded model, then this model is also the single stable model of S. Conversely, if a rule set S has a single stable model, then this model is also the well-founded model of S and it is total.

If a rule set S has a partial well-founded model I that is not total, i.e., in which some ground atoms have the truth value undefined, then S has either no stable model or more than one stable model.

In the latter case, a ground atom is true (or false, respectively) in all stable models of S if and only if it is true (or false, respectively) in I.

In other words, if a rule set S has a partial (non-total) well-founded model I and at least one stable model, then a ground atom A is undefined in I if and only if it has different truth values in different stable models of S.

Furthermore, if a rule set has no stable model, then some ground atoms are undefined in its well-founded model.

Roughly speaking, the stable model semantics and the well-founded semantics tend to agree with each other and with the intuition, when there is a unique minimal Herbrand model that conveys the intuitive meaning.

When there are several minimal Herbrand models that convey the intuitive meaning, such as for $S_2 = \{ (p \leftarrow \neg q), (q \leftarrow \neg p) \}$ with minimal models $HI(\{p\})$ and $HI(\{q\})$, then these tend to be exactly the stable models, and the well-founded model tends to be partial, because it represents their "merge" (being defined where they agree and undefined where they disagree).

When no minimal Herbrand model clearly conveys the intuitive meaning, such as for $S_3 = \{ (p \leftarrow \neg p) \}$ with minimal model $HI(\{p\})$, then there tends to exist no stable model (corresponding to the "justification postulate") whereas the well-founded model exists (corresponding to the "consistency postulate"), but tends to leave the truth values of all atoms undefined.

Thus, the well-founded semantics cannot differentiate between the two critical cases, although they are quite different.

5.3.5   Inflationary Semantics

In this subsection, we restrict our attention to *datalog¬* programs. Thus, in this case, the Herbrand universe is always a finite universe denoted as **dom** and the Herbrand base *HB* is finite, too. A *datalog¬* program P is a finite set of normal clauses. Recall from Definition 21 that a *normal clause* is a rule r of the form

$$A \leftarrow L_1, \ldots, L_m$$

where $m \geq 0$ and A is an atom $R_0(\boldsymbol{x}_0)$. Each L_i is an atom $R_i(\boldsymbol{x}_i)$ or a negated atom $\neg R_i(\boldsymbol{x}_i)$. The arguments $\boldsymbol{x}_0, \ldots, \boldsymbol{x}_m$ are vectors of variables or constants (from **dom**). Every variable in $x_0, \ldots, x_m$ must occur in some unnegated atom $L_i = R_i(x_i)$, i.e., the clause must be range restricted (Definition 23).

We denote the head (consequent) of a rule r as $H(r)$, and the body (antecedent) of r as $B(r)$. We further distinguish the positive and negative literals in the body as follows:

$$B^+(r) = \{R(x) \mid \exists i\, L_i = R(x)\}, \quad B^-(r) = \{R(x) \mid \exists i\, L_i = \neg R(x)\}$$

Let us now extend the definition of the *immediate consequence operator*

$$\mathbf{T}_P(\mathbf{I}) : \mathcal{P}(HB) \to \mathcal{P}(HB)$$

(cf. Definition 153) to rules containing negated atoms. Note that since HB is finite, so is $\mathcal{P}(HB)$.

Definition 188 (Immediate consequence operator $\mathbf{T}_P(\mathbf{I})$ for datalog$^\neg$).
Given a datalog$^\neg$ program P and an instance $\mathbf{I}$ over its schema $sch(P)$, a fact $R(t)$ is an immediate consequence *for $\mathbf{I}$ and P (denoted as $\mathbf{T}_P(\mathbf{I})$), if either R is an extensional predicate symbol of P and $R(t) \in \mathbf{I}$, or there exists some ground instance r of a rule in P such that*

- $H(r) = R(t)$,
- $B^+(r) \subseteq \mathbf{I}$, *and*
- $B^-(r) \cap \mathbf{I} = \emptyset$.

The *inflationary semantics* [5,2] is inspired by inflationary fixpoint logic [86]. In place of the immediate consequence operator $\mathbf{T}_P$, it uses the *inflationary operator* $\widetilde{\mathbf{T}}_P$, which (for any datalog$^\neg$ program P) is defined as follows:

$$\widetilde{\mathbf{T}}_P(\mathbf{I}) = \mathbf{I} \cup \mathbf{T}_P(\mathbf{I})$$

Definition 189 (Inflationary semantics of datalog$^\neg$). *Given a datalog$^\neg$ program P and an instance $\mathbf{I}$ over the extensional predicate symbols of P, the inflationary semantics of P w.r.t. $\mathbf{I}$, denoted as $P_{inf}(\mathbf{I})$, is the limit of the sequence $\{\widetilde{\mathbf{T}}_P^i(\mathbf{I})\}_{i \geq 0}$, where $\widetilde{\mathbf{T}}_P^0(\mathbf{I}) = \mathbf{I}$ and $\widetilde{\mathbf{T}}_P^{i+1}(\mathbf{I}) = \widetilde{\mathbf{T}}_P(\widetilde{\mathbf{T}}_P^i(\mathbf{I}))$.*

By the definition of $\widetilde{\mathbf{T}}_P$, the following sequence of inclusions holds:

$$\widetilde{\mathbf{T}}_P^0(\mathbf{I}) \subseteq \widetilde{\mathbf{T}}_P^1(\mathbf{I}) \subseteq \widetilde{\mathbf{T}}_P^2(\mathbf{I}) \subseteq \ldots$$

Furthermore, each set in this sequence is a subset of the finite set HB, such that the sequence clearly reaches a fixpoint $P_{inf}(\mathbf{I})$ after a finite number of steps. However, $HI(P_{inf}(\mathbf{I}))$ is a model of P containing $\mathbf{I}$, but not necessarily a *minimal* model containing $\mathbf{I}$.

Example 190. Let P be the program: $\{\,(p \leftarrow s \wedge \neg q),\ (q \leftarrow s \wedge \neg p)\,\}$. Let $\mathbf{I} = \{s\}$. Then $P_{inf}(\mathbf{I}) = \{s, p, q\}$. Although $HI(P_{inf}(\mathbf{I}))$ is a model of P, it is not minimal. The minimal models containing $\mathbf{I}$ are $HI(\{s, p\})$ and $HI(\{s, q\})$.

The above example shows that given an instance $\mathbf{I}$, the inflationary semantics $P_{inf}(\mathbf{I})$ of P w.r.t. $\mathbf{I}$ may not yield any of the minimal models that convey the intuitive meaning of P. Moreover, $P_{inf}(\mathbf{I})$ is not necessarily the least fixpoint of $\widetilde{\mathbf{T}}_P$ containing $\mathbf{I}$, either. In fact, the inflationary operator $\widetilde{\mathbf{T}}_P$ is not monotonic. With the above example, let I_1 be $\{s\}$, and I_2 be $\{s, p\}$. Then $\widetilde{\mathbf{T}}_P(I_1) = \{s, p, q\}$, and $\widetilde{\mathbf{T}}_P(I_2) = \{s, p\}$.

Thus the existence of a least fixpoint cannot be guaranteed by the Knaster-Tarski Theorem 148, but then it might be guaranteed by the finiteness of $\mathcal{P}(HB)$. However, the problem is[12] that there may be different minimal fixpoints. In the example above, both $\{s, p\}$ and $\{s, q\}$ are fixpoints of $\widetilde{\mathbf{T}}_P$ containing $\{s\}$, but none of their proper subsets is.

Let us now see how the inflationary semantics behaves with the examples used earlier to illustrate and compare the other approaches.

Example 191. $S_1 = \{(q \leftarrow r \wedge \neg p),\ (r \leftarrow s \wedge \neg t),\ (s \leftarrow \top)\}$
$$\widetilde{\mathbf{T}}_{S_1}^1(\emptyset) = \{s\},$$
$$\widetilde{\mathbf{T}}_{S_1}^2(\emptyset) = \{s, r\},$$
$$\widetilde{\mathbf{T}}_{S_1}^3(\emptyset) = \{s, r, q\} = \widetilde{\mathbf{T}}_{S_1}^4(\emptyset).$$
Thus the inflationary fixpoint of S_1 is $\{s, r, q\}$, which agrees with the stable and the well-founded semantics and with the intuitive meaning.

Example 192. $S_2 = \{(p \leftarrow \neg q),\ (q \leftarrow \neg p)\}$
$$\widetilde{\mathbf{T}}_{S_2}^1(\emptyset) = \{p, q\} = \widetilde{\mathbf{T}}_{S_2}^2(\emptyset).$$
Thus the inflationary fixpoint of S_2 is $\{p, q\}$, which is not minimal and disagrees with the stable and the well-founded semantics and with the intuitive meaning. It represents the union of all minimal models.

Example 193. $S_3 = \{(p \leftarrow \neg p)\}$
$$\widetilde{\mathbf{T}}_{S_3}^1(\emptyset) = \{p\} = \widetilde{\mathbf{T}}_{S_3}^2(\emptyset).$$
The inflationary fixpoint of S_3 is $\{p\}$, which corresponds to the intuitive understanding based on the "consistency postulate", but differs from both the stable model semantics (there is no stable model) and the well-founded semantics (the well-founded model leaves the truth value of p undefined).

Example 194. $S_4 = \{(p \leftarrow \neg p),\ (p \leftarrow \top)\}$
$$\widetilde{\mathbf{T}}_{S_4}^1(\emptyset) = \{p\} = \widetilde{\mathbf{T}}_{S_4}^2(\emptyset).$$
The inflationary fixpoint of S_4 is $\{p\}$, which agrees with the stable and the well-founded semantics and with the intuitive meaning.

These examples may give the impression that the inflationary semantics just handles the critical cases differently from the other approaches, but agrees with them in uncritical cases. However, this is not so.

Example 195. $S_5 = \{(r \leftarrow \neg q),\ (q \leftarrow \neg p)\}$ has two minimal models $HI(\{q\})$ and $HI(\{p, r\})$, of which only the first conveys the intuitive meaning under the

---

[12] Another problem is that even if a least fixpoint exists, Lemma 150 is not applicable. If $\widetilde{\mathbf{T}}_P^n(\mathbf{I}) = \widetilde{\mathbf{T}}_P^{n+1}(\mathbf{I})$, this might not be the least fixpoint.

closed world assumption. This model coincides with the only stable model and with the well-founded model, which is total. Note that the set is stratifiable.

The inflationary fixpoint of S_5 is $\widetilde{\mathbf{T}}^1_{S_5}(\emptyset) = \{q, r\}$, which is neither intuitive nor related to the minimal models in any systematic way.

The inflationary semantics gives up a fundamental principle, which the other approaches do keep: that models are preserved when adding logical consequences, that is, if a formula φ is true in all "canonical" models of S, then each "canonical" model of S is also a model of $S \cup \{\varphi\}$. In the previous example, q is true in the only inflationary model $HI(\{q, r\})$ of S_5, but $HI(\{q, r\})$ is not an inflationary model of $S_5 \cup \{q\}$.

This may be the deeper reason why in spite of its attractive complexity properties (Section 8) the inflationary semantics is not very much being used in practice.[13]

5.4   RDF Model Theory

5.4.1   Introduction to RDF

"The *Resource Description Framework* (*RDF*) is a language for representing information about 'resources' on the world wide web" [114].

Resources. How is the concept of "resource" to be understood? While RDF data representing information *about* resources is supposed to be accessible on the Web, the resources themselves do not necessarily have to be accessible. Thus, a "resource" is not necessarily a Web site or service. A resource is any (tangible or intangible) entity one represents information about.

Each resource is assumed to be uniquely identified by a *uniform resource identifier (URI)*, and everything identified by a URI is a resource.[14] A URI only plays the role of a unique identifier comparable to a bar code. In contrast to a *uniform resource locator (URL)*, a URI identifying a resource is not assumed to point to a Web page representing this resource – even though in practice this is often the case.

Triples and graphs. RDF data is represented in the form of *triples* consisting of a *subject*, a *predicate* and an *object* with the predicate representing a binary relation between the subject and the object. Instead of triples, one might just as well express RDF data in the form of atoms where the predicate is written as a binary relation symbol with the subject and the object as arguments.

Definition 196 (RDF syntax)

– *There are two classes of RDF symbols:*

---

[13] But it does integrate imperative constructs into logic, and there are indications that it may be useful for querying relational databases, see Section 14.5 in [2].

[14] Note the circularity of this definition.

- *An* RDF Vocabulary $V = U \cup L$ *consists of two disjoint subsets:*
  a set U *of so-called* URI references *and a set* L *of so-called* literals.
  Both URI references and literals are also called names.
- B *is a set disjoint from* V *containing so-called* blank nodes *or* b-nodes.

  − *From these symbols the following complex structures may be formed:*

  - *An* RDF triple *or* RDF statement *in* V *and with blank nodes in* B *is an expression of the form* (s, p, o) *where*
    $s \in U \cup B$ *is called the* subject *of the triple,*
    $p \in U$ *is called the* predicate *or* property *of the triple,*
    $o \in U \cup B \cup L$ *is called the* object *of the triple.*
    An RDF triple is ground *if it contains no blank node.*
  - *An* RDF graph *in* V *and with blank nodes in* B *is a finite or infinite or empty subset of* $(U \cup B) \times U \times (U \cup B \cup L)$, *i.e., a set of RDF triples. An RDF graph is* ground *if the triples it contains are all ground.*

In the context of RDF (and throughout this subsection) the word *literal* is not used as in logic (see Definition 19), but as in programming languages, where *literal* means a textual representation of a value.

In order to make the intention of the RDF notions easier to grasp, let us draw some rough analogies to first-order predicate logic.

An RDF vocabulary $V = U \cup L$ is analogous to a signature (Definition 3) and the blank nodes in B are analogous to variables, which belong to the logical symbols (Definition 2). The literals in L are analogous to constants, but with the intention that they should not be arbitrarily interpreted, but as strings or numbers or similar values. The URI references in U are also analogous to constants, but, being permitted in predicate position, also to relation symbols. In the terminology of Section 3, the signature is overloaded.

A triple is analogous to an atomic formula, but there are restrictions how it may be constructed: URI references from U may occur in all three positions, literals from L may only occur in object position, blank nodes from B may occur in subject or object position, but not in predicate position.

An RDF graph is analogous to a formula or set of formulas. A finite RDF graph corresponds to the existential closure of the conjunction of its triples. An infinite RDF graph corresponds to the appropriate generalisation, which does not have a direct counterpart in first-order predicate logic.

A slightly different analogy explains the terminology "RDF graph". Given a set of triples, the set of members of $U \cup L \cup B$ occurring in subject or object position can be regarded as "nodes", and each triple (s, p, o) can be regarded as a directed edge from s to o that is labelled with p. Thus an RDF graph corresponds to a graph in the mathematical sense.

Moreover, the URI references occurring in subject or object position of triples can also be regarded as pointers to the actual data representing the resource, which can be used in efficient implementations for a fast data access. This view illustrates the advantage of distinguishing between identifiers and resources in RDF (compare also Section 9.2.4) in spite of the slightly more involved formalism. The same distinction is made in object-oriented databases, and as pointed out in [23], storing RDF data as graphs in object-oriented databases may be preferable over storing them as relational tuples, as far as data retrieval and query answering are concerned.

5.4.2   Formal Semantics of RDF

The *formal semantics of RDF* [87] is specified similarly to that of first-order predicate logic by a Tarski style model theory. The concepts of interpretation and model serve to define a notion of logical consequence, or entailment, of an RDF graph.

However, there is not a single notion of an RDF interpretation, but several ones, each imposing additional constraints to the previous one:

- *Simple RDF Interpretations*
- *RDF Interpretations*
- *RDFS Interpretations*

Simple RDF interpretation is the basic notion: RDF interpretations and RDFS interpretations are simple RDF interpretations satisfying further conditions.

RDF interpretations give special meaning to predefined URI references such as `rdf:type`, `rdf:Property` and `rdf:XMLLiteral`: the URI reference `rdf:type` expresses a notion of instance relationship between the instance of a type and the type class itself (named in analogy to object-oriented type systems), `rdf:Property` expresses the type class of all predicates and `rdf:XMLLiteral` expresses the type class of all XML literals.[15]

RDFS interpretations are RDF interpretations that give special meaning to some additional URI references related to domain and range of properties or to subclass relationship (which, remarkably, may be cyclic).

Simple RDF Interpretations. It is convenient to distinguish between "untyped" (or "plain") and "typed literals". The former are syntactic representations of values that cannot be represented by other literals, such as the boolean value `true`; such literals are to be interpreted as "themselves", i.e., they are element of the domain. The latter are syntactic representations of values that may also be represented by other literals, such as the floating point number 0.11, which according to XML Schema, the reference for RDF scalar datatypes, can be represented by the literals `".11"^^xsd:float` and `"0.110"^^xsd:float`, among others.[16]

Definition 197 (Simple RDF interpretation of an RDF vocabulary). *A simple RDF interpretation $I = (IR, IP, IEXT, IS, IL, LV)$ of an RDF Vocabulary $V = U \cup L^T \cup L^U$ where U is a set of URIs, L^T a set of typed literals, and L^U a set of untyped literals (with $L^T \cap L^U = \emptyset$), is defined as follows:*

- *IR is a set of resources, called the domain of I*

---

[15] Following a widespread practice, `rdf` is the namespace prefix for the XML namespace of RDF and used here for conciseness instead of the actual namespace URI.

[16] Following a widespread practice, `xsd` stands for the namespace of XML Schema.

- *IP is a set, called the* set of properties[17] *of I*
- *IEXT : IP → P(IR × IR) is a total function*
- *IS : U → IR ∪ IP is a total function*
- *IL : L^T → IR is a total function*
- *LV ⊆ IR, called the* set of literal values *of I. Recall, that the untyped literals are interpreted as "themselves", i.e., L^U ⊆ LV.*

The main difference between the above definition and the corresponding part of the definition of an interpretation for first-order predicate logic are as follows:

- In simple RDF interpretations, a predicate symbol in U is not directly associated with a binary relation, but with an arbitrary domain element that refers, by means of *IEXT* to the actual binary relation. Note that no conditions are put on how such a "relation representative" may occur in relations. Thus, in a simple RDF interpretation, a domain element d may well occur in the relation it "represents". As a consequence, this additional level of "relation representatives" is no stringent deviation from Tarski model theory for first-order predicate logic.

  Furthermore, this tie between the "relation representative" and the actual relation in a simple RDF interpretation is used in none of the other concepts of RDF semantics – RDF semantics keeps an account of all overloaded symbols, but does not make use of this book-keeping. Indeed, following [50], the classical model theory for RDF introduced below does not maintain this tie between "relation representative" and actual relation.
- Simple RDF interpretations of RDF *vocabularies* do not interpret blank nodes, since they are not part of an RDF vocabulary. Only the extension of simple RDF interpretations to RDF *graphs* (Definition 199) needs to consider blank nodes, and does so in the spirit of Tarski model theory for first-order predicate logic in the case of existentially quantified variables.

Thus, simple RDF interpretations of RDF vocabularies are, in spite of "stylistic" peculiarities, very much in line with Tarski model theory for first-order predicate logic.[18]

Simple RDF Interpretations of Ground RDF Graphs. The notion of simple RDF interpretation of RDF vocabularies introduced above is extended to RDF graphs such that a ground RDF graph is interpreted as the conjunction of its (ground) RDF triples, which are interpreted like ground atoms. Note, however, that this intuitive view may lead to infinite formulas (not considered in first-order predicate logic) as an RDF graph may contain infinitely many triples.

---

[17] The denomination "set of property representatives" would be more accurate.

[18] In the document introducing RDF Model theory, the notions "interpretation" and "denotation" do not seem to be clearly distinguished. Whereas the table of contents and the definitions suggest that denotations are defined on graphs and interpretations on vocabularies only, in later sections the parlance changes to "denotations of names" and to interpretations that assign truth values to graphs. In this tutorial, only the name "interpretation" is used both for vocabularies and for RDF graphs.

As a minor detail, RDF makes it possible to specify the language of an untyped literal `lit` using the widespread ISO 639 and IETF 1766 standardised language codes: `lit@en` means that `lit` is in English, `lit@de` means that `lit` is in German, etc.

Definition 198 (Simple RDF interpretations of ground RDF graphs).
Let $I = (IR, IP, IEXT, IS, IL, LV)$ be a simple RDF interpretation of an RDF vocabulary $V = U \cup L^T \cup L^U$ with set of URIs U, set of typed literals L^T and set of untyped literals L^U, where $L^T \cap L^U = \emptyset$.

I is extended to ground RDF graphs as follows:

- $I(lit) = lit$ *(untyped literal in V)*
- $I(lit@lang) = (lit, lang)$ *(untyped literal with language in V)*
- $I(lit\char94\char94 type) = IL(lit)$ *(typed literal in V)*
- $I(uri) = IS(uri)$ *(URI in V)*
- $I((s, p, o)) = true$ *(ground RDF triple)*
  iff $s, p, o \in V,$ $I(p) \in IP,$ $(I(s), I(o)) \in IEXT(I(p))$
- $I(G) = true$ *(ground RDF graph)*
  iff $I((s, p, o)) = true$ *for all triples* (s, p, o) *in G.*

Note that the empty graph is true in all simple RDF interpretations.

Note furthermore that a ground RDF graph G is false in a simple RDF interpretation of a vocabulary V as soon as the subject, predicate or object of a triple in G does not belong to the vocabulary V. This is a slight (though entirely benign) deviation from the model theory of first-order predicate logic, which does not assign truth values to formulas composed of symbols from another vocabulary, or signature, than that of the interpretation considered.

Extended Simple RDF Interpretations of RDF Graphs. Simple RDF interpretation only apply to *ground* RDF graphs. This notion is extended to RDF graphs containing blank nodes such that an RDF graph is interpreted as the existential closure (the blank nodes representing variables) of the conjunction of its triples. As pointed out above, this intuition may lead to infinite formulas with, in presence of blank nodes, possibly even infinitely many variables, a case not considered in first-order predicate logic. The technique of the extension is to add to an interpretation I a mapping A that corresponds to a variable assignment.

Definition 199 (Extended simple RDF interpretation). *Let V be an RDF vocabulary and B a set of blank nodes with $V \cap B = \emptyset$. Furthermore, let $I = (IR, IP, IEXT, IS, IL, LV)$ be a simple RDF interpretation of V.*

A blank node assignment for B in I is a total function $A : B \to IR$ mapping each blank node to a member of the domain of I.

For any blank node assignment A the extended simple RDF interpretation $[I + A]$ is defined as follows:

- $[I + A](bnode) = A(bnode)$ *(bnode)*
- $[I + A](lit) = I(lit)$ *(untyped literal in V)*
- $[I + A](lit@lang) = I(lit@lang)$ *(untyped literal with language in V)*

- $[I + A](\text{lit\^\^type}) = I(\text{lit\^\^type})$ *(typed literal in V)*
- $[I + A](\text{uri}) = I(\text{uri})$ *(URI in V)*
- $[I + A]((s, p, o)) = \text{true}$ *(ground or non-ground RDF triple)*
  iff $s, o \in V \cup B$, $p \in V$, $I(p) \in IP$ and $([I + A](s), [I + A](o)) \in IEXT(I(p))$
- $[I + A](G) = \text{true}$ *(ground or non-ground RDF graph)*
  iff $[I + A]((s, p, o)) = \text{true}$ for all triples (s, p, o) in G

The simple RDF interpretation I satisfies a ground or non-ground RDF graph G, iff there exists a blank node assignment A with $[I + A](G) = \text{true}$.

Definition 200 (Simple RDF entailment). *Let G_1 and G_2 be two arbitrary RDF graphs. The simple RDF entailment relation $\models_{simply}$ is defined as follows: $G_1 \models_{simply} G_2$, read G_1 simply entails G_2, if and only if all simple RDF interpretations satisfying G_1 also satisfy G_2.*

A Classical Model Theory for Simple RDF Entailment. The RDF model theory has been criticised for its non-standardness and several problems have been identified in the context of layering more expressive ontology or rule languages on top of RDF. In this section, we propose a model theory which is closer to classical logics to characterise simple RDF entailment.[19] This characterisation shows that simple RDF entailment on finite RDF graphs is the same as entailment for first-order predicate logical formulas that

- are existential[20],
- are conjunctive[21],
- contain only binary relation symbols, and
- contain no function symbols of arity ≥ 1

For infinite RDF graphs it is an obvious generalisation of entailment for first-order predicate logic.

First, *classical RDF interpretations* and models are introduced, and the entailment relation $\models_{classical}$ is defined based on the notion of classical RDF models. Furthermore a one-to-one mapping between classical RDF interpretations and extended simple RDF interpretations is established. Finally we show that for two arbitrary RDF graphs G_1 and G_2 holds $G_1 \models_{simply} G_2$ if and only if $G_1 \models_{classical} G_2$.

Definition 201 (Classical RDF interpretation). *Let $V = U \cup B \cup L$ be an RDF Vocabulary where U is a set of URI references, B a set of blank node identifiers and Li a set of literals. We call elements in U also in analogy to first-order predicate logic constant symbols and distinguish the set of predicate symbols $U_P \subset U$. Note, that here a predicate symbol is necessarily also a constant symbol (in contrast to standard first-order predicate logic, cf. Section 3.1, where predicate and constant symbols are allowed but not required to overlap). A classical RDF interpretation $I = (D, M^c, M^p, M^l, A)$ consists of*

---

[19] Note that this theory does not characterise the other forms of RDF entailment such as non-simple RDF entailment or RDFS entailment.

[20] I.e. a formula the negation of which is universal.

[21] I.e. the matrix of their prenex normal form is a conjunction of atoms.

- a domain of discourse $D \subset L^U$ where $L^U \subset L$ is the set of untyped literals in L,
- a total function M^c from URI references (constant symbols) in U to elements of the domain D,
- a total function M^p from predicate symbols in U_P to elements in $\mathcal{P}(D \times D)$
- a total function M^l from literals in L to elements of the domain D, plain literals are mapped to themselves,
- and a blank node assignment function A from B to $U \cup L$.

The main deviation from standard first-order predicate logic interpretations are the specific treatment of literals and that predicate symbols are required to be a subset of the constant symbols. The latter is required for equivalence with the notion of extended simple RDF interpretation from [87] as explained in the previous section and could otherwise be dropped.

Definition 202 (Classical RDF model). Let G be an RDF graph and $I = (D, M^c, M^p, M^l, A)$ a classical RDF interpretation of the vocabulary $V = U \cup B \cup L$ where U is a set of URIs, B is a set of blank node identifiers, and L is a set of literals. I is a model of G, if for every triple $(s, p, o) \in G$, s is in $U \cup B$, p is in U, o is in $U \cup B \cup L$, and the tuple $(M^c(s), M^c(o))$ is in the relation $M^p(p)$ interpreting the predicate symbol p.

We define the *classical RDF entailment* relation $\models_{classical}$ in the expected way: A graph G_1 entails a graph G_2 if and only if every classical model of G_1 is also a classical model of G_2.

Definition 203 (Classical interpretation corresponding to an extended simple RDF interpretation). Let $V = U \cup B \cup L^T \cup L^U$ be an RDF vocabulary where U is a set of URI references, B a set of blank node identifiers, L^T a set of typed, and L^U a set of untyped literals. Let $I = [(IR, IP, IEXT, IS, IL, LV) + A]$ be an extended simple RDF interpretation of V. The corresponding classical interpretation $class(I) = (D, M^c, M^p, M^l, A')$ of the same vocabulary V is defined as follows:

- $D := IR$
- $M^c(c) := IS(c)$ for all $c \in U$
- $M^p(p) := IEXT(IS(p))$ for all $p \in P$ such that $IEXT(IS(p))$ is defined.
- $M^l(l) := IL(l)$ for all typed literals in L^T
- $A' := A$

Lemma 204. Let G be an RDF graph, and I an extended simple RDF interpretation of the vocabulary V. Let $class(I)$ be the corresponding classical interpretation of the vocabulary V. If $I \models_{simply} G$ then $class(I) \models_{classical} G$.

Proof. Let $I = [(IR, IP, IEXT, IS, IL, LV) + A]$ and $class(I) = (D, M^c, M^p, M^l, A)$. Let $V = U \cup B \cup L^T \cup L^U$ where U is the set of URIs, B the set of blank node identifiers, L^T the set of typed literals, and L^U the set of untyped literals of V. It suffices to show that for any triple (s, p, o) in G the following conditions hold:

- $s \in U \cup B$: (s, p, o) is in G, I is a model of G, hence $s \in U \cup B$: by definition
- $p \in U$: by definition
- $o \in U \cup B \cup L$: by definition
- $(M^c(s), M^c(o)) \in M^p(p)$: (s, p, o) is in G, I is a model of G, therefore the tuple $(IS(s), IS(o))$ is in $IEXT(IS(p))$, hence $(M(s), M(o)) \in M^p(p)$. $\square$

In the following definition $dom(f)$ denotes the domain of a function f.

Definition 205 (Extended simple RDF interpretation corresponding to a classical RDF interpretation). Let $V = U \cup B \cup L^T \cup L^U$ be an RDF vocabulary where U is a set of URI references, B a set of blank node identifiers, L^T a set of typed literals, and L^U a set of untyped literals. Let $I_c = (D, M^c, M^p, M^l, A)$ be a classical RDF interpretation over V. The extended simple RDF interpretation $RDF(I_c) = [(IR, IP, IEXT, IS, IL, LV) + A']$ corresponding to I_c is defined as follows:

- $IR := D$
- $IP := \{ M^c(p) \mid p \in dom(M^p) \text{ and } p \in dom(M^c) \}$
- $IEXT : IP \rightarrow (IR \times IR)$, $IEXT(M^c(p)) := M^p(p)$ for all p in U such that both M^c and M^p are defined on p.
- $IS : U \rightarrow IR \cup IP$, $IS(u) := M^c(u)$ for all c in U.
- $IL := M^l$
- LV is the set of untyped literals L^U
- $A'(x) := A(x)$ for all $x \in B$

Lemma 206. Let G be an RDF graph, I_c a classical interpretation of the vocabulary V, and $RDF(I_c)$ its corresponding RDF interpretation. If $I_c \models_{classical} G$ then $RDF(I_c)$ is a simple RDF model of G.

Proof. We have to show that $RDF(I_c) \models_{simply} G$. Hence $RDF(I_c) \models_{simply} t$ must be true for every triple t in G. Let $t := (s, p, o)$ be a triple in G. Then $I_c \models_{classical} t$ is true by assumption. Therefore s is in $C \cup B$, p is in U and o is in $U \cup B \cup L$. Moreover $(M^c(s), M^c(o)) \in M^p(p)$. Hence $(IS(s), IS(o)) \in IEXT(IS(p))$, and thus $RDF(I_c) \models_{simply} G$. $\square$

Lemma 207. Let I_s be an extended simple RDF interpretation and I_c a classical RDF interpretation of the same vocabulary. Then $RDF(class(I_s)) = I_s$ and $class(RDF(I_c)) = I_c$.

Proof. This lemma is a direct consequence of the Definitions 203 and 205. $\square$

From Lemmata 204, 206 and 207 we can immediately conclude the following corollary:

Corollary 208 (Equivalence of classical RDF entailment and simple RDF entailment). Let G_1 and G_2 be two RDF graphs. $G_1 \models_{simply} G_2$ if and only if $G_1 \models_{classical} G_2$.

In [50], a more involved reformulation of RDF interpretation and entailment is presented that also extends to RDFS interpretations and entailment. However, for consistency with the rest of this article, we have chosen the above presentation.

6   Operational Semantics: Positive Rule Sets

6.1   Semi-naive Evaluation of Datalog Programs

The fixpoint semantics of a positive logic program P directly yields an operational semantics based on canonical forward chaining of the immediate consequence operator $\mathbf{T}_P$ introduced in Section 5 (Definition 153) until the least fixpoint is reached.

Let us quickly recapitulate the definition of the fixpoint of a datalog program P given the example program in Listing 6_1.

Listing 6_1. An example program for fixpoint calculation

```
feeds_milk(betty).
lays_eggs(betty).
has_spines(betty).

monotreme(X) ← lays_eggs(X), feeds_milk(X).
echidna(X) ← monotreme(X), has_spines(X).
```

The *intensional* predicate symbols of a datalog program P are all those predicate symbols that appear within the head of a rule, as opposed to the *extensional* predicate symbols which appear only in the bodies of rules of a program. With this definition `feeds_milk`, `lays_eggs` and `has_spines` are extensional predicate symbols, whereas `monotreme` and `echidna` are intensional predicate symbols. The set of all extensional and intensional predicate symbols of a datalog program P (denoted $ext(P)$ and $int(P)$ respectively) is called the schema of P. An *instance* over a schema of a logic program is a set of sets of tuples $s_1, \ldots, s_k$, where each set of tuples $s_i, 1 \leq i \leq k$ is associated with a predicate symbol p in the schema and s_i is the extension of p. The set of base facts of the program 6_1 corresponds to an instance over the extensional predicate symbols, where the set $\{betty\}$ is the set associated with each of the symbols `feeds_milk`, `lays_eggs` and `has_spines`.

Based on these definitions the semantics of a logic program P is defined as a mapping from extensions over $ext(P)$ to extensions over $int(P)$. There are several possibilities to define this function. The fixpoint semantics uses the *immediate consequence operator* $\mathbf{T}_P$ for this aim.

Given a datalog program P and an instance I over its schema $sch(P)$, an atom A is an *immediate consequence* of P and I if it is either already contained in I or if there is a rule $A \leftarrow cond_1, \ldots, cond_n$ in P where $cond_i \in I$ $\forall 1 \leq i \leq n$. The immediate consequence operator $\mathbf{T}_P(I)$ maps an instance over the schema $sch(P)$ to the set of immediate consequences of P and I.

A fixpoint over the operator $\mathbf{T}_P$ is defined as an instance I such that $\mathbf{T}_P(I) = I$. It turns out that any fixpoint for a datalog program is a model of the (conjunction of clauses of the) program. Furthermore, the model-theoretic semantics $P(I)$ of a logic program P on an input instance I, which is defined as the minimum model of P that also contains I, is the minimum fixpoint of $\mathbf{T}_P$.

As mentioned above, this fixpoint semantics for datalog programs, which may be extended to non-datalog rules[69], gives directly rise to a constructive algorithm to compute the minimum model of a program.

Consider again Listing 6.1. The set of immediate consequences of this program with the initial instance[22] $I_0 = \{\{\}_{f\_m}, \{\}_{l\_e}, \{\}_{h\_s}, \{\}_{mon}, \{\}_{ech}\}$ is $I_1 :=$ $\mathbf{T}_P(I_0) = \{\{betty\}_{f\_m}, \{betty\}_{l\_e}, \{betty\}_{h\_s}, \{\}_{mon}, \{\}_{ech}\}$. The second application of the fixpoint operator yields $I_2 := \mathbf{T}_P^2(I_0) = \{\{betty\}_{f\_m}, \{betty\}_{l\_e}, \{betty\}_{h\_s}, \{betty\}_{mon}, \{\}_{ech}\}$.

I_3 is defined analogously and the extension of echidna is set to $\{betty\}$. Finally the application of $\mathbf{T}_P$ to I_3 does not yield any additional facts such that the condition $I_3 = I_4$ is fulfilled, and the fixpoint is reached.

The above procedure can be implemented with the pseudo-algorithm in Listing 6.2, which is called *naive evaluation* of datalog programs, because for the computation of I_i all elements of I_{i-1} are recomputed. As suggested by its name, the function ground_facts returns all the ground facts of the program which is to be evaluated. The function instantiations takes as a first argument a rule R, which may contain variables, and as a second argument the set of facts I_{i-1} which have been derived in the previous iteration. It finds all instantiations of the rule R which can be satisfied with the elements of I_{i-1}.

Listing 6.2. Naive evaluation of a datalog program P

```
I₀  := ∅
I₁  := ground_facts(P)
i   := 1
while Iᵢ ≠ Iᵢ₋₁ do
   i  := i + 1
   Iᵢ := Iᵢ₋₁
   while (R = Rules.next())
      Insts := instantiations(R, Iᵢ₋₁)
      while (inst = Insts.next())
         Iᵢ := Iᵢ ∪ head(inst)
return Iᵢ
```

The central idea underlying the so-called *semi-naive* evaluation of datalog programs is that all facts that can be newly derived in iteration i must use one of the facts that were newly derived in iteration $i - 1$ – otherwise they have already been derived earlier. To be more precise, the rule instantiations that justify the derivation of a new fact in iteration i must have a literal in their rule body which was derived in iteration $i - 1$. In order to realize this idea one must keep track of the set of newly derived facts in each iteration. This method is also called *incremental forward chaining* and is specified by Listing 6.3. In line 2 the increment Ink is initialized with all facts of the datalog program. In line

---

[22] the predicate symbols in subscript position indicate that the first set is the extension of feeds_milk, the second one the one of lays_eggs, and so on.

4 the set Insts of instantiations of rules that make use of at least one atom of the increment Ink is computed at the aid of the function instantiations. The function instantiations does not yield ground rules that are justified by the set KnownFacts only, such that the call instantiations({ p(a), q(a) }, { }) for a program consisting of the rule r(x) ←p(X), q(X) would *not* yield the instantiation i_1 := r(a) ←p(a), q(a). In contrast, i_1 would be returned by the call instantiations({ p(a) }, { q(a) }) with respect to the same program.

Once these fresh rule instantiations have been determined, the distinction between facts in the increment and older facts is no longer necessary, and the two sets are unified (line 5). The new increment of each iteration is given by the heads of the rule instantiations in Insts.

Listing 6_3. Semi-naive evaluation of a datalog program P

```
1   KnownFacts := ∅
2   Ink := { Fact | (Fact ← true) ∈ P }
3   while (Ink ≠ ∅)
4     Insts := instantiations(KnownFacts, Ink)
5     KnownFacts := KnownFacts ∪ Ink
6     Ink := heads(Insts)
7   return KnownFacts
```

Although the semi-naive evaluation of datalog programs avoids a lot of redundant computations that the naive evaluation performs, there are still several ways of optimizing it.

- In the case that besides a program P also a query q is given, it becomes apparent that a lot of computations, which are completely unrelated to q, are carried out. This is a general problem of forward chaining algorithms when compared to backward chaining. However, it is possible to write logic programs that, also when executed in a forward-chaining manner, are in a certain sense goal-directed. In fact it is possible to transform any datalog program P and query q into a logic program P' such that the forward chaining evaluation of P' only performs computations that are necessary for the evaluation of q. In Section 6.2 these so-called *magic templates transformations* are presented.
- A second source of inefficiency is that in each iteration i, it is tested from scratch whether the body of a rule is satisfied. It is often the case that a rule body completely satisfied in iteration i was almost completely satisfied in iteration $i-1$, but the information about which facts contributed to the satisfaction of rule premises in iteration $i-1$ must be recomputed in iteration i. It is therefore helpful to store complete and partial instantiations of rules during the entire evaluation of the program.
- Storing partial instantiations of rule bodies gives rise to another optimization if the rules of the program share some of their premises. In this case, the partial rule instantiations are shared among the rules. Both this and the

previous optimization are realized by the Rete algorithm, which is introduced in Section 6.3.

6.2   The Magic Templates Transformation Algorithm

The magic templates algorithm [51] is a method of introducing a goal directed search into a forward chaining program, thereby benefiting both from the termination of forward chaining programs and from the efficiency of goal directed search. It is important to emphasize that the evaluation of the transformed program is performed in the ordinary forward chaining way or can be combined with the semi-naive algorithm as described above.

The magic templates rewriting transforms a program P and a query q in two steps: a transformation of the program into an adorned version, and a rewriting of the adorned program into a set of rules that can be efficiently evaluated with a bottom up strategy.

6.2.1   Adornment of Datalog Programs

In the first step, the program is rewritten into an *adorned* version according to a *sideways information passing strategy*, often abbreviated sip.

A sideways information passing strategy determines how variable bindings gained from the unification of a rule head with a goal or sub-goal are passed to the body of the rule, and how they are passed from a set of literals in the body to another literal. The ordinary evaluation of a Prolog program implements a special sideways information passing strategy, in which variable bindings are passed from the rule head and all previously occurring literals in the body to the body literal in question. There are, however, many other sips which may be more convenient in the evaluation of a datalog or Prolog program. In this survey, only the standard Prolog sip is considered, and the interested reader is referred to [18] for a more elaborate discussion of sideways information passing strategies.

The construction of an adorned program is exemplified by the transformation of the transitive closure program in Listing 6_4 together with the query t(a,Answer) into its adorned version in Listing 6_5. In order to better distinguish the different occurrences of the predicate t in the second rule, they are labeled t-1, t-2 and t-3, but they still denote the same predicate.

Listing 6_4. Transitive closure computation

```
t(X,Y) ← r(X, Y).
t-3(X,Z) ← t-1(X, Y), t-2(Y, Z).

r(a, b).
r(b, c).
r(c, d).
```

When evaluated in a backward chaining manner, the query $Q := $t(a,Answer) is first unified with the head of the first rule, generating the binding X=a which is passed to the rule body. This sideways information passing can be briefly expressed by $t \hookrightarrow_X r$. The query Q is also unified with the head of the second rule, generating once more the binding X=a, which would be used to evaluate the literal t-1(X,Y) by a Prolog interpreter. In the remaining evaluation of the second rule, the binding for Y computed by the evaluation of t-1(X,Y) is passed over to the predicate t-2. This can be briefly expressed by the sips $t-3 \hookrightarrow_X t-1$ and $t-1 \hookrightarrow_Y t-2$.

From this information passing strategy an adorned version of Listing 6.4 can be derived. Note that all occurrences of the predicate t (and its numbered versions) are evaluated with the first argument bound and the second argument free when Q is to be answered. In the magic templates transformation it is important to differentiate between different call-patterns for a predicate. This is where adornments for predicates come into play. An adornment a for a predicate p of arity n is a word consisting of n characters which are either 'b' (for bound) or 'f' (for free). Since the first argument of t is always bound in the program and the second argument is always free, the only adornment for t is bf. Since the evaluation of literals of *extensional* predicates amounts to simply looking up the appropriate values, adornments are only introduced for *intensional* predicate symbols.

It is interesting to note that the choice of the information passing strategy strongly influences the resulting adorned program. In the case that one chooses to evaluate the literal t-2 before t-1, both arguments of t-2 would be unbound yielding the sub-query $t-2^{ff}$, and thus an additional adorned version of the second rule would have to be introduced for this sub-query. This additional adorned rule would read $t-3^{ff}(X,Z) \leftarrow t-1^{fb}(X, Y), t-2^{ff}(Y, Z)..$ For the sake of simplicity, the following discussion refers to the shorter version depicted in Listing 6.5 only.

Listing 6.5. The adorned version of the program in Listing 6.4

```
t^{bf}(X,Y) ← r(X, Y).
t-3^{bf}(X,Z) ← t-1^{bf}(X, Y), t-2^{bf}(Y, Z).

r(a, b).
r(b, c).
r(c, d).
```

6.2.2   Goal-Directed Rewriting of the Adorned Program

Given an adorned datalog program P^{ad} and a query q, the general idea of the magic templates rewriting is to transform P^{ad} into a program P^{ad}_m in a way such that all sub-goals relevant for answering q can be computed from additional rules in P^{ad}_m. Slightly alternated versions of the original rules in P^{ad} are included in P^{ad}_m, the bodies of which ensure that the rule is only fulfilled if the head of the rule belongs to the set of relevant sub-goals.

Hence the magic template transformation generates two kinds of rules: The first set of rules controls the evaluation of the program by computing all relevant sub-goals from the query, and the second set of rules is an adapted version of the original program with additional premises in the bodies of the rules, which ensure that the rules are only evaluated if the result of the evaluation contributes to the answer of q.

The functioning of the magic templates transformation and the evaluation of the transformed program is again exemplified by the transitive closure computation in Listings 6_4 and 6_5.

1. In a first step, a predicate $\texttt{magic\_p}^a$ of arity $nb(p^a)$ is created for each adorned predicate $\mathbf{p}^a$ that occurs in the adorned program, where $nb(p^a)$ denotes the number of bound arguments in p^a – in other words the number of 'b's in the adornment a. Thus for the running example, the predicate $\texttt{magic\_t}^{bf}$ with arity one is introduced. The intuition behind magic predicates is that their extensions during bottom-up evaluation of the program, often referred to as *magic sets*, contain all those sub-goals that need to be computed for p^a. In the transitive closure example, the only initial instance of $\texttt{magic\_t}^{bf}$ is $\texttt{magic\_t}^{bf}(\texttt{a})$, which is directly derived from the query $\texttt{t(a,Answer)}$. This initial magic term is added as a seed[23] to the transformed program in Listing 6_6.

2. In a second step, rules for computing sub-goals are introduced reflecting the sideways information passing within the rules. Let r be a rule of the adorned program P^{ad}, let h^a be the head of r, and $l_1 \ldots l_k$ the literals in the body of r. If there is a query that unifies with the head of the rule, if queries for $l_1 \ldots l_i$ ($i < k$) have been issued and if they have been successful, the next step in a backward chaining evaluation of P^{ad} would be to pursue the sub-goal l_{i+1}. Thus a control rule $l_{i+1} \leftarrow \texttt{magic\_h}^a, l_1 \ldots l_i$ is included in P_m^{ad}. For the running example the rule $\texttt{magic\_t}^{bf}(\texttt{Y}) \leftarrow \texttt{magic\_t}^{bf}(\texttt{X}), \texttt{t(X,Y)}$ is added.

3. In a third step, the original rules of P^{ad} are adapted by adding some extra conditions to their bodies in order to evaluate them only if appropriate sub-goals have already been generated by the set of control rules. Let r be a rule in P^{ad} with head h^a and with literals $l_1, \ldots, l_n$. r shall only be evaluated if there is a sub-goal $magic\_h^a$ for the head, and if there are sub-goals for each of the derived predicates of the body. For the adorned version of the transitive closure program (Listing 6_5) both the first and the second rule must be rewritten. Since there is no derived predicate in the first rule, the only literal which must be added to the rule body is $\texttt{magic\_t}^{bf}(X)$, yielding the transformed rule $\texttt{t}^{bf}(\texttt{X,Y}) \leftarrow \texttt{magic\_t}^{bf}(X), \texttt{r(X,Y)}$. With the second rule having two derived predicates in the rule body, one might expect that three additional magic literals would have to be introduced in the rule body. But since $\texttt{t-1}$ and $\texttt{t-3}$ have the same adornment and the same variables for their bound arguments, they share the same magic predicate.

---

[23] It is called the *seed*, because all other magic terms are directly or indirectly derived from it.

The evaluation of the magic transitive closure program is presented in Listing 6_7 for the goal t(a, Answer). Note that in contrast to the naive and semi-naive bottom-up algorithms, only those facts are derived, which are potentially useful for answering the query. In particular, the facts r(1, 2), r(2, 3), and r(3, 1) are never used. Moreover the sub-goal r(d,X) corresponding to the magic predicate magic_t^{bf}(d) is never considered.

Listing 6_6. The magic templates transformation of the program in Listing 6_5 for the query t(a,X)

```
1  magic_t^bf(Y) ← magic_t^bf(X), t(X,Y).
2  t^bf(X,Y) ← magic_t^bf(X), r(X,Y).
3  t-3^bf(X,Z) ← magic_t^bf(X),t-1^bf(X,Y),magic_t^bf(Y), t-2^bf(Y,Z).
4  magic_t^bf(a). // the seed
5
6  r(a, b).   r(b, c).   r(c, d).
7  r(1, 2).   r(2, 3).   r(3, 1).
```

Listing 6_7. Evaluation of program 6_6

```
t(a,b)          // derived by the seed and rule 2
magic_t^bf(b)   // derived by the seed, t(a,b) and rule 1
t(b,c)          // derived by magic_t^bf(b), and rule 2
magic_t^bf(c)   // derived by magic_t^bf(b), t(b,c) and rule 1
t(c,d)          // derived by magic_t^bf(c) and rule 2
t(a,c)          // derived by rule 3
t(a,d)          // derived by rule 3
t(b,d)          // derived by rule 3
```

6.3   The Rete Algorithm

The Rete algorithm [72,56] was originally conceived by Charles L. Forgy in 1974 as an optimized algorithm for inference engines of rule based expert systems. Since then several optimizations of Rete have been proposed, and it has been implemented in various popular expert systems such as Drools, Soar, Clips, JRules and OPS5.

The Rete algorithm is used to process rules with a conjunction of conditions in the body and one or more actions in the head, that are to be carried out when the rule fires. These rules are stored in a so-called *production memory*. The other type of memory that is used by the Rete algorithm is the *working memory*, which holds all the facts that make up the current configuration the rule system is in. A possible action induced by a rule may be the addition of a new fact to the working memory, which may itself be an instance of a condition of a rule, therefore triggering further actions to be carried out in the system.

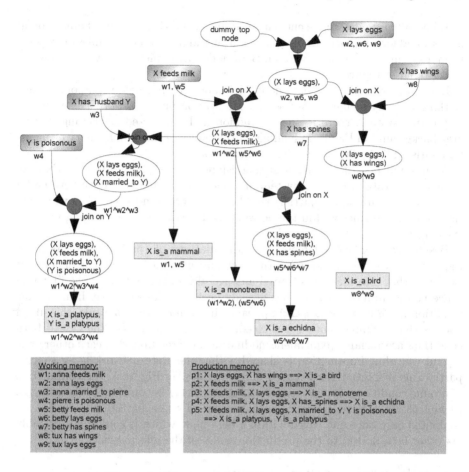

Fig. 1. A Rete Network for Animal Classification

Avoiding redundant derivations of facts and instances of rule precedents, the Rete algorithm processes production rules in a so-called *Rete network* consisting of *alpha-nodes*, *beta-nodes*, *join-nodes* and *production-nodes*.

Figure 1 illustrates the way a Rete network is built and operates. It serves as an animal classification system relying on characteristics such as has wings, has spikes, is poisonous, etc. The example rules exhibit overlapping rule bodies (several atomic conditions such as X lays eggs are shared among the rules).

For each atomic condition in the body of a rule, the Rete network features one alpha-node containing all the elements of the working memory that make this atomic condition true. Alpha-nodes are distinguished by shaded rectangles with round corners in Figure 1. Although the same atomic condition may occur multiple times distributed over different production rules, only one single alpha node is created in the Rete network to represent it. Therefore the condition X lays eggs, which is present in the conditions of all rules except for p2, is represented by a single alpha-node in Figure 1.

While alpha-nodes represent single atomic conditions of rule bodies, beta-nodes stand for conjunctions of such conditions, and hold sets of tuples of working memory elements that satisfy them. Beta-nodes are depicted as ovals with white background in Figure 1.

In contrast to alpha and beta nodes, join nodes do not hold tuples of or single working memory elements, but serve computation purposes only. For each rule in the rule system, there is one production node (depicted as rectangles with grey background in Figure 1) holding all the tuples of working memory elements that satisfy all the atomic conditions in its body.

Alpha- and beta-nodes are a distinguishing feature of Rete in that they remember the state of the rule system in a fine grained manner. With beta-nodes storing instantiations of (partial) rule bodies, there is no need of reevaluating the bodies of all rules within the network in the case that the working memory is changed.

Besides *storing* derived facts and instantiations of (partial) rule premises, the Rete network also allows information *sharing* to a large extent. There are two ways that information is shared among rules in the network. The first way concerns the alpha-nodes and has already been mentioned above. If an atomic condition (such as X feeds milk) appears within more than one rule, this alpha node is shared among both rules. Needless to say, this is also the case if both conditions are variants (equivalent modulo variable renaming) of each other. The second way that information is shared within the Rete network is by sharing partial rule instantiations between different rules. In Figure 1, the conjunction of atomic conditions (X lays eggs), (X feeds milk) is common to the rules p3, p4 and p5. In a Rete network, instantiations of these partial rule bodies are computed only once and saved within a beta node which is connected (possibly via other beta nodes) to the production nodes of the affected rules.

6.4   Basic Backward Chaining: SLD-Resolution

Resolution proofs are refutation proofs, i.e. they show the unsatisfiability of a set of formulas. As it holds that the set of formulas $P \cup \{\neg\varphi\}$ is unsatisfiable iff $P \models \varphi$, resolution may be used to determine entailment (compare Theorem 35). Observe that a goal $\leftarrow a_1, \ldots, a_n$ is a syntactical variant of the first order sentence $\forall x_1 \ldots x_m (\bot \leftarrow a_1 \wedge \ldots \wedge a_n)$ where $x_1, \ldots, x_m$ are all variables occurring in $a_1, \ldots a_n$. This is equivalent to $\neg \exists x_1 \ldots x_m (a_1 \wedge \ldots \wedge a_n)$. If we use SLD-resolution[24] to show that a logic program P and a goal $\leftarrow a_1, \ldots, a_n$ are unsatisfiable we can conclude that $P \models \exists x_1 \ldots x_m (a_1 \wedge \ldots \wedge a_n)$.

Definition 209 (SLD Resolvent). *Let C be the clause $b \leftarrow b_1, \ldots, b_k$, G a goal of the form $\leftarrow a_1, \ldots, a_m, \ldots, a_n$, and let θ be the mgu of a_m and b. We assume that G and C have no variables in common (otherwise we rename the variables of C). Then G' is an SLD resolvent of G and C using θ if G' is the goal $\leftarrow (a_1, \ldots a_{m-1}, b_1, \ldots b_k, a_{m+1}, \ldots a_n)\theta$.*

---

[24] SLD is an acronym for Selected Literal Definite Clause.

Definition 210 (SLD Derivation). *A* SLD derivation *of* $P \cup \{G\}$ *consists of a sequence* $G_0, G_1, \ldots$ *of goals where* $G = G_0$, *a sequence* $C_1, C_2, \ldots$ *of variants of program clauses of* P *and a sequence* $\theta_1, \theta_2, \ldots$ *of mgu's such that* G_{i+1} *is a resolvent from* G_i *and* C_{i+1} *using* θ_{i+1}. *An* SLD-refutation *is a finite SLD-derivation which has the empty goal as its last goal.*

Definition 211 (SLD Tree). *An* SLD tree T *w.r.t. a program* P *and a goal* G *is a labeled tree where every node of* T *is a goal and the root of* T *is* G *and if* G *is a node in* T *then* G *has a child* G' *connected to* G *by an edge labeled* (C, θ) *iff* G' *is an SLD-resolvent of* G *and* C *using* θ.

Let P be a definite program and G a definite goal. A *computed answer* θ for $P \cup \{G\}$ is the substitution obtained by restricting the composition of $\theta_1, \ldots \theta_n$ to the variables occurring in G, where $\theta_1, \ldots \theta_n$ is the sequence of mgu's used in an SLD-refutation of $P \cup \{G\}$.

Observe that in each resolution step the selected literal a_m and the clause C are chosen non-deterministically. We call a function that maps to each goal one of its atoms a *computation rule*. The following proposition shows that the result of the refutation is independent of the literal selected in each step of the refutation.

Proposition 212 (Independence of the Computation Rule). *[111] Let* P *be a definite Program and* G *be a definite goal. Suppose there is an SLD-refutation of* $P \cup \{G\}$ *with computed answer* θ. *Then, for any computation rule* R, *there exists an SLD-refutation of* $P \cup \{G\}$ *using the atom selected by* R *as selected atom in each step with computed answer* θ' *such that* $G\theta$ *is a variant of* $G\theta'$.

The independence of the computation rule allows us to restrict the search space: As a refutation corresponds to a branch of in an SLD-tree, to find all computed answers we need to search all branches of the SLD-tree. The independence of the computation rule allows us to restrict our search to branches constructed using some (arbitrary) computation rule.

Example 213. Consider the logic program 6_8 with query $q = \leftarrow \mathtt{t(1,2)}$:

Listing 6_8. Transitive Closure

```
t(x,y) ← e(x,y).
t(x,y) ← t(x,z), e(z,y).
e(1,2) ← .
e(2,1) ← .
e(2,3) ← .
← t(1,2) .
```

An SLD-tree for program 6_8 and q is shown in the following figure. We label the edges of an SLD tree with the number of a rule instead of a rule. We denote by (n') the rule number n where each variable x occurring in rule n is replaced by x'.

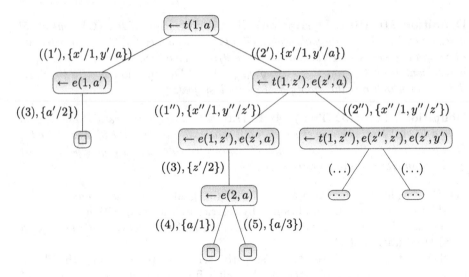

Fig. 2. An SLD tree for program 6_8

If we want to compare the operational semantics of a program P to its declarative semantics we need a declarative notion of an answer of program P. A *correct answer* for a program P and goal G is a substitution θ such that $P \models G\theta$. Using this notion we can define the soundness and completeness of logic programming.

Proposition 214 (Soundness and Completeness of Logic Programming).
[111] Let P be a program and let Q be a query. Then it holds that

- *every computed answer of P and G is a correct answer and*
- *for every correct answer σ of P and G there exists a computed answer θ such that θ is more general that σ.*

Observe that to find a computed answers of a program P and goal G operationally one has to visit the leaf of a finite branch in the SLD-tree w.r.t. P and G. The order in which we visit these nodes is not determined by the definition of an SLD-refutation. We call such an order a *search strategy*. An *SLD-procedure* is a deterministic algorithm which is an SLD-resolution constrained by a computation rule and a search strategy.

As SLD-trees are infinite in general, the completeness of an SLD-procedure depends on the search strategy. To be complete, an SLD-procedure must visit every leaf of a finite branch of an SLD-tree within a finite number of steps. A search strategy with this property is called *fair*. Obviously not every search strategy is fair. For example the depth first search strategy used by Prolog is not fair. An example of a fair search strategy is breath first search.

6.5   Backward Chaining with Memorization: OLDT-Resolution

As stated in the previous section not every search strategy is complete. This is due to the fact that an SLD-tree is infinite in general. As we only consider finite programs, an SLD-tree may only be infinite if it has an infinite branch. As a branch in an SLD-tree corresponds to an SLD-derivation we denote a branch as $[G_1, G_2, \ldots]$ where $G_1, G_2 \ldots$ are the goals of the corresponding derivation.

A branch $B = [G_1, G_2, \ldots]$ in an SLD-tree may be infinite if there is a subsequence $[G_{i_1}, G_{i_2}, \ldots]$ ($i_j < i_k$ if $j < k$) of B such that

- for all $j, k \in \mathbb{N}$ G_{i_j} and G_{i_k} contain an equal (up to renaming of variables) atom or
- for all $j \in \mathbb{N}$ G_{i_j} contains an atom which is a real instance of an atom in $G_{i_{j+1}}$.

Non-termination due to the first condition is addressed by a evaluation technique called *tabling* or *memorization*. The idea of tabling is the idea of dynamic programming: store intermediate results to be able to look these results up instead of having to recompute them. In addition to the better termination properties, performance is improved with this approach.

The OLDT algorithm [150] is an extension of the SLD-resolution with a left to right computation rule. Like SLD-resolution, it is defined as a non-deterministic algorithm.

A subset of the predicate symbols occurring in a program are classified as *table predicates*. A goal is called a *table goal* if its leftmost atom has a table predicate. Solutions to table goals are the intermediate results that are stored. Table goals are classified as either *solution goals* or *look-up goals*. The intuition is that a solution goal 'produces' solutions while a look-up goal looks up the solutions produced by an appropriate solution goal.

An *OLDT-structure* (T, T_S, T_L) consists of an SLD-tree T and two tables, the solution table T_S and the look-up table T_L. The *solution table* T_S is a set of pairs $(a, T_S(a))$ where a is an atom and $T_S(a)$ is a list of instances of a called the *solutions* of a. The *look-up table* T_L is a set of pairs $(a, T_L(a))$ where a is an atom and p is a pointer pointing to an element of $T_S(a')$ where a is an instance of a'. T_L contains one pair $(a, T_L(a))$ for an atom a occurring as a leftmost atom of a goal in T.

The *extension of an OLDT structure* (T, T_S, T_L) consists of three steps:

1. a resolution step,
2. a classification step, and
3. a table update step.

In the resolution step a new goal is added to the OLDT-tree, in the classification step this new goal is classified as either non-tabled goal or solution goal or look-up goal and in the table update step the solution table and the update table are updated. While step one is equal for non-tabled and solution goals, step two and three are equal for tabled nodes while there is nothing to do in these steps for non-tabled nodes.

Let (T, T_S, T_L) be an OLDT structure and $G = \leftarrow a_1, \ldots, a_n$ a goal in T. If G is a non-tabled goal or a solution goal then in the resolution step a new goal G' is added to T which is connected to G with an edge labeled (C, θ) where G'

is the SLD-resolvent of G and C using θ. If G is a look-up node then in the resolution step the new node G' is added to T with an edge labeled $(a \leftarrow, \theta)$ where a is the atom in the solution table that the pointer $T_L(a_1)$ points to and the substitution θ is the mgu of a and a_1. Finally the pointer $T_L(a_1)$ is set to point to the next element of the list it points to.

In the classification step the new goal G' is classified as a non-table goal if its leftmost atom is not a table predicate and a table goal otherwise. If G' is a table goal then G' is classified as a look-up node if there is a pair $(a, T_S(a))$ in the solution table and a is more general than the leftmost atom a' of G'. In this case a new pair (a', p) is added to the look-up table and p points to the first element of $T_S(a)$. If G' is not classified as a look-up node then it is classified as a solution node and a new pair $(a', [])$ is added to the solution table.

In the table update step new solutions are added to the solution table. Recall that the problem we want to tackle here is the recurrent evaluation of equal (up to renaming of variables) atoms in goals. Therefore the 'solutions' we want to store in the solution table are answers to an atom in a goal.

In SLD-resolution the term answer is defined only for goals. This notion can be extended to atoms in goals in the following way. OLDT-resolution uses a left to right computation rule. If the derivation of a goal $G =\leftarrow a_1, \ldots, a_n$ is finite, then there is a finite number n of resolution steps such that the nth resolvent G_n on G is $\leftarrow a_2, \ldots, a_n$. We call the sequence $[G_1, \ldots, G_n]$ a *unit sub-refutation* of a_1 and the restriction of $\theta_1 \ldots \theta_n$ to the variables occurring in a_1 is called an *answer for a_1*.

Now if the goal G produced in the resolution step is the last goal of a unit sub-refutation of a with answer θ then the update step consists in adding θ to the list $T_S(a)$.

Example 215. Reconsider the program from Example 213

Listing 6_9. Transitive Closure

```
t(x,y) ← e(x,y) .
t(x,y) ← t(x,z), e(z,y) .
e(1,2) ← .
e(2,1) ← .
e(2,3) ← .
← t(1,2) .
```

After a sequence of OLDT-resolutions of solution goals or non-tabled goals the OLDT-tree in Figure 3 is constructed. To indicate which nodes are solution nodes and which are look-up nodes we prefix solution nodes with 'S:' and look-up nodes with 'L:'.

As the left branch is a unit sub-refutation of $t(1, a)$ with solution $\{a/2\}$ the entry $t(1, 2)$ is added to the solution table. As $t(1, a)$ is more general than the leftmost atom of the goal $t(1, z'), e(z', a)$ this goal is classified as a look-up node. Instead of using resolution to compute answers for the first atom of this goal we use the solutions stored in the solution table. The final OLDT-tree is depicted in 4:

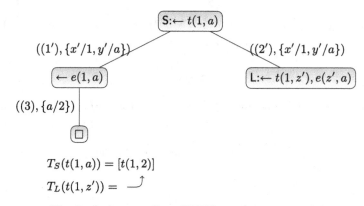

$$T_S(t(1, a)) = [t(1, 2)]$$
$$T_L(t(1, z')) = \quad \rule{0pt}{0pt}$$

Fig. 3. An intermediary OLDT tree for program 6_9

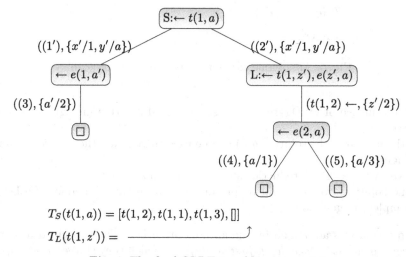

$$T_S(t(1, a)) = [t(1, 2), t(1, 1), t(1, 3), []]$$
$$T_L(t(1, z')) = \quad \rule{0pt}{0pt}$$

Fig. 4. The final OLDT tree for program 6_9

Observe that the program of example 215 does not terminate with SLD-resolution while it does terminate with OLDT-resolution. The following example shows that OLDT-resolution is not complete in general.

Example 216. Consider the program 6_10 and query $q = \leftarrow p(x)$

Listing 6_10. Program for which OLDT resolution is incomplete

```
p(x) ← q(x), r .
q(s(x)) ← q(x) .
q(a) ← .
r ← .
← p(x) .
```

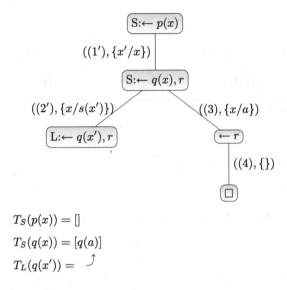

$$T_S(p(x)) = []$$
$$T_S(q(x)) = [q(a)]$$
$$T_L(q(x')) = \; \curvearrowleft$$

Fig. 5. An intermediary OLDT tree for program 6_10

After a sequence of OLDT-resolution steps the OLDT-tree in Figure 5 is constructed

In the next step the solution $q(a)$ can be used to generate the solution $q(s(a))$ (see Figure 6).

It is easy to see that if reduction steps are only applied to the node L:$\leftarrow q(x'), r$ then no solutions for $p(x)$ will be produced in finite time. Therefore OLDT is not complete in general.

This problem was addressed by the authors of OLDT. They specified a search strategy called *multistage depth-first strategy* for which they showed that OLDT becomes complete if this search strategy is used. The idea of this search strategy is to order the nodes in the OLDT-tree and to apply OLDT-resolution-steps to the nodes in this order. If the node that is the biggest node with respect to that ordering is reduced then a stage is complete and a new stage starts where reduction is applied to the smallest node again. Therefore it is not possible to apply OLDT-steps twice in a row if there are other nodes in the tree which are resolvable.

In the above example it would therefore not be possible to repeatedly apply reductions to the node L:$\leftarrow q(x'), r$ without reducing the node $\leftarrow r$ which yields a solution for $p(x)$.

6.6   The Backward Fixpoint Procedure

The last sections have shown bottom up and top down methods for answering queries on Horn logic programs. While the naive and semi-naive bottom up methods suffer from an undirected search for answering queries, the top

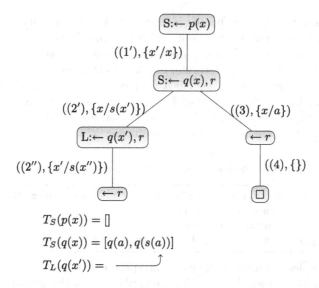

$$T_S(p(x)) = []$$
$$T_S(q(x)) = [q(a), q(s(a))]$$
$$T_L(q(x')) = \quad\underline{\qquad}^{\uparrow}$$

Fig. 6. An intermediary OLDT tree for program 6_10

down methods such as SLD resolution (Section 6.4) may often not terminate although the answer can be computed in finite time by a bottom up procedure. Non-termination of top down procedures is addressed by tabling (storing the encountered sub-queries and their solutions) in OLDT resolution (Section 6.5) and other advanced top down methods such as QSQ or SLDAL-Resolution[158], the ET^* and ET_{interp}[54,67] algorithms and the RQA/FQI[122] strategy. The problem of undirected search in forward chaining methods is solved by rewriting the rules such that special atoms representing encountered sub-goals are represented by custom-built atoms and by requiring an appropriate sub-goal to be generated before a rule of the original program is fired. Two representatives of this second approach are the Alexander[97] and the Magic Set methods (Section 6.2).

In [27] a sound and complete query answering method for recursive databases based on meta-interpretation called *Backward Fixpoint Procedure*, is presented, and it is shown that the Alexander and Magic Set methods can be interpreted as *specializations* of the Backward Fixpoint Procedure (BFP) and that also the efficient top down methods based on SLD resolution implement the BFP. Studying the BFP reveals the commonalities and differences between top down and bottom up processing of recursive Horn logic programs and is thus used to top of this chapter.

The backward fixpoint procedure is specified by the meta interpreter in Listing 6_11, which is intended to be evaluated by a bottom up rule engine. Facts are only generated in a bottom up evaluation of the interpreter if a query has been issued for that fact or if an appropriate sub-query has been generated by the meta-interpreter itself (Line 1). Sub-queries for rule bodies are generated if a sub-query for the corresponding rule head already exists (Line 2). Sub-queries for conjuncts are generated from sub-queries of conjunctions they appear in (Line 3 and 4). The predicate `evaluate` consults the already generated facts, and may take a single atom or a conjunction as its argument, returning true if all of the conjuncts have already been generated. It must be emphasized that using a *bottom up* rule engine for evaluating the BFP meta-interpreter for an object rule program is equivalent to evaluating this object program *top down*, thereby not generating any facts which are irrelevant for answering the query. For the correctness of the meta-interpreter approach for fixpoint computation and for an example for the evaluation of an object program with the BFP meta-interpreter see [27].

Listing 6_11. The backward fixpoint procedure meta interpreter

```
1   fact(Q) ← query_b(Q) ∧ rule(Q ← B) ∧ evaluate(B)
2   query_b(B) ← query_b(Q) ∧ rule(Q ← B)
3   query_b(Q_1) ← query_b(Q_1 ∧ Q_2)
4   query_b(Q_2) ← query_b(Q_1 ∧ Q_2) ∧ evaluate(Q_1)
```

A direct implementation of the meta-interpreter may lead to redundant computations of facts. To see this consider the application of the meta-interpreter to the object program p ←q, r and the query p. The relevant instantiated rules of the meta-interpreter contain the ground queries `evaluate(q,r)` and `evaluate(q)`, thereby accessing the fact q twice. Getting rid of these redundant computations is elegantly achieved by specifying a bottom up evaluation of a binary version of the predicate `evaluate` as shown in Listing 6_12. The first argument of `evaluate` contains the conjuncts which have already been proved, while the second argument contains the rest of the conjunction. Therefore a fact `evaluate($\emptyset, Q$)` represents a conjunction which has not yet been evaluated at all, while `evaluate($Q,\emptyset$)` represents a completely evaluated conjunction. With this new definition of `evaluate` the atoms `evaluate($B$)` and `evaluate($Q_1$)` in Listing 6_11 must be replaced by `evaluate($B,\emptyset$)` and `evaluate($Q_1,\emptyset$)`, respectively. With this extension, the BFP meta-interpreter of Listing 6_11 becomes redundant. A non-redundant version is obtained by only considering rules (1, 5 to 11) of Listings 6_11, 6_12 and 6_13. For the proofs for the redundancy of the rules (1 to 9) on the one hand and for the equivalence of the interpreters made up of rules (1 to 4) and (1, 5 to 11) on the other hand see [27].

Listing 6_12. Implementation of the predicate `evaluate`

```
5   evaluate(∅,B) ← query_b(Q) ∧ rule(Q ← B)
6   evaluate(B_1,B_2) ← evaluate(∅,B_1 ∧ B_2) ∧ fact(B_1)
7   evaluate(B_1 ∧ B_2,B_3) ← evaluate(B_1,B_2 ∧ B_3) ∧ B_1 ≠ ∅ ∧ fact(B_2)
8   evaluate(B,∅) ← fact(B)
9   evaluate(B_1 ∧ B_2,∅) ← evaluate(B_1,B_2) ∧ B_1 ≠ ∅, fact(B_2)
```

Listing 6_13. Replacement rules for the rules 2 to 4 in Listing 6_11

```
10  query_b(B_2) ← evaluate(B_1,B_2) ∧ B_2 ≠ (C_1 ∧ C_2)
11  query_b(B_2) ← evaluate(B_1,B_2 ∧ B_3)
```

The implementation of the backward fixpoint procedure gives rise to two challenges exemplified by the sub-goal $query_b(r(x,a))$, which may be generated during the evaluation of a program by the BFP meta-interpreter. The sub-goal is both nested and non-ground. The main problem with non-ground terms generated by the application of the BFP meta-interpreter to an object program is that for deciding whether a newly derived fact is a logical duplicate of an already derived fact it is not sufficient to perform string matching, but full unification is needed. With *specialization*[74], a common partial evaluation technique used in logic programming, one can get rid of these problems.

Specialization is applied to the BFP meta-interpreter with respect to the rules of the object program. For each rule of the meta-interpreter that includes a premise referring to a rule of the object program, one specialized version is created for each rule of the object program. The first rule of the BFP meta-interpreter (Listing 6.11) specialized with respect to the rule $p(x) \leftarrow q(x) \wedge r(x)$ results in the following partially evaluated rule:

$$fact(p(x)) \leftarrow query_b(p(x)) \wedge evaluate(q(x) \wedge r(x))$$

Similarly, the specialization of the second rule of the meta-interpreter with respect to the same object rule yields the partially evaluated rule $query_b(q(x) \wedge r(x)) \leftarrow query_b(p(x))$.

Another specialization which can be applied to the BFP meta-interpreter is the specialization of the $query_b$ predicate with respect to the predicates of the object program, transforming a fact $query_b(p(a))$ into the fact $query_b\text{-}p(a)$ and eliminating some of the nested terms generated during the evaluation. With this transformation the first rule of the BFP is further simplified to:

$$fact(p(x)) \leftarrow query_b\text{-}p(x) \wedge evaluate(q(x) \wedge r(x))$$

Getting rid of non-ground terms can also be achieved by specialization resulting in an adorned version of the program. Adornment of logic programs is described in the context of the magic set transformation in Section 6.2. [27] also discusses the *faithfulness* of representations of sub-queries as facts. Adornments of sub-queries are not completely *faithful* in the sense that the adornment of the distinct queries $p(X,Y)$ and $p(X,X)$ results in the same adorned predicate p^{ff}. As described in Section 6.2, multiple adorned versions for one rule of the original program may be generated.

In [27] it is shown that the above specializations of the meta-interpreter made up of the rules (1, 5 to 11) with respect to an object program P and the omittance of the meta-predicates evaluate and fact yields exactly the supplementary magic set transformation and the Alexander method applied to P. Therefore both of these methods implement the BFP.

Not only can bottom up processing methods be specialized from the BFP, but it can also be used to specify top down procedures such as ET^*, ET_{interp}, QSQ, etc. The difference between SLD resolution and the BFP is explained in [27] in terms of the employed data structures. SLD resolution uses a hierarchical data structure which relates sub-queries and proved facts to the queries they belong to. On the other hand, the BFP employs relations – i.e. a flat data structure – for memorizing answers to queries, and therefore allows to share computed answers between queries that are logically equivalent. SLD resolution and the hierarchical resolution tree can be simulated by the BFP by introducing identifiers for queries, thus allowing to relate facts and sub-queries with queries to the answers of which they contribute. See [27] for details. This simulation prevents sharing of answers between queries and thus makes the evaluation less efficient. One conclusion that can be drawn from the BFP is that it does not make sense to hierarchically structure queries according to their generation. In contrast it makes sense to rely on a static rewriting such as the Alexander or Magic Set rewriting and process the resulting rules with a semi-naive bottom-up rule engine.

7   Operational Semantics: Rule Sets with Non-monotonic Negation

In the previous chapter evaluation methods for logic programs without negation are examined. This chapter considers a more general form of logic programs, namely ones that use negation. The rules considered in this chapter are all of the form

$$A \leftarrow L_1, \ldots, L_n$$

where the $L_i, 1 \leq i \leq n$ are literals, and A is an atom. Thus negative literals are allowed in the bodies of rules, but not in their heads. It is important to note that augmenting logic programming with negation increases expressivity and is necessary for deriving certain information from a database.

In Section 5 two important semantics for logic programming with negation have been described: The *stable model semantics* (See Section 5.3.2) and the *well-founded model semantics* (Section 5.3.3). However, this declarative semantics does not provide an easy to implement algorithm neither for computing the entailments of a logic program with negation nor for answering queries with respect to such programs. In fact the greatest unfounded sets in the definition of the well-founded semantics and the stable models in the stable models theory must be guessed.

In this section constructive algorithms for computing the so-called *iterative fixpoint semantics*, the stable model semantics and the well-founded model semantics are described and applied to example programs to better illustrate their functioning.

The kind of negation which is generally used in logic programming is called negation as failure and can be described as follows: A negated literal $\neg A$ is true, if its positive counterpart A cannot be derived from the program. A possible application of negation as failure is given in Listing 7_14. Since male(eduard) is given and married(eduard) cannot be derived, bachelor(eduard) is logical consequence of the program, while bachelor(john) is not. Negation as failure is also known under the term *non-monotonic* negation, because the addition of new facts to a program may cause some of its entailments to be no longer true: The addition of married(eduard) to the program in Listing 7_14 invalidates the conclusion bachelor(eduard).

Listing 7.14. An Illustration for the Use of Negation as Failure

```
married(john).
male(john).
male(eduard).
bachelor(X) ← male(X), not married(X)
```

The adoption of negation as failure brings about several interesting, not to say intricate questions. Consider the program in Listing 7.15. If the literal q is assumed to be false, then the literal p must be true according to the second rule. This, however, causes the literal q to be true. On the other hand there is no possibility of deriving the literal q. Hence the semantics of Program 7.15 is not clear. Therefore syntactical restrictions on logic programs have been proposed, to ensure that all programs satisfying these restrictions have an intuitive declarative semantics.

Listing 7.15. A program with Recursion through negation

```
q ← p.
p ← not q.
```

7.1 Computation of the Iterative Fixpoint Semantics for Stratified Logic Programs with Negation as Failure

One possibility of limiting the use of negation is by *stratification* (see Definition 164 in Subsection 5.3.1).

It is easy to see that for some programs no stratification can be found. Since in Program 7.15 q depends on p by the first rule and p depends on q by the second rule, they would have to be defined in the same stratum. Since q depends *negatively* on p, this case is precluded by the third premise above. A program for which no stratification can be found is called *non-stratifiable*, programs for which a stratification exists are called *stratifiable*. The iterative fixpoint semantics does not provide a semantics for non-stratifiable programs.

[9] defines the semantics for stratified logic programs as an iterated fixpoint semantics based on the immediate consequence operator $\mathbf{T}_P$ (Definition 153) as follows. Let $S_1, \ldots, S_n$ be a stratification for the program P. Recall that $\mathbf{T}_P^i(I)$ denotes the i-fold application of the immediate consequence operator to the database instance I. Then the semantics of the program P is the set M_n where M_0 is defined as the initial instance over the extensional predicate symbols of P, and the M_i are defined as follows:

$$M_1 := \mathbf{T}_{S_1}^{\omega}(M_0), \quad M_2 := \mathbf{T}_{S_2}^{\omega}(M_1), \quad \ldots, \quad M_n := \mathbf{T}_{S_n}^{\omega}(M_{n-1})$$

This procedure shall be illustrated at the example program in Listing 7.16. The intensional predicate symbols has_hobbies, has_child, married, and bachelor can be separated into the strata $S_1 := \{\texttt{has\_hobbies}\}$, $S_2 := \{\texttt{has\_child}, \texttt{married}\}$,

$S_3 := \{\texttt{bachelor}\}$. The initial instance $M_0 = \{\{john\}_{human}, \{john\}_{plays\_the\_piano}, \{john\}_{male}\}$ is directly derived from the facts of the program. Since $\texttt{has\_hobbies}$ is the only element of S_1, only the first rule is relevant for the computation of $M_1 := M_0 \cup \{\{john\}_{has\_hobbies}\}$. The second and the third rule are relevant for the computation of M_2, which is the same instance as M_1. Finally, the fourth rule allows to add the fact $\texttt{bachelor(john)}$ yielding the final instance $M_3 := M_2 \cup \{\{john\}_{bachelor}\}$.

Listing 7_16. A stratifiable program with negation as failure

```
human(john).
male(john).
plays_the_piano(john).

has_hobbies(X) ← plays_the_piano(X).
has_child(X) ← human(X), not has_hobbies(X).
married(X) ← human(X), has_child(X).
bachelor(X) ← male(X), not married(X).
```

7.2   Magic Set Transformation for Stratified Logic Programs

While the computation of the iterative fixpoint of a stratified logic program allows to answer an arbitrary query on the program, it is inefficient in the sense that no goal-directed search is performed. One method for introducing goal-directedness into logical query answering, that is also relatively easy to implement, is the magic set rewriting as introduced in Section 6.2. The task of transferring the magic set approach to logic programs with negation has therefore received considerable attention [41], [98], [16], [139], [15].

The main problem emerging when applying the magic set method to programs with negative literals in rule bodies is that the resulting program may not be stratified. There are two approaches to dealing with this situation. The first one is to use a preprocessing stage for the original program in order to obtain a stratified program under the magic set transformation and is pursued by [41]. The second one is to accept the unstratified outcome of the magic set transformation and to compute some other semantics which deals with unstratified programs. This second approach is employed by [19], which proposes to compute the well-founded model by Kerisit's *weak consequence operator* at the aid of a new concept called *soft stratification*.

Because of its simplicity and straightforwardness, only the first approach is presented in this article.

In [41] three causes for the unstratification of a magic-set transformed program are identified:

- both an atom $\texttt{a}$ and its negation $\texttt{not a}$ occur within the body of the same rule of the program to be transformed.

- a negative literal occurs multiple times within the body of a rule of the original program
- a negative literal occurs within a recursive rule

With b occurring both positively and negatively in the body of the first rule, Listing 7_17 is an example for the first cause of unstratification. The predicate symbol c is an extensional one, and therefore no magic rules are created for it, a and b are intensional ones. When the magic set transformation from the last chapter is naively applied to the program and the query a(1), which means that negated literals are transformed in the very same way as positive ones, the magic set transformed program in Listing 7_18 is not stratified, because it contains a negative dependency cycle among its predicates: magic_b^b negatively depends on b^b, which again depends on magic_b^b.

Listing 7_17. A program leading to unstratification under the naive magic set transformation

```
a(x) ← not b(x), c(x,y), b(y).
b(x) ← c(x,y), b(y).
```

Listing 7_18. The unstratified outcome of the magic set transformation applied to Program 7_17

```
magic_aᵇ(1).
magic_bᵇ(x) ← magic_aᵇ(x).
magic_bᵇ(y) ← magic_aᵇ(x), not bᵇ(x), c(x,y).
a(x) ← magic_aᵇ(x), not bᵇ(x), c(x,y), bᵇ(y).
magic_bᵇ(y) ← magic_bᵇ(x), c(x,y).
b(x) ← magic_bᵇ(x), c(x,y), b(y).
```

[41] proposes to differentiate the contexts in which a negative literal is evaluated by numbering the occurrences of the literal in the rule body before the magic set transformation is applied. The numbered version of Listing 7_17 is displayed in Listing 7_19 where the two occurrences of b have been numbered. Additionally, for each newly introduced numbered predicate symbol p_i its defining rules are copies from the definition of the unnumbered symbol p, with all occurrences of p replaced by p_i. In this way, the semantics of the program remains unchanged, but the program becomes stratified under the magic set transformation, as can be verified in Listing 7_20.

Listing 7_19. Program 7_17 with differentiated contexts for the literal b

```
a(x) ← not b_1(x), c(x,y), b_2(y).
b_1(x) ← c(x,y), b_1(y).
b_2(x) ← c(x,y), b_2(y).
```

Listing 7_20. The stratified outcome of the magic set transformation applied to program 7_19

```
magic_a^b(1).
magic_b_1^b(x) ← magic_a^b(x).
magic_b_2^b(y) ← magic_a^b(x), not b_1^b(x), c(x,y).
a^b(x) ← magic_a^b(x), not b_1^b(x), c(x,y), b_2^b(y).
magic_b_1^b(y) ← magic_b_1^b(x), c(x,y).
b_1(x) ← magic_b_1^b(x), c(x,y), b_1(y).
magic_b_2^b(y) ← magic_b_2^b(x), c(x,y).
b_2(x) ← magic_b_2^b(x), c(x,y), b_2(y).
```

Also for the second and third source of unstratification, elimination procedures can be specified that operate on the adorned rule set, but are carried out prior to the magic set transformation. For more details and a proof, that the resulting programs are indeed stratified see [41].

7.3   Computation of the Stable Model Semantics

While the iterative fixpoint semantics provides an intuitive and canonical semantics for a subset of logic programs with negation as failure, several attempts have been made to assign a semantics to programs which are not stratifiable. One of these attempts is the *stable model semantics* (see Section 5.3.2).

An example for a program which is not stratifiable but is valid under the stable model semantics is given in Listing 7_21.

Listing 7_21. A non-stratifiable program with a stable model semantics

```
married(john, mary).
male(X) ← married(X,Y), not male(Y).
```

The stable model semantics for a program P is computed as follows: In a first step all rules containing variables are replaced by their ground instances. In a second step the program is transformed with respect to a given model M into a program $GL_M(P)$ by deleting all those rules which contain a negative literal $not(L)$ in their body where L is contained in M, and by deleting all those negative literals $not(L)$ from the rules for which L is not contained in M. Clearly, the semantics of the program P remains unchanged by both of these transformations with respect to the particular model M. Since this transformation has first been proposed by Gelfond and Lifschitz in [77], it is also known under the name *Gelfond-Lifschitz-Transformation* (See also Definition 165).

An Herbrand interpretation M is a *stable set* of P if and only if it is the unique minimal Herbrand model of the resulting negation-free program $GL_M(P)$. See Definition 166 and Lemma 167. The stable model semantics for a program P (written $S_\Pi(P)$) is defined as the stable set of P, and remains undefined if there is none or more than one of them.

The Gelfond-Lifschitz-Transformation of Listing 7_21 with respect to the set $M := \{\texttt{married(john, mary)}, \texttt{male(John)}\}$ results in the Program in Listing 7_22. Rule instances and negative literals of rule instances have been crossed out according to the rules mentioned above. Since the unique minimal Herbrand model of the resulting Program is also $M = \{\texttt{married(john, mary)}, \texttt{male(John)}\}$, M is a stable set of the original program in 7_21. Since there are no other stable sets of the program, M is its stable model.

Listing 7_22. Listing 7_21 transformed with respect to the set {`married(john, mary)`, `male(John)`}

```
married ( john , mary ).
male ( john )  ←  married ( john , mary ), not  male(mary).
male(mary)  ←  married(mary, john), not male(john).
male ( mary )  ←  married ( mary , mary ), not  male(mary).
male(john)  ←  married(john, john), not male(john).
```

An efficient implementation of the stable model semantics (and also the well-founded model semantics) for range-restricted and function-free normal logic programs is investigated in [123] and its performance is compared to that of SLG resolution in [40].

7.4   A More Efficient Implementation of the Stable Model Semantics

The approach of [123] recursively constructs all possible stable models by adding one after another positive and negative literals from the set of *negative antecedents* (Definition 217) to an intermediate candidate full set B (see Definition 219). The algorithm (see Listing 7_23) makes use of backtracking to retract elements from B and to find all stable models of a program. In addition to the program P itself and the intermediate candidate set B, the algorithm takes a third argument which is a formula ϕ that is tested for validity whenever a stable model is found. The algorithm returns true if there is a stable model of ϕ and false otherwise. Moreover it can be adapted to find all stable models of a program or to determine whether a given formula is satisfied in all stable models.

Definition 217 (Negative Antecedents). *Given a logic program P, the set of its negative antecedents $NAnt(P)$ is defined as all those atoms a such that $not(a)$ appears within the body of a rule of P.*

Definition 218 (Deductive closure). *The deductive closure $Dcl(P, L)$ of a program P with respect to a set of literals L is the smallest set of atoms containing the negative literals L^- of L, which is closed under the following set of rules:*

$$R(P, L) := \{\, c \leftarrow a_1, \ldots, a_n \mid c \leftarrow a_1, \ldots, a_n, not(b_1), \ldots, not(b_m) \in P, \quad (1)$$
$$\{not(b_1), \ldots, not(b_m) \subseteq L^-\}\}$$

Definition 219 (Full Sets (from [123])). *A set Λ of not-atoms (negated atoms) is called P-full iff for all $\phi \in NAnt(P)$, $not(\phi) \in \Lambda$ iff $\phi \notin Dcl(P, \Lambda)$.*

Example 220. Consider the logic program $P := \{q \leftarrow not(r).q \leftarrow not(p).r \leftarrow q.\}$ The negative antecedents of the program are $NAnt(P) = \{r, p\}$. $\Lambda_1 := \{not(r), not(p)\}$ is not a full set with respect to P because $not(r)$ is in Λ_1, but r is in the deductive closure $Dcl(P, \Lambda_1)$. The only full set with respect to P is $\Lambda_2 := \{not(p)\}$: $not(p) \in \Lambda_2$ and $p \notin Dcl(P, \Lambda_2)$ holds for p and $not(r) \notin \Lambda_2$ and $r \in Dcl(P, \Lambda_2)$ holds for the other element r of $NAnt(P)$.

Theorem 221 (Relationship between full sets and stable models ([123])). *Let P be a ground program and Λ a set of not-atoms (negated atoms). (i) If Λ is a full set with respect to P then $Dcl(P, \Lambda)$ is a stable model of P. (ii) If Δ is a stable model of P then $\Lambda = not(NAnt(P) - \Delta)$ is a full set with respect to P such that $Dcl(P, \Lambda) = \Delta$.*

According to theorem 221 it is sufficient to search for full sets instead of for stable models, because stable models can be constructed from these full sets. This approach is pursued by the algorithm in Listing 7.23.

Definition 222 (L covers A). *Given a set of ground literals L and a set of ground atoms A, L is said to cover A, iff for every atom a in A either $a \in L$ or $not(a) \in L$ holds.*

Listing 7.23. Efficient computation of the stable model semantics for a logic program

```
function stable_model(P,B,φ)
  let B' = expand(P,B) in
    if conflict(P,B') then false
    else
      if (B' covers NAnt(P)) then test(Dcl(P,B'),φ)
      else
        take some χ ∈ NAnt(P) not covered by B'
        if stable_model(P, B'∪{not(χ)},φ) then true
          else stable_model(P, B'∪{χ},φ)
```

The algorithm is not fully specified, but relies on the two functions **expand** and **conflict**, which undergo further optimization. The idea behind the function expand is to derive as much further information as possible about the common part B of the stable models that are to be constructed without losing any model. One could also employ the identity function as an implementation for **expand**, but by burdening the entire construction of the full sets on the backtracking search of the function **stable_model**, this approach would be rather inefficient. A good choice for the **expand** function is to return the least fixpoint of the *Fitting operator* $F_P(B)$:

Definition 223 (Fitting operator F_P). *Let B be a set of ground literals, and P a ground logic program. The set $F_P(B)$ is defined as the smallest set including B that fulfills the following two conditions: (i) for a rule $h \leftarrow a_1, \ldots, a_n, not(b_1), \ldots, not(b_m)$ with $a_i \in B, 1 \leq i \leq n$ and*

$not(b_j), \in B, 1 \leq j \leq m$, h is in $F_P(B)$.

(ii) if for an atom a such that for all of its defining rules, a positive premise p is in its body and $not(p)$ is in B, or a negative literal $not(p)$ is in its body with p in B, then a is in $F_P(B)$.

The function `conflict` returns true whenever (i) B covers $NAnt(P)$, and (ii) if there is an atom a in the set B such that $a \notin Dcl(P, B)$ or a literal $not(a) \in B$ such that $a \in Dcl(P, B)$. In this way, `conflict` prunes the search for full sets (and therefore the search for stable models) by detecting states in which no stable model can be constructed as early as possible. For further optimizations regarding the computation of the stable model semantics with the function `stable_model` the reader is referred to [123].

7.5   Computation of the Well-Founded Model Semantics

Another approach to defining a semantics for logic programs that are neither stratifiable nor locally stratifiable is the *well-founded model approach* [152] (see Section 5.3.3).

Recall that in this context the term *interpretation* refers to a set of positive or negative literals $\{p_1, \ldots, p_k, not(n_1), \ldots, not(n_i)\}$ and that the notation $\overline{S}$, with $S = \{s_1, \ldots, s_n\}$ being a set of atoms, refers to the set $\{\neg s_1, \ldots, \neg s_n\}$ in which each of the atoms is negated.

An *unfounded set* (see Section 5.3.3) of a logic program P with respect to an interpretation I is a set of (positive) atoms U, such that for each instantiated rule in P which has head $h \in U$, at least one of the following two conditions applies.

- the body of the rule is not fulfilled, because it contains either a negative literal `not(a)` with a$\in I$ or a positive literal a with `not(a)`$\in I$.
- the body of the rule contains another (positive) atom $a \in U$ of the unfounded set.

The greatest unfounded set turns out to be the union of all unfounded sets of a program. Note that the definition above does not immediately provide an algorithm for finding the greatest unfounded set. In this subsection, however, a straight-forward algorithm is derived from the definition and in the following subsection, a more involved algorithm for computing the well-founded semantics is introduced.

The computation of the well founded semantics is an iterative process mapping interpretations to interpretations and involving the computation of immediate consequences and greatest unfounded sets. The initial interpretation is the empty set, which reflects the intuition that at the beginning of the program examination, nothing is known about the entailments of the program. The iteration uses the following three kinds of mappings:

- the immediate consequence mapping $\mathbf{T}_P(I)$ of the program with respect to an interpretation I

- the greatest unfounded set mapping $\mathbf{U}_P(I)$, which finds the greatest unfounded set of a program with respect to an interpretation I
- $\mathbf{W}_P(I) := \mathbf{T}_P(I) \cup \overline{\mathbf{U}_P(I)}$ which maps an interpretation to the union of all of its immediate consequences and the set of negated atoms of the greatest unfounded set.

The well-founded semantics (see Section 5.3.3) of a logic program is then defined as the least fixpoint of the operator $\mathbf{W}_P(I)$. The computation of well founded sets and of the well founded semantics is best illustrated by an example (see Listing 7_24). The set of immediate consequences $\mathbf{T}_P(\emptyset)$ of the empty interpretation of the program 7_24 is obviously the set $\{c(2)\}$. The greatest unfounded set $\mathbf{U}_P(\emptyset)$ of the program with respect to the empty interpretation is the set $\{d(1), f(2), e(2), f(1)\}$. $f(1)$ is in $\mathbf{U}_P(\emptyset)$, because there are no rules with head $f(1)$, and therefore the conditions above are trivially fulfilled.

Note that the fact a(1) is not an unfounded fact with respect to the interpretation $\emptyset$, although one is tempted to think so when reading the program as a logic program with negation as failure semantics.

The three atoms $\{d(1), f(2), e(2)\}$ form an unfounded set, because the derivation of any of them would require one of the others to be already derived. There is no possibility to derive any of them first. Hence, according to the well-founded semantics, they are considered false, leading to $I_1 := \mathbf{W}_P(\emptyset) = \mathbf{T}_P(\emptyset) \cup \overline{\mathbf{U}_P(\emptyset)} = \{c(2)\} \cup \overline{\{d(1), f(2), e(2), f(1)\}} = \{c(2), \neg d(1), \neg f(2), \neg e(2), \neg f(1)\}$.

In the second iteration a(1) is an immediate consequence of the program, but still neither one of the atoms a(2) and b(2) can be added to the interpretation (also their negated literals cannot be added). After this second iteration the fixpoint $\{c(2), \neg d(1), \neg f(2), \neg e(2), \neg f(1), a(1)\}$ is reached without having assigned a truth value to the atoms a(2) and b(2).

Listing 7_24. Example program for the well-founded semantics

```
b(2) ← ¬ a(2).
a(2) ← ¬ b(2).

d(1) ← f(2), ¬ f(1).
e(2) ← d(1).
f(2) ← e(2).

a(1) ← c(2), ¬ d(1).
c(2).
```

The computation of this partial well-founded model involves guessing the unfounded sets of a program P. If P is finite, all subsets of the atoms occurring in P can be tried as candidates for the unfounded sets. In practice those atoms that have already been shown to be true or false do not need to be reconsidered, and due to the fact that the union of two unfounded sets is an unfounded set itself, the greatest unfounded set can be computed in a bottom up manner, which decreases the average case complexity of the problem. Still, in the worst case $O(2^a)$ sets have to be tried for each application of the operator $\mathbf{U}_P$, with a being the number of atoms in the program. In [154] a deterministic algorithm for computing the well-founded semantics of a program is described.

7.6   Computing the Well-Founded Semantics by the Alternating Fixpoint Procedure

The central idea of the alternating fixpoint procedure[154] is to iteratively build up a set of negative conclusions $\tilde{A}$ of a logic program, from which the positive conclusions can be derived at the end of the process in a straightforward way. Each iteration is a two-phase process transforming an underestimate of the negative conclusions $\tilde{I}$ into a temporary overestimate $\mathbf{S}_P(\tilde{I})$ and back to an underestimate $\mathbf{A}_P(\tilde{I}) := \tilde{\mathbf{S}}_P(\tilde{\mathbf{S}}_P(\tilde{I}))$. Once this two-phase process does not yield further negative conclusions, a fixpoint is reached. The set of negative conclusions of the program is then defined as the least fixpoint $\tilde{A} := \mathbf{A}_P^\omega(\emptyset)$ of the monotonic transformation $\mathbf{A}_P$.

In each of the two phases of each iteration the fixpoint $S_P(\tilde{I}) := \mathbf{T}_{P'}^\omega(\emptyset)$ of an adapted version of the immediate consequence operator corresponding to the ground instantiation of the program P_H plus the set $\tilde{I}$ of facts that are already known to be false, is computed.

In the first phase the complement $\tilde{\mathbf{S}}_P(\tilde{I}) := \overline{(H - \mathbf{S}_P(\tilde{I}))}$ of this set of derivable facts constitutes an overestimate of the set of negative derivable facts, and in the second phase the complement $\tilde{\mathbf{S}}_P(\tilde{\mathbf{S}}_P(\tilde{I}))$ is an underestimate.

Let's now turn to the adapted immediate consequence operator. As in the previous sections, the algorithm does not operate on the program P itself, but on its Herbrand instantiation P_H. Based on the Herbrand instantiation P_H and a set of negative literals $\tilde{I}$ a derived program $P' := P_H \cup \tilde{I}$ and a slightly altered version of the immediate consequence operator $\mathbf{T}_{P'}$ of P' are defined.

A fact f is in the set $\mathbf{T}_{P'}(I)$ of immediate consequences of the program P' if all literals l_i in the body of a rule with head f are fulfilled. The difference to the previous definition of the immediate consequence operator is that the bodies of the rules are not required to be positive formulas, but may contain negative literals as well. A negative literal in the rule body is only fulfilled, if it is explicitly contained in the program P' (stemming from the set $\tilde{I}$ which is one component of P'). A positive literal in the body of P' is fulfilled if it is in the interpretation I.

For the proof of the equivalence of the partial models computed by the well-founded model semantics and the alternating fixpoint algorithm the reader is referred to [154].

The computation of the well-founded semantics of the program in Listing 7_24 with the alternating fixpoint procedure is achieved without guessing well-founded sets by the following steps.

- $\mathbf{S}_P(\emptyset) = \{c(2)\}$. The fact $a(1)$ cannot be derived because negation is not treated as negation as failure, but only if the negated literal is in $\tilde{I}$. Similarly, neither one of the facts $b(2)$ and $a(2)$ are in $\mathbf{S}_P(\emptyset)$.

- $\tilde{\mathbf{S}}_P(\emptyset) = \overline{(H - \mathbf{S}_P(\emptyset))} = \overline{\{a(2), b(2), f(2), f(1), d(1), e(2), f(2), c(2), a(1)\}}$-
  $\overline{\{c(2)\}} = \{\neg a(2), \neg b(2), \neg f(2), \neg f(1), \neg d(1), \neg e(2), \neg f(2), \neg a(1)\}$ is the first
  overestimate of the derivable negative facts.
- $\mathbf{S}_P(\tilde{\mathbf{S}}_P(\emptyset)) = \{c(2), a(1), b(2), a(2)\}$ and thus $\mathbf{A}_P(\emptyset) = \tilde{\mathbf{S}}_P(\tilde{\mathbf{S}}_P(\emptyset)) = \{\neg f(2),$
  $\neg f(1), \neg d(1), \neg e(2)\}$ is the second underestimate of the derivable negative
  literals (the first one was the emptyset).
- $\tilde{\mathbf{S}}_P(\tilde{A}_P(\emptyset)) = \{\neg a(2), \neg b(2), \neg f(2), \neg f(1), \neg d(1), \neg e(2)\}$
- $\mathbf{A}_P(\mathbf{A}_P(\emptyset)) = \{\neg f(2), \neg f(1), \neg d(1), \neg e(2)\} = \mathbf{A}_P(\emptyset)$ means that the fixpoint has been reached and $\tilde{A} = \mathbf{A}_P(\emptyset)$ is the set of of negative literals
  derivable from the program.
- The well founded partial model of the program is given by $\tilde{A} \cup \mathbf{S}_P(\tilde{A}) =$
  $\{\neg f(2), \neg f(1), \neg d(1), \neg e(2), c(2), a(1)\}$, which is the same result as in the
  previous section.

For finite Herbrand universes the partial well-founded model is computable
in $O(h)$ with h being the size of the Herbrand Universe [154].

7.7 Other Methods for Query Answering for Logic Programs with Negation

While this chapter gives a first idea on methods for answering queries on stratified and general logic programs with negation, many approaches have not been
mentioned. The previous sections have shown different ways of implementing the
stable model semantics and the well-founded model semantics for general logic
programs mainly in a forward chaining manner (except for the magic set transformation, which is a method of introducing goal-directed search into forward
chaining).

The best known backward chaining method for evaluating logic programs
with negation is an extension of SLD resolution with negation as failure, and is
called SLDNF [33][10][145][58]. SLDNF is sound with respect to the completion
semantics [42] of a logic program and complete for Horn logic programs [93].

Przymusinski introduced SLS resolution[135] as a backward chaining operational semantics for general logic programs under the perfect model semantics
[132]. SLS resolution was extended by Ross to global SLS-resolution[140], which
is a procedural implementation of the well-founded model semantics.

8   Complexity and Expressive Power of Logic Programming Formalisms

8.1 Complexity Classes and Reductions

In this section we recall what is meant by the complexity of logic programming.
Moreover, we provide definitions of the standard complexity classes encountered
in this survey and provide other related definitions. For a detailed exposition of
the complexity notions, the reader is referred to e.g., [94,126].

8.1.1   Decision Problems

In this section, we only deal with *decision problems*, i.e., problems where the answer is "yes" or "no". Formally, a decision problem is a language L over some alphabet Σ. An *instance* of such a decision problem is given as a word $x \in \Sigma^*$. The question to be answered is whether $x \in L$ holds. Accordingly, the answer is "yes" or "no", respectively. The resources (i.e., either time or space) required in the worst case to find the correct answer for any instance x of a problem L is referred to as the *complexity* of the problem L.

8.1.2   Complexity of Logic Programming

There are three main kinds of decision problems (and, thus, three main kinds of complexity) connected to plain datalog and its various extensions [156]:

- The **data complexity** is the complexity of the following decision problem: Let P be some *fixed* datalog program.

  Instance. An input database D_{in} and a ground atom A.
  Question. Does $D_{in} \cup P \models A$ hold?

- The **program complexity** (also called *expression complexity*) is the complexity of the following decision problem: Let D_{in} be some *fixed* input database.

  Instance. A datalog program P and a ground atom A.
  Question. Does $D_{in} \cup P \models A$ hold?

- The **combined complexity** is the complexity of the following decision problem:

  Instance. A datalog program P, an input database D_{in}, and a ground atom A.
  Question. Does $D_{in} \cup P \models A$ hold?

Note that for all versions of datalog considered in this paper, the combined complexity is equivalent to the program complexity with respect to polynomial-time reductions. This is due to the fact that with respect to the derivation of ground atoms, each pair $\langle D_{in}, P \rangle$ can be easily reduced to the pair $\langle D_\emptyset, P^* \rangle$, where $D_\emptyset$ is the empty database instance associated with a universe of two constants c_1 and c_2, and P^* is obtained from $P \cup D_{in}$ by straightforward encoding of the universe $U_{D_{in}}$ using n-tuples over $\{c_1, c_2\}$, where $n = \lceil |U_{D_{in}}| \rceil$. For this reason, we mostly disregard the combined complexity in the material concerning datalog.

As for logic programming in general, a generalization of the combined complexity may be regarded as the main complexity measure. Below, when we speak about the **complexity** of a fragment of logic programming, we mean the complexity of the following decision problem:

Instance. A datalog program P and a ground atom A.
Question. Does $P \models A$ hold?

8.1.3 Complexity Classes

Normally, the time complexity of a problem is expressed in terms of the steps needed by a Turing machine which decides this problem. Likewise, the space complexity corresponds to the number of cells visited by a Turing machine. However, the complexity classes we are interested in here can be defined by any "reasonable" machine model, e.g. random access machines, which are more closely related to real-world computers.

We shall encounter the following complexity classes in this survey.

$$\mathsf{L} \subseteq \mathsf{NL} \subseteq \mathsf{P} \subseteq \mathsf{NP} \subseteq \mathsf{PSPACE} \subseteq \mathsf{EXPTIME} \subseteq \mathsf{NEXPTIME}$$

These are the classes of problems which can be solved in logarithmic space (L), non-deterministic logarithmic space (NL), polynomial time (P), non-deterministic polynomial time (NP), polynomial space (PSPACE), exponential time ($\mathsf{EXPTIME}$), and non-deterministic exponential time ($\mathsf{NEXPTIME}$).

Any complexity class $\mathcal{C}$ has its *complementary class* denoted by co-$\mathcal{C}$, which is defined as follows. For every language $L \subseteq \Sigma^*$, let $\overline{L}$ denote its *complement*, i.e. the set $\Sigma^* \setminus L$. Then co-$\mathcal{C}$ is $\{\overline{L} \mid L \in \mathcal{C}\}$.

Another interesting kind of complexity classes are the classes of the polynomial hierarchy. Formally, they are defined in terms of oracle Turing machines. Intuitively, an oracle is a subroutine for solving some sub-problem where we do not count the cost of the computation. Let $\mathcal{C}$ be a set of languages. For a language L, we say that $L \in \mathsf{P}^{\mathcal{C}}$ (or $L \in \mathsf{NP}^{\mathcal{C}}$) if and only if there is some language $A \in \mathcal{C}$ such that L can be decided in polynomial-time (resp. in non-deterministic polynomial-time) by an algorithm using an oracle for A. The *polynomial hierarchy* consists of classes Δ_i^p, Σ_i^p, and Π_i^p defined as follows:

$$\Delta_0^p = \Sigma_0^p = \Pi_0^p = \mathsf{P}$$
$$\Delta_{i+1}^p = \mathsf{P}^{\Sigma_i^p}$$
$$\Sigma_{i+1}^p = \mathsf{NP}^{\Sigma_i^p}$$
$$\Pi_{i+1}^p = \text{co-}\Sigma_{i+1}^p$$

for all $i \geq 0$. The class PH is defined as

$$\mathsf{PH} = \bigcup_{i \geq 0} \Sigma_i^p.$$

8.1.4 Reductions

Let L_1 and L_2 be decision problems (i.e., languages over some alphabet Σ). Moreover, let $R : \Sigma^* \to \Sigma^*$ be a function which can be computed in logarithmic space and which has the following property: for every $x \in \Sigma^*$, $x \in L_1$ if and only if $R(x) \in L_2$. Then R is called a *logarithmic-space reduction* from L_1 to L_2 and we say that L_1 is *reducible* to L_2.

Let $\mathcal{C}$ be a set of languages. A language L is called $\mathcal{C}$-*hard* if any language L' in $\mathcal{C}$ is reducible to L. If L is $\mathcal{C}$-hard and $L \in \mathcal{C}$ then L is called *complete for* $\mathcal{C}$ or simply $\mathcal{C}$-*complete*.

Besides the above notion of a reduction, complexity theory also considers other kinds of reductions, like polynomial-time reductions or Turing reductions (which are more liberal kinds of reductions). In this paper, unless otherwise stated, a reduction means a logarithmic-space reduction. However, we note that in several cases, results that we shall review have been stated for polynomial-time reductions, but the proofs establish that they hold under logarithmic-space reductions as well.

8.1.5   Turing Machines

As was already mentioned above, the complexity classes considered here are usually defined in terms of Turing machines. On the other hand, as soon as one has several complete problems for some complexity class $\mathcal{C}$, further $\mathcal{C}$-hardness results are usually obtained by reducing one of the already known $\mathcal{C}$-hard problems to the new problem under investigation. In other words, Turing machines are no longer needed explicitly. However, in the context of logic programming, a great portion of the hardness results recalled below have very intuitive proofs "from first principles" (i.e., via reductions from the computations of Turing machines rather than via reductions from other problems). We therefore briefly recall the definition of deterministic and non-deterministic Turing machines.

A *deterministic Turing machine (DTM)* is defined as a quadruple (S, Σ, δ, s_0) with the following meaning: S is a finite set of *states*, Σ is a finite alphabet of *symbols*, δ is a *transition function*, and $s_0 \in S$ is the *initial state*. The alphabet Σ contains a special symbol $\sqcup$ called the *blank*. The transition function δ is a map

$$\delta: \quad S \times \Sigma \quad \rightarrow \quad (S \cup \{\text{yes}, \text{no}\}) \times \Sigma \times \{\text{-1}, \ 0, \ \text{+1}\},$$

where **yes**, and **no** denote two additional states not occurring in S, and -1, 0, +1 denote *motion directions*. It is assumed here, without loss of generality, that the machine is well-behaved and never moves off the tape, i.e., $d \neq$ -1 whenever the cursor is on the leftmost cell; this can be easily ensured by proper design of δ (or by a special symbol which marks the left end of the tape).

Let T be a DTM (Σ, S, δ, s_0). The tape of T is divided into *cells* containing symbols of Σ. There is a *cursor* that may move along the tape. At the start, T is in the initial state s_0, and the cursor points to the leftmost cell of the tape. An *input string* I is written on the tape as follows: the first $|I|$ cells $c_0, \ldots, c_{|I|-1}$ of the tape, where $|I|$ denotes the length of I, contains the symbols of I, and all other cells contain $\sqcup$.

The machine takes successive *steps* of computation according to δ. Namely, assume that T is in a state $s \in S$ and the cursor points to the symbol $\sigma \in \Sigma$ on the tape. Let

$$\delta(s, \sigma) = (s', \sigma', d).$$

Then T changes its current state to s', overwrites σ' on σ, and moves the cursor according to d. Namely, if $d =$ -1 or $d =$ +1, then the cursor moves to the previous cell or the next one, respectively; if $d = 0$, then the cursor remains in the same position.

When any of the states **yes** or **no** is reached, T halts. We say that T *accepts* the input I if T halts in **yes**. Similarly, we say that T *rejects* the input in the case of halting in **no**.

A *non-deterministic Turing machine (NDTM)* is defined as a quadruple (S, Σ, Δ, s_0), where S, Σ, s_0 are the same as before. Possible operations of the machine are described by Δ, which is no longer a function. Instead, Δ is a relation:

$$\Delta \subseteq (S \times \Sigma) \times (S \cup \{\textbf{yes}, \textbf{no}\}) \times \Sigma \times \{\texttt{-1, 0, +1}\}.$$

A tuple whose first two members are s and σ respectively, specifies the action of the NDTM when its current state is s and the symbol pointed at by its cursor is σ. If the number of such tuples is greater than one, the NDTM non-deterministically chooses any of them and operates accordingly.

Unlike the case of a DTM, the definition of acceptance and rejection by a NDTM is asymmetric. We say that an NDTM *accepts* an input if there is at least one sequence of choices leading to the state **yes**. An NDTM *rejects* an input if no sequence of choices can lead to **yes**.

8.2 Propositional Logic Programming

We start our complexity analysis of logic programming with the simplest case, i.e., propositional logic programming.

Theorem 224. *(implicit in [95,156,89]) Propositional logic programming is P-complete.*

Proof. Membership. Let a program P be given. Recall from Section 6.1 that the semantics of P can be defined as the least fixpoint of the immediate consequence operator $\mathbf{T}_P$) and that this least fixpoint $lfp(\mathbf{T}_P)$ can be computed in polynomial time even if the "naive" evaluation algorithm from Listing 6_2 is applied. Indeed, the number of iterations (i.e. applications of $\mathbf{T}_P$) is bounded by the number of rules plus one. Moreover, each iteration step is clearly feasible in polynomial time.

Hardness. Let A be an arbitrary language in P. Thus A is decidable by a deterministic Turing machine (DTM) T in at most $q(|I|)$ steps for some polynomial q, for any input I. We show that the computation of the Turing machine T on any input I can be simulated by a propositional logic program as follows: Let $N = q(|I|)$. W.l.o.g., we assume that the computation of T on input I takes exactly N steps.

The transition function δ of a DTM with a single tape can be represented by a table whose rows are tuples $t = \langle s, \sigma, s', \sigma', d \rangle$. Such a tuple t expresses the following if-then-rule:

> **if** at some time instant τ the DTM is in state s, the cursor points to cell number π, and this cell contains symbol σ
> **then** at instant $\tau + 1$ the DTM is in state s', cell number π contains symbol σ', and the cursor points to cell number $\pi + d$.

It is possible to describe the complete evolution of a DTM T on input string I from its initial configuration at time instant 0 to the configuration at instant N by a propositional logic program $L(T, I, N)$. To achieve this, we define the following classes of propositional atoms:

symbol$_\alpha[\tau, \pi]$ for $0 \leq \tau \leq N$, $0 \leq \pi \leq N$ and $\alpha \in \Sigma$. Intuitive meaning: at instant τ of the computation, cell number π contains symbol α.

cursor$[\tau, \pi]$ for $0 \leq \tau \leq N$ and $0 \leq \pi \leq N$. Intuitive meaning: at instant τ, the cursor points to cell number π.

state$_s[\tau]$ for $0 \leq \tau \leq N$ and $s \in S$. Intuitive meaning: at instant τ, the DTM T is in state s.

accept Intuitive meaning: T has reached state **yes**.

Let us denote by I_k the k-th symbol of the string $I = I_0 \cdots I_{|I|-1}$. The initial configuration of T on input I is reflected by the following *initialization facts* in $L(T, I, N)$:

$$\begin{aligned}
symbol_\sigma[0, \pi] &\leftarrow & \text{for } 0 \leq \pi < |I|, \text{ where } I_\pi = \sigma \\
symbol_{\sqcup}[0, \pi] &\leftarrow & \text{for } |I| \leq \pi \leq N \\
cursor[0, 0] &\leftarrow & \\
state_{s_0}[0] &\leftarrow &
\end{aligned}$$

Each entry $\langle s, \sigma, s', \sigma', d \rangle$ of the transition table δ is translated into the following propositional Horn clauses, which we call the *transition rules*. We thus need the following clauses for each value of τ and π such that $0 \leq \tau < N$, $0 \leq \pi < N$, and $0 \leq \pi + d$.

$$\begin{aligned}
symbol_{\sigma'}[\tau + 1, \pi] &\leftarrow state_s[\tau], symbol_\sigma[\tau, \pi], cursor[\tau, \pi] \\
cursor[\tau + 1, \pi + d] &\leftarrow state_s[\tau], symbol_\sigma[\tau, \pi], cursor[\tau, \pi] \\
state_{s'}[\tau + 1] &\leftarrow state_s[\tau], symbol_\sigma[\tau, \pi], cursor[\tau, \pi]
\end{aligned}$$

These clauses almost perfectly describe what is happening during a state transition from an instant τ to an instant $\tau + 1$. However, it should not be forgotten that those tape cells which are not changed during the transition keep their old values at instant $\tau + 1$. This must be reflected by what we term *inertia rules*. These rules are asserted for each time instant τ and tape cell numbers π, π', where $0 \leq \tau < N$, $0 \leq \pi < \pi' \leq N$, and have the following form:

$$\begin{aligned}
symbol_\sigma[\tau + 1, \pi] &\leftarrow symbol_\sigma[\tau, \pi], cursor[\tau, \pi'] \\
symbol_\sigma[\tau + 1, \pi'] &\leftarrow symbol_\sigma[\tau, \pi'], cursor[\tau, \pi]
\end{aligned}$$

Finally, a group of clauses termed *accept rules* derives the propositional atom *accept*, whenever an accepting configuration is reached.

$$accept \leftarrow state_{\textbf{yes}}[\tau] \qquad \text{for } 0 \leq \tau \leq N.$$

Denote by L the logic program $L(T, I, N)$. Note that $\mathbf{T}_L^0 = \emptyset$ and that $\mathbf{T}_L^1$ contains the initial configuration of T at time instant 0. By construction, the least fixpoint $lfp(\mathbf{T}_L)$ of L is reached at $\mathbf{T}_L^{N+2}$, and the ground atoms added to $\mathbf{T}_L^\tau$, $2 \leq \tau \leq N + 1$, i.e., those in $\mathbf{T}_L^\tau \setminus \mathbf{T}_L^{\tau-1}$, describe the configuration of T on the input I at the time instant $\tau - 1$. The least fixpoint $lfp(\mathbf{T}_L)$ contains *accept* if and only if an accepting configuration has been reached by T in at most N computation steps. Hence, $L(T, I, N)) \models accept$ if and only if T has reached an accepting state within $q(N)$ steps with $N = |I|$.

The translation from I to $L(T, I, N)$ with $N = q(|I|)$ is very simple and is clearly feasible in logarithmic space, since all rules of $L(T, I, N))$ can be generated independently of each other and each has size logarithmic in $|I|$; note that the numbers τ and π have $O(\log |I|)$ bits, while all other syntactic constituents of a rule have constant size. We have thus shown that every language A in P is logspace reducible to propositional logic programming. Hence, propositional logic programming is P-hard. □

Note that the the polynomial-time upper bound can be even sharpened to a *linear time* upper bound, as was shown in [57,120]. As far as the lower bound is concerned, the above proof could be greatly simplified by using reductions from other P-complete problems like, e.g., from the monotone circuit value problem (see [126]). However, the proof from first principles provides a basic framework from which further results will be derived by slight adaptations in the sequel.

An interesting kind of syntactical restrictions on programs is obtained by restricting the number of atoms in the body. Let $\mathrm{LP}(k)$ denote logic programming where each clause has at most k atoms in the body. Then, by results in [156,90], one easily obtains that $\mathrm{LP}(1)$ is NL-complete. Indeed, the correspondence between the well-known NL-complete reachability problem of directed graphs and $\mathrm{LP}(1)$ is immediate. On the other hand, observe that the DTM encoding in the proof of Theorem 224 can be easily modified to programs in $\mathrm{LP}(2)$. Hence, $\mathrm{LP}(k)$ for any $k \geq 2$ is P-complete.

8.3   Conjunctive Queries

For the complexity analysis of conjunctive queries (CQs), we restrict ourselves to *boolean* conjunctive queries (cf. Definition 25), i.e. the queries under consideration are of the form

$$Q : ans() \leftarrow r_1(\mathbf{u}_1) \wedge \ldots \wedge r_n(\mathbf{u}_n)$$

where $n \geq 0$; $r_1, \ldots, r_n$ are (not necessarily distinct) extensional relation symbols and $ans()$ is a 0-ary intensional relation symbol; moreover, $\mathbf{u}_1, \ldots, \mathbf{u}_n$ are lists of terms of appropriate length.[25]

Query Q evaluates to *true* if there exists a substitution θ such that $r_i(\mathbf{u}_i)\theta \in D_{in}$ for all $i \in \{1, \ldots, n\}$; otherwise, the query evaluates to *false*.

---

[25] Note that without this restriction to boolean CQs, the head literal of a conjunctive query would have the form $ans(\mathbf{u})$, where $\mathbf{u}$ is a list of terms. However, as far as the complexity of query evaluation is concerned, this difference is inessential.

Theorem 225. *The program complexity of conjunctive queries is* NP-*complete [37].*

This problem appears as Problem SR31 in Garey and Johnson's book [76].

Proof. Membership. We guess an assignment for each variable of the query and check whether all the resulting ground atoms in the query body exist in D_{in}. This check is obviously feasible in polynomial time.

Hardness. We reduce the NP-complete 3-SAT problem to our problem. For this purpose, we consider the following input database (over a ternary relation symbol c and a binary relation symbol v) as fixed:

$$D_{in} = \{ c(1,1,1),\, c(1,1,0),\, c(1,0,1),\, c(1,0,0),$$
$$c(0,1,1),\, c(0,1,0),\, c(0,0,1),\, v(1,0),\, v(0,1) \}$$

Now let an instance of the 3-SAT problem be given through the 3-CNF formula

$$\Phi = \bigwedge_{i=1}^{n} l_{i,1} \vee l_{i,2} \vee l_{i,3}$$

over propositional atoms $x_1, \ldots, x_k$. Then we define a conjunctive query Q as follows:

$$ans() \leftarrow c(l^*_{1,1}, l^*_{1,2}, l^*_{1,3}), \ldots, c(l^*_{1,1}, l^*_{1,2}, l^*_{1,3}), v(x_1, \bar{x}_i), \ldots, v(x_k, \bar{x}_k)$$

where $l^* = x$ if $l = x$, and $l^* = \bar{x}$ if $l = \neg x$. By slight abuse of notation, we thus use x_i to denote either a propositional atom (in Φ) or a first-order variable (in Q).

It is straightforward to verify that the 3-CNF formula Φ is satisfiable if and only if $D_{in} \cup Q \models ans()$ holds.   □

8.4   First-Order Queries

Recall from Definition 6 that we are mainly considering first-order queries *without* equality here. Hence, atoms are of the form $r(\mathbf{u})$ for some relational symbol r from the signature $\mathcal{L}$ and a list of terms $\mathbf{u}$ whose length corresponds to the arity of r. Compound formulae are constructed from simpler ones by means of quantification (with $\forall$ and $\exists$) and the conjuncts $\wedge, \vee, \neg$. Note however that the following complexity result also holds if we consider first-order predicate logic *with* equality.

Theorem 226. *(implicit in [90,156]) First-order queries are program-complete for* PSPACE. *Their data complexity is in the class* AC^0, *which contains the languages recognized by unbounded fan-in circuits of polynomial size and constant depth [94].*

Proof. We only prove the PSPACE-completeness. Actually, we show that the combined complexity is PSPACE-complete. However, by the considerations in

Section 8.1, the PSPACE-completeness of the program-complexity follows immediately.

Membership. Let φ be a first-order sentence and D_{in} be an input database with domain elements **dom**. Let $n = |D_{in}| + |\mathbf{dom}|$ and $m = |\varphi|$. There are maximal m alternations of $\forall$ and $\exists$ (because the number of variables in φ is less than m), thus the evaluation has maximal m nested loops. In each loop we need to store

1. the position of the currently processed variable, and
2. for each variable with the assigned value in **dom**, its position in **dom**.

The space for these operations is then $O(m)$, hence in PSPACE.

Hardness. The PSPACE-hardness can be shown by a reduction from the QBF problem. Assume that ϕ is the quantified Boolean formula

$$Qx_1 \ldots Qx_n \alpha(x_1, \ldots, x_n)$$

where Q is either $\forall$ or $\exists$ and α is a quantifier-free Boolean formula.

We first define the signature $\mathcal{L} = \{\mathsf{istrue}, \mathsf{isequal}, \mathsf{or}, \mathsf{and}, \mathsf{not}\}$ The predicates and, or, not are used to define the operators of Boolean algebra. The predicate istrue is unary and defines the truth value *true*, whereas the predicate isequal is binary and defines the equality of two values.

For each sub-formula β of α, we define a quantifier-free, first-order formula $T_\beta(z_1, \ldots, z_n, x)$ with the following intended meaning: if the variables x_i have the truth value z_i, then the formula $\beta(x_1, \ldots, x_n)$ evaluates to the truth value x. Note that $T_\beta(z_1, \ldots, z_n, x)$ can be defined inductively w.r.t. the structure of α as follows:

Case $\beta =$

$$
\begin{aligned}
x_i \ (\text{with } 1 \leq i \leq n): \quad & T_\beta(\bar{z}, x) \equiv \mathsf{isequal}(x, z_i) \\
\neg \beta': \quad & T_\beta(\bar{z}, x) \equiv \exists t_1 T_{\beta'}(\bar{z}, t_1) \wedge \mathsf{not}(x, t_1) \\
\beta_1 \wedge \beta_2: \quad & T_\beta(\bar{z}, x) \equiv \exists t_1, t_2\ T_{\beta_1}(\bar{z}, t_1) \wedge T_{\beta_2}(\bar{z}, t_2) \wedge \mathsf{and}(t_1, t_2, x) \\
\beta_1 \vee \beta_2: \quad & T_\beta(\bar{z}, x) \equiv \exists t_1, t_2\ T_{\beta_1}(\bar{z}, t_1) \wedge T_{\beta_2}(\bar{z}, t_2) \wedge \mathsf{or}(t_1, t_2, x)
\end{aligned}
$$

Finally, we define the input database as $D_{in} = \{\mathsf{istrue}(1), \mathsf{isequal}(0,0), \mathsf{isequal}(1, 1), \mathsf{or}(1,1,1), \mathsf{or}(1,0,1), \mathsf{or}(0,1,1), \mathsf{or}(0,0,0), \mathsf{and}(1,1,1), \mathsf{and}(1,0,0), \mathsf{and}(0,1,0), \mathsf{and}(0,0,0), \mathsf{not}(1,0), \mathsf{not}(0,1)\}$, and the first-order query φ is defined as follows:

$$\varphi \equiv \exists x\ Qz_1 \ldots Qz_n\ \mathsf{istrue}(x) \wedge T_\alpha(\bar{z}, x)$$

It is then straightforward to show that the formula ϕ is satisfiable if and only if the evaluation of φ returns *true*. $\qquad\square$

8.5 Unification

Unification is used extensively in several areas of computer science, including theorem proving, database systems, natural language processing, logic programming, computer algebra, and program verification. We briefly introduce the basic notions here. Additional material can be found in [13] or [52].

Recall from Definition 50 that two atoms or terms s and t are called *unifiable* if there exists a substitution σ with $s\sigma = t\sigma$. Such a substitution σ is called a *unifier* of s and t. A unifier σ of s and t is called *most general* if any other unifier σ' of s and t is an instance of σ, i.e., there exists a substitution η with $\sigma' = \sigma\eta$.

The **unification problem** is the following decision problem: given terms s and t, are they unifiable?

Robinson described an algorithm that solves this problem and, if the answer is positive, computes a most general unifier of given two terms (see [138]). His algorithm had exponential time and space complexity mainly because of the representation of terms by strings of symbols. However, by using more sophisticated data structures (like directed acyclic graphs), unification was later shown to be feasible in polynomial time. In fact, even linear time suffices (see [116,130]).

Theorem 227. *([59,162,60]) The unification problem is* P-*complete.*

Note that in the above definition of unification, a unifier σ of s and t makes the terms $s\sigma$ and $t\sigma$ syntactically equal. More generally, one may look for so-called *E-unifiers* which make the terms $s\sigma$ and $t\sigma$ equal modulo some equational theory.

Equational theories are usually presented by finite sets E of identities of the form $l = r$, which are referred to as *equational axioms*. The *equational theory* $Th(E)$ presented by E is the smallest congruence relation over terms (for a given signature $\mathcal{L}$) containing E and closed under substitutions, i.e., $Th(E)$ is the smallest congruence containing all pairs $l\rho = r\rho$, where $l = r$ is in E and ρ is a substitution. We write $s =_E t$ to denote that the pair (s,t) of terms is a member of $Th(E)$. In this survey, we only consider the equationl axioms (for some function symbol f) depicted in Figure 7.

Associativity	A(f)	$f(f(x,y),z) = f(x,f(y,z))$
Commutativity	C(f)	$f(x,y) = f(y,x)$
Idempotence	I(f)	$f(x,x) = x$
Existence of Unit	U(f)	$f(x,1) = x,\ f(1,x) = x$

Fig. 7. Equational Axioms

An *E-unifier* of s and t is a substitution ρ such that $s\rho =_E t\rho$ holds. Whenever such an *E*-unifier exists, we say that the terms s and t are *E-unifiable*. For every equational theory E, the **E-unification problem** is the following decision problem: given terms s and t, are they E-unifiable, i.e., is there a substitution ρ, such that $s\rho =_E t\rho$?

By examining the signature $\mathcal{L}$ over which the terms of unification problems in the theory $Th(E)$ have been built, we distinguish between three different kinds of *E*-unification. Let $sig(E)$ be the set of all function and constant symbols occurring in the equational axioms of E. If $\mathcal{L} = sig(E)$ holds, then we speak about *elementary* E-*unification.* If the signature $\mathcal{L}$ contains in addition free constant symbols, but no free function symbols, then we speak about *E-unification with constants.* Finally, if the signature $\mathcal{L}$ contains free function symbols of arbitrary arities, then we speak about *general* E-*unification.* Figure 8 summarizes the complexity results for some equational unification decision problems. The entry ⟵ means that upper bounds carry over to the simpler case.

theory	complexity		
	elementary	with constants	general
∅	⟵	⟵	linear [116,130]
A	⟵	NP-hard [20] and in NEXPTIME [131]	NP-hard
C		NP-complete (folkore, see e.g. [76,13])	NP-complete
AC	NP-complete	NP-complete	NP-complete [96]
ACI	⟵	in P	NP-complete [96]
ACIU	⟵	in P	NP-complete [121]

Fig. 8. Complexity Results for Equational Unification Decision Problems

8.6   Positive Definite Rule Sets

Let us now turn to datalog. We first consider the data complexity.

Theorem 228. *(implicit in [156,89]) Datalog is data complete for* P.

Proof. (Sketch) Grounding P on an input database D yields polynomially many clauses in the size of D; hence, the complexity of propositional logic programming is an upper bound for the data complexity.

The P-hardness can be shown by writing a simple datalog *meta-interpreter* for propositional LP(k), where k is a constant.

Represent rules $A_0 \leftarrow A_1, \ldots, A_i$, where $0 \leq i \leq k$, by tuples $\langle A_0, \ldots, A_i \rangle$ in an $(i+1)$-ary relation R_i on the propositional atoms. Then, a program P in LP(k) which is stored this way in a database $D(P)$ can be evaluated by a fixed datalog program $P_{MI}(k)$ which contains for each relation R_i, $0 \leq i \leq k$, a rule

$$T(X_0) \leftarrow T(X_1), \ldots, T(X_i), R_i(X_0, \ldots, X_i).$$

$T(x)$ intuitively means that atom x is true. Then, $P \models A$ just if $P_{MI} \cup P(D) \models T(A)$. P-hardness of the data complexity of datalog is then immediate from Theorem 224.   □

The program complexity is exponentially higher.

Theorem 229. *(implicit in [156,89])*   *Datalog is program complete for* EXPTIME.

Proof. Membership. Grounding P on D leads to a propositional program P' whose size is exponential in the size of the fixed input database D. Hence, by Theorem 224, the program complexity is in EXPTIME.

Hardness. In order to prove EXPTIME-hardness, we show that if a DTM T halts in less than $N = 2^{n^k}$ steps on a given input I where $|I| = n$, then T can be simulated by a datalog program over a fixed input database D. In fact, we use $D_\emptyset$, i.e., the empty database with the universe $U = \{0, 1\}$.

We employ the scheme of the DTM encoding into logic programming from Theorem 224, but use the predicates $symbol_\sigma(X, Y)$, $cursor(X, Y)$ and $state_s(X)$ instead of the propositional letters $symbol_\sigma[X, Y]$, $cursor[X, Y]$ and $state_s[X]$ respectively. The time points τ and tape positions π from 0 to $2^m - 1$, $m = n^k$, are represented by m-ary tuples over U, on which the functions $\tau + 1$ and $\pi + d$ are realized by means of the successor $Succ^m$ from a linear order $\leq^m$ on U^m.

For an inductive definition, suppose $Succ^i(\mathbf{X}, \mathbf{Y})$, $First^i(\mathbf{X})$, and $Last^i(\mathbf{X})$ tell the successor, the first, and the last element from a linear order $\leq^i$ on U^i, where $\mathbf{X}$ and $\mathbf{Y}$ have arity i. Then, use rules

$$Succ^{i+1}(Z, \mathbf{X}, Z, \mathbf{Y}) \leftarrow Succ^i(\mathbf{X}, \mathbf{Y})$$
$$Succ^{i+1}(Z, \mathbf{X}, Z', \mathbf{Y}) \leftarrow Succ^1(Z, Z'), Last^i(\mathbf{X}), First^i(\mathbf{Y})$$
$$First^{i+1}(Z, \mathbf{X}) \leftarrow First^1(Z), First^i(\mathbf{X})$$
$$Last^{i+1}(Z, \mathbf{X}) \leftarrow Last^1(z), Last^i(\mathbf{X})$$

Here $Succ^1(X, Y)$, $First^1(X)$, and $Last^1(X)$ on $U^1 = U$ must be provided. For our reduction, we use the usual ordering $0 \leq^1 1$ and provide those relations by the ground facts $Succ^1(0, 1)$, $First^1(0)$, and $Last^1(1)$.

The initialization facts $symbol_\sigma[0, \pi]$ are readily translated into the datalog rules

$$symbol_\sigma(\mathbf{X}, \mathbf{t}) \leftarrow First^m(\mathbf{X}),$$

where $\mathbf{t}$ represents the position π, and similarly the facts $cursor[0, 0]$ and $state_{s_0}[0]$. The remaining initialization facts $symbol_\sqcup[0, \pi]$, where $|I| \leq \pi \leq N$, are translated to the rule

$$symbol_\sqcup(\mathbf{X}, \mathbf{Y}) \leftarrow First^m(\mathbf{X}), \leq^m(\mathbf{t}, \mathbf{Y})$$

where $\mathbf{t}$ represents the number $|I|$; the order $\leq^m$ is easily defined from $Succ^m$ by two clauses

$$\leq^m(\mathbf{X}, \mathbf{X}) \leftarrow$$
$$\leq^m(\mathbf{X}, \mathbf{Y}) \leftarrow Succ^m(\mathbf{X}, \mathbf{Z}), \leq^m (\mathbf{Z}, \mathbf{Y})$$

The transition and inertia rules are easily translated into datalog rules. For realizing $\tau + 1$ and $\pi + d$, use in the body atoms $Succ^m(\mathbf{X}, \mathbf{X}')$. For example, the clause

$$symbol_{\sigma'}[\tau + 1, \pi] \leftarrow state_s[\tau], symbol_\sigma[\tau, \pi], cursor[\tau, \pi]$$

is translated into

$$symbol_{\sigma'}(\mathbf{X'}, \mathbf{Y}) \leftarrow state_s(\mathbf{X}), symbol_{\sigma}(\mathbf{X}, \mathbf{Y}), cursor(\mathbf{X}, \mathbf{Y}), Succ^m(\mathbf{X}, \mathbf{X'}).$$

The translation of the accept rules is straightforward.

For the resulting datalog program P', it holds that $P' \cup D_{\emptyset} \models accept$ if and only if T accepts input I in at most N steps. It is easy to see that P' can be constructed from T and I in logarithmic space. Hence, datalog has EXPTIME-hard program complexity.   □

Note that, instead of using a generic reduction, the hardness part of this theorem can also be obtained by applying complexity upgrading techniques [127,17].

8.7 Stratified Definite Rule Sets (stratified Datalog)

Recall from Definition 21 that a *normal clause* is a rule of the form

$$A \leftarrow L_1, \ldots, L_m \qquad (m \geq 0)$$

where A is an atom and each L_i is a literal. A *normal logic program* is a finite set of normal clauses. As was explained in Section 7, if a normal logic program P is *stratified*, then the clauses of P can be partitioned into disjoint sets $S_1, \ldots, S_n$ s.t. the semantics of P is computed by successively computing fixpoints of the immediate consequence operators $\mathbf{T}_{S_1}, \ldots, \mathbf{T}_{S_n}$. More precisely, let $\mathbf{I}_0$ be the initial instance over the extensional predicate symbols of P and let $\mathbf{I}_i$ (with $1 \leq i \leq n$) be defined as follows:

$$\mathbf{I}_1 := \mathbf{T}_{S_1}^{\omega}(\mathbf{I}_0), \quad \mathbf{I}_2 := \mathbf{T}_{S_2}^{\omega}(\mathbf{I}_1), \quad \ldots, \quad \mathbf{I}_n := \mathbf{T}_{S_n}^{\omega}(\mathbf{I}_{n-1})$$

Then the semantics of program P is given through the set $\mathbf{I}_n$.

Note that in the propositional case, $\mathbf{I}_n$ is clearly polynomially computable. Hence, stratified negation does not increase the complexity. Analogously to Theorems 224, 228, and 229, we thus have:

Theorem 230. *(implicit in [9]) Stratified propositional logic programming with negation is* P-*complete. Stratified datalog with negation is data complete for* P *and program complete for* EXPTIME.

Note that nonrecursive logic programs with negation are trivially stratified since, in this case, the dependency graph is acyclic and the clauses can be simply partitioned into strata according to a topological sort of the head predicates. Actually, any nonrecursive datalog program with negation can be easily rewritten to an equivalent first-order query and vice versa (cf. Theorem 243). Hence, analogously to Theorem 226, we have the following complexity results.

Theorem 231. *(implicit in [90,156]) Nonrecursive propositional logic programming with negation is* P-*complete. Nonrecursive datalog with negation is program complete for* PSPACE. *Its data complexity is in the class* AC[0], *which contains the languages recognized by unbounded fan-in circuits of polynomial size and constant depth [94].*

8.8   Well-Founded and Inflationary Semantics

In Section 7.6, an *alternating fixpoint* procedure for computing the well-founded semantics was presented. This computation aims at iteratively building up a set of negative conclusions $\tilde{A}$ of a logic program. It starts with an underestimate of the negative conclusions $\tilde{I} = \emptyset$ from which an overestimate $\tilde{\mathbf{S}}_P(\tilde{I})$ is computed which is in turn used to move back to an underestimate $\mathbf{A}_P(\tilde{I}) := \tilde{\mathbf{S}}_P(\tilde{\mathbf{S}}_P(\tilde{I}))$, etc. The iteration of this monotonic transformation $\mathbf{A}_P$ leads to a least fixpoint $\tilde{A} := lfp(\mathbf{A}_P)$. The well-founded semantics of the program P is given through the set $\tilde{A} \cup \tilde{\mathbf{S}}_P(\tilde{A})$. Clearly, for a propositional logic program, this fixpoint computation can be done in polynomial time. Together with Theorem 224, we thus get.

Theorem 232. *(implicit in [154,155]) Propositional logic programming with negation under well-founded semantics is* P*-complete. Datalog with negation under well-founded semantics is data complete for* P *and program complete for* EXPTIME.

As was mentioned in Section 5.3.5, the *inflationary semantics* is defined via the *inflationary operator* $\tilde{\mathbf{T}}_P$, which is defined as $\tilde{\mathbf{T}}_P(I) = I \cup \mathbf{T}_{P^I}(I)$ (cf. Definition 189). Clearly, the limit $\tilde{\mathbf{T}}_P^\omega(\mathbf{I})$ is computable in polynomial time for a propositional program P. Therefore, by the above results, we have

Theorem 233. *([5]; implicit in [86]) Propositional logic programming with negation under inflationary semantics is* P*-complete. Datalog with negation under inflationary semantics is data complete for* P *and program complete for* EXPTIME.

8.9   Stable Model Semantics

An interpretation I of a normal logic program P is a *stable model* of P [77] if I is the (unique) minimal Herbrand model of P^I. As was mentioned in Section 5.3.2, a program P may have zero, one, or multiple stable models.

Note that every stratified program P has a unique stable model, and its stratified and stable semantics coincide. Unstratified rules increase the complexity as the following theorem illustrates.

Theorem 234. *([115], [22]) Given a propositional normal logic program P, deciding whether P has a stable model is* NP*-complete.*

Proof. Membership. Clearly, P^I is polynomial time computable from P and I. Hence, a stable model M of P can be guessed and checked in polynomial time.

Hardness. Modify the DTM encoding in the proof of Theorem 224 for a nondeterministic Turing machine T as follows.

1. For each state s and symbol σ, introduce atoms $B_{s,\sigma,1}[\tau], \ldots, B_{s,\sigma,k}[\tau]$ for all $1 \leq \tau < N$ and for all transitions $\langle s, \sigma, s_i, \sigma_i', d_i \rangle$, where $1 \leq i \leq k$.

2. Add $B_{s,\sigma,i}[\tau]$ in the bodies of the transition rules for $\langle s, \sigma, s_i, \sigma'_i, d_i \rangle$.
3. Add the rule

$$B_{s,\sigma,i}[\tau] \leftarrow \neg B_{s,\sigma,1}[\tau], \ldots, \neg B_{s,\sigma,i-1}[\tau], \neg B_{s,\sigma,i+1}[\tau], \ldots, \neg B_{s,\sigma,k}[\tau].$$

Intuitively, these rules non-deterministically select precisely one of the possible transitions for s and σ at time instant τ, whose transition rules are enabled via $B_{s,\sigma,i}[\tau]$.

4. Finally, add a rule

$$accept \leftarrow \neg accept.$$

It ensures that *accept* is true in every stable model.

It is immediate from the construction that the stable models M of the resulting program correspond to the accepting runs of T.   □

Notice that, as shown in [115], the hardness part of this result holds even if all rules in P have exactly one literal in the body and, moreover, this literal is negative. As an easy consequence of Theorem 234, we obtain

Theorem 235. *([115]; [142] and [102]) Propositional logic programming with negation under stable model semantics is* co-NP-*complete. Datalog with negation under stable model semantics is data complete for* co-NP *and program complete for* co-NEXPTIME.

The co-NEXPTIME result for program complexity, which is not stated in [142], follows from an analogous result for datalog under fixpoint models in [102] and a simple, elegant transformation of this semantics to the stable model semantics [142].

8.10   Disjunctive Rule Sets

A *disjunctive logic program* is a set of clauses

$$A_1 \vee \cdots \vee A_k \leftarrow L_1, \ldots, L_m \text{ with } (k \geq 1, m \geq 0),$$

where each A_i is an atom and each L_j is a literal, see [112,119]. The semantics of negation-free disjunctive logic programs is based on *minimal* Herbrand models. As was pointed out in Section 5.1.4, in general, disjunctive logic programs do not have a unique minimal Herbrand model.

Denote by $\mathrm{MM}(P)$ the set of all minimal Herbrand models of P. The *Generalized Closed World Assumption (GCWA)* [118] for negation-free P amounts to the meaning $\mathcal{M}_{GCWA}(P) = \{L \mid \mathrm{MM}(P) \models L\}$.

Theorem 236. *([62,64])   Let P be a propositional negation-free disjunctive logic program and A be a propositional atom. Deciding whether $P \models_{GCWA} A$ is* co-NP-*complete.*

Proof. (Sketch) It is not hard to argue that for an atom A, we have $P \models_{GCWA} A$ if and only if $P \models_{PC} A$, where $\models_{PC}$ is the classical logical consequence relation. In addition, any set of clauses can be clearly represented by a suitable disjunctive logic program. Hence, the co-NP-hardness follows from the well-known NP-completeness of SAT.   □

Stable negation naturally extends to disjunctive logic programs, by adopting that I is a *(disjunctive) stable model* of a disjunctive logic program P if and only if $I \in \mathrm{MM}(P^I)$ [133,78]. The disjunctive stable model semantics subsumes the disjunctive stratified semantics [132]. For well-founded semantics, no such natural extension is known; the semantics in [24,134] are the most appealing attempts in this direction.

Clearly, P^I is easily computed, and $P^I = P$ if P is negation-free. Thus,

Theorem 237. *([63,64,65]) Propositional disjunctive logic programming under stable model semantics is Π_2^p complete. Disjunctive datalog under stable model semantics is data complete for Π_2^p and program complete for* co-NEXPTIME^{NP}.

8.11   Rule Sets with Function Symbols

If we allow function symbols, then logic programs become undecidable.

Theorem 238. *([8,151]) Logic programming is r.e.-complete.*[26]

Proof. (Sketch) On the one hand, the undecidability can be proved by a simple encoding of (the halting problem of) Turing machines similar to the encoding in the proof of Theorem 229 (use terms $f^n(c)$, $n \geq 0$, for representing cell positions and time instants). This reduction from the halting problem also establishes the r.e.-hardness. On the other hand, the least fixpoint $lfp(\mathbf{T}_P)$ of any logic program P is clearly a recursively enumerable set. This shows the r.e.-membership and, thus, in total, the r.e.-completeness of logic programming.   □

A natural decidable fragment of logic programming with functions are *nonrecursive programs*. Their complexity is characterized by the following theorem.

Theorem 239. *([47]) Nonrecursive logic programming is* NEXPTIME-*complete.*

Proof. (Sketch) The NEXPTIME-membership is established by applying SLD-resolution with constraints. The size of the derivation turns out to be exponential. The NEXPTIME-hardness is proved by reduction from the tiling problem for the square $2^n \times 2^n$.   □

---

[26] In the context of recursion theory, reducibility of a language (or problem) L_1 to L_2 is understood in terms of a Turing reduction, i.e., L_1 can be decided by a DTM with oracle L_2, rather than logarithmic-space reduction.

8.12   Expressive Power

The expressive power of query languages such as datalog is a topic common to database theory [2] and finite model theory [61] that has attracted much attention by both communities. By the expressive power of a (formal) *query language*, we understand the set of all queries expressible in that language.

In general, a *query* q defines a mapping $\mathcal{M}_q$ that assigns to each suitable input database D_{in} (over a fixed input schema) a result database $D_{out} = \mathcal{M}_q(D_{in})$ (over a fixed output schema); more logically speaking, a query defines global relations [85]. For reasons of representation independence, a query should, in addition, be *generic*, i.e., invariant under isomorphisms. This means that if τ is a permutation of the domain $Dom(\mathcal{D})$, then $\mathcal{M}(\tau(D_{in})) = \tau(D_{out})$. Thus, when we speak about queries, we always mean generic queries.

Formally, the *expressive power* of a query language Q is the set of mappings $\mathcal{M}_q$ for all queries q expressible in the language Q by some *query expression* (program) E; this syntactic expression is commonly identified with the semantic query it defines, and simply (in abuse of definition) called a query.

There are two important research tasks in this context. The first is comparing two query languages Q_1 and Q_2 in their expressive power. One may prove, for instance, that $Q_1 \subsetneq Q_2$, which means that the set of all queries expressible in Q_1 is a proper subset of the queries expressible in Q_2, and hence, Q_2 is strictly more expressive than Q_1. Or one may show that two query languages Q_1 and Q_2 have the same expressive power, denoted by $Q_1 = Q_2$, and so on.

The second research task, more related to complexity theory, is determining the absolute expressive power of a query language. This is mostly achieved by proving that a given query language Q is able to express exactly all queries whose evaluation complexity is in a complexity class $\mathcal{C}$. In this case, we say that Q *captures* $\mathcal{C}$ and write simply $Q = \mathcal{C}$. The *evaluation complexity* of a query is the complexity of checking whether a given atom belongs to the query result, or, in the case of Boolean queries, whether the query evaluates to *true* [156,85].

Note that there is a substantial difference between showing that the query evaluation problem for a certain query language Q is $\mathcal{C}$-complete and showing that Q captures $\mathcal{C}$. If the evaluation problem for Q is $\mathcal{C}$-complete, then *at least one* $\mathcal{C}$-hard query is expressible in Q. If Q captures $\mathcal{C}$, then Q expresses *all* queries evaluable in $\mathcal{C}$ (including, of course, all $\mathcal{C}$-hard queries).

To prove that a query language Q captures a machine-based complexity class $\mathcal{C}$, one usually shows that each $\mathcal{C}$-machine with (encodings of) finite structures as inputs that computes a generic query can be represented by an expression in language Q. There is, however, a slight mismatch between ordinary machines and logical queries. A Turing machine works on a string encoding of the input database D. Such an encoding provides an implicit *linear order* on D, in particular, on all elements of the universe U_D. The Turing machine can take profit of this order and use this order in its computations (as long as genericity is obeyed). On the other hand, in logic or database theory, the universe U_D is a pure set and thus unordered. For "powerful" query languages of inherent non-deterministic nature at the level of NP this is not a problem, since an ordering on U_D can be non-deterministically guessed. However, for many query languages, in particular, for those corresponding to complexity classes below NP, generating a linear order is not feasible. Therefore, one often assumes that a linear ordering of the universe elements is predefined, i.e., given explicitly in the input database. More specifically, by *ordered databases* or *ordered finite structures*, we mean databases whose schemas contain special relation symbols *Succ*, *First*, and *Last*, that are always interpreted such that $Succ(x, y)$ is a successor relation of some linear order and $First(x)$ determines the first element and $Last(x)$ the last element in this order. The importance of predefined linear orderings becomes evident in the next two theorems.

Before coming to the theorems, we must highlight another small mismatch between the Turing machine and the datalog setting. A Turing machine can consider each input bit independently of its value. On the other hand, a plain datalog program is not able to detect that some atom is *not* a part of the input database. This is due to the representational peculiarity that only positive information is present in a database, and that the negative information is understood via the closed world assumption. To compensate this deficiency, we will slightly augment the syntax of datalog. *Throughout this section, we will assume that input predicates may appear negated in datalog rule bodies; the resulting language is* datalog$^+$. This extremely limited form of negation is much weaker than stratified negation, and could be easily circumvented by adopting a different representation for databases.

The difference between unordered and ordered databases becomes apparent in the next two theorems:

Theorem 240. *(cf. [36])* datalog$^+$ $\subsetneqq$ P.

Proof. (Hint.) Show that there exists no datalog$^+$ program P that can tell whether the universe U of the input database has an even number of elements. $\qquad\square$

Theorem 241. *([125,80]; implicit in [156,89,106])* On ordered databases, datalog$^+$ captures P.

Proof. (Sketch) By Theorem 230, query answering for a fixed datalog$^+$ program is in P. It thus remains to show that each polynomial-time DTM T on finite input databases D can be simulated by a datalog$^+$ program. This is shown by a simulation similar to the ones in the proofs of Theorems 224 and 229. $\qquad\square$

Next, we compare the expressive power of nonrecursive datalog and, in particular, nonrecursive range-restricted datalog with well-known database query languages. Recall that in datalog with negation, the rules are of the form:

$$q : S(\boldsymbol{x}_0) \leftarrow L_1, \ldots, L_m.$$

where $m \geq 0$ and S is an intensional predicate symbol. Each L_i is an atom $R_i(\boldsymbol{x}_i)$ or a negated atom $\neg R_i(\boldsymbol{x}_i)$. $\boldsymbol{x}_0, \ldots, \boldsymbol{x}_m$ are vectors of variables or constants (from dom). Moreover, this rule is *range-restricted* if every variable in $x_0, \ldots, x_m$ occurs in some unnegated atom $L_i = R_i(x_i)$ in the body.

A datalog program is called range-restricted if all its rules are range-restricted. Nonrecursive range-restricted datalog is referred to as *nr-datalog⁻*. An nr-datalog⁻ *query* is a query defined by some nr-datalog⁻ program with a specified target relation.

Note that equality may be incorporated into nr-datalog⁻ by permitting literals of the form $s = t$ and $s \neq t$ for terms s and t. However, as the following proposition shows, any nr-datalog⁻ program with equality can be simulated by an nr-datalog⁻ program not using equality.

Proposition 242. *Any nr-datalog⁻ program with equality can be simulated by an nr-datalog⁻ program not using equality.*

Proof. Assume that an nr-datalog⁻ contains literals of the form $s = t$ and $s \neq t$. It suffices to describe the construction for a single nr-datalog⁻ rule.

We consider the unnegated equalities $s = t$ first. We can easily get rid of equalities where one of the terms (say s) is a variable and the other one is a constant. In this case, we simply replace all occurrences of the variable s by the constant t. It remains to consider the case of equalities $s = t$ where both s and t are variables. In this case, we can partition all the variables occurring in equations into l disjoint sets $C_1, \ldots, C_l$, such that for each $C_i = \{x_{i1}, x_{i2} \ldots, x_{ik}\}$ where $(1 \leq i \leq l)$, the equalities $x_{i1} = x_{i2} = \ldots = x_{ik}$ can be derived from the body of the rule. Without loss of generality, we choose x_{i1} from each partition C_i and whenever a variable $x \in C_i$ occurs in the rule, we replace it with x_{i1}. We apply this transformation also to all literals of the form $s \neq t$: if $s \in C_i$ or $t \in C_i$, we replace it with x_{i1} too.

After this transformation, we obtain a rule with equality literals only in negated form $s \neq t$ as follows:

$$S(u) \leftarrow L_1, \ldots, L_n, D_1, \ldots, D_m.$$

where every $D_i, (1 \leq i \leq m)$ is an inequality $s_i \neq t_i$. Now let $G_1, \ldots, G_m$ be m new relation symbols. Then we add the following rules:

$$G_1(u_1) \leftarrow L_1, \ldots, L_n, s_1 = t_1$$
$$G_2(u_2) \leftarrow L_1, \ldots, L_n, s_2 = t_2$$
$$\ldots$$
$$G_m(u_m) \leftarrow L_1, \ldots, L_n, s_m = t_m$$

Where $u_{i(1 \leq i \leq m)} = var(L_1) \cup \ldots \cup var(L_n)$. With the above method of eliminating the equality literals, we can easily obtain m new rules with rule heads $G'_1, \ldots, G'_m$ in which no equality literal occurs. Finally we rewrite the original rule as follows:

$$S(u) \leftarrow L_1, \ldots, L_n, \neg G'_1, \ldots, \neg G'_m.$$

Now all equality literals (either unnegated or negated) have indeed been removed from our nr-datalog⁻ program.   □

Theorem 243. *(cf. [2]) Nonrecursive range-restricted datalog with negation = relational algebra = domain-independent relational calculus. Nonrecursive datalog with negation = first-order logic (without function symbols).*

Proof. We prove here only the first equivalence: Nonrecursive range-restricted datalog (nr-datalog$^\neg$) and relational algebra have the equivalent expressive power. Proofs of the other equivalence results can be found in Chapter 5 of [2].

"⇒": We have to show that, given any range-restricted nr-datalog$^\neg$ program, there is an equivalent relational algebra expression. By Proposition 242, we may restrict ourselves w.l.o.g. to nr-datalog$^\neg$ programs not using equality. It suffices to show how the construction of an equivalent relational algebra expression works for a single nr-datalog$^\neg$ rule. Since relational algebra is closed under composition, the simulation of the program with a relational algebra expression is then straightforward.

Consider an nr-datalog$^\neg$ rule of the following form:

$$S(u) \leftarrow P_1(u_1), \ldots, P_n(u_n), \neg N_1(v_1), \ldots, \neg N_m(v_m).$$

where the P_i's are unnegated atoms and the $\neg N_j$'s are negated ones. We need first to construct a new relation A as $A = P_1 \bowtie \ldots \bowtie P_n$. Now the relational algebra expression for S is as follows:

$S = \pi_u(P_1 \bowtie \ldots \bowtie P_n \bowtie (\pi_{v_1} A - N_1) \bowtie \ldots \bowtie (\pi_{v_m} A - N_m))$

Note that if the same relation symbol (for example S) occurs in more than one rule head (for example $r_1, \ldots, r_l$), then we have to rename the algebra expressions for $r_1, \ldots, r_l$ as $S_1, \ldots, S_l$ and thus S can be written as $S = S_1 \cup \ldots \cup S_l$.

Due to the ordering of the rules in the program, we can start with the rules with the smallest ordering number and simulate the rules one by one until all the rules containing the target relation are processed.

"⇐": It remains to show that, given a relational algebra expression, we can construct an equivalent range-restricted nr-datalog$^\neg$ program. We consider here only the six primitive operators: selection, projection, Cartesian product, rename, set union, and set difference. One algebra fragment, the so-called SPJR algebra, consists of the first 4 operators, namely selection, projection, Cartesian product, and rename.

In [2] (page 61) the simulation of SPJR algebra by conjunctive queries is given. Since conjunctive queries are a fragment of nr-datalog$^\neg$, we only need to consider the remaining 2 operators: set union and set difference. The simulation is trivial: for set union we construct two rules with the same rule head. The set difference operation $R - S$ corresponds to $ans(x) \leftarrow R(x), \neg S(x)$. $\qquad \square$

The expressive power of relational algebra is equivalent to that of a fragment of the database query language SQL (essentially, SQL without grouping and aggregate functions). The expressive power of SQL is discussed in [108,55,107].

On ordered databases, Theorem 241 together with the Theorems 230, 232, and 233 implies

Theorem 244. *On ordered databases, the following query languages capture* P: *stratified datalog, datalog under well-founded semantics, and datalog under inflationary semantics.*

Syntactical restrictions allow us to capture classes within P. Let datalog$^+$(1) be the fragment of datalog$^+$ where each rule has at most one non-database predicate in the body, and let datalog$^+$(1, d) be the fragment of datalog$^+$(1) where each predicate occurs in at most one rule head.

Theorem 245. *([80,157]) On ordered databases, datalog$^+$(1) captures* NL *and the fragment datalog$^+$(1, d) captures* L.

Due to the inherent non-determinism, the stable model semantics is much more expressive.

Theorem 246. *([142]) Datalog under stable model semantics captures* co-NP.

Note that for this result an order on the input database is not needed. Informally, in each stable model such an ordering can be guessed and checked by the program.

Finally, we briefly address the expressive power of disjunctive logic programs.

Theorem 247. *([64,65]) Disjunctive datalog under stable model semantics captures Π_2^p.*

9   Optimization

This section concludes the thread on evaluation and operational semantics beginning with Section 6. Where Sections 6 and 7 focus on the evaluation of entire query programs containing many rules and the interaction or chaining of such rules, this section's focus is on the evaluation of individual queries (cf. Section 3 for the definition of conjunctive and first-order queries). Where appropriate, though, we also remind of related results on query programs.

We focus on two aspects of query evaluation only, viz., query rewriting and containment and (logical) query algebras. A more complete picture of challenges and techniques for efficient query evaluation can be found, e.g., in [75], Chapters 15–16, or in [82].

Conjunctive or first-order queries are useful tools for the declarative specification of one's query intent. Figuring out the details of how such queries are evaluated is left to the query engine. For actual evaluation, however, a query engine needs to determine a detailed specification on how to evaluate a given query. Such a specification is commonly called a *query plan*. Query plans are typically expressed in an algebra, i.e., a set of operators on the domain of discourse. Query algebras thus serve to demonstrate how to specify and optimize evaluation plans for queries and are the focus of the first part of this section (Section 9.1).

Both on the level of the declarative query and on the level of a query plan for that query, we might want to find semantically equivalent queries that are better suited for execution. Furthermore, given a set of queries (e.g., resulting from the bodies of several rules) we might want to avoid doing the same or similar work for different queries several times. Rather we would like to compare these queries to find common sub-queries that can be evaluated once and then shared for the execution of multiple other queries. Such problems are considered in the second part (Section 9.3) of this section on query rewriting and containment.

9.1 An Algebraic Perspective on Queries

The relational algebra, introduced in [43,44] and refined in [37], has long been the formal foundation for relational database systems. Though practical systems often deviate notably (see Section 9.2.2), it has proved to be an invaluable tool for understanding formal properties of query languages (primarily, completeness, complexity, and semantics), for query planning and optimization, and for implementing query engines.

In the following, we give a brief definition of (a variant of) the relation algebra and its relation to rule-based query languages. For a more detailed discussion of the relational algebra see, e.g., [75]. An outlook on extensions of the relational algebra covering two aspects (duplicates and order) of query languages mostly ignored in the rest of this article follows. We conclude this section with some remarks on algebras for complex values, where the limitation to constants as attribute values is relaxed.

Let $\mathcal{L}$ be a signature (cf. Section 3, Definition 3), $\mathcal{D}$ a database schema over $\mathcal{L}$ (cf. Section 3, and I a database instance for $\mathcal{D}$. In the following, we use the relational view of logic as described in Section 3.3. In particular, we use the unnamed or ordered perspective of relations: Attributes in a relation are identified by position (or index) not by name. For a tuple $t = (x_1, \ldots, x_n)$ we use $t[i]$ to denote the value of the i-th attribute in t, i.e., x_i. We assume a finite domain and, where convenient, the presence of a domain relation enumerating the elements of the domain.

Definition 248 (Selection). *Let P be an n-ary relation from I and C be a conditional expression $i = c$ with $i \leq n$ and c a constant from $\mathcal{L}$ or $i = j$ with $i, j \leq n$.*

The relational selection $\sigma_C(P)$ returns the set of tuples from P that fulfill C, viz. $\sigma_{i=c}(P) = \{t \in P : t[i] = c\}$ and $\sigma_{i=j}(P) = \{t \in P : t[i] = t[j]\}$.

As discussed in Section 3.3, relations can be seen as tables with each tuple forming a row and each attribute forming a column. Selection can than be seen as a "vertical" restriction of such a table, where some rows (i.e., tuples) are omitted. From a perspective of first-order queries, selection corresponds to body atoms containing some constants c if C is $i = c$ and to multiple occurrences of the same variable if C is $i = j$.

In practice, C is often extended to allow further conditional expression over elements of the domain, e.g., on ordered sorts comparisons such as $i \leq c$ are possible.

Definition 249 (Projection). *Let P be an n-ary relation from I and $i_1, \ldots, i_m \leq n$ with $k < l \implies i_k < i_l$.*

The relational projection $\pi_{i_1,...,i_m}(P) = \{(t_1,...,t_m) : \exists t_i \in \mathcal{D} : t[i_1] = t_1 \wedge ... \wedge t[i_m] = t_m\}$ returns the m-ary relation made up of tuples from P dropping all but the $i_1,...,i_m$-th attributes.

Projection can be seen as "horizontal" restriction of a relation (imagined as a table). In contrast to the selection, relational projection however may incur additional cost beyond the linear "slicing" off of a few columns: Dropping columns may lead to duplicates that are not allowed in a (pure) relation.

The first-order correspondent of relational projection is the body-only occurrence of variables.

Definition 250 (Cartesian product). *Let P be an n-ary, Q an m-ary relation from I.*

The Cartesian (or cross) product $P \times Q = \{(t_1,...,t_n,t_{n+1},...,t_{n+m}) : (t_1,...,t_n) \in P \wedge (t_{n+1},...,t_{n+m}) \in Q\}$ returns the $(n+m)$-ary relation of all tuples consisting of concatenations of first tuples from P and second tuples from Q.

Cartesian product can be seen as table multiplication as the name indicates and corresponds to the conjunction of atoms (with no shared variables) in first-order queries.

The relational algebra is completed by standard set operations on relations:

Definition 251 (Relational union, intersection, and difference). *Let P and Q be n-ary relations.*

The relational union $P \cup Q = \{t \in \mathcal{D}^n : t \in P \vee t \in Q\}$, intersection $P \cap Q = \{t \in \mathcal{D}^n : t \in P \wedge t \in Q\}$, and difference $P - Q = \{t \in \mathcal{D}^n : t \in P \wedge t \notin Q\}$ are specialisations of standard set operations to sets of relations.

Notice that all three operations require that P and Q have the same arity. As usual either union or intersection can be defined in terms of the other two (at least under the assumption of a domain relation enumerating all elements of the domain).

Two more operators are commonly used in relational algebra expressions though they can be defined by means of the previous ones: relational join and division.

Definition 252 (Join). *Let P be an n-ary, Q be an m-ary relation from I, $f : \{1,...,n\} \rightarrow \{1,...,m\}$ a partial, injective function, and $k = |f^{-1}(\{1,...,m\}|$ the number of pairs in f.*

The relational join $P \bowtie_f Q = \{(t_1,...,t_{n+m-k}) : (t_1,...,t_n) \in P \wedge \exists t \in Q : \forall n < i \leq n+m-k : t[i-n] = t_i \wedge \forall(i,j) \in f : t_i = t[j]\}$ returns the $(n+m-k)$-ary relation of all tuples from P combined with those tuples from Q where the i-th attribute value in P is equal to the f(i)-th in Q (omitting the f(i)-th attribute from the result).

Often f is small and we write directly $P \bowtie_{i \rightarrow j,...} Q$ instead of giving f separately. Relational join corresponds to multiple occurrences of a variable in a conjunctive query.

A join over k attributes can be rewritten to k selections on a Cartesian product: Let $f : \{(i_1, j_1), \ldots, (i_k, j_k)\}$ and P be an n-ary relation.

$$P \bowtie_f Q = \sigma_{i_k = j_k + n}(\sigma_{i_{k-1} = j_{k-1} + n}(\ldots \sigma_{i_1 = j_1 + n}(P \times Q) \ldots))$$

Definition 253 (Division). *Let P be an n-ary, Q be an m-ary relation from I with $m < n$.*
The relational division (or quotient)

$$P \div Q = \{(t_1, \ldots, t_{n-m}) : \forall (t_{n-m+1}, \ldots, t_n) \in Q : (t_1, \ldots, t_n) \in P\}$$

returns the $n - m$-ary relation of all tuples t such that any combination of t with a tuples from Q forms a tuple from P

The division is the relational algebra's counterpart to universal quantification in bodies of first-order queries.

Division can be rewritten to an expression using only projection, difference, and Cartesian product:

$$P \div Q = \pi_{A_1, \ldots, A_n}(P) - \pi_{A_1, \ldots, A_n}((\pi_{A_1, \ldots, A_n}(P) \times Q) - P)$$

In early formulations of the relational algebra including Codd's original proposal, additional operators such as the permutation are provided:

Definition 254 ([44,37] Permutation). *Let P be an n-ary relation from I and $f : \{1, \ldots, n\} \to \{1, \ldots, n\}$ a bijection.*
The permutation

$$\mathsf{Perm}_f(P) = \{(t_1, \ldots, t_n) : \exists t \in P : t[f(1)] = t_1, \ldots, t[f(n)] = t_n\}$$

returns an n-ary relation containing all permutations of tuples of P.

However, permutation is usually not considered as part of the relational algebra due to its undesirable complexity (the size of $\mathsf{Perm}_f(P)$ may be exponentially higher than the size of P, viz. in $O(|P| \times n^n)$) and as it can be expressed as $\pi_{2,\ldots,n+1}(\sigma_{n=n+1}(\ldots \pi_{2,\ldots,n+1}(\sigma_{2=n+1}(\pi_{2,\ldots,n+1}(\sigma_{1=n+1}(P \times \pi_1(P))) \times \pi_2(P))) \times \ldots \pi_n(P)))$. Notice, however, that the equivalence is of another quality than the equivalences for join and division: It depends on the schema of P and its size is linear in the arity of P (compensating for the lower complexity of π, σ, and $\times$ compared to Perm).

Another common extension of the relational algebra is the semi-join operator.

Definition 255 (Semi-join). *Let P be an n-ary, Q an m-ary relation from I, $f : \{1, \ldots, n\} \to \{1, \ldots, m\}$ a partial, injective function, and $k = |f^{-1}(\{1, \ldots, m\}|$ the number of pairs in f.*
The relational semi-join $P \ltimes_f Q = \{(t_1, \ldots, t_n) : (t_1, \ldots, t_n) \in P \wedge \exists t \in Q : \forall (i, j) \in f : t_i = t[j]\}$ returns the n-ary relation of all tuples from P for which a tuple from Q exists such that the i-th attribute value in P is equal to the $f(i)$-th in Q.

Intuitively, the semi-join corresponds to a filter on P that only retains tuples from P with join partners from Q. In contrast to the Cartesian product and the normal join its result is thus always linear in P and no trace of Q occurs in the result.

Let P be an n-ary relation, $i_1, \ldots, i_k$ be the attributes from Q occurring in f, then $P \ltimes_f Q = \pi_{1,\ldots,n}(P \bowtie_f Q) = P \bowtie_f \pi_{i_1,\ldots,i_k}(Q)$. Thus the semi-join can be expressed using only projection and join or only projection, selection, and Cartesian product (as join can be expressed using selection and Cartesian product only).

However, a rewriting of semi-joins is often not desirable. To the contrary [21] proposes to use semi-joins to reduce query processing in some cases (tree queries) even to polynomial time complexity. Recent work [105] shows that the semi-join algebra, i.e., relational algebra with the join and Cartesian product replaced by the semi-join is equivalent to the guarded fragment of first-order logic.

The semi-join operator is an example for an operator that though actually weaker than the existing operators in the relational algebra might actually be exploited to obtain equivalent, but faster formulations for a restricted class of queries.

A similar observation can be made for the usual handling of universal quantification as division (with or without subsequent rewriting) as well as existential quantification as projection may result in poor performance as intermediary results are unnecessary large. This has lead to the development of several (more efficient, but also more involved) direct implementations of division as well as of alternatives such as the semi- and complement-join:

Definition 256 (Complement-Join). *(cf. [26]) Let P be an n-ary, Q be an m-ary relation from I, $f : \{1, \ldots, n\} \rightarrow \{1, \ldots, m\}$ a partial, injective function, and $k = |f^{-1}(\{1, \ldots, m\})|$ the number of pairs in f.*

The relational semi-join $P \overline{\ltimes}_f Q = \{(t_1, \ldots, t_n) : (t_1, \ldots, t_n) \in P \wedge \nexists t \in Q : \forall(i,j) \in f : t_i = t[j]\}$ returns the n-ary relation of all tuples from P for which no tuple from Q exists such that the i-th attribute value in P is equal to the $f(i)$-th in Q.

Obviously, $P \overline{\ltimes}_f Q = P - \pi_{1,\ldots,n}(P \bowtie_f Q)$ and thus $P \overline{\ltimes}_f Q = P - P \ltimes_f Q$.

For details on the use of the complement- and semi-join for realizing quantification, see [26].

9.1.1 Translating First-Order Queries

Chandra and Merlin [37] show that

Theorem 257. *([37]) For each relational expression there is an equivalent first order query, and vice versa.*

There is one caveat: This result only holds if, as Chandra and Merlin assume, the domain is finite or the queries are domain independent. In the following, the former is assumed (an exhaustive discussion of domain independence can be found, e.g., in [2]). Assuming a finite domain allows "domain closure" for queries such as $ans(x) \leftarrow \neg q(x, y)$. Such a query is transformed into the expression $\pi_1(\mathcal{D}^2 - Q)$ with $\mathcal{D}$ domain of the query and Q the relation corresponding to the predicate symbol q.

Proof (Sketch). The equivalence proof from [37] is a fairly straightforward structural induction over relational expressions and first-order queries respectively. Instead of a full proof, we give a number of illustrative translation:

1. $ans(x) \leftarrow q(x, y) \wedge r(y, z)$ is equivalent to $\pi_1(Q \bowtie_{2\to1} R)$ as well as to $\pi_1(\sigma_{2=3}(Q \times R))$ as well as to $\pi_1(Q \bowtie_{2\to1} \pi_1(R))$.
2. $ans(x) \leftarrow \neg q(x, y)$ is equivalent to $\pi_1(\mathcal{D}^2 - Q)$ as well as to $\mathcal{D} - \pi_1(Q)$.
3. $ans(x, y) \leftarrow (p(x, y) \wedge \neg q(y)) \vee (p(x, y) \wedge \forall z : s(x, y, z)$ is equivalent to $\pi_{1,2}((P - (\mathcal{D} \times Q)) \cup (P \bowtie_{1\to1, 2\to2} \pi_{1,2}(S \div \mathcal{D})))$.

Theorem 258. *(cf. [37]) Conjunctive queries and relational expressions formed only from selection, projection, Cartesian product, intersection, and join have the same expressiveness. This extends trivially to expressions formed only from selection, projection, and Cartesian product, as join can be rewritten as above and, for n-ary relations P and Q, $P \cap Q = \pi_{1,\ldots,n}(\sigma_{1=n+1}(\sigma_{2=n+2}(\ldots\sigma_{n=n+n}(P \times Q)\ldots)))$.*

For illustration, see equivalence (1) in the proof of Theorem 257.

9.1.2 Query Rewriting

It is important to notice in the above examples of equivalent relational algebra expressions for a given first-order query, that there are always several reasonable expressions for the same query. Consider, e.g., again the query $ans(x, y) \leftarrow p(x, y) \wedge (\neg q(y, z) \vee \neg r(y, w))$. This query is equivalent to, e.g.,

- $\pi_{1,2}(P \bowtie_{2\to1} ((\mathcal{D}^2 - Q) \cup (\mathcal{D}^2 - R)))$
- $\pi_{1,2}(P \bowtie_{2\to1} (\pi_1(\mathcal{D}^2 - (Q \cap R))))$
- $\pi_{1,2}(P \bowtie_{2\to1} (\mathcal{D} - \pi_1(Q \cap R)))$

Of these three equivalent queries only the application of de Morgan's law carries over to the first-order queries. Many other equivalences have no correspondence in first-order queries. In this respect, first-order queries are more declarative and more succinct representations of the query intent than relational expressions. However, that relational expressions allow such fine differences has shown to be of great value for query optimization, i.e., determining which of the equivalent formulations of a query should be used for evaluation: The relational algebra allows the separation of this planning phase from the actual evaluation. A query planner or optimizer can decide, based, e.g., on general equivalences as discussed here and on estimated costs of different relational expressions which variant to use.

Equivalence Laws. Equivalence laws between relational algebra expressions comprise common laws for set operators $\cup, \cap$, and $-$. In particular, $\cup$ and $\cap$ are associative and commutative, de Morgan's law and distribute laws for intersection and union apply.

More interesting are equivalence laws for the additional operators such as $\bowtie$, $\times$, σ, and π:

Cartesian Product and Join. The Cartesian product $\times$ is commutative and associative just as $\cup$ and $\cap$. For the relational $\bowtie$ a proper adjustment of the join condition is required[27]. If the join expression is flipped, $\bowtie$ is commutative, i.e., $P \bowtie_{1=2} Q \equiv Q \bowtie_{2=1} P$. For associativity, the join condition needs to be adapted, e.g., $P \bowtie_{1=3} (R \bowtie_{1=2} S) \equiv (P \times R) \bowtie_{1=1,3=2} S$ (assuming all relations are binary) since both join conditions involve attributes from S.

Selection. Selection is generally a good candidate for optimization, pushing selections (a fast but possibly fairly selective operation) inside of an expression thus limiting the size of intermediary results. Also selection can generally be propagated "down" into an expression: Selection distributes over $\times$, $\bowtie$ and the set operators. For $-$ and $\cap$ it suffices to propagate the selection to the first relation, e.g., $\sigma_C(P - Q) = \sigma_C(P) - \sigma_C(Q) = \sigma_C(P) - \sigma_C(Q)$. For Cartesian product and Join it suffices to propagate the selection to those sub-expressions that contain the attributes referenced in C. Let P be an n-ary relation. Then

$$\sigma_{i=c}(P \times Q) = \begin{cases} \sigma_{i=c}(P) \times Q & \text{if } i \leq n \\ P \times \sigma_{i=c}(Q) & \text{if } i > n \end{cases}$$

Projection. In contrast to selection, we can only propagate selection "down" in an expression to the point where the attributes dropped by the projection are last referenced in the expression. Conversely, an expression might benefit from introducing additional projections to get rid of attributes not used in the remainder of an expression as early as possible, viz. immediately after the innermost expression referencing them. Moreover, since as a result of a projection some tuples may become duplicates and thus be dropped in the set semantics considered so far, projection can in general not be distributed over any of the set operators. It can be propagated over join and Cartesian product: Let P be an n-ary, Q an m-ary relation and $i_1, \ldots, i_k \leq n$, $i_{k+1}, \ldots, i_{k+l} > n$ then

$$\pi_{i_1,\ldots,i_{k+l}}(P \times Q) = \pi_{i_1,\ldots,i_k}(P) \times \pi_{i_{k+1},\ldots,i_{k+l}}(Q).$$

9.2 "Real" Queries

"Real" relational databases and queries deviate in a few, but important points from both the relational algebra, first-order queries, and datalog. Some of these are highlighted in the remainder of this section.

We start by moving from relations as sets to relations as bags (then called multi-relations). Bag semantics is in practice often faster as it allows to ignore

---

[27] Note, that this when using the named perspective of the relational algebra (where attributes are identified by name rather than position) no adjustment is necessary and $\bowtie$ is trivially associative.

duplicates except when specifically noted rather than an implicit and costly elimination of duplicates at each relational operator (though, of course, only projection and union can actually create new duplicates).

9.2.1   From Sets to Bags

The need for multi-relations is evident when considering aggregation queries like *"what is the sum of the values of some column"*. In a set relational algebra the projection to the aggregation column collapses all same value tuples and thus makes this query impossible to express. The same argument can be made for any query that returns just a projection of the columns of queried relations, as the number of duplicates may be significant to the user (e.g., in *"what are the titles of all first and second level sections"*). Also, many practical systems support multi-relations to save the cost of duplicate handling. Indeed, neither QUEL [148] nor SQL [11], the now dominating "relational" query language, are (set) relational query languages, but rather possess features that are not expressible in (set) relational algebra, viz. aggregation, grouping, and duplicate elimination. The semantic of these expressions assumes that the underlying data structure is a bag (or even a sequence) rather than a set.

Therefore, in practical query languages duplicate handling must be addressed. Based on the control over duplicate creation and elimination, one can distinguish relational query languages into *weak* and *strong* duplicate controlling languages. QUEL [148] and SQL [11] provide little control over duplicates (essentially just the DISTINCT operator and GROUP-BY clauses) and thus fall into the first class. The only means is an explicit duplicate elimination. Similarly, Prolog's operational semantics [160] also contains operations for explicit duplicate handling (e.g., bagof vs. setof).

In contrast, DAPLEX [146] is based on "iteration semantics" and gives precise control over the creation and elimination of duplicates. An example of a DAPLEX query is shown in the following listing:

```
FOR EACH Student
   SUCH THAT FOR SOME Course(Student)
      Name(Dept(Course)) = "EE" AND
      Rank(Instructor(Course)) = "ASSISTANT PROFESSOR"
   PRINT Name(Student)
```

A first formal treatment of this "iteration semantics" for relational databases is found in [49], where a *generalization of the relational algebra* to multi-relations is proposed. This extension is not trivial and raises a number of challenges for optimizations: joins are no longer idempotent, the position of projections and selections is less flexible, as $\pi_R(R \times S) \neq R$ and $\sigma_P(R) \uplus \sigma_Q(R) \neq \sigma_{P \vee Q}(R)$ due to duplicates in the first expression[28]. Though this algebra provides a useful

---

[28] Assuming π and σ to be the multi-set generalizations of their relational counterparts. $\uplus$ is understood here as *additive union*, i.e., t occurs n times in $R \cup S$, if t occurs i times in R and j times in S and $n = i + j$. [84] considers additionally maximal union (i.e., where $n = \max(i, j)$), which does not exhibit this particular anomaly.

theoretical foundation, it does little to address the concerns regarding efficient processing of "iteration semantics" expressions.

[84] shows that (nested) relational algebra on multi-relations (i.e., relations as bags) is strictly more expressive than on relations as sets. Unsurprisingly, the core difference lies in the "counting power" of the bag algebra. More precisely, the bag algebra no longer exhibits a $0-1$ law (i.e., the property that queries are either on almost all input instances true or on almost all input instances false). E.g., the query that tests whether, given two relations, the cardinality of R is bigger than the cardinality of S can be expressed as $(\pi_1(R \times R) - \pi_1(R \times S)) \neq 0$ where π is a bag algebra projection *without* duplicate elimination and $-$ is difference on multi-sets, where the multiplicity of a tuple t in the result is the multiplicity of t in the first argument minus the multiplicity in the second argument. Observe, that $\pi_1(R \times R)$ and $\pi_1(R \times S)$ contain the same tuples but if $R > S$, $\pi_1(R \times R)$ contains those tuples with greater multiplicity than $\pi_1(R \times S)$ and vice verse if $R < S$. This query observes no $0-1$ law: For each instance on which it is true we can construct an instance on which it is true. Unsurprisingly, it can not be expressed in set relational algebra.

Similarly, [109] proposes a query language called $\mathcal{BQL}$ over bags whose expressiveness amounts to that of a relational language with aggregates. This approach provides a formal treatment of aggregations and grouping as found, e.g., in SQL (GROUP-BY clause and aggregation operators such as AVG, COUNT, and SUM). $\mathcal{BQL}$ is "seen as a rational reconstruction of SQL" that is fully amenable to formal treatment. [109] also considers extensions of $\mathcal{BQL}$ with power operators, structural recursion, or loops and shows that the latter two extensions are equivalent.

[100] proposes a different view of multi-relations as *incomplete information*: though conceptually "a relation represents a set of entities", one tuple per entity, and thus does not contain duplicates, the concept of a multi-relation allows a formal treatment of partial information about entities. A multi-relation is a projection of a complete relation, i.e., it consists of a subset of columns within some relation (without duplicates). Thus it may contain duplicates in contrast to the relation. [100] considers multi-relations only as output of queries not as first class data items in the database. Semantically, they can not exist independently of the base relation. No (base or derived) relation should contain duplicates.

Moving from sets to bags (or multi-sets) in the relational algebra, obviously affects query containment and optimization. Most notably many of the algebraic laws mentioned in the previous section do no longer apply. For more details, see [38] and, more recently, [91].

9.2.2 From Bags to Sequences

Basic relational algebra (and first order logic) are fundamentally order agnostic. This is a desirable property as it allows understanding and implementation of operators without considering a specific order of the result. However, it limits the *expressiveness* of the algebra: We can not (conveniently) express a query asking for the "five students with the highest marks" nor a query asking for every second student nor a query testing if a certain set is even (e.g., the participants in a chess competition).

Moreover, queries involving order occur in many *practical* applications, in particular where reporting (presentation) and analysis is concerned. Reporting is certainly the most common use for order (return the results in some order, return only top k results, etc.). This has lead to the addition of order as an "add on" to the usual query evaluation frameworks, e.g., in SQL where the `ORDER BY` clause may not be used as part of a view definition but only at the outer-most (or reporting) level of a query.

Finally, the *physical* algebra (i.e., the actual algorithms used for evaluating a query) of most relational database systems (including all major commercial systems) is based on the concept of iterators (or streams or pipelines): A physical query plan is a hierarchy of operators, each iterating over the output of its dependent operators and creating its own result on demand. Conceptually, such operators support (aside of `open` and `close` for initialization and destruction) only one operation, viz. `next`, which returns the next element in the operator's result. Note, that such a design intrinsically supports order. However, if used for the evaluation of pure relational expressions, the order in which an operator produces its results is up to the implementation of that operator and we can choose to implement the same logical operator with physical operators that produce results in different orders. This flexibility (in choosing an efficient operator implementation regardless of the result order) is lost, if the logical operators already require a specific order. Nevertheless, exploiting the ability of physical operators to manage order to provide that concept also to the query author is tempting. For more details on physical operators and order see the seminal survey [82].

These considerations have, more recently, revived interest in a proper treatment of order in an algebra driven by two main areas: analytical queries (OLAP-style) and queries against (intrinsically ordered) XML data and their realization in relational databases.

List-based Relational Algebra. Focused on the first aspect, [147] proposes a list-based recasting of the relational algebra.

First, we redefine a relation to be a *finite sequence* of tuples over a given relation schema (consisting as usual in a finite set of attributes and associated domains). A relation may, in particular, contain duplicates (if key attributes are present, the values of the key attributes of every two tuples *must* be distinct as usual).

Under this definition, *selection* and *projection* remain essentially unchanged except that they are now order and duplicate preserving. Only projection may introduce *new* duplicates, if the same tuple results from more than one input tuple.

Union is, obviously, affected considerably by ordered relations. [147] proposes standard list append as union, appending the tuples of the second relation in order after the tuples of the first relation.

Similar, *Cartesian product* $A \times B$ is defined as the result of appending for each tuple of A (in order) the product with each tuple of B (again in order). Thus the result contains first the combination of the first tuple of A with each tuple of B (preserving B's order), followed by the combination of the second tuple of A with each tuple of B, etc. *Join* is defined as usual as combination of selection and product. Note that this definition is immediately consistent with a nested loop implementation. However, other join and product operators (such as sort-merge or hash join) produce tuples in different orders and are no longer correct physical realisations of the logical join or product.

Difference $A \setminus B$ becomes order-preserving, multi-set difference, i.e., for each distinct tuple $t \in A$ with m occurrences in A and n occurrences in B, the last $m - n$ occurrences of t in A are preserved. We could also choose to preserve the first $m - n$ occurrences, however, preserving the *last* occurrences leads immediately to an implementation where the tuples of A must be visited only once.

As in the case of bags or multi-sets, we introduce two additional operations duplicate elimination and grouping. *Duplicate elimination* retains, as difference, the *last* occurrence. Aggregation is treated analogously to projection. For details on duplicate elimination and grouping see [75] on multi-sets and [147] on sequences.

In additional to these adapted standard or multi-set operators, we need two additional operators to properly support order: sorting and top k.

Definition 259 (Sort). *Let P be an ordered n-ary relation and $<_S$ some order relation on $\mathcal{D}^n$. Let $<_P$ denote the (total) order of tuples in P.*

The $<_s$-sorted relation $sort_S(P) = [t_1, \ldots, t_n]$ such that for all $t_i : \forall t_j : i < j \implies t_i <_s t_j \lor \neg(t_i <_s t_j) \land t_i <_p t_j$ returns the tuples in P ordered by $<_s$. If $<_s$ is not a total order, the order of P is preserved on any "gaps" in $<_s$.

In practical cases, S might, e.g., consist of a list of attributes and order specifications of the form "ASCENDING" or "DESCENDING" as in the case of SQL's ORDER BY.

Definition 260 (Top k). *Let $P = [t_1, \ldots t_n]$ be an ordered n-ary relation and $k \in \mathbb{N}$ some positive integer.*

The top-k relation $top_k(P) = [s_1, \ldots, s_l]$ with $l = \min(k, n)$ such that $s_i \in top_k(P) \implies P = [t_1, \ldots, t_{i-1}, s_i, t_{i+1}, \ldots t_n]$ returns the k first entries of P (or all entries of P if P has less than k entries).

The top k operation is available, e.g., in Microsoft's SQL Server (TOP N clause), in IBM's DB2 (FETCH FIRST N ROWS ONLY), and in Oracle DBMS (using a selection on the pseudo-column ROWNUM).

With this sequence algebra, we can now express *all* SQL constructs including ORDER BY, GROUP BY, and DISTINCT which were not expressible in the standard relational set algebra. To also cover null values some additional modifications (mostly to selection) are needed, see, e.g., [159]. For more details on translating SQL into relational algebra (and/or relational calculus) see [34].

However, this comes at the price of considerably more involved equivalences (cf. [147]). Many of the associativity and commutativity laws for the relational (set) algebra no longer hold in the bag or set case. Therefore, practical optimizers often go to considerable length to find order-agnostic parts of queries even if some ordering is required, e.g., at the end result. For those parts, we can then use standard relational algebra optimization. This desire is reflected in the limitations of the ORDER BY clause in SQL and, to give just one more recent example, the introduction of **unordered** contexts in XQuery, where the usual strictly ordered semantics of XQuery is (temporarily) "disabled". Handling order only where necessary, is an important aim of XML and XQuery optimization and algebras, see, e.g., [128] for details.

9.2.3   From Constants to Complex Values

So far, we have considered the values contained in an attribute of a relation as atomic or simple, i.e., without further *structure*. Examples of such values are, of course, numbers, strings, truth values, and enumerated values.

In many applications, we are, however, concerned also with values of another nature: structured or hierarchical values such as sets, lists, or trees. Though such data may be decomposed and stored in first-normal form, such an approach may not be desirable if the values are very irregular, often considered as a single "value", or their shape is dictated by application or other external requirements [113].

Research on complex values has been a focus of the database community in the first half of the 1990s, see, e.g., [84,25,103,32,1]. They have seen renewed interest in the context of XML and other semi-structured data and its querying and storing (both natively and in relational databases). They serve, e.g., as an expressive foundation for a large fragment of XQuery [101].

Complex values: Tuples and Sets. There are several variant definitions in the literature for complex values. In this section, we follow mostly [1] as its notions are conveniently simple and yet expressive enough to discuss important variations.

First, we need to define a complex value:

Definition 261 (Complex value). *Let* $\mathcal{D}_1, \ldots, \mathcal{D}_n$ *be domains for* atomic *values. Then*

- *each* $a \in \mathcal{D}_i$ *for* $i \leq n$ *is a (atomic) value of type* D_i.
- *each* $[v_1, \ldots, v_n]$ *is a (tuple) value of type* $[T_1, \ldots, T_n]$ *if* $v_1, \ldots, v_n$ *are values of types* $T_1, \ldots, T_n$, *respectively, and* $n \in \mathbb{N}$.
- *each finite* $S \in \mathcal{P}(\mathsf{values}(T))$ *is a (set) value of type* $\{T\}$ *if* T *is a type and* $\mathsf{values}(T)$ *is the set of all values of* T.

A complex value is either an atomic, a tuple, or a set value.

Note that the definition allows *only finite* values (both tuples and sets are required to be finite and there are *no cycles*. Furthermore, values do not carry identity (as in the case of object- or object-relational databases), i.e., there are no two distinct values with the same structure.

Example 262. Examples of complex values (for simplicity using strings and integers as only domains):

- "Caesar", 17, "Flamen Dialis", 44 are all atomic values of type string or integer, respectively.
- ["Caesar", 44], [44], [], ["Caesar", [17, "Flamen Dialis"]] are all tuple types.
- {["Caesar", 44], [44], {[]}, {}} is a set type.

Obviously there are infinitely more complex values (actually, even if the domains for atomic values are empty that is the case).

Often, for complex values a named perspective on tuples is often preferred. It has the additional advantage of highlighting the close relationship to XML and other semi-structured data models. In a named perspective, we would, e.g., obtain [Name: "Caesar", Office: [AtAge: 17, Title: "Flamen Dialis"]]. However, for consistency with the rest of this article we use the unnamed perspective in the following.

A well-known variant of this definition of complex values is the nested relations model, see, e.g., [92]. The idea is to allow entire relations to occur as values of attributes of other relations. In the terms of our above definition this means that sets and tuples constructors must alternate in any complex value: A set may contain only tuples (but not sets) and a tuple may contain only sets or atomic values (but not tuples). However, this limitation does not affect the expressiveness of the data model and is not considered further.

An algebra for complex values. For an algebra, the main difference if we consider not only atomic but also complex values are operators that allow the construction and destruction of set and tuple values as well as there restructuring.

The first addition to the algebra may be surprising: It is essentially a higher-order function to apply some restructuring operation to all elements of a set:

Definition 263 (Map (Replace)). *Let R be a set type and f a restructuring function. Then $map\langle f \rangle(R) = \{f(r) : r \in R\}$ is the set of elements of R restructured according to f, i.e., the application of f to all elements of R. This can be considered a higher-order function familiar from functional programming.*

Restructuring functions are, e.g., projections, set and tuples construction, and their compositions. For details see [1] and Example 264.

Note that, in particular, $map\langle f \rangle$ itself is a restructuring function allowing, which allows for restructuring of nested elements. However, restructuring is limited to a depth fixed in the query (no recursive tree transformations).

In some ways, $map\langle\rangle$ can be considered a generalization of relational project, which restructures each tuple in a relation by retaining only some of its attributes.

In a similar generalization of the relational select, *select* on complex values allows arbitrary boolean functions as predicates including comparators $=$, $\in$, and $\subset$.

The basic set operations ($\cup$, $\cap$, and, $\setminus$) are defined as usual. Both arguments must be sets of the same type. The *cross product* is changed to an n-ary operation on set types $\times(R_1, \ldots, R_n) = \{[t_1, \ldots, t_n] : t_1 \in R_1, \ldots, t_n \in R_n\}$ such that the result tuples obtain each component from one of the parameter sets.

Note, that in particular binary cross product no longer combines the components of the tuples of the two parameter sets (relations) but rather creates simply a set of binary tuples containing as components the unchanged elements of the original sets. To obtain classical product, a compound expression is needed: Let R, S be two binary relations, then $\mathsf{map}\langle[1.1, 1.2, 2.1, 2.2]\rangle(\times(R, S))$ computes the classical product of R and S: First the compute a set of binary tuples with the first component a tuple from R and the second a tuple from S ($\times(R, S)$, then we transform that result using the restructuring function $[1.1, 1.2, 2.1, 2.2]$, a shorthand for the function that creates from each binary tuple in the parameter set a new tuple with the first components first attribute (1.1) followed by the first components second attribute (1.2) etc.

Finally, we add a "flattening" or "set collapse" operation collapse that takes a set of sets as argument and returns the union of all members in that set.

Example 264. Let S of type $\{[Int, \{Int\}]\}$, i.e., S is a nested relation with the second attribute containing sets of integers as values.

- Select from S tuples where the first component is a member of the second component: $\sigma\langle 1 \in 2\rangle(S)$.
- Select pairs sets of (set) values in S where the first is a subset of the second: $\mathsf{map}\langle[1.2, 2.2]\rangle(\sigma\langle 1.2 \subseteq 2.2\rangle(\times(S, S)))$ which is equivalent to the expression $\sigma\langle 1 \subseteq 2\rangle(\times(\mathsf{map}\langle[1.2]\rangle(S), \mathsf{map}\langle[1.2]\rangle(S)))$ where the restructuring (in this case a projection) is pushed to the leaves of the expression.
- The Join of R and S on the first attribute again is expressed as a compound expression $\sigma\langle 1 = 3\rangle(\mathsf{map}\langle[1.1, 1.2, 2.1, 2.2]\rangle(\times(R, S)))$ in analogy to the standard equivalence $R \bowtie_C S = \sigma_C(R \times S)$.
- Unnesting (as introduced in [92]) creates from a relation like S a set of flat tuples containing combinations of the first attribute of the original tuples and one of the elements of the second attribute. It can be expressed as $\mathsf{collapse}(\mathsf{map}\langle\times(\{1\}, 2)\rangle(S))$: First the restructuring function $\times(\{1\}, 2)$ is applied to all elements of S creating sets of tuples with the first attribute from the values of the first attribute of S and the second attribute from the members of the set values of the second attribute of S. Then all these sets are collapsed into a single one.
- To add the value of the first attribute of S to the second, we can use $\mathsf{map}\langle\{1\} \cup 2\rangle(S)$.

Note, that all queries are also functions, either boolean or restructuring functions and can thus be used as parameters for $\mathsf{map}\langle\rangle$ or $\sigma\langle\rangle$, respectively.

[1] also establishes a calculus that is, for safe queries, equivalent to the above algebra. In particular, it is shown that queries in this algebra are domain-independent in the sense of Section 3.2.3).

A possible extension to the above algebra to allow in particular the expression of recursive queries such as the transitive closure of a relation directly in the algebra, is the *powerset* operator: Given a set as parameter, powerset returns the set of all subsets of R.

The idea of expressing transitive closure in the above algebra is to first construct the powerset of a relation and then eliminate all sets that do not (1) contain the original relation and (2) are not transitively closed. For details on the complex expression for computing transitive closure, see [1].

The price of the powerset operator is further examined in [149]. They show that any algorithm in the above algebra for expressing transitive closure using powerset (which is the required for expressing transitive closure, cf. [129]) needs *exponential space*. In fact, they even prove that result for deterministic transitive closure, i.e., transitive closure of a graph with out-degree ≤ 1. This contrasts with PSPACE algorithms for transitive closure using, e.g., relational algebra and a fixpoint operator such as WHILE. It is an open problem, whether there are queries expressible with powerset that are not expressible without

[25] shows that the above algebra (and equivalent or similar proposed query languages such as the nested relational algebra [92]) without powerset operator can be elegantly formalized as monad algebra, studied in the context of category theory and programming languages, and based, unsurprisingly, on structural recursion on sets.

Combining complex values with bags (as discussed for flat relational algebra in Section 9.2.1) is discussed in [83]. As expected, the nested bag algebra is more expressive than the nested set algebra (as introduced above), however, with increasing nesting depth the expressiveness difference becomes fairly subtle.

Combining complex values with sequences (as discussed for flat relational algebra in Section 9.2.2) leads sequences of complex values very similar to the data model of the W3C XQuery language. [101] shows that a core of that language can indeed be formalized in notions similar to monad algebra (which, as mentioned above, is equivalent to the algebra discussed in this section without powerset operator) and gives complexity of various sublanguages of (non-recursive) XQuery.

The rest of this section considers adding complex values to relational algebra. How about adding them to, e.g., non-recursive datalog? [48] shows that non-recursive datalog (or Prolog) with trees and lists is equivalent to first-order logic over lists and trees and that, in the non-recursive case, this addition is benign w.r.t. data complexity (it remains in AC_0).

9.2.4   From Values to Objects

Managing structured or semi-structured data involves the determination of what defines the identity of a data item (be it a node in a tree, graph, or network, an object, a relational tuple, a term, or an XML element). Identity of data items is relevant for a variety of concepts in data management, most notably for joining, grouping and aggregation, as well as for the representation of cyclic structures.

"What constitutes the identity of a data item or entity?" is a question that has been answered, both in philosophy and in mathematics and computer science, essentially in two ways: based on the extension (or structure and value) of the entity or separate from it (and then represented through a surrogate).

Extensional Identity. Extensional identity defines identity based on the extension (or structure and value) of an entity. Variants of extensional identity are

Leibniz's law[29] of the *identity of indiscernibles*, i.e., the principle that if two entities have the same properties and thus are indiscernible they must be one and the same. Another example of this view of identity is the *axiom of extensionality* in Zermelo-Fraenkel or von Neumann-Bernays-Gödel set theory stating that a set is uniquely defined by its members.

Extensional identity has a number of desirable properties, most notably the compositional nature of identity, i.e., the identity of an entity is defined based on the identity of its components. However, it is insufficient to reason about identity of entities in the face of changes, as first pointed out by Heracleitus around 500 BC: *You cannot step twice into the same river; for fresh waters are flowing in upon you.* (Fragment 12).

He postulates that the composition or extension of an object defines its identity and that the composition of any object changes in time. Thus, nothing retains its identity for any time at all, there are no persistent objects.

This problem has been addressed both in philosophy and in mathematics and computer science by separating the extension of an object from its identity.

Surrogate Identity. Surrogate identity defines the identity of an entity independent from its value as an external surrogate. In computer science surrogate identity is more often referred to as *object identity.* The use of identity separate from value has three implications (cf. [12] and [99])

- In a model with surrogate identity, naturally two notions of object *equivalence* exist: two entities can be identical (they are the same entity) or they can be equal (they have the same value).
- If identity is separate from value, identity is no longer necessarily compositional and it is possible that two distinct entities *share* the same (meaning identical, not just same value) properties or sub-entities.
- *Updates* or changes on the value of an entity are possible without changing its identity, thus allowing the tracking of changes over time.

In [12] value, structure, and location independence are identified as essential attributes of surrogate identity in data management. An identifier or identity surrogate is value and structure independent if the identity is not affected by changes of the value or internal structure of an entity. It is location independent if the identity is not affected by movement of objects among physical locations or address spaces.

Object identity in object-oriented data bases following the ODMG data model fulfill all three requirements. Identity management through primary keys as in relational databases violates value independence (leading to Codd's extension to the relation model [45] with separate surrogates for identity). Since object-oriented programming languages are usually not concerned with persistent data, their object identifiers often violate the location independence leading to anomalies if objects are moved (e.g., in Java's RMI approach).

---

[29] So named and extensively studied by Willard V. Quine.

Surrogate or object identity poses, among others, two challenges for query and programming languages based on a data model supporting this form of identity: First, where for extensional identity a single form of equality (viz. the value and structure of an entity) suffices, object identity induces at least two, often three flavors of *equality* (and thus three different *joins*): Two entities may be equal w.r.t. identity (i.e., their identity surrogates are equivalent) or value. If entities are complex, i.e., can be composed from other objects, one can further distinguish between "shallow" and "deep" value equality: Two entities are "shallow" equivalent if their value is equal and their components are the same objects (i.e., equal w.r.t. identity) and "deep" equivalent if their value is equal and the values of their components are equal. Evidently, "shallow" value-based equality can be defined on top of identity-based and "deep" value-based equality.

The same distinction also occurs when *constructing* new entities based on entities selected in a query: A selected entity may be linked as a component of a constructed entity (object sharing) or a "deep" or "shallow" copy may be used as component.

Summarizing, surrogate or object identity is the richer notation than extensional identity addressing in particular object sharing and updates, but conversely also requires a slightly more complex set of operators in query language and processor.

The need for surrogate identity in contrast to extensional identity as in early proposals for relational databases has been argued for [45], as early as 1979 by Codd himself. He acknowledges the need for unique and permanent identifiers for database entities and argues that user-defined, user-controlled primary keys as in the original relational model are not sufficient. Rather permanent *surrogates* are suggested to avoid anomalies resulting from user-defined primary keys with external semantics that is subject to change.

In [99] an extensive review of the implications of object identity in data management is presented. The need for object identity arises if it is desired to "distinguish objects from one another regardless of their content, location, or addressability" [99]. This desire might stem from the need for dynamic objects, i.e., objects whose properties change over time without loosing their identity, or versioning as well as from object sharing.

[99] argues that identity should neither be based on address (-ability) as in imperative programming languages (variables) nor on data values (in the form of identifier keys) as in relational databases, but rather a separate concept maintained and guaranteed by the database management system.

Following [99], programming and query languages can be classified in two dimensions by their support for object identity: the first dimension represents to what degree the identity is managed by the system vs. the user, the second dimension represents to what degree identity is preserved over time and changes.

Problems of user defined identity keys as used in relational databases lie in the fact that they cannot be allowed to change, although they are user-defined descriptive data. This is especially a problem if the identifier carries some external semantics, such as social security numbers, ISBNs, etc. The second problem is that identifiers can not provide identity for some subsets of attributes.

The value of object identities (OIDs) as query language primitives is investigated in [3]. It is shown that OIDs are useful for

- object sharing and cycles in data,
- set operations,
- expressing any computable database query.

The data model proposed in [3] generalizes the relational data model, most complex-object data models, and the logical data model [103]. At the core of this data model stands a mapping from OIDs to so-called o-values, i.e., either constants or complex values containing constants or further OIDs. Repeated applications of the OID-mapping yield *pure values* that are regular infinite trees. Thus trees with OIDs can be considered finite representations of infinite structures.

The OID-mapping function is partial, i.e., there may be OIDs with no mapping for representing incomplete information.

It is shown that "a primitive for OID invention must be in the language ... if unbounded structures are to be constructed" [3]. Unbounded structures include arbitrary sets, bags, and graph structures.

Lorel [4] represents a semi-structured query language that supports both extensional and object identity. Objects may be shared, but not all "data items" (e.g., paths and sets) are objects, and thus not all have identity. In Lorel construction defaults to object sharing and grouping defaults to duplicate elimination based on OIDs.

9.3   Optimal Views: Equivalence and Containment

9.3.1   Beyond Relational Containment

For Web queries against semi-structured data early research on query containment and optimization has focused on regular path expressions [6], short RPEs. More recently, XPath has been in the focus of research with its central role in upcoming Web query standards becoming apparent.

(Regular) path queries (or expressions, short RPEs) are regular expressions over the label alphabet of some tree or graph. They select all nodes in a tree or graph that are reachable from the root via a path (with nodes) whose labels form a word in the language given by the regular (path) expression. *Path (inclusion) constraints* (e.g., $p_1 \subset p_2$ or $p_1 \equiv p_2$ indicating that the nodes selected by p_1 are a subset, resp. identical to the nodes selected by p_2) can be exploited to rewrite regular path expressions. [6] shows that equivalence of RPEs under path inclusion constraints is, in fact, decidable in EXPSPACE. [71] extends this result to conjunctive queries with regular expressions (a subset of STRUQL) and shows that it is still decidable and in EXPSPACE.

[68] gives a practical algorithm for rewriting RPEs containing wildcards and a closure axis like XPath's **descendant**. They employ, as we do in this work,

graph schemata and automata for processing such schemata. However, as the queries they consider are only regular path expressions, they can also use an automaton for (each of) the regular path expressions to be rewritten. The product of the query with the schema automaton is computed and the resulting product automaton is "pruned" to obtain a (query) automaton equivalent to the original one under the given graph schema. In effect, this allows the rewriting of regular path expressions such as `*.a.*.b.c`. If the schema specifies that there is at most one `a` and at most one `b` on the path from the root to a `c`, this can be specialized to `(not(a))*.a.((not(b))*.b.c`, an expression that prunes some search paths in the data graph earlier than the original one.

[31] shows that a restriction to a deterministic semi-structured data model where the labels of all children of a node are distinct, for paths without closure axes (i.e., with only child axis), to decidable containment and minimization, but remains undecidable for general regular expressions.

XPath containment and minimization differs from containment and minimization of RPEs in that basic XPath expressions are simpler than RPEs, (no `(a.b)*`) but full XPath contains additional constructs such as node identity join that easily make containment and minimization undecidable. Other additions of XPath such as reverse axes have been shown [124] to be reducible to a core XPath involving only forward axes and can thus be safely ignored in the following. Therefore, various subsets have been considered, for a more complete survey of the state-of-the-art in XPath query containment in ab- or presence of schema constraints see [143].

The essential results are positive results if only tree pattern queries (understood as XPath queries with only child and descendant axis and no wildcard labels) are considered (e.g., [7] presenting an $O(N^4)$, with n the number of nodes in the query, algorithm for minimizing in the absence of integrity constraints; [136] proposed an $O(n^2)$ algorithm for the same problem and an $O(n^4)$ algorithm in the presence of required-child, required-descendant, and subtype integrity constraint). In the latter paper, an $O(n^2)$ algorithm is given for the case that only required-child and required-descendant constraints are allowed. Miklau and Suciu [117] show that the problem becomes CO-NP complete if the tree patterns may also contain wildcards. [35] shows how to obtain wildcard free XPath expressions but needs to introduce new language constructs ("layer" axes) for restricted rather than arbitrary-length path traversals in the document tree (thus not contradicting the results from [117]). [143] refines this result showing that adding disjunction does not affect this complexity.

If arbitrary regular path expressions are allowed (for vertical navigation), query minimization becomes PSPACE-hard, as subsumption of regular expressions r_1 and r_2 is equivalent to testing whether $L(r_1) \subseteq L(r_2)$ which is known to be PSPACE-hard.

Whereas early work on minimization under DTDs, e.g., [161] focused on simple structural constraints (basically only child and parent constraints) and weak subsets of XPath for optimizing XML queries, Deutsch and Tannen [53] show that the problem of XPath containment in the presence of DTDs and simple integrity constraints (such as key or foreign key constraints from XML Schema) is undecidable in general and that this result holds for a large class of integrity constraints. If only DTDs are considered [143] shows that containment of XPath with only horizontal axes but including wildcards, union, filters, and descendant axes is EXPTIME-complete. [143] further shows that even for XPath with only child axis and filters containment in presence of DTDs is already CONP-complete. Adding node-set inequality to the mix makes the containment problem immediately undecidable, using XPath expressions with variables even PSPACE-complete (in the absence of DTDs)

[70] discusses also the minimization of XPath queries with only child and descendant axes (as well as filters and wildcards), focusing in particular on the effect of the wildcard operator. It proposes a polynomial algorithm for computing minimal XPath queries of limited branched XPath expressions, i.e., XPath expressions where filters (XPath predicates []) occur only in one of the branches under each XPath step.

Recently, attention has turned to optimization of full *XQuery* as well: In [39], where a heuristic optimization technique for XQuery is proposed: Based on the PAT algebra, a number of normalizations, simplification, reordering, and access path equivalences are specified and a deterministic algorithm developed. Though the algorithm does not necessarily return an optimal query plan it is expected and experimentally verified to return a reasonably good one.

References

1. Abiteboul, S., Beeri, C.: The Power of Languages for the Manipulation of Complex Values. VLDB Journal 4(4), 727–794 (1995)
2. Abiteboul, S., Hull, R., Vianu, V.: Foundations of Databases. Addison-Wesley Publishing Co. Reading (1995)
3. Abiteboul, S., Kanellakis, P.C.: Object Identity as a Query Language Primitive. Journal of the Association for Computing Machinery 45(5), 798–842 (1998)
4. Abiteboul, S., Quass, D., McHugh, J., Widom, J., Wienerm, J.L.: The Lorel Query Language for Semistructured Data. International Journal on Digital Libraries 1(1), 68–88 (1997)
5. Abiteboul, S., Vianu, V.: Datalog Extensions for Database Queries and Updates. Journal of Computer and System Sciences 43, 62–124 (1991)
6. Abiteboul, S., Vianu, V.: Regular Path Queries with Constraints. In: Proc. ACM SIGACT-SIGMOD-SIGART Symposium on Principles of Database Systems (PODS), pp. 122–133. ACM Press, New York (1997)
7. Amer-Yahia, S., Cho, S., Lakshmanan, L.V.S., Srivastava, D.: Minimization of Tree Pattern Queries. In: Proc. ACM SIGMOD Symposium on the Management of Data (SIGMOD), pp. 497–508. ACM Press, New York (2001)
8. Andréka, Németi: The Generalized Completeness of Horn Predicate Logic as a Programming Language. Acta Cybernetica 4, 3–10 (1978) (This is the published version of a 1975 report entitled "General Completeness of PROLOG")
9. Apt, K., Blair, H., Walker, A.: Towards a Theory of Declarative Knowledge. In: Minker, J. (ed.) Foundations of Deductive Databases and Logic Programming, pp. 89–148. Morgan Kaufmann, San Francisco (1988)

10. Apt, K., Doets, K.: A New Definition of SLDNF-Resolution. Journal of Logic Programming 18, 177–190 (1994)
11. Astrahan, M.M., Blasgen, M.W., Chamberlin, D.D., Eswaran, K.P., Gray, J.N., Griffiths, P.P., King, W.F., Lorie, R.A., McJones, P.R., Mehl, J.W., Putzolu, G.R., Traiger, I.L., Wade, B.W., Watson, V.: System R: Relational Approach to Database Management. ACM Transactions on Database Systems 1(2), 97–137 (1976)
12. Atkinson, M., DeWitt, D., Maier, D., Bancilhon, F., Dittrich, K., Zdonik, S.: The Object-oriented Database System Manifesto. In: Bancilhon, F., Delobel, C., Kanellakis, P. (eds.) Building an Object-oriented Database System: The Story of O2, ch. 1, pp. 1–20. Morgan Kaufmann Publishers Inc. San Francisco (1992)
13. Baader, F., Snyder, W.: Unification Theory. In: Robinson, J.A., Voronkov, A. (eds.) Handbook of Automated Reasoning, vol. 1, pp. 447–533. Elsevier, Amsterdam (2001)
14. Bailey, J., Bry, F., Furche, T., Schaffert, S.: Web and Semantic Web Query Languages: A Survey. In: Eisinger, N., Małuszyński, J. (eds.) Reasoning Web. LNCS, vol. 3564, Springer, Heidelberg (2005)
15. Balbin, I., Meenakshi, K., Ramamohanarao, K.: A Query Independent Method for Magic Set Computation on Stratified Databases. In: Proc. International Conference on Fifth Generation Computer Systems, pp. 711–718 (1988)
16. Balbin, I., Port, G., Ramamohanarao, K., Meenakshi, K.: Efficient Bottom-Up Computation of Queries of Stratified Databases. Journal of Logic Programming 11, 295–344 (1991)
17. Balcázar, J., Lozano, A., Torán, J.: The Complexity of Algorithmic Problems on Succinct Instances. In: Baeta-Yates, R., Manber, U. (eds.) Computer Science, pp. 351–377. Plenum Press, New York, USA (1992)
18. Beeri, C., Ramakrishnan, R.: On the Power of Magic. In: Proc. ACM SIGACT-SIGMOD-SIGART Symposium on Principles of Database Systems (PODS), pp. 269–283. ACM Press, New York (1987)
19. Behrend, A.: Soft Stratification for Magic set based Query Evaluation in Deductive Databases. In: Proc. ACM SIGACT-SIGMOD-SIGART Symposium on Principles of Database Systems (PODS), pp. 102–110. ACM Press, New York (2003)
20. Benanav, D., Kapur, D., Narendran, P.: Complexity of Matching Problems. In: Jouannaud, J.-P. (ed.) Rewriting Techniques and Applications. LNCS, vol. 202, pp. 417–429. Springer, Heidelberg (1985)
21. Bernstein, P.A., Chiu, D.-M.W.: Using Semi-Joins to Solve Relational Queries. Journal of the Association for Computing Machinery 28(1), 25–40 (1981)
22. Bidoit, N., Froidevaux, C.: Negation by Default and Unstratifiable Programs. Theoretical Computer Science 78, 85–112 (1991)
23. Bönström, V., Hinze, A., Schweppe, H.: Storing RDF as a Graph. In: Proc. Latin American Web Congress, pp. 27–36 (2003)
24. Brass, S., Dix, J.: Disjunctive Semantics Based upon Partial and Bottom-Up Evaluation. In: Sterling, L. (ed.) International Conference on Logic Programming, pp. 199–213. MIT Press, Cambridge (1995)
25. Breazu-Tannen, V., Buneman, P., Wong, L.: Naturally Embedded Query Languages. In: Hull, R., Biskup, J. (eds.) ICDT 1992. LNCS, vol. 646, pp. 140–154. Springer, Heidelberg (1992)
26. Bry, F.: Towards an Efficient Evaluation of General Queries: Quantifier and Disjunction Processing Revisited. In: Proc. ACM SIGMOD Symposium on the Management of Data (SIGMOD), pp. 193–204. ACM Press, New York (1989)

27. Bry, F.: Query Evaluation in Recursive Databases: Bottom-up and Top-down Reconciled. Data and Knowledge Engineering 5(4), 289–312 (1990)
28. Bry, F., Pătrânjan, P.-L., Schaffert, S.: Xcerpt and XChange: Logic Programming Languages for Querying and Evolution on the Web. In: Demoen, B., Lifschitz, V. (eds.) ICLP 2004. LNCS, vol. 3132, Springer, Heidelberg (2004)
29. Bry, F., Schaffert, S.: Towards a Declarative Query and Transformation Language for XML and Semistructured Data: Simulation Unification. In: Stuckey, P.J. (ed.) ICLP 2002. LNCS, vol. 2401, Springer, Heidelberg (2002)
30. Bry, F., Schaffert, S., Schröder, A.: A Contribution to the Semantics of Xcerpt, a Web Query and Transformation Language. In: Seipel, D., Hanus, M., Geske, U., Bartenstein, O. (eds.) Applications of Declarative Programming and Knowledge Management. LNCS (LNAI), vol. 3392, pp. 258–268. Springer, Heidelberg (2005)
31. Buneman, P., Fan, W., Weinstein, S.: Query Optimization for Semistructured Data Using Path Constraints in a Deterministic Data Model. In: Proc. International Workshop on Database Programming Languages (DBLP), pp. 208–223. Springer, Heidelberg (2000)
32. Buneman, P., Naqvi, S., Tannen, V., Wong, L.: Principles of Programming with Complex Objects and Collection Types. Theoretical Computer Science 149(1), 3–48 (1995)
33. Cavedon, L., Lloyd, J.: A Completeness Theorem for SLDNF-Resolution. Journal of Logic Programming 7, 177–191 (1989)
34. Ceri, S., Gottlob, G.: Translating SQL into Relational Algebra: Optimization, Semantics, and Equivalence of SQL Queries. IEEE Transactions on Software Engineering 11(4), 324–345 (1985)
35. Chan, C.-Y., Fan, W., Zeng, Y.: Taming XPath Queries by Minimizing Wildcard Steps. In: Aberer, K., Koubarakis, M., Kalogeraki, V. (eds.) Databases, Information Systems, and Peer-to-Peer Computing. LNCS, vol. 2944, Springer, Heidelberg (2004)
36. Chandra, A., Harel, D.: Structure and Complexity of Relational Queries. Journal of Computer and System Sciences 25, 99–128 (1982)
37. Chandra, A.K., Merlin, P.M.: Optimal Implementation of Conjunctive Queries in Relational Data Bases. In: ACM Symposium on Theory of Computing (STOC), pp. 77–90. ACM Press, New York (1977)
38. Chaudhuri, S.: Optimization of Real Conjunctive Queries. In: Proc. ACM SIGACT-SIGMOD-SIGART Symposium on Principles of Database Systems (PODS), pp. 59–70. ACM Press, New York (1993)
39. Che, D., Aberer, K., Özsu, T.: Query Optimization in XML Structured-document Databases. The VLDB Journal 15(3), 263–289 (2006)
40. Chen, W., Warren, D.S.: Tabled Evaluation with Delaying for General Logic Programs. Journal of the Association for Computing Machinery 43(1), 20–74 (1996)
41. Chen, Y.: A Bottom-up Query Evaluation Method for Stratified Databases. In: Proc. International Conference on Data Engineering (ICDE), pp. 568–575. IEEE Computer Society Press, Los Alamitos (1993)
42. Clark, K.: Negation as Failure. In: Gallaire, H., Minker, J. (eds.) Logic and Data Base, pp. 293–322. Plenum Press, New York, USA (1978)
43. Codd, E.F.: A Relational Model of Data for Large Shared Data Banks. Communications of the ACM 13(6), 377–387 (1970)
44. Codd, E.F.: Relational Completeness of Data Base Sublanguages. Database Systems, pp. 65–98 (1972)
45. Codd, E.F.: Extending the Database Relational Model to Capture more Meaning. ACM Transactions on Database Systems 4(4), 397–434 (1979)

46. Dantsin, E., Eiter, T., Gottlob, G., Voronkov, A.: Complexity and Expressive Power of Logic Programming. In: Proc. IEEE Conference on Computational Complexity, pp. 82–101 (1997)

47. Dantsin, E., Voronkov, A.: Complexity of Query Answering in Logic Databases with Complex Values. In: Adian, S., Nerode, A. (eds.) LFCS 1997. LNCS, vol. 1234, pp. 56–66. Springer, Heidelberg (1997)

48. Dantsin, E., Voronkov, A.: Expressive Power and Data Complexity of Nonrecursive Query Languages for Lists and Trees. In: Proc. ACM SIGACT-SIGMOD-SIGART Symposium on Principles of Database Systems (PODS), pp. 157–165. ACM Press, New York (2000)

49. Dayal, U., Goodman, N., Katz, R.H.: An Extended Relational Algebra with Control over Duplicate Elimination. In: Proc. ACM SIGACT-SIGMOD-SIGART Symposium on Principles of Database Systems (PODS), pp. 117–123. ACM Press, New York (1982)

50. de Bruijn, J., Franconi, E., Tessaris, S.: Logical Reconstruction of RDF and Ontology Languages. In: Fages, F., Soliman, S. (eds.) PPSWR 2005. LNCS, vol. 3703, Springer, Heidelberg (2005)

51. Debray, S., Ramakrishnan, R.: Abstract Interpretation of Logic Programs Using Magic Transformations. Journal of Logic Programming 18, 149–176 (1994)

52. Dershowitz, N., Jouannaud, J.-P.: Rewrite Systems. In: van Leeuwen, J. (ed.) Handbook of Theoretical Computer Science B: Formal Methods and Semantics ch. 6, pp. 243–309. Elsevier Science, Amsterdam (1990)

53. Deutsch, A., Tannen, V.: Containment and Integrity Constraints for XPath Fragments. In: Proc. Int'l. Workshop on Knowledge Representation meets Databases (KRDB) (2001)

54. Dietrich, S.W.: Extension Tables: Memo Relations in Logic Programming. In: Proc. Symposium on Logic Programming (SLP), pp. 264–272 (1987)

55. Dong, G., Libkin, L., Wong, L.: Local Properties of Query Languages. In: Afrati, F.N., Kolaitis, P.G. (eds.) ICDT 1997. LNCS, vol. 1186, pp. 140–154. Springer, Heidelberg (1996)

56. Doorenbos, R.B.: Production Matching for Large Learning Systems. PhD thesis, Carnegie Mellon University, Pittsburgh, PA, USA (1995)

57. Dowling, W.F., Gallier, J.H.: Linear-Time Algorithms for Testing the Satisfiability of Propositional Horn Formulae. Journal of Logic Programming 1(3), 267–284 (1984)

58. Drabent, W.: Completeness of SLDNF-Resolution for Non-Floundering Queries. In: Proc. International Symposium on Logic Programming, p. 643 (1993)

59. Dwork, C., Kanellakis, P., Mitchell, J.: On the Sequential Nature of Unification. Journal of Logic Programming 1, 35–50 (1984)

60. Dwork, C., Kanellakis, P., Stockmeyer, L.: Parallel Algorithms for Term Matching. SIAM Journal of Computing 17(4), 711–731 (1988)

61. Ebbinghaus, H.-D., Flum, J.: Finite Model Theory. Perspectives in Mathematical Logic. Springer, Heidelberg (1995)

62. Eiter, T., Gottlob, G.: Propositional Circumscription and Extended Closed World Reasoning are Π_2^P-complete. Theoretical Computer Science 114(2), 231–245 (1993)

63. Eiter, T., Gottlob, G.: On the Computational Cost of Disjunctive Logic Programming: Propositional Case. Annals of Mathematics and Artificial Intelligence 15(3/4), 289–323 (1995)

64. Eiter, T., Gottlob, G., Mannila, H.: Adding Disjunction to Datalog. In: Proc. ACM SIGACT-SIGMOD-SIGART Symposium on Principles of Database Systems (PODS), pp. 267–278. ACM Press, New York (1994)
65. Eiter, T., Gottlob, G., Mannila, H.: Disjunctive Datalog. ACM Transactions on Database Systems 22(3), 364–418 (1997)
66. Fagin, R.: Finite-Model Theory — a Personal Perspective. Theoretical Computer Science 116, 3–31 (1993)
67. Fan, C., Dietrich, S.W.: Extension Table Built-ins for Prolog. Software — Practice and Experience 22(7), 573–597 (1992)
68. Fernandez, M.F., Suciu, D.: Optimizing Regular Path Expressions Using Graph Schemas. In: Proc. International Conference on Data Engineering (ICDE), pp. 14–23. IEEE Computer Society Press, Los Alamitos (1998)
69. Fitting, M.: Fixpoint Semantics For Logic Programming – A Survey. Theoretical Computer Science 278, 25–51 (2002)
70. Flesca, S., Furfaro, F., Masciari, E.: On the Minimization of XPath Queries. In: Aberer, K., Koubarakis, M., Kalogeraki, V. (eds.) Databases, Information Systems, and Peer-to-Peer Computing. LNCS, vol. 2944, pp. 153–164. Springer, Heidelberg (2004)
71. Florescu, D., Levy, A., Suciu, D.: Query Containment for Conjunctive Queries with Regular Expressions. In: Proc. ACM SIGACT-SIGMOD-SIGART Symposium on Principles of Database Systems (PODS), pp. 139–148. ACM Press, New York (1998)
72. Forgy, C.L.: Rete: a Fast Algorithm for the Many Pattern/Many Object Pattern Match Problem. Expert systems: a software methodology for modern applications, pp. 324–341 (1990)
73. Furche, T., Linse, B., Bry, F., Plexousakis, D., Gottlob, G.: RDF Querying: Language Constructs and Evaluation Methods Compared. In: Barahona, P., Bry, F., Franconi, E., Henze, N., Sattler, U. (eds.) Reasoning Web. LNCS, vol. 4126, Springer, Heidelberg (2006)
74. Gallagher, J.P.: Tutorial on Specialisation of Logic Programs. In: Proc. ACM SIGPLAN Symposium on Partial Evaluation and Semantics-based Program Manipulation (PEPM), pp. 88–98. ACM Press, New York (1993)
75. Garcia-Molina, H., Ullman, J.D., Widom, J.: Database Systems: The Complete Book. Prentice-Hall, Englewood Cliffs (2002)
76. Garey, M., Johnson, D.: Computers and Intractability. Freeman, New York (1979)
77. Gelfond, M., Lifschitz, V.: The Stable Model Semantics for Logic Programming. In: Proc. International Conference and Symposium on Logic Programming, pp. 1070–1080. MIT Press, Cambridge (1988)
78. Gelfond, M., Lifschitz, V.: Classical Negation in Logic Programs and Disjunctive Databases. New Generation Computing 9, 365–385 (1991)
79. Gottlob, G., Papadimitriou, C.: On the Complexity of Single-rule Datalog Queries. Information and Computation 183, 104–122 (2003)
80. Grädel, E.: Capturing Complexity Classes with Fragments of Second Order Logic. Theoretical Computer Science 101, 35–57 (1992)
81. Grädel, E., Otto, M.: On Logics with Two Variables. Theoretical Computer Science 224(1-2), 73–113 (1999)
82. Graefe, G.: Query Evaluation Techniques for Large Databases. ACM Computing Surveys 25(2), 73–169 (1993)
83. Grumbach, S., Milo, T.: Towards Tractable Algebras for Bags. In: Proc. ACM SIGACT-SIGMOD-SIGART Symposium on Principles of Database Systems (PODS), pp. 49–58. ACM Press, New York (1993)

84. Grumbach, S., Vianu, V.: Tractable Query Languages for Complex Object Databases. In: Proc. ACM SIGACT-SIGMOD-SIGART Symposium on Principles of Database Systems (PODS), pp. 315–327. ACM Press, New York (1991)

85. Gurevich, Y.: Logic and the Challenge of Computer Science. In: Börger, E. (ed.) Current Trends in Theoretical Computer Science. ch. 1, pp. 1–57. Computer Science Press (1988)

86. Gurevich, Y., Shelah, S.: Fixpoint Extensions of First-Order Logic. Annals of Pure and Applied Logic 32, 265–280 (1986)

87. Hayes, P.: RDF Model Theory. Recommendation, W3C (2004)

88. Hinrichs, T., Genesereth, M.: Herbrand Logic. Technical Report LG-2006-02, Stanford Logic Group, Computer Science Department, Stanford University (November 2006)

89. Immerman, N.: Relational Queries Computable in Polynomial Time. Information and Control 68, 86–104 (1986)

90. Immerman, N.: Languages that Capture Complexity Classes. SIAM Journal of Computing 16, 760–778 (1987)

91. Ioannidis, Y.E., Ramakrishnan, R.: Containment of Conjunctive Queries: Beyond Relations as Sets. ACM Transactions on Database Systems 20(3), 288–324 (1995)

92. Jaeschke, G., Schek, H.J.: Remarks on the Algebra of Non First Normal Form Relations. In: Proc. ACM SIGACT-SIGMOD-SIGART Symposium on Principles of Database Systems (PODS), pp. 124–138. ACM Press, New York (1982)

93. Jaffar, J., Lassez, J.-L., Lloyd, J.: Completeness of the Negation as Failure Rule. In: Proc. International Joint Conference on Artificial Intelligence (IJCAI), pp. 500–506 (1983)

94. Johnson, D.S.: A Catalog of Complexity Classes. In: van Leeuwen, J. (ed.) Handbook of Theoretical Computer Science, vol. A, ch. 2, Elsevier, Amsterdam (1990)

95. Jones, N., Laaser, W.: Complete Problems in Deterministic Polynomial Time. Theoretical Computer Science 3, 105–117 (1977)

96. Kapur, D., Narendran, P.: Complexity of Unification Problems with Associative-commutative Operators. Journal of Automated Reasoning 9(2), 261–288 (1992)

97. Kerisit, J.-M.: A Relational Approach to Logic Programming: the Extended Alexander Method. Theoretical Computer Science 69, 55–68 (1989)

98. Kerisit, J.-M., Pugin, J.-M.: Efficient Query Answering on Stratified Databases. In: Proc. International Conference on Fifth Generation Computer Systems, pp. 719–726 (1988)

99. Khoshafian, S.N., Copeland, G.P.: Object Identity. In: Proc. International Conference on Object-oriented Programming Systems, Languages and Applications, pp. 406–416. ACM Press, New York (1986)

100. Klausner, A., Goodman, N.: Multirelations — Semantics and Languages. In: Proc. International Conference on Very Large Data Bases (VLDB), vol. 11, pp. 251–258. Morgan Kaufmann, San Francisco (1985)

101. Koch, C.: On the Complexity of Nonrecursive XQuery and Functional Query Languages on Complex Values. ACM Transactions on Database Systems 31(4) (2006)

102. Kolaitis, P., Papadimitriou, C.: Why Not Negation by Fixpoint? Journal of Computer and System Sciences 43, 125–144 (1991)

103. Kuper, G.M., Vardi, M.Y.: The Logical Data Model. ACM Transactions on Database Systems 18(3), 379–413 (1993)

104. Le Bars, J.-M.: Counterexamples of the 0-1 Law for Fragments of Existential Second-order Logic: an Overview. Bulletin of Symbolic Logic 6(1), 67–82 (2000)

105. Leinders, D., Marx, M., Tyszkiewicz, J., den Bussche, J.V.: The Semijoin Algebra and the Guarded Fragment. Journal of Logic, Language and Information 14(3), 331–343 (2005)
106. Leivant, D.: Descriptive Characterizations of Computational Complexity. Journal of Computer and System Sciences 39, 51–83 (1989)
107. Libkin, L.: On the Forms of Locality over Finite Models. In: Proc. IEEE Conference on Logic in Computer Science (LICS), pp. 204–215. IEEE Computer Society Press, Los Alamitos (1997)
108. Libkin, L., Wong, L.: New Techniques for Studying Set Languages, Bag Languages and Aggregate Functions. In: Proc. ACM SIGACT-SIGMOD-SIGART Symposium on Principles of Database Systems (PODS), pp. 155–166. ACM Press, New York (1994)
109. Libkin, L., Wong, L.: Query Languages for Bags and Aggregate Functions. Journal of Computer and System Sciences 55(2), 241–272 (1997)
110. Lindström, P.: On Extensions of Elementary Logic. Theoria 35 (1969)
111. Lloyd, J.: Foundations of Logic Programming, 2nd edn. Springer, Heidelberg (1987)
112. Lobo, J., Minker, J., Rajasekar, A.: Foundations of Disjunctive Logic Programming. Logic Programming Series. MIT Press, Cambridge (1992)
113. Makinouchi, A.: A Consideration of Normal Form of Not-necessarily-normalized Relations in the Relational Data Model. In: Proc. International Conference on Very Large Data Bases (VLDB), pp. 447–453 (1977)
114. Manola, F., Miller, E.: RDF Primer. Recommendation, W3C (2004)
115. Marek, W., Truszczyński, M.: Autoepistemic Logic. Journal of the Association for Computing Machinery 38(3), 588–619 (1991)
116. Martelli, A., Montanari, U.: Unification in Linear Time and Space: a Structured Presentation. Technical Report B 76-16, University of Pisa (1976)
117. Miklau, G., Suciu, D.: Containment and Equivalence for a Fragment of XPath. Journal of the Association for Computing Machinery 51(1), 2–45 (2004)
118. Minker, J.: On Indefinite Data Bases and the Closed World Assumption. In: Loveland, D.W. (ed.) 6th Conference on Automated Deduction. LNCS, vol. 138, pp. 292–308. Springer, Heidelberg (1982)
119. Minker, J.: Overview of Disjunctive Logic Programming. Annals of Mathematics and Artificial Intelligence 12, 1–24 (1994)
120. Minoux, M.: LTUR: A Simplified Linear-Time Unit Resolution Algorithm for Horn Formulae and Computer Implementation. Information Processing Letters 29(1), 1–12 (1988)
121. Narendran, P.: Unification Modulo ACI+1+0. Fundamenta Informaticae 25(1), 49–57 (1996)
122. Nejdl, W.: Recursive Strategies for Answering Recursive Queries - The RQA/FQI Strategy. In: Proc. International Conference on Very Large Data Bases (VLDB), pp. 43–50. Morgan Kaufmann Publishers Inc. San Francisco (1987)
123. Niemelä, I., Simons, P.: Efficient Implementation of the Well-founded and Stable Model Semantics. In: Proc. Joint International Conference and Symposium on Logic Programming, pp. 289–303 (1996)
124. Olteanu, D., Meuss, H., Furche, T., Bry, F.: XPath: Looking Forward. In: Chaudhri, A.B., Unland, R., Djeraba, C., Lindner, W. (eds.) EDBT 2002. LNCS, vol. 2490, Springer, Heidelberg (2002)
125. Papadimitriou, C.: A Note on the Expressive Power of Prolog. Bulletin of the EATCS 26, 21–23 (1985)

126. Papadimitriou, C.: Computational Complexity. Addison-Wesley Publishing Co. Reading (1994).
127. Papadimitriou, C., Yannakakis, M.: A Note on Succinct Representations of Graphs. Information and Control 71, 181–185 (1985)
128. Paparizos, S., Jagadish, H.V.: Pattern Tree Algebras: Sets or Sequences. In: Proc. International Conference on Very Large Data Bases (VLDB), pp. 349–360. VLDB Endowment (2005)
129. Paredaens, J., Gucht, D.V.: Converting Nested Algebra Expressions into Flat Algebra Expressions. ACM Transactions on Database Systems 17(1), 65–93 (1992)
130. Paterson, M., Wegman, M.: Linear Unification. Journal of Computer and System Sciences 16, 158–167 (1978)
131. Plandowski, W.: Satisfiability of Word Equations with Constants is in PSPACE. In: Proc. Annual Symposium on Foundations of Computer Science (FOCS), pp. 495–500 (1999)
132. Przymusinsik, T.: On the Declarative Semantics of Deductive Databases and Logic Programs. In: Minker, J. (ed.) Foundations of Deductive Databases and Logic Programming. ch. 5, pp. 193–216. Morgan Kaufmann, San Francisco (1988)
133. Przymusinski, T.: Stable Semantics for Disjunctive Programs. New Generation Computing 9, 401–424 (1991)
134. Przymusinski, T.: Static Semantics for Normal and Disjunctive Logic Programs. Annals of Mathematics and Artificial Intelligence 14, 323–357 (1995)
135. Przymusinski, T.C.: On the Declarative and Procedural Semantics of Logic Programs. Journal of Automated Reasoning 5(2), 167–205 (1989)
136. Ramanan, P.: Efficient Algorithms for Minimizing Tree Pattern Queries. In: Proc. ACM SIGMOD Symposium on the Management of Data (SIGMOD), pp. 299–309. ACM Press, New York (2002)
137. Reiter, R.: On Closed World Data Bases. In: Gallaire, H., Minker, J. (eds.) Logic and Data Base, pp. 55–76. Plenum Press, New York, USA (1978)
138. Robinson, J.: A Machine-Oriented Logic Based on the Resolution Principle. Journal of the Association for Computing Machinery 12(1), 23–41 (1965)
139. Ross, K.: Modular Stratification and Magic Sets for Datalog Programs with Negation. In: Proc. ACM SIGACT-SIGMOD-SIGART Symposium on Principles of Database Systems (PODS), ACM Press, New York (1990)
140. Ross, K.: A Procedural Semantics for Well-Founded Negation in Logic Programs. Journal of Logic Programming 13, 1–22 (1992)
141. Schaffert, S., Bry, F.: Querying the Web Reconsidered: A Practical Introduction to Xcerpt. In: Proc. Extreme Markup Languages (2004)
142. Schlipf, J.: The Expressive Powers of the Logic Programming Semantics. Journal of Computer and System Sciences 51(1), 64–86 (1995)
143. Schwentick, T.: XPath Query Containment. SIGMOD Record 33(1), 101–109 (2004)
144. Schwichtenberg, H.: Logikprogrammierung. Institute for Mathematics, University of Munich (1993)
145. Sheperdson, J.: Unsolvable Problems for SLDNF-Resolution. Journal of Logic Programming 10, 19–22 (1991)
146. Shipman, D.W.: The Functional Data Model and the Data Languages DAPLEX. ACM Transactions on Database Systems 6(1), 140–173 (1981)
147. Slivinskas, G., Jensen, C.S., Snodgrass, R.T.: Bringing Order to Query Optimization. SIGMOD Record 31(2), 5–14 (2002)
148. Stonebraker, M., Held, G., Wong, E., Kreps, P.: The Design and Implementation of INGRES. ACM Transactions on Database Systems 1(3), 189–222 (1976)

149. Suciu, D., Paredaens, J.: Any Algorithm in the Complex Object Algebra with Powerset needs Exponential Space to Compute Transitive Closure. In: Proc. ACM SIGACT-SIGMOD-SIGART Symposium on Principles of Database Systems (PODS), pp. 201–209. ACM Press, New York (1994)

150. Tamaki, H., Sato, T.: OLDT Resolution with Tablulation. In: International Conference on Logic Programming, pp. 84–98 (1986)

151. Tärnlund, S.-A.: Horn Clause Computability. BIT Numerical Mathematics 17, 215–216 (1977)

152. van den Bussche, J., Paredaens, J.: The Expressive Power of Structured Values in Pure OODBs. In: Proc. ACM SIGACT-SIGMOD-SIGART Symposium on Principles of Database Systems (PODS), pp. 291–299. ACM Press, New York (1991)

153. van Emden, M., Kowalski, R.: The Semantics of Predicate Logic as a Programming Language. Journal of the Association for Computing Machinery 23(4), 733–742 (1976)

154. van Gelder, A.: The Alternating Fixpoint of Logic Programs With Negation. In: Proc. ACM SIGACT-SIGMOD-SIGART Symposium on Principles of Database Systems (PODS), pp. 1–10. ACM Press, New York (1989)

155. van Gelder, A., Ross, K., Schlipf, J.: The Well-Founded Semantics for General Logic Programs. Journal of the Association for Computing Machinery 38(3), 620–650 (1991)

156. Vardi, M.: The Complexity of Relational Query Languages. In: ACM Symposium on Theory of Computing (STOC), pp. 137–146, San Francisco (1982)

157. Veith, H.: Logical Reducibilities in Finite Model Theory. Master's thesis, Information Systems Department, TU Vienna, Austria (September 1994)

158. Vieille, L.: A Database-Complete Proof Procedure Based on SLD-Resolution. In: International Conference on Logic Programming, pp. 74–103 (1987)

159. von Bültzingsloewen, G.: Translating and Optimizing SQL Queries Having Aggregates. In: Proc. International Conference on Very Large Data Bases (VLDB), pp. 235–243, San Francisco, CA, USA (1987)

160. Warren, D.H.D., Pereira, L.M., Pereira, F.: Prolog - the Language and its Implementation compared with Lisp. In: Proc. Symposium on Artificial Intelligence and Programming Languages, pp. 109–115 (1977)

161. Wood, P.T.: Optimising Web Queries using Document Type Definitions. In: Proc. ACM Int'l. Workshop on Web Information and Data Management (WIDM), pp. 28–32. ACM Press, New York (1999)

162. Yasuura, H.: On Parallel Computational Complexity of Unification. In: Proc. International Conference on Fifth Generation Computer Systems, pp. 235–243. ICOT (1984)

Reasoning in Description Logics:
Basics, Extensions, and Relatives

Ulrike Sattler

University of Manchester
http://www.cs.man.ac.uk/~sattler/

Abstract. This tutorial covers the very basics of Description Logics (DLs): first, we present the primary DL $\mathcal{ALC}$, namely its syntax, semantics, and reasoning problems, making use of a running example. Next, we discuss a few important extensions and explain DL's relationship with first order logic, with modal logic, with OWL, and with rule-based formalisms, and give a brief sketch of tableau-based reasoning algorithms for DLs.

1 Introduction

Description logics (DLs) [7,10,20] are a family of logic-based knowledge representation formalisms designed to represent and reason about the knowledge of an application domain in a structured and well-understood way. They are descendants of semantic networks and frames, and are equipped with a formal, Tarski-style semantics. Recently, they have attracted increased attention since they form the logical basis of the Web Ontology Language OWL [43]: OWL comes in three OWL flavours, and two of these flavours, namely OWL Lite, OWL DL, as well as OWL 1.1 [33], are based on DLs.

In computer science, an ontology is an explicit, formal specification of a shared conceptualisation [34,17], where "a conceptualisation" means an abstract model of some aspect of the world. In this abstract model, relevant concepts of the aspect in question are defined, including a description of the vital properties of their instances. For example, if we are concerned with transportation means, relevant concepts are "bicycle" and "power unit", and the description of bicycles contains a statement such as "a bicycle is powered by a human through pedalling". In the last decade, ontologies became rather popular not only due to their role in the Semantic Web [14], but also due to their usage in enterprise knowledge management systems [74], medical terminology systems [72,61,71], and biology [76,15].

An ontology is an artefact and thus has to be *built* by (possibly a group of) domain experts—and it will *evolve* over time in any application that changes over time. Moreover, it is advisable to *integrate* existing ontologies if a larger aspect of the world is to be covered—instead of building a new one from scratch. Finally, if an ontology is *deployed*, knowledge is shared using the concepts defined in this ontology, e.g., concrete objects are described using the vocabulary fixed in an

G. Antoniou et al. (Eds.): Reasoning Web 2007, LNCS 4636, pp. 154–182, 2007.

ontology and this fixed vocabulary is used to provide more transparent access to data. Each of these tasks is rather complex: e.g. building involves a huge amount of creativity, integration requires knowledge in a large aspect. Moreover, all four ontology engineering tasks might involve co-operation, which increases the risk of misunderstanding, redundancy, etc. Thus if an ontology is to be engineered or used by more than one user, the use of an *unambiguous* language such as OWL makes it possible to agree upon a specification and thus decreases the risk of misunderstandings.

The increasing importance of ontologies and their processing in computers has led to the development of ontology editors such as OntoEdit, Protégé , OilEd, and SWOOP [73,60,38,13]. Due to the above mentioned complexity of ontology engineering tasks, it is highly desirable that these editors support the user in the design, evolution, integration, and deployment of ontologies through corresponding, intelligent system services. This automatic processing of ontologies has further implications on the ontology language. In addition to the reduction of misunderstandings, an unambiguous language enables the precise definition of the behaviour of system services, i.e., we can *define* what a system service is supposed to do on a given input. This enables the investigation of the soundness, completeness, and termination of the algorithms underlying the system services.

Moreover, if an ontology language is based on a logic, this yields further possibilities: we can base system services on logical reasoning problems, and thus we can profit from the huge amount of work in computer science and logic-based knowledge representation. There exists a large variety of decidability and complexity results for DLs (see Chapter 3 of [7]) and related logics (see [67,23]). We can also use a variety of results in model theory to learn more about the expressive power [5] of an ontology language [16,75].

For the design of an ontology language, knowing about the decidability and computational complexity of the reasoning problems that underly system services is important. It gives insight into the sources of complexity, and thus might allow to devise certain fragments of the ontology language for which the corresponding algorithms show more desirable properties or better performance.

Recently, the ontology editors Protégé OWL and SWOOP [38,51] have been developed which provide system services based on logical reasoning problems to support the user in the above mentioned ontology engineering tasks. For example, in the design phase, the computation of the taxonomy[1] taking into account the description of the concepts defined so far might help to detect modelling flaws in an early design phase: missing or unintended specialisation links are signs of incomplete or erroneous concept descriptions. In all tasks, singling out synonymous concepts helps reducing redundancy and thus misunderstandings. Finally, checking the consistency of concept description also helps detecting modelling flaws.

However, since ontology engineering is still a rather new field, various other such services will need to be devised to provide optimal support. For example, one would like to see an explanation for unintended specialisation links or

---

[1] The specialisation hierarchy of the concepts defined so far.

inconsistencies and be supported in debugging such flaws; one would like to extract, from an ontology, the "sub-ontology" that "covers" a given term or concept; one would like to ask the editor to propose a new concept description as (the most specific) generalisation of a given set of instances; one would like to find a concept description that follows a certain "pattern" of a concept; or one would like to see a user-friendly approximation of a concept description, for instance in a frame-based notation. These services are provided by so-called *non-standard inference services* such as the least common subsumer and most specific concept, matching of concepts, or computing the approximation of a concept expressed in a more expressive logic in a less expressive logic [52,22,53,6,11,18].

2   A Basic DL and Its Extensions

In this section, we introduce and explain the basic notions of Description Logics including syntax, semantics, and reasoning services. We will explain how the latter are used in applications, and describe the relationship between DLs and other logics.

We define the syntax and semantics of the basic DL $\mathcal{ALC}$ [69] with general TBoxes and ABoxes, and explain them using our running example. We will also define different forms of TBoxes including acyclic ones.

Definition 1. *Let* **C** *be a set of* concept names *and* **R** *be a set of* role names *disjoint from* **C**. *The set of* $\mathcal{ALC}$ concepts *over* **C** *and* **R** *is inductively defined as follows:*

- *every concept name is an* $\mathcal{ALC}$ *concept description,*
- $\top$ *and* $\bot$ *are* $\mathcal{ALC}$ *concept descriptions,*
- *if* C *and* D *are* $\mathcal{ALC}$ *concept descriptions and* r *is a role name, then the following are also* $\mathcal{ALC}$ *concept descriptions:*
  - $C \sqcap D$ *(conjunction),*
  - $C \sqcup D$ *(disjunction),*
  - $\neg C$ *(negation),*
  - $\exists r.C,$ *(existential restriction), and*
  - $\forall r.C$ *(value restriction).*

As usual, we use parenthesis to clarify the structure of concepts.

Definition 1 fixes the *syntax* of $\mathcal{ALC}$ concepts, that is, it allows us to distinguish between expressions that are "well-formed", i.e., $\mathcal{ALC}$ concept descriptions, and those that are not. For example $A \sqcap \exists r. \forall s.(E \sqcap \neg F)$ is an $\mathcal{ALC}$ concept description, whereas $\forall s.s$ is not since s cannot be both a concept and a role name.

Next, we will introduce some DL parlance and abbreviations. If a concept description is a concept name, $\top$, or $\bot$, we also call it *atomic*, and if it is constructed using at least one of the above operators, we call it *complex*. Also, we often use "$\mathcal{ALC}$ concept" as an abbreviation of "$\mathcal{ALC}$ concept description" and, if it is clear from the context that we talk about $\mathcal{ALC}$ concepts, we may even drop the $\mathcal{ALC}$ and use "concepts" for "$\mathcal{ALC}$ concepts".

Remark: Please note that a *concept description* is, basically, a string, and it is not to be confused with the general "concept" in the sense of an abstract or general idea from philosophy. When we use DLs in applications, we may use a concept name or construct a concept description to describe a relevant "concept", yet the latter is far more intricate than the former.

Also, when clear from the context, **C** and **R** are not mentioned explicitly. In the following, we will use upper case letters A, B, etc. for concept names, upper case letters C, D, etc. for possibly complex concepts, and lower case letters r, s, etc. for role names.

Next, we define the semantics of $\mathcal{ALC}$ by means of an interpretation and then provide an example.

Definition 2. *An* interpretation $\mathcal{I} = (\Delta^{\mathcal{I}}, \cdot^{\mathcal{I}})$ *consists of a non-empty set* $\Delta^{\mathcal{I}}$, *called the* interpretation domain, *and a mapping* $\cdot^{\mathcal{I}}$ *that maps every*

- *concept name* $A \in \mathbf{C}$ *to a set* $A^{\mathcal{I}} \subseteq \Delta^{\mathcal{I}}$, *and every*
- *role name* $r \in \mathbf{R}$ *to a binary relation* $r^{\mathcal{I}} \subseteq \Delta^{\mathcal{I}} \times \Delta^{\mathcal{I}}$.

The mapping $\cdot^{\mathcal{I}}$ *is extended to complex concepts as follows:*

$$
\begin{aligned}
\top^{\mathcal{I}} &:= \Delta^{\mathcal{I}}, \\
\bot^{\mathcal{I}} &:= \emptyset, \\
(C \sqcap D)^{\mathcal{I}} &:= C^{\mathcal{I}} \cap D^{\mathcal{I}}, \\
(C \sqcup D)^{\mathcal{I}} &:= C^{\mathcal{I}} \cup D^{\mathcal{I}}, \\
(\neg C)^{\mathcal{I}} &:= \Delta^{\mathcal{I}} \setminus C^{\mathcal{I}}, \\
(\exists r.C)^{\mathcal{I}} &:= \{d \in \Delta^{\mathcal{I}} \mid \text{there is an } e \in \Delta^{\mathcal{I}} \text{ with } \langle d, e \rangle \in r^{\mathcal{I}} \text{ and } e \in C^{\mathcal{I}}\}, \\
(\forall r.C)^{\mathcal{I}} &:= \{d \in \Delta^{\mathcal{I}} \mid \text{for all } e \in \Delta^{\mathcal{I}}, \text{ if } \langle d, e \rangle \in r^{\mathcal{I}}, \text{ then } e \in C^{\mathcal{I}}\}.
\end{aligned}
$$

We call

- $C^{\mathcal{I}}$ *the* extension of C *in* $\mathcal{I}$,
- $a \in \Delta^{\mathcal{I}}$ *an* instance of C *in* $\mathcal{I}$ *if* $a \in C^{\mathcal{I}}$, *and*
- $b \in \Delta^{\mathcal{I}}$ *an* r-filler of a *in* $\mathcal{I}$ *if* $\langle a, b \rangle \in r^{\mathcal{I}}$.

Again, if $\mathcal{I}$ is clear from the concept, we omit "in $\mathcal{I}$". Please note that $A^{\mathcal{I}}$ denotes the result of applying the mapping $\cdot^{\mathcal{I}}$ to the concept name A; this might be considered to be an unusual way of writing mappings, yet it is quite helpful and ink-saving. In the past, DL researchers have used different notations such as $\mathcal{I}(A)$ or $[[A]]_{\mathcal{I}}$, but the one used here is the one that "stuck".

Let us consider the following example interpretation $\mathcal{I}$:

$$
\begin{aligned}
\Delta^{\mathcal{I}} &= \{m, c6, c7, et\}, \\
\mathsf{Employee}^{\mathcal{I}} &= \{m\}, \\
\mathsf{Company}^{\mathcal{I}} &= \{c6, c7, et\}, \\
\mathsf{Person}^{\mathcal{I}} &= \{m, et\}, \\
\mathsf{Incorporation}^{\mathcal{I}} &= \{c7\} \\
\mathit{worksFor} &= \{\langle m, c6 \rangle, \langle m, c7 \rangle, \langle et, et \rangle\}
\end{aligned}
$$

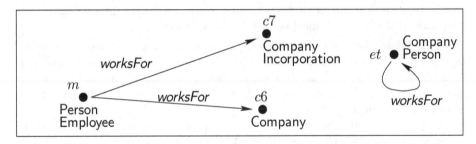

Fig. 1. A graphical representation of the example interpretation $\mathcal{I}$

We can easily modify $\mathcal{I}$ to obtain other interpretations $\mathcal{I}_1$, $\mathcal{I}_2$, etc., by adding or removing elements and changing the interpretation of concept and role names. An interpretation is often conveniently drawn as a directed, labelled graph with a node for each element of the interpretation domain and labelled as follows: a node is labelled with all concept names the corresponding element of the interpretation domain is an instance of, and we find an edge from one node to another labelled with r if the element corresponding to the latter node is an r-filler of the element corresponding to the former node. As an example, Figure 1 shows a graphical representation of $\mathcal{I}$.

Let us take a closer look at $\mathcal{I}$. By definition, all elements are instances of $\top$, and no element is an instance of $\bot$. The elements m and et are instances of Person, and et is a *worksFor*-filler of itself. For Boolean concepts, m is an instance of Person ⊓ Employee, and $c6$ is an instance of Company ⊓ ¬Person because $c6$ is *not* an instance of Person. For existential restrictions, m and et are instances of ∃*worksFor*.Company, but only m is an instance of ∃*worksFor*.¬Person. For value restrictions, all elements are instances of ∀*worksFor*.Company: for m and et, this is clear, and for $c6$ and $c7$, this is due to the fact that they do not have *any* *worksFor*-fillers, and hence *all* their *worksFor*-fillers satisfy whatever condition we may have. In general, if an element has no r-filler, then it is an instance of ∀$r.C$ for any concept C. In contrast, m is *not* an instance of ∀*worksFor*.(Company ⊓ Incorporation) because m has $c6$ as its *worksFor*-filler who is *not* an instance of Company⊓Incorporation since it is not an instance of Incorporation. At this stage, we invite the reader to consider some more interpretations and concepts and determine which element is an instance of which concept.

So far, we have defined syntax and semantics of the concept language $\mathcal{ALC}$. Next, we define knowledge bases and their semantics, starting with *terminological knowledge bases*, so-called TBoxes.

Definition 3. *For C and D possibly complex $\mathcal{ALC}$ concepts, an expression of the form $C \sqsubseteq D$ is called an $\mathcal{ALC}$ general concept inclusion and abbreviated GCI. A finite set of GCIs is called an $\mathcal{ALC}$ TBox.*

An interpretation $\mathcal{I}$ satisfies a GCI $C \sqsubseteq D$ if $C^{\mathcal{I}} \subseteq D^{\mathcal{I}}$. An interpretation that satisfies each GCI in a TBox $\mathcal{T}$ is called a model *of $\mathcal{T}$.*

Again, if it is clear that we are talking about $\mathcal{ALC}$ concepts and TBoxes, we omit "$\mathcal{ALC}$" and use simply TBox or GCI. For example, the interpretation $\mathcal{I}$ given in Figure 1 satisfies each of the GCIs in

$$\mathcal{T}_1 := \{ \text{Employee} \sqsubseteq \text{Person},$$
$$\text{Incorporation} \sqsubseteq \neg\text{Person},$$
$$\text{Employee} \sqsubseteq \exists worksFor.\text{Company},$$
$$\exists worksFor.\text{Company} \sqsubseteq \text{Person} \}$$

and thus $\mathcal{I}$ is a model of $\mathcal{T}_1$. To verify this, for each GCI $C \sqsubseteq D$, we determine $C^{\mathcal{I}}$ and $D^{\mathcal{I}}$ and then check whether $C^{\mathcal{I}}$ is indeed a subset of $D^{\mathcal{I}}$. For the first GCI, we observe that $\text{Employee}^{\mathcal{I}} = \{m\} \subseteq \{m, et\} = \text{Person}^{\mathcal{I}}$. Similarly, for the second one, we have $\text{Incorporation}^{\mathcal{I}} = \{c7\} \subseteq \{c6, c7\} = (\neg\text{Person})^{\mathcal{I}}$. For the third one, m is the only instance of Employee and also an instance of $\exists worksFor.\text{Company}$, hence it is also satisfied by $\mathcal{I}$. Finally $(\exists worksFor.\text{Company})^{\mathcal{I}} = \{m, et\}$ and both m and et are instances of Person.

In contrast, $\mathcal{I}$ does not satisfy the GCI

$$\exists worksFor.\text{Company} \sqsubseteq \text{Employee} \tag{1}$$

because et *worksFor* some Company, but is not a Employee.

In general, a TBox $\mathcal{T}$ allows us to distinguish between those interpretations that are and those that aren't models of $\mathcal{T}$. This means that we should aim at devising a TBox all of whose models indeed fit our intuition. For example, Equation 1 should be in our TBox if we think that only Employees can work for Companys. In general, the more GCIs our TBox contains, the fewer models we have.

Next, in Figure 2, we define a TBox $\mathcal{T}$ that indeed partially captures our intuition of working. The first GCI states that no Company can be a Person and also implies that no Person can be a Company. The fourth GCI states that every Employee is a Person who *worksFor* a Company and, vice versa, the fifth GCI states that any Person who *worksFor* a Company is an Employee. The sixth GCI ensures that only Persons can work for something.

Next, we define the *assertional* part of a knowledge base, the so-called ABox, and knowledge bases.

$$\mathcal{T} := \{ \text{Company} \sqsubseteq \neg\text{Person},$$
$$\text{PrivateComp} \sqsubseteq \text{Company},$$
$$\text{Incorporation} \sqsubseteq \text{Company},$$
$$\text{Employee} \sqsubseteq \text{Person} \sqcap \exists worksFor.\text{Company},$$
$$\text{Person} \sqcap \exists worksFor.\text{Company} \sqsubseteq \text{Employee},$$
$$\exists worksFor.\top \sqsubseteq \text{Person},$$
$$\text{Entrepreneur} \sqsubseteq \text{Person} \sqcap \exists owns.\text{Company},$$
$$\text{Person} \sqcap \exists owns.\text{Company} \sqsubseteq \text{Entrepreneur},$$
$$\exists owns.\top \sqsubseteq \text{Person} \}$$

Fig. 2. An example TBox

$$\mathcal{A} := \{\mathsf{Mary} : \mathsf{Person},$$

$\mathcal{A} := \{\mathsf{Mary} : \mathsf{Person},$	$\langle\mathsf{Mary, comp1}\rangle : \textit{worksFor},$
$\mathsf{comp1} : \mathsf{Company},$	$\langle\mathsf{Hugo, comp2}\rangle : \textit{worksFor},$
$\mathsf{comp2} : \mathsf{Company} \sqcap \mathsf{Incorporation},$	$\langle\mathsf{Betty, comp2}\rangle : \textit{owns},$
$\mathsf{Hugo} : \mathsf{Person},$	$\langle\mathsf{Mary, comp2}\rangle : \textit{owns},$
$\mathsf{Betty} : \mathsf{Person} \sqcap \mathsf{Employee} \}$	

Fig. 3. An example ABox

Definition 4. *Let* **I** *be a set of* individual names *disjoint from* **R** *and* **C***. For* $a, b \in \mathbf{I}$ *individual names,* C *a possibly complex* $\mathcal{ALC}$ *concept, and* $r \in \mathbf{R}$ *a role name, an expression of the form*

- $a{:}\,C$ *is called an* $\mathcal{ALC}$ concept assertion, *and*
- $\langle a, b\rangle{:}\,r$ *is called an* $\mathcal{ALC}$ role assertion.

A finite set of $\mathcal{ALC}$ *concept and role assertions is called an* $\mathcal{ALC}$ *ABox.*

An interpretation function $\cdot^{\mathcal{I}}$*, additionally, is required to map every individual name* $a \in \mathbf{I}$ *to an element* $a^{\mathcal{I}} \in \Delta^{\mathcal{I}}$*. An interpretation* $\mathcal{I}$ *satisfies*

- *a concept assertion* $a{:}\,C$ *if* $a^{\mathcal{I}} \in C^{\mathcal{I}}$*, and*
- *a role assertion* $\langle a, b\rangle{:}\,r$ *if* $\langle a^{\mathcal{I}}, b^{\mathcal{I}}\rangle \in r^{\mathcal{I}}$*.*

An interpretation that satisfies each concept assertion and each role assertion in an ABox $\mathcal{A}$ *is called a* model *of* $\mathcal{A}$ *.*

Again, if it is clear that we are talking about $\mathcal{ALC}$ concepts and ABoxes, we omit "$\mathcal{ALC}$" and use simply ABox, concept assertion, etc.. Moreover, we use $C \equiv D$ as an abbreviation for the two GCIs $C \sqsubseteq D$ and $D \sqsubseteq C$.

In Figure 3, we present an example ABox with concept and role assertions, and the following interpretation $\mathcal{I}$ is a model of this ABox:

$$\Delta^{\mathcal{I}} = \{h, m, c6, c4\}$$
$$\mathsf{Mary}^{\mathcal{I}} = m, \ \mathsf{Betty}^{\mathcal{I}} = \mathsf{Hugo}^{\mathcal{I}} = h, \ \mathsf{comp1}^{\mathcal{I}} = c6, \mathsf{comp2} = c4$$
$$\mathsf{Person}^{\mathcal{I}} = \{h, m, c6, c4\}$$
$$\mathsf{Employee}^{\mathcal{I}} = \{h, m\}$$
$$\mathsf{Company}^{\mathcal{I}} = \{c6, c4\}$$
$$\mathsf{Incorporation}^{\mathcal{I}} = \{c4\}$$
$$\mathsf{Entrepreneur}^{\mathcal{I}} = \emptyset$$
$$\textit{worksFor}^{\mathcal{I}} = \{\langle m, c6\rangle, \langle h, c4\rangle\}$$
$$\textit{owns}^{\mathcal{I}} = \{\langle h, c4\rangle, \langle m, c4\rangle\}$$

Please observe that the individual names Hugo and Betty are interpreted as the same element, h and that, for example, $\mathsf{Employee}$ has more instances than strictly required by $\mathcal{A}$.

Finally, we take the natural step and combine TBoxes and ABoxes in knowledge bases.

Definition 5. *An* $\mathcal{ALC}$ *knowledge base* $\mathcal{K} = (\mathcal{T}, \mathcal{A})$ *consists of an* $\mathcal{ALC}$ *TBox* $\mathcal{T}$ *and an* $\mathcal{ALC}$ *ABox* $\mathcal{A}$*. An interpretation that is both a model of* $\mathcal{A}$ *and of* $\mathcal{T}$ *is called a* model *of* $\mathcal{K}$*.*

Hence for an interpretation to be a model of $\mathcal{K}$, it has to satisfy all assertions in $\mathcal{K}$'s ABox and all GCIs in $\mathcal{K}$'s TBox. As an example, consider $\mathcal{K}$ consisting of the TBox $\mathcal{T}$ from Figure 2 and the ABox $\mathcal{A}$ from Figure 3. Please note that the interpretation $\mathcal{I}$ given above is *not* a model of $\mathcal{K}$: $\mathcal{I}$ is a model of $\mathcal{A}$, but not of $\mathcal{T}$ since $\mathcal{I}$ does not satisfy two GCIs in $\mathcal{T}$:

1. m and h are Persons owning a Company, $c4$, but they are not instances of Entrepreneur in $\mathcal{I}$, thereby violating the last-but-one GCI in $\mathcal{T}$.
2. $c6$ and $c4$ are both instances of Person and of Company, thereby violating the first GCI in $\mathcal{T}$.

We can easily obtain a model $\mathcal{I}'$ of $\mathcal{K}$ from $\mathcal{I}$ as follows: $\mathcal{I}'$ is identical to $\mathcal{I}$, apart from the interpretation of Entrepreneur and of Person, which are defined as follows: $\text{Person}^{\mathcal{I}'} = \text{Entrepreneur}^{\mathcal{I}'} = \{h, m\}$. We leave it to the reader to verify that $\mathcal{I}'$ is indeed a model of $\mathcal{T}$ and $\mathcal{A}$.

An important difference to databases and other formalisms can be illustrated by the following example. Consider the TBox from Figure 2 and an ABox that only contains the assertion Mary: Employee. In contrast to what one would think with a database in mind, this knowledge base is perfectly "ok", i.e., we can say that Mary stands for an instance of Employee, thereby implying that she must work for a Company—*without* mentioning such a company. That is, a knowledge base may contain *partial* knowledge: Mary stands for an element that is *worksFor*-related to some instance of Company, but we do not know to which. Similarly, consider a knowledge base $\mathcal{K}$ containing the following statements:

1. the following GCIs for an Inc-Entrepreneur:

$$\text{Inc-Entrepreneur} \sqsubseteq \text{Entrepreneur} \sqcap \forall \textit{owns}.\text{Incorporation},$$

2. the assertions $\langle \text{John}, \text{C4} \rangle$: *owns* and C4: Incorporation, and
3. the assertions $\langle \text{Mary}, \text{C3} \rangle$: *owns* and Mary: Inc-Entrepreneur.

Now, who of John and Mary are Inc-Entrepreneurs? $\mathcal{K}$'s ABox states that John represents something that has one *owns*-filler, and this is an Incorporation, hence one could think that John is an Inc-Entrepreneur. By definition of the semantics of ABoxes, though, there are models $\mathcal{I}$ of $\mathcal{K}$ in which $\text{John}^{\mathcal{I}}$ has other *owns*-fillers than the one given explicitly, and some of them may *not* be instances of Incorporation. That is, our ABox contains some information about one *owns*-filler of an element called John, but this element might have other *owns*-fillers about which we do not know (or did not say) anything. Thus John cannot be said to be a Inc-Entrepreneur. In the general AI literature, this principal is referred to as the *open world assumption*, and we will come back to that later. In contrast, we have said in $\mathcal{K}$ that Mary is an Inc-Entrepreneur, and thus in every model $\mathcal{I}$ of $\mathcal{K}$, it must be the case that $\text{C3}^{\mathcal{I}}$ is an instance of Incorporation—despite the fact that this is not stated explicitly in the ABox. Hence, Mary is indeed an Inc-Entrepreneur, and we can infer that C3 is an Incorporation; we will be more precise on this "inference" in Section 3.

2.1   Restricted TBoxes and Concept Definitions

In general, a TBox may contain two kinds of information: general "background knowledge" and concept definitions. So far, our TBox contains, however, only general concept inclusion axioms. In our example in Figure 2, we have used the fourth and the fifth GCIs two define the meaning of Employee. In general, if we want to make sure C and D always have the same instances, then we need to introduce two GCIs $C \sqsubseteq D$ and $D \sqsubseteq C$. Hence we have introduced $C \equiv D$ as an abbreviation for $C \sqsubseteq D$ and $D \sqsubseteq C$, and we call an expression of the form $A \equiv C$ with A a concept name a *concept definition* of the concept A. Now consider the concept definition

$$\text{Happy} \equiv \text{Person} \sqcap \forall \text{likes.Happy.} \tag{2}$$

First, observe that this concept definition is *cyclic*: the definition of Happy involves the concept Happy. Next, we consider an interpretation $\mathcal{I}$ with

$$\{\langle p, m \rangle, \langle m, p \rangle\} = \text{likes}^{\mathcal{I}} \text{ and } \{p, m\} = \text{Person}^{\mathcal{I}},$$

and ask ourselves whether p is an instance of Happy in $\mathcal{I}$. Since Happy is a defined concept, we could expect that we can determine this by simply considering the interpretation of other concepts and roles. This is, however, not the case: we can choose either $\text{Happy}^{\mathcal{I}} = \{p, m\}$ or $\text{Happy}^{\mathcal{I}} = \emptyset$, and both choices would make $\mathcal{I}$ a model of the concept definition 2.

To give TBoxes more "definitorial power", we need to restrict them so as to avoid cyclic references as in the example above.

Definition 6. *An $\mathcal{ALC}$ concept definition is an expression of the form $A \equiv C$ or $A \sqsubseteq C$ for A a concept name and C a possibly complex $\mathcal{ALC}$ concept. We call $A \equiv C$ an exact concept definition and $A \sqsubseteq C$ a primitive concept definition.*

Let $\mathcal{T}$ be a finite set of concept definitions. We say that A directly uses B if there is a concept definition $A \equiv C \in \mathcal{T}$ such that B occurs in C. We use uses for the transitive closure of "directly uses".

We call a finite set $\mathcal{T}$ of concept definitions an acyclic TBox if

– *there is no concept name in $\mathcal{T}$ that uses itself and*
– *if no concept name occurs more than once on the left hand side of a concept definition in $\mathcal{T}$.*

If $\mathcal{T}$ is an acyclic TBox with $A \equiv C \in \mathcal{T}$, we say that A is defined in $\mathcal{T}$ and that C is the definition of A in $\mathcal{T}$.

By definition, in an acyclic TBox, we cannot have a situation such as follows:

$$A_1 \equiv \ldots A_2 \ldots$$
$$A_2 \equiv \ldots A_3 \ldots$$
$$\vdots \quad \vdots$$
$$A_n \equiv \ldots A_1 \ldots$$

$$\begin{aligned}
\mathcal{T}_1 := \{ &\mathsf{Company} \sqsubseteq \neg\mathsf{Person}, \\
&\exists \textit{worksFor}.\top \sqsubseteq \mathsf{Person}, \\
&\exists \textit{owns}.\top \sqsubseteq \mathsf{Person} \ \} \\
\mathcal{T}_2 := \{ &\mathsf{Incorporation} \sqsubseteq \mathsf{Company}, \\
&\mathsf{PrivateComp} \sqsubseteq \mathsf{Company}, \\
&\mathsf{Employee} \equiv \mathsf{Person} \sqcap \exists \textit{worksFor}.\mathsf{Company}, \\
&\mathsf{Entrepreneur} \equiv \mathsf{Person} \sqcap \exists \textit{owns}.\mathsf{Company} \ \}
\end{aligned}$$

Fig. 4. A combined TBox where Employee and Entrepreneur are defined

Since acyclic TBoxes are a syntactic restriction of TBoxes, we do not need to define their semantics since it follows directly from those for (general) TBoxes.

If one wants to make use both of GCIs to represent background knowledge and of concept definitions, then we can combine them. That is, we can simply consider a TBox to consist of two parts, say a set of GCIs $\mathcal{T}_1$ and a set of concept definitions $\mathcal{T}_2$. In order to preserve the above mentioned "definitorial power" of $\mathcal{T}_2$ one only has to make sure that concepts defined in $\mathcal{T}_2$ do not occur in $\mathcal{T}_1$. As an example, consider Figure 4.

Please note that this "splitting" of a TBox in a definitorial part and a background part has no consequences on the definition of its semantics—it merely allows us to talk about those concepts *defined* in a TBox.

3   Basic Reasoning Problems and Services

So far, we have defined the components of a DL knowledge base and what it means for an interpretation to be a model of such a knowledge base. Next, we define the reasoning problems commonly considered in DLs, and discuss their relationships. We start by defining the basic reasoning problems in DLs upon which the basic system services of a DL *reasoner* are built, and then provide a number of examples.

Definition 7. *Let $\mathcal{K} = (\mathcal{T}, \mathcal{A})$ be an $\mathcal{ALC}$ knowledge base, C, D possibly complex $\mathcal{ALC}$ concepts, and a an individual name. We say that*

1. *C is* satisfiable *w.r.t. $\mathcal{T}$ if there exists a model $\mathcal{I}$ of $\mathcal{T}$ and some $d \in \Delta^{\mathcal{I}}$ with $d \in C^{\mathcal{I}}$,*
2. *C is* subsumed *by D w.r.t. $\mathcal{T}$, written $C \sqsubseteq_{\mathcal{T}} D$, if $C^{\mathcal{I}} \subseteq D^{\mathcal{I}}$ for each model $\mathcal{I}$ of $\mathcal{T}$,*
3. *C and D are* equivalent *w.r.t. $\mathcal{T}$, written $C \equiv_{\mathcal{T}} D$, if $C^{\mathcal{I}} = D^{\mathcal{I}}$ for each model $\mathcal{I}$ of $\mathcal{T}$,*
4. *$\mathcal{K}$ is* consistent *if there exists a model of $\mathcal{K}$, and*
5. *a is an* instance *of C w.r.t. $\mathcal{K}$ if $a^{\mathcal{I}} \in C^{\mathcal{I}}$ for each model $\mathcal{I}$ of $\mathcal{K}$.*

Please note that satisfiability and subsumption are defined w.r.t. a TBox, whereas consistency and instance are defined w.r.t. a TBox and an ABox. Moreover, we already use the notion of "being an instance of a concept" for elements of an interpretation domain—here, we have defined this notion for individual names. This might be slightly confusing, but is quite natural: an individual name a can be interpreted in many different ways, and $a^{\mathcal{I}_1}$ can have quite different properties from $a^{\mathcal{I}_2}$. A knowledge base can, however, enforce that $a^{\mathcal{I}}$ is an instance of some concept in *every* model $\mathcal{I}$ of its models, which is why we define the notion of an instance for individual names as well. All our reasoning problems are defined w.r.t. some knowledge base. We can always assume that these are empty: in this case, "all models of $\mathcal{K}$ (or $\mathcal{T}$)" becomes simply "all interpretations".

We give a few example inferences and invite the reader to explain them to make sure that they understand the notions defined in Definition 7:

- $A \sqcap \neg A$ is *unsatisfiable*,
- $\bot$ and $A \sqcap \neg A$ are equivalent (w.r.t. the empty TBox),
- $\exists r.A \sqcap \forall r.\neg A$ is unsatisfiable,
- Company $\sqcap \exists worksFor.$Company is *not* satisfiable w.r.t. the TBox $\mathcal{T}$ from Figure 2,
- $A \sqcap B$ is subsumed by A (w.r.t. the empty TBox),
- $\exists r.A \sqcap \forall r.B$ is subsumed by $\exists r.B$
- Incorporation $\sqsubseteq_{\mathcal{T}} \neg$Person w.r.t. TBox $\mathcal{T}$ from Figure 2,
- $\exists worksFor.$Company $\sqsubseteq_{\mathcal{T}} \neg$Company w.r.t. TBox $\mathcal{T}$ from Figure 2,
- the knowledge base consisting of the TBox $\mathcal{T}$ from Figure 2 and the ABox $\mathcal{A}$ from Figure 3 is consistent,
- the knowledge base $(\mathcal{T}, \mathcal{A}_2)$ with $\mathcal{A}_2$ defined as follows is not consistent:

$$\mathcal{A}_2 = \{\text{ET: Company}, \langle \text{ET, Foo} \rangle: worksFor\},$$

and removing any of the two assertions from $\mathcal{A}_2$ results in an ABox that is consistent with $\mathcal{T}$, and
- Mary and Hugo are instances of Employee w.r.t. $\mathcal{T}$ from Figure 2 and $\mathcal{A}$ from Figure 3.

Next, we would like to point out that it is possible for a knowledge base $(\mathcal{T}, \mathcal{A})$ to be consistent and, at the time, for a concept C to be unsatisfiable w.r.t. $\mathcal{T}$: clearly, $\bot$ is unsatisfiable w.r.t. every TBox since, by Definition 2, $\bot^{\mathcal{I}} = \emptyset$ for every interpretation $\mathcal{I}$. Even if C is defined in $\mathcal{T}$ (see Definition 6), it is possible that C is unsatisfiable w.r.t. $\mathcal{T}$ while $\mathcal{T}$ is consistent; consider, for example, the TBox $\mathcal{T} = \{A \equiv B \sqcap \neg B\}$ which has infinitely many models, none of which has an instance of A.

To help the reader understanding the reasoning problems defined, we mention three important properties of the subsumption relationship which follow directly from Definition 7.

Lemma 1. *Let C, D, and E be concepts, a an individual name, and $(\mathcal{T}, \mathcal{A})$ a knowledge base.*

1. $C \sqsubseteq_{\mathcal{T}} C$.
2. *If $C \sqsubseteq_{\mathcal{T}} D$ and $D \sqsubseteq_{\mathcal{T}} E$, then $C \sqsubseteq_{\mathcal{T}} E$.*

3. *If a is an instance of C w.r.t. $(\mathcal{T}, \mathcal{A})$ and $C \sqsubseteq_{\mathcal{T}} D$, then a is an instance of D w.r.t. $(\mathcal{T}, \mathcal{A})$.*

Please note that Lemma 1.(1) and (2) says that the subsumption relationship is reflexive and transitive.

Next, we formalise some of the implicit relationships between DL reasoning problems that we have used intuitively in our considerations above, and which should be proved as an exercise by the reader.

Theorem 1. *Let $\mathcal{K} = (\mathcal{T}, \mathcal{A})$ be an $\mathcal{ALC}$ knowledge base, C, D possibly complex $\mathcal{ALC}$ concepts, and a an individual name. Then*

1. *C and D are equivalent w.r.t. $\mathcal{T}$ iff $C \sqsubseteq_{\mathcal{T}} D$ and $D \sqsubseteq_{\mathcal{T}} C$.*
2. *C is subsumed by D w.r.t. $\mathcal{T}$ iff $C \sqcap \neg D$ is not satisfiable w.r.t. $\mathcal{T}$.*
3. *C is satisfiable w.r.t. $\mathcal{T}$ iff C is not subsumed by $\bot$.*
4. *C is satisfiable w.r.t. $\mathcal{T}$ iff $(\mathcal{T}, \{a\!:\!C\})$ is consistent.*
5. *a is an instance of C w.r.t. $\mathcal{K}$ iff $(\mathcal{T}, \mathcal{A} \cup \{a\!:\!\neg C\})$ is not consistent.*

As a consequence of this theorem, we can restrict our attention to knowledge base consistency since all other reasoning problems can be *reduced* to it: to decide these other reasoning problems, we can simply use an algorithm for consistency.

In general, when designing or changing a knowledge base, it is helpful to see the *effects* of the statements so far. We will use the reasoning problems defined so far to formalise some of these effects and formulate them in terms of *reasoning services*. The following is a list of the most basic DL reasoning services: given a knowledge base $(\mathcal{T}, \mathcal{A})$, concepts C and D, and an individual name a, check whether

- C is *satisfiable* w.r.t. $\mathcal{T}$,
- C is *subsumed by* D w.r.t. T,
- C and D are *equivalent* w.r.t. T,
- $(\mathcal{T}, \mathcal{A})$ is *consistent*,
- a is an *instance of* C w.r.t. $(\mathcal{T}, \mathcal{A})$.

Please note that these basic reasoning services correspond one-to-one to the basic reasoning problems from Definition 7. As a consequence, we know exactly *what* each of these reasoning services should do, even though we might not know *how* such a service could be implemented—this will be discussed in Section 6. To put it differently, the behaviour of a service has been described independently from a specific implementation, and thus we can expect that, for example, every satisfiability checker for $\mathcal{ALC}$ gives the same answer when asked whether a certain concept is satisfiable w.r.t. a certain TBox—regardless of how this satisfiability checker works.

Clearly, we might be able to compute these services "by hand", yet this is unfeasible for larger knowledge bases, and it has turned out to be quite useful to have implementations of these services. In the past, numerous DLs have been investigated w.r.t. their *decidability* and *complexity*, i.e., whether or which of the reasoning problems are decidable and, if they are, how complex they are in terms of computation time and space.

Using these basic reasoning services, we can specify slightly more sophisticated reasoning services as follows:

- *classification* of a TBox: given a TBox $\mathcal{T}$, compute the subsumption hierarchy of all concept names occurring in $\mathcal{T}$ w.r.t. $\mathcal{T}$. That is, for each pair A, B of concept names occurring in $\mathcal{T}$, check whether A is subsumed by B w.r.t. $\mathcal{T}$ and whether B is subsumed by A w.r.t. $\mathcal{T}$.
- checking the *satisfiability* of concepts in $\mathcal{T}$: given a TBox $\mathcal{T}$, for each concept name A in $\mathcal{T}$, test whether A is satisfiable w.r.t. $\mathcal{T}$. If it is not, then this is a clear indication of a modelling error.
- *instance retrieval*: given a concept C and a knowledge base $\mathcal{K}$, return all those individual names a such that a is an instance of C w.r.t. $\mathcal{K}$. That is, for each individual name a occurring in $\mathcal{K}$, check whether it is an instance of C w.r.t. $\mathcal{K}$, and return the set of those individual names that are.
- *realisation* of an individual name: given an individual a and a knowledge base $\mathcal{K}$, check, for each concept name A occurring in $\mathcal{T}$, whether a is an instance of A w.r.t. $\mathcal{K}$, and then return all those A that are.

The result of the classification is usually presented in form of the *subsumption hierarchy*, that is, a graph whose nodes are labelled with concept names from $\mathcal{T}$ and where we find an edge from a node labelled A to a node labelled B if A is subsumed by B w.r.t. $\mathcal{T}$. We may want to choose a slightly more succinct representation: from Lemma 1, we know that the subsumption relationship $\sqsubseteq_{\mathcal{T}}$ is a *pre-order*, i.e., a reflexive and transitive relation. It is common practice to consider the induced *strict partial order* $\sqsubset_{\mathcal{T}}$, i.e., an irreflexive and transitive (and therefor anti-symmetric) relation, by identifying all concepts participating in a cycle $C \sqsubseteq_{\mathcal{T}} ... \sqsubseteq_{\mathcal{T}} C$—or collapsing them all into a single node in our graphical representation. In addition, we might want to show only "direct edges", that is, we might not want to draw an edge from a node labelled C to a node labelled E in case there is a node labelled D such that $C \sqsubseteq_{\mathcal{T}} D \sqsubseteq_{\mathcal{T}} E$: this is commonly known as the *Hasse diagram* of a partial order. We cordially invite the reader to compute the the the subsumption hierarchy for the TBox from Figure 2.

3.1 Applications of Reasoning Services

Here, we sketch how DL reasoning services can be used in an application. Assume we want to design a DL knowledge base about companies, employees, entrepreneurs, etc. First, we would need to fix some set of interesting *terms* and decide which of them are concept names and which are role names. Then we could explicate some background knowledge, for example that Companys and Persons are disjoint and that only a Person ever *worksFor* somebody, see $\mathcal{T}_1$ in Figure 4. Next, we could define some relevant concepts, for example Incorporation, Employee, and Entrepreneur in $\mathcal{T}_2$ in Figure 4. Then it might be useful to see the subsumption hierarchy of our TBox. In our example, we can easily compute this hierarchy by hand.

Now assume that somebody adds the following concept definition to $\mathcal{T}_2$:

$$\text{Inc-Employee} \equiv \exists worksFor.\text{Incorporation}.$$

For $\mathcal{T}'$ this extended TBox, it is a bit more tricky to see that, in addition to the subsumptions above, we also have Inc-Employee $\sqsubseteq_{\mathcal{T}'}$ Person. Yet, this still fits our intuition and we can continue extending our knowledge base. Assume we extend $\mathcal{T}'$ with the following statement that expresses that a LazyEntrepreneur does not *own* any Companys:

$$\text{LazyEntrepreneur} \sqsubseteq \forall \textit{owns}.\neg\text{Company}.$$

Let $\mathcal{T}''$ be the result of this extension. It might be a bit more tricky to see but— in contrast to what our concept names suggest—a LazyEntrepreneur is *not* an Entrepreneur, i.e., LazyEntrepreneur $\not\sqsubseteq_{\mathcal{T}''}$ Entrepreneur. If we want to fix this, we could now try to modify this GCI, for example, by turning it into the following concept definition:

$$\text{LazyEntrepreneur} \equiv \text{Entrepreneur} \sqcap \forall \textit{owns}.\neg\text{Company}.$$

This modification would, unfortunately, make LazyEntrepreneur unsatisfiable w.r.t. the resulting TBox since an Entrepreneur necessarily *owns* some Company.

Now assume we add to $\mathcal{T}'$ some knowledge about individuals, for example, we add our ABox from Figure 3. Then it would be quite helpful to learn that Mary and Hugo are instances of Employee and that Hugo is an instances of Inc-Employee w.r.t. $\mathcal{T}'$. Even though this knowledge is not explicitly stated in our knowledge base, it follows from it, and thus should be made available to the user. For example, if one would ask to see all Employees, then Betty, Mary, and Hugo should be returned.

Currently, the design of ontology editors that help users to build, maintain, and use a DL knowledge base is a rather active research area, partially due to the fact that the Web Ontology Language OWL is based on DLs; we will discuss this relationship and tools in more detail in Section 7.1.

4   Important Extensions of the Basic DL $\mathcal{ALC}$

We introduce important extensions of the basic DL $\mathcal{ALC}$: inverse roles, number restrictions, and some more operators on roles.

Consider our running example and assume that we want to add to our TBox from Figure 2 the following GCIs to express that Idlers are Employees, and that Companys do not employ Idlers:

$$\text{Idler} \sqsubseteq \text{Employee},$$
$$\text{Company} \sqsubseteq \forall \textit{employs}.\neg\text{Idler}.$$

Let us call the resulting TBox $\mathcal{T}'$. Intuitively, Idler should be unsatisfiable w.r.t. $\mathcal{T}'$: due to the first GCI above, an instance p of Idler would also need to be an instance of Employee, and hence the fourth GCI from $\mathcal{T}$ implies that p has a *worksFor*-filler, say c, that is an instance of Company. Now, if p *worksFor* c, then c employs p, and thus the second statement above implies that p is an instance of

¬Idler, contradicting our assumption. Now this argumentation contains a serious flaw: due to the definition of the semantics, *worksFor* and *employs* are interpreted as some arbitrary binary relations, and thus it is *not* the case that, if p *worksFor* c, then c *employs* p. Indeed, Idler is satisfiable w.r.t. $\mathcal{T}'$: any model $\mathcal{I}$ of $\mathcal{T}$ in which $\mathsf{Idler}^{\mathcal{I}} \subseteq \mathsf{Employee}^{\mathcal{I}}$ holds and *employs*$^{\mathcal{I}} = \emptyset$ is a model of $\mathcal{T}'$.

In order to relate roles such as *worksFor* and *employs* in the obvious way, DLs have been extended with *inverse roles*. The fact that a certain DL allows for inverse roles is usually indicated by the letter $\mathcal{I}$ in its name; see the Appendix of [7] for an explanation of DL naming schemes.

Definition 8. *For R a role name, R^- is an* inverse role. *The set of $\mathcal{ALCI}$ concepts over* **C** *and* **R** *is inductively defined as follows:*

- *every concept name is an $\mathcal{ALCI}$ concept,*
- *if C and D are $\mathcal{ALCI}$ concepts and r is a role name, then the following are also $\mathcal{ALCI}$ concepts:*
  - $C \sqcap D, C \sqcup D, \neg C,$
  - $\exists r.C$ *and* $\exists r^-.C,$ *and*
  - $\forall r.C$ *and* $\forall r^-.C.$

In addition, an interpretation $\mathcal{I}$ also maps inverse roles to binary relations as follows:

$$(r^-)^{\mathcal{I}} = \{\langle y, x \rangle \mid \langle x, y \rangle \in r^{\mathcal{I}}\}.$$

As a consequence, we now have indeed that $\langle x, y \rangle \in r^{\mathcal{I}}$ if and only if $\langle y, x \rangle \in (r^-)^{\mathcal{I}}$, and we can thus rephrase our new constraints using *worksFor*$^-$ instead of *employs*:

$$\mathsf{Idler} \sqsubseteq \mathsf{Employee},$$
$$\mathsf{Company} \sqsubseteq \forall \textit{worksFor}^-.\neg\mathsf{Idler}.$$

We use $\mathcal{T}''$ for the extension of the TBox $\mathcal{T}$ from Figure 2 with the above two GCIs. Please verify that Idler is indeed unsatisfiable w.r.t. $\mathcal{T}''$.

In any system based on a DL with inverse roles, it would clearly be beneficial to allow the user to introduce "names" for inverse roles, such as "employs" for *worksFor*$^-$, "child-of" for *has-child*$^-$, or "part-of" for *has-part*$^-$. Indeed, as we will see in Section 7.1, OWL provides means to make such statements.

The above line of reasoning has been repeated numerous times in DL related research:

- we want to express something, e.g., that company does not employ idlers;
- this seems to be not possible in a satisfactory way: in contrast to our intuition, Idler was satisfiable w.r.t. $\mathcal{T}'$;
- we extend our DL with a new constructor, e.g., inverse roles.

Please note that the latter involves extending the syntax (i.e., allowing roles r^- in the place of role names r) *and* the semantics (i.e., fixing $(r^-)^{\mathcal{I}}$).

Next, assume we want to restrict the number of companies owned by entrepreneurs to, say, at least 3 and at most 7: so far, we have only said that each entrepreneur owns at least one company in the eighth GCI in Figure 2. Again, we can try hard, e.g., using the following GCI:

$$\text{Entrepreneur} \sqsubseteq \exists \textit{owns}.(\text{Company} \sqcap A) \sqcap$$
$$\exists \textit{owns}.(\text{Company} \sqcap \neg A \sqcap B) \sqcap$$
$$\exists \textit{owns}.(\text{Company} \sqcap \neg A \sqcap \neg B).$$

This will ensure that any instance of Entrepreneur *owns* at least three Companys due to the usage of the mutually contradictory concepts A, $\neg A \sqcap B$, and $\neg A \sqcap \neg B$. It can be shown, however, that we cannot use a similar trick to ensure that an Entrepreneur owns at most seven Companys. As a consequence, *number restrictions* were introduced in DLs:

Definition 9. *For n a non-negative number, r a role name and C a (possibly complex) concept description, a number restriction is a concept description of the form $(\leqslant n\, r.C)$ or $(\geqslant n\, r.C)$. The DLs $\mathcal{ALCQ}$ and $\mathcal{ALCQI}$ are obtained from $\mathcal{ALC}$ and $\mathcal{ALCI}$, respectively, by allowing number restrictions as additional concept forming constructors.*

For an interpretation $\mathcal{I}$, its mapping $\cdot^{\mathcal{I}}$ is extended as follows, where $\#M$ is used to denote the cardinality of a set M:

$$(\leqslant n\, r.C) := \{d \in \Delta^{\mathcal{I}} \mid \#\{e \mid \langle d, e \rangle \in r^{\mathcal{I}} \text{ and } e \in C^{\mathcal{I}}\} \leq n\}$$
$$(\geqslant n\, r.C) := \{d \in \Delta^{\mathcal{I}} \mid \#\{e \mid \langle d, e \rangle \in r^{\mathcal{I}} \text{ and } e \in C^{\mathcal{I}}\} \geq n\}$$

We cordially invite the reader to check, for example, which elements of the example interpretation $\mathcal{I}$ given in Figure 1 are instances of $(\leqslant 2\ \textit{worksFor}.\text{Company})$ or $(\geqslant 2\ \textit{worksFor}.\text{Company})$.

It might seem odd that the presence of number restrictions in a DL is indicated by a $\mathcal{Q}$ in their name: this is due to the fact that these number restrictions are *qualified*, i.e., they allow to restrict the number of r-fillers that are *in the extension of* a concept C. In contrast, *unqualified* number restrictions are of the form $(\leqslant n\, r.\top)$ and $(\geqslant n\, r.\top)$, and thus only allow to restrict the number of r-fillers—regardless of what concept they are an instance of. Traditionally, the presence of unqualified number restrictions in a DL is indicated by an $\mathcal{N}$ in their name, and the letter $\mathcal{Q}$ stands for qualifying number restrictions. For a more detailed description of the naming conventions of DLs, see the appendix of [7].

Next, assume that we want to make use of two roles *sibling* and *partOf* between companies, e.g., in a GCI as follows:

$$\mathcal{T} = \{\text{Company} \sqcap \exists \textit{sibling}.\text{Company} \sqsubseteq \exists \textit{partOf}.\text{Conglomerate}\}$$

Now, after a bit of thinking, we should expect to have the following entailments w.r.t. $\mathcal{T}$:

$$\text{Dodgy} \sqcap \text{Company} \sqcap \exists \textit{sibling}.\text{Company} \sqsubseteq_{\mathcal{T}} \exists \textit{sibling}.\exists \textit{sibling}.\text{Dodgy}$$
$$\text{Conglomerate} \sqcap \exists \textit{partOf}^-.\exists \textit{partOf}^-.\text{Dodgy} \sqsubseteq_{\mathcal{T}} \exists \textit{partOf}^-.\text{Dodgy}$$

The first one should hold because an element d's *sibling*-filler e should have d as a *sibling*-filler, i.e., the extension of the *sibling* should be symmetric. Similarly, the extension of the role *partOf* (and thereby of *partOf*$^-$) should be transitive. However, these two statements are *not* entailed by $\mathcal{T}$. We could add the above statements as GCIs to our TBox $\mathcal{T}$, but still this would not imply, e.g., that

$$\mathsf{Fair} \sqcap \mathsf{Company} \sqcap \exists \textit{sibling}.\mathsf{Company} \sqsubseteq_{\mathcal{T}} \exists \textit{sibling}.\exists \textit{sibling}.\mathsf{Fair},$$

i.e., we would need to add similar GCIs for all relevant concepts in addition to the one for Dodgy. This would obviously "clutter" our TBox $\mathcal{T}$ and still not yield the desired result since we might not be able to foresee which possibly complex concept descriptions might be relevant for a user of $\mathcal{T}$.

To overcome these problems, DLs have been extended with various role inclusions [48,40]: means to express that

- a role is *transitive*, e.g., to capture *hasAncestor* and *partOf*,
- one role is a *sub-role* of another role, e.g., *worksFor* is a sub-role of *involvedWith* and *hasBranch* is a sub-role *partOf*$^-$,
- a role is *symmetric*, which can be done using a combination of inverse and sub-roles: to say, e.g., that *sibling* is symmetric is equivalent to saying that *sibling*$^-$ is a sub-role of *sibling*,
- one role transfers through another one, e.g., the owner of something also owns that thing's parts: this can be achieved using so-called complex role inclusions [40] such as *owns* ∘ *partOf*$^-$ ⊑ *owns* or *hasParent* ∘ *hasBrother* ⊑ *hasUncle*,
- and other statements such as reflexivity and irreflexivity.

For more details on these extensions, please consult [48,40].

The final extension we mention here concerns *nominals*: so far, individual names are restricted to occur in ABox assertions, and thus we make statements "about" individuals, but we cannot use individuals to describe concepts. For example, we can say that the BillG *owns* a Company, but we cannot define the concept of those people working in a company owned by BillG. To overcome this, nominals have been introduced in DLs [66]: roughly speaking, a nominal is an individual name that is used as a concept. For example, if BillG is an individual name, we can say that

$$\mathsf{BillGWorker} \equiv \mathsf{Employee} \sqcap \exists \textit{worksFor}.(\mathsf{Company} \sqcap \exists \textit{owns}^-.\{\mathsf{BillG}\}).$$

Now this definition is inconsistent with the following ABox

$$\begin{aligned} \mathcal{A} = \{ \; &\mathsf{Mary} : \mathsf{BillGWorker} \sqcap \forall \textit{worksFor}.\mathsf{GreatCompany} \; \} \\ &\mathsf{Mike} : \mathsf{BillGWorker} \sqcap \forall \textit{worksFor}.\neg \mathsf{GreatCompany} \\ &\mathsf{BillG} : (\leqslant 1 \; \textit{owns}.\mathsf{Company}) \end{aligned}$$

because BillG owns at most 1 Company, and thus the two BillGWorkers have to work in the same Company, which is not possible since this company cannot be both an instance of GreatCompany and its negation.

As we have seen above, the extension of $\mathcal{ALC}$ with inverse roles and number restrictions is called $\mathcal{ALCQI}$, and the extension of $\mathcal{ALCQI}$ with transitive roles and sub-roles[2] is called $\mathcal{SHIQ}$ [48]. The extension of $\mathcal{SHIQ}$ with nominals is called $\mathcal{SHOIQ}$ [46] and forms the logicical basis of OWL DL—apart from concrete datatypes, which are a restricted form of concrete domains, a topic for which we refer the reader to [8,55]. The extension of $\mathcal{SHOIQ}$ with complex role inclusions mentioned above is called $\mathcal{SROIQ}$ [40] and forms the logicical basis of OWL 1.1, see [33]. We will come back to the relationship between DLs and OWL in Section 7.1.

5 DLs and Other Logics

This section explains the close relationship between DLs and other logics, namely first order logic and modal logic. Due to space limitations, we cannot introduce these logics, and we write this section for readers familiar with one or both of these logics. Also, we concentrate on the basic DL $\mathcal{ALC}$ and some extensions; for a more detailed analysis, see Chapter 4 of [7].

5.1 DLs as Decidable Fragments of First Order logic

Most DLs can be seen as decidable fragments of first-order predicate logic, although some provide operators such as transitive closure of roles or fixpoints that make them decidable fragments of second-order logic [16]. Viewing role names as binary relations and concept names as unary relations, we define two translation functions, π_x and π_y, that inductively map $\mathcal{ALC}$-concepts into first order formulae with one free variable, x or y:

$$\begin{aligned}
\pi_x(A) &:= A(x), & \pi_y(A) &:= A(y),\\
\pi_x(C \sqcap D) &:= \pi_x(C) \wedge \pi_x(D), & \pi_y(C \sqcap D) &:= \pi_y(C) \wedge \pi_y(D),\\
\pi_x(C \sqcup D) &:= \pi_x(C) \vee \pi_x(D), & \pi_y(C \sqcup D) &:= \pi_y(C) \vee \pi_y(D),\\
\pi_x(\exists r.C) &:= \exists y.r(x,y) \wedge \pi_y(C), & \pi_y(\exists r.C) &:= \exists x.r(y,x) \wedge \pi_x(C),\\
\pi_x(\forall r.C) &:= \forall y.r(x,y) \Rightarrow \pi_y(C), & \pi_y(\forall r.C) &:= \forall x.r(y,x) \Rightarrow \pi_x(C).
\end{aligned}$$

To translate a TBox, we observe that a GCI $C \sqsubseteq D$ enforces each instance of C to be an instance of D, i.e., a GCI corresponds to a universally quantified implication and a TBox corresponds to the conjunction of its GCIs. To translate an ABox, we observe that it makes assertions about elements "known by name", i.e., constants. So, we translate a TBox $\mathcal{T}$ and an ABox $\mathcal{A}$ as follows, where $\psi[x/a]$ is the formula obtained from ψ by replacing all free occurrences of x with a:

$$\pi(\mathcal{T}) = \bigwedge_{C \sqsubseteq D \in \mathcal{T}} \forall x.(\pi_x(C) \Rightarrow \pi_x(D))$$

$$\pi(\mathcal{A}) = \bigwedge_{a:C \in \mathcal{A}} \pi_x(C)[x/a] \wedge \bigwedge_{(a,b):r \in \mathcal{A}} r(a,b).$$

---

[2] Sub-role statements are traditionally made in a role hierarchy, which leads to the $\mathcal{H}$ in the DL's name.

This translation preserves the semantics: we can easily view DL interpretations as first order interpretations and, vice versa, first order interpretations as DL interpretations.

Theorem 2. *Let* $(\mathcal{T}, \mathcal{A})$ *be an $\mathcal{ALC}$-knowledge base, C, D possibly complex $\mathcal{ALC}$-concepts, and a an individual name. Then*

1. *$(\mathcal{T}, \mathcal{A})$ is satisfiable iff $\pi(\mathcal{T}) \wedge \pi(\mathcal{A})$ is satisfiable,*
2. *$C \sqsubseteq_{\mathcal{T}} D$ iff $\pi(\mathcal{T}) \Rightarrow \forall x.(\pi_x(C) \Rightarrow \pi_x(D))\})$ is valid, and*
3. *a is an instance of C w.r.t. $(\mathcal{T}, \mathcal{A})$ iff $(\pi(\mathcal{T}) \wedge \pi(\mathcal{A})) \Rightarrow \pi_x(C)[x/a]$ is valid.*

This translation not only provides an alternative way of defining the semantics of $\mathcal{ALC}$, but also tells us that all reasoning problems for $\mathcal{ALC}$ knowledge bases are decidable: the translation of a knowledge base uses only variables x and y, and thus yields a formula in the *two variable fragment of first order logic*, for which satisfiability is known to be decidable in non-deterministic exponential time [32]. Similarly, the translation of a knowledge base uses quantification only in rather restricted way, and therefore yields a formula in the *guarded fragment* [1], for which satisfiability is known to be decidable in deterministic exponential time [30]. As we can see, the exploration of the relationship between DLs and first order logics even gives us upper complexity bounds "for free".

The translation of more expressive DLs may be straightforward, or more difficult, depending on the additional constructs: inverse roles can be captured easily in both the guarded and the two variable fragment by simply swapping the variable places; e.g., $\pi_x(\exists R^-.C) = \exists y.R(y, x) \wedge \pi_y(C)$. Number restrictions can be captured using (in)equality or so-called *counting quantifiers*. It is known that the two-variable fragment with counting quantifiers is still decidable in non-deterministic exponential time [59]. Transitive roles, however, cannot be expressed with two variables only, and the three variable fragment is known to be undecidable. The guarded fragment, when restricted carefully to the so-called *action guarded fragment* [29], can still capture a variety of features such as number restrictions, inverse roles, and fixpoints, while remaining decidable in deterministic exponential time.

5.2   DLs as Cousins of Modal Logic

Description Logics are closely related to Modal Logics, yet they have been developed independently. This close relationship was discovered only rather late [67], and has been exploited quite successfully to transfer complexity and decidability results as well as reasoning techniques [68,24,49,2]. It is not hard to see that $\mathcal{ALC}$-concepts can be viewed as syntactical variants of formula of multi modal $\mathbf{K_{(m)}}$: Kripke structures can easily be viewed as DL interpretations and, vice versa, DL interpretations as Kripke structures; we can then view concept names as propositional variables, and role names as modal parameters, and realize this correspondence through the mapping π as follows:

$$\pi(A) := A, \text{ for concepts names } A$$

$$\pi(C \sqcap D) := \pi(C) \wedge \pi(D),$$
$$\pi(C \sqcup D) := \pi(C) \vee \pi(D),$$
$$\pi(\neg C) := \neg\pi(C),$$
$$\pi(\forall r.C) := [r]\pi(C),$$
$$\pi(\exists r.C) := \langle r \rangle \pi(C).$$

Now, the translation of DL knowledge bases is slightly more tricky: a TBox $\mathcal{T}$ is satisfied only in those structures where, for each $C \sqsubseteq D$, $\neg\pi(C) \vee \pi(D)$ holds *globally*, i.e., in each world of our Kripke structure (or equivalently, in each element of our interpretation domain). We can express this using the universal modality, that is, a special modal parameter U that is interpreted as the total accessbility relation in all Kripke structures.

Theorem 3. *Let $\mathcal{T}$ be an $\mathcal{ALC}$-TBox and E, F possibly complex $\mathcal{ALC}$-concepts. Then*

1. *F is satisfiable iff $\pi(F)$ is satisfiable,*
2. *F is satisfiable w.r.t. $\mathcal{T}$ iff $\pi(F) \wedge \bigwedge_{C \sqsubseteq D \in \mathcal{T}} [U](\pi(C) \Rightarrow \pi(D))$ is satisfiable,*
3. *$E \sqsubseteq_{\mathcal{T}} F$ iff $\bigwedge_{C \sqsubseteq D \in \mathcal{T}} [U](\pi(C) \Rightarrow \pi(D)) \Rightarrow (\pi(E) \Rightarrow \pi(F))$ is valid.*

Like TBoxes, ABoxes do not have a direct correspondence in modal logic, but they can be seen as a special case of a modal logic constructor, namely *nominals* [3], which is where the DL nominals got their name from. In contrast to nominals in DLs, in modal logics, nominals tend to come with additional operators, e.g., the @ operator.

6   Tableau-Based Reasoning Algorithms

For several expressive DLs, there exist efficient implementations of the reasoning services described in Section 3 [39,36,70,50,56], most of which are tableau-based. For an extensive survey of tableau algorithms for description logics, see, e.g., [10]. In the following, we will give an intuitive description of description logic tableau algorithms, and we invite the reader to generate some illustrations of our explanations while reading them, similar to the illustration given in Figure 1. In general, these algorithms work on trees whose nodes stand for elements of an interpretation domain, and the input is assumed to be in negation normal form.[3] Nodes are labelled with sets of concepts, namely those they are assumed to be an instance of. Edges between nodes are labelled with role names or sets of role names, namely those that hold between the corresponding elements.

Intuitively, to decide the satisfiability of a concept C, a tableau algorithm starts with an instance x_0 of C, i.e., a tree consisting of a root node x_0 only

---

[3] A concept is in negation normal form if negation occurs in front of concept names only. It is not hard to see that each concept can be transformed into an equivalent one in negation normal form by pushing negation inwards, using de Morgan's rules and the duality between existential and universal restrictions.

with C as its node label (written $\mathcal{L}(x_0) = \{C\}$). Then the algorithm breaks down concepts in node labels syntactically, thus inferring new constraints on the model of C to be built, and possibly generating new elements, i.e., new nodes. In general, a tableau algorithm employs a set of *completion rules*, and often it uses one such completion rules per syntactic construct. For example, the completion rules for $\sqcap$, $\exists$, and $\forall$ roughly work as follows:

($\sqcap$) if it finds a conjunction $D \sqcap E \in \mathcal{L}(y)$, it adds both D and E to $\mathcal{L}(y)$;

($\exists$) if it finds $\exists r.F \in \mathcal{L}(y)$, it generates a new r-successor node of y, say z, and sets $\mathcal{L}(z) = \{F\}$;

($\forall$) if a node y has some r-successor z and it finds $\forall r.G \in \mathcal{L}(y)$, then it adds G to $\mathcal{L}(z)$.

In the presence of a TBox $\mathcal{T}$, we can employ a rule that adds, for each GCI $C_i \sqsubseteq D_i \in \mathcal{T}$, and for each node y, the (negation normal form of the) concept $(\neg C_i \sqcup D_i)$ to $\mathcal{L}(y)$. Now, for logics with disjunctions, various tableau algorithms non-deterministically choose whether to add D or E to $\mathcal{L}(y)$ for $(D \sqcup E) \in \mathcal{L}(y)$. The answer behaviour is as follows: if this "completion" can be carried out exhaustively without encountering a node with both a concept and its negation in its label—a so-called *clash*—then the algorithm answers that the input concept was satisfiable, and unsatisfiable, otherwise.

Since we are talking about decision procedures, *termination* is an important issue. Even though tableau algorithms for some DLs terminate "automatically", this is not the case for more expressive ones. For example, consider the algorithm sketched above on the input concept A and TBox $\{A \sqsubseteq \exists r.A\}$: it would create an infinite r-chain of nodes with labels $\{A, \exists r.A\}$. To guarantee termination, the tableau algorithm needs to be stopped explicitly. Intuitively, the processing of an element z is stopped if all "relevant" concepts in the label of z are also present in the label of an "older" element z'. In this case, z' is said to *block* z. The definition of "relevant" has to be chosen carefully since it is crucial for the correctness of the algorithm [9,47,48] and for the efficiency of the implementation [44,37].

Correctness of DL tableau algorithms are often proved as follows: first, termination is proved by showing that the algorithm builds a (tree) structure of bounded size in a monotonic manner. Soundness is proved by constructing a model (or an abstraction of a model) of the input concept (and TBox) in case that the algorithm stops without having generated a clash. If a blocking situation has occurred, this often yields either a finite, cyclic model or an "unravelled" infinite tree model (or an abstraction thereof). Completeness can be proved by using a model of the input concept and TBox to steer the application of the non-deterministic rules and proving that no clash occurs using this control.

In the tableau sketched above and in various other tableau algorithms, disjunction is treated non-deterministically. When implementing tableau algorithms or designing an optimal tableau algorithm for a logic that is complete for a deterministic complexity class, this non-determinism has to be circumvented. A natural solution is back-tracking and its various optimisations such as dependency-directed back-jumping. For DLs, a variety of optimisations have been developed that concern all aspects of the algorithm, including pre-processing, early clash-detection, partial mode re-use, etc., see [39,48,35,36,44] for descriptions of these optimisations.

7 DLs, OWL, and Rules

In this section, we very briefly review the relationship between DLs and OWL and DLs and rules. We do not present any details, but merely point the reader to the relevant literature.

7.1 DLs and OWL

The Semantic Web Ontology Language OWL[4] comes in three increasingly expressive flavours, namly OWL Lite, OWL DL, and OWL Full. The first two flavours are based on DLs: OWL Lite is based on the DL $\mathcal{SHIN}(D)$, which is the extension of $\mathcal{ALC}$ with inverse roles, unqualified number restrictions, transitive roles, role hierarchies, and datatypes, and OWL Lite is based on the DL $\mathcal{SHOIQ}(D)$, which is the further extension with qualified number restrictions and nominals [43].

In Table 1, we present some OWL constructors and their DL counterparts.

Table 1. OWL constructors

Constructor	DL Syntax	Example
intersectionOf	$C_1 \sqcap \ldots \sqcap C_n$	Human $\sqcap$ Male
unionOf	$C_1 \sqcup \ldots \sqcup C_n$	Doctor $\sqcup$ Lawyer
complementOf	$\neg C$	$\neg$Male
oneOf	$\{x_1 \ldots x_n\}$	{john, mary}
allValuesFrom	$\forall P.C$	$\forall$hasChild.Doctor
someValuesFrom	$\exists r.C$	$\exists$hasChild.Lawyer
hasValue	$\exists r.\{x\}$	$\exists$citizenOf.{USA}
minCardinality	$\geqslant nr$	$\geqslant$2hasChild
maxCardinality	$\leqslant nr$	$\leqslant$1hasChild
inverseOf	r^-	hasChild$^-$

An important feature of OWL is that, besides "abstract" classes, i.e., those that correspond to DL concepts, one can also use XML Schema *datatypes* (e.g., string, decimal and float) in someValuesFrom, allValuesFrom, and hasValue restrictions. E.g., the class Adult could be asserted to be equivalent to Person $\sqcap$ $\exists$age.over17, where over17 is an XML Schema datatype based on decimal, but with the added restriction that values must be at least 18. This is a rather restricted form of what is known in DLs as *concrete domains* [8]. In addition to XML Schema, OWL makes use of RDF,[5] the W3C base for the Semantic Web, to state some basic facts. Using these building blocks, the class Adult could be written as:

---

[4] http://www.w3.org/2004/OWL/

[5] See http://www.w3.org/RDF/

```
<xsd:simpleType name="over17">
  <xsd:restriction base="xsd:positiveInteger">
  <xsd:minInclusive value="18"/>
  </xsd:restriction>
</xsd:simpleType>

<owl:Class rdf:ID="Adult">
  <owl:intersectionOf rdf:parseType="Collection">
    <owl:Class rdf:about="#Person"/>
    <owl:Restriction>
      <owl:onProperty rdf:resource="#age"/>
      <owl:someValuesFrom rdf:resource="#over17"/>
    </owl:Restriction>
  </owl:intersectionOf>
</owl:Class>
```

Table 2. OWL axioms

Axiom	DL Syntax	Example
subClassOf	$C_1 \sqsubseteq C_2$	Human $\sqsubseteq$ Animal $\sqcap$ Biped
equivalentClass	$C_1 \equiv C_2$	Man $\equiv$ Human $\sqcap$ Male
subPropertyOf	$P_1 \sqsubseteq P_2$	hasDaughter $\sqsubseteq$ hasChild
equivalentProperty	$P_1 \equiv P_2$	cost $\equiv$ price
disjointWith	$C_1 \sqsubseteq \neg C_2$	Male $\sqsubseteq$ ¬Female
sameAs	$\{x_1\} \equiv \{x_2\}$	{President_Bush} $\equiv$ {G_W_Bush}
differentFrom	$\{x_1\} \sqsubseteq \neg\{x_2\}$	{john} $\sqsubseteq$ ¬{peter}
TransitiveProperty	$P \in \mathbf{R}_+$	hasAncestor$^+$ $\in \mathbf{R}_+$
FunctionalProperty	$\top \sqsubseteq {\leqslant}1P$	$\top \sqsubseteq {\leqslant}1$hasMother
InverseFunctionalProperty	$\top \sqsubseteq {\leqslant}1P^-$	$\top \sqsubseteq {\leqslant}1$isMotherOf$^-$
SymmetricProperty	$P \equiv P^-$	isSiblingOf $\equiv$ isSiblingOf$^-$

The OWL counterpart of a DL knowledge base is called an *ontology* and consists of a set of axioms. A DL knowledge base further distinguishes between a TBox to contain "class-level" statements and an ABox to contain "individual-level" statements, but an OWL ontology does not make this distinction. In Table 2, we give some OWL axioms together with their DL counterparts.

7.2   DLs and Rules

As we have seen, most DLs are *decidable* fragments of first-order logic, as are decidable rule-based formalisms such as function-free Horn rules. The reason for why these families of logics are decidable are, however, quite different. Like modal logics, most DLs enjoy some form of *tree model property* [31,75], that is, every satisfiable concept or knowledge base has a model whose relational structure is tree shaped.[6] This is not to say that it does not have other, non-tree shaped models, yet it tells us that we can concentrate on tree-shaped ones in algorithms to decide satisfiability. In contrast, function-free Horn rules are decidable because they lack existential quantification (and thus full negation) and therefore can be said to have a (very) *small model property*: a satisfiable set of such rules has a model whose elements all occur explicitly (i.e., as individual names) in the rule set. The relational structure of models, however, cannot be restricted. In contrast to the *open world assumption* of DLs mentioned in Section 2, many rule-based formalisms employ the so-called *closed world assumption*, i.e., if a statement α does not follow from a given knowledge base, then we assume that its negation $\mathsf{not}\,\alpha$ is true—which is closely related to "negation as failure". Please note that the use of negation as failure in rule bodies leads to a non-monotonic logic: e.g., consider the rule $\mathsf{not}\,\alpha \wedge \beta \rightarrow \gamma$ which, together with the (only) fact β, implies γ. Now, if we add α to our fact base, we can no longer infer γ. Hence learning more (facts) might lead to fewer deductions, which is why this kind of logic is called non-monotonic. In the AI literature, various forms of non-monotonic formalisms have been investigated, including circumscription, negation as failure, and defaults; see, e.g., [65] for an overview.

There are various reasons for combining DLs with rules, some of which indeed require such a combinations, other that can be (partially) adressed within DLs:

- we want to add a form of non-monotonicity to DLs, e.g., in the form we find in logic programs with negation as failure [28]: this has been discussed, e.g., in [12,25],
- we want to express epistemic queries over our DL knowledge base: this allows for a form of closed-world reasoning over a knowledge base that is weaker than the one in the item above and has been adressed, e.g., in [19],
- we want to increase DLs' expressive power to be stronger when it comes to role operators: this has motivated the design of the DLs $\mathcal{RIQ}$ and $\mathcal{SROIQ}$ [45,40] and influence the design of OWL 1.1 [33], yet these DLs still impose certain syntactic restrictions so as to to remain decidable,
- we want to express integrity constraints [62], i.e., constrain the form of assertions in our ABox: this has been discussed, e.g., in [25,19,41].

In the last decade, various combinations of DLs with rules have been proposed [54,26,63,58,64,27,42]. To retain decidability, such a combination has to be restricted [54,58], yet there are various options for these restrictions. First decidable (and undecidable) combinations are described in [54,26] and, recently, these approaches have been generalised to more powerful settings in so-called (weakly) DL-safe rules [58,57]. In this combination, concepts and roles are allowed to occur in both rule bodies and heads as unary, respectively binary predicates in atoms, but each variable of a rule is required to occur in some body literal whose predicate is neither a concept nor a role. Roughly speaking, this condition makes

---

[6] In fact, in the presence of ABoxes, we rather have "forest shaped" than "tree shaped", and in the presence of transitive roles, we rather have "with a tree skeleton".

rules applicable only to known individuals, i.e., those that are mentioned explicitly in the knowledge base. This preserves satisfiability even for more expressive, non-monotonic rule formalisms such as hybrid MKNF knowledge bases [57]. Another approach is the one followed in the DL-programs approach [27]: there, non-monotonic logic programs (that are read with answer set or well-founded semantics) can contain queries to a DL knowledge base in rule bodies. Even though information can "flow" from rules to the DL knowledge base and back, this information flow is limited in scope, basically because the semantics of this combination is defined in such a way that the rule set and the DL knowledge do not "operate" on the same interpretation domain.

8   Last Words

We have tried to give a brief overview of some notions in DLs and thus had to leave out numerous interesting aspects such as other historical and philosophical aspects, other reasoning techniques, non-standard inference problems, other applications of DLs, other extensions and restrictions of DLs, results and techniques concerning the computational complexity, etc. There is a rather large amount of literature available, and we only want to mention a few that we find helpful as a starting point:

- the Description Logic web page at `http://dl.kr.org/` with interesting links, e.g., to the DL workshop series and their proceedings, most of which are available on-line;
- the DL Handbook [7];
- some articles that provide an overview over a larger aspect: [21] describes how DLs can be applied to reason about database conceptual models, [55] provides an overview of concrete domains in DLs, [10] provides an overview of tableau algorithms in DLs, [4] provides an overview of temporal extension to DLs.

References

1. Andréka, H., van Benthem, J., Németi, I.: Modal languages and bounded fragments of predicate logic. Journal of Philosophical Logic 27(3), 217–274 (1998)
2. Areces, C.: Logic Engineering. The Case of Description and Hybrid Logics. PhD thesis, ILLC, University of Amsterdam (2000)
3. Areces, C., Blackburn, P., Marx, M.: A road-map on complexity for hybrid logics. In: Flum, J., Rodríguez-Artalejo, M. (eds.) CSL 1999. LNCS, vol. 1683, pp. 307–321. Springer, Heidelberg (1999)
4. Artale, A., Franconi, E.: A survey of temporal extensions of description logics. Annals of Mathematics and Artificial Intelligence 30(1-4), 171–210 (2000)
5. Baader, F.: A formal definition for the expressive power of terminological knowledge representation languages. Journal of Logic and Computation 6(1), 33–54 (1996)
6. Baader, F., Brandt, S., Küsters, R.: Matching under side conditions in description logics. In: Nebel, B. (ed.) Proc. of the 17th Int. Joint Conf. on Artificial Intelligence (IJCAI-01), Seattle, Washington, pp. 213–218. Morgan Kaufmann, Los Altos (2001)

7. Baader, F., Calvanese, D., McGuinness, D., Nardi, D., Patel-Schneider, P.F. (eds.): The Description Logic Handbook: Theory, Implementation, and Applications. Cambridge University Press, Cambridge (2003)

8. Baader, F., Hanschke, P.: A schema for integrating concrete domains into concept languages. In: Proc. of the 12th Int. Joint Conf. on Artificial Intelligence (IJCAI-91), Sydney, pp. 452–457 (1991)

9. Baader, F., Sattler, U.: Expressive number restrictions in description logics. Journal of Logic and Computation 9(3), 319–350 (1999)

10. Baader, F., Sattler, U.: An overview of tableau algorithms for description logics. TABLEAUX 2000 69, 5–40 (2000) An abridged version appeared in Tableaux 2000, vol. 1847 of LNAI, 2000. Springer-Verlag

11. Baader, F., Turhan, A.-Y.: On the problem of computing small representations of least common subsumers. In: Jarke, M., Koehler, J., Lakemeyer, G. (eds.) KI 2002. LNCS (LNAI), vol. 2479, Springer, Heidelberg (2002)

12. Baader, F., Hollunder, B.: How to prefer more specific defaults in terminological default logic. In: Proc. of the 13th Int. Joint Conf. on Artificial Intelligence (IJCAI-93), Chambery, France, pp. 669–674. Morgan Kaufmann, Los Altos (1993)

13. Bechhofer, S., Horrocks, I., Goble, C., Stevens, R.: OilEd: a reason-able ontology editor for the semantic web. In: Proc. of the 2001 Description Logic Workshop (DL 2001), pp. 1–9. CEUR (2001), http://ceur-ws.org/

14. Berners-Lee, T., Hendler, J., Lassila, O.: The semantic Web. Scientific American 284(5), 34–43 (2001)

15. Bodenreider, O., Stevens, R.: Bio-ontologies: current trends and future directions. Briefings in Bioinformatics 7(3), 256–274 (2006)

16. Borgida, A.: On the relative expressive power of Description Logics and Predicate Calculus. Artificial Intelligence Journal 82(1) (1996)

17. Borst, P., Akkermans, H., Top, J.: Engineering ontologies. International Journal of Human-Computer Studies 46, 365–406 (1997)

18. Brandt, S., Küsters, R., Turhan, A.-Y.: Approximation and difference in description logics. In: Fensel, D., Giunchiglia, F., McGuiness, D., Williams, M.-A. (eds.) Proc. of the 8th Int. Conf. on the Principles of Knowledge Representation and Reasoning (KR-02), pp. 203–214. Morgan Kaufmann, Los Altos (2002)

19. Calvanese, D., De Giacomo, G., Lembo, D., Lenzerini, M., Rosati, R.: Epistemic first-order queries over description logic knowledge bases. In: Proc. of the 2006 Description Logic Workshop (DL 2006). CEUR (2006)

20. Calvanese, D., De Giacomo, G., Lenzerini, M., Nardi, D.: Reasoning in expressive description logics. In: Robinson, A., Voronkov, A. (eds.) Handbook of Automated Reasoning, Elsevier Science Publishers (North-Holland), Amsterdam (2001)

21. Calvanese, D., Lenzerini, M., Nardi, D.: Description logics for conceptual data modeling. In: Chomicki, J., Saake, G. (eds.) Logics for Databases and Information Systems, pp. 229–263. Kluwer Academic Publishers, Dordrecht (1998)

22. Cuenca Grau, B., Horrocks, I., Kazakov, Y., Sattler, U.: Just the right amount: Extracting modules from ontologies. In: Proc. of the Sixteenth International World Wide Web Conference (WWW2007) (to appear)

23. De Giacomo, G.: Decidability of Class-Based Knowledge Representation Formalisms. PhD thesis, Università degli Studi di Roma "La Sapienza" (1995)

24. De Giacomo, G., Lenzerini, M.: Boosting the correspondence between description logics and propositional dynamic logics (extended abstract). In: Proc. of the 12th Nat. Conf. on Artificial Intelligence (AAAI-94), AAAI Press, Stanford, California, USA (1994)

25. Donini, F., Nardi, D., Rosati, R.: Description logics of minimal knowledge and negation as failure. ACM Trans. Comput. Log. 3(2), 177–225 (2002)
26. Donini, F.M., Lenzerini, M., Nardi, D., Schaerf, A.: AL-log: Integrating Datalog and Description Logics. J. of Intelligent Information Systems 10(3), 227–252 (1998)
27. Eiter, T., Lukasiewicz, T., Schindlauer, R., Tompits, H.: Combining answer set programming with description logics for the semantic web. In: Proc. of the 9th Int. Conf. on the Principles of Knowledge Representation and Reasoning (KR-04), pp. 141–151 (2004)
28. Gelfond, M., Lifschitz, V.: The stable model semantics for logic programming. In: Kowalski, R., Bowen, K. (eds.) Proc. of the 5th Int. Conf. on Logic Programming, pp. 1070–1080. The MIT Press, Cambridge (1988)
29. Gonçalvès, E., Grädel, E.: Decidability issues for action guarded logics. In: Proc. of the 2000 Description Logic Workshop (DL 2000), pp. 123–132. CEUR (2000), http://ceur-ws.org/
30. Grädel, E.: On the restraining power of guards. Journal of Symbolic Logic 64(4), 1719–1742 (1999)
31. Grädel, E.: Why are modal logics so robustly decidable. In: Paun, G. Rozenberg, G., Salomaa, A. (eds.) Current Trends in Theoretical Computer Science. Entering the 21st Century, pp. 393–408. World Scientific (2001)
32. Grädel, E., Kolaitis, P., Vardi, M.: On the Decision Problem for Two-Variable First-Order Logic. Bulletin of Symbolic Logic 3, 53–69 (1997)
33. Cuenca Grau, B., Horrocks, I., Parsia, B., Patel-Schneider, P., Sattler, U.: Next steps for owl. In: Proc. of OWL: Experiences and Directions. CEUR (2006), http://ceur-ws.org/
34. Gruber, T.R.: Towards Principles for the Design of Ontologies Used for Knowledge Sharing. In: Guarino, N., Poli, R. (eds.) Formal Ontology in Conceptual Analysis and Knowledge Representation, Deventer, The Netherlands, Kluwer Academic Publishers, Dordrecht (1993)
35. Haarslev, V., Möller, R.: Consistency testing: The RACE experience. In: Dyckhoff, R. (ed.) TABLEAUX 2000. LNCS, vol. 1847, pp. 1–18. Springer, Heidelberg (2000)
36. Haarslev, V., Möller, R.: RACER system description. In: Goré, R.P., Leitsch, A., Nipkow, T. (eds.) IJCAR 2001. LNCS (LNAI), vol. 2083, Springer, Heidelberg (2001)
37. Hladik, J.: Implementation and optimisation of a tableau algorithm for the guarded fragment. In: Egly, U., Fermüller, C. (eds.) TABLEAUX 2002. LNCS (LNAI), vol. 2381, Springer, Heidelberg (2002)
38. Horridge, M., Tsarkov, D.: Supporting early adoption of OWL 1.1 with Protege-OWL and FaCT++. In: Proc. of OWL: Experiences and Directions. CEUR (2006), http://ceur-ws.org/
39. Horrocks, I.: Using an Expressive Description Logic: FaCT or Fiction? In: Proc. of the 6th Int. Conf. on the Principles of Knowledge Representation and Reasoning (KR-98), Morgan Kaufmann, Los Altos (1998)
40. Horrocks, I., Kutz, O., Sattler, U.: The even more irresistible $\mathcal{SROIQ}$. In: Proc. of the 10th International Conference of Knowledge Representation and Reasoning (KR-2006), Morgan Kaufmann, Los Altos (2006)
41. Horrocks, I., Motik, B., Sattler, U.: Bridging the gap between owl and relational databases. In: Proc. of the Sixteenth International World Wide Web Conference (WWW, 2007) (to appear)
42. Horrocks, I., Patel-Schneider, P.F.: A Proposal for an OWL Rules Language. In: Proc. of the Thirteenth Int'l World Wide Web Conf. (WWW 2004), ACM, New York (2004)

43. Horrocks, I., Patel-Schneider, P.F., van Harmelen, F.: From SHIQ and RDF to OWL: The making of a web ontology language, vol. 1(1). John Wiley & Sons, Chichester (2003)

44. Horrocks, I., Sattler, U.: Optimised reasoning for $\mathcal{SHIQ}$. In: Proc. of the 15th European Conf. on Artificial Intelligence (ECAI 2002) (2002)

45. Horrocks, I., Sattler, U.: Decidability of SHIQ with complex role inclusion axioms. In: Proc. of the 18th Int. Joint Conf. on Artificial Intelligence (IJCAI-03), Morgan Kaufmann, Los Altos (2003)

46. Horrocks, I., Sattler, U.: A tableau decision procedure for $\mathcal{SHOIQ}$. Journal of Automated Reasoning, (2006) (to appear)

47. Horrocks, I., Sattler, U., Tobies, S.: Practical reasoning for expressive description logics. In: Ganzinger, H., McAllester, D., Voronkov, A. (eds.) LPAR 1999. LNCS, vol. 1705, pp. 161–180. Springer, Heidelberg (1999)

48. Horrocks, I., Sattler, U., Tobies, S.: Practical reasoning for very expressive description logics. Logic Journal of the IGPL 8(3), 239–264 (2000)

49. Horrocks, I., Patel-Schneider, P.F.: Optimising propositional modal satisfiability for description logic subsumption. In: Calmet, J., Plaza, J. (eds.) AISC 1998. LNCS (LNAI), vol. 1476, Springer, Heidelberg (1998)

50. Hustadt, U., Schmidt, R.A.: Issues of decidability for description logics in the framework of resolution. In: Caferra, R., Salzer, G. (eds.) Automated Deduction in Classical and Non-Classical Logics. LNCS (LNAI), vol. 1761, pp. 191–205. Springer, Heidelberg (2000)

51. Kalyanpur, A., Parsia, B., Sirin, E., Cuenca-Grau, B., Hendler, J.: Swoop: A 'Web' ontology editing browser, vol. 4(2). John Wiley & Sons, Chichester (2005)

52. Kalyanpur, A., Parsia, B., Sirin, E., Hendler, J.: Debugging unsatisfiable classes in owl ontologies, vol. 3(4). John Wiley & Sons, Chichester (2005)

53. Küsters, R.: Non-Standard Inferences in Description Logics. In: Küsters, R. (ed.) Non-Standard Inferences in Description Logics. LNCS (LNAI), vol. 2100, Springer, Heidelberg (2001)

54. Levy, A.Y., Rousset, M.-C.: Combining Horn rules and description logics in CARIN. Artificial Intelligence 104(1-2), 165–209 (1998)

55. Lutz, C.: Description logics with concrete domains—a survey. In: Advances in Modal Logics, vol. 4, World Scientific Publishing Co. Pte. Ltd. (2003)

56. Motik, B.: Reasoning in Description Logics using Resolution and Deductive Databases. PhD thesis, Universität Karlsruhe (TH) (2006)

57. Motik, B., Rosati, R.: A faithful integration of description logics with logic programming. In: Proc. of the 20th Int. Joint Conf. on Artificial Intelligence (IJCAI-07), pp. 477–482 (2007)

58. Motik, B., Sattler, U., Studer, R.: Query answering for OWL-DL with rules, vol. 3(1), pp. 41–60. John Wiley & Sons, Chichester (2005)

59. Pacholski, L., Szwast, W., Tendera, L.: Complexity results for first-order two-variable logic with counting. SIAM Journal of Computing 29(4), 1083–1117 (2000)

60. Protégé (2003) Homepage at http://protege.stanford.edu/

61. Rector, A., Horrocks, I.: Experience building a large, re-usable medical ontology using a description logic with transitivity and concept inclusions. In: Proc. of the WS on Ontological Engineering, AAAI Spring Symposium (AAAI'97), AAAI Press, Stanford, California, USA (1997)

62. Reiter, R.: What should a database know? Journal of Logic Programming 14, 127–153 (1990)

63. Rosati, R.: Towards expressive KR systems integrating datalog and description logics: preliminary report. In: Proc. of the 1999 Description Logic Workshop (DL'99). CEUR (1999), http://ceur-ws.org/

64. Rosati, R.: Dl+log: Tight integration of description logics and disjunctive datalog. In: Proc. of the 10th Int. Conf. on the Principles of Knowledge Representation and Reasoning (KR-06), pp. 68–78 (2006)

65. Russell, S., Norvig, P.: Artificial Intelligence. A Modern Approach. Prentice-Hall, Englewood Cliffs (1995)

66. Schaerf, A.: Reasoning with individuals in concept languages. Data and Knowledge Engineering 13(2), 141–176 (1994)

67. Schild, K.: A correspondence theory for terminological logics: Preliminary report. In: Proc. of the 12th Int. Joint Conf. on Artificial Intelligence (IJCAI-91), Sydney, pp. 466–471 (1991)

68. Schild, K.: Terminological cycles and the propositional μ-calculus. In: Doyle, J., Sandewall, E., Torasso, P. (eds.) Proc. of the 4th Int. Conf. on the Principles of Knowledge Representation and Reasoning (KR-94), Bonn, pp. 509–520. Morgan Kaufmann, Los Altos (1994)

69. Schmidt Schauß, M., Smolka, G.: Attributive concept descriptions with complements. Artificial Intelligence 48(1), 1–26 (1991)

70. Sirin, E., Parsia, B., Cuenca Grau, B., Kalyanpur, A., Katz, Y.: Pellet: A practical owl-dl reasoner. John Wiley & Sons, Chichester (to appear)

71. Spackman, K.A.: Managing clinical terminology hierarchies using algorithmic calculation of subsumption: Experience with SNOMED-RT. Journal of the American Medical Informatics Association, Fall Symposium Special Issue (2000)

72. Stevens, R., Horrocks, I., Goble, C., Bechhofer, S.: Building a bioinformatics ontology using OIL. IEEE Information Technology in Biomedicine. special issue on Bioinformatics. 6(2), 135–141 (2002)

73. Sure, Y., Staab, S., Angele, J.: OntoEdit: Guiding ontology development by methodology and inferencing. In: Meersman, R., Tari, Z., et al. (eds.) CoopIS 2002, DOA 2002, and ODBASE 2002. LNCS, vol. 2519, Springer, Heidelberg (2002)

74. Uschold, M., King, M., Moralee, S., Zorgios, Y.: The enterprise ontology. The Knowledge Engineering Review 13 (1998)

75. Vardi, M.Y.: Why is modal logic so robustly decidable? In: Immerman, N., Kolaitis, P.G. (eds.) Descriptive Complexity and Finite Models. DIMACS: Series in Discrete Mathematics and Theoretical Computer Science, vol. 31, American Mathematical Society (1997)

76. Wolstencroft, K., Brass, A., Horrocks, I., Lord, P., Sattler, U., Turi, D., Stevens, R.: A little semantic web goes a long way in biology. In: Gil, Y., Motta, E., Benjamins, V.R., Musen, M.A. (eds.) ISWC 2005. LNCS, vol. 3729, Springer, Heidelberg (2005)

Reactive Rules on the Web

Bruno Berstel[1], Philippe Bonnard[1], François Bry[2], Michael Eckert[2],
and Paula-Lavinia Pătrânjan[2]

[1] ILOG
9, rue de Verdun, 94250 Gentilly, France
{berstel,bonnard}@ilog.fr — http://www.ilog.com
[2] University of Munich, Institute for Informatics
Oettingenstr. 67, 80538 München, Germany
{bry,eckert,patranjan}@pms.ifi.lmu.de — http://www.pms.ifi.lmu.de

Abstract. *Reactive rules* are used for programming rule-based, reactive systems, which have the ability to detect events and respond to them automatically in a timely manner. Such systems are needed on the Web for bridging the gap between the existing, passive Web, where data sources can only be accessed to obtain information, and the dynamic Web, where data sources are enriched with reactive behavior. This paper presents two possible approaches to programming rule-based, reactive systems. They are based on different kinds of reactive rules, namely *Event-Condition-Action rules* and *production rules*. Concrete reactive languages of both kinds are used to exemplify these programming paradigms. Finally the similarities and differences between these two paradigms are studied.

1 Introduction

Reactivity on the Web, the ability to detect events and respond to them automatically in a timely manner, is needed for bridging the gap between the existing, passive Web, where data sources can only be accessed to obtain information, and the dynamic Web, where data sources are enriched with reactive behavior. Reactivity is a broad notion that spans Web applications such as e-commerce platforms that react to user input (e.g., putting an item into the shopping basket), Web Services that react to notifications or service requests (e.g., SOAP messages), and distributed Web information systems that react to updates in other systems elsewhere on the Web (e.g., update propagation among biological Web databases).

The issue of enriching (relational or object-oriented) database systems with reactive features has been largely discussed in the literature and software solutions (called active database systems) have been employed for some years by now. Differences between (generally centralized) active databases and the Web, where a central clock, a central management are missing and new data formats (such as XML and RDF) are used, give reasons for developing new approaches. Moreover, approaches that cope with existing and upcoming Semantic Web technologies (by gradually evolving together with these technologies) are more likely

G. Antoniou et al. (Eds.): Reasoning Web 2007, LNCS 4636, pp. 183–239, 2007.

to leverage the Semantic Web endeavor. Along this line, of crucial importance for the Web is the usability of (Semantic) Web technologies that should be approachable also by users with little programming experience.

The rule-based approach to realizing reactivity on the Web is discussed in this lecture as an example of an easy to use (Semantic) Web technology. Compared with general purpose programming languages and frameworks, rule-based programming brings in declarativity, fine-grain modularity, and higher abstraction. Moreover, modern rule-based frameworks add natural-language-like syntax and support for the life cycle of rules. All these features make it easier to write, understand, and maintain rule-based applications, including for non-technical users.

The *Event-Condition-Action (ECA) rules* and *production rules* fall into the category of *reactive rules*, which are used for programming rule-based, reactive systems. In addition to the inherent benefits of rule-based programming mentioned above, the interest of reactive rules and rule-based technology for the Web is underlined by the current activity within W3C working groups on these subjects.[1]

Due to the emphasis they put on events, ECA rules have traditionally been used in reactive systems such as telecommunication network management. As such, they are well-suited for the reactive, event-based aspect of (distributed) Web applications. Production rules originate from non-monotonous expert systems, where they were used to encode the behavior of a system based on domain-specific knowledge. This makes them relevant to address the stateful, expertise-based aspect of (higher-end) Web applications.

ECA rules have the structure *ON Event IF Condition DO Action* and specify to execute the *Action* automatically when the *Event* happens, provided the *Condition* holds. Production rules are of the form *WHEN Condition DO Action* and specify to execute the *Action* if an update to the (local) data base makes the *Condition* true. This shows that the similarities in the structure of these two kinds of rules come with similarities, but also some differences, in the semantics of the two rule paradigms.

Since most Web applications have both an event-based and an expertise-based aspect, and because the two paradigms are semantically close to each other, Web applications can choose one paradigm or the other, depending on where they put the emphasis. They can also leverage the advantages of both, by choosing to implement a part of their logic using ECA rules, and another part using production rules.

This paper provides an introduction to programming Web systems with reactive rules, by discussing concrete reactive languages of both kinds, thus trying to reveal differences and similarities between the two paradigms. To illustrate the two approaches to realizing reactive behavior, the ECA rules language XChange and the ILOG Rule Language (IRL) have been chosen. XChange is an ongoing research project at the University of Munich and part of the work in the Network

---

[1] The W3C Rule Interchange Format Working Group is chartered to develop a format for rules that should enable rules to be translated between different rule systems, http://www.w3.org/2005/rules/wg.html

of Excellence REWERSE[2] (Reasoning on the Web with Rules and Semantics), which is a research project mainly funded by the European Commission. IRL is a production rule language marketed by ILOG[3] as part of their production rules system ILOG JRules.

2   Reactive Behavior on the Web: Application Examples

The Web has traditionally been perceived as a distributed repository of hypermedia documents and data sources with clients (in general browsers) that retrieve documents and data, and servers that store them. Although reflecting a widespread use of the Web, this perception is not accurate.

With the emergence of Web applications, Web Services, and Web 2.0, the Web has become much more dynamic. Such Web nodes (applications, sites, services, agents, etc.) constantly react to events bringing new information or making existing information outdated and change the content of data sources. Programming such reactive behavior entails (1) detecting situations that require a reaction and (2) responding with an appropriate state-changing action [BE06b].

We present in this section several application example of such reactive behavior on the Web.

2.1   Distributed Information Portal

Many data sources on the Web are evolving in the sense that they change their content over time in reaction to events bringing new information or making existing information outdated. Often, such changes must be mirrored in data on other Web nodes – updates need to be propagated. For Web applications, such as distributed information portals, where data is distributed over the Web and part of it is replicated, update propagation is a prerequisite for keeping data consistent.

As a concrete application example, consider the setting of several distributed Web sites of a fictitious scientific community of historians called the Eighteenth Century Studies Society (ECSS). ECSS is subdivided into participating universities, thematic working groups, and project management. Universities, working groups, and project management have each their own Web site, which is maintained and administered locally. The different Web sites are autonomous, but cooperate to evolve together and mirror relevant changes from other Web sites.

The ECSS Web sites maintain (XML or RDF) data about members, publications, meetings, library books, and newsletters. Data is often shared, for example a member's personal data is present at his home university, at the management node, and in the working groups he participates in. Such shared data needs to be kept consistent among different nodes. This can be realized by communicating changes as events between the different nodes using reactive rules. Events that occur in this community include changes in the personal data of members, keeping track of the inventory of the community-owned library, or simply announcing

---

[2] http://rewerse.net
[3] http://ilog.com

information from email newsletters to interested working groups. These events require reactions such as updates, deletion, alteration, or propagation of data, which can also be implemented using reactive rules.

Full member management of the ECSS community, a community-owned and distributed virtual library (e.g., lending books, monitions, reservations), meeting organization (e.g., scheduling panel moderators), and newsletter distribution are desirable features of such a Web-based information portal. And all these can be elegantly implemented by means of reactive rules.

2.2   E-Shopping Web Site

Shopping Cart Example. This example shows how a simple reactive rule set calculates the shopping discount of a customer. The business rules describing the discount allocation policy are listed hereafter:

1. If the total amount of the customer's shopping is higher than 100, then perform a discount of 10%.
2. If it is the first shopping of the customer, then perform a discount of 5%.
3. If the client has a gold status and buys more than 5 discounted items, then perform an additional discount of 2%.
4. Rule 1 and 2 must not be applied for the same customer, the first rule has the priority against the second. The third rule is applied only if rule 1 or rule 2 have been applied.

Those policies might be taken into account by a reactive rule service (Web service, procedural application, etc.). This service receives the customer and his shopping cart information as input. The discount calculation is then processed following the previous rules and returns the discount value to the service caller.

Credit Analysis Example. This second example shows how a simple reactive ruleset defines a loan acceptance service. It determines whether a loan is accepted, depending on the client's history and the loan request duration. A client's score is calculated according to the following business policy. If the client's score is high enough, the loan is accepted and its rate is calculated.

1. If the loan duration is lower than five years then set the loan rate to 4.0% and add 5 to the score, else set it to 6.0%.
2. If the client has filed a bankruptcy, subtract 5 to the score.
3. If the client's salary is between 20000 and 40000, add 10 to the score.
4. If the client's salary is greater than 40000, add 15 to the score.
5. If the score is upper than 15, then the loan is accepted.

Those policies are usually implemented by a rule service (Web service, application). This service receives the loan request as input information, applies the rule on them in order to check the acceptance, and finally returns to the caller the loan characteristics.

3   Event-Condition-Action Rules

3.1   General Ideas

Many Web-based systems need to have the capability to *update data* found at (local or remote) Web resources, to *exchange information* about events (such as executed updates), and to *detect and react* not only to simple events but also to situations represented by a temporal combinations of events. The issue of updating data plays an important role, for example, in e-commerce applications receiving and processing buying or reservation orders. The issues of notifying, detecting, and reacting upon events of interest begin to play an increasingly important role within business strategy on the Web and event-driven applications are being more widely deployed.

Different approaches can be followed for implementing Web applications having the capabilities touched on above. Section 1 has discussed the advantages of a rule-based approach for realizing reactive applications compared to general purpose programming languages and frameworks. Event-Condition-Action rules are high-level, elegant means to implement reactive Web applications whose architecture imply more than one Web components/nodes and their communication is based on exchanging events.

For communicating events on the Web two strategies are possible: the *push* strategy, i.e. a Web node informs (possibly) interested Web nodes about events, and the *pull* strategy, i.e. interested Web nodes query periodically (poll) persistent data found at other Web nodes in order to determine changes. Both strategies are useful. A push strategy has several advantages over a strategy of periodical polling: it allows faster reaction, avoids unnecessary network traffic, and saves local resources.

3.2   ECA-Language Design Issues

Rules. In the introduction, it has already been mentioned that ECA rules have the general form *ON Event IF Condition DO Action*. Before going into depth on events, conditions, and actions, we examine the notion of an ECA rule as a whole.

Rule Execution Semantics. The general idea for interpreting a single ECA rule is to execute the *Action* automatically when the *Event* happens, provided the *Condition* holds. However, things become more complex when we consider not just a single rule but a set of rules (also called a rule base).

Consider the following example of two (informally specified) rules:

```
ON item out of stock
DO set item's status to ''not available''

ON item out of stock
IF item is in stock at one of the shop's suppliers
DO reorder item and set status to ''reordered''
```

188   B. Berstel et al.

These two rules are in a conflict when we try to execute both in response to an out of stock event for an item that is in stock at one of its suppliers. A language's rule execution semantics, determine what happens in such a situation. Possible rule execution semantics include (see also [Pat98, WC96]):

- Selecting *one single* rule (or rather rule instance) from the so-called conflict set, the set of executable rules, for execution. This requires a selection principle in the language such as numeric priorities which are assigned to rules, a priority relation between rules, the textual order of rules in their definition, or the temporal order in which rules have been added to the rule base. (The last two are also often used as a "tie-breaker" when two rules have the same priority.) Some languages are simply non-deterministic, i.e., select a rule randomly or by an unspecified principle. The principle by which rules are chosen is often called the conflict resolution strategy.
- Executing *all* rules (or rule instances) from the conflict set sequentially in some order, which is determined similar to the selection above. When during the execution another event is generated by a rule, one can either suspend the execution of the other rules in the current conflict set to (recursively) execute any rules triggered by that event or first execute the complete conflict set and then (iteratively) turn to any rules triggered by any events generated in the meantime.
- Simply rejecting the execution of any rule (instance), possibly reporting an exception.

Usually, it is possible to avoid such conflicts by writing the rules differently. In the above example, the first rule could be modified to include a condition "item is *not* in stock at supplier." Unfortunately, when rule sets grow larger, this can lead to quite lengthy conjunctions of conditions. If, in the above example, we also want to consider the case that an item is in stock at a different branch, we might have to add the negation of this condition to all other rules.

This short discussion has only scratched the surface of execution semantics for ECA rules. While they have been studied quite extensively in the area of Active Database Management Systems [Pat98, WC96], i.e., in the context of typically closed and centralized systems, rule execution semantics have not been explored very much for the Web as an open and distributed system.

Flow on Information in a Rule. ECA Rules exhibit a flow of information between their three parts. In the earlier example, the "out of stock" event part has to provide some identifier for the item. The condition part of the second rule makes use of this identifier in determining whether there is a supplier for the item, possibly providing the supplier's name to the action part.

A common way to provide for such a flow of information in an ECA language is to use variables, which are bound and exchanged between the different parts. This requires that the "sub-languages" in which the different parts are written share the same notion of a variable binding or at least that there is some conversion mechanism if different notions are used.

Variants of ECA Rules. In some cases, especially when reasonably complex decisions are involved, the same piece of knowledge must be distributed over several rules. We've already seen an example of this with the two rules processing out of stock events. To support a better modeling of such cases, some languages offer extended forms of ECA rules such as so-called ECAA rules [KEP00]. ECAA rules have the form *ON Event IF Condition DO Action ELSE Alternative-Action*, specifying to execute *Alternative-Action* when the *Event* happens but the *Condition* does not hold. The example rules can be thus merged into one:

```
ON    item out of stock
IF    item is in stock at one of the shop's suppliers
DO    reorder item and set status to ''reordered''
ELSE set item's status to ''not available''
```

Note that any ECAA rule can generally be rewritten as two ECA rules, one with the original condition and one with the negated condition. A further variant are EC^nA^n rules, which specify a number of condition-action pairs; typically only the first action whose condition holds is executed.

Rule Base Modifications. Some ECA rule-based systems allow to modify the rule base at run-time without restarting the system. The modifications are adding rules, by either registering a completely new rule or enabling a previously deactivated rule, removing rules, by either unregistering or disabling an existing rule, as well as replacing a rule. Often it is necessary to apply a number of modifications in an atomic fashion, i.e., all changes come into effect at the same time.

Events. Event drive the execution of ECA rule programs, which makes the event part an important determinant for expressivity and ease-of-use of an ECA language or system.

The Notion of an Event. It is hard to give a clear definition of what is an event. Often, an event is defined as an observable and relevant state change in a system; however with this definition, what is observable depends on the boundary and abstraction level of the system (which is particularly hard to grasp in an open system such as the Web), and what is relevant depends on the considered application. For processing purposes, an event is usually given a *representation* as an object or a message, and for the purpose of ECA languages this gives a practical definition of what is an event.

Examples of events one might want to react to include:

- Updates of local or remote data.
- Messages (or notifications) coming from some external source such as a human user (e.g., by filling out a Web form), another program (e.g., a request or reply from a Web service), or sensors (e.g., RFIDs).
- System events such as reports of the system status (e.g., CPU load) or of exceptions and errors (e.g., broken network connections, hardware failures).

- Timer events such as an alarm at a particular date and time or a periodic alarm (e.g., every day at 7am). A particular form of timer events are dynamic events (a term coined in [Ron97]), where the time is specified not directly in the event part of a rule, but given by some entry in a database.
- Composite events, that is a combinations of events occurring over time. In contrast to so-called atomic or primitive events, which include the previous examples, composite events are usually not represented by a single object or message in the stream of events. Rather, they are just a collection of atomic events that satisfy some pre-defined pattern. The pattern is often called a composite event query, and accordingly composite events can be seen as answers to such composite event queries. Composite events will be discussed in more detail later.

Events, or rather their representations, usually contain information detailing the circumstances of the event such as:

- Who has generated the event (*generator*, sender)?
- When has the event happened (*occurrence time*, sending time) and when was it detected (*detection time*, receiving time)? Note that these times are often not the same due to delays in transmission and often given according to different clocks that are not (and cannot be) perfectly synchronized.
- Which kind of event has happened (*event type*, class)? Event types are ultimately application-dependent and of varying abstraction levels; examples could be an insertion of an element into an XML document (quite low-level in the data layer) or a customer putting an item into the shopping cart (higher-level in the application layer). Event-driven systems often employ a type system for events (e.g., a class hierarchy), but the example of XChange shows that this is not a necessity. (Note though that XChange does not preclude typing event messages with XML schema or a similar mechanism.)
- What data has been affected by the event (*event data*)? In the above example of an insertion, the event could include information about where the insertion has taken place (document URI, position in the document) and what (XML fragment) has been inserted. In the example of putting an item into the shopping cart, the event could include information about that item (product name, quantity) and the customer (name or another identifier).
- Why has the event happened, i.e., which previous events are responsible for making the current event happen (*causality information*)?

The Event Part of a Rule. The event part of an ECA rule has a two-fold purpose: it determines when to react, i.e., specifies a class (or set) of events that trigger the rule, and extracts data from the event (usually in the form of variable bindings) that can then be used in the condition and action part. Accordingly, the event part of a rule is in essence a query against (the stream of) incoming events. In contrast to answers to traditional database queries, however, answers to event queries are associated with an occurrence time, mirroring the temporal nature of events.

Composite Events and Composite Event Queries. Often, a situation that requires a reaction cannot be detected from a single atomic event. Such situations are called *composite events* (as opposed to single atomic events), and they are especially important on the Web: in a carefully developed application, atomic events might suffice as designers have the freedom to choose events according to their goal. On the Web, however, many different applications are integrated and have to cooperate. Situations which have not been considered in an application's design must then be inferred from several atomic events.

There are at least the following four complementary dimensions that need to be considered for an event query language:

- Data extraction: As mentioned above, event carry data that is relevant to whether and how to react. The data must be provided (typically as bindings for variables) to the condition and action part of an ECA rule.
- Event composition: To support composite events, event queries must support composition constructs such as the conjunction, disjunction, and negation of events (or more precisely of event queries).
- Temporal conditions: Time plays an important role in many reactive Web applications. Event queries must be able to express temporal conditions such as "events A and B happen within 1 hour and A happens before B."
- Event accumulation: Event queries must be able to accumulate events of the same type to aggregate data or detect repetitions. For example, a stock market application might require notification if "the average over the last 5 reported stock prices raises by 5%," or a service level agreement might require a reaction when "3 server outages have been reported within 1 hour."

The most prevalent style for event query languages uses composition operators such as conjunction and sequence to combine primitive event queries into composite event queries. We will see an example of this in Section 3.3 on XChange. This approach is not without problems, though: for the sequence operator alone, four different interpretations are conceivable as suggested in [ZS01]. We will therefore also look at an alternative approach called XChange^{EQ} in Section 3.3.

Conditions. The condition part of an ECA rule expresses usually a query to persistent data sources. As with event queries, condition queries have the twofold purpose of determining whether the rule fires (i.e., the action is executed) and extracting data in the form of variable bindings that is then used in the reaction. Querying XML, RDF, and other Web data is well-studied and a multitude of query languages have been devised [BBFS05]. Criteria to be considered for the Web query language used to express the condition part include:

- What is the query language's notion of answers (variable bindings, newly constructed data)?
- How are answers delivered, can they be used to "parameterize" further queries or the action? Can, for example, a variable bound in an event query be a parameter in a condition query, i.e., the value delivered by the event query be accessed and used in the condition query?

- What evaluation methods for queries are possible (backward chaining, forward chaining)?
- Which data models are supported (XML, RDF, OWL)? Is it possible to access data in different data models within one query?
- How does the query language deal with object identity?
- Which reasoning or deductive capabilities does the query language provide (views, deductive rules, etc.)?

The choice of a query language has significant influence on the design of a reactive language and should thus be made carefully. While the primary purpose of the query language is to query persistent data (in the condition part), event messages often come in the same formats as persistent data. Accordingly, the query language is often also be used to query data in atomic events in the event part of ECA rules.

Actions. While the event and condition part of an ECA rule only detect that a system has (entered) a certain state without affecting it, the action part intends to modify the current state and yield a new state. Typical actions are:

- Updating persistent data on the Web. For example, the event that a customer puts an item into her shopping basket requires recomputing the total price.
- Raising new events to communicate with other agents on the Web (Web sites, Web services, etc.). Usually the new event message is sent as a notification in an *asynchronous* manner and execution of the current rule or other rules proceeds immediately without waiting for an answer. For example, upon a checkout event, a new event containing a list with the bought items and the customer's address is sent to the warehouse to initiate delivery.
- Procedure calls to some host environment or a Web service. In contrast to raising new events, a procedure call is usually *synchronous* and the rule has to wait for the call to complete before execution is continued.
- Modifications to the rule base. This includes the possibility to enable and disable rules[4] or to register (add) new rules and unregister (delete) existing rules. Such modifications of the rule base are not without problems, however, as self-modifying programs are generally conceived to be hard to analyze and understand.

Updates. Updates modify the contents of Web resources by inserting, deleting, or replacing data items. Depending on the data format of the Web resources such data items are XML fragments, RDF triples, or OWL facts.

Updates can be specified conveniently in some update language. There is a strong connection between update languages and query languages, and most existing update languages are based on a query language. The query language

---

[4] Note, however, that alternatively to a specific enable/disable action, this can also be modeled by adding a condition on some object (a boolean value or similar), which signals whether the rule is "enabled" or "disabled," to rules and modifying this object through and update

can be used to locate items or positions in the resource where an update should be performed as well as to construct new data that will be inserted or used to replace old data.

Combinations of Actions. Being able to execute only one primitive action such as a single update or raising one new event is usually far too limiting. Actions that have to be taken can be quite complex and require several primitive actions to be performed. The most common way to put together several primitive actions into a compound action is to perform them in a sequence. However other ways to form compound actions such as a specification of alternatives (if one action can fail) or a conditional execution are useful, too.

Usually we expect a compound action to be executed in a transactional manner, i.e., either the whole compound action takes effect or it has no effect at all. In a distributed setting such as the Web this requires that all participants involved in a compound action agree on a commit protocol such as the two-phase commit (2PC; see, e.g., [CDK01]).

Solutions to realize compound actions based on specifying a compensating action for each action have not been investigated deeply in the framework of ECA rules on the Web. Such issues have been investigated for databases, e.g., Sagas [GMS87] (and a myriad of follow-up work on advanced transaction models), as well as in Web Services, e.g., with the notion of a "Business Activity" in WS-Transaction [C+04]. However it should be noted that the primary aim of these proposals is increasing parallelism for long running transactions. They still require two-phase commits (in particular at the end of the transaction) to give transactional guarantees in a distributed setting.

3.3   XChange as an Example of ECA Rules Language

This section presents *XChange*, a high-level, ECA rules-based language for realizing reactivity on the Web. We first introduce the paradigms upon which the language XChange relies and then present and exemplify the core constructs of the language.

Paradigms. Clear paradigms that a programming language follows provide a better language understanding and ease programming. Hence, explicitly stated paradigms are essential for Web languages, since these languages should be easy to understand and use also by practitioners with little programming experience.

Event vs. Event Query. As discussed in Section 3.2, one can conceive every kind of changes on the Web as events. For processing them, XChange represents each event as one XML document. Event queries are queries against the XML data representing events. Event query specifications differ considerably from event representations, e.g. event queries may contain variables for event data items. Most proposals dealing with reactivity do not significantly differentiate between event and event query. Overloading the notion of event precludes a clear language semantics and thus, makes the implementation of the language and its usage much more difficult. Event queries in XChange serve a double purpose: detecting events of interest and temporal combinations of them, and selecting data items from events' representation.

Volatile vs. Persistent Data. The development of the XChange language – its design and its implementation – reflects the view over the Web data that differentiates between *volatile data* (event data communicated on the Web between XChange programs) and *persistent data* (data of Web resources such as XML or HTML documents). Volatile data *cannot* be updated but persistent data can. To inform about, correct, complete, or invalidate former volatile data, new messages containing information about events that have occurred are communicated between Web nodes.

Pattern-Based Approach. XChange is a *pattern-based language*: Event queries describe *patterns* for events requiring a reaction. Web queries describe patterns for persistent Web data. Action specifications build also upon pattern specifications, as we will see later. Patterns are templates that closely resemble the structure of the data to be queried, constructed, or modified, thus being very intuitive and also straight forward to visualize [BBB+04].

Strategy for Event Communication. Possible communication strategies (i.e. pull and push) have been touched on in Section 3.1. The pull strategy is supported by languages for Web queries (e.g. XQuery [B+05] or Xcerpt [SB04]). XChange uses the *push* strategy for communicating events.

Processing of Events. Event queries are evaluated locally at each Web node. Each such Web node has its own local *event manager* for processing incoming events and evaluating event queries against the incoming event stream (volatile data). For efficiency reasons, an incremental evaluation is used for detecting composite events.

Bounded Event Lifespan. Event queries are such that no data on any event has to be kept forever in memory, i.e. the event lifespan should be bounded. Hence, design enforces that volatile data remains volatile. If for some applications it is necessary to make part of volatile data persistent, then the applications should turn events into persistent Web data by explicitly saving events.

Rules. An XChange program is located at one Web node and consists of one or more ECA rules of the form *Event query – Web query – Action*. Events are communicated between XChange programs by ECA rules that raise and send them as event messages. Every incoming event (i.e., event message) is queried using the *event query* (introduced by keyword ON). If an answer is found and the *Web query* (introduced by keyword FROM) has also an answer, then the specified action (introduced by keyword DO) is executed.

Rule parts communicate through variable substitutions. Substitutions obtained by evaluating the event query can be used in the Web query and the action part, those obtained by evaluating the Web query can be used in the action part.

The following example rule shows the structure and the information passing mechanism of an XChange ECA rule. Concrete examples of event queries, Web queries, and actions are given in the next sections.

```
ON <new discounts for books of type T applied by supplier S>
FROM <stock of books of type T low>
DO <send new order of books of type T to S >
```

The next sections introduce the Web query, event query, and action part of an XChange ECA rule. We start with the Web queries since XChange event queries and updates build upon and extend the Web queries.

Web Queries. XChange embeds the Web query language Xcerpt [BS02a, Sch04] for expressing the *Web query* part of ECA rules and for specifying deductive rules in XChange programs. Using Xcerpt one can query and reason with tree- or graph-structured data such as XML or RDF documents. A deductive rule has the following form in Xcerpt[5]:

```
CONSTRUCT construct-term
FROM query-term
END
```

Such deductive rules allow for constructing views over (possibly heterogeneous) Web resources that can be further queried in the *Web query* part of XChange ECA rules.

Xcerpt is a *pattern-based language*: it uses query patterns, called *query terms*, for querying Web data and construction patterns, called *construct terms*, for re-assembling data selected by queries into new data items. For conciseness, Xcerpt represents data, query terms, and construct terms in a term-like syntax; the same approach is also taken in XChange. For example, for representing XML documents as terms, element names become term labels and child elements are represented as subterms surrounded by curly braces or square brackets (in case of ordered child elements).

Both partial (i.e. incomplete) or total (i.e. complete) query patterns can be specified. A query term t using a partial specification denoted by double brackets or braces) for its subterms matches with all such terms that (1) contain matching subterms for all subterms of t and that (2) might contain further subterms without corresponding subterms in t. In contrast, a query term t using a total specification (denoted by single square brackets [ ] or curly braces { }) does not match with terms that contain additional subterms without corresponding subterms in t.

Query terms contain *variables* for selecting subterms of data items that are bound to variables. In Xcerpt and XChange, variables are placeholders for data, very much like logic programming variables are. Variables are preceded by the keyword **var**. Variable restrictions can be also specified, by using the construct

---

[5] XChange integrates the Web query language Xcerpt – XChange constructs are based on and extend Xcerpt constructs and the prototypical implementation of XChange uses a prototypical implementation of Xcerpt. The keyword **FROM** has been used instead of **IF** for introducing the condition part of XChange ECA rules for achieving language uniformity without changing Xcerpt's language design and implementation.

-> (read *as*), which restricts the bindings of the variables to those terms that are matched by the restriction pattern (given on the right hand side of ->). The following Xcerpt query term queries the list of suppliers at http://suppliers.com to determine the names and URIs of companies supplying books. This information is used e.g. when some books are out of stock and need to be reordered.

```
in { resource {"http://suppliers.com/list.xml", XML},
  desc supplier {{
    items {{ desc type { "Book" } }},
    contact {{
      name { var N },
      URI { var U }
    }}
  }}
}
```

Xcerpt query terms may be augmented by additional constructs like *subterm negation* (keyword without), *optional subterm specification* (keyword optional), and *descendant* (keyword desc) [SB04]. Query terms are "matched" with data or construct terms by a non-standard unification method called *simulation unification* dealing with partial and unordered query specifications. More detailed discussions on simulation unification can be found in [BS02b, Sch04]. In the above given example, the variable substitutions N ↦ "Springer" and U ↦ "www.springer.de" could be obtained as result of simulation unifying the query term with the given XML document.

Event Queries. *Event messages* denote XChange event representations and communicate events between (same or different) Web nodes. An XChange *event message* is an XML document with a root element labelled event and the five parameters (represented as child elements as they may contain complex content): raising-time (i.e. the time of the event manager of the Web node raising the event), reception-time (i.e. the time at which a node receives the event), sender (i.e. the URI of the Web node where the event has been raised), recipient (i.e. the URI of the Web node where the event has been received), and id (i.e. a unique identifier given at the recipient Web node).

Each XChange-aware Web node monitors such incoming event messages to check if they match an event query of one of its XChange ECA rules. Differences between volatile and persistent data make Web query languages not sufficient as candidates for querying event data: Many situations need for their detection not just one event to occur, but more than one event to occur. The temporal order of these (component) events and the specified temporal restrictions on their occurrence time need also to be taken into account in detecting situations. Mirroring these practical requirements, XChange offers not only *atomic event queries* but also *composite event queries*.

Atomic Event Queries. Atomic event queries detect occurrences of single, atomic events. They are query patterns for the XML representation of events and may be

accompanied by an absolute time restriction, which are used to restrict the events
that are considered relevant for an event query to those that have occurred in a
specified (finite) time interval. Such a time interval may be given by fixed start
and end time points (keyword **in**) or just by an end time point (keyword **before**),
in which case the interval starts with the time point of event query definition.

The following XChange atomic event query detects announcements of discounts applied by a supplier. The information about the supplier (sender URI)
and the discount for a type of items are to be bound to the variables S, D, and
T, respectively.

```
xchange:event {{
  xchange:sender { var S },
  discount {{
    items {{
      type { var T },
      discount { var D }
    }}
  }}
}}
```

Composite Event Queries using Composition Operators. The need for detecting
not only atomic events but also composite events has been motivated in Section 3.2. XChange offers *composite event queries* for specifying and detecting
composite events of interest.

A composite event query consists of (1) a connection of (atomic or composite)
event queries with event composition operators and (2) an optional temporal
range limiting the time interval in which events are relevant to the composite
event query. Composition operators are denoted with keywords such as **and** (both
events have to happen), **andthen** (the events have to happen in sequence), **or**
(either event can happen), **without** (non-occurrence of the event in a given time
frame). Limiting temporal ranges can be specified with keywords such as **before**
(all events have to happen before a certain time point), **in** (all events have to
happen in an absolute time interval), **within** (all events have to happen within
a given length of time). For a more in-depth discussion of XChange composite
event queries see [Eck05, Pö5, BEP06a].

Composite events (detected using composite event queries) do not have time
stamps, as atomic events do. Instead, a composite event inherits from its components a start time (i.e. the reception time of the first received constituent event
that is part of the composite event) and an end time (i.e. the reception time of
the last received constituent event that is part of the composite event). That is,
in XChange composite events have a *duration* (a length of time).

The following composite event query evaluates successfully if no acknowl-
edgment for the order s-rw2007-0023 is received between the 1st and 15th of
October 2007:

```
without {
  xchange:event {{
```

```
    acknowledgement {{
      order {{ id { "s-rw2007-0023" } }}
    }}
  }}
} during [ 2007-10-01T10:00:00 .. 2007-10-15T14:00:00 ]
```

Composite Event Queries using XChange^{EQ}. Querying composite events based on composition operators (as presented above) has been well-investigated in active databases systems and works well with small queries. However, queries involving a larger number of events can sometimes become difficult to express and to understand.

Consider and example where we want for events a, b, c and d to happen and have the constraints that a happens before b, a also happens before c, and c before d. Note that the query cannot be expressed as and{ andthen[a, b], andthen[a, c], andthen[c, d]}, since this query would allow different instances of a and c events to be used. A correct way to express the query would be: andthen[a, and{b, andthen[c, d]}]. If we now only add an additional constraint that b happens before d, the new query bears only little resemblance to the old: andthen[a, and{b, c}, d]. In fact, even though we *added* a constraint in our specification, the query has one operator *less*.

Composition operators mix the event querying dimensions explained in Section 3.2 (in the case of andthen event composition and temporal relationships are mixed). It can be argued that this leads to the exemplified difficulties in expressing and understanding queries and also to a certain incompleteness in the expressivity of such event query languages.

An alternative to using composition operators in XChange is investigated with the high-level event query language XChange^{EQ}. In XChange^{EQ}, the four orthogonal event querying dimensions are treated separately. The above example can be expressed as: and{event i: a, event j: b, event k: c, event l: d} where {i before j, i before k, k before l, j before l} . (Keep in mind that a, b, c, d are generally multi-line atomic event queries, so that the increase in length compared to the composition-based approach is insignificant and outweighed by better readability.)

XChange^{EQ} also adds support for deductive rules on events, relative temporal event (e.g., "five days longer than event i, " written extend[i, 5 days]), and enforces a clear separation between time specifications that are used as events (and waited for) or only as restrictions (conditions in the where-part). The following example rule detects an overdue event when an order that has been received before October 15 has not been acknowledged within 5 days.

```
DETECT
  overdue { var I }
ON
  and {
    event i: order {{ id { var I } }},
    event j: extend[i, 5 days],
```

```
    while j: not acknowledgment{{ id{ var I } }}
  } where { i before datetime("2007-10-15:14:00") }
END
```

More detail on XChange^{EQ} can be found in [BE06a, BE07].

Actions. XChange rules support the following primitive actions: executing simple updates to persistent Web data (such as the insertion of an XML element) and raising new events (i.e., sending a new event message to a remote Web node or oneself). To specify more complex actions, compound actions can be constructed as from the primitive actions.

Updating Web Data. An XChange *update term* is a (possibly incomplete) pattern for the data to be updated, augmented with the desired update operations (i.e., an update term is an Xcerpt query term enriched with update specifications). An update term may contain different types of update operations: An *insertion operation* specifies an Xcerpt construct term that is to be inserted, a *deletion operation* specifies an Xcerpt query term for deleting all data terms matching it, and a *replace operation* specifies an Xcerpt query term to determine data terms to be modified and an Xcerpt construct term as their new value. The following XChange update term updates the `offer.xml` document upon arrival of new books:

```
in { resource {"http://myshop.de/offer.xml", XML},
  offer {{
    books {{
      items {{
        type { var T },
        insert new-arrival { var B }
      }}
    }}
  }}
}
```

Raising New Events. Events to be raised are specified as (complete) patterns for the event messages, called *event terms*. An event term is simply an Xcerpt construct term restricted to having a root labelled **event** and at least one subterm **recipient** specifying the URI of the recipient. The following XChange event term is used to order 50 Reasoning Web 2007 books at Springer:

```
xchange:event {
  xchange:recipient {"http://www.springer.de"},
  order {
    id { "s-rw2007-0023" },
    book { "Reasoning Web -- Third International Summer School
            2007, Tutorial Lectures" },
    count { "50" }
```

```
},
delivery-info {
  company { ... }, address{ ... }
}
}
```

Specifying Compound Actions. The primitive actions described by update terms and event terms can become powerful by combining them. XChange hence allows specifying complex actions as combinations of (primitive and compound) actions. Actions can be combined with disjunctions and conjunctions. Disjunctions specify alternatives, only one of the specified actions is to be performed successfully. (Note that actions such as updates can be unsuccessful, i.e., fail.) Conjunctions in turn specify that all actions need to be performed. The combinations are indicated by the keywords or and **and**, followed by a list of the actions enclosed in braces or brackets. The list of the actions can be ordered (indicated by square brackets, []) or unordered (indicated by curly braces, {}). If the actions are ordered, their execution order is specified to be relevant. If the actions are unordered, their execution order is specified as irrelevant, thus giving more freedom for parallelization.

Declarative and Operational Semantics. XChange combines an event language, a query language, and an update language into ECA-rules. Accordingly, the declarative and operational semantics are given separately for each rule part. The semantics of an XChange ECA-rule follows immediately from the semantics of its parts; the "glue" between the parts is given by the substitutions for the variables. The semantics of event queries is the most interesting aspect of XChange semantics and is discussed in [Eck05, Pŏ5, BEP06b]. Semantics of XChange^{EQ} are provided as a model theory and fixpoint theory and discussed in [BE07]. The underlying ideas for the semantics of Web queries and updates can be found in [BEP06b] and their detailed description is given in [Sch04] and [Pŏ5], respectively.

Current Status. XChange is an ongoing research project. The design, the core language constructs, and the semantics of XChange are completed. For revealing the strengths and limits of the language, a couple of use cases have been developed: Travel organization as an application of Web-based reactive travel planning and support and e-Book store as a simple Semantic Web scenario are presented in [Pŏ5]. XChange has also been used for determining the suitability of the ECA rules approach for business process modeling and in paticular for implementing the EU-Rent case study [Rom06, BEPR06].

A proof-of-concept implementation[6] exists, which follows a modular approach that mirrors the operational semantics. The XChange prototype has been implemented in Haskell, a functional programming language; chosing Haskell has been strongly motivated by an existing Xcerpt prototype implementation, which has been extended for implementing XChange. The XChange prototype has been

---

[6] XChange Prototype, http://reactiveweb.org/xchange/prototype.html

employed for implementing the application scenario *Distribuited Information Portal* described in Section 2; the developed demonstration of XChange is presented in [Gra06, BEGP06]. Issues of efficiency of the implementation, esp. for event detection and update execution, have not been a priority in developing the prototype and are subject to future work.

There are a couple of further research issues that deserve attention within the XChange project, such as the automatic generation of XChange rules (e.g. based on the dependencies between Web resources' data) or the development of a visual counterpart of the textual language (along this line, the visual rendering of Xcerpt programs – visXcerpt [BBSW03] – is to be extended).

3.4 Implementation of ECA Systems

Implementation and architecture of ECA rules systems have been studied extensively in the area of Active Database Management Systems (see [WC96] for an overview). Unlike the Web, which is open, distributed, and decentralized, active databases are rather closed and centralized systems. It is therefore not clear how well their architectures would transfer to a Web context and there has not been much research on this issue. We therefore concentrate in this section mainly on the algorithms used in implementations of the event, condition, and action part, respectively, rather than overall architectural issues.

Event Part – Atomic Events. The evaluation of atomic event queries has two main issues, mainly with regard to efficiency: the detection of updates in documents and databases (mainly XML, but also other Web data formats) that satisfy given (update) event queries and the evaluation of a potentially large number of event queries against events that are received from other Web nodes as messages.

Detection of relevant updates has been studied extensively in relational databases [WC96, HCH+99], often under the term "trigger processing." The only work we are aware of where this issue has been studied from an XML perspective is Active XQuery [BBCC02], which will be described in Section 3.5.

The other issue is that when an event message (an XML document) is received, a potentially large number of atomic event queries (e.g., XPath expressions or Xcerpt/XChange query terms) have to be evaluated against this message. From an optimization perspective, this is the inverse of the classical database query optimization: instead of evaluating a single query against a relatively large amount of data, we have to evaluate a large amount of queries against relatively small data. Therefore, atomic event query evaluation requires multi-query optimization where queries (rather than data) are indexed and similarities between queries exploited. A number of approaches for multi-query optimization of XPath expressions have been devised, which are based on finite state machines [DAF+03, GMOS03]. However, the issue has been treated only in isolation and not as part of a full ECA rule engine.

Event Part – Composite Events. For the evaluation of composite event queries, a data-driven approach is best-suited. Since it can work incrementally, it is preferable for efficiency reasons: work done in one evaluation step of an event query should not be redone in future evaluation steps. For example, the composite event query "events A and B happen" requires to check every incoming event if it is A or B and thus multiple evaluation steps. When event A is detected, we want to remember this for later when B is detected to signal the composite event. In contrast, a non-incremental, query-driven (backward-chaining-like) evaluation would have to check the entire history of events for an A when a B is detected. Popular data-driven approaches used in the past include finite automata [GJS92, SSSM05, BC06] and event trees (or graphs) [CKAK94, MS97, ME01, AE04, AC05, BEP06a].

In the finite automata approach, states signify the "progress" made in detecting a composite event and state transitions are caused by incoming atomic events. This simple intuition is complicated though by the need to backtrack or reset the automata after the first event has been detected in order to detect further events. Further, when data is correlated between events, automata have to be extended to accommodate this, too.

The event tree approach is similar to the Rete algorithm, which will be described in detail in Section 4.4 in the context of production rules. The basic idea is to represent an event query as an operator tree where leaf nodes correspond to atomic event queries and inner nodes to composition operators such as conjunction or sequence. New events (or event data) flow bottom up in this tree and inner nodes have a storage to memorize previously detected events. When an inner node detects a composite event from the new and the memorized events, it "forwards" this composite event to its parent node. When event queries share subexpressions, this can be exploited by using a directed acyclic graph instead of a tree. So far, this is also the basic idea of Rete; however, certain operators such the sequence allow to disable evaluation of subtrees depending on the stored events: for example, to evaluate the sequence of events E_1 followed by E_2, the subtree for E_2 must only be evaluated after an E_1 instance has been detected.

Another approach discussed in the literature are (special types of) Petri nets [GD93]. However this can be seen as a variant of the event tree approach, since for each possible operator a separate Petri net is given and for a given event query the Petri nets for all its operators are then connected in essentially the same manner as the inner nodes in the event tree.

Condition Part – Query Evaluation. For the evaluation of Web queries in the condition part, ECA rules systems usually rely on existing query evaluation engines. Accordingly, query processing takes only place whenever a rule is triggered by an event. This means that even though the condition part of an ECA rule can be considered a standing query (whose result could be precomputed whenever the underlying data changes), it is not treated this way but only posed as a spontaneous query whenever necessary. This kind of evaluation of a (single) Web query is a well-researched issue, see, e.g., [BEE+07].

We will see in Section 4.4 that evaluating the condition part only when an event triggers an ECA rule is in contrast to the continual evaluation of the condition part in production rule systems.[7] An advantage of treating conditions as spontaneous queries is that no restrictions are being posed on the accessed data sources, they can be any resources anywhere on the Web and event queries that "crawl" from Web resource to Web resource are conceivable. In contrast, precomputing query answers would usually be restricted to a local and closed set of resources.

Action Part – Update Execution. For specifying the updates in the `Action` part of ECA rules, a update language is employed. Due to the absence of a standard update language for XML or RDF data, each ECA rule language uses its own update language and the supported updates are usually implemented in an ad-hoc fashion.

At least for the path-based update languages for XML, good chances exist to change this situation as the W3C works towards standardizing a update extension to XQuery. The W3C XQuery Update Facility[8] Working Draft, released in July 2006, presents the syntax and semantics of such an XQuery extension. The draft defines update primitives such as insertion or deletion of a node, modification of a node while preserving its identity, or creation of a updated node with a new identity. Variants of these primitives are also proposed, e.g. insert after or insert as last. The notion of *pending update list* is defined as an unordered collection of update primitives, which is the base for update execution. Guidelines for constructing the pending update list are also given.

The issue of *snapshot semantics* is currently discussed in the W3C XML Query Working Group for processing the specified updates. The following snapshot semantics is used for the UpdateX [SHS04] language, an XQuery-based update language for XML: A first processing step determines the scope of the updates (i.e. for a FLWUpdate expression, the variables declared in the FOR and LET XQuery clauses are bound) and evaluate (not apply) each update primitive; the list of update primitives is thus formed. A checking step follows, where different kinds of constraints (e.g. given by a DTD) are performed. If their execution would not give invalid results, the updates in the constructed list are applied sequentially. Following these steps, the UpdateX has been implemented within the Galax[9] project.

An interesting implementation approach is followed in the Active XQuery language [BBCC02], which uses the update extensions to XQuery proposed in [TIHW01]. The main notions of SQL [KK00] triggers are used here but the execution model of SQL-3 is revised so as to cope with the hierarchical nature of XML data. Active XQuery update specifications may involve insertion or deletion of (whole) fragments of XML documents. These statements are called *bulk*

---

[7] It would of course be conceivable to use the condition query evaluation techniques of production rules for the evaluation of conditions of ECA rules. However we are not aware of any systems doing this.

[8] XQuery Update Facility, http://www.w3.org/TR/xqupdate/

[9] Galax, http://www.cise.ufl.edu/research/mobility/

update statements in this work. Problems may occur when executing such bulk updates directly: Consider the example of inserting a whole subtree S into an XML tree T. An ECA rule whose `Event` part waits for insertions of portions of S into T to fire would not detect the insertion without a mechanism supporting this. Thus, bulk update statements in Active XQuery are transformed (i.e. expanded) into equivalent collections of simple update operations. An algorithm for update expansion is outlined in [BBCC02]. The output of the algorithm is a list of simple update operations together with evaluation directives, which guide the language processor in firing all triggered ECA rules.

Alternative techniques for implementing the update operations are presented in [TIHW01] for the case when XML data is stored in a relational database (i.e. XML update statements are translated into SQL statements). This is the only work on updates for the Web that reports on implementation performance. Using three sets of test data (i.e. synthesized data with fixed structure, synthesized data with random structure, and real life data from the DBLP [dbl] bibliography database) experimental results were done in order to compare the techniques proposed for the core update operations (here, insert and delete).

3.5 An Overview of Existing ECA Languages and Systems

There are not great many ECA languages developed so far or under development at moment and most of them are results of research efforts done in the academia in the last couple of years.

The *General Semantic Web ECA Framework* [BFMS06a, MSvL06, BFMS06b] is a research endeavor that proposes a general framework[10] for reactive behavior on the Semantic Web. The generality here is given by the heterogeneity of the ECA rule components, which can be specified by using different event, condition, and action languages. Just the information flow between the rule components in form of variable substitutions constrains the languages of choice. The language used in writing an ECA component is given by means of the ECA-ML markup language for ECA rules offered by the framework; e.g. the URI of the languages is given as an attribute:

```
<eca:rule xmlns:eca="http://.../eca/2006/eca-ml">
  ...
</eca:rule>
```

ECA rule components are processed at Web nodes where a processor for the given language exists. For determining whom to forward the processing task, a Language and Service Registry is queried. A reference implementation for determining an appropriate Web processing node together with an event detection module based on a SNOOP-like event specifications have been completed. An action component given by a process algebra, the Calculus of Communicating Systems (CCS) [Mil83], has been proposed and its implementation is underway.

---

[10] General Semantic Web ECA Framework,
http://www.dbis.informatik.uni-goettingen.de/eca/

Also, an ontology of behavior is under development with the aim of using it as basis for reasoning and for easing the editing of ECA rules. As basis for it, the OWL-DL ontology[11] of the Resourceful Reactive Rules[12] (r3) project is considered. The goal of the r3 project is to develop a prototypical implementation of a Semantic Web reactive rule engine based on the ideas of the General Semantic Web ECA Framework.

Prova[13] is a combination of Java with Prolog-style rules. It employs ECA rules as means for distributed and agent programming. ECA rules react to incoming messages or pro-actively poll for state changes. By using Prova, composite events can be detected and different kinds of actions can be executed. Complex workflows can be specified in the action part as all BPEL constructs are directly available in the language. Prova has been used in a number of academic projects and also as basis for a commercial product for information integration.

The ruleCore[14] system provides an engine for executing ECA rules and also a couple of GUI tools such as the ruleCore Monitor, which gives run-time status information on the engine. The ruleCore engine detects situations specified by means of composite events. One can detect for example sequences, conjunctions, disjunctions, and negation of events. The engine supports also the detection of events that happen within a given time interval. Several event sources and of different kinds can be connected to the ruleCore engine, which processes events represented as XML documents. The action part of ECA rules can contain a number of action items, which specify that scripts are to be executed or events are to be generated. ruleCore has been developed by Analog Software. It can be used in research projects and can also be licensed for commercial use.

The Reaction RuleML[15] effort of the RuleML Initiative[16] aims at a general language that should enable inter-operation between industrial products and academic research results following different approaches to reactivity. The work on the ECA Logic Programming language (ECA-LP) and the ECA Rule Markup language (ECA-RuleML) as its XML serialization syntax has started during 2006. These languages are general enough to support ECA rules and their variant ECAP rules, but also production rules. They allow the specification of composite events to be detected and of different kinds of actions (notifications, updates and sequences of updates, etc.) to be executed.

An ECA rule language for XML data is proposed in [BPW02] and adapted for RDF data as the RDF Triggering Language (RDF-TL) [PPW03]. These languages have the capability to react only to single events and do not provide constructs for querying for complex combinations of events. As actions, simple insertions or deletions to XML or RDF data and sequences thereof are supported. At moment of writing these two research projects are not developed further.

---

[11] r3 Ontology, http://rewerse.net/I5/r3/DOC/2005/index.html

[12] Resourceful Reactive Rules,http://rewerse.net/I5/r3/

[13] Prova, http://www.prova.ws

[14] ruleCore, http://www.rulecore.com/index.html

[15] Reaction RuleML, http://ibis.in.tum.de/research/ReactionRuleML/

[16] RuleML Initiative, http://www.ruleml.org

ECA rules are discussed in the context of XSL [xsl01] and Lorel [AQM+97] as means to realize active document management systems, i.e. XML repositories with reactive capabilities [BCP00]. An ECA rule consists here of an event part and a condition-action part, which mixes the condition and the action specifications. Events considered here are just simple modifications of XML documents and there is no support for composite events. Conditions are (XSL or Lorel) queries to XML documents, and actions consist of constructing new documents and/or modifying existing documents in the document base, and then placing them into folders, publishing them on the Web, or sending them by e-mail.

Active XQuery [BBCC02] extends the Web query language XQuery by ECA rules, which are adapted from SQL-3 and thus called triggers in this work. The event part of such a trigger specifies an affected XML fragment by means of an XPath expression and the update operation (insert, delete, replace, or rename) on this fragment. The condition part is given by an XQuery WHERE clause. The actions available are the previously mentioned, simple update operations and external operations such as sending of messages.

Before and after triggers can be specified in Active XQuery: Before triggers consider the condition and action parts before the given event actually occurs. For after triggers the occurrence of the event is a prerequisite of evaluating the condition and action parts. The trigger components communicate through transition variables – two system-defined variables referring to the old and new nodes and additional variables defined by means of an XQuery LET clause. One can also associate priorities to Active XQuery triggers and specify a triggering granularity for the triggers – statement-level triggers fire once for each set of nodes affected by the change and node-level triggers fire for each node in such a set.

A research work supporting a path-based specification and the detection of composite events *for XML documents* [BKK04] has been also proposed. How this approach does (or even would) scale to the Web is unclear; for example, one cannot relate (primitive or composite) events that have occurred in XML documents distributed on the Web, as the communication of event data is not supported. It does not represent a full reactive language for the Web, but it could be extended and integrated into a reactive language.

4   Production Rules

4.1   General Ideas

What Is a Production Rule?. A production rule is a piece of knowledge organized along an *WHEN condition DO action* structure. The intent of a rule is to evolve the state of the system by executing the action. To guide this evolution, the action will only be applied from a state where the condition is true. The state that results from the execution of the action of a production rule can be incompatible with the state in which the rule was applied. This is common in production rule programs, and can be seen as a noticeable difference with other, monotonic rule programming paradigms such as logic rules.

Production Rules Based Software Applications. Production rules are used in software applications to encode their logic, or parts of it. As a result, an industrial application may rely on thousands of rules, each rule representing a piece of the knowledge of the company policy. Since industrial applications have a rich life cycle, spanning over several years and involving dozens of persons with various roles, production rule systems have to provide the support for managing this huge amount of information in the long term. This is the purpose of a Business Rule Management System such as ILOG JRules, as illustrated in Section 4.3.

Production Rules Based Web Applications. Business (production) rules is not the only paradigm on which real-world applications rely. Examples of other paradigms are a multi-tier architecture, and the Web. Web applications will typically use production rules to encode their policy-intensive aspects, that is, the part of their logic that requires the complex handling of the system state, based on the business knowledge of the company. The use of production rules will thus ease the implementation of Web applications with several agents playing different roles.

Production Rules Versus Integrity Rules. Integrity rules are introduced in a relational data base to enforce its correctness and its consistency. In order to maintain referential integrity between primary and foreign keys as data is inserted or deleted from the database, certain insert and delete rules must be defined. Like production rules, integrity rules have a condition part determining in which context they are executed. In fact, integrity rules might be implemented by a production rules system adapted to RDBMS environment. However, specialized integrity system are likely to be more efficient to process huge amount of data characterizing actual databases. On the other hand, the purpose of PR systems is not limited to DB referential integrity and could be applied on various domains.

4.2   Description of a Production Rules System

The Working Memory and the Underlying Data Model. As programs handle data, a programming language defines (more or less implicitly) a data model. Being in essence reactive, rule-based programming languages must ensure, either in the definition of the data model or through specific constructs of the rule language itself, that a rule-based program is able to react to changes in the data. While ECA rule languages introduce the concept of event in the data model and the rule language to this end, production rule languages introduce the concept of *working memory* in the data model, and an *update* statement in the rule language.

The working memory is the finite set of data items (facts, objects... names vary) against which the rules are executed. Data items are explicitly added to, and removed from, this set by the program through dedicated statements (usually *assert* and *retract*). Since changes in data are explicitly notified to the rule engine through the *update* statement, the data can follow basically any data model. Some production rule languages, such as OPS5, include a custom data metamodel in their definitions. Most modern production rule languages are designed to operate on foreign data models, such as those of other programming languages (e.g. Java or .NET's CLR) or XML dialects. Their data model then heavily relies on the introspection mechanisms provided by the foreign data models, such as reflection in programming languages, or the XML schemata.

Relation with RDF Concepts. In the same manner than a production rule language can be adapted to an XML dialect or to a programmation language model, it can process RDF models and data. However, some specificities of RDF induce new constraints on the rule language and on the rule engine. For example, RDF resources are type-mutable, and new type labels may be added to a resource during the execution of the rules. Moreover, the model itself could change at runtime through the addition of new properties or types. Another example can be found in RDF with subproperties, or in OWL with transitive, commutative, or inverse relations. To support these additional modeling features, the rule engine must elaborate its handling of the type system, and extend its pattern matching function to take the specific capabilities of properties into account. Depending on the production rule system considered, all or only part of these features will be supported, by additional constructs in the rule language and abilities of the rule engine. This will represent an element of choice for the users, depending on their actual need of RDF specific features.

Structure and Semantics of a Production Rule. As mentioned before, the overall structure of a production rule is *WHEN condition DO action*. The condition part expresses in which situation the rule should be elected for execution; the action part describes what should be performed as part of executing the rule.

The condition part of a rule contains patterns describing the data that will trigger the rule. When evaluating a rule condition, the production rule engine will search the working memory for data that match all the patterns of the rule condition. The nature of the constraints expressed by these patterns depends on the data model; typical examples are constraints on the class of objects, constraints on the value of attributes of objects, or constraints on elements of an XML document. Constraints that involve a single data item from the working memory are called *discrimination tests*; constraints that involve several data items from the working memory are called *join tests*. The data items involved in the condition part can be bound to variable names, for reference in the action part.

Each collection of data items from the working memory that match all the patterns of a rule condition gives birth to a *rule instance*. Executing a rule instance consists in interpreting the statements in the rule action on these data items. The statements that can be found in the action part of a production rule usually are those that can be found in any procedural language: assignments, conditionals, loops.

If the production rule language relies on a foreign data model borrowed from a programming language, it may naturally also borrow its statements: for instance a production rule language using the Java object model is likely to express the action parts of its rules in Java, or a Java-like scripting language. If the production rule language matches XML documents, specific statements have to be introduced to express the action parts of rules. Here again, programming or scripting languages can be reused, provided that a mapping is established between the XML data model and the underlying data model of the language used. In all cases, specific statements must be added to handle the working memory: *assert, retract,* and *update.* Note that production rule languages that use a custom data model can save the *update* statement if their interpretation of assignment integrates the notification to the rule engine.[17]

```
rule highValuePurchaseByYoungCustomer {
  when {
    c: Customer(age < 21);
    s: ShoppingCart(owner == c; value > 1000.0);
  } then {
    s.manualCheck = true;
    update s;
  }
}
```

Fig. 1. Example of a production rule (using the IRL language)

The example in Fig. 1 demonstrates the basic elements of a production rule, here formulated in the ILOG Rule Language (IRL), which is detailed in Section 4.3. In this example, the rule matches two objects in its condition part: an instance of the `Customer` class and an instance of the `ShoppingCart` class. The condition of the rule will be satisfied iff: the value of the `age` attribute of the customer is less than 21, the value of the `value` attribute of the shopping cart is greater than 1,000 (these are discrimination tests), and the value of the `owner` attribute of the shopping cart is a reference to the customer (this is a join test). Note that `Customer` and `ShoppingCart` can be classes of any language such as Java or C#; they can as well be element types from an XML schema.

For each pair of a customer and a shopping cart from the working memory that match all the discrimination and join tests, an instance of the rule is created. In any such instance, the c and s variables are bound to the customer and shopping cart of the instance. When the action part is executed for one rule instance, the `manualCheck` attribute of the shopping cart is set to true, and the rule engine is notified that the shopping cart has been modified, with an *update* statement.

It must be noted that, although the condition part of the rule is still satisfied by the customer and shopping cart after the rule is executed, the rule will not be executed again. This fundamental principle of production rules, called the *refraction principle*, states that once a rule instance has been executed, the

---

[17] This is true also with foreign programming languages that provide a mechanism for extending the access to their data model with notifications, such as the daemons in some dialects of Lisp.

condition of the rule must become false **on the data items of the instance** before the rule can be considered again for execution on these data items. The implementation of this principle is discussed in Section 4.4. As one can imagine, this principle is key in avoiding trivial loops.

Two additional constructs of interest can be used in the condition part of a production rule, namely *not* and *collect*. These construct leverage the finiteness of the working memory to allow the rule author to express conditions on either the *absence* of objects matching a given pattern, or the *collection* of all objects matching a pattern. Rule `tooManyCarts` of Fig. 2 detects a situation where a customer is the owner of two shopping carts or more, while rule `noCart` detects when a customer has no associated cart in working memory.

```
rule tooManyCarts {
  when {
    c: Customer();
    carts: collect ShoppingCart(owner == c) where (size() > 1);
  } then {
    out.println("Customer " + c.name + " has too many (" +
                carts.size() + ") carts.");
  }
}

rule noCart {
  when {
    c: Customer();
    not ShoppingCart(owner == c);
  } then {
    out.println("Customer " + c.name + " has no cart.");
  }
}
```

Fig. 2. Example of the *collect* and *not* constructs

Stateless and Stateful Semantics of a Production Rule Engine. We have described above the semantics of the basic operations on a rule, namely: evaluating the condition part of a rule against a working memory, creating a rule instance on a matching tuple of data items, and executing a rule instance. Similarly the *assert, retract,* and *update* respectively add or remove an item to/from the working memory, and notify the rule engine that a data item has changed in the working memory. Defining how these operations on rules and on the working memory interact, defines the semantics of the rule engine, and thus of the execution of a rule program. And there are several possible combinations. We present here the two most useful ones, which are related to a stateless and a stateful usage of a rule engine.

The *stateful* case corresponds to applications that correlate data items, or that infer information from the existing data items. A typical example is network or plant supervision, where data from various sources is correlated to synthesize a global picture. In these applications, and in contrast with the stateless case described below, the action of one rule may heavily influence the eligibility of other rules, by modifying the values of attributes involved in the condition parts. As a consequence, the rule engine must carefully take *update* notifications into account in order to ensure that the truth value of the rule conditions, and thus the list of eligible rules, is known at any time. How to efficiently implement this is the cornerstone of the many variants of the Rete algorithm, described in Section 4.4.

The principle of the rule execution algorithm in the stateful case is to maintain at all times which rules are eligible for execution, based on the state of the working memory. The set of these candidate rule instances is called the *conflict set*. As described in Fig. 3, the rule engine picks a rule instance from this set and executes its actions. This may affect the working memory, either by adding data items to it, or by removing items from it, or by updating items that are in working memory. In reaction to this the rule engine updates the conflict set, that is, it creates rule instances for the rules whose condition parts become true, and removes the rule instances whose condition parts become false. The engine operates in this way until the conflict set is empty.

> **Algorithm** STATEFULPRENGINE
> 1. compute conflict set CS from working memory WM
> 2. **while** CS is not empty **do**
> 3.   pick a rule instance (r, t) from CS
> 4.   execute the actions of r on the tuple t of data items
> 5.   update CS from the updated WM
> 6. **end**

Fig. 3. Production rule execution algorithm in a stateful context

The *stateless* case corresponds to what is called filtering applications, where the rules are used to scan a flow of objects on a one-by-one, or tuple-by-tuple, basis. Examples include data validation, call dispatching, or even some simple form of scoring. In these applications, all the rules typically have the same signature, that is, they match the same number of objects of the same classes. More important, the attributes involved in the patterns of the condition parts of the rules are **never** modified by the action parts of the rules. This property of the rules entails that the eligibility of the rules on a given tuple of data items will not vary during the execution of the rules. In other words, given a tuple of data items, the engine can evaluate each rule condition in turn, and immediately execute the rule actions if the condition is satisfied. This will yield the same results as the conflict set approach, where all the rule conditions would first be evaluated on the tuple, and then instances of the matching rules would be executed. Furthermore in the stateless case working memory updates can be ignored, or at least delayed until the processing of all the rules on the tuple. This approach is followed by the Sequential algorithm exposed in Section 4.4. Under the conditions stated above on the rules, the stateless semantics can be viewed as an optimization of the stateful one.

The rule execution algorithm in the stateless case, described in Fig. 4, thus relies on an inner loop working on a given tuple of data items, where the rule engine evaluates the condition part of each rule against the tuple, and if satisfied executes the action part of the rule. In an outer loop the tuples of data items are formed, and fed to the inner loop. How these tuples are formed may vary: they may come from the content of the working memory, in which case the rule engine will have to take care in the outer loop of the *assert, retract,* and *update* operations; or they may be handled outside of the rule program, in particular in the rather common case where the rule actions do not add nor remove data items to/from the working memory.

Algorithm STATELESSPRENGINE
1. **for each** tuple t of data items **do**
2.   **for each** rule r **do**
3.   **if** t satisfies the condition part of r **then**
4.   execute the actions of r on t
5.   **end**
6. **end**

Fig. 4. Production rule execution algorithm in a stateless context

4.3   ILOG JRules as an Example of a Production Rules System

ILOG JRules[18] is a complete Business Rules Management System (BRMS), that is, a collection of development tools and runtime libraries that help both IT and business people in writing business rules, maintaining them over time and across the enterprise, and deploying them for execution. This section details the concepts leading to the introduction of *business rules*, and then presents the *tools* and *languages* in ILOG JRules that provide support in addressing the challenges arising in the life cycle of a business rules application.

Business Policies and Business Rules. Business policies gather the knowledge of a company, an organization, etc. describing how operations are to be conducted. They are *a priori* not meant to be processed by a computer, but rather by humans (or business people). As such, they are typically worded in natural language, and stored on paper.

When automation of business policies is considered, a more software-centric embodiment is introduced as business rules, and an unambiguous and executable form of rules is looked for, for instance production rules. Yet, the desire to preserve the interesting property of business policies to be usable by non-technical people has led to the design of Business Rule Management Systems, where domain experts can author rules in a business-friendly format, which is then automatically translated into a format suitable for execution, namely a programming language.

---

[18] ILOG, http://www.ilog.com/

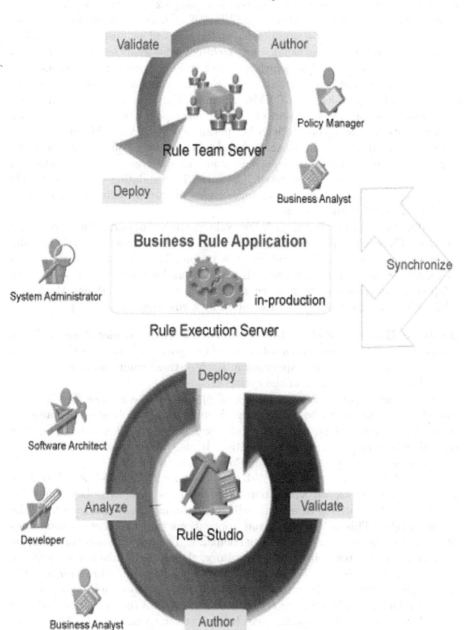

Fig. 5. The life cycle of a production rules based software application

The Life Cycle of a Business Rules Application. The development and the maintenance of a real production system is a complex activity involving several actors throughout the life cycle of the application, and of the rules themselves. The life cycle of the rules can be summarized as follows, and as illustrated in Fig. 5.

The first protagonist is usually an Architect who analyzes the application and builds the data model on which the rules will be expressed. This model will typically derive from the application's underlying data model, such as a Java object model or a collection of XML schemas. The rules themselves are then authored based on a description of the company policy, for instance a paper documentation. The authoring is either performed by a Policy Manager, or the rules are drafted by a Business Analyst and validated by a Policy Manager. Once the rules are ready they are deployed by an Administrator to the production machine where they will be executed. The authoring-validation-deployment cycle can be repeated as the policies change. Rules may eventually be retired and archived away from the system.

As illustrated in Fig. 5, this rich life cycle has to be supported by a collection of tools. These tools are designed to be used by the various actors in the life cycle, that is, both technical and business people. This also leads to the design of various levels of rule languages, all with a sound semantics, but some more adapted to being handled by non-technical rule authors such as Policy Managers, while others are more suited for execution by a rule engine.

Tools for Business Rules Management. The ILOG JRules Business Rules Management System provides a collection of components to support the complex life cycle of a business rules application. Each of these components is targetted toward some specific actors in the cycle.

ILOG Rule Studio is made of a set of plugins to the Eclipse development platform. It is meant to be used by the Architect and the Business Analyst to build the data model on which the rules will be expressed and to define the overall architecture of the rule application. It also allows them to author rules, as well as to create templates for the Policy Manager to fill.

ILOG Rule Team Server is a Web application with a Web-based interface. It serves as a workspace where non-technical users such as Policy Managers can work collaboratively to author, edit, validate, organize, and search for the business rules. This is key in evolved applications that can contain thousands of rules and may involve dozens of participants. The projects and the elements they contain are stored in a rule repository, that is, a database connected to ILOG Rule Team Server. Authentification and privilege procedures ensure that actors have rights to perform modification or deployment on the rule repository.

ILOG Rule Execution Server is targetted at System Administrators that need to push rule sets to J2EE applications. It allows them to monitor the deployment of rules and to define versions of rule sets.

ILOG Rule Scenario Manager is a component accessible both from ILOG Rule Execution Server and ILOG Rule Team Server, and designed to help users test their rules against real data.

From Business Policies to Executable Rules. If for example a company has the policy "When a customer under 21 buys for more than $ 1,000 the transaction must be manually checked", this policy could be expressed by the business rule in Fig. 6. This rule would typically be authored using ILOG Rule Team Server. In order to be executed, it would first be translated into the IRL rule given in Fig. 1, then pushed to an application embedding a rule engine.

```
definitions
  set c to a customer;
  set s to a shopping cart;
if all of the following conditions are true:
  - the age of c is less than 21
  - the value of s is greater than 1,000
  - c is the owner of s
then
  make it true that s must be manually checked;
```

Fig. 6. Example of a business rule (using the BAL language)

Business Rule Languages. ILOG JRules defines several formats for business rules: the Business Action Language (BAL), the Decision Tables, and the Decision Trees. The Business Action Language, illustrated in Fig. 6, provides a great level of expresiveness, while allowing non-technical users to author rules with a minimal learning curve.

Decision tables and trees provide a concise view of a set of business rules as a spreadsheet or tree. Spreadsheets and trees help the rule author navigate and manage large sets of business rules. Decision tables are rules composed of rows and columns and are used to lay out in tabular form all possible situations which a business decision may encounter, and to specify which action to take in each of these situations. Decision tables allow the user to view and manage large sets of business rules with homogeneous conditions. Decision trees provide the same functionality, but are composed of branches that have decision nodes as their inner nodes, and action nodes as their leaves. Decision trees allow the user to manage a large set of rules with some conditions in common but not all.

ILOG JRules even provides a framework for defining new, specialized business rule languages; this Business Rule Language Definition Framework (BRLDF) will be used by software engineers to taylor a dedicated rule language for business experts to author rules in a specific domain or application.

Ruleflow. ILOG JRules introduces an additional concept, which is only remotely connected to production rules, but which acknowledges the fact that any program of a reasonable size has both declarative and procedural aspects. This concept is named *ruleflow*, and is used to describe the flow of execution of a program. A ruleflow can be edited using a graphical editor, and is eventually translated into an IRL representation. A ruleflow is composed of tasks, which can be of three kinds:

- A *rule task* is made of a selection from the set of all rules. It also has a number of parameters, among which the choice of the stateless or stateful semantics (see Section 4.2). When a rule task is executed, the corresponding algorithm is activated on the rules composing the task.
- A *function task* executes a function, that is, in essence a series of actions as could be found in the action part of a rule.
- A *flow task* orchestrates a collection of other task (rule, function, and flow tasks) using standard statements such as sequence, conditionals, loops, fork-join, etc.

In addition to the tasks, a ruleflow contains global variables (known as "ruleset variables") that can be used to vehiculate data between rules and tasks, and marks one of the tasks (usually a flow task) as the main task. Organizing rules into a ruleflow allows the user to handle larger rule-based programs, and to better master their operational semantics. As a result, executing a ILOG JRules program amounts to populating the working memory and then launching the main task of the ruleflow.

Executable Rules. ILOG JRules defines one language for executable rules, named ILOG Rule Language (IRL). All kinds of business rules are eventually translated in IRL for execution. However rules can be directly authored in IRL using ILOG Rule Studio (but not using ILOG Rule Team Server, which is aimed at non-technical users). They are then referred to as technical rules. As illustrated by the examples in Fig. 1 and 2, the ILOG Rule Language ressembles classical programming languages. It allows to use more advanced constructs, such as loops in the action part of the rules.

Integration in an Application. The rules encode usually only part of the logic of an application. And beyond the logic there is also the logistics, that is, the user interface, the connection to other software such as databases, etc. The interaction and co-operation of various parts of an application, including the part that is implemented using rules, has to be addressed by any rule-based system.

ILOG JRules is a system written in Java, and as such is designed to be interfaced with Java applications, or as a consequence with any programming language that a Java program can be interfaced with. As far as Java is concerned, the main two cases are standard J2SE applications, and J2EE-based systems. In both cases, the principle is that the application embedding the rule engine is the master of the control flow. It is responsible for providing the rules and ruleflow to the engine, of populating the working memory, and of triggerring the execution of the rules. The engine then performs the rule execution and returns the control to the application. Since the working memory has been populated with **references** (as opposed to copies) to the Java objects of the host application, the execution of the rules directly implements the application logic on the actual objects handled by the application.

In the J2SE case, this co-operation scheme between the application and the rule engine is implemented using simple Java calls to an Application Programming Interface (API) defined in the ILOG JRules documentation.

J2EE Deployment. For the integration of rules into a J2EE-based application, the ILOG Rule Execution Server (RES) provides, for the main application servers, ready-to-use J2EE rule execution services that implements this behavior. In addition, the Web-based console of the RES allows system administrators to manage rule-based applications by deploying new versions of rule sets to rule execution services, by enabling or disabling them, and through basic monitoring and statistical analysis tools.

The console provides remote management and monitoring through the JMX technology. The model persists all changes made to a ruleset. The version log maintained by ILOG JRules records the details of the different versions of the ruleset including information on the user who modified data, time of modification, and any comments that have been made.

Generating Web Services From Rules. An additional feature of ILOG JRules is the ability for the user to generate a Web Service implementation from a rule set. Deploying production rule sets as Web Services allows users to define and change the behavior of Web servers during their execution. As Web Services are commonly used over the Web to process information in a stateless or a stateful context, this deployment helps bringing production rules into Web applications.

The deployment itself consists in generating a specific Web Service operation for the rule set. The signature of the operation is based upon the signature of the rule set, described in ILOG JRules with formal variables called *ruleset parameters*. As Web Services operates only on XML data, the types in the signature should be compliant with the XML-XSD type system. A binding between XML types and and their related object types (Java, C++, C#) may help to adapt the rules to XML information. The execution of the operation is composed of the following steps: providing the input parameter values to the engine, executing the rules, and returning the output parameter values to the Web Service caller as XML documents. In order to cope with scalability in terms of number of operation calls, ILOG JRules provides the way for pools of rule engines to be managed inside the application server embedding the Web Service.

Processing Web Data With ILOG JRules. ILOG JRules provides two way to process Web data inside rules by the mean of two automatic bindings: the XML Binding and the Web Service Binding.

Most Web data is defined through XML documents, modeled by XML Schemata. The XML Binding feature transforms a schema into a runtime object model, in such a way that an XML document can be deserialized into a memory object. ILOG JRules enables to execute production rules against such memory objects. Hence, most of XML documents coming from the Web can be processed.

The Web Service Binding feature enables a programmer to invoke external Web Service operations from a production rule as if they were usual Java methods. The WSDL model of the Web Service is first translated into an object model.

The port types and their operations are mapped onto classes and methods. As soon as this mapping is achieved, ILOG JRules is able to send or retrieve data automatically represented as objects, to or from the Web Services. This feature is important as Web Services are identified as a usual source of information and processing over the Web.

Validating and Testing Rules. The ILOG Rule Studio and ILOG Rule Team Server components provide a number of rule validation services based on static analysis techniques. In addition, the ILOG Rule Scenario Manager (RSM) component is an execution test tool to dynamically verify deployable rules. The RSM console is intended for policy managers to manage the rule testing environment, to run rulesets on predefined sets of input data, or to monitor sets of performance tests. Using the RSM console, the users define and manage scenarios, organize them into scenario suites, and set up simulations that compare scenario suites.

Each scenario specifies deployed rulesets to execute and input data to execute the rules on. A set of tests can be applied to track the performance of the execution of the rules. Testing against a baseline report allows for non-regression testing of the rules as they evolve. In scenario suites and simulations, the user can specify key performance indicators to follow the performance evolution of scenarios over modifications to the rules.

4.4   Implementation of a Production Rule Engine

Overview of the Rete Algorithm. Forward-chaining inference algorithms, including Rete ([For82]), use a match-select-execute cycle. During the *match* stage, the engine creates rule instances by evaluating the rule conditions against the data in the working memory. The *select* stage consists in choosing one of the above-created rule instances. In the *execute* stage, the actions of the selected rule instance are executed, which may modify the working memory and trigger a new *match* stage. This cycle follows the stateful semantics described in Section 4.2 by Fig. 3.

A characteristics of the Rete algorithm is to perform the *match* stage each time the working memory is modified. As a result, the set of potentially executable rule instances is always up-to-date relative to the working memory. A naive implementation of this stage may be time-consuming, due to the huge number of combinations between the data items to be considered. To address this risk, Rete compiles the rule conditions into a *network* so as to minimize the number of patterns that need to be evaluated. The two underlying mechanisms are the sharing of patterns that are common to serval rules, and the incrementality of change propagation.

Rete also defines a selection strategy for choosing a rule instance in the conflict set that results from the evaluation of the rule conditions. The conflict set is implemented as an *agenda* of rule instances which are sorted according to this strategy. The engine cycle ends only when the agenda is empty.

The Rete Network Structure and Behavior. The Rete network is a compact representation of all the patterns expressed in the conditions of the rules. It is a directed acyclic graph structured in four layers, namely:

- The discrimination tree, where the nodes represent the discrimination tests found in the rule conditions;
- The alpha nodes, which form the data item tuples from the individual items;
- The join network, in which the nodes represent the join tests found in the rule conditions; and
- The rule nodes, which form the rule instances.

The input of the graph is the working memory; the output is the agenda. Each node in the network is equiped with a local memory, in which are stored all the data items or tuples that satisfy the pattern associated with the node, as well as the ones associated with the ancestor nodes in the network.

The network reacts to three kinds of events coming from the working memory: insertion of a data item into the working memory, modification of a data item in the working memory, and removal of a data item from the working memory. The events are propagated throughout the network by tokens; the first two kinds of events use *positive* tokens, while the last kind uses *negative* tokens. The tokens also carry the data item concerned by the event.

When a node in the Rete network receives a positive token for a data item, the rule engine evaluates on the data item the pattern represented by the node. If the data item satisfies the pattern, and[19] the data item is not already present in the local memory of the node, it is stored and the positive token is forwarded down the network. If the data item was already stored in the node memory and does not satisfy the pattern (any longer), it is removed from the local memory of the node and a negative token is sent to the children nodes.

When a node receives a negative token for a data item, and[19] the data item is present in the local memory of the node, it removes the data item from its local memory and propagates down the negative token.

The layers of a Rete network are depicted in Fig. 7 and detailed below.

The Discrimination Tree. The discrimination tree in the Rete network performs the evaluation of the discrimination tests of the rule conditions.[20] The first level of nodes in the discrimination tree operates a classification of the objects. Below these classification of nodes are discrimination nodes, which test the patterns expressed on the properties of the data items.

Like all nodes in the Rete network, the nodes in the discrimination tree maintain a local memory of data items satisfying the pattern that they test, and

---

[19] This implements the refraction principle which, as mentioned on page 209, states that when a rule is executed on a tuple of data items, its condition part must become false on this very tuple, and then of course true again, for the rule to be eligible for execution on the tuple.

[20] Let us remind (from the discussion on page 208) that *discrimination tests* are patterns that express a constraint involving a single data item from the working memory, while patterns involving several data items are called *join tests*.

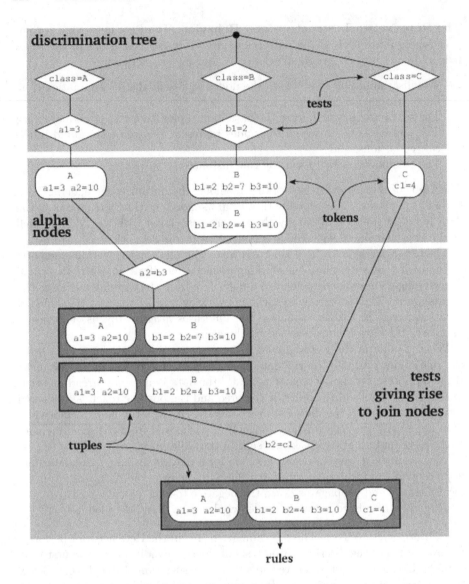

Fig. 7. An example of a Rete network

propagate positive and negative tokens according to the principles mentioned above.

The Alpha Nodes. The alpha nodes gather the tokens that successfully passed the discrimination tests, and prepare them as tuples for the join network. There is thus no pattern evaluation performed by alpha nodes. The local memory of each node stores one or several tokens (or equivalently the data items carried by the tokens), which are represented by round-cornered rectangles in Fig. 7. There are three alpha nodes in the figure: one alpha node contains two items of class B, while the other two alpha nodes contain only one data item each: one of class A and one of class C, respectively.

The Join Network. This layer is in charge of performing the Cartesian product between the alpha nodes by applying join tests. It is composed of two alternating kinds of nodes: join nodes and beta nodes.

The role of a join node is to evaluate a join test on a tuple of data items. To this end, a join node makes the cross-product of two different tuple memory nodes (alpha or beta nodes). Note that the standard Rete involves binary join nodes with a left upper branch linked to an alpha node, and a right upper branch linked to either an alpha or a beta node. On the resulting tuples, the rule engine evaluates the join test represented by the join node. Each satisfying tuple is stored in the local memory and propagated to the descendant beta nodes.

The role of a beta node is to memorize all tuples satisfying a join predicate. Special variants of the beta nodes are also used to implement the *not* and *collect* constructs. The output of a beta node is either a subsequent join node, or a rule node which will form a rule instance on the tuple of data items, and insert it into the agenda.

The Rete Agenda. The agenda stores rule instances that are entitled to be fired. A rule instance is the association between a rule and a tuple of data items that passes through the whole Rete network, and thus satisfies all the patterns in the condition of the rule. Rule instances placed in the agenda are said to be eligible.

Unless the agenda is empty, in which case the execution cycle of the engine is stopped, it often happens that there are several eligible rules. Consequently, the rule engine has to have some way of deciding which particular rule in the agenda should be fired. A conflict resolution strategy is then applied. In the agenda, rule instances are ordered according to several criteria that determine which rule should be fired first. Additional execution control can be offered for the implementation of more complex features.

– Priority: The first criterion that is taken into account to decide at which position a rule instance should be placed in the agenda is the rule priority, a numerical quantity associated with the rule. The rule priority may depend on values of properties of the data items matched by the rule: the priority is then actually dependent on the rule instance, and is said to be dynamic.
– Recency: If two rule instances have the same priority, the rule that matches the most recent object (that is, the most recently inserted or modified object) will be fired first. This principle is often named LIFO, as the last rule instance in agenda is executed the first, given the same priority.
– Specificity: This criterion states that the most specialized rules must be executed before more general rules. How it is implemented varies with the rule engine.

Priority, recency, and specificity are used to resolve conflicts when several rule instances are candidate for firing at the same time. If, after using this conflict resolution method, several rule instances remain candidates, then the engine should use internal metarules to ensure that the same sequence of rule firing will always be followed, given the same conditions.

The Sequential Algorithm. The previous sections explained Rete as a powerful and complex algorithm, able to perform efficiently incremental inference chaining. However, the inference chaining feature is costly in time and memory. An important part of industrial production rules applications only operate a simple matching on inputs without any modification nor inference chaining on the working memory. These filtering applications are the target of the stateless semantics of a production rule engine (see Section 4.2), which is implemented by the Sequential algorithm.

In the Sequential algorithm, tuples of data items are submitted to rules. The structure of the tuples (in terms of object classes) is computed from the structure of the rule conditions which, as explained in Section 4.2, all match the same number of objects of the same classes. The data items in the tuples are fetched from the working memory.

The conditions of the rules are then evaluated on each tuple, in an order following the rule priorities.[21] The satisfied rules are immediately executed. There is no agenda that collects the rule instances before executing them.

This simplification of the engine cycle permits to enhance the sharing of tests between rules. The evaluation is very similar to a decision tree applied on a single tuple. The algorithm is quicker than Rete on filtering problems.

LEAPS Algorithm. As mentioned above, Rete-like algorithms materialize the whole set of tuples satisfying a rule set. The computation occurring during the matching part of the engine cycle results in synchronizing the internal engine state of the Rete network and the real object state of the working memory. Nevertheless, the Rete propagation by saturation is memory and time consuming. In fact, on some rule sets the incremental inference may lead to huge modifications of the Rete network. Some matching evaluations done at one time are never used later.

The main contribution of LEAPS is to introduce a lazy evaluation of the satisfying tuples. They are calculated only when needed.

Instead of being memorized in local memories of the network nodes, the tuples are stored in containers that are iterated by means of complex cursors. Every data item addition to, or removal from, a container is assigned a timestamp. The iteration on containers performed by cursors is based on the timestamps. The system maintains an internal stack of insertion/retraction events ordered by their timestamps. During a rule execution cycle, the top level of the stack is selected and used to constitute a seed of tuples for a rule. If the seeded tuple satisfies the rule, then it is executed. Otherwise, the next rule is examined against the current top element of the stack. After a rule is fired, the next top element takes place. When the stack is empty, the execution stops.

An important distinction between LEAPS and Rete concerns the conflict set determination. While Rete proceeds by saturation and determines the conflict

---

[21] As a consequence, the Sequential algorithm does not support dynamic priorities.

set completely at each modification of the working memory, LEAPS only selects the first rule instance to be executed, without constituting the complete conflict set. This lazy evaluation explains deeply the difference in performance of the two algorithms.

4.5   Production Rule Samples

Shopping Cart Example. This section proposed a simple implementation of the shopping cart sample (described in Section 2.2). The discount policies specifying how to calculate the discount of a customer are listed hereafter:

1. if the total amount of the customer's shopping is higher than 100, then perform a discount of 10
2. if it is the first shopping of the customer, then perform a discount of 5
3. if the client has a gold status and buys more than 5 discounted items, then perform an additional discount of 2
4. the rule 1 and 2 could not be applied for the same customer, the first rule having the priority against the second. The third rule is applied only if rule 1 or rule 2 have been applied.

We propose to show some elements of implementation of such policies based upon ILOG JRules language.

Firstly, the object model must be defined and might be composed of the following classes:

- the *Customer* class defines the customer's characteristics (status, first shopping...),
- the *ShoppingCart* class memorizes the current shopping of a customer as a list of items and their global amount.
- the *Item* class represents an article order and its price.
- the *Discount* contains the final discount of the shopping.

Secondly, we propose a production rule implementation of the policies using the previous object model. Observe that the discounting policies should be evaluated in a specific order. This order will be ensured by the priority of the rules. In ILOG JRules, a rule priority is an integer expression: the greater the more important. Note that there is not always an isomorphic mapping between the policies and their production rule implementation. For example, the fourth policy has no production rule implementation, but is shared among the others.

The first step is to determine if the first policy is satisfied, Fig. 8. The HIGH priority ensures that the rule be the first to be evaluated.

At this point, Fig. 9, the second rule is activated if there is no discount, that is to say if the first rule has not been executed.

Finally, Fig. 10, the third rule is potentially applied. It requires that a discount instance exists in the working memory, infering that one of the previous rule has been executed. The LOW priority ensures that this rule be executed at last.

At the ruleset level, a *Customer* and a *ShoppingCart* instances must be inserted in the working memory to activate the discount rules. Those instances

```
rule giveGlobalAmountDiscount {

  priority = HIGH;

  when {

   cart: ShoppingCart ( getTotalAmount()>100 );

   not Discount ();

  }

  then {

    insert Discount ( ) {

     value = .1;

    }

  }

}
```

Fig. 8. giveGlobalAmountDiscount rule

might be seen as the inputs of a rule service that executes the shopping cart ruleset and performs the discounting policies. The result of the service execution is the output discount instance, if exists. We have then identified a service, *computeDiscount* relying on the following signature:

$$computeDiscount : Customer \times ShoppingCart \rightarrow Discount$$

As soon as the input and output parameters of the ruleset are identified, ILOG JRules helps to generate a Web service embedding the ruleset execution. This Web service is then declared and managed by an application server. By this way, production rulesets are easily deployed in Web environments.

Credit Analysis Example. Here is a simple implementation based on ILOG JRules of the credit analysis sample (described in Section 2.2). A loan acceptance is determined depending on the client's history and his demand. The acceptance process follows the listed policies:

1. if the loan duration is lower than five years then set the loan rate to 4.0% and add 5 to the score, else set it to 6.0%,
2. if the client has filed a bankrupcy, substract 5 to the score,
3. if the client's salary is between 20000 and 40000, add 10 to the score,
4. if the client's salary is greater than 40000, add 15 to the score,
5. if the score is upper than 15, then the loan is accepted.

```
rule giveFirstShoppingDiscount {

  priority = MEDIUM;

  when {

   Customer ( isFirstShopping() );

   cart: ShoppingCart ( );

   not Discount ();

  }

  then {

   insert Discount ( ); {

     discount = .05;

   }

  }

}
```

Fig. 9. giveFirstShoppingDiscount rule

Firstly, the object model, used later by the production rules, must be defined:

1. the *Borrower* class provides the client's characteristics (salary, bankrupcy),
2. the *Loan* class is composed of the loan parameters (duration, rate, client's score).

An instance of a borrower and a loan instance, the inputs of the service, must be inserted in the working memory before the rules are executed. Those insertions might be performed by other production rules not presented in this section. The result of the execution, the output, is provided by the loan instance (acceptance, rate, score).

The first rule, Fig. 11, corresponding to the first policy, declares two rule bodies: a *then* and an *else* body. The last *evaluate* condition determines which body is executed when the upper conditions are satisfied.

The second rule, Fig. 12, calculates the bankrupcy score, if necessary.

The third rule, Fig. 13, calculates the score depending on the borrower's salary. Observe that this rule implements both the third and the fourth policy.

The fourth rule, Fig. 14, determines if the loan is accepted. The execution order of the previous rules does not impact the final result. However, this last

```
rule giveGoldDiscount {

  priority = LOW;

  when {

   Customer ( isGold() );

   cart: ShoppingCart ( );

   collect Item ( isDiscounted() ) where ( size()>=5 ) in cart.getItems();

   discount: Discount();

  }

  then {

   modify discount {

     value += .02;

   }

  }

}
```

Fig. 10. giveFiveOverFiveItemsGoldDiscount rule

rule must be executed after the others as soon as the score computation is completed. It is ensured by its LOWER priority.

The loan acceptance service might be deployed as a Web service operation presenting the following informal signature:

$computeLoanAcceptance : Borrower \times Loan \rightarrow Loan$

4.6 Overview of Existing Production Rules Languages and Systems

OPS5. The OPS (Official Production System) language family has been designed in the 70th by Charles Forgy. OPS5 was the first production rule language to be used in an expert system.

OPS5 uses a forward-chaining inference engine; programs execute by scanning "working memory elements". OPS5 stores data in working memory, and if-then rules in production memory. If the data in working memory matches the conditions of a rule in production memory, the rule actions take place.

The engine architecture, based on the Rete algorithm, is especially efficient to scale up to large problems involving hundreds or thousands of rules.

```
rule computeLoanRate {

  when {

    loan: Loan ( );

    evaluate ( loan.duration < 5 );

  }

  then {

    modify loan {

      score += 5;

      rate = .04;

    }

  }

  else {

    modify loan {

      rate = .06;

    }

  }

}
```

Fig. 11. computeLoanRate rule

The OPS5 rule named **rule1** shown in Fig. 15 is composed of three conditions and one action. The last two conditions match locations that are not connected to any place of the same name. The action part inserts a new **place** instance in the working memory.

JBoss Rules. Previously named Drools, JBoss Rules[22] is a Java open source business engine (Apache Software Foundation open source license). It has implementations for the Rete and for the LEAPS pattern matching algorithms. The conflict resolution of the agenda is based on the priority and the LIFO principles. The rule structure takes benefit of the underlying Java object model. Fig. 16 gives an example of a JBoss Rules rule.

---

[22] JBoss rule, http://www.jboss.com/products/rules

```
rule computeBankrupcyScore {

  when {

    Borrower ( hasBankrupcy() );

    loan: Loan ( );

  }

  then {

    modify loan {

      score -= 5;

    }

  }

}
```

Fig. 12. computeBankrupcyScore rule

In addition the JBoss rules environment provides a way to declare rules as a decision table spreadsheet (Excel). A dedicated compiler analyses the spreadsheet and translates it into rules.

Blaze Advisor. Blaze Advisor, developped by FairIsaac[23], includes a visual development environment for writing, editing, and testing business rule services that are executed using a sophisticated rule server.

The rule repository enables developers to work in a coordinated manner as teams and leverage each others work by sharing and reusing rules, rule sets, rule flows and object models. It can be stored as an XML file, database or LDAP directory.

It offers a simple English-like Structured Rule Language (SRL) for writing rules.

At the same time sophisticated ruleset metaphors (decision tables, decision trees and scorecards) provide a way for nonprogrammers to author rules as well.

PegaRules. PegaRules, developed by PegaSystems[24], introduces different types of rules: declarative rules (computing values or enforcing constraints), Decision Tree rules, Integration Rules (interfacing different system and application), transformation rules (data) and process rules (Managing the receiving, assignment, routing, and tracking of work).

---

[23] FairIsaac, http://www.fairisaac.com

[24] PegaSystems, http://www.pegasystems.com/

```
rule computeSalaryScore {

  when {

    borrower: Borrower ( s: getSalary(); s>20000);

    loan: Loan ( );

    evaluate ( s<40000);

  }

  then {

    modify loan {

      score += 10;

    }

  else {

    modify loan {

      score += 15;

    }

  }

}
```

Fig. 13. computeSalaryScore rule

It provides convenient HTML rule forms to build, manage and configure rules.

An execution environment provides both forward chaining (procedural logic) and backward chaining (goal-based logic) to determine known and unknown dependent facts.

Jess. Jess[25], a rule engine for the Java platform, is a superset of CLIPS programming language, developed by Ernest Friedman-Hill of Sandia National Labs. It was first written in late 1995.

It provides backward and forward chaining on facts executed by a Rete algorithm.

A last type of rules with no body, the defquery construct, are used to search the fact knowledge base under direct program control. This query returns the list of all fact tuples of the working memory matching the rule condition.

---

[25] Jess, http://www.jessrules.com/

```
rule computeLoanAcceptance {

  priority = LOWER;

  when {

    loan: Loan ( );

  }

  then {

    modify loan {

      acceptance = (score>15);

    }

  }

}
```

Fig. 14. computeLoanAcceptance rule

```
(p orderItemWhenOutOfStock
  (item ^id <itemId>)
  - (stock ^itemId <itemId>)
  (supplierStock ^supplierId <supplierId> ^itemId <itemId>)
  -->
  (make order ^itemId <itemId> ^supplierId <supplierId>)
)
```

Fig. 15. Example of an OPS5 rule

```
rule "order item when out of stock"
  when
    item: Item ( )
    not Stock ( this.item == item );
    supplier: Supplier ( hasItemInStock ( item ) );
  then
    assert( new Order(item,supplier) );
end
```

Fig. 16. Example of a JBoss Rules rule

```
rule discount is
  if shoppingCart.items.count is between 2 and 4
  then
    shoppingCart.discount = 10;
```

Fig. 17. Example of a Blaze advisor rule

```
(defrule orderItemWhenOutOfStock
  (item ?itemId)
  (not (stock ?itemId) )
  (supplierStock ?supplierId ?itemId)
 =>
  (assert ( order ?itemId ?supplierId ) )
)
```

Fig. 18. Example of a Jess rule

5 ECA and Production Rules: Similarities and Differences

The introduction of this paper highlighted that ECA rules and production rules address two complementary but different parts of software applications. ECA rules naturally apply in distributed applications, while production rules naturally apply in logically rich applications. As a result, beyond a minimal level of complexity both approaches are beneficial to Web applications.

This different positioning of ECA and production rules can probably be perceived in Sections 3.2 and 4.2, in that the ECA rules are naturally presented to address the distributed nature of Web applications, whereas the presentation of production rules naturally tends to focus on the management of the state system for one node in a distributed Web application.

This section addresses the similarities and differences between the ECA rules and production rules approaches. The positioning of both approaches is studied on the support they provide for distribution, for managing the state of the system, for managing the control flow of the program, for detecting and handling events, and with respect to the current market.

5.1 Distributed Applications

In a distributed system, the architecture requires a dedicated description that is not addressed by rules. Because of the absence of features dedicated to distributed applications in production rules, implementing distributed algorithms using only production rules requires to resort to classical distributed algorithms. On the other hand, the fact that ECA rules are well adapted for distributed applications comes with an associated price: ECA rules have to tackle the challenges of all distributed applications, in particular they are sensitive to the performance of the communication network and protocol they rely on.

5.2 Managing State

Three levels of a state can be distinguished in a rule-based Web application:

1. The state defined by the objects (and events) matched by a rule. This "rule-local state" has a life time spanning from the beginning of the evaluation of the rule conditions, to the end of the execution of the rule actions.

2. The state of the rule engine. This state will be thought of as local to the rule engine when the engine is seen as one of the node in the Web application; it will be thought of as global to the rule engine from the viewpoint of the individual rules managed by the engine. This "engine state" is where ECA and production rule systems differ.
3. The state of the whole Web application. As in all distributed applications, the definition of such a global state is a problem in itself, and neither ECA nor production rules do reify this state in their implementations.

The engine state includes the rule-local states of all the rules being currently under evaluation or execution. In production rule systems, it will additionally include the working memory, and optionally global registers.[26] The working memory and the optional global registers provide the capability of exchanging data between rules, thus augmenting the expression power.

ECA rules usually do not have an engine-level state that is specific and internal to the current process instance. ECA rules have to explicitly maintain this state in events and databases. Consider the example of handling a book order: a process instance is created each time a book order from a customer is received. Such an incoming order could contain information such as the customer's address. This information is not needed immediately, but only late in the process for sending rejection back or acknowledging and delivering the requested books. The customer's data has to be either saved in a database or passed along through all rules as part of event data.

This difference with respect to state management between the ECA and production rule approaches is quite characteristic and has reflections in a number of other differences detailed below.

5.3   Control Flow of Rule Programs

Event-Driven vs. State-Driven Execution. Probably the most salient difference between ECA and production rules is what drives their execution. ECA rules are executed due to an explicit event. In contrast, production rules are executed due to some condition on the state becoming true; while this is usually caused by some event, the event is implicit and not available in the production rule.

To give an example, a production rule might have a condition expressing that a customer is of legal age (18 years or older). When the condition becomes true, it can in general not distinguish whether the customer has had a birthday or whether there has been a manual correction in the data. For an ECA rule this would be different and distinguishable events (and its reaction can include sending a birthday card in the former case).

This also illustrates a more subtle difference between production rules and ECA rules. It might seem at first that the production rule WHEN *age* $\geq$ *18* DO *notify customer service* and the ECA rule ON *change of age* IF *age* $\geq$ *18* DO

---

[26] Such global registers are known as "ruleset variables" in ILOG JRules.

notify customer service specify the same behavior. In fact however, they do not: the production rule will send only *one* notification when the customer becomes 18; the ECA rule will send a notification on *every* birthday once the customer is over 18.[27] Encoding the behavior of the production rule with ECA rules is not necessarily simple. (A possible solution is to encode as part of the data an assertion whether the customer service has already been notified or not, and to query this in the condition part.)

To summarize, ECA rules often allow a more fine-grained control of behavior because they are driven by events not states, but this more fine-grained control comes at a price requiring more complicated programs than production rules in some cases (in particular the cases where the state is more relevant than events).

The Current State of the Computation. The declarative aspect of rules is an advantage for implementing algorithms that rely on case-based reasoning. However it can rapidly occur that some algorithms, or parts of them, introduce a sequential aspect, for which the declarativity is of little help. In these cases the programmer will need to define and maintain a "current state of the computation", which will indicate the parts of the rules that should be considered for implementing each step of the algorithm. There are several ways for a rule language to support this requirement.

Global Objects. The control of the flow of execution can be achieved by adding to each rule a condition on a context object denoting the current state of the computation. However such an object would be a global object (from the viewpoint of the rules): production rule systems provide at least the working memory for storing this global object. However it can be argued that such an implementation is rather an applicative one, as opposed to a support from the language.

This solution is even harder to consider in ECA rule systems due to the lack of an "engine-global state". As a result, there is no clear notion in ECA rule-based specifications of which events are expected next. ECA rules are triggered by every incoming event matching the event query, regardless of whether this event is expected or not. This might entail unexpected behavior, especially if events are generated "out-of-order" by faulty or malicious behavior of systems.

Activation and Deactivation of Rules. Both ECA and production rule systems may provide constructs in the rule languages to activate rules, that is, to make them potential candidates for execution, or to deactivate them, that is, to instruct the engine no longer to consider them for potential execution. This (de)activation of rules being provided by language constructs, they can be invoked by the rule actions and thus will occur at runtime.

Dynamic enabling and disabling of rules provides a solution on a meta-level for controlling the flow of execution. However this method of implementing the control flow is clearly fragile in terms of understanding the program behavior, and as such will cause maintainance issues as soon as the number of rules exceeds a few dozens.

---

[27] In both cases, the behavior might be changed by applying different rule execution semantics, though.

XChange doesn't provide constructs for dynamically (de)activate rules from rule programs. ILOG JRules used to provide an API that could be invoked from rule programs, for that purpose. It has been replaced by the introduction "of rule-flows", described hereafter.

Error and Exception Handling. The ability to specify exceptional conditions and their consequences, including recovery measures, are as important for realizing complex applications as the ability to define "normal behavior." An exceptional situation in the online shop example used throughout this paper could, for example, occur if the credit card of a customer has expired. Possible means for recovery include asking the customer for updated information or canceling the whole order request.

Since exceptions can be conveniently expressed as (special) events, ECA rules are a convenient mechanism for handling exceptions. They allow to treat exceptions like any other event. This approach has quite successfully been employed for exception handling e.g. in [BCCT05].

Production rules typically rely on the sub-language used for the rule actions. For instance, ILOG JRules includes a `try-catch` construct. However, in practice handling an exception requires knowledge about the context in which it occurred, and often involves taking some action to modify the flow of execution. In other words, the notion of a engine-global state may prove missing.

5.4 Detection of Events and of Composite Events

Many ECA rule languages have a strong support for temporal notions through their composite event querying facilities. Application examples where there is a strong need for this include dealing with sensor data (e.g., compute sliding averages), monitoring applications (e.g., correlation of different alarm signals within some time frame), work-flow applications (e.g., waiting for a number of parallel events to finish), and applications involving "time-outs" (e.g., detection of overdue orders).

In their original form, production rules do not allow references to time and events as are necessary in these applications examples. However, efforts have been made to extend production rules in this direction. In particular, ILOG JRules has been augmented with event management capabilities, that is, the recognition of chronicles [Gha96, DM07].

A chronicle is a pattern describing a sequence of events, with time constraints on these events. It is thus expressive enough to support the detection of composite events. In addition, the integration of chronicle recognition with production rules allows to relate the payload of events with state information maintained by regular facts. However, integrating chronicle recognition to the Rete algorithm [Ber02] requires to precisely define the semantics of the pattern matching engine in presence of both timed events and regular facts.

5.5 Maturity of Existing Implementations

As already mentioned in Section 3.5, most of the existing ECA rule languages for the Web are outcomes of research projects. Their implementations are usually just proof-of-concept ones, where efficiency was not considered a priority. However, stable implementations are offered for the Prova language and the ruleCore engine. The Prova language has an open source implementation as Prova 2.0 Beta 3 at moment. Prova has been succesfully employed in the development of the Xcalia[28] product Xcalia Core for Services 4.3.0[29] for efficiently computing global execution plans in a distributed environment.

Contrary to the current status of ECA rules-based systems, the production rules approach has been succesfully employed for developing (commercial and open source) software products. OPS5, JBoss Rules, Blaze Advisor, PegaRules, and Jess have been given as examples of such systems in Section 3.5. The interest in production rules has been influenced by (but has not arisen out of) the need of reactive systems in the new setting – the Web. It might be the case that the Web will accelerate the development of stable implementations also for ECA rules sytems.

6 Conclusion

This paper has discussed the use of different kinds of reactive rules for programming Web-based systems with reactive capabilities. Its main intent is to provide a good foundation towards deciding on the type of reactive rules (systems) to be used for implementing the desired Web application.

Enriching IT systems, such as database management systems not connected to the Web, with reactive features is not a new research and development concern. Reactive rules, as means to realize such systems, have been well-studied in the literature and also have successfully been used in commercial software products. Through the application examples given in this paper, we have motivated the need for employing reactive systems on the Web. We have also stressed the need for adapting existing reactive rules-based approaches to the Web's peculiarities.

The two kinds of reactive rules – Event-Condition-Action rules and production rules – have been discussed in detail and concrete languages of both kinds have been used to exemplify the concepts and their suitability for programming Web applications. By choosing an ECA rules-based language coming from the academia – XChange – and a software product offered by ILOG – ILOG JRules – for illustrating reactive rules systems, we have offered insights in the work done in the academia and industry, which may play a role for those readers which are at the beginning of their careers.

Though not an easy task, we have tried to reveal similarities and differences between the two kinds of reactive rule sytems, so as to guide programmers in choosing the suitable rule system for their Web applications. ECA rules are well-suited for applications where the focus is on the distributed nature of Web and there is a need to refer to events and/or detect composite events. Production rules are well-suited for logically rich applications where the focus is rather on the management of the state system for each Web node than on the distribution

---

[28] Xcalia, http://www.xcalia.com/

[29] Xcalia Core for Services 4.3.0, http://www.xcalia.com/products/core.jsp

aspects. These views reflect the current status of research and development on reactive rules systems and, thus, some of the stated differences might progressively become obsolete in the near or farther future.

Acknowledgments

This research has been partly funded by the European Commission and by the Swiss Federal Office for Education and Science within the 6th Framework Programme project REWERSE number 506779 (http://rewerse.net).

References

[AC05]   Adaikkalavan, R., Chakravarthy, S.: SnoopIB: Interval-Based Event Specification and Detection for Active Databases. Data and Knowledge Engineering (2005) (In press)

[AE04]   Adi, A., Etzion, O.: Amit — the situation manager. Int. J. on Very Large Data Bases 13(2), 177–203 (2004)

[AQM+97]   Abiteboul, S., Quass, D., McHugh, J., Widom, J., Wiener, J.: The Lorel Query Language for Semistructured Data. Proc. Int. Journal on Digital Libraries (1997)

[B+05]   Boag, S., et al.: XQuery 1.0: An XML Query Language. W3C candidate recommendation, World Wide Web Consortium (2005)

[BBB+04]   Berger, S., Bry, F., Bolzer, O., Furche, T., Schaffert, S., Wieser, C.: Xcerpt and visXcerpt: Twin Query Languages for the Semantic Web. In: Proc. Int. Semantic Web Conf (Demos track) (2004)

[BBCC02]   Bonifati, A., Braga, D., Campi, A., Ceri, S.: Active XQuery. In: 18th Int. Conf. on Data Engineering (ICDE2002), San Jose, California (2002)

[BBFS05]   Bailey, J., Bry, F., Furche, T., Schaffert, S.: Web and Semantic Web Query Languages: A Survey. In: Eisinger, N., Małuszyński, J. (eds.) Reasoning Web. LNCS, vol. 3564, pp. 35–133. Springer, Heidelberg (2005)

[BBSW03]   Berger, S., Bry, F., Schaffert, S., Wieser, C.: Xcerpt and visXcerpt: From Pattern-Based to Visual Querying of XML and Semistructured Data. In: Proc. Int. Conf. on Very Large Databases, pp. 1053–1056. Morgan Kaufmann, San Francisco (2003)

[BC06]   Barga, R.S., Caituiro-Monge, H.: Event Correlation and Pattern Detection in CEDR. In: Grust, T., Höpfner, H., Illarramendi, A., Jablonski, S., Mesiti, M., Müller, S., Patranjan, P.-L., Sattler, K.-U., Spiliopoulou, M., Wijsen, J. (eds.) EDBT 2006. LNCS, vol. 4254, pp. 919–930. Springer, Heidelberg (2006)

[BCCT05]   Brambilla, M., Ceri, S., Comai, S., Tziviskou, C.: Exception Handling in Workflow-Driven Web Applications. In: Proc. Int. Conference on World Wide Web, ACM, New York (2005)

[BCP00]   Bonifati, A., Ceri, S., Paraboschi, S.: Active Rules for XML: A New Paradigm for E-Services. In: First Workshop on Technologies for E-Services, colocated with VLDB2000 (2000)

[BE06a]   Bry, F., Eckert, M.: A High-Level Query Language for Events. In: Proc. Int. Workshop on Event-driven Architecture, Processing and Systems, IEEE, Los Alamitos (2006)

[BE06b]   Bry, F., Eckert, M.: Twelve Theses on Reactive Rules for the Web. In: Proc. Int. Workshop Reactivity on the Web, Springer, Heidelberg (2006)

[BE07]   Bry, F., Eckert, M.: Rule-Based Composite Event Queries: The Language XChange^{EQ} and its Semantics. In: Proc. Int. Conf. on Web Reasoning and Rule Systems, Springer, Heidelberg (2007)

[BEE$^+$07] Bry, F., Eisinger, N., Eiter, T., Furche, T., Gottlob, G., Ley, C., Linse, B., Pichler, R., Wei, F.: Foundations of Rule-Based Query Answering. Reasoning Web Summer School 2007 (2007)

[BEGP06]   Bry, F., Eckert, M., Grallert, H., Pătrânjan, P.-L.: Reactive Web Rules: A Demonstration of XChange. In: Proc. Int. Conf. on Rules and Rule Markup Languages (RuleML) for the Semantic Web, Posters and Demonstrations (2006)

[BEP06a]   Bry, F., Eckert, M., Pătrânjan, P.-L.: Querying Composite Events for Reactivity on the Web. In: Shen, H.T., Li, J., Li, M., Ni, J., Wang, W. (eds.) Advanced Web and Network Technologies, and Applications. LNCS, vol. 3842, pp. 38–47. Springer, Heidelberg (2006)

[BEP06b]   Bry, F., Eckert, M., Pătrânjan, P.-L.: Reactivity on the Web: Paradigms and Applications of the Language XChange. J. of Web Engineering 5(1), 3–24 (2006)

[BEPR06]   Bry, F., Eckert, M., Pătrânjan, P.-L., Romanenko, I.: Realizing Business Processes with ECA Rules: Benefits, Challenges, Limits. In: Proc. Int. Workshop on Principles and Practice of Semantic Web. LNCS, Springer, Heidelberg (2006)

[Ber02]   Berstel, B.: Extending the RETE Algorithm for Event Management. In: TIME, pp. 49–51 (2002)

[BFMS06a]   Behrends, E., Fritzen, O., May, W., Schenk, F.: Combining ECA Rules with Process Algebras for the Semantic Web. In: Proceedings of Second International Conference on Rules and Rule Markup Languages for the Semantic Web, Athens, Georgia, USA, November 10-11, 2006, pp. 29–38 (2006)

[BFMS06b]   Behrends, E., Fritzen, O., May, W., Schubert, D.: An ECA Engine for Deploying Heterogeneous Component Languages in the Semantic Web. In: Proceedings of Workshop Reactivity on the Web, Munich, Germany LNCS (2006)

[BKK04]   Bernauer, M., Kappel, G., Kramler, G.: Composite Events for XML. In: Proc. Int. World Wide Web Conf. pp. 175–183. ACM, New York (2004)

[BPW02]   Bailey, J., Poulovassilis, A., Wood, P.T.: An Event-Condition-Action Language for XML. In: Proc. Int. World Wide Web Conf. pp. 486–495. ACM, New York (2002)

[BS02a]   Bry, F., Schaffert, S.: A Gentle Introduction into Xcerpt, a Rule-based Query and Transformation Language for XML. In: Proceedings of International Workshop on Rule Markup Languages for Business Rules on the Semantic Web, Sardinia, Italy, June 14, 2002 (2002)

[BS02b]   Bry, F., Schaffert, S.: Towards a Declarative Query and Transformation Language for XML and Semistructured Data: Simulation Unification. In: Stuckey, P.J. (ed.) ICLP 2002. LNCS, vol. 2401, Springer, Heidelberg (2002)

[C$^+$04]   Cox, W. et al.: Web Services Transaction (WS-Transaction) (2004), http://dev2dev.bea.com/pub/a/2004/01/ws-transaction.html

[CDK01]   Coulouris, G., Dollimore, J., Kindberg, T.: Distributed Systems: Concepts and Design, 3rd edn. Addison-Wesley, Reading (2001)

[CKAK94] Chakravarthy, S., Krishnaprasad, V., Anwar, E., Kim, S.-K.: Composite Events for Active Databases: Semantics, Contexts and Detection. In: Proc. Int. Conf. on Very Large Data Bases, pp. 606–617. Morgan Kaufmann, San Francisco (1994)

[DAF+03] Diao, Y., Altinel, M., Franklin, M.J., Zhang, H., Fischer, P.M.: Path Sharing and Predicate Evaluation for High-Performance XML Filtering. ACM Trans. Database Syst. 28(4), 467–516 (2003)

[dbl] University of Trier DBLP Bibliography,
http://www.informatik.uni-trier.de/~ley/db/

[DM07] Dousson, C., Le Maigat, P.: Chronicle Recognition Improvement Using Temporal Focusing and Hierarchization. In: IJCAI, pp. 324–329 (2007)

[Eck05] Eckert, M.: Reactivity on the Web: Event Queries and Composite Event Detection in XChange. Diplomarbeit/diploma thesis, Institute of Computer Science, LMU, Munich (2005)

[For82] Forgy, C.L.: A Fast Algorithm for the Many Pattern/Many Object Pattern Match Problem. Artif. Intelligence 19(1), 17–37 (1982)

[GD93] Gatziu, S., Dittrich, K.R.: Events in an Active Object-Oriented Database System. In: Proc. Int. Workshop on Rules in Database Systems, pp. 23–39. Springer, Heidelberg (1993)

[Gha96] Ghallab, M.: On Chronicles: Representation, On-line Recognition and Learning. In: KR, pp. 597–606 (1996)

[GJS92] Gehani, N.H., Jagadish, H.V., Shmueli, O.: Composite Event Specification in Active Databases: Model & Implementation. In: Proc. Int. Conf. on Very Large Data Bases, pp. 327–338. Morgan Kaufmann, San Francisco (1992)

[GMOS03] Green, T.J., Miklau, G., Onizuka, M., Suciu, D.: Processing XML Streams with Deterministic Automata. In: Calvanese, D., Lenzerini, M., Motwani, R. (eds.) ICDT 2003. LNCS, vol. 2572, pp. 173–189. Springer, Heidelberg (2002)

[GMS87] Garcia-Molina, H., Salem, K.: Sagas. In: Proc. ACM SIGMOD Int. Conf. on Management of Data, pp. 249–259. ACM Press, New York (1987)

[Gra06] Grallert, H.: Propagation of Updates in Distributed Web Data: A Use Case for the Language XChange. Project thesis, Inst. f. Informatics, U. of Munich (2006)

[HCH+99] Hanson, E.N., Carnes, C., Huang, L., Konyala, M., Noronha, L., Parthasarathy, S., Park, J.B., Vernon, A.: Scalable Trigger Processing. In: Proc. of the 15th Int. Conf. on Data Engineering, pp. 266–275 (1999)

[KEP00] Knolmayer, G., Endl, R., Pfahrer, M.: Modeling Processes and Workflows by Business Rules. In: van der Aalst, W.M.P., Desel, J., Oberweis, A. (eds.) Business Process Management. LNCS, vol. 1806, pp. 16–29. Springer, Heidelberg (2000)

[KK00] Kline, K., Kline, D.: SQL in a Nutshell. O'Reilly Associates (2000)

[ME01] Moreto, D., Endler, M.: Evaluating Composite Events using Shared Trees. IEE Proceedings — Software 148(1), 1–10 (2001)

[Mil83] Milner, R.: Calculi for Synchrony and Asynchrony. Theoretical Computer Science 25, 267–310 (1983)

[MS97] Mansouri-Samani, M., Sloman, M.: GEM: A Generalised Event Monitoring Language for Distributed Systems. Distributed Systems Engineering 4(2), 96–108 (1997)

[MSvL06]   May, W., Schenk, F., von Lienen, E.: Extending an OWL Web Node with
            Reactive Behavior. In: Alferes, J.J., Bailey, J., May, W., Schwertel, U.
            (eds.) PPSWR 2006. LNCS, vol. 4187, pp. 134–148. Springer, Heidelberg
            (2006)

[Pat98]   Paton, N.W. (ed.): Active Rules in Database Systems. Springer, Heidel-
            berg (1998)

[PPW03]   Papamarkos, G., Poulovassilis, A., Wood, P.T.: Event-Condition-Action
            Rule Languages for the Semantic Web. In: Proc. Int. Workshop on Se-
            mantic Web and Databases (co-located with VLDB), pp. 309–327 (2003)

[Pǎ05]   Pǎtrânjan, P.-L.: The Language XChange: A Declarative Approach to
            Reactivity on the Web. Dissertation/Ph.D. thesis, Institute of Computer
            Science, LMU, Munich, 2005. PhD Thesis, Institute for Informatics, Uni-
            versity of Munich (2005)

[Rom06]   Romanenko, I.: Use Cases for Reactivity on the Web: Using ECA Rules
            for Business Process Modeling. Master's thesis, Inst. f. Informatics, U. of
            Munich (2006)

[Ron97]   Roncancio, C.: Toward Duration-Based, Constrained and Dynamic Event
            Types. In: Andler, S.F., Hansson, J. (eds.) ARTDB 1997. LNCS,
            vol. 1553, pp. 176–193. Springer, Heidelberg (1999)

[SB04]   Schaffert, S., Bry, F.: Querying the Web Reconsidered: A Practical Intro-
            duction to Xcerpt. In: Proc. Extreme Markup Languages (2004)

[Sch04]   Schaffert, S.: Xcerpt: A Rule-Based Query and Transformation Language
            for the Web. PhD thesis, Institute for Informatics, University of Munich,
            Germany (2004)

[SHS04]   Sur, G.M., Hammer, J., Siméon, J.: An XQuery-Based Language for
            Processing Updates in XML. In: Informal Proc. PLAN-X 2004 (2004)

[SSSM05]   Sánchez, C., Slanina, M., Sipma, H.B., Manna, Z.: Expressive Complete-
            ness of an Event-Pattern Reactive Programming Language. In: Wang, F.
            (ed.) FORTE 2005. LNCS, vol. 3731, pp. 529–532. Springer, Heidelberg
            (2005)

[TIHW01]   Tatarinov, I., Ives, Z.G., Halevy, A.Y., Weld, D.S.: Updating XML. In:
            Proc. ACM SIGMOD 2001, Santa Barbara, California, USA (2001)

[WC96]   Widom, J., Ceri, S.: Active Database Systems: Triggers and Rules for
            Advanced Database Processing. Morgan Kaufmann, San Francisco (1996)

[xsl01]   World Wide Web Consortium (W3C) Extensible Stylesheet Language
            (XSL) (October 2001), http://www.w3.org/TR/xsl/

[ZS01]   Zhu, D., Sethi, A.S.: SEL, A New Event Pattern Specification Language
            for Event Correlation. In: Proc. Int. Conf. on Computer Communications
            and Networks, pp. 586–589. IEEE, Los Alamitos (2001)

Rule-Based Policy Representation and Reasoning for the Semantic Web

Piero A. Bonatti[1] and Daniel Olmedilla[2]

[1] Università di Napoli Federico II, Napoli, Italy
bonatti@na.infn.it
[2] L3S Research Center and University of Hannover
olmedilla@L3S.de

Abstract. The Semantic Web aims at enabling sophisticated and autonomic machine to machine interactions without human intervention, by providing machines not only with data but also with its meaning (semantics). In this setting, traditional security mechanisms are not suitable anymore. For example, identity-based access control assumes that parties are known in advance. Then, a machine first determines the identity of the requester in order to either grant or deny access, depending on its associated information (e.g., by looking up its set of permissions). In the Semantic Web, any two strangers can interact with each other automatically and therefore this assumption does not hold. Hence, a semantically enriched process is required in order to regulate an automatic access to sensitive information. Policy-based access control provides sophisticated means in order to support protecting sensitive resources and information disclosure.

However, the term policy is often overloaded. A general definition might be "a statement that defines the behaviour of a system". However, such a general definition encompasses different notions, including security policies, trust management policies, business rules and quality of service specifications, just to name a few. Researchers have mainly focussed on one or more of such notions separately but not on a comprehensive view. Policies are pervasive in web applications and play crucial roles in enhancing security, privacy, and service usability as well. Interoperability and self-describing semantics become key requirements and here is where Semantic Web comes into play. There has been extensive research on policies, also in the Semantic Web community, but there still exist some issues that prevent policy frameworks from being widely adopted by users and real world applications.

This document aims at providing an overall view of the state of the art (requirements for a policy framework, some existing policy frameworks/ languages, policy negotiation, context awareness, etc.) as well as open research issues in the area (policy understanding in a broad sense, integration of trust management, increase in system cooperation, user awareness, etc.) required to develop a successful Semantic Policy Framework.

G. Antoniou et al. (Eds.): Reasoning Web 2007, LNCS 4636, pp. 240–268, 2007.
© Springer-Verlag Berlin Heidelberg 2007

1   Introduction

Information provided in the current Web is mainly human oriented. For example, HTML pages are human understandable but a computer is not able to understand the content and extract the right concepts represented there, that is, the meaning of the data. The Semantic Web [1] is a distributed environment in which information is self-describable by means of well-defined semantics, that is, machine understandable, thus providing interoperability (e.g., in e-commerce) and automation (e.g., in search). In such an environment, entities which have not had any previous interaction may now be able to automatically interact with each other. For example, imagine an agent planning a trip for a user. It needs to search for and book a plane and a hotel taking into account the user's schedule. When the user's agent contacts a hotel's website, the latter needs to inform the former that it requires a credit card in order to confirm a reservation. However, the user may probably want to restrict the conditions under which her agent automatically discloses her personal infomation. Due to such exchange of conditions and personal information, as well as its automation, security and privacy become yet more relevant and traditional approaches are not suitable anymore. On the one hand, unilateral access control is now replaced by bilateral protection (e.g., not only the website states the conditions to be satisfied in order to reserve a room but also the user agent may communicate conditions under which a credit card can be disclosed). On the other hand, identity-based access control cannot be applied anymore since users are not known in advance. Instead, entities' properties (e.g., user's credit card or whether a user is a student) play a central role. Both these properties and conditions stating the requirements to be fulfilled by the other party, must be described in a machine-understandable language with well-defined semantics allowing other entities to process them. Systems semantically annotated with policies enhance their authorisation process allowing, among others, to regulate information disclosure (privacy policies), to control access to resources (security policies), and to estimate trust based on parties' properties (trust management policies) [2].

Distributed access control has addressed some of these issues though not completely solved them yet. Examples like KeyNote [3] or PolicyMaker [4] provide a separation between enforcement and decision mechanisms by means of policies. However, policies are bound to public keys (identities) and are not expressive enough to deal with Semantic Web scenarios. RBAC (Role-Based Access Control) also does not meet Semantic Web requirements since it is difficult to assign roles to users which are not known in advance. Regarding to user's privacy protection, Platform for Privacy Preferences (P3P) provides a standard vocabulary to describe Web server policies. However, it is not expressive enough (it is a schema, not a language, and only describes purpose for the gathered data) and it does not allow for enforcement mechanisms. On the other hand, there is a wide offer of policy languages that have been developed to date [5,6,7,8], addressing the general requirements for a Semantic Web policy language: expressiveness, simplicity, enforceability, scalability, and analyzability [9]. These policies can be exchanged between entities on the Semantic Web and therefore they are described using languages with well-founded semantics.

The policy languages listed above differ in expressivity, kind of reasoning required, features and implementations provided, etc. For the sake of simplicity, they are divided according to their protocol for policy exchange between parties, depending on the sensitivity of policies. On the one hand, assuming that all policies are public and accessible (typical situation in many multi-agent systems), the process of evaluating whether two policies from two different entities are compatible or not consists in gathering the relevant policies (and possibly relevant credentials) from the involved entities and checking whether they *match* (e.g., [10]). On the other hand, if policies may be private (typical situation for business rules [11]), it implies that not all policies are known in advance but they may be disclosed at a later stage. Therefore, a *negotiation* protocol in which security and trust is iteratively established is required [12].

However, specifying policies is as difficult as writing imperative code, getting a policy right is as hard as getting a piece of software correct, and maintaining a large number of them is even harder. Fortunately, ontologies and policy reasoning may help users and administrators on specification, conflict detection and resolution of such policies [5,13].

As it can be seen, there has been extensive research in the area, including the Semantic Web community, but several aspects still exist that prevent policy frameworks from widespread adoption and real world application. This manuscript incorporates and merges the ideas of previously published papers [14,2,15] and aims at providing an overall view of the state of the art (requirements for a policy framework, some existing policy frameworks/languages, policy negotiation, context awareness, etc.) as well as open research issues in the area (policy understanding in a broad sense, integration of trust management, increase in system cooperation, user awareness, etc.) required to develop a successful Semantic Policy Framework. Section 2 describes how policies are exchanged and how they interact among parties on the Semantic Web, with a brief description of the main Semantic Web policy languages and how ontologies may be used in policy specification, conflict detection and validation. Some examples of application scenarios are presented in Section 3, where policy based security and privacy are used. Section 4 discusses important requirements and open research issues in this context, focusing on policies in general and their integration into trust management frameworks, as well as on approaches to increase system cooperation, usability and user-awareness of policy issues. This manuscript finally concludes with a last section (Section 5) in which the most important isssues presented are summarized.

2   Policy Based Interaction and Evaluation

Policies allow for security and privacy descriptions in a machine understandable way. More specifically, service or information providers may use security policies to control access to resources by describing the conditions a requester must fulfil (e.g., a requester to resource A must belong to institution B and prove it by means of a credential). At the same time, service or information consumers may regulate the information they are willing to disclose by protecting it with privacy policies (e.g., an entity is willing to disclose its employee card credential only to the web server of its employer). Given two sets of policies, an engine may check whether they are compatible, that is, whether they match. The complexity of this process varies depending on the sensitivity of policies (and the expressivity of the policies). If all policies are public at both sides (typical situation in many multi-agent systems), provider and requester, the requester may initially already provide the relevant policies together with the request and the evaluation process can be performed in a one-step evaluation by the provider policy engine (or an external trusted matchmaker) and return a final decision. Otherwise, if policies may be private, as it is, for example, typically the case for sensitive business rules, this process may consist of several steps negotiation in which new policies and credentials are disclosed at each step, therefore advancing after each iteration towards a common agreement. In this section we give an overview of both types of languages. The main features of these languages are shown in Table 1. Additionally, we use the running policy "only employees of institution XYZ may retrieve a file" to illustrate an example of each language.

2.1 One-Step Policy Evaluation

Assuming that policies are publicly disclosable, there is no reason why a requester should not disclose its relevant applicable policies together with its request. This way, the provider's policy engine (or a trusted external matchmaker in case the provider does not have one) has all the information needed to make an authorisation decision. The KAOS and REI frameworks, specially designed using Semantic Web features and constructs, fall within this category of policy languages, those which do not allow policies themselves to be protected.

Table 1. Comparison of KAOS, REI, PeerTrust and Protune[1]

Policy Language	Authorization Protocol	Reasoning Paradigm	Conflict Detection	Meta-policies	Loop Detection
KAOS	One-step	DL	Static detection & resolution		
REI	One-step	DL + variables	Dinamyc detection & resolution	Used for conflict resolution	
PeerTrust	Negotiation	LP + ontologies			Distributed Tabling
Protune	Negotiation	LP + ontologies		Used for driving decisions	

KAOS Policy and Domain Services. KAOS Services [5,16] provide a framework for specification, management, conflict resolution and enforcement of policies allowing for distributed policy interaction and support for dynamic policy changes. It uses OWL [17] ontologies (defining e.g. actors, groups and actions) to describe the policies and the application context, and provides administration tools (KAOS Administration Tool - KPAT) to help administrators to write down their policies and hide the complexity of using OWL directly. A policy in KAOS may be a positive (respectively negative) authorisation, i.e., constraints that permit (respectively forbid) the execution of an action, or a positive (respectively negative) obligation, i.e., constraints that require an action to be executed (respectively waive the actor from having to execute it). A policy is then represented as an instance of the appropriate policy type, associating values to its properties, and giving restrictions on such properties (Figure 1 sketches part of a KAOS policy).

```
<owl:Class rdf:ID="RetrieveFileAction">
   <owl:intersectionOf>
      <owl:Class rdf:about="#AccessAction"/>
         <owl:Class>
            <owl:Restriction>
               <owl:onProperty rdf:resource="#performedBy"/>
               <owl:someValuesFrom>
                  <owl:Class>
                     <owl:oneOf rdf:parseType="Collection">
                        <owl:Thing rdf:about="#EmployeeInstitutionXYZ"/>
                     </owl:oneOf>
                  </owl:Class>
               </owl:someValuesFrom>
            </owl:Restriction>
         </owl:Class>
      </owl:Restriction>
   </owl:intersectionOf>
</owl:Class>

<policy:PosAuthorizationPolicy rdf:ID="PolicyRetrieveFileAction">
   <policy:controls rdf:resource="#RetrieveFileAction"/>
   <policy:hasPriority>1</policy:hasPriority>
</policy:PosAuthorizationPolicy>
```

Fig. 1. Example of KAOS policies

KAOS benefits from the OWL representation and description logic based subsumption mechanisms [18]. Thus, it allows to, for example, obtain all known subclasses or instances of a class within a given range (used during policy specification to help users choosing only valid classes or instances) or detect policy conflicts (by checking disjointness of subclasses of the action class controlled by policies). KAOS is able to detect three types of conflicts, based on the types of policies that are allowed in the framework: positive vs. negative authorisation (a policy allows access and but another denies it), positive vs. negative obligation (a policy obliges to execute an action while another dispensates from such obligation) and positive

---

[1] DL refers to Description Logic while LP stands for Logic Programming.

obligation vs. negative authorisation (a policy obliges to execute an action but another denies authorisation for such execution). KAOS resolves such conflicts (also called harmonisation) based on assigning preferences to policies and resolving in favour of the policies with higher priority (Section 2.3 will later extend on this).

Finally, KAOS assumes a default authorisation mechanism in case no policy applies to a request. It can be either "permit all actions not explicitly forbidden" or "forbid all actions not explicitly authorised".

REI. REI 2.0 [19,10] expresses policies according to what entities can or cannot do and what they should or should not do. They define an independent ontology which includes the concepts for permissions, obligations, actions, etc. Additionally, as in KAOS, they allow the import of domain dependent ontologies (including domain dependent classes and properties). REI 2.0 is represented in OWL-Lite and includes logic-like variables in order to specify a range of relations.

REI policies (see Figure 2 for an example) are described in terms of deontic concepts: permissions, prohibitions, obligations and dispensations, equivalently to the positive/negative authorisations and positive/negative obligations of KAOS. In addition, REI provides a specification of speech acts for the dynamic exchange of rights and obligations between entities: delegation (of a right), revocation (of a previously delegated right), request (for action execution or delegation) and cancel (of a previous request).

```
<policy:Policy rdf:ID="RetrieveFilePolicy">
  <policy:grants rdf:resource="#Perm_Employee_XYZ">
</policy:Policy>

<policy:Granting rdf:ID=#Perm_Employee_XYZ">
  <policy:to rdf:resource="#PersonVar">
  <policy:deontic rdf:resource="Perm_Retrieve_File">
</policy:Granting>

<deontic:Permission rdf:ID="Perm_Retrieve_File">
  <deontic:actor rdf:resource="#PersonVar">
  <deontic:action rdf:resource="&action;RetrieveFile">
  <deontic:constraint rdf:resource="#IsEmployeeXYZ">
</deontic:Permission>

<constraint:SimpleConstraint rdf:ID="IsEmployeeXYZ">
  <constraint:subject rdf:resource="#PersonVar">
  <constraint:predicate rdf:resource="&emp;affiliation">
  <constraint:object rdf:resource="&emp;XYZ">
</constraint:SimpleConstraint>
```

Fig. 2. Example of REI policies

As in the KAOS framework, REI policies may conflict with each other (right vs. prohibition or obligation vs. dispensation). REI provides mechanisms for conflict detection and constructs to resolve them, namely, overriding policies (similar to the prioritisation in KAOS) and definition at the meta-level of the global modality (positive or negative) that holds (see Section 2.3 for more details).

2.2   Policy-Driven Negotiations

In the approaches presented previously, policies are assumed to be publicly disclosable. This is true for many scenarios but there exist other scenarios where
it may not hold. For example, imagine a hospital revealing to everyone that in
order to receive Alice's medical report, the requester needs an authorisation from
Alice's psychiatrist. Another example, imagine Tom wants to share his holiday
pictures on-line only with his friends. If he states publicly that policy and Jes-
sica is denied access, she may get angry because of Tom not considering her as a
friend. Moreover, policy protection becomes even more important when policies
protects sensitive business rules.

These scenarios require the possibility to protect policies (policies protecting
policies) and the process of finding a match between requester and provider becomes more complex, since not all relevant policies may be available at the time.
Therefore, this process may consist of a several steps negotiation, by disclosing
new policies and credentials at each step, and therefore advancing after each iteration towards a common agreement [12]. For example, suppose Alice requests
access to a resource at e-shop. Alice is told that she must provide her credit card
to be granted access. However, Alice does not want to disclose her credit card just
to anyone and she communicates to e-shop that before it gets her credit card, it
should provide its Better Business Bureau certification. Once e-shop discloses it,
Alice's policy is fulfilled and she provides the credit card, thus fulfilling e-shop's
policy and receiving access to the requested resource (see Figure 3).

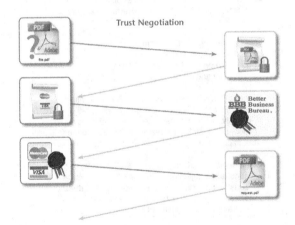

Fig. 3. Policy-driven negotiation between Alice and e-shop

Below, the two most recent languages for policy-driven negotiation are presented. They are also specially designed for the Semantic Web. However, we refer
the interested reader to other languages for policy based negotiations [20,21,22],
which may be applied to the Semantic Web.

PeerTrust. PeerTrust [7] builds upon previous work on policy-based access control and release for the Web and implements automated trust negotiation for such a dynamic environment.

PeerTrust's language is based on first order Horn rules (definite Horn clauses), i.e., rules of the form "$lit_0 \leftarrow lit_1, \ldots, lit_n$" where each lit_i is a positive literal $P_j(t_1, \ldots, t_n)$, P_j is a predicate symbol, and the t_i are the arguments of this predicate. Each t_i is a term, i.e., a function symbol and its arguments, which are themselves terms. The head of a rule is lit_0, and its body is the set of lit_i. The body of a rule can be empty.

Definite Horn clauses can be easily extended to include negation as failure, restricted versions of classical negation, and additional constraint handling capabilities such as those used in constraint logic programming. Although all of these features can be useful in trust negotiation, here are only described other more unusual required language extensions. Additionally, PeerTrust allows the import of RDF based meta-data therefore allowing the use of ontologies within policy descriptions.

```
retrieveFile(fileXYZ) $ Requester ←
    employed(Requester) @ institutionXYZ.
```

Fig. 4. Example of PeerTrust policies

References to Other Peers. PeerTrust's ability to reason about statements made by other peers is central to trust negotiation. To express delegation of evaluation to another peer, each literal lit_i is extended with an additional *Authority* argument, that is

$$lit_i @ \text{Authority}$$

where *Authority* specifies the peer who is responsible for evaluating lit_i or has the authority to evaluate lit_i. The *Authority* argument can be a nested term containing a sequence of authorities, which are then evaluated starting at the outermost layer.

A specific peer may need a way of referring to the peer who asked a particular query. This is accomplished by including a *Requester* argument in literals, so that now literals are of the form

$$lit_i @ \text{Issuer} \$ \text{Requester}$$

The *Requester* argument can also be nested, in which case it expresses a chain of requesters, with the most recent requester in the outermost layer of the nested term.

Using the *Issuer* and *Requester* arguments, it is possible to delegate evaluation of literals to other parties and also express interactions and the corresponding negotiation process between parties (see Figure 4 for an example).

Signed Rules. Each peer defines a policy for each of its resources, in the form of a set of definite Horn clause rules. These and any other rules that the peer defines on its own are its *local* rules. A peer may also have copies of rules defined by other peers, and it may use these rules to generate proofs, which can be sent to other entities in order to give evidence of the result of a negotiation.

A signed rule has an additional argument that says who signed the rule. The cryptographic signature itself is not included in the policy, because signatures are very large and are not needed by this part of the negotiation software. The signature is used to verify that the issuer really did issue the rule. It is assumed that when a peer receives a signed rule from another peer, the signature is verified before the rule is passed to the DLP evaluation engine. Similarly, when one peer sends a signed rule to another peer, the actual signed rule must be sent, and not just the logic programmatic representation of the signed rule. More complex signed rules often represent delegations of authority.

Loop Detection Mechanisms. In declarative policy specification, loops may easily occur and should not be considered as errors. For example, declarative policies may state at the same time that "anyone with write permissions can read a file" and "anyone with read permissions can write a file". If not handled accordingly, such loops may end up in non-terminating evaluation [23]. In practice, policies, including for instance business rules, are complex and large in number (and typically not under control of a single person) which increases the risk of loops and non-termination during dynamic policy evaluation. A distributed tabling algorithm can handle safely mutual recursive dependencies (loops) in distributed environments. Due to the security context, other aspects like private and public policies and proof generation must be taken into account [23].

Protune. The PRovisional TrUst NEgotiation framework Protune [8] aims at combining distributed trust management policies with provisional-style business rules and access-control related actions. Protune's rule language extends two previous languages: PAPL [20], which until 2002 was one of the most complete policy languages for trust negotiation, and PeerTrust [7], which supports distributed credentials and a more flexible policy protection mechanism. In addition, the framework features a powerful declarative meta-language for driving some critical negotiation decisions, and integrity constraints for monitoring negotiations and credential disclosure.

Protune provides a framework with:

- A trust management language supporting general provisional-style[2] actions (possibly user-defined).
- An extendible declarative meta-language for driving decisions about request formulation, information disclosure, and distributed credential collection.
- A parameterised negotiation procedure, that gives a semantics to the meta-language and provably satisfies some desirable properties for all possible meta-policies.

---

[2] Authorizations involving actions and side effects are sometimes called provisional.

```
access('fileXYZ') ←
    credential(employee, C),
    C.type :employee_id,
    C.affiliation :'XYZ'.

access(_).type:decision.
access(_).sensitivity :public.
```

Fig. 5. Example of Protune policies

- Integrity constraints for negotiation monitoring and disclosure control.
- General, ontology-based techniques for importing and exporting meta-policies and for smoothly integrating language extensions.
- Advanced policy explanations in order to answer why, why-not, how-to, and what-if queries [24]

The Protune rule language is based on normal logic program rules "$A \leftarrow L_1, \ldots, L_n$" where A is a standard logical atom (called the *head* of the rule) and $L_1, \ldots, L_n$ (the *body* of the rule) are literals, that is, L_i equals either B_i or $\neg B_i$, for some logical atom B_i.

A *policy* is a set of rules (see Figure 5 for an example), such that negation is applied neither to *provisional predicates* (defined below), nor to any predicate occurring in a rule head. This restriction ensures that policies are *monotonic* on credentials and actions, that is, as more credentials are released and more actions executed, the set of permissions does not decrease.

The vocabulary of predicates occurring in the rules is partitioned into the following categories: *Decision Predicates* (currently supporting "allow()" which is queried by the negotiation for access control decisions and "sign()" which is used to issue statements signed by the principal owning the policy, *Abbreviation Predicates* (as described in [20]), *Constraint Predicates* (which comprise the usual equality and disequality predicates) and *State Predicates* (which perform decisions according to the state). State Predicates are further subdivided in *State Query Predicates* (which read the state without modifying it) and *Provisional Predicates* (which may be made true by means of associated actions that may modify the current state like e.g. *credential*(), *declaration*(), *logged*(X, *logfile_name*)).

Furthermore, meta-policies consist of rules similar to object-level rules. They allow to inspect terms, check groundness, call an object-level goal G against the current state (using a predicate *holds*(G)), etc. In addition, a set of reserved attributes associated to predicates, literals and rules (e.g., whether a policy is public or sensitive) is used to drive the negotiator's decisions. For example, if p is a predicate, then p.sensitivity : private means that the extension of the predicate is private and should not be disclosed. An assertion p.type : provisional declares p to be a provisional predicate; then p can be attached to the corresponding action α by asserting p.action :α. If the action is to be executed locally, then we assert p.actor : self, otherwise assert p.actor : peer.

2.3 Policy Specification, Conflict Detection and Resolution

Previous sections described how the Semantic Web may benefit from the protection of resources with policies specifying security and privacy constraints. However, specifying policies may be as difficult as writing imperative code, getting a policy right is as hard as getting a piece of software correct, and maintaining a large number of them is only harder. Fortunately, the Semantic Web can help administrators with policy specification, and detection and resolution of conflicts.

Policy Specification. Tools like the KAOS Policy Administration Tool (K-PAT) [5] and the PeerTrust Policy Editor provide an easy to use application to help policy writers. This is important because the policies will be enforced automatically and therefore errors in their specification or implementation will allow outsiders to gain inappropriate access to resources, possibly inflicting huge and costly damages. In general, the use of ontologies on policy specification reduces the burden on administrators, helps them with their maintenance and decreases the number of errors. For example, ontology-based structuring and abstraction help maintain complex software, and so do they with complex sets of policies. In the context of the Semantic Web, ontologies provide a formal specification of concepts and their interrelationships, and play an essential role in complex web service environments, semantics-based search engines and digital libraries. Nejdl et al. [13] suggest using two strategies to compose and override policies, building upon the notions of mandatory and default policies, and formalising the constraints corresponding to these kinds of policies using F-Logic. A prototype implementation as a Protégé plug-in shows that the proposed policy specification mechanism is implementable and effective.

Conflict Detection and Resolution. Semantic Web policy languages also allow for advanced algorithms for conflict detection and its resolution. For example, in Section 2.1 it was briefly described how conflicts may arise between policies, either at specification time or runtime. A typical example of a conflict is when several policies apply to a request and one allows access while another denies it (positive vs. negative authorisation). Description Logic based languages may use subsumption reasoning to detect conflicts by checking if two policies are instances of conflicting types and whether the action classes, that the policies control, are not disjoint. Both KAOS and REI handle such conflicts (like right vs. prohibition or obligation vs. dispensation) within their frameworks and both provide constructs for specifying priorities between policies, hence the most important ones override the less important ones. In addition, REI provides a construct for specifying a general modality priority: positive (rights override prohibitions and obligations override dispensations) or negative (prohibitions override rights and dispensations override obligations). KAOS also provides a conflict resolution technique called "policy harmonisation'. If a conflict is detected the policy with lower priority is modified by refining it with the minimum degree necessary to remove the conflict. This process may generate zero, one or several policies as a refinement of the previous one (see [5] for more information). This process is performed statically at policy specification time ensuring that no conflicts arise at runtime.

3 Applying Policies on the Semantic Web

The benefits of using semantic policy languages in distributed environments with automated machine-machine interaction have been described extensible in previous sections. This section aims at providing some examples of its use in the context of the Web, (Semantic) Web Services and the (Semantic) Grid. In all cases, different solutions have been described addressing different scenarios from the point of view of one-step authorization or policy-driven negotiations.

3.1 Policies on the Web

The current Web infrastructure does not allow the enforcement of user policies while accessing web resources. Web server authentication is typically based on authentication mechanisms in which users must authenticate themselves (either by means of certificates or typing a user name and password). Semantic Web policies overcome such limitations of the Web.

Kagal et al. [6] describe how the REI language can be applied in order to control access to web resources. Web pages are marked up with policies specifying which credentials are required to access such pages. A policy engine (bound to the web server) decides whether the request matches the credentials requested. In case it does not, the web server could show which credentials are missing. Furthermore, Kolari et al. [25] presents an extension to the Platform for Privacy Preferences (P3P) using the REI language. The authors propose enhancements using REI policies to increase the expressiveness and to allow for existing privacy enforcement mechanisms.

PeerTrust can be used to provide advanced policy-driven negotiations on the Web in order to control access to resources [7,26]. A user receives a signed (by a trusted authority) applet after requesting access to a resource. Such an applet includes reasoning capabilities and is loaded in the Web browser. The applet automatically imports the policies specified by the user and starts a negotiation. If the negotiation succeeds, the applet simply retrieve the resource requested or, if necessary, redirects the user to the appropriate repository.

3.2 Semantic Web Services

Semantic Web Services aim at the automation of discovery, selection and composition of Web Services. Denker et al. [27] and Kagal et al. [10] suggest extending OWL-S with security policies, written in REI, like e.g. whether a service requires or is capable of providing secure communication channels. An agent may then submit a request to the registry together with its privacy policies. The match-maker at the registry will filter out non-compatible service descriptions and select only those whose security requirements of the service match the privacy policies of the requester.

Differently, Olmedilla et al. [28] propose the use of the PeerTrust language to decide if trust can be established between a requester and a service provider during runtime selection of web services. Modelling elements are added to the Web Service Modeling Ontology (WSMO) in order to include security information in the description of Semantic Web Services. In addition, the authors discuss different registry architectures and their implications for the matchmaking process.

3.3 Semantic Grid

Grid environments provide the middleware needed for access distributed computing and data resources. Distinctly administrated domains form virtual organisations and share resources for data retrieval, job execution, monitoring, and data storage. Such an environment provides users with seamless access to all resources they are authorised to access. In current Grid infrastructures, in order to be granted access at each domain, user's jobs have to secure and provide appropriate digital credentials for authentication and authorisation. However, while authentication along with single sign-on can be provided based on client delegation of X.509 proxy certificates to the job being submitted, the authorisation mechanisms are still mainly identity-based. Due to the large number of potential users and different certification authorities, this leads to scalability problems calling for a complementary solution to the access control mechanisms specified in the current Grid Security Infrastructure (GSI) [29].

Uszok et al. [30] presents an integration of the KAOS framework into Globus Tookit 3. Its authors suggest offering a KAOS grid service and providing an interface so grid clients and services may register and check whether a specific action is authorised or not. The KAOS grid service uses the KAOS policy services described in Section 2.1 and relies on the Globus local enforcement mechanisms.

Alternatively, Constandache et al. [31] describe an integration of policy driven negotiations for the GSI, using semantic policies and enhancing it providing automatic credential fetching and disclosure. Policy-based dynamic negotiations allow more flexible authorisation in complex Grid environments, and relieve both users and administrators from up front negotiations and registrations. Constandache et al. [31] introduces an extension to the GSI and Globus Toolkit 4.0 in which policy-based negotiation mechanisms offer the basis for overcoming these limitations. This extension includes property-based authorisation mechanisms, automatic gathering of required certificates, bidirectional and iterative trust negotiation and policy based authorisation, ingredients that provide advanced self-explanatory access control to grid resources.

4   Requirements and Open Research Issues for a Semantic Web Policy Framework

Policies are pervasive in web applications. They play crucial roles in enhancing security, privacy and usability of distributed services, and indeed may determine the success (or failure) of a web service. However, users will not be able to benefit from these protection mechanisms unless they understand and are able to personalize policies applied in such contexts. For web services this includes policies for access control, privacy and business rules, among others.

This section summarizes research performed over the past years on semantic policies and especially aim to analyse those aspects that did not receive so much attention so far. We will focus our discussion on the following strategic goals and lines of research:

- *Rules-based policy representation*: Rule-based languages are commonly regarded as the best approach to formalizing policies due to its flexibility, formal semantics and closeness to the way people think.
- Adoption of a *broad notion of policy*, encompassing not only access control policies, but also privacy policies, business rules, quality of service, and others. We believe that all these different kinds of policies should eventually be integrated into a single framework.
- *Strong and lightweight evidence*: Policies make decisions based on properties of the peers interacting with the system. These properties may be strongly certified by cryptographic techniques, or may be reliable to some intermediate degree with lightweight evidence gathering and validation. A flexible policy framework should try to merge these two forms of evidence to meet the efficiency and usability requirements of web applications.
- These desiderata imply that trust negotiation, reputation models, business rules, and action specification languages have to be integrated into a single framework at least to some extent. It is crucial to find the right tradeoff between generality and efficiency. *So far, no framework has tried to merge all aspects into a coherent system.*
- *Automated trust negotiation* is one of the main ingredients that can be used to make heterogeneous peers effectively interoperate. This approach relies on and actively contributes to advances in the area of *trust management*.
- *Lightweight knowledge representation and reasoning* does not only refer to computational complexity; it should also reduce the effort to specialize general frameworks to specific application domains; and the corresponding tools should be easy to learn and use for common users, with no particular training in computers or logic. We regard these properties as crucial for the success of a semantic web framework.
- The last issue cannot be tackled simply by adopting a rule language. Solutions like *controlled natural language syntax for policy rules*, to be translated by a parser into the internal logical format, will definitely ease the adoption of any policy language.
- *Cooperative policy enforcement*: A secure cooperative system should (almost) never say *no*. Web applications need to help new users in obtaining the services that the application provides, so potential customers should not be discouraged. Whenever prerequisites for accessing a service are not met, web applications should explain what is missing and help the user in obtaining the required permissions.

- As part of cooperative enforcement, advanced *explanation mechanisms* are necessary to help users in understanding policy decisions and obtaining the permission to access a desired service.

In the remainder of this section we describe the current state of the art on these issues, expand on them and point out several interesting research directions related to them: the need for an flexible and easy policy representation, the different types of policies which must be considered in order to address real world scenarios, the need for strong and lightweight evidence on the information that policies require, the importance of trust management as part of a policy framework, describing in detail negotiations and provisional actions and how cooperative systems which explain their decisions to users as well as policy specification in natural language increase user awareness and understanding.

4.1 Rule-Based Policy Representation

Rule-based languages are commonly regarded as the best approach to formalizing security policies. In fact, most of the systems we use every day adopt policies formulated as rules. Roughly speaking, the access control lists applied by routers are actually rules of the form: *"if a packet of protocol X goes from hosts Y to hosts Z then [don't] let it pass"*. Some systems, like Java, adopt procedural approaches. Access control is enforced by pieces of code scattered around the virtual machine and the application code; still, the designers of Java security felt the need for a method called *implies*, reminiscent of rules, that causes certain authorizations to entail other authorizations [32].

The main advantages of rule-based policy languages can be summarized as follows:

- People (including users with no specific training in computers or logic) spontaneously tend to formulate security policies as rules.
- Rules have precise and relatively simple formal semantics, be it operational (rewrite semantics), denotational (fixpoint-based), or declarative (model theoretic). Formal semantics is an excellent help in implementing and verifying access control mechanisms, as well as validating policies.
- Rule languages can be flexible enough to model in a unified framework the many different policies introduced along the years as ad-hoc mechanisms. Different policies can be harmonized and integrated into a single coherent specification.

In particular, logic programming languages are particularly attractive as policy specification languages. They enjoy the above properties and have efficient inference mechanisms (linear or quadratic time). This property is important as in most systems policies have to manage a large number of users, files, and operations—hence a large number of possible authorizations. And for those applications where linear time is too slow, there exist well-established compilation techniques (materialization, partial evaluation) that may reduce reasoning to pure retrieval at run time.

Another fundamental property of logic programs is that their inference is *nonmonotonic*, due to *negation-as-failure*. Logic programs can make default decisions in the absence of complete specifications. Default decisions arise naturally in real-world security policies. For example, *open* policies prescribe that authorizations by default are granted, whereas *closed* policies prescribe that they should be denied unless stated otherwise. Other nonmonotonic inferences, such as authorization inheritance and overriding, are commonly supported by policy languages.

For all of these reasons, rule languages based on nonmonotonic logics eventually became the most frequent choice in the literature. A popular choice consists of *normal logic programs*, i.e. sets of rules like

$$A \leftarrow B_1, \ldots, B_m, \text{not } C_1, \ldots, \text{not } C_n$$

interpreted with the *stable model semantics* [33]. In general, each program may have one stable model, many stable models, or none at all. There are opposite points of view on this feature.

Some authors regard multiple models as an opportunity to write nondeterministic specifications where each model is an acceptable policy and the system makes an automatic choice between the available alternatives [34]. For instance, the models of a policy may correspond to all possible ways of assigning permissions that preserve a *Chinese Wall* policy [35]. However, the set of alternative models may grow exponentially, and the problem of finding one of them is NP-complete. There are exceptions with polynomial complexity [36,37], though.

Some authors believe that security managers would not trust the system's automatic choice and adopt restrictions such as *stratifiability* [38] to guarantee that the canonical model be unique. The system rejects non-stratified specifications, highlighting nonstratified rules to help the security administrator in reformulating the specifications. As a further advantage, stratifiability-like restrictions yield PTIME semantics.

4.2 A Broad Notion of Policy

Policies are pervasive in all web-related contexts. Access control policies are needed to protect any system open to the internet. Privacy policies are needed to assist users while they are browsing the web and interacting with web services. Business rules specify which conditions apply to each customer of a web service. Other policies specify constraints related to Quality of Service (QoS). In E-government applications, visas and other documents are released according to specific eligibility policies. This list is not exhaustive and is limited only by the class of applications that can be deployed in the world wide web.

Most of these policies make their decisions based on similar pieces of information [39] – essentially, properties of the peers involved in the transaction. For example, age, nationality, customer profile, identity, and reputation may all be considered both in access control decisions, and in determining which discounts are applicable (as well as other eligibility criteria). It is appealing to integrate these kinds of policies into a coherent framework, so that (i) a common in-frastructure can be used to support interoperability and decision making, and (ii) the policies themselves can be harmonized and synchronized.

In the general view depicted above, policies may also establish that some events must be logged (audit policies), that user profiles must be updated, and that when a transaction fails, the user should be told how to obtain missing permissions. In other words, policies may specify *actions* whose execution may be interleaved with the decision process. Such policies are called *provisional policies*. In this context, *policies act both as decision support systems and as declarative behavior specifica-tions.* An effective user-friendly approach to policy specification could give com-mon users (with no training in computer science or logic) better control on the behavior of their own system (see the discussion in Section 4.5).

Of course, the extent to which this goal can be achieved depends on the policy's ability to *interoperate* with legacy software and data – or more generally, with the rest of the system. Then a policy specification language should support suitable primitives for interacting with external packages and data in a flexible way.

The main challenges raised by these issues are then the following:

– Harmonizing security and privacy policies with business rules, provisional policies, and other kinds of policy is difficult because their standard for-malizations are based on different derivation strategies, and even different reasoning mechanisms (cf. Section 4.4). Deduction, abduction, and event-condition-action rule semantics need to be integrated into a coherent frame-work, trying to minimize subtleties and technical intricacies (otherwise the framework would not be accessible to common users).
– Interactions between a rule-based theory and "external" software and data have been extensively investigated in the framework of logic-based mediation and logic-based agent programming [40,41]. However, there are novel issues re-lated to implementing high-level policy rules with low-level mechanisms such as firewalls, web server and DBMS security mechanisms, and operating sys-tem features, that are often faster and more difficult to bypass than rule inter-preters [42]. A convincing realization of this approach might boost the appli-cation of the rich and flexible languages developed by the security community.

4.3 Strong and Lightweight Evidence

Currently two major approaches for managing trust exist: policy-based and reputation-based trust management. The two approaches have been developed within the context of different environments and target different requirements. On the one hand, policy-based trust relies on "strong security" mechanisms such as signed certificates and trusted certification authorities (CAs) in order to reg-ulate access of users to services. Moreover, access decisions are usually based on mechanisms with well defined semantics (e.g., logic programming) providing strong verification and analysis support. The result of such a policy-based trust management approach usually consists of a binary decision according to which the requester is trusted or not, and thus the service (or resource) is allowed or denied. On the other hand, reputation-based trust relies on a "soft computational" approach to the problem of trust. In this case, trust is typically computed from local experiences together with the feedback given by other entities in the network. For instance, eBay buyers and sellers rate each other after each transaction. The ratings pertaining to a certain seller (or buyer) are aggregated by eBay's reputation system into a number reflecting seller (or buyer) trustworthiness as judged by the eBay community. The reputation-based approach has been favored for environments such as Peer-to-Peer or Semantic Web, where the existence of certifying authorities can not always be assumed but where a large pool of individual user ratings is often available.

Another approach – very common in today's applications – is based on forcing users to commit to contracts or copyrights by having users click an "accept" button on a pop-up window. This is perhaps the lightest approach to trust, that can be generalized by having users utter *declarations* (on their e-mail address, on their preferences, etc.) e.g. by filling an HTML form.

Real life scenarios often require to make decisions based on a combination of these approaches. Transaction policies must handle expenses of all magnitudes, from micropayments (e.g. a few cents for a song downloaded to your iPod) to credit card payments of a thousand euros (e.g. for a plane ticket) or even more. The cost of the traded goods or services contributes to determine the risk associated to the transaction and hence the trust measure required.

Strong evidence is generally harder to gather and verify than lightweight evidence. Sometimes, a "soft" reputation measure or a declaration in the sense outlined above is all one can obtain in a given scenario. We believe that the success of a trust management framework will be determined by the ability of *balancing trust levels and risk levels* for each particular task supported by the application, adding the following to the list of interesting research directions:

– How should different forms of trust be integrated? Some hints on modelling context aware trust, recommendation and risk with rules is given in [26] and a first proposal for a full integration in a policy framework can be found in [43]. However, new reputation models are being introduced, and there is a large number of open research issues in the reputation area (e.g., vulnerability to coalitions). Today, it is not clear which of the current approaches will be successful and how the open problems will be solved. Any proposal should therefore aim at maximal modularity in the integration of numerical and logical trust.
– How many different forms of evidence can be conceived? In principle, properties of (and statements about) an individual can be extracted from any – possibly unstructured – web resource. Supporting such a variety of information in policy decisions is a typical semantic web issue – and an intriguing one. However, such general policies are not even vaguely as close to become real as the policies based on more "traditional" forms of evidence (see the discussion in the next section).

4.4 Trust Management

During the past few years, some of the most innovative ideas on security policies arose in the area of *automated trust negotiation* [44,8,45,7,46,47,48,49,50].

That branch of research considers peers that are able to automatically negotiate credentials according to their own declarative, rule-based policies. Rules specify for each resource or credential request which properties should be satisfied by the subjects and objects involved. At each negotiation step, the next credential request is formulated essentially by *reasoning* with the policy, e.g. by inferring implications or computing abductions.

Since about five years frameworks exist where credential requests are formulated by exchanging *sets of rules* [8,45]. Requests are formulated *intensionally* in order to express compactly and simultaneously all the possible ways in which a resource can be accessed — shortening negotiations and improving privacy protection because peers can choose the best option from the point of view of sensitivity. It is not appealing to request *"an ID and a credit card"* by enumerating all possible pairs of ID credentials and credit card credentials; it is much better to *define* what IDs and credit cards are and send the definition itself. Another peer may use it to check whether some subset of its own credentials fulfills the request. This boils down to gathering the relevant concept definitions in the policy (so-called *abbreviation rules*) and sending them to the other peer that reasons with those rules locally.

In [8,45] *peers communicate by sharing their ontologies*. Interestingly, typical policies require peers to have a common a priori understanding only of the predicate representing credentials and arithmetic predicates, as any other predicate can be understood by sharing its definition. The only nontrivial knowledge to be shared is the X.509 standard credential format. In this framework, interoperability based on ontology sharing is already at reach! This is one of the aspects that make policies and automated trust negotiation a most attractive application for semantic web ideas.

Another interesting proposal of [45] is the notion of *declaration*, that has already been discussed in Section 4.3. This was the first step towards a more flexible and lightweight approach to policy enforcement, aiming at a better tradeoff between protection efforts and risks. According to [51], this framework was one of the most complete trust negotiation systems. The major limitation was the lack of distributed negotiations and credential discovery, which are now supported as specified in [8].

Negotiations. In response to a resource request, a web server may ask for credentials proving that the client can access the resource. However, the credentials themselves can be sensitive resources. So the two peers are in a completely symmetrical situation: the client, in turn, asks the server for credentials (e.g. proving that it participates in the Better Business Bureau program) before sending off the required credentials. Each peer decides how to react to incoming requests according to a local policy, which is typically a set of rules written in some logic programming dialect. As we pointed out, requests are formulated by selecting some rules from the policies. This basic schema has been refined along the years taking several factors into account [44,8,45,7,46,47,48,49,50].

First, policy rules may possibly inspect a *local state* (such as a legacy database) that typically is not accessible by other peers. In that case, in order to make rules intelligible to the recepient, they are partially evaluated with respect to the current state.

Second, *policies themselves are sensitive resources*, therefore not all relevant rules are shown immediately to the peer. They are first filtered according to policy release rules; the same schema may be applied to policy release rules themselves for an arbitrary but finite number of levels. As a consequence, some negotiations that might succeed, in fact fail just because the peers do not tell each other what they want. The study of methodologies and properties that guarantee negotiation success is an interesting open research issue.

Moreover, *credentials are not necessarily on the peer's host.* It may be necessary to locate them on the network [52]. As part of the automated support to *cooperative enforcement*, peers may give each other hints on where a credential can be found [53]. There are further complications related to actions (cf. Section 4.4). In order to tune the negotiation strategy to handle these aspects optimally, we can rely on a *metapolicy language* [8] that specifies which predicates are sensitive, which are associated to actions, which peer is responsible for each action, and where credentials can be searched for, guiding negotiation in a declarative fashion and making it more cooperative and interoperable. Moreover, the metapolicy language can be used to instantiate the framework in different application domains and link predicates to the ontologies where they are defined.

Provisional Policies. Policies may state that certain requests or decisions have to be logged, or that the system itself should search for certain credentials. In other words, policy languages should be able to specify *actions*. Event-condition-action (ECA) rules constitute one possible approach. Another approach consists in labelling some predicates as *provisional*, and associating them to actions that (if successful) make the predicate true [8]. We may also specify that an action should be executed by some other peer; this results in a request.

A cooperative peer tries to execute actions under its responsibility whenever this helps in making negotiations succeed. For example, provisional predicates may be used to encode business rules. The next rule[3] enables discounts on low-selling articles in a specific session:

$$\texttt{allow}(Srv) \leftarrow \ldots, \texttt{session}(ID),$$
$$\texttt{in}(X, \texttt{sql:query}(\texttt{'select} * \texttt{from low\_selling'})),$$
$$\texttt{enabled}(\texttt{discount}(X), ID).$$

Intuitively, if $\texttt{enabled}(\texttt{discount}(X), ID)$ is not yet true but the other conditions are verified, then the negotiator may execute the action associated to $\texttt{enabled}$ and the rule becomes applicable (if $\texttt{enabled}(\texttt{discount}(X), ID)$ is already true, no action is executed). The (application dependent) action can be defined and associated to $\texttt{enabled}$ through the metapolicy language. With the metalanguage one can also specify when an action is to be executed.

Some actions would be more naturally expressed as ECA rules. However, it is not obvious how the natural bottom-up evaluation schema of ECA rules should

---

[3] Formulated in PROTUNE's language.

be integrated with the top-down evaluation adopted by the current core policy language. The latter fits more naturally the abductive nature of negotiation steps. So integration of ECA rules is still an interesting open research issue.

Stateful vs. Stateless Negotiations. Negotiations as described above are in general stateful, because (i) they may refer to a local state – including legacy software and data – and (ii) the sequence of requests and counter requests may become more efficient if credentials and declarations are not submitted again and again, but kept in a local negotiation state. However, negotiations are not *necessarily* stateful because

- the server may refuse to answer counter-requests, or – alternatively – the credentials and declarations disclosed during the transaction may be included in every message and need not be cached locally;
- the policy does not necessarily refer to external packages.

Stateless protocols are just special cases of the frameworks introduced so far. Whether a stateless protocol is really more efficient depends on the application. Moreover, efficiency at all costs might imply less cooperative systems.

Are stateful protocols related to scalability issues? We do not think so. The web started as a stateless protocol, but soon a number of techniques were implemented to simulate stateful protocols and transactions in quite a few real world applications and systems, capable of answering a huge number of requests per time unit. We observe that if the support for stateful negotiations had been cast into http, probably many of the intrinsic vulnerabilities of simulated solutions (like cookies) might have been avoided.

New Issues. Existing approaches to trust management and trust negotiation already tackle the need for flexible, knowledge-based interoperability, and take into account the main idiosyncrasies of the web – because automated trust negotiation frameworks have been designed with exactly that scenario in mind. Today, to make a real contribution (even in the context of a policy-aware web), we should further perform research on the open issues of trust management, including at least the following topics:

- Negotiation success: how can we guarantee that negotiations succeed despite all the difficulties that may interfere: rules not disclosed because of lack of trust; credentials not found because their repository is unknown. What kind of properties of the policy protection policy and of the *hints* (see Section 4.4) guarantee a successful termination when the policy "theoretically" permits access to a resource?
- Optimal negotiations: which strategies optimize information disclosure during negotiation? Can reasonable preconditions prevent unnecessary information disclosure?
- In the presence of multiple ways of fulfilling a request, how should the client choose a response? We need both a language for expressing preferences, and efficient algorithms for solving the corresponding optimization problem.

While this negotiation step is more or less explicitly assumed by most approaches on trust negotiation, there is no concrete proposal so far.

Additionally, integration of abductive semantics and ECA semantics is an open issue, as we have pointed out in a previous section.

4.5   Cooperative Policy Enforcement

Cooperative enforcement involves both machine-to-machine and human-machine aspects. The former is handled by negotiation mechanisms: published policies, provisional actions, hints, and other metalevel information (see Section 4.4) can be interpreted by the client to identify what information is needed to access a resource, and how to obtain that information.

Let us discuss the human-machine interaction aspect in more detail: One of the most important causes of the enormous number of computer security violations on the Internet is the users' lack of technical expertise. Users are typically not aware of the security policies applied by their system, neither of course about how those policies can be changed and how they might be improved by tailoring them to specific needs. As a consequence, most users ignore their computer's vulnerabilities and the corresponding countermeasures, so the system's protection facilities cannot be effectively exploited.

It is well known that the default, generic policies that come with system installations – often biased toward functionality rather than protection – are significantly less secure than a policy specialized to a specific context, but very few users know how to tune or replace the default policy. Moreover, users frequently do not understand what the policy really checks, and hence are unaware of the risks involved in many common operations.

Similar problems affect privacy protection. In trust negotiation, credential release policies are meant to achieve a satisfactory tradeoff between privacy and functionality – many interesting services cannot be obtained without releasing some information about the user. However, we cannot expect such techniques to be effective unless users are able to understand and possibly personalize the privacy policy enforced by their system.

A better understanding of a web service's policy makes it also easier for a first-time user to interact with the service. If denied access results simply in a "*no*" answer, the user has no clue on how he or she can possibly acquire the permission to get the desired service (e.g., by completing a registration procedure, by supplying more credentials or by filling in some form). This is why we advocate *cooperative policy enforcement*, where negative responses are enriched with suggestions and other explanations whenever such information does not violate confidentiality (sometimes, part of the policy itself is sensitive).

For these reasons, *greater user awareness and control on policies* is one of our main objectives, making policies easier to understand and formulate to the common user in the following ways:

- Adopt a *rule-based policy specification language*, because these languages are flexible and at the same time structurally similar to the way in which policies are expressed by nontechnical users.

- Make the policy specification language more friendly by e.g. developing a *controlled natural language* front-end to translate natural language text into executable rules (see next section).
- Develop *advanced explanation mechanisms* [24,54,55] to help the user understand what policies prescribe and control.

Inference Web (IW) [54,55] is a toolkit that aims at providing useful explanations for the behavior of (Semantic-) Web based systems. In particular, [54] propose support for knowledge provenance information using metadata (e.g., Dublin Core information) about the distributed information systems involved in a particular reasoning task. [54] also deals with the issue of representing heterogeneous reasoning approaches, domain description languages and proof representations; the latter issue is addressed by using PML, the OWL-based Proof Markup Language [56].

Specifically applied to policies, [24] contains a requirements analysis for explanations in the context of automated trust negotiation and defines explanation mechanisms for *why, why-not, how-to,* and *what-if* queries. Several novel aspects are described:

- Adoption of a *tabled explanation structure* as opposed to more traditional approaches based on single derivations or proof trees. The tabled approach makes it possible to describe infinite failures, which is essential for *why not* queries.
- Explanations show simultaneously different possible proof attempts and allow users to see both local and global proof details at the same time. This combination of local and global (intra-proof and inter-proof) information facilitates navigation across the explanation structures.
- Introduction of suitable heuristics for focussing explanations by removing irrelevant parts of the proof attempts. A second level of explanations can recover missing details, if desired.
- Heuristics are *generic*, i.e. domain independent, they require no manual configuration.
- The combination of tabling techniques and heuristics yields a novel method for explaining failure.

Explanation mechanisms should be *lightweight* and *scalable* in the sense that (i) they do not require any major effort when the general framework is instantiated in a specific application domain, and (ii) most of the computational effort can be delegated to the clients. Queries are answered using the same policy specifications used for negotiation. Query answering is conceived for the following categories of users:

- Users who try to understand how to obtain access permissions;
- Users who monitor and verify their own privacy policy;
- Policy managers who verify and monitor their policies.

Currently, advanced queries comprise *why/why not, how-to,* and *what-if* queries. Why/why not queries can be used by security managers to understand why some specific request has been accepted or rejected, which may be useful for debugging purposes. Why-not queries may help a user to understand what needs to be done in order to obtain the required permissions, a process that in general may include a combination of automated and manual actions. Such features are absolutely essential to enforce security requirements without discouraging users that try to connect to a web service for the first time. How-to queries have a similar role, and differ from why-not queries mainly because the former do not assume a previous query as a context, while the latter do.

What-if queries are hypothetical queries that allow to predict the behavior of a policy before credentials are actually searched for and before a request is actually submitted. What-if queries are good both for validation purposes and for helping users in obtaining permissions.

Among the technical challenges related to explanations, we mention:

- Find the right tradeoff between explanation quality and the effort for instantiating the framework in new application domains. Second generation explanation systems [57,58,59] prescribe a sequence of expensive steps, including the creation of an independent domain knowledge base expressly for communicating with the user. This would be a serious obstacle to the applicability of the framework.

Natural Language Policies. Policies should be written by and understandable to users, to let them control behavior of their system. Otherwise the risk that users keep on adopting generic hence ineffective built-in policies, and remain unaware of which controls are actually made by the system is extremely high – and this significantly reduces the benefits of a flexible policy framework.

Most users have no specific training in programming nor in formal logics. Fortunately, they spontaneously tend to formulate policies as rules; still, logical languages may be intimidating. For this reason, the design of front ends based on graphical formalisms as well as *natural language interfaces* are crucial to the adoption of formal policy languages. We want policy rules to be formulated like: *"Academic users can download the files in folder historical_data whenever their creation date precedes 1942"*.

Clearly, the inherent ambiguity of natural language is incompatible with the precision needed by security and privacy specifications. Solutions to that can be the adoption of a *controlled* fragment of English (e.g., the ATTEMPTO system[4]) where a few simple rules determine a unique meaning for each sentence. This approach can be complemented with a suitable interface that clarifies what the machine understands.

5   Conclusions

Policies are really knowledge bases: a single body of declarative rules used in many possible ways, for negotiations, query answering, and other forms of system behavior control. As far as trust negotiation is concerned, we further argue

---

[4] http://www.ifi.unizh.ch/attempto/

that transparent interoperation based on ontology sharing can become "everyday technology" in a short time, and trust negotiation especially will become a success story for semantic web ideas and techniques.

In addition to stateless negotiation [60], we need stateful negotiation as well [45]. Even the Web, which started as a stateless protocol, now implements a number of techniques to simulate stateful protocols and transactions, especially in applications for accessing data other than web pages.

Cooperative policy enforcement and trust management gives common users better understanding and control on the policies that govern their systems and the services they interact with. The closer we get to this objective, the higher the impact of our techniques and ideas will be.

Policies will have to handle decisions under a wide range of risk levels, performance requirements, and traffic patterns. It is good to know that the rule-based techniques that different research communities are currently converging to are powerful enough to effectively address such a wide spectrum of scenarios. This is the level of flexibility needed by the Semantic Web.

About This Manuscript. This manuscript provides an introduction to policy representation and reasoning for the Semantic Web. It describes the benefits of using policies and presents four of the most relevant policy languages. These four languages are classified according to whether policies are assumed to be public or else may be protected. The former consists of a single evaluation step where a policy engine or a matchmaker decides whether two policies are compatible or not. Examples of this kind of evaluation are the KAOS and REI frameworks. If policies may be protected (by e.g. other policies), the process is not anymore a one-step evaluation. In this case, policies guide a negotiation in which policies are disclosed iteratively increasing the level of security at each step towards a final agreement. Examples of these kind of frameworks are PeerTrust and Protune. Furthermore, Semantic Web techniques can be used to ease and enhance the process of policy specification and validation. Conflicts between policies can be found and even resolved automatically (either by meta-policies or by harmonisation algorithms).

In order to demonstrate the benefits and feasibility of Semantic Web policies, several application scenarios are briefly described, namely the (Semantic) Web, (Semantic) Web Services and the (Semantic) Grid. Finally a list of open research issues that prevent existing policy languages from being widely adopted are introduced. This list is intended to help new researchers in the area to focus on those crucial problems which are still unsolved.

References

1. Berners-Lee, T., Hendler, J., Lassila, O.: The Semantic Web. Scientific American (May 2001)
2. Antoniou, G., Baldoni, M., Bonatti, P.A., Nejdl, W., Olmedilla, D.: Rule-based policy specification. In: Yu, T., Jajodia, S. (eds.) Secure Data Management in Decentralized Systems. Advances in Information Security, vol. 33, Springer, Heidelberg (2007)

3. Blaze, M., Feigenbaum, J., Keromytis, A.D.: Keynote: Trust management for public-key infrastructures (position paper). In: Christianson, B., Crispo, B., Harbison, W.S., Roe, M. (eds.) Security Protocols. LNCS, vol. 1550, pp. 59–63. Springer, Heidelberg (1999)
4. Blaze, M., Feigenbaum, J., Strauss, M.: Compliance checking in the policymaker trust management system. In: Hirschfeld, R. (ed.) FC 1998. LNCS, vol. 1465, pp. 254–274. Springer, Heidelberg (1998)
5. Uszok, A., Bradshaw, J.M., Jeffers, R., Suri, N., Hayes, P.J., Breedy, M.R., Bunch, L., Johnson, M., Kulkarni, S., Lott, J.: KAoS policy and domain services: Toward a description-logic approach to policy representation, deconfliction, and enforcement. In: POLICY, p. 93 (2003)
6. Kagal, L., Finin, T.W., Joshi, A.: A policy based approach to security for the semantic web. In: Fensel, D., Sycara, K.P., Mylopoulos, J. (eds.) ISWC 2003. LNCS, vol. 2870, pp. 402–418. Springer, Heidelberg (2003)
7. Gavriloaie, R., Nejdl, W., Olmedilla, D., Seamons, K.E., Winslett, M.: No registration needed: How to use declarative policies and negotiation to access sensitive resources on the semantic web. In: Bussler, C.J., Davies, J., Fensel, D., Studer, R. (eds.) ESWS 2004. LNCS, vol. 3053, pp. 342–356. Springer, Heidelberg (2004)
8. Bonatti, P.A., Olmedilla, D.: Driving and monitoring provisional trust negotiation with metapolicies. In: 6th IEEE International Workshop on Policies for Distributed Systems and Networks (POLICY 2005), Stockholm, Sweden, pp. 14–23. IEEE Computer Society Press, Los Alamitos (2005)
9. Tonti, G., Bradshaw, J.M., Jeffers, R., Montanari, R., Suri, N., Uszok, A.: Semantic web languages for policy representation and reasoning: A comparison of KAoS, Rei, and Ponder. In: International Semantic Web Conference, pp. 419–437 (2003)
10. Kagal, L., Paolucci, M., Srinivasan, N., Denker, G., Finin, T.W., Sycara, K.P.: Authorization and privacy for semantic web services. IEEE Intelligent Systems 19(4), 50–56 (2004)
11. Taveter, K., Wagner, G.: Agent-oriented enterprise modeling based on business rules. In: Kunii, H.S., Jajodia, S., Sølvberg, A. (eds.) ER 2001. LNCS, vol. 2224, pp. 527–540. Springer, Heidelberg (2001)
12. Winsborough, W.H., Seamons, K.E., Jones, V.E.: Automated trust negotiation. In: DARPA Information Survivability Conference and Exposition, IEEE Press, Los Alamitos (2000)
13. Nejdl, W., Olmedilla, D., Winslett, M., Zhang, C.C.: Ontology-based policy specification and management. In: Gómez-Pérez, A., Euzenat, J. (eds.) ESWC 2005. LNCS, vol. 3532, pp. 290–302. Springer, Heidelberg (2005)
14. Bonatti, P.A., Duma, C., Fuchs, N., Nejdl, W., Olmedilla, D., Peer, J., Shahmehri, N.: Semantic web policies - a discussion of requirements and research issues. In: Sure, Y., Domingue, J. (eds.) ESWC 2006. LNCS, vol. 4011, Springer, Heidelberg (2006)
15. Olmedilla, D.: Security and privacy on the semantic web. In: Petkovic, M., Jonker, W. (eds.) Security, Privacy and Trust in Modern Data Management, Springer, Heidelberg (to appear)
16. Bradshaw, J.M., Uszok, A., Jeffers, R., Suri, N., Hayes, P.J., Burstein, M.H., Acquisti, A., Benyo, B., Breedy, M.R., Carvalho, M.M., Diller, D.J., Johnson, M., Kulkarni, S., Lott, J., Sierhuis, M., von Hoof, R.: Representation and reasoning for DAML-based policy and domain services in KAoS and nomads. In: The Second International Joint Conference on Autonomous Agents & Multiagent Systems (AAMAS), Melbourne, Victoria, Australia (2003)

17. Dean, M., Schreiber, G.: OWL web ontology language reference (2004)
18. Baader, F., Calvanese, D., McGuinness, D.L., Nardi, D., Patel-Schneider, P.F. (eds.): The Description Logic Handbook: Theory, Implementation, and Applications. Cambridge University Press, Cambridge (2003)
19. Kagal, L.: A Policy-Based Approach to Governing Autonomous Behaviour in Distributed Environments. PhD thesis, University of Maryland Baltimore County (2004)
20. Bonatti, P., Samarati, P.: Regulating Service Access and Information Release on the Web. In: Conference on Computer and Communications Security (CCS'00), Athens (2000)
21. Li, N., Mitchell, J.C.: RT: A Role-based Trust-management Framework. In: DARPA Information Survivability Conference and Exposition (DISCEX), Washington, D.C (2003)
22. Trevor, J., Suciu, D.: Dynamically distributed query evaluation. In: Proceedings of the twentieth ACM SIGMOD-SIGACT-SIGART Symposium on Principles of Database Systems, Santa Barbara, CA, USA, ACM, New York (2001)
23. Alves, M., Damásio, C.V., Nejdl, W., Olmedilla, D.: A distributed tabling algorithm for rule based policy systems. In: 7th IEEE International Workshop on Policies for Distributed Systems and Networks (POLICY 2006), London, Ontario, Canada, pp. 123–132. IEEE Computer Society, Los Alamitos (2006)
24. Bonatti, P.A., Olmedilla, D., Peer, J.: Advanced policy explanations on the web. In: 17th European Conference on Artificial Intelligence (ECAI 2006), Riva del Garda, Italy, pp. 200–204. IOS Press, Amsterdam (2006)
25. Kolari, P., Ding, L., Ganjugunte, S., Joshi, A., Finin, T.W., Kagal, L.: Enhancing web privacy protection through declarative policies. In: 6th IEEE International Workshop on Policies for Distributed Systems and Networks (POLICY 2005), Stockholm, Sweden, pp. 57–66. IEEE Computer Society, Los Alamitos (2005)
26. Staab, S., Bhargava, B.K., Lilien, L., Rosenthal, A., Winslett, M., Sloman, M., Dillon, T.S., Chang, E., Hussain, F.K., Nejdl, W., Olmedilla, D., Kashyap, V.: The pudding of trust. IEEE Intelligent Systems 19(5), 74–88 (2004)
27. Denker, G., Kagal, L., Finin, T.W., Paolucci, M., Sycara, K.P.: Security for daml web services: Annotation and matchmaking. In: Fensel, D., Sycara, K.P., Mylopoulos, J. (eds.) ISWC 2003. LNCS, vol. 2870, pp. 335–350. Springer, Heidelberg (2003)
28. Olmedilla, D., Lara, R., Polleres, A., Lausen, H.: Trust negotiation for semantic web services. In: Cardoso, J., Sheth, A.P. (eds.) SWSWPC 2004. LNCS, vol. 3387, pp. 81–95. Springer, Heidelberg (2005)
29. Grid Security Infrastructure, http://www.globus.org/security/overview.html
30. Uszok, A., Bradshaw, J.M., Jeffers, R.: Kaos: A policy and domain services framework for grid computing and semantic web services. In: Jensen, C., Poslad, S., Dimitrakos, T. (eds.) iTrust 2004. LNCS, vol. 2995, pp. 16–26. Springer, Heidelberg (2004)
31. Constandache, I., Olmedilla, D., Nejdl, W.: Policy based dynamic negotiation for grid services authorization. In: Semantic Web Policy Workshop in conjunction with 4th International Semantic Web Conference, Galway, Ireland (2005)
32. Li Gong: Inside Java 2 Platform Security: Architecture, API Design, and Implementation. Addison-Wesley, Reading (1999)
33. Gelfond, M., Lifschitz, V.: The stable model semantics for logic programming. In: Proc. of the 5th ICLP, pp. 1070–1080. MIT Press, Cambridge (1988)

34. Bertino, E., Ferrari, E., Buccafurri, F., Rullo, P.: A logical framework for reasoning on data access control policies. In: Proc. of the 12th IEEE Computer Security Foundations Workshop (CSFW'99), pp. 175–189. IEEE Computer Society, Los Alamitos (1999)

35. Brewer, D.F.C., Nash, M.J.: The chinese wall security policy. In: IEEE Symposium on Security and Privacy, pp. 206–214. IEEE Computer Society Press, Los Alamitos (1989)

36. Palopoli, L., Zaniolo, C.: Polynomial-time computable stable models. Ann. Math. Artif. Intell. 17(3-4), 261–290 (1996)

37. Saccà, D., Zaniolo, C.: Stable models and non-determinism in logic programs with negation. In: Proc. of the Ninth ACM SIGACT-SIGMOD-SIGART Symposium on Principles of Database Systems (PODS'90), pp. 205–217. ACM, New York (1990)

38. Apt, K.R., Blair, H.A., Walker, A.: Towards a theory of declarative knowledge. In: Foundations of Deductive Databases and Logic Programming, pp. 89–148. Morgan Kaufmann, San Francisco (1988)

39. Bonatti, P.A., Shahmehri, N., Duma, C., Olmedilla, D., Nejdl, W., Baldoni, M., Baroglio, C., Martelli, A., Patti, V., Coraggio, P., Antoniou, G., Peer, J., Fuchs, N.E.: Rule-based policy specification: State of the art and future work. Technical report, Working Group I2, EU NoE REWERSE (August 2004), http://rewerse.net/deliverables/i2-d1.pdf

40. Subrahmanian, V.S., Adali, S., Brink, A., Emery, R., Lu, J.J., Rajput, A., Rogers, T.J., Ross, R., Ward, C.: Hermes: Heterogeneous reasoning and mediator system, http://www.cs.umd.edu/projects/publications/abstracts/hermes.html

41. Subrahmanian, V.S., Bonatti, P.A., Dix, J., Eiter, T., Kraus, S., Ozcan, F., Ross, R.: Heterogenous Active Agents. MIT Press, Cambridge (2000)

42. Rosenthal, A., Winslett, M.: Security of shared data in large systems: State of the art and research directions. In: Proceedings of the ACM SIGMOD International Conference on Management of Data, Paris, France, June 13-18, 2004, pp. 962–964. ACM, New York (2004)

43. Bonatti, P.A., Duma, C., Olmedilla, D., Shahmehri, N.: An integration of reputation-based and policy-based trust management. In: Semantic Web Policy Workshop in conjunction with 4th International Semantic Web Conference, Ireland (2005)

44. Blaze, M., Feigenbaum, J., Strauss, M.: Compliance Checking in the PolicyMaker Trust Management System. In: Financial Cryptography, British West Indies (February 1998)

45. Bonatti, P.A., Samarati, P.: A uniform framework for regulating service access and information release on the web. Journal of Computer Security 10(3), 241–272 (2000) Short version in the Proc. of the Conference on Computer and Communications Security (CCS'00), Athens (2000)

46. Winsborough, W., Seamons, K., Jones, V.: Negotiating Disclosure of Sensitive Credentials. In: Second Conference on Security in Communication Networks, Amalfi, Italy (September 1999)

47. Winsborough, W., Seamons, K., Jones, V.: Automated Trust Negotiation. In: DARPA Information Survivability Conference and Exposition, Hilton Head Island, SC (2000)

48. Winslett, M., Yu, T., Seamons, K.E., Hess, A., Jacobson, J., Jarvis, R., Smith, B., Yu, L.: Negotiating trust on the web. IEEE Internet Computing 6(6), 30–37 (2002)

49. Yu, T., Winslett, M., Seamons, K.E.: Supporting structured credentials and sensitive policies through interoperable strategies for automated trust negotiation. ACM Trans. Inf. Syst. Secur. 6(1), 1–42 (2003)

50. Becker, M.Y., Sewell, P.: Cassandra: distributed access control policies with tunable expressiveness. In: 5th IEEE International Workshop on Policies for Distributed Systems and Networks, Yorktown Heights (2004)
51. Seamons, K., Winslett, M., Yu, T., Smith, B., Child, E., Jacobsen, J., Mills, H., Yu, L.: Requirements for Policy Languages for Trust Negotiation. In: 3rd International Workshop on Policies for Distributed Systems and Networks, Monterey, CA (2002)
52. Li, N., Winsborough, W., Mitchell, J.C.: Distributed Credential Chain Discovery in Trust Management (Extended Abstract). In: ACM Conference on Computer and Communications Security, Philadelphia, Pennsylvania, ACM, New York (2001)
53. Zhang, C., Bonatti, P.A., Winslett, M.: Peeraccess: A logic for distributed authorization. In: 12th ACM Conference on Computer and Communication Security (CCS 2005), Alexandria, VA, USA, ACM Press, New York (2005)
54. McGuinness, D.L., da Silva, P.P.: Explaining answers from the semantic web: The inference web approach. Journal of Web Semantics 1(4), 397–413 (2004)
55. McGuinness, D.L., da Silva, P.P.: Trusting answers from web applications. In: New Directions in Question Answering, pp. 275–286 (2004)
56. da Silva, P.P., McGuinness, D.L., Fikes, R.: A proof markup language for semantic web services. Technical Report KSL Tech Report KSL-04-01 (January 2004)
57. Swartout, W., Paris, C., Moore, J.: Explanations in knowledge systems: Design for explainable expert systems. IEEE Expert: Intelligent Systems and Their Applications 6(3), 58–64 (1991)
58. Tanner, M.C., Keuneke, A.M.: Explanations in knowledge systems: The roles of the task structure and domain functional models. IEEE Expert: Intelligent Systems and Their Applications 6(3), 50–57 (1991)
59. Wick, M.R.: Second generation expert system explanation. In: David, J.-M., Krivine, J.-P., Simmons, R. (eds.) Second Generation Expert Systems, pp. 614–640. Springer, Heidelberg (1993)
60. Kolovski, V., Katz, Y., Hendler, J., Weitzner, D., Berners-Lee, T.: Towards a policy-aware web. In: Semantic Web Policy Workshop in conjunction with 4th International Semantic Web Conference, Galway, Ireland (2005)

Rule Interchange on the Web

Harold Boley[1], Michael Kifer[2], Paula-Lavinia Pătrânjan[3],
and Axel Polleres[4]

[1] University of New Brunswick, Faculty of Computer Science
Institute for Information Technology - e-Business, NRC
46 Dineen Drive, Fredericton, Canada
harold.boley@nrc-cnrc.gc.ca
http://www.cs.unb.ca/ boley/
[2] State University of New York at Stony Brook
Department of Computer Science
Stony Brook, New York 11794-4400, USA
kifer@cs.sunysb.edu
http://www.cs.sunysb.edu/ kifer/
[3] University of Munich, Institute for Informatics
Oettingenstr. 67, D-80538 München
paula.patranjan@ifi.lmu.de
http://www.pms.ifi.lmu.de
[4] Digital Enterprise Research Institute
National University of Ireland, Galway
axel.polleres@deri.org
http://www.polleres.net/

Abstract. Rules play an increasingly important role in a variety of Semantic Web applications as well as in traditional IT systems. As a universal medium for publishing information, the Web is envisioned to become the place for publishing, distributing, and exchanging rule-based knowledge. Realizing the importance and the promise of this vision, W3C has created the Rule Interchange Format Working Group (RIF WG) and chartered it to develop an interchange format for rules in alignment with the existing standards in the Semantic Web architecture stack.

However, creating a generally accepted interchange format is by no means a trivial task. First, there are different understandings of what a "rule" is. Researchers and practitioners distinguish between deduction rules, normative rules, production rules, reactive rules, etc. Second, even within the same category of rules, systems use different (often incompatible) semantics and syntaxes. Third, existing Semantic Web standards, such as RDF and OWL, show incompatibilities with many kinds of rule languages at a conceptual level.

This article discusses the role that different kinds of rule languages and systems play on the Web, illustrates the problems and opportunities in exchanging rules through a standardized format, and provides a snapshot of the current work of the W3C RIF WG.

G. Antoniou et al. (Eds.): Reasoning Web 2007, LNCS 4636, pp. 269–309, 2007.
© Springer-Verlag Berlin Heidelberg 2007

1 Introduction

Rule interchange on the Web has become an increasingly important issue during the last couple of years in both industry and academia. Offering a flexible, adaptive approach towards applications development on a high level of abstraction, declarative rules languages have already been developed by different communities and deployed in various application domains. Companies manage and specify their business logic in the form of rules [The00]. Rules are also being used for modeling security policies in cooperative systems [Bon05], and they are gaining popularity as a means of reasoning about Web data [BS04, EIP+06, Ros06].

To exploit the full potential of rule-based approaches, the business rules and the Semantic Web communities have started to develop solutions for reusing and integrating knowledge specified in different rule languages. The Rule Markup Initiative[1], which started in 2000, focused its efforts on defining a shared Rule Markup Language (RuleML) that tries to encompass different types of rules. The European Network of Excellence REWERSE [BS04] (Reasoning on the Web with Rules and Semantics) proposes R2ML [WGL06], the REWERSE I1 Rule Markup Language, which offers a solution for interchanging rules between heterogeneous systems combining RuleML, SWRL, and OCL. Moreover, three member submissions for Web rule languages, namely the Semantic Web Rule Language (SWRL) [HPSB+04], the Web Rules Language (WRL) [ABdB+05], and SWSL Rules [BBB+] (a rule language proposed by the Semantic Web Services Language Committee[2]) were submitted independently to the World Wide Web Consortium (W3C) as starting points for standardization in the rules area.

Finally, at the end of 2005, W3C launched the Rule Interchange Format Working Group (RIF WG) which has been chartered to standardize a common format for rule interchange on the Web.

In this article, we start with a general discussion of problems related to rule interchange on the Web and outline the role of rules in realizing the Semantic Web vision. Then, we present the results of the W3C RIF WG achieved so far and outline future work to be done. In particular, we will discuss the first two public working drafts released by the Working Group—the *Use Cases and Requirements* [GHMe] document and the technical design of a core rule interchange format, the *RIF Core* [BK07].

1.1 Running Example: A Simple Movie Scenario

To illustrate the main ideas, we use an example where several movie databases interoperate through the Web.

Example 1. The fictitious International Movie Datastore (IMD) publishes its database through its Web site `http://imd.example.org/`. This database is shown in Figure 1(a). Likewise, John Doe Sr., who owns a DVD Rental Store, MoviShop, makes his movie rental services available on the Web. His site is supported by a similar database shown in Figure 1(b).

---

[1] Rule Markup Initiative, `http://www.ruleml.org`

[2] http://www.daml.org/services/swsl/

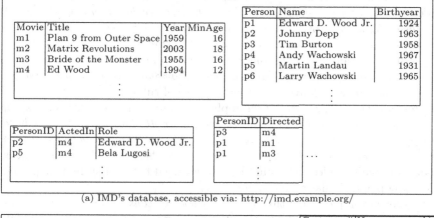

Movie	Title	Year	MinAge
m1	Plan 9 from Outer Space	1959	16
m2	Matrix Revolutions	2003	18
m3	Bride of the Monster	1955	16
m4	Ed Wood	1994	12

Person	Name	Birthyear
p1	Edward D. Wood Jr.	1924
p2	Johnny Depp	1963
p3	Tim Burton	1958
p4	Andy Wachowski	1967
p5	Martin Landau	1931
p6	Larry Wachowski	1965

PersonID	ActedIn	Role
p2	m4	Edward D. Wood Jr.
p5	m4	Bela Lugosi

PersonID	Directed
p3	m4
p1	m1
p1	m3

(a) IMD's database, accessible via: http://imd.example.org/

DVD#	Movie
dvd1	m1
dvd2	m1

Customer#	DVD#	RentalDate	ReturnDate
c1	dvd2	2007-09-01	2007-09-01
c2	dvd5	2007-01-01	

Customer#	Name	Age
c1	Joanna Doe	31
c2	Johnny Dough	12
c3	John Doe Jr.	16

((b) MoviShop's database

Fig. 1. IMD, a fictitious movie database, and MoviShop, a fictitious DVD rental store

By employing Web formats such as XML, RDF, and OWL, John can share data over the Web. John also uses Semantic Web technologies for implementing some of the services MoviShop is offering. For instance, MoviShop provides customers with information about the newest movies by importing data from http://imd.example.org/. It also publishes the information about available movies and links to other Web sources that provide reviews and recommendations (such as IMD). MoviShop also supports online ordering of movies, which can later be picked up in a branch office of MoviShop.

Recently John has become fascinated by the new business opportunities, which could arise if MoviShop could import and exchange not only data but also business rules. He is thus very excited about W3C's ongoing efforts towards a common rules interchange format.

1.2 Rules and Rule Types

Creating a format for rule interchange on the Web, which could help John conduct his business, is not a trivial task. First, there are different ideas about what *types* of rules are of interest: one might get different views depending on whether you talk to a production rule vendor, a database vendor, or a Semantic Web researcher. This is because the term "rule" is an umbrella for a number of related, but still quite different concepts.

A simple example of a rule is a CSS selector, i.e. a statement that defines how browsers should render elements on an HTML page, such as the list of available movies in John's MoviShop. At the business level, John might be interested to enforce *constraint rules* such as "*credit cards accepted by MoviShop are VISA and MasterCard.*" Moreover, rules can define implicit data, e.g. "*Customers who have rented more than 100 movies are priority customers.*"

Integrity constraints on the structure of the data in databases, such as "*each movie has a single production year,*" or "*each MoviShop customer has a unique identification number,*" provide another example of rules.

Statements specifying parts of an application's dynamic behavior such as '*if an item is perishable and it is delivered more than 10 days after the scheduled delivery date then the item will be rejected*' or '*if a customer is blacklisted then deny the customer's request to booking a movie*' are also rules. The second rule is a good example for rules that could be interchanged between systems deployed by MoviShop and similar online shops.

The above examples show that rules may specify *constraints, (implicit) construction of new data, data transformations, updates on data* or, more general, *event-driven actions*. Rules are also used for *reasoning* with Web and Semantic Web data. From a high-level view, rules are statements that express static or dynamic relationships among different data items, the logic of applications, and more generally of business processes within enterprises.

Rules may differ significantly not only in their purpose (*e.g.*, transforming data), but also in their form. Consider, for example, the following rules:

```
(R1)  IF movie ?M was produced before 1930
      THEN ?M is a black and white movie
```

```
(R2)  ON request from customer ?C to book a movie
      IF customer ?C is blacklisted
      DO deny ?C's request
```

Rule *R1* has two components: The IF part searches for movies produced before 1930 and binds the variable M to such movies. The THEN part of the rule uses the retrieved information to construct new data—a view over the movie data. Rule *R2* has a different structure: The ON part waits for a request for booking a movie to come in, i.e. an event. The IF part of rule *R2* is similar to the IF part of rule *R1*—it checks a condition about the customer requesting a movie. The DO part specifies the action to be executed on a request from a blacklisted customer.

Different kinds of rules present different requirements to the implementor. *R2* needs a richer language and a more complex execution semantics than *R1*, since its ON part requires support for detecting incoming events and its DO part needs support for executing actions. However, both types of rules share the need to support conditions in the IF part. This commonality among different types of rules suggest a way of approaching the development of a rule interchange format by starting with common parts (such as the IF part) and extending this support to various features of different types of rules. To better understand the similarities among different types of rules, we divide them into three categories: *deduction rules, normative rules, and reactive rules* (see [TW01, BM05]).

Deduction Rules are statements of how to derive knowledge from other knowledge by using logical inference. Deduction rules are also called derivation rules in the business rules community, constructive rules by logicians, and views in the database community.

One could say that deduction rules describe *static* dependencies among entities which might be used to infer additional implicit knowledge from what is explicitly stated in a knowledge base or database. Deductive rules are often specified as implications of the form head ← body: The head gives a specification of the data to be constructed/inferred and the body queries the underlying database(s). Both rule parts may and usually share variables. Variables get bound to data items in the body and these bindings are then used in the head to infer new data. In the previous example, rule *R1* is a deductive rule. Its body is introduced by the keyword IF and the head by THEN. The head and the body share the variable M, which is a placeholder for a movie object.

The actual syntax and the nature of the parts in a rule depend on the chosen rule language. Some languages divide the body into a query part, which selects data from one or more databases, and a condition part, which acts as a filter for the results obtained by evaluating the query part. Consider the rule *R1*, which constructs a view of black and white movies from a movie database at http://imd.example.org/movies.xml. The body of the rule searches for movies in a database and then filters out the movies produced before 1930. As a concrete example of a rule language, let us consider rule R1 expressed in Xcerpt[3], an XML rule language based on deductive rules:

```
CONSTRUCT
   black-and-white { all var Title }
FROM
   in { resource { "http://imd.example.org/movies.xml", XML},
        moviedb {{
            movie {{
                title { var Title },
                year { var Year }
            }}
        }}
   } WHERE var Year < 1930
END
```

Rule components specify patterns for the data to be constructed or queried. The rule head, introduced by CONSTRUCT, gathers *all* substitutions for the variable *Title*. The rule body, introduced by FROM gives an incomplete pattern for the *movies.xml* data and retrieves the movie titles and years as substitutions for the variables *Title* and *Year*. The WHERE part specifies the desired filter condition.

The given Xcerpt rule exemplifies a deductive rule with *selection and filtering* of data in the body and *grouping* of data items in the head. Data is retrieved from a single data source—an XML document—but more than one data source can be

---

[3] Xcerpt, http://xcerpt.org

queried within one deductive rule. The data source may be explicitly given, as in this case, or given implicitly (e.g. upon loading a ruleset). Depending on the rule language used to specify and evaluate deductive rules, other features may also be supported. Join queries over multiple data sources, which correlate pieces of data found in the data sources, may also be specified in a deductive rule's body. Other features, such as aggregation of data (e.g. by means of aggregate functions like count, which counts the substitutions for a given variable), or external function calls may or may not be allowed to be used in rules.

Other examples of rule languages based on deductive rules are SQL views, Datalog, Prolog, and most other logical rules languages.

Normative Rules are rules that pose constraints on the data or on the logic of an application. Such rules ensure that changes made to a database do not cause inconsistencies and that the business logic of a company is obeyed. Normative rules are also called structural rules in the business rules community and integrity constraints in databases.

Normative rules describe disallowed inconsistencies rather than inferring new knowledge. A simple constraint is that each customer must have a unique identification number. Two different identification numbers for the same person are an indication of corrupted data. Similar examples arise in E-R models in the form of key declarations and cardinality restrictions. XML's DTDs also provide rudimentary capabilities to express such key constraints in the form of ID and IDREF attributes, and XML Schema provides rich support for key and foreign key constraints.

In some cases, deductive rules can be used to implement normative rules[4]. In other cases, reactive rules (discussed next) can be used to implement certain types of normative rules. The decision largely depends on the application and on the available support for different rule types. For example, in [FFLS99] constraints are used to describe the structure of Web sites and deductive rules are used as a specification and implementation mechanism. Deductive rules are also used to specify assertion-style constraints in databases. In addition, database implementors often use triggers—a form of reactive rules—as a technique for implementing integrity constraints.

Reactive Rules offer means to describe reactive behavior and implement reactive systems, i.e. to automatically execute specified actions when events of interest occur and/or certain conditions become true. Reactive rules are also called active rules and dynamic rules. Unlike deduction rules, reactive rules talk about state changes. Events represent changes in the state of the world and rules specify further changes that must occur in reaction to the events (hence the name *reactive rules*). Reactive rules usually have the form of Event-Condition-Action (ECA) rules or production rules.

ECA rules are rules of the form ON Event IF Condition DO Action. This means that the Action should be executed if the Event occurs, provided that

---

[4] More details on the proposed classification of rules can be found at http://www.w3.org/2005/rules/wg/wiki/Classification_of_Rules

the `Condition` also holds. The `Event` part serves a twofold purpose: detecting events of interest and selecting data items from their representations (by binding variables as discussed above). Different kinds of events may be supported, ranging from low-level, data-driven events, such as the deletion of a subtree of an XML tree, to high-level more abstract events, such as the delay of a flight. Depending on the rule language, only single occurrences of events (*atomic events*) may be allowed to be specified and detected, or temporal combinations of events (*composite events*) may be permitted. The events mentioned previously are all atomic. The following is an example of a composite event: "*customer ?C requests booking a movie AND no response from ?C on bringing back movie M1.*"

The `Condition` part queries the state of the world—e.g. XML and RDF data in Web applications or a legacy database—and may be expressed in a query language such as XPath[5], Xcerpt[6], or SPARQL[7]. Like the `Event` part, the `Condition` also selects data items that can be further used in executing the `Action`. Different kinds of actions may be supported by reactive systems: updates to data (e.g., insertion of a subtree into an XML tree), changes to the rule set itself (e.g., removal of a rule), new events to be triggered, or procedure calls (e.g., calling an external function which sends an email message). Actions can also be combined to ease the programming of complex applications.

The following example gives a possible implementation of the rule *R2* previously mentioned in this section. We use XChange[8] here, a language which is based on ECA rules:

```
ON
   xchange:event {{
     xchange:sender { var S },
     order {{
       customer { var C }
     }}
   }}
FROM
   in { resource { "http://MoviShop.org/blacklisted.xml", XML },
     desc var C
   }
DO
   xchange:event {
     xchange:recipient { var S },
     message { "Your request can not be processed,
               since you are blacklisted" }
   }
END
```

---

[5] XPath, http://www.w3.org/TR/xpath
[6] Xcerpt, http://xcerpt.org
[7] http://www.w3.org/TR/rdf-sparql-query/
[8] XChange, http://reactiveweb.org/xchange/intro.html

XChange [BBEP05, BEP06b, PÖ5] integrates the query language Xcerpt for specifying the condition part (introduced by FROM) of reactive rules. XChange assumes that each reactive Web node has reactive rules in place and that the communication of Web nodes is realized through event messages—messages carrying information on the events that have occurred. XChange reactive rules react upon such event messages, which are labelled xchange:event. The ON part of the example reactive rule gives a pattern for incoming event messages that represent booking requests. The FROM part is an Xcerpt query; the descendant construct in the example is used for searching at a variable depth in *blacklisted.xml* for the customer requesting the order. The DO part sends an event message to the customer announcing the reasons for denying the request.

Examples of other ECA rule languages and systems are the General Semantic Web ECA Framework,[9] [BFMS06, MSvL06] Prova,[10], ruleCore[11], and Active XQuery [BBCC02]. Another ECA rule language for XML data is proposed in [BPW02] and adapted for RDF data as the RDF Triggering Language (RDF-TL) [PPW03]. Reaction RuleML[12] was recently launched as part of the RuleML Initiative.[13] Its aim is the development of a markup language for the family of reactive rules.

Triggers are a form of ECA rules employed in database management systems: The E part specifies the database update operation to react to, the C part specifies the condition that needs to hold for executing the database update operations specified in the A part. Triggers combined with relational or object-oriented database systems give rise to so-called active database systems. Most of the active database systems support triggers where all three rule parts – E, C, and A – are explicitly specified; proposals also exist where the E or the C part is either missing or implicit. Examples of active database systems include Starburst [Wid96], Postgres [PS96], and the systems based on SQL:1999 [Mel02].

It is worthwhile to also mention other, less popular, variations of ECA rules. Event-Condition-Action-Alternative (ECAA) rules extend the ECA rules by specifying the action to be executed when the given condition doesn't hold. Note that an ECAA rule can be rewritten into two ECA rules, where the condition part of one rule is the negation of the other. An EC^nA^{n+1} rule is a generalization of an ECAA rule. Yet another form of ECA rules are the Event-Condition-Action-Postcondition (ECAP) rules, which extend ECA rules by specifying a (post)condition that needs to hold after the action has been executed. These kinds of restrictions make sense, for instance, when considering action execution frameworks supporting transactions.

Production rules are rules of the form IF Condition DO Action. They say that the Action part must be executed whenever a change to the underlying

[9] General Semantic Web ECA Framework,
http://www.dbis.informatik.uni-goettingen.de/eca/

[10] Prova, http://www.prova.ws

[11] ruleCore, www.rulecore.com

[12] Reaction RuleML, http://ibis.in.tum.de/research/ReactionRuleML/

[13] RuleML Initiative, http://www.ruleml.org

database makes `Condition` true. The `Condition` queries the working memory, which contains the data on which the rules operate. Selected data is then used to execute the actions specified in the `Action` part. An action usually contains operations on the working memory (e.g., assert a new data item) but also statements à la procedural programming (e.g., assignment, loop).

As an example, consider a different incarnation of the reactive rule $R2$ – this time using ILOG's commercial production rules system JRules.[14] Other production rules systems include OPS5,[15] JBoss Rules,[16] and Jess.[17]

```
rule denyBlacklistedCustomers {
    when {
        c: Customer (blacklisted == yes);
        m: MoviesCart (owner == c; value > 0);
    } then {
        out.println ("Customer "+c.name+" is blacklisted!");
        retract m;
    }
}
```

The condition part of the rule (introduced by `when`) gives a pattern for instances of classes `Customer` and `MoviesCart`. It matches `Customer` instances whose attribute `blacklisted` is set to `yes` and whose `MoviesCart`'s attribute `value` is greater than zero (meaning that the customer wants to order at least one movie). The two classes used in the example rule may be Java or C classes or element types from an XML Schema. The action part (introduced by `then`) announces the reason of denying the request and updates the working memory removing the `MoviesCart` object for the respective `Customer` instance (by the statement `retract m`).

ECA and production rules are discussed in [BBB+07], where an in-depth presentation of both approaches to reactive behavior is given. The work also tries to reveal similarities and differences between the two approaches to programming reactive applications on the Web. The structure and semantics of the two kinds of rules indicate that the ECA rule approach is well suited for distributed applications which rely on event-based communication between components, while the production rule approach is more appropriate for coding the logic of stateful applications.

A considerable number of rule languages that can be employed for programming Semantic Web applications have been proposed, which we will discuss in more detail in Section 2. An overview of current rule languages and systems that were considered of interest by the participants of the W3C RIF WG can be found at http://www.w3.org/2005/rules/wg/wiki/List_of_Rule_Systems. In

---

[14] ILOG JRules, http://www.ilog.com/products/jrules/

[15] Official Production System 5, http://www.cs.gordon.edu/local/courses/cs323//OPS5/ops5.html

[16] JBoss Rules, http://www.jboss.com/products/rules

[17] Jess, http://www.jessrules.com/

this section we presented a classification of rules that can be a basis for discovering commonalities between rule languages. However, as the examples have shown, they also reveal considerable differences with respect to syntax, supported features, and semantics. Thus, to determine whether language constructs have the same effect in different rule languages, an analysis based on the language semantics is needed. A standard interchange format should be geared for exchanging rules with different structure, constructs, and semantics.

1.3 W3C RIF WG Charter

The charter of the W3C RIF WG[18] gives guidelines and requirements for the rule interchange format to be developed within the Working Group. This document and the particular interests of the participants of the W3C RIF WG will influence the ultimate shape RIF is going to take.

The W3C RIF WG is chartered to develop an exchange format for rules that should enable rules to be translated between different rule languages and, thus, to be used in different rule systems. This is to be achieved through two phases corresponding to the development of an extensible core interchange format and a set of extensions (called standard dialects). Each of these work phases is chartered for up to two years.

Phase I focuses essentially on Horn rules for a core rule interchange format. The RIF Core development should build a stable backbone and allow extensions in the second phase. For Phase II, the charter just gives starting points for possible extensions. For example, the core format might be extended in the direction of first-order rules, (possibly non-monotonic) logic programming rules, and particularly ECA and production rules, neither of which to be fully covered in the core.

The charter also emphasizes compatibility with Web and Semantic Web technologies such as XML, RDF, SPARQL, and OWL. It states that the primary normative syntax of a general rule interchange format must be based on XML. Moreover, it states that RIF must support interoperability with RDF data and be compatible with OWL and SPARQL.

1.4 Outline

The subsequent sections are structured as follows. In Section 2 we describe in more detail the role of rules and rule interchange in the Semantic Web architecture.

Then we turn to a discussion of the early working draft documents published by the RIF WG. The use cases for rule interchange described in the Second W3C Public Working Draft of *Use Cases and Requirements* are discussed in Section 3. The requirements for RIF that follow from these initial use cases are discussed in Section 4. The first public Working Draft on *RIF Core Design* [BK07] will be discussed in Section 5, where we present the current syntax and semantics of the RIF Core using an example.

---

[18] http://www.w3.org/2005/rules/wg/charter.html

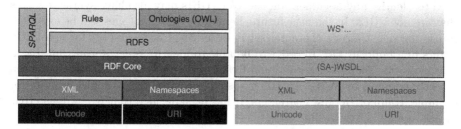

Fig. 2. The role of rules in the Semantic-Web layer cake

A comprehensive classification system, called RIF Rule Arrangement Framework (RIFRAF), is currently under development and is being populated with existing rule languages and systems. The status of this study and impact on possible extensions to RIF Core are also briefly discussed in Section 5.

2   Rules in the Semantic Web Architecture: Where Do Rules Belong?

Recent versions of the often cited "Semantic Web Layer Cake" [BL05] position rules as a central component (see Figure 2).

We have already pointed out in the introduction that rule interchange, and thus RIF, will not be restricted to Semantic Web applications. It is expected, for example, that rules will affect Web Services standards, such as SA-WSDL,[19] which merge the Semantic Web and Web services worlds by allowing semantic annotations within WSDL documents. However, since the role of rules within the Web services layer is yet to be clearly defined by the standards bodies, we will focus on the "core" semantic Web architecture and discuss the applications of rules to the existing Semantic Web standards: XML, RDF, RDFS, OWL, and SPARQL. Note that the presented version of the Semantic Web architecture stack in Figure 2 leaves out layers such as "Proof," "Security," "Encryption," and "Trust." Rules are certainly going to play an important role within these layers as well, but here we will focus on the layers that already have recommendations endorsed by W3C.

2.1   URIs and Unicode

The Semantic Web is based on the idea of *Uniform Resource Identifiers (URIs)* as unique identifiers for documents that live on the Web, but also for real-world or abstract objects. Following this paradigm, RIF will support and require the use of URIs for objects, relations, and other components of rules. The main difference between URIs and URLs is that, for instance, `http://imd.example.org#m1` might be a URI that identifies a movie stored at IMD, but it does not necessarily

---

[19] http://www.w3.org/2002/ws/sawsdl/

need to identify any document on the Web. URIs may also have syntactic forms that are not URLs. In the near future, Semantic Web languages will be expected to use the rich *Unicode* character set in order to provide support for non-Latin letters in a uniform way. In order to be able to identify objects using non-Latin character sets, the IRI (International Resource Identifier) specification has been recently adopted by W3C. An IRI is just like a URI, but it might include, for example, Kanji or Hebrew characters. It has been decided that RIF will use IRIs to denote globally accessible objects.

2.2 XML and Namespaces

The *eXtensible Markup Language* (XML) has been chosen as the standard exchange syntax for data and messages on the Web and, consequently, will likely also be the basis for the exchange of rules on the Web.

Example 2 (Running example continued). In order to support movie enthusiasts and other people like John, our video store owner, IMD makes its movie data available in an XML document, as shown in Figure 3.

```
<?xml version="1.0"  encoding="UTF-8"?>
<moviedb xmlns="http://imd.example.org/ns/">
  <movie ID="m1">
    <title>Plan 9 from Outer Space</title>
    <directedBy IDref="p1"/>
    ...
    <year>1959</year>
    <age>16</age>
  </movie>

  ...

  <person ID="p1">
    <name>Edward D. Wood Jr.</name>
    <dateOfBirth>1924-10-10</dateOfBirth>
  </person>

  ...

</moviedb>
```

Fig. 3. IMD's XML dump, available at `http://imd.example.org/movies.xml`

In XML, URIs also serve to denote unique identifiers. For example, identifiers in `http://imd.example.org/movies.xml`, such as `http://imd.example.org/movies.xml#m1`, can be used to denote objects described in the document. Moreover, URIs serve to denote "scopes" of element or attribute names within XML documents using XML's *namespace* mechanism. For instance, the XML document in Figure 3 has the default namespace `http://imd.example.org/ns/`. An element named `name` in the figure refers to "the `name` element associated with the URI `http://imd.example.org/ns/`," which is used to specify the name of a person. Namespaces are used to disambiguate references to element or attribute names that appear in the same document, but have different meaning and are typically defined externally. For instance, the `name` element that describes a person could have a different structure from the name element that is used for companies. The latter may be defined in an external document using some other namespace.

Sometimes, notably in RDF, however, the term "namespace" is used to refer to prefixes of full URLs. For instance, `<imd:age>` is treated as an abbreviation of the URI `http://imd.example.org/ns/age`, if `imd` is defined as a "macro" for `http://imd.example.org/ns/`. Reusing the term "namespace" in this situation is unfortunate and causes confusion. A more appropriate term, *compact URI* (or *curi*), has recently been adopted for the abbreviation schemes like `<imd:age>` above. RIF will support compact URIs as well.

Semantic Web languages are required to support an XML exchange syntax and so will RIF. Since XML is verbose and is hard for humans to write and understand, it is used mostly for machine-to-machine exchange. Semantic Web languages, such as RDF or OWL, also support more human-friendly *abstract syntaxes*, and RIF will provide such a human-oriented syntax as well.

XML comes with several accompanying standards: for querying XML documents (XPath and XQuery); for transforming XML documents to XML and other formats (XSLT); for specifying document structure (XML Schema); and so on. Although XPath, XQuery, and XSLT are the most common query and transformation tools for XML, many XML rule languages based on logic programming have been developed. These include eLog [BFG+01], Xcerpt [Sch04] and XChange [BEP06a], and Prolog systems with extensive XML support like Ciao Prolog [CH01] or SWI Prolog [WHvdM06]. Examples of Xcerpt and XChange were given in the introduction and similar examples can be worked out for the other languages on the above list. These examples and overlapping expresive features of these rule languages suggest that at least some rules could be exchanged among dissimilar systems. However, it is not yet clear how far this can be taken and to what extent (query, transformation, or validation) rules on top of XML can be interchanged in general.

2.3   RDF and RDFS

The *Resource Description Framework* (RDF) is the basic data model for the Semantic Web. It is built upon one of the simplest structures for representing data—a directed labeled graph. An RDF graph is typically described by a set of triples of the form ⟨*Subject Predicate Object*⟩, also called *statements*, which represent the edges of the graph. In the RDF terminology, predicates are called *properties* and are identified by URIs. Subjects and Objects can be either URIs denoting real or abstract *resources*, datatype literals (e.g., 1.2, "abc"), or XML literals (i.e. well-formed XML snippets).[20] Besides a normative RDF/XML syntax, several more readable syntaxes for RDF have been devised, we use here the more terse Turtle [Bec06] syntax.

---

[20] Strictly speaking, RDF does not allow literals in subject positions, but languages like SPARQL lift this restriction.

Example 3 (Running example continued). IMD also exports its movie data in RDF, see Figure 4 (a) and additionally provides some structural information on its data as an RDFS hierarchy Figure 4(b).

```
@prefix imd: <http://imd.example.org/ns/>
@prefix foaf: <http://xmlns.com/foaf/0.1/>
@prefix bio: <http://purl.org/vocab/bio/0.1/>
@prefix rdf: <http://www.w3 ...rdf-syntax-ns#>

<imd:m1> <imd:title> "Plan 9 from Outer Space".
<imd:m1> <imd:directedBy> <imd:p1> .
<imd:m1> <imd:year> "1959" .
    ...


<imd:m29> <imd:year> "1929" .

    ...

<imd:p1> <foaf:name> "Edward D. Wood Jr.";
         <bio:event> _:p1Birth.

_:p1Birth a <bio:Birth>;
          <bio:date> "1924-10-10".
          <bio:place> "Poughkeepsie, NY, USA".
    ...
```

```
@prefix imd: <http://imd.example.org/ns/>
@prefix foaf: <http://xmlns.com/foaf/0.1/>
@prefix bio: <http://purl.org/vocab/bio/0.1/>
@prefix rdf: <http://www.w3 ...rdf-syntax-ns#>
@prefix rdfs: <http://www.w3 ...rdf-schema#>


    ...


<imd:directedBy> <rdfs:domain> <imd:Movie>.
<imd:directedBy> <rdfs:range> <imd:Director>.
<imd:Director> <rdfs:subclassOf> <foaf:person>.


    ...
```

(a) Movie data in RDF   (b) Structural metadata in RDF Schema (RDFS)

Fig. 4. IMD's data in RDF(S)

John imports this metadata to process it for MoviShop, finding it more flexible and easier to combine with his own data than a fixed XML scheme. John's customers are often interested in additional information about movies, such as, whether old movies are color or black-and-white—information that is *not* explicitly provided by the exported IMD's metadata. In order to avoid labeling every movie explicitly as color or black-and-white, John wants his system to *automatically* infer that all movies produced before 1930 are black and white, and that the movies produced after, say, 1950 are likely to be color movies. Then he would have to label explicitly only the movies produced in-between.

(R1)   Every movie at http://movishop.example.org/ produced
       before 1930 is black and white.

(R1') Every movie at http://movishop.example.org/ produced
       after 1950 is color unless stated otherwise.

He finds out that there are several rule languages which he could use and again to process such rules, but not really any format which allows him to publish this rule.

Rule Languages for RDF. Several rule engines can process rules of the form (R1) and some also rules of the form (R1').[21]

---

[21] Rule (R1') is using so-called "default reasoning" and its treatment requires non-first-order logic. It can be handled by systems such as FLORA-2 and dlvhex, which are briefly described here.

TRIPLE[22] allows to access RDF data and manipulate it by Horn rules defined in F-Logic [KLW95] syntax. The engine is based on XSB[23].

JENA[24] has its own rule language and execution engine, which allows forward (RETE-style [For82]) and backward chaining (tabled SLG resolution[SW94]) evaluation of rules on top of RDF.

cwm[25] is a simple forward chaining reasoner, which uses Notation3 (N3), a rule language that extends RDF's widely used turtle syntax [Bec06]. The semantics of N3 is not, however, defined formally, so the results of rule evaluation are implementation-dependent.

FLORA-2[26] is a very powerful rule-based system, which is capable of representing and efficiently executing logic programming style rules. It is based on F-logic, but in addition has support for higher-order modeling via HiLog [CKW93a] and for declarative state changes via Transaction Logic [BK98, BK94]. It uses XSB as its rule evaluation engine.

Finally, dlvhex[27] is a flexible framework for developing extensions to the declarative Logic Programming Engine DLV,[28] which supports RDF import and provides rules on top of RDF. DLV's [LPF+06] rules language is disjunctive Datalog [EGM97], i.e., it is based on logic programming with disjunctions in rule heads, negation as failure in rule bodies, and several other extensions—all based on the so-called answer set semantics (see [Bar03]).

As can be seen by this short list of the available engines, they cover a plethora of different languages and semantics. However, they all also support a common sublanguage, i.e., function-free Horn rules. Most of these systems would for instance allow to express and process rule (R1) from the above example, which can be written as a Horn rule as follows:

$$\forall D, M, Y. \; (triple(D, rdf : type, moviShop : Dvd) \land triple(D, moviShop : shows, M) \land \\ triple(M, rdf : type, imd : Movie) \land triple(M, imd : year, Y) \; \land \; Y < 1930 \\ \rightarrow triple(M, rdf : type, moviShop : BWMovie))$$

A common sublanguage that underlies most of the rule systems is the basic idea behind RIF Core, the core dialect of RIF. However, not all languages support all types of rules. For instance, even within the category of languages that are based on deduction rules not all the languages support rule (R1'). To support exchange between languages that are more expressive than the core, RIF will provide dialects that extend the RIF Core dialect. For instance, rule (R1') could be supported by a logic programming dialect of RIF.

RDF Schema. RDF itself was not designed to express schema information – this job was given to a separate specification known as *RDF Schema* (RDFS).

---

[22] http://triple.semanticweb.org/

[23] http://xsb.sourceforge.net/

[24] http://jena.sourceforge.net/

[25] http://www.w3.org/2000/10/swap/doc/cwm

[26] http://flora.sourceforge.net

[27] http://con.fusion.at/dlvhex/

[28] http://www.dlvsystem.com/

RDFS is a very simple ontology language for specifying taxonomies of resources and properties, as well as domain and range restrictions for properties, such as the ones shown in Figure 4(b). Our IMD site uses RDFS to express some of the axioms about the movie domain. For instance, an axiom might say that each subject of a triple with the <imd:directedBy> property is a member of the class <imd:Movie>.

These structural axioms can themselves be interpreted as rules. In fact the above-mentioned RDF engines often approximate RDF and RDFS semantics with Datalog rules [tH05, EIP$^+$06].

For instance, the RDFS entailment rule (rdfs3) from [Hay04], which states

If an RDF graph contains triples (P rdfs:range C) and (S P O) then the triple O rdf:type C is entailed.

can be written as a Horn rule as follows:

$$\forall S, P, O, C. triple(P, rdf : range, C) \wedge triple(S, P, O) \rightarrow triple(O, rdf : type, C)$$

The following examples show how this rule is represented in TRIPLE's F-Logic style, JENA's rule syntax, N3, FLORA-2, and dlvhex.

TRIPLE:

```
rdf := 'http://www.w3.org/1999/02/22-rdf-syntax-ns#'.
rdfs := 'http://www.w3.org/2000/01/rdf-schema#'.
type := rdf:type.
range := rdfs:range.

FORALL O,C O[type->C] <- EXISTS  S,P (S[P->O] AND P[range->C]).
```

JENA:

```
@prefix rdf: <http://www.w3.org/1999/02/22-rdf-syntax-ns#>.
@prefix rdfs: <http://www.w3.org/2000/01/rdf-schema#>.

[rdfs3: (?s ?p ?o) (?p rdfs:range ?c) -> (?o rdf:type ?c)]
```

N3:

```
@prefix rdf: <http://www.w3.org/1999/02/22-rdf-syntax-ns#>.
@prefix log: <http://www.w3.org/2000/10/swap/log#> .
@prefix rdfs: <http://www.w3.org/2000/01/rdf-schema#> .

{ <#p> rdfs:range <#c>. <#s> <#p> <#o> . }
                log:implies { <#o> rdf:type <#c> }.
```

FLORA-2:

```
:- iriprefix rdf = 'http://www.w3.org/2000/01/rdf-schema#'.

?O[rdf#type->?C] :- ?S[?P->?O], ?P[rdf#range->?C]).
```

dlvhex:
```
#namespace("rdf","http://www.w3.org/1999/02/22-rdf-syntax-ns#")
#namespace("rdfs","http://www.w3.org/2000/01/rdf-schema#")

triple(O,rdf:type,C) :- triple(P,rdfs:range,C), triple(S,P,O).
triple(S,P,O) :-
       &rdf["http://UrlWithRdfData.example.org/data.rdf"](S,P,O)
```

As we can see, all these languages have syntactic differences, but they express the RDFS axiom in our example in similar ways. A common exchange format like RIF would enable interchange of such rules between the various systems.

RDF enhanced with rules may be useful in several other contexts: for defining mappings between RDF vocabularies, for specifying implicit metadata, for integrating information from different sources, and so on.

2.4 OWL

RDFS is good only for very simple ontologies and a more expressive language based on Description Logic was recommended by W3C. The *Web Ontology Language* [DSB+04] (OWL) adds several features to the simple class hierarchies of RDFS. First, it provides an algebra for constructing complex classes out of simpler ones. Second, it extends what one can do with properties by allowing transitive, symmetric, functional, and inverse properties. It also supports restrictions on property values and cardinality.

Still, OWL proved to be insufficient for many applications on the Semantic Web and the need to add rules became evident early on. Unfortunately, OWL is not easily combinable with most rule-based formalisms. For one thing, OWL allows disjunctive and existential information, while most rule systems do not. For another, OWL is entirely based on first-order logic, while many rule-based formalisms support so-called *default reasoning*, which is not first-order.

To illustrate, the following statement is easily within OWL's competence:

```
Every movie has at least one director.
```

Using the abstract syntax [PSHH04] of OWL, one can write it as follows:

```
Class( imd:movie partial
              restriction (imd:directedBy minCardinality 1) )
```

But representing the same as a logical rule

$$\forall M. \ (\ triple(M, rdf:type, imd:movie) \ \rightarrow \ \exists D.triple(M, imddirectedBy, D) \ )$$

requires existential quantification in the rule head, which places such a rule squarely outside of most rule systems.[29]

---
[29] Existentials in rule heads are beyond Horn rules, though in many cases, rule systems can approximate such existential information using Skolem functions.

Even a simple extension of OWL by Horn rules, such as SWRL [HPSB+04], raises several non-trivial semantic issues and the language quickly looses its most attractive asset – decidability. Moreover, as already mentioned, many rule systems support so-called default negation as opposed to classical negation. Rule (R1') in Example 3 uses precisely this kind of negation. Such a rule cannot be represented in OWL or its rule-based extension SWRL and yet this kind of statements are commonplace.

Default negation goes beyond RIF Core, but it is expected to be supported by at least one of the future dialects of RIF, which will be developed as part of Phase II work. We refer the reader to [dBEPT06, EIP+06, Ros06] for further details on the issues concerning the integration of OWL and rules.

2.5 SPARQL

SPARQL [Pe06] is a forthcoming RDF query language standard, which is still under development by the W3C Data Access Working Group (DAWG).[30] Other RDF query languages with interesting features were proposed as well [FLB+06].

SPARQL is interesting in connection with rules and RIF for several reasons:

1. The RIF Working Group promises in its charter to "ensure that the rule language is compatible with the use of SPARQL as a language for querying of RDF datasets." This could be achieved by allowing SPARQL queries in rule bodies.
2. SPARQL's CONSTRUCT queries can be viewed as deductive rules, which create new RDF triples from RDF datasets [Pol07, SS07].
3. SPARQL queries can be represented as Datalog rules [Pol07].

SPARQL allows querying RDF *datasets* via simple and complex graph patterns. A graph pattern is a graph some of whose nodes and arcs are labeled with variables instead of resources. Besides graph patterns, SPARQL has several interesting features, such as optional graph patterns, filtering values, and unions of patterns.

Example 4 (Running example continued). Although John could choose any number of systems for his shop, he was concerned with being locked into one of the systems without a possibility to switch. So, he decided to try his luck with SPARQL, as this language is expected to get W3C's stamp of approval soon. Suppose that the RDF dataset from Figure 4(a) is accessible via URI `http://imd.example.org/movies.rdf` and that RDF data about the movies in John's MoviShop is accessible through `http://movishop.example.org/store.rdf`. Then he could ask a query about all movies produced before 1930 as follows:

```
@prefix imd: <http://imd.example.org/ns/>
@prefix moviShop: <http://movishop.example.org/ns/>
@prefix rdf: <http://www.w3 ...rdf-syntax-ns#>
```

---

[30] `http://www.w3.org/2001/sw/DataAccess/`

```
SELECT ?M
FROM <http://imd.example.org/movies.rdf>
FROM <http://movishop.example.org/store.rdf>
WHERE { ?D rdf:type moviShop:Dvd . ?D movShop:shows ?M .
        ?M rdf:type imd:Movie . ?M imd:year ?Y .
        FILTER (?Y < 1930) }
```

Since this was easy, John feels glad that RIF WG has decided to ensure SPARQL compatibility.

Then suddenly John stumbled upon a brilliant idea: to express the above query as a rule using SPARQL's CONSTRUCT statement:

```
CONSTRUCT { ?M rdf:type moviShop:BWMovie }
FROM <http://imd.example.org/movies.rdf>
FROM <http://movishop.example.org/store.rdf>
WHERE { ?D rdf:type moviShop:Dvd . ?D movShop:shows ?M .
        ?M rdf:type imd:Movie . ?M imd:year ?Y .
        FILTER (?Y < 1930) }
```

However, an insider told John that the Data Access Working Group, which is in charge of SPARQL, is not planning to position SPARQL as a rule language and the semantics of the rules expressed using the CONSTRUCT statement is not fully defined. The insider also suggested that John look into the ways of translating complex SPARQL queries into Datalog rules and process them with one of the earlier mentioned rule engines [Pol07].

We thus see that rules play (or can play) an important role in several layers of the Semantic Web architecture. In turn, the Semantic Web architecture has influenced the design of RIF inspiring such design decisions as the use of IRIs, the compact URI scheme, XML, and the use of XML data types. The Semantic Web imposed a number of other requirements on RIF, which will be discussed further in Sections 4 and 5. However, in order to get a better idea of practical scenarios which defined these requirements, we will first discuss some of the use cases for rule interchange, which served as input to RIF design.

3   W3C Use Cases on Rule Interchange

Close to fifty use cases[31] for rule interchange on the Web have been submitted by the W3C RIF WG participants. These use cases depict a wide variety of scenarios where rules are useful or even indispensable. Scenarios range from life sciences, to e-commerce to business rules and Semantic Web rules. Other scenarios involve fuzzy reasoning, automated trust establishment, rule-based service level agreement, etc.

The W3C RIF WG collected use cases for both phases of its chartered work, but the Use Cases document does not group them according to the work phases.

---

[31] http://www.w3.org/2005/rules/wg/wiki/Use_Cases

Such a classification would be difficult in many cases, since different implementations of the same use case might be possible. Some of these implementations might require Phase II features but some might be realizable completely within Phase I.

Each use case presents requirements to be acknowledged by the rule interchange format to be developed by the working group. Some of these requirements are stated explicitly, others are implied.

The submitted use cases were analyzed and classified into eight categories.[32] Seven use cases were chosen and edited for publication as the First W3C Public Working Draft of *Use Cases and Requirements*,[33] which was released in March 2006.

The first draft did not include the requirements to RIF – these were included in the second draft along with two new use cases. In this paper we present four of the use cases from the second draft. The requirements to rule interchange are discussed in Section 4.

3.1   Negotiating eBusiness Contracts Across Rule Platforms

The first two use cases motivate the need for a rule interchange format towards facilitating automated, Web-based negotiations where rules are to be exchanged between involved parties. The first use case presented in this section shows the importance of such interchange for the reuse of electronic business documents (such as order requests and business policies) that are made available online.

Jane and Jack negotiate an electronic business contract on the supply of items by Jane's company. The negotiation process involves exchange of contract-related data and rules. Since the two companies may use different technologies, Jane and Jack agree upon the data model and use RIF for interchanging rules. The data is transmitted as XML documents using an agreed-upon format, together with the rules to run simulations, and the results of these simulations are also represented as XML data.

A purchase order from Jack's company contains XML documents describing information on the desired goods, packaging, and delivery location and date. The associated rules describe delivery and payment policies. An example of such a rule is

```
If an item is perishable and it is
delivered more than 10 days after the scheduled
delivery date then the item will be rejected.
```

Jane's company wants a relaxation of the delivery policy proposed by Jack. Thus, Jane proposes for acceptance and sends to Jack the following rule expressing the result of the negotiation carried out so far:

---

[32] Use case categories, http://www.w3.org/2005/rules/wg/wiki/General_Use_Case_Categories

[33] First   W3C   Public   Working   Draft   of   *Use   Cases   and   Requirements* http://www.w3.org/2005/rules/wg/ucr/draft-20060323.html

```
If an item is perishable and
it is delivered more than 7 days after the scheduled
delivery date but less than 14 days after the scheduled
delivery date then a discount of 18.7 percent will be
applied to this delivery.
```

Jack's company defines future requests for items in form of an appropriate XML schema document and a set of rules. This information is then published on their Web site, so as to give supply companies the possibility to respond electronically by sending XML cost sheets. Just like shown in the example scenario above, companies send rules expressed using RIF and Jack's company analyzes them for negotiation of electronic contracts.

Reactive rule-based systems (discussed already in Section 1) offer elegant means for implementing rules such as those exemplified in this use case. Rule-based negotiation frameworks or languages such as Protune[34] could be used for implementing this use case.

3.2   Negotiating eCommerce Transactions Through Disclosure of Buyer and Seller Policies and Preferences

This use case shows that a higher degree of interoperability can be gained by employing a rule interchange format within the process of establishing trust between the parties offering and those requesting a service in eCommerce scenarios. Automated trust establishment is possible when policies for every credential and every service can be codified. So as to minimize user intervention, the policies should be checked automatically whenever possible. The notion of policies is a quite general one referring to access control policies, privacy policies, business rules, etc. (see e.g. [BO05] for a more in-depth discussion of trust negotiation). Policies and credentials are themselves subject to access control. Thus, rule interchange is necessarily done during negotiation and disclosure of rules (in general) depends on the current level of trust that negotiating systems have achieved.

The interchange of rules is exemplified here with the negotiation between an online shop (eShop) and a customer (Alice) who wants to buy a device at eShop, a scenario that very similarly could apply to our running MoviShop example. Both Alice and eShop employ systems (agents) for establishing trust through negotiation with the goal of successful completion of the desired transaction. The negotiation is based on policies which describe which partners are trusted for what purposes, the credentials each system has, and which it will disclose if a certain level of trust is achieved.

Upon Alice's request to buy the desired device, eShop's agent sends parts of its policy back to Alice's agent. The two agents involved in the negotiation interchange a set of rules implementing the policies. Such an example rule is:

```
A buyer must provide credit card information together with
delivery information (address, postal code, city, country).
```

---

[34] Protune, http://www.l3s.de/~olmedilla/pub/2005/2005_policy_protune.pdf

Alice's agent evaluates its own policies and the received ones for determining whether eShop's information request is consistent with her own policies. The agent uses policy rules such as:

```
Disclose Alice's credit card information only to
online shops belonging to the Better Business Bureau.
```

By disclosing the above given rule, Alice's agent asks eShop's agent to provide credentials stating that it belongs to the Better Business Bureau, Alice's most trusted source of information on online shops. Since eShop has such a credential and its policy states to release it to any potential customer, eShop's agent passes the credential to Alice's agent. Before disclosing credit card and delivery information to eShop, Alice's agent checks whether release of this information would not break Alice's denial constraints. These constraints are given by the following two rules:

```
Never disclose two different credit cards to the same
online shop.

For anonymity reasons, never provide both birth
date and postal code.
```

For this purchase, the birth date is not an issue and only information on one credit card is requested. Thus, Alice's constraints are respected. Alice's negotiation system therefore provides her credit card and delivery information to eShop. eShop checks that Alice is not in its client black list, then confirms the purchase transaction, generates an email notification to Alice that contains information about the purchase, and notifies eShops's delivery department.

3.3   Access to Business Rules of Supply Chain Partners

This use case shows that the existence of a rule interchange format would ease the integration of different business processes by offering business process designers a unified view over the used business rules while still allowing each involved company to work with their own technology of choice.

The focus of the use case is on the integration of supply chain business processes of multiple partners across company boundaries. Similar scenarios can be encountered also within a single company that is organized into semi-independent business units. Each business unit might use different strategies (i.e., the logic behind the decisions taken in a process) and technologies.

Such situations as addressed by this use case occur usually when companies merge and their business processes need to be integrated. *Business processes* are "structured, measured sets of activities designed to produce a specific output for a particular customer or market" [Dav93]. A business process can span activities of a single company or of multiple companies. Often the strategies followed by an organization are specified by means of *business rules* [The00, Hal05]. In contrast to procedural code, business rules are easier to comprehend and use for business process designers, since they are declarative and high-level specifications.

For integrating supply chain business processes where multiple organizations are involved, part of the business processes' logic needs to be exposed (for determining the best strategy for integrating the processes) and, furthermore, business rules defined by different (partner) organizations need to be executed. There are two possible solutions for using such business rules and the decision of implementing one of them depends also on ownership constraints: Different rule sets could be merged into a single set of business rules, which can be then processed in a uniform manner on one side. The other possibility consists in accessing the other parties' rule sets only by invoking remote engines and (locally) processing their results only.

Consider an inspection of a damaged vehicle and the corresponding insurance adjustment process as examples of two processes that need to be integrated. Since the inspection of the vehicle is usually performed by independent inspectors, the inspection process can not be directly integrated into the adjustment process. The following business rules defines a decision point within the processes:

```
If inspector believes vehicle-is-repairable
then process-as-repair
otherwise process-as-total-loss.
```

The choice of sub-processes to be performed after the inspector's work depends on the decision taken using the above rule. In terms of business process modeling, the example given is an instance of the *exclusive choice pattern* [vdAtHKB03]; the insurance adjustment process branches into two alternative paths and exactly one of them can be chosen. Systems supporting *Event-Condition-Action-Alternative Action (ECAA)* offer an elegant solution for implementing such rules. As already noted in Section 1, for obtaining the same effect with a system supporting reactive rules of the *Event-Condition-Action* form, two ECA rules can be used where the condition of one rule is the negated condition of the other.

3.4   Managing Inter-organizational Business Policies and Practices

This use case demonstrates the need for supporting annotation of rules in a rule interchange format, where rules or rulesets are labeled with tags carrying meta-information.

The use case addresses the need for interchanging rules that may not be directly executed by machines, i.e. rules that need input in form of a decision or confirmation from a person. The setting is somewhat similar to the use case of Section 3.3 – multiple organizations and/or multiple units of a single organization – but the focus here is on the management of their business policies and practices. Another similarity consists in the fact that policies and practices are specified as business rules.

The scenario is based on the EU-Rent case study [EU-05], a specification of business requirements for a car rental company, promoted by the European

Business Rules Conference [Eur05] and the Business Rules Group [Bus05]. EU-Rent operates in different EU countries. Thus, the company needs to comply with existing EU regulations and each of its branches needs to comply also with the regulations of the country it operates in.

CarWise and AutoLaw are consultancy companies that offer different services like, for instance, clarifying regulations on managing fleets of vehicles by negotiating with EU regulators and UK regulators, respectively. The outcome of such a service are interpreted regulations and rules that can be directly used by rule systems. CarWise and AutoLaw advise EU-Rent of rules that are to be used at European and UK level, respectively.

EU-Rent has a set of rules in place that implement the companies' policies and the EU regulations. Part of these rules are distributed to all EU-Rent branches. Thus, for example EU-Rent UK needs to integrate the received rules with the existing ones at the UK level. The rule set might change at the company level (case in which rules need to be propagated to the branches), but also at national (branches) level due to new national regulations. Changes of the rule set could be updates (modifications) or deletions (removal) of existing rules, or insertions of new rules into the rule set.

A concrete example rule that the EU-Rent corporate HQ could add is the following:

```
Each electronic compliance document must have its
required electronic signatures 48 hours before its
filing deadline.
```

Such kinds of (business) rules can be implemented by means of reactive rules. The event part of the reactive rule specifies the event *48 hours before the filing deadline*. The condition part queries for the existence of the electronic signatures. The action part reports an out-of-compliance situation.

All three different types of rules discussed in Section 1 are usually encountered in specifications of use cases for managing business policies and practices. The following example gives three (business) rules of the EU-Rent case study: the rule R1 is a deductive rule, R2 a normative rule, and R3 a reactive rule.

```
(R1) A customer who spends more than 1000 EUR per year
     is a Gold customer.
(R2) A customer can rent at most one car at a time.
(R3) A rental reservation must not be accepted if the
     customer is blacklisted.
```

Section 1 has also presented two possible implementations of rule *R3* using reactive rules. More generally, the article [BEPR06] analyzes the realization of business processes by means of ECA rules. With a focus on control flow, a concrete EU-Rent business process scenario is implemented using the reactive rule-based language XChange. This work has led to the introduction of a procedure notion in XChange which is absent in most other rule languages. The work has also shown that constructs for structuring rule sets are desirable in rule-based languages.

3.5   Other Use Cases

Apart from the four use cases, which we described in detail, let us briefly recap the other use cases specified in the RIF WG's use cases document. The complete use case descriptions, as published by the Working Group, can be found at http://www.w3.org/TR/2006/WD-rif-ucr-20060710/.

Collaborative Policy Development for Dynamic Spectrum Access. This use case shows that by using a rule interchange format and deploying third-party systems, the flexibility in matching the goals of end-users of a service or device with the ones of providers and regulators of such services and devices can be increased.

The use case concentrates on examples from the dynamic spectrum access for wireless communication devices. It is assumed that the policies of a region and the protocols for dynamically accessing available spectrums are defined by rules. The goal is to have reconfigurable devices that can operate legally in various regulatory and service environments. One of the technical preconditions of making this possible relies on the format in which the rules are expressed and the ability of devices to understand and use these rules.

To be able to use the advantages of a rule interchange format in this setting, a third-party group should be formed, which is responsible for translating regional policies and protocols into the interchange format.

Ruleset Integration for Medical Decision Support. This use case motivates the need for merging rule sets written in different rule languages. This allows for inferring data that could not be obtained without the merge. This is an important task of expert systems based on reasoning with rules. Complex decision making systems use different data bases, ontologies, and rules written in different rule languages.

The use case gives examples from the medical domain, where different data sources come into play, such as pharmaceutical, patient data bases, and medical ontologies.

Interchanging Rule Extensions to OWL. The use case gives a concrete motivation for a rule interchange format that is compatible with OWL (as required also by the W3C RIF WG charter). This is the shortest use case in the Second W3C Public Working Draft of *Use Case and Requirements*, yet a considerable number of application domains such as medicine, biology, and e-Science, which partly adopted OWL already, could benefit from the combination of rules with ontologies. The domain of labeling brain cortex structures in MRI (Magnetic Resonance Imaging) images is chosen here for illustration purposes. A deductive rule is exemplified by use of which implicit knowledge, i.e. dependencies between ontology properties, is inferred which cannot be expressed directly in OWL itself.

Vocabulary Mapping for Data Integration. Different application domains such as health care, travel planning, and IT management often need solutions to the problems raised by integrating information from multiple data sources with different data representation models. The idea of this use case relies on the reusability of rules that implement mappings between such data models.

The use case gives examples from IT systems management. The concrete example uses three different data sources, which are taken as basis for analyzing the flexibility of a division's business processes with respect to changes of their IT management contracts. In many cases, the simple solution of mapping the information of the three data sources to a single data format such as RDF does not offer satisfactory results. One of the problems lies in the different granularities of the contained data, which might be either too detailed or too coarse grained. Thus, deductive rules – possibly involving aggregation of fine-grained data – are used for defining simple and usable views over the data sources. The implemented deductive rules are then published so as to be reused across the company, where similar views are needed.

BPEL Orchestration of Web Services. The use case exemplifies a commercial credit approval Web service implemented as a BPEL orchestration of two Web services, a credit history service and a rule-based decision service. A rule interchange format would allow the re-use of rules for evaluating credit histories. Moreover, rule editing and customization tools from different RIF compatible vendors would ease the rule specification task.

Three rule sets for credit evaluation are used, which are executed sequentially. The first two sets of rules calculate threshold values and a credit score, while the third set of rules compares these values and makes the decision to approve or deny the credit. The outcome of the decision system is in form of an XML document informing about the decision and the reason(s) for it. The need for querying and constructing XML data comes here into play, since for replying to the customer, the answer needs to be constructed based on the XML data received from the Web Service.

Publishing Rules for Interlinked Metadata. The use case stresses the importance of specifying implicit knowledge in form of rules and publishing them for re-use, so as to allow interlinking (meta-)data and rules from different Web sources. Semantic Web technologies such as RDF allow publishing metadata expressing the semantics of data in machine-readable form. Often, such (explicit) knowledge is supplemented by rules capturing implicit knowledge. Thus, a more concise representation of data is obtained, maintenance of meta-data is simplified, and storage requirements are reduced.

The role of a rule interchange format is exemplified by means of the movie database scenario presented in Section 1.1 that we have already used throughout this paper. The example rule *R1* given in Section 1.2, which constructs a view of black and white movies, captures such implicit knowledge that can be further used. However, also more complex rules implicitly linking and cross-referencing between several online sources or involving (scoped) negation are covered, e.g.

(R3)

```
IF movie M is  listed at http://AlternativeMDB.example.org
   but not listed at http://imd.example.org
THEN M is an independent movie
```

4 W3C Requirements on a Rule Interchange Format

As already mentioned in Section 3, each use case imposes certain requirements that should be taken into account when developing RIF. Consider again our running example shortly described in Section 1.1. John Doe's MoviShop uses data on movies, customers, etc., expressed in XML, RDF, RDFS, and OWL. Thus, to exchange rules over this data, RIF should offer support for XML, RDF, and OWL. More details on what *support* means in such a context are given by the corresponding requirements on data representation models discussed in this section. If RIF (core or some dialect of it) meets the requirements posed by MoviShop's rules and the rule language R used for implementing them, John needs a translator from R to RIF for interchanging (part of) its rules. For developing such translators, one of the general requirements for RIF concerns the precise syntax and semantics, which are to become starting points for correct translator implementations.

This section shortly discusses the requirements on RIF, which have been approved by the W3C RIF WG and published in the Second Public Working Draft of 'RIF Use Cases and Requirements'. The process of gathering and deciding upon requirements on RIF has taken into account three sources of requirements: Firstly, we have considered the (explicit and implicit) requirements posed by the RIF use cases in the above mentioned document; we have determined a set of requirements that are posed by each of these use cases—we call them *general requirements*. Secondly, each WG participant have had the possibility to propose requirements that she or he considered relevant for RIF. The third source of requirements is the so-called RIF Rulesystems Arrangement Framework[35] (RIFRAF), a framework that classifies rule systems based on a set of discriminators. RIFRAF is to be used also as basis for determining desired RIF dialects. The outcome of the work on RIF requirements is presented next by dividing the requirements into *general*, *Phase I*, and *Pase II requirements*. The focus is more on the general and Phase I requirements, since the Phase II requirements are ongoing work at moment of writing.

4.1 General Requirements

The following requirements on RIF have a general character in the sense that they express high-level conditions that RIF and the translators from and to RIF need to meet.

---

[35] RIFRAF,   http://www.w3.org/2005/rules/wg/wiki/Rulesystem_Arrangement_Framework

- *Implementability:* RIF must be implementable using well understood techniques, and should not require new research in e.g. algorithms or semantics in order to implement translators.
- *Semantic precision:* RIF core must have a clear and precise syntax and semantics. Each standard RIF dialect must have a clear and precise syntax and semantics that extends RIF core.
- *Extensible Format:* It must be possible to create new dialects of RIF and extend existing ones upwardly compatible.
- *Translators:* For every standard RIF dialect it must be possible to implement translators between rule languages covered by that dialect and RIF without changing the rule language.
- *Standard components:* RIF implementations must be able to use standard support technologies such as XML parsers and other parser generators, and should not require special purpose implementations when reuse is possible.

4.2   Phase I Requirements

The list of requirements given next refers to the RIF developed within Phase I. It consists of requirements on the core interchange format.

- *Compliance model:* RIF must define a compliance model that will identify required/optional features.
- *Default behavior:* RIF must specify at the appropriate level of detail the default behavior that is expected from a RIF compliant application that does not have the capability to process all or part of the rules described in a RIF document, or it must provide a way to specify such default behavior.
- *Different semantics:* RIF must cover rule languages having different semantics.
- *Embedded comments:* RIF must be able to pass comments.
- *Embedded metadata:* RIF must support metadata such as author and rule name.
- *Limited number of dialects:* RIF must have a standard core and a limited number of standard dialects based upon that core.
- *OWL data:* RIF must cover OWL knowledge bases as data where compatible with Phase I semantics.
- *RDF data:* RIF must cover RDF triples as data where compatible with Phase I semantics.
- *Rule language coverage:* RIF must cover the set of languages identified in the Rulesystem Arrangement Framework (RIFRAF). This requirement acts as an umbrella for a set of requirements, which are expected as outcome of the work on RIFRAF.
- *Dialect Identification:* RIF must have a standard way to specify the dialect of the interchanged rule set in a RIF document. As the rule interchange format developed within the W3C RIF WG—RIF—will come in form of a core (RIF Core) and a set of dialects extending the core interchange format, a mechanism is needed for specifying which RIF dialect is used for a set

of rules to be interchanged. This plays a role for example in the case that incompatible RIF dialects exist.

- *XML syntax:* RIF must have an XML syntax as its primary normative syntax.
- *XML types:* RIF must support an appropriate set of scalar datatypes and associated operations as defined in XML Schema part 2 and associated specifications. This requirement is also stated in the W3C RIF WG charter.
- *Merge Rule Sets:* RIF should support the ability to merge rule sets. The big interest in a standardized interchange format for rules is also determined by the possibility of merging rule sets written in different rule languages through RIF. This requirement is also explicitly stated e.g. in the use case 'Ruleset Integration for Medical Decision Support'.
- *Identify Rule Sets:* RIF will support the identification of rule sets.

4.3   Phase II Requirements

The *Second Public Working Draft of 'RIF Use Cases and Requirements'* contains one single requirement for the second phase of RIF development, namely that *RIF must be able to accept XML elements as data.* The list of Phase II requirements will of course be extended in the near future. At moment of writing, the WG started the work on gathering other requirements for the RIF dialects to be developed within Phase II. Under discussion are requirements such as the full coverage of RDF and OWL, or the support for external calls (e.g. to a SPARQL query processor). For an elegant implementation of rule R2 of our running example, which is employed for denying requests from blacklisted MoviShop customers, a RIF dialect is needed where e.g. action specifications are allowed in the rules head. In other words, a RIF dialect for reactive rules or just a form of them (such as production or ECA rules) is desirable. Whether or not the RIF WG will develop such a RIF dialect depends largely on the interest of its participants, their willingness to work towards a *'reactive'* dialect, and its acceptance by the WG as a whole.

5   The Rule Interchange Format: Current Core and Possible Extensions

This section discusses the current work of the W3C RIF WG on the RIF Core and means for determining the RIF standard dialects that will extend this core interchange format.

In the first phase, the working group agreed on defining a deliberately inexpressive core language which covers features available in most common rule languages and devise a first proposal for a common exchange syntax for this language.

Going back to our classification of rules from the introduction, where we divided rule languages into deductive, normative, and reactive rules, let us briefly recap the common ingredients which are necessary to model these rules.

All the rules we mentioned were in some sense checking a *condition* on a (static or dynamic) knowledge base. In our examples from the introduction, we called this the IF part for deduction rules and production rules; queries and normative rules can, as a whole be viewed as checking a condition. This common feature of RIF rules is acknowledged in that RIF Core will provide a simple logic language to specify such conditions.

The *RIF Condition Language* (which at present is a working title for a simple language fragment to express these common conditions) is the fundamental layer shared by Logic Programming rules (based on the Horn subset of first-order logic), production (Condition-Action) rules, Event-Condition-Action rules, normative rules (integrity constraints), and queries.

This RIF Condition Language will thus provide means to exchange basic conditions, consisting of simple conjunctions and disjunctions of atomic formulas with existential variables, as well as a distinguished equality predicate. Starting from the requirement to support sorted constants and variables, this core dialect is developed as a general multisorted logic, whose sorts can be "webized", i.e. referenced by IRIs and aligned with relevant XML standards for typing, such as XML Schema datatypes, as well as, later on, OWL and RDFS classes. Other constructs of this language (constants, functions, predicates, etc.) can also be identified by IRIs.

As an example of an extension layer on top of the RIF Condition Language, the first working draft of RIF Core introduces the *RIF Horn Rule Language* as chartered for RIF Phase 1. Because of the underlying "Condition Logic with Equality and Sorts" we obtain a "Multi-Sorted Horn Logic with Equality". It will turn out that, given the former, only a small extra effort is required to obtain the latter: the main part of a Horn rule is its body, and this is exactly a condition in our sense and already sufficient for expressing simple rules. The Horn rule layer will allow simple inference of atomic formulae, given that the respective condition holds, thus it covers deductive rules and assert-only production rules. The definition of dynamic aspects, namely event and non-assert action parts, is currently under discussion.

Next steps will include extensions such as built-ins and negation, which are useful features not only for the Horn Rule dialect, but also for a potential Production Rule dialect of RIF. Moreover, it is planned to define adequate (RDF) metadata for RIF rules and rulesets, to specify how RDF data can be processed by RIF rules, and to embed RIF rules into RDF statements.

Now let us have a closer look at the condition language as it is defined in the first working draft.

5.1   The RIF Core Condition Language – Syntax

The basis of the language in Phase 1 is formed by conjunctive conditions that can appear in the bodies of Horn-like rules with equality. Disjunctions of these conditions are also allowed because such generalized rules are known to reduce to the pure Horn case.

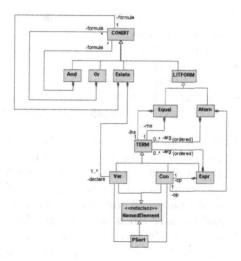

Fig. 5. The RIF Core condition meta-model

The first working draft of the RIF Core document [BK07] develops a syntax and semantics for such RIF conditions, which also supports a basic set of primitive data types (such as xsd:long, xsd:string, xsd:decimal, xsd:time, xsd:dateTime, taken from the respective XML Schema datatypes [BM04]).

In order to support a general approach, as well as possible future higher-order dialects based on HiLog [CKW93b] and Common Logic [ed06], the RIF Core language does not separate symbols used to denote constants from symbols used as names for functions or predicates. Instead, all these symbols are drawn from the same universal domain. When desired, separation between the different kinds of symbols is introduced through the mechanism of *sorts*, which will also be used for "typing" arguments as mentioned before. In logic, the mechanism of sorts is used to classify symbols into separate subdomains. One can decide that certain sorts are disjoint (for example, decimal and dateTime) and others are not (for example, integer could be a subsort of the sort decimal). Control of what sorts can be used for predicate (or concept) names, for function symbols, and so on, shall, by the general mechanism introduced in RIF Core, be upon agreement between the rule exchanging parties, or the ones defining a specific RIF dialect.

Figure 5 shows a snapshot of the current RIF condition meta-model.

Based on this metamodel, two syntaxes are currently proposed for simple conditions. A preliminary XML syntax, as well as a more readable syntax which is similar in style to what in OWL is called the Abstract Syntax [PSHH04]. This latter syntax, which resembles other standard syntaxes for (variants of) first-order logic, is based on the following EBNF, used in examples of the first RIF Core working draft:

```
CONDITION   ::= CONJUNCTION | DISJUNCTION | EXISTENTIAL | ATOMIC
CONJUNCTION ::= 'And' '(' CONDITION* ')'
DISJUNCTION ::= 'Or' '(' CONDITION* ')'
```

```
EXISTENTIAL ::= 'Exists' Var+ '(' CONDITION ')'
ATOMIC      ::= Uniterm | Equal
Uniterm     ::= Const '(' TERM* ')'
Equal       ::= TERM '=' TERM
TERM        ::= Const | Var | Uniterm
Const       ::= CONSTNAME | '"'CONSTNAME'"'''^^'SORTNAME
Var         ::= '?'VARNAME | '?'VARNAME'^^'SORTNAME
```

The terminal and non-terminal symbols in this EBNF should be largely self-explanatory and we refer the reader to [BK07] for details. Note that the productions for constants (Const) and variables (Var) include optionally sorted versions. Most knowledge representation, programming and rule languages allow/require "typing" of constants and also of variables: take for example typed literals in RDF, or variables in common programming languages, which is accounted for by the *Multisorted RIF Logic*, to be discussed in more detail below. At this point we do not commit to any particular vocabulary for the names of constants, variables, or sorts.

Example 5 (Running example (cont'd)). For instance, in John's rule for classifying old movies as black-and-white, the condition part written in first-order logic looks as follows:

$$\exists D, Y.\ MoviShopDvd(D) \land shows(D, M) \land$$
$$IMDMovie(M) \land IMDYear(M, Y)\ \land\ before(Y, 1930)$$

In RIF's EBNF syntax, he could write this straightforwardly:

```
Exists ?D ?Y (
    And ( "moviShop:Dvd"( ?D ) "imd:shows"( ?D ?M )
          "imd:Movie"( ?M ) "imd:Year"( ?M ?Y )
          "op:date-less-than"( ?Y "1930-01-01T00:00:00Z"^^dateTime ) ) )
```

Note that the names of the predicates are IRIs and thus are "webized." In the future, builtin predicates, like `"op:date-less-than"` will be also standardized around XPath and XQuery functions [MMe07].

Note that in the above condition there is one free (i.e. non-quantified) variable. Free variables arise because we are dealing with formulas that might occur in a rule IF part. When this happens, the free variables in a condition formula shall also occur in the rule THEN part. We will see that such variables are quantified universally outside the rule, and the scope of such quantification is the entire rule.

An XML syntax for this condition language is currently under discussion, where element names will be close to the metamodel/EBNF. Let us turn now to the model theory behind RIF's Condition Language.

5.2   The RIF Core Condition Language – Semantics

The first step in defining a model-theoretic semantics for a logic-based language is to define the notion of a semantic structure, also known as an interpretation.

RIF takes here, in order to be general and extensible, an approach common to systems that not only cover classical first-order logic, but also uncertainty or inconsistency (which are clearly important in the open Web environment), i.e., multi-valued logics. Here, truth values are not only f ("false") and t ("true"), but a set of truth values TV, which has a total or partial order, called the truth order (denoted with $<_t$). For instance, in classical logic this order is simply $false <_t true$, whereas logics dealing with uncertainty or inconsistency often are four-valued logics, e.g. with a partial order $f <_t u <_t t$ and $f <_t i <_t t$, where u and i denote "unknown" and "inconsistent", respectively.[36]

Moreover, since RIF on the syntactic level does not distinguish between constants, functions, and predicates, a semantic structure, I, is defined as a tuple of mappings $\langle I_C, I_V, I_F, I_R \rangle$, which determines the truth value of every formula, as explained below. Here, I_C, I_V, I_F, and I_R denote the interpretation of the domain elements as, respectively, constants, variables, functions, and relations.

Definition 1 (Interpretation). *Let D be a non-empty set of elements called the domain of I, Const the set of constants, predicate names, and function symbols, and Var the set of variables.*

An interpretation $I = \langle I_C, I_V, I_F, I_R \rangle$ consists of four mappings:

- $I_C : Const \to D$
- $I_V : Var \to D$[37]
- $I_F :$ *from Const to functions from $D^* \to D$, where D^* is a set of all tuples of any length over the domain D*
- $I_R :$ *from Const to truth-valued mappings $D^* \to TV$*

Using these mappings, we can define a more general mapping, I, as follows:

- $I(k) = I_C(k)$ *if $k \in$ Const*
- $I(?v) = I_V(?v)$ *if $?v \in$ Var*
- $I(f(t_1...t_n)) = I_F(f)(I(t_1), ..., I(t_n))$

Finally, the mapping $I_{Truth} : \phi \to TV$ for conditions ϕ is defined inductively:

- *Atomic formulas: $I_{Truth}(r(t_1...t_n)) = I_R(r)(I(t_1), ..., I(t_n))$*
- *Equality: $I_{Truth}(t_1 = t_2) = t$ iff $I(t_1) = I(t_2)$; $I_{Truth}(t_1 = t_2) = f$ otherwise.*
- *Conjunction: $I_{Truth}($ And $(c_1 ... c_n)) = min_t(I_{Truth}(c_1), ..., I_{Truth}(c_n))$, where min_t is minimum with respect to the truth order.*
- *Disjunction: $I_{Truth}($ Or $(c_1 ... c_n)) = max_t(I_{Truth}(c_1), ..., I_{Truth}(c_n))$, where max_t is maximum with respect to the truth order.*
- *Quantification: $I_{Truth}($ Exists $?v_1 ... ?v_n (c)) = max_t(I'_{Truth}(c))$ where max_t is taken over all interpretations $I' = < I_C, I'_V, I_F, I_R >$, which agree with I everywhere except possibly in the interpretation I'_V of the variables $?v_1, ..., ?v_n$.*

---

[36] Such logics can also be given another partial order $<_k$, called the knowledge order: $u <_k t <_k i$ and $u <_k f <_k i$. See, e.g., [Fit02] for details.

[37] This is also often called variable assignment elsewhere in the literature.

Multisorted RIF Logic As mentioned earlier and also seen in the EBNF, one may attach *sorts* from a set of primitive sorts (defined for a RIF dialect) to constants and variables. The list of supported primitive sorts in RIF Core (which probably will be extended later on) is: `long`, `string`, `decimal`, `time`, and `dateTime`. Signatures for function and relation symbols specify their arity and argument (and value) sorts. The current syntax to declare function sorts is:

$$':- \text{ signature' '"'NAME'"'} \; s_1 \; '*' \ldots '*' \; s_n \; '\rightarrow' \; s \; ',' $$
$$r_1 \; '*' \ldots '*' \; r_k \; '\rightarrow' \; r \; ',' \ldots$$

Relation (or predicate) sorts are declared similarly:

$$':- \text{ signature' '"'NAME'"'} \; s_1 \; '*' \ldots '*' \; s_n \; ',' $$
$$r_1 \; '*' \ldots '*' \; r_k \; ',' \ldots$$

For instance, the sorts of the XPath/XQuery relation `op:date-less-than` used above could be defined by this signature:

```
:- signature "op:date-less-than" dateTime * dateTime
```

Interpretations of multi-sorted RIF dialects extend Definition 1 by new functions to assign primitive sorts and function sorts assign a set of allowed primitive sorts to the symbols of `Const`. The details of multi-sorted interpretations are currently being worked out, but they seem to be an important feature, as many languages (including RDF, Prolog, HiLog and F-Logic, Common Logic) support signature declarations and/or typed literals and variables.

5.3   RIF Core Horn Rules

As a first simple core format for a complete but minimal rules interchange language, the RIF WG defined a *RIF Core Rule Language* by extending the RIF Core Condition Language, where conditions become rule bodies. RIF Phase 1 covers only the expressivity of Horn Rules, i.e. rules with one positive derived atomic formula in the head (or THEN part).[38]. This simple rules dialect extends the EBNF syntax for Core Conditions by the following productions:

```
Ruleset  ::= RULE*
RULE     ::= 'Forall' Var* CLAUSE
CLAUSE   ::= Implies | ATOMIC
Implies  ::= ATOMIC ':-' CONDITION
```

The symbol `:-` denotes the implication connective used in rules. The statement `ATOMIC :- CONDITION` should be informally read as if `CONDITION` is true then `ATOMIC` is also true. We deliberately avoid using the connective ← here because in some RIF dialects, such as Logic Programming dialects and Production Rules dialects, the implication `:-` will have different meaning from the meaning of the first-order implication ←.

---

[38] Note, that the minor extensions such as allowing existentials and disjunctions in the body via RIF Core conditions do not increase the expressive power of the language above Horn.

The upcoming envisioned RIF dialects will extend this core rule language by generalizing the positive RIF conditions in the bodies, and probably they will also allow more expressive rule heads.

RIF Core Horn Rules – Semantics. In Section 5.2 above we already defined the notion of semantic structures and the truth value of a RIF condition in such a semantic structure (interpretation).

While semantic structures can be multivalued, rules are typically two-valued even in logics that support inconsistency and uncertainty: a rule is either satisfied in an Interpretation I (true) or not (false). We can define satisfaction of a rule '*head* :- *body*' in Interpretation I, denoted by $I \models head$:- *body* simply as follows:

$$I \models head \text{ :- } body \text{ iff } I_{Truth}(head) \geq_t I_{Truth}(body)$$

Note that, since in RIF Core we consider Horn clauses, where free variables are assumed to be universally quantified over the whole rule, strictly speaking, we need to refine this to: $I \models clause$ iff $I' \models clause$ for every I' that agrees with I everywhere except possibly on some variables free in *clause*. In this case, we also say that I is a model of the clause. I is a model of a rule set R iff it is a model of every rule in R.

The notion of a model is only the basic ingredient in the definition of a semantics of a rule set. In general, the semantics of a rule set R is the set of its *intended* models (see e.g. [Sho87]). There are different theories of what the intended sets of models are supposed to look like depending on the features of the particular rule sets.

For Horn rules, which we use in this section, the intended set of models of R is commonly agreed upon: it is the set of *all* models of R. However, in (future) rule dialects which allow constructs such as nonmonotonic negation (aka negation-as-failure) in rule bodies, only some of the models of a rule set are viewed as intended. This issue will be addressed in the appropriate dialects of RIF. The two most common theories of intended models are based on the so called well-founded models [GRS88] and stable models [GL88].

Future extensions of the presented RIF Core will need to enable the provider of a rule set to be interchanged to declare explicitly what notion of intended models are assumed in this rule set.

Example 6 (Running example (cont'd)). Finally, John Doe can publish and exchange his rule

(R1)

```
    IF movie M was produced before 1930
    THEN M is a black and white movie
```

which declares his definition of black and white movies using RIF Core:

```
"moviShop:BWMovie" ( ?M ) :-
  Exists ?D ?Y (
    And ( "moviShop:Dvd"( ?D ) "imd:shows"( ?D ?M )
          "imd:Movie"( ?M ) "imd:Year"( ?M ?Y )
          "op:date-less-than"( ?Y "1930-01-01T00:00:00Z"^^dateTime ) ) )
```

Not too bad, but John waits what's next and when he will be able to exchange more complex rules such as

```
(R2)
   IF movie M is  listed at http://altmd.example.org but not
      listed at http://imd.example.org
   THEN M is an independent movie
(R3)
   ON request from customer C to book a movie
   IF customer C is blacklisted
   DO deny C's request
```

and he is eagerly waiting for a complete RIF which will enable him to do so. The current core does not yet provide this feature, but is carefully designed to enable plugging in of different forms of negation or various models of events and actions in RIF dialects to be defined in the future.

5.4   What's Next?

The core rules fragment we have seen so far will provide the basis for further dialects to cover richer features and express rules and rulesets beyond simple Horn. The current efforts towards a very general model theory, catering for multi-sorted and multi-valued logic extensions do not seem necessary for simple Horn rules, but will enable upward compatible extensions of this common basis.

Currently, the underlying metamodel, introduced at the beginning of this section, is also being extended towards a base ontology for describing the available features of existing rule languages and systems. The working group has analyzed this feature space and collected a list of discriminators (distinguishing features) in the so called RIF Rules Arrangement Framework[39] (RIFRAF). Aligning the RIF Core Metamodel with RIFRAF in a common ontology will help RIF users to classify their rule sets and features with respect to the upcoming family of possibly diverging RIF dialects. We point out here again, that it is not the goal of RIF to provide a one-for-all rule language which can cover all of these features. Distinct features of different rule systems are often simply incompatible. Rather, the concept of RIF dialects will enable the exchange of rules within common fragments or variable feature sets between various parties in a modular fashion.

6   Conclusion

This paper has presented a snapshot of the current working drafts of the W3C RIF Working Group, which is working on the development of an interchange format for rules. The need for such a format has been motivated by the use cases of the Second Public Working Draft of the RIF WG, which we have described briefly. We illustrated the main ideas behind rule interchange using an example of a DVD rental store. The example illustrates that in order to adequately

---

[39] http://www.w3.org/2005/rules/wg/wiki/Rulesystem_Arrangement_Framework

represent the services provided by MoviShop we need different types of rules: *deductive*, *normative*, and *reactive*. MoviShop's rules work with the data obtained from different data sources. These data may be expressed using XML, RDF, and/or OWL. The types of rules and the data (and metadata) representation models needed for the task pose a number of requirements to the interchange format for MoviShop's rules. These requirements drive the development of a core interchange format for rules—the *RIF Core*—and its extensions—*RIF dialects*.

As of this writing, the RIF WG has released the First Public Working Draft of `RIF Core`. It includes the *RIF Condition Language* and its extension to the *RIF Horn Rule Language*. The RIF Condition Language is expected to be used for expressing the part of rules that is common to deductive, normative, and reactive rules, namely the `IF` part, as shown via examples. The *RIF Horn Rule Language* is intended to allow exchanging Horn-style deductive rules. This core language is clearly not sufficient for interchanging many kinds of rules, but it offers the basis for future extensions most of which will be developed as RIF dialects.

Acknowledgments

This research has been partly funded by the European Commission and by the Swiss Federal Office for Education and Science within the EU FP6 Network of Excellence REWERSE[40] (IST-506779). This work was done while Michael Kifer was visiting DERI Innsbruck. His work was supported in part by the BIT Institute, NSF grants CCR-0311512 and IIS-0534419, and by US Army Research Office under a subcontract from BNL. The work of Axel Polleres was partly supported by the EU FP6 project inContext (IST-034718)[41] as well as by the Spanish MEC and Universidad Rey Juan Carlos under the project SWOS (URJC-CM-2006-CET-0300). We also thank NSERC for its support through the discovery grant of Harold Boley.

References

[ABdB+05]   Angele, J., Boley, H., de Bruijn, J., Fensel, D., Hitzler, P., Kifer, M., Krummenacher, R., Lausen, H., Polleres, A., Studer, R.: Web Rule Language (WRL), W3C member submission (September 2005)

[Bar03]   Baral, C.: Knowledge Representation, Reasoning and Declarative Problem Solving. Cambridge University Press, Cambridge (2003)

[BBB+]   Battle, S., Bernstein, A., Boley, H., Grosof, B., Grüninger, M., Hull, R., Kifer, M., Martin, D., McGuinness, D.L., McIlraith, S., Su, J., Tabet, S.: Semantic web services framework (SWSF)

[BBB+07]   Berstel, B., Bonnard, P., Bry, F., Eckert, M., Pătrânjan, P.-L.: Reactive Rules on the Web. In: Reasoning Web – Third International Summer School 2007, Tutorial Lectures (2007) In preparation.

---

[40] `http://rewerse.net/`

[41] `http://www.in-context.eu/`

[BBCC02]   Bonifati, A., Braga, D., Campi, A., Ceri, S.: Active XQuery. In: 18th
            Int. Conf. on Data Engineering (ICDE2002), San Jose, California
            (2002)

[BBEP05]   Bailey, J., Bry, F., Eckert, M., Pătrânjan, P.-L.: Flavours of XChange,
            a rule-based reactive language for the (Semantic) Web. In: Adi, A.,
            Stoutenburg, S., Tabet, S. (eds.) RuleML 2005. LNCS, vol. 3791,
            Springer, Heidelberg (2005)

[BM04]   Biron, P.V., Malhotra, A. (eds): XML Schema Part 2: Datatypes, 2 nd
            edn. W3C Recommendation (October 2004)

[BK07]   Boley, H., Kifer, M. (eds.): RIF Core Design, W3C Editor's Draft (30
            March 2007)

[Bec06]   Beckett, D.: Turtle - Terse RDF Triple Language (April 2006) Available
            at http://www.dajobe.org/2004/01/turtle/

[BEP06a]   Bry, F., Eckert, M., Patranjan, P.-L.: Reactivity on the web: Paradigms
            and applications of the language xchange. Journal of Web Engineer-
            ing 5(1), 3–24 (2006)

[BEP06b]   Bry, F., Eckert, M., Pătrânjan, P.-L.: Reactivity on the Web: Para-
            digms and applications of the language XChange. J. of Web Engineer-
            ing 5(1), 3–24 (2006)

[BEPR06]   Bry, F., Eckert, M., Pătrânjan, P.-L., Romanenko, I.: Realizing busi-
            ness processes with eca rules: Benefits, challenges, limits. In: Alferes,
            J.J., Bailey, J., May, W., Schwertel, U. (eds.) PPSWR 2006. LNCS,
            vol. 4187, pp. 10–11. Springer, Heidelberg (2006)

[BFG⁺01]   Baumgartner, R., Flesca, S., Gottlob, G., Nieuwenhuis, R., Voronkov,
            A.: The elog web extraction language. In: Nieuwenhuis, R., Voronkov,
            A. (eds.) LPAR 2001. LNCS (LNAI), vol. 2250, Springer, Heidelberg
            (2001)

[BFMS06]   Behrends, E., Fritzen, O., May, W., Schenk, F.: Combining ECA Rules
            with Process Algebras for the Semantic Web. In: Proceedings of Second
            International Conference on Rules and Rule Markup Languages for the
            Semantic Web, Athens, Georgia, USA, November 10-11, 2006, pp. 29–
            38 (2006)

[BK94]   Bonner, A.J., Kifer, M.: Transaction logic programming (or a logic
            of declarative and procedural knowledge). Technical Report CSRI-
            270, University of Toronto, April 1992, Revised: (February 1994),
            http://www.cs.toronto.edu/~bonner/transaction-logic.html

[BK98]   Bonner, A.J., Kifer, M.: A logic for programming database transac-
            tions. In: Chomicki, J., Saake, G. (eds.) Logics for Databases and In-
            formation Systems. ch. 5, pp. 117–166. Kluwer Academic Publishers,
            Dordrecht (1998)

[BL05]   Berners-Lee, T.: Web for Real People, April 2005. Keynote Speech at
            the 14th World Wide Web Conference (WWW2005). Slides available
            at http://www.w3.org/2005/Talks/0511-keynote-tbl/

[BM05]   Bry, F., Marchiori, M.: Ten theses on logic languages for the Semantic
            Web. In: Fages, F., Soliman, S. (eds.) PPSWR 2005. LNCS, vol. 3703,
            Springer, Heidelberg (2005)

[BO05]   Bonatti, P.A., Olmedilla, D.: Driving and monitoring provisional trust
            negotiation with metapolicies. In: IEEE Int. Workshop on Policies for
            Distributed Systems and Networks, IEEE Computer Society Press, Los
            Alamitos (2005)

[Bon05]   Bonatti, P.A.: Rule languages for security and privacy in cooperative systems. In: 29th Annual International Computer Software and Applications Conference (COMPSAC 2005), Edinburgh, Scotland, UK, July 25-28, 2005, pp. 268–269 (2005)

[BPW02]   Bailey, J., Poulovassilis, A., Wood, P.T.: An event-condition-action language for XML. In: Proc. Int. World Wide Web Conf. pp. 486–495. ACM, New York (2002)

[BS04]   Bry, F., Schwertel, U.: REWERSE – reasoning on the Web. AgentLink News, 15 (2004)

[Bus05]   Business Rules Group (2005), www.businessrulesgroup.org

[CH01]   Cabeza, D., Hermenegildo, M.: Distributed www programming using (ciao-)prolog and the pillow library. Theory and Practice of Logic Programming 1(3), 251–282 (2001)

[CKW93a]   Chen, W., Kifer, M., Warren, D.S.: HiLog: A foundation for higher-order logic programming. Journal of Logic Programming 15(3), 187–230 (1993)

[CKW93b]   Chen, W., Kifer, M., Warren, D.S.: HILOG: A foundation for higher-order logic programming. Journal of Logic Programming 15(3), 187–230 (1993)

[Dav93]   Davenport, T.H.: Process Innovation: Reengineering Work through Information Technology. Havard Business School Press, Boston, Massachusetts (1993)

[dBEPT06]   de Bruijn, J., Eiter, T., Polleres, A., Tompits, H.: On representational issues about combinations of classical theories with nonmonotonic rules. In: Lang, J., Lin, F., Wang, J. (eds.) KSEM 2006. LNCS (LNAI), vol. 4092, Springer, Heidelberg (2006)

[DSB+04]   Dean, M., Schreiber, G., Bechhofer, S., Harmelen, F.v., Hendler, J., Horrocks, I., McGuinness, D.L., Patel-Schneider, P.F., Stein, L.A.: OWL Web Ontology Language Reference, W3C Recommendation (February 2004)

[ed06]   Delugach, H. (ed.): Iso common logic (2006) available at http://philebus.tamu.edu/cl/

[EGM97]   Eiter, T., Gottlob, G., Mannila, H.: Disjunctive datalog. ACM Transactions on Database Systems 22(3), 364–418 (1997)

[EIP+06]   Eiter, T., Ianni, G., Polleres, A., Schindlauer, R., Tompits, H.: Reasoning with rules and ontologies. In: Barahona, P., Bry, F., Franconi, E., Henze, N., Sattler, U. (eds.) Reasoning Web. LNCS, vol. 4126, pp. 93–127. Springer, Heidelberg (2006)

[EU-05]   EU-Rent Case Study (2005), www.eurobizrules.org/ebrc2005/eurentcs/eurent.htm

[Eur05]   European Business Rules Conference (2005), www.eurobizrules.org

[FFLS99]   Fernandez, M.F., Florescu, D., Levy, A.Y., Suciu, D.: Verifying integrity constraints on web sites. In: IJCAI, pp. 614–619 (1999)

[Fit02]   Fitting, M.: Fixpoint semantics for logic programming – a survey. Theoretical Computer Science 278(1-2), 25–51 (2002)

[FLB+06]   Furche, T., Linse, B., Bry, F., Plexousakis, D., Gottlob, G.: Rdf querying: Language constructs and evaluation methods compared. In: Barahona, P., Bry, F., Franconi, E., Henze, N., Sattler, U. (eds.) Reasoning Web. LNCS, vol. 4126, pp. 1–52. Springer, Heidelberg (2006)

[For82]   Forgy, C.: RETE: A fast algorithm for the many pattern/many object pattern match problem. Artificial Intelligence 19, 17–37 (1982)

[GHMe]   Ginsberg, A., Hirtle, D., McCabe, F., Patranjan, P.-L. (eds.): RIF Core Design. W3C Working Draft

[GL88]   Gelfond, M., Lifschitz, V.: The stable model semantics for logic programming. In: Kowalski, R.A., Bowen, K. (eds.) 5th Int'l Conf. on Logic Programming, pp. 1070–1080. The MIT Press, Cambridge, Massachusetts (1988)

[GRS88]   Van Gelder, A., Ross, K., Schlipf, J.S.: Unfounded sets and well-founded semantics for general logic programs. In: 7th ACM Symposium on Principles of Database Systems, Austin, Texas, pp. 221–230. ACM, New York (1988)

[Hal05]   Hall, J.: Business rules boot camp. In: Tutorial at the European Business Rules Conference (2005)

[Hay04]   Hayes, P.: RDF semantics. Technical report, W3C, W3C Recommendation (February 2004), http://www.w3.org/TR/rdf-mt/

[HPSB+04]   Horrocks, I., Patel-Schneider, P.F., Boley, H., Tabet, S., Grosof, B., Dean, M.: SWRL: A semantic web rule language combining OWL and RuleML, W3C Member Submission (2004)

[KLW95]   Kifer, M., Lausen, G., Wu, J.: Logical foundations of object-oriented and frame-based languages. Journal of the ACM 42(4), 741–843 (1995)

[LPF+06]   Leone, N., Pfeifer, G., Faber, W., Eiter, T., Gottlob, G., Perri, S., Scarcello, F.: The dlv system for knowledge representation and reasoning. ACM Transactions on Computational Logic 7(3), 499–562 (2006)

[Mel02]   Melton, J.: Advanced SQL 1999: Understanding Object-Relational, and Other Advanced Features. Elsevier Science Inc. New York, USA (2002)

[MMe07]   Malhotra, A., Melton, J., Walsh, N. (eds.): XQuery 1.0 and XPath 2.0 Functions and Operators, W3C Recommendation (January 2007), available at http://www.w3.org/TR/xpath-functions/

[MSvL06]   May, W., Schenk, F., von Lienen, E.: Extending an OWL Web Node with Reactive Behavior. In: Alferes, J.J., Bailey, J., May, W., Schwertel, U. (eds.) PPSWR 2006. LNCS, vol. 4187, pp. 134–148. Springer, Heidelberg (2006)

[Pe06]   Prud'hommeaux, E., Seaborne, A. (eds.): SPARQL Query Language for RDF, W3C Candidate Recommendation (2006), available at http://www.w3.org/TR/rdf-sparql-query/

[Pol07]   Polleres, A.: From SPARQL to rules (and back). In: Proceedings of the 16th World Wide Web Conference (WWW 2007) Banff, Canada, May 2007. Accepted for publication, technical report version (2007), available at http://www.polleres.net/publications/GIA-TR-2006-11-28.pdf

[PPW03]   Papamarkos, G., Poulovassilis, A., Wood, P.T.: Event-condition-action rule languages for the Semantic Web. In: Bressan, S., Chaudhri, A.B., Lee, M.L., Yu, J.X., Lacroix, Z. (eds.) CAiSE 2002 and VLDB 2002. LNCS, vol. 2590, pp. 309–327. Springer, Heidelberg (2003)

[PS96]   Potamianos, S., Stonebraker, M.: The postgres rule system. In: Widom, J., Ceri, S. (eds.) Active Database Systems - Triggers and Rules for Advanced Database Processing, pp. 44–61. Springer, Berlin, (1996)

[PSHH04]   Patel-Schneider, P.F., Hayes, P., Horrocks, I.: OWL Web Ontology Language Semantics and Abstract Syntax, W3C Recommendation (February 2004)

[Pŏ5]   Pătrânjan, P.-L.: The Language XChange: A Declarative Approach to
             Reactivity on the Web. Dissertation/Ph.D. thesis, Institute of Com-
             puter Science, LMU, Munich, 2005. PhD Thesis, Institute for Infor-
             matics, University of Munich (2005)
[Ros06]   Rosati, R.: Integrating Ontologies and Rules: Semantic and Computa-
             tional Issues. In: Barahona, P., Bry, F., Franconi, E., Henze, N., Sat-
             tler, U. (eds.) Reasoning Web. LNCS, vol. 4126, pp. 128–151. Springer,
             Heidelberg (2006)
[Sch04]   Schaffert, S.: Xcerpt: A Rule-Based Query and Transformation Lan-
             guage for the Web. PhD thesis, University of Munich (October 2004)
[Sho87]   Shoham, Y.: Nonmonotonic logics: Meaning and utility. In: Proceed-
             ings of the 10th International Joint Conference on Artificial Intelligence
             (IJCAI-87), pp. 388–393. Morgan Kaufmann, San Francisco (1987)
[SS07]   Schenk, S., Staab, S.: Networked rdf graphs. Technical Report Arbeits-
             berichte des Fachbereichs Informatik 3/2007, Institut für Informatik,
             Universität Koblenz-Landau (2007)
[SW94]   Swift, T., Warren, D.S.: Efficiently implementing slg resolution (Janu-
             ary 1994)
[tH05]   ter Horst, H.J.: Completeness, decidability and complexity of entail-
             ment for rdf schema and a semantic extension involving the owl vo-
             cabulary. Journal of Web Semantics 3(2) (2005)
[The00]   The Business Rules Group. Defining business rules – what are they
             really? (2000) Available at www.businessrulesgroup.org
[TW01]   Taveter, K., Wagner, G.: Agent-oriented enterprise modeling based on
             business rules. In: ER, pp. 527–540 (2001)
[vdAtHKB03] van der Aalst, W.M.P., ter Hofstede, A.H.M., Kiepuszewski, B., Bar-
             ros, A.P.: Workflow patterns. Distributed and Parallel Databases 14(1)
             (2003)
[WGL06]   Wagner, G., Giurca, A., Lukichev, S.: A Usable Interchange Format
             for Rich Syntax Rules Integrating OCL, RuleML and SWRL. In: Hit-
             zler, P., Wache, H., Eiter, T. (eds.) RoW2006 Reasoning on the Web
             Workshop at WWW2006 (2006)
[WHvdM06]   Wielemaker, J., Huang, Z., van der Meij, L.: Swi-prolog and the
             web. manuascript (2006), http://hcs.science.uva.nl/projects/
             SWI-Prolog/articles/TPLP-plweb.pdf
[Wid96]   Widom, J.: The starburst active database rule system. Knowledge and
             Data Engineering 8(4), 583–595 (1996)

Reasoning in Semantic Wikis

Markus Krötzsch[1], Sebastian Schaffert[2], and Denny Vrandečić[1]

[1] AIFB, Universität Karlsruhe (TH), Karlsruhe, Germany
{kroetzsch,vrandecic}@aifb.uni-karlsruhe.de
[2] Salzburg Research Forschungsgesellschaft, Salzburg, Austria
sebastian.schaffert@salzburgresearch.at

Abstract. Semantic wikis combine the collaborative environment of a classical wiki with features of semantic technologies. Semantic data is used to structure information in the wiki, to improve information access by intelligent search and navigation, and to enable knowledge exchange across applications. Though semantic wikis hardly support complex semantic knowledge and inferencing, we argue that this is not due to a lack of practical use cases. We discuss various tasks for which advanced reasoning is desirable, and identify open challenges for the development of inferencing tools and formalisms. Our goal is to outline concrete options for overcoming current problems, since we believe that many problems in semantic wikis are prototypical for other Semantic Web applications as well. Throughout the paper, we refer to our semantic wiki implementations *IkeWiki* and *Semantic MediaWiki* for practical illustration.

1 Introduction

Semantic wikis enrich wiki systems for collaborative content management with semantic technologies. Annotations added to wiki pages are stored in a knowledge base, and possibly connected with background ontologies. Based on these annotations, semantic wikis provide enhanced navigation, search, and retrieval, and often also contextual adaptation of the presentation of the content. Collaborative authored semantic content is exported to the Semantic Web in standard formats, such as RDF [1] and OWL [2].

Semantic wikis have been successfully applied in real-world scenarios, and various implementations exist – see [3] for an overview of current research. Prominent systems like Semantic MediaWiki [4,5], IkeWiki [6,7], and SemperWiki [8] managed to disseminate semantic technologies among a broad audience, and many of the emerging semantic wikis resemble "small Semantic Webs." Indeed, wikis are characterised by their dynamic, open nature with many different contributors who independently create different "pieces of knowledge" that need to be integrated.

In spite of their success, semantic wikis often use very simple semantic structures and hardly employ complex inferencing procedures. We argue that this is not at all due to a lack of practical applications of advanced reasoning: though a little semantics might go a long way, we believe that many worthwhile goals won't be reached without additional expressivity. There are, of course, complications when moving from shallow semantic data to more complex ontologies, and we will discuss requirements, existing challenges, and open problems. Motivated by concrete use cases for inferencing within semantic wikis, we outline viable ways for improving reasoning support in wikis. Based

G. Antoniou et al. (Eds.): Reasoning Web 2007, LNCS 4636, pp. 310–329, 2007.

on our experience with developing IkeWiki and Semantic MediaWiki, we provide many examples for simple inferencing within these systems, and give an outlook on upcoming enhancements related to reasoning.

The goal of this article is on the one hand to introduce into semantic wikis as an interesting testbed for evaluating Semantic Web technologies, including reasoning, and on the other hand to illustrate in practical application scenarios – based on semantic wikis – where reasoning can lead to interesting applications and where reasoning still faces challenges that need to be addressed.

After giving a short outline of semantic wikis in Section 2, we briefly describe our two semantic wiki systems, Semantic MediaWiki and IkeWiki, with a particular focus on the way knowledge is represented. We then show general uses of reasoning for enhancing *browsing, querying, editing,* and *validating* in Section 4. In Section 5, we outline three different concrete application scenarios for reasoning in semantic wikis and from that derive selected challenges that we consider as relevant for future reasoning systems. In Section 7, we conclude by sketching next steps towards improving reasoning support in our wiki systems.

2   Semantic Wikis

The term "semantic wiki" encompasses a broad range of applications that are using machine-readable data with a well-defined semantics to augment the functionality of a wiki-based content management system. To clarify this rather unsharp definition, we now present some ways of classifying semantic wikis and present typical implementations and usage scenarios. Possibly the most important characteristic of each semantic wiki is its approach towards collecting semantic data. Classical wikis are primarily designed for collecting textual information, and the collaborative creation of this content is supported in many ways, e.g. through simple user interfaces, extensive versioning support, or discussion pages. Semantic wikis need to find ways of also obtaining machine-readable data, without sacrificing the core strengths of classical wikis. Three main sources for semantic data are usually considered:

Manually provided content. Virtually all current semantic wikis enable users to directly enter and modify semantic data via the wiki's editing interface or an extension thereof. Implementations range from providing text-forms for RDF data, over the use of a simplified wiki-markup within existing texts, to the use of additional interactive user interfaces that support annotation. Basically all classical wikis provide simple annotation support in the form of tagging or categorisation. Semantic wikis extend these capabilities.

Automatically collected metadata. Many wikis already collect large amounts of metadata that is required for normal operation. This includes details about authors, version histories, licensing, and hyperlinks. This data can be converted into machine-readable formats that enable interchange and reuse, as was done, e.g., with Wikipedia's metadata in the *Wikipedia*[3] project[1]. Another source of metadata is information associated with multimedia files, used e.g. in IkeWiki to gather information on uploaded images.

---

[1] http://labs.systemone.at/wikipedia3

External background knowledge. Semantic wikis are not always the only source for semantic data, and can be used in conjunction with other semantic data sets. In this case, the wiki should be able to import and reuse ontologies or RDF datasets, in order to take this background-knowledge into account for editing and presentation. A prototypical implementation of such functionality was described in [9].

Semantic wikis often use more than one of those sources, but some way of manually providing semantic content appears to be a core feature of all current implementations. Independent of its source, the use of the available semantic data can be very different. Though the boundaries are not strict, the following two approaches are prominent:

"Wikis for semantic data." Wikis that sufficiently support the editing of ontological information can be used as collaborative ontology editors. The system in this case can help domain experts and ontologists to cooperate in one system, while the text-content of each wiki page is used to create a human-readable specification in parallel to the formal ontology. Even if the wiki does not provide means of editing complex schema information, it can still be used to develop and document ontological vocabularies in a similar way. The use of wikis for such tasks facilitates the dynamic, evolutionary development of ontologies, and supports the gradual lifting of informal textual descriptions to formal conceptualisations. In the project *Dynamont*[2], IkeWiki is used for this purpose.

"Semantic data for wikis." Wikis are already used successfully in many applications where the primary task is to collect textual content. In those cases, semantic data is used to support the current usage of the wiki, e.g. by simplifying the retrieval of information through semantic search functions. Semantic data in this case either is used to make some of the wiki's contents machine-processable, or to simplify wiki maintenance by exploiting metadata. A major goal is to retain the known working principles of the wiki, and thus to not introduce too many new interfaces or functions. Examples of this use are given by many sites running Semantic MediaWiki, such as ontoworld.org [4]. Another typical scenario for wiki usage is internal knowledge management in working groups.

3   Knowledge Representation in Wikis

In this section, we briefly introduce two popular semantic wiki systems, *IkeWiki* and *Semantic MediaWiki*, which will also be our main objects of examples in later sections. Here, we are mainly interrested in the forms of semantic knowledge that each of those applications supports, and on the approaches for representing this data within the wiki. Advanced uses of this data will be discussed in later sections.

3.1   Semantic MediaWiki

Semantic MediaWiki (SMW) [4] is an extension of the popular wiki software *MediaWiki*[3] that is used by Wikipedia and many other sites. SMW is typically used as a modular enhancement to existing MediaWiki installations, and thus aims at a seamless

---

[2] http://dynamont.factlink.net
[3] http://www.mediawiki.org

integration of semantic features into the existing user interfaces. The internal knowledge model of SMW is closely related to OWL DL, although just a small fragment of the expressive means of this language is actually available within the wiki.

The necessary collection of semantic data in SMW is achieved by letting users add annotations to the wiki-text of articles via a special markup. Every article corresponds to exactly one ontological element (including classes and properties), and every annotation in an article makes statements about this single element. This locality is helpful for maintenance: if knowledge is reused in many places, users must still be able to understand where the information originally came from. Furthermore, all annotations refer to the (abstract) concept represented by a page, not to the HTML document. Formally, this is implemented by providing strictly separate URIs for the article and its topic.

Most of the annotations that occur in SMW correspond to simple *ABox statements* in OWL DL, i.e. they describe certain individuals by asserting relations between them, annotating them with data values, or classifying them. The schematic information (*TBox*) representable in SMW is intentionally shallow. The wiki is not intended as a general purpose ontology editor, since distributed ontology engineering and large-scale reasoning still faces various open challenges, some of which we will consider below.

Categories are a simple form of annotation that allows users to classify pages. Categories are already available in MediaWiki, and SMW merely endows them with a formal interpretation as OWL classes. To state that the article `ESWC2006` belongs to the category `Conference`, one just writes `[[Category:Conference]]` within the article `ESWC2006`.

Relations describe relationships between two articles by assigning annotations to existing links. For example, there is a relation `program chair` between `ESWC2006` and `York Sure`. To express this, users just edit the page `ESWC2006` to change the normal link `[[York Sure]]` into `[[program chair::York Sure]]`.

Attributes allow users to specify relationships of articles to things that are not articles. For example, one can state that `ESWC2006` started at June 11 2006 by writing `[[start date:=June 11 2006]]`. In most cases, a relation to a new page `June 11 2006` would not be desired. Also, the system should understand the meaning of the given date, and recognise equivalent values such as `2006-06-11`.

Annotations are usually not shown at the place where they are inserted. Category links appear only at the bottom of a page, relations are displayed like normal links, and attributes just show the given value. A *factbox* at the bottom of each page enables users to view all extracted annotations, but the main text remains undisturbed.

It is obvious that the processing of Attributes requires some further information about the *Type* of the annotations. Integer numbers, strings, and dates all require different handling, and one needs to state that an attribute has a certain type. As explained above, every ontological element is represented as an article, and the same is true for categories, relations, and attributes. This also has the advantage that a *user documentation* can be written for each element of the vocabulary, which is crucial to enable consistent use of annotations.

The types that are available for attributes also have dedicated articles. In order to assign a type in the above example, we just need to state a relationship between

`Attribute:start date` and `Type:Date`. This relation is called `has type` (in the English version of SMW) and has a special built-in meaning.[4] SMW has a number of similar *special properties* that are used to specify certain technical aspects of the system, but most users can reuse existing annotations and do not have to worry about underlying definitions.

When using SMW as a wiki, users rarely are confronted with complete URIs. Instead, SMW generates unique URIs from the titles of the respective articles whenever this is necessary, especially for exporting semantic data as OWL/RDF. URIs of entities within the wiki thus are typically "local" to the given wiki, and are generated dynamically as the wiki is extended. It is also possible for users to assign given existing URIs to concepts that occur in the wiki, e.g. to associate a wiki's category `Category:Person` with the URI of the concept `foaf:Person` provided by the FOAF vocabulary. Such reuse of existing URIs is constraint to vocabularies that have been explicitly *imported* by the wiki's administrators, such that no abuse of existing URIs is possible (e.g. `foaf:Person` should never be used as the URI of a binary property).

Besides such explicit annotations, SMW does not consider any other sources of semantic data. Prototypes for using expressive ontologies within SMW have been studied [9], but the usual approach is to export semantic content from the wiki, and to further process it within some other semantic system that can also incorporate additional ontologies.

3.2 IkeWiki

IkeWiki is a complete reimplementation of a semantic wiki as a Java web application. The name *IkeWiki* is derived from the Hawaiian words *ike* – meaning "knowledge" – and *wiki* – meaning "quick". Although now also considered in different settings, IkeWiki has originally been developed as a prototype tool to support knowledge workers in collaboratively formalising knowledge. IkeWiki's design principles are an easy to use, interactive interface, compatibility with Semantic Web standards, immediate exploitation of semantic annotations, support for different levels of formal expressiveness (from RDF to OWL), and reasoning support.

IkeWiki uses the Java-based Semantic Web framework *Jena* as a backend and therefore offers support not only for plain RDF but also for the representation of different kinds of ontologies (RDFS and OWL). Different reasoning mechanisms can be employed; the default installation uses OWL-RDFS reasoning (essentially subclass and type inference), but we have also successfully integrated the Pellet reasoner with full OWL-DL support. We are also experimenting with a rule-based reasoning engine that would allow users to add user-defined rules to the knowledge base. One of the goals of IkeWiki is to support the formalisation of knowledge all the way from informal texts to formal ontologies.

In contrast to Semantic MediaWiki, IkeWiki relies on background ontologies that are pre-loaded in the knowledge base. As a consequence, it is not possible to annotate a link with a predicate that is not defined as an OWL ObjectProperty in the knowledge base. Likewise, IkeWiki only offers AnnotationProperties and DatatypeProperties as textual

---

[4] Also, it is treated as an owl:AnnotationProperty in order to stay in OWL DL.

metadata fields. This can be seen as a "restrictive" approach as compared to Semantic MediaWikis "open" approach.

Every page in IkeWiki corresponds to a resource in the knowledge base and is associated with a type (concept). A new page in general has the page `rdfs:Resource`, which can be further refined by the user. IkeWiki's reasoning component automatically infers all types of a page that follow by subclass relationships or relations to other pages. As this can be somewhat confusing to users, IkeWiki by default only offers link annotations that are compatible with the currently associated page types.

Unlike Semantic MediaWiki, IkeWiki stores all semantic metadata separately from the page content. When rendering a page, a so called *rendering pipeline* assembles content from the article database and metadata from the knowledge base to create an "enriched article" that contains the relevant semantic annotations. This approach has the advantage to make the maintenance of the knowledge base easier, but on the other hand does not allow versioning of the metadata and the locality of metadata is abandoned.

The IkeWiki interface makes heavy use of AJAX[5] technologies to provide an interactive interface. Page content is entered using a WYSIWYG editor. Semantic annotations are created in a separate "annotations editor"; the rationale behind this decision is that IkeWiki was designed as a collaborative tool that allows users with different levels of experience to work on the data in a defined workflow, and that editing content and metadata are separate processes in such settings.

The annotations editor allows to add types to a page and the links it contains via a guided, dialogue-based interface (see Figure 2 on page 319). When a user clicks on the +-symbol behind a link or behind the page types, he is presented with a list of all applicable properties or classes from which he can choose what he thinks appropriate. Reasoning is used to restrict this list to only the relevant ontology concepts. IkeWikis interface therefore prohibits to add link or page types that are not applicable, but supports the user by showing those types that *are* applicable. This conflicts to some extent with the "wiki philosophy" but results in a more homogeneous knowledge base with no inconsistencies with respect to the ontologies.

In addition to normal page annotations, IkeWiki's annotation editor also supports to modify or extend the loaded ontologies themselves. Specific support is given for adding sub-/superclasses, range/domain of properties, inverse relations, etc. There is currently no support for advanced OWL concepts like cardinality constraints and other restrictions.

3.3 Maintaining Ontologies in Wikis

Since advanced reasoning features are typically based on information that is more complex than simple RDF data, semantic wikis need to provide means for editing ontological axioms or logical rules as well. This is not a trivial task, since wikis and ontological knowledge bases are structured in different ways. In this section, we discuss how ontological information can still be maintained in wikis, and which kinds of such information are most suggestive for seamless integration in current usage.

---

[5] AJAX = *Asynchronous JavaScript and XML*, a technology that allows Web-applications to look and feel like desktop applications.

Semantic assertions in wikis typically refer to the contents of the wiki, which usually are represented by wiki pages or parts thereof. Simple assertions can thus be made at the place in the wiki to which they refer: assertions truly are annotations to the text of the wiki. If more complex axioms are taken into account, it becomes apparent that the structural models of ontologies and wikis do not match so nicely any more:

- Wikis are based on the notion of *articles* which might be further separated into sections.
- Ontologies are based on the notion of *axioms* or *rules*.

So how should ontological axioms be distributed among articles? Wiki articles often play the role of the underlying *vocabulary* used in ontological axioms, but each axiom might refer to many different articles. Different approaches towards solving this problem exist:

- **Decoupling pages and axioms.** Instead of treating axioms as annotations of wiki pages, it is also possible to consider them as independent content in their own right. Some semantic wikis therefore provide two input forms for each page: one for page text and one for axioms. While this allows users to freely organise axioms within the wiki, it has the disadvantage that there is no direct way of finding the page within which a particular axiom was given.
- **Strict coupling of pages and axioms.** If the possible kinds of ontological axioms are known, and if their structure is sufficiently simple, then it makes sense to couple them with one of the affected pages. For example, MediaWiki allows users to state subsumption relationships between categories.[6] Although two categories are involved in each subsumption, the axiom must be stated on the page of the subsumed category. Similar solutions can be found for many typical types of axioms. For complex axioms that could be expressed in syntactically different ways, however, the assignment of pages could still be ambiguous.
- **Loose coupling of pages and axioms.** Another solution is to couple a particular axiom to all pages that it affects. Thus, one axiom might be displayed on many pages, while being separated from the wiki text, and each page displays all axioms that are directly relevant for it. This solution is attractive for keeping an overview of all axioms, but it significantly affects the architecture of the wiki. Axioms do no longer belong to articles, and editing, versioning, and discussion of particular axioms needs additional mechanisms. For simplicity, axioms should be editable by editing the article in which they appear – but then concurrently editing two different articles might yield editing conflicts.

Each of the above solutions has its advantages and disadvantages, and a major future design task for semantic wikis will be to develop combined solutions that further push the expressivity of semantic wikis without sacrificing simplicity and usability.

4   Using Reasoning in Wikis

Reasoning is the process of deriving conclusions from formal symbolic knowledge, as constituted by the semantic content of a semantic wiki. In the case of a semantic

---

[6] Which, in some of their uses, can be viewed as ontological classes.

wiki, the premises are the underlying knowledge base together with the actual page content. Reasoning can be applied in semantic wikis for various different effects and benefits. The "conclusions" of reasoning can be of many different kinds, e.g. deriving of additional relations, but also the adaptation of the presentation based on information in the knowledge base. In the following, we describe four areas where reasoning could provide actual benefit to wiki users. Note that all four areas have been investigated separately in other contexts; however, semantic wikis provide a useful testbed to show the possible benefits of all areas in a single application.

4.1 Browsing and Displaying the Wiki Contents

Knowledge that is made explicit within the wiki enables the system to provide additional ways to browse, explore, and display the wiki's content. This is relevant not only as a support for finding information within the wiki, but also as a basic way for inspecting its semantic contents. In contrast to advanced search functions that are discussed in the following section, browsing generally relies on information that is *local* to the data that is currently displayed.

Displaying semantic data. A typical way of browsing data is to simply display, for every page in the wiki, the pages and concepts that it directly relates to. Often, this is done in textual form to inform users about the semantic contents of a page without requiring them to view the page source. For instance, Semantic MediaWiki inserts a *Factbox* below every article, showing related articles and attribute values, and displaying links to those elements, as well as to specific search functions and the article's RDF export. It also provides a browsing feature that displays incoming and outgoing relationships as well as filtering by relations and attributes.

Domain specific visualisations. Besides generic browsing functions, there are cases in which semantic information can be used to generate customised displays for specific types of data. For example, IkeWiki displays symbols for indicating licensing information, and provides special display for EXIF metadata that is extracted from image files. Semantic MediaWiki supports conversions between units of measurement which in turn are specified by semantic annotations within the wiki. In each of those examples, it is necessary that the wiki is aware of certain domain specific annotations that are treated in a special way. Existing vocabularies are suggestive as a basis for such special features, and it might be necessary to incorporate further ontological background knowledge to properly support those knowledge models within the wiki.

Graphical visualisation. Besides textual displays of a resource's semantic context, graphical visualisations can be helpful for exploring a wiki's content. IkeWiki, for example, can render a graph that shows all resources within a certain relational distance to the current one. The main advantage of graphical displays is their ability to convey more information directly without lengthy textual descriptions. Colours, shapes, and spacial grouping can carry relevant information. The main problem, on the other hand, is that automatically generated layouts of graphs are easily confusing if many resources are involved: visualisations often do not scale to larger amounts of data.

Filtering and selection. The above ways of displaying data are challenged when the amount of semantic content is large. For example, the article "Germany" in English Wikipedia has more than 30,000 incoming links, many of which could represent certain semantic relations. Filtering, grouping, and ordering of results is needed to usefully display such information. While ordering often requires extralogical information, filtering and grouping correspond to semantic retrieval and classification. Criteria for those operations might be provided by the given usage context, user preferences (i.e. semantic statements about the user), or by explicit queries (e.g. as in faceted browsers).

Some of the above visualisation methods could be realised with little or no reasoning effort. But as soon as semantic wikis incorporate semantic knowledge that is not restricted to the most simple facts, even the immediate relationships of some resource need to be computed first. The reason is that browsing should usually visualise the semantic model of the wiki, not just statements given explicitly by editors.

4.2 Querying the Knowledge

Besides the individual display of wiki pages, semantic wikis provide mechanisms to directly query their knowledge base. The query language used in IkeWiki is SPARQL. Semantic MediaWiki provides its own simple query language whose syntax is based on MediaWiki's mark-up language for editing. Semantically, this built-in language is easily seen to correspond to concepts of the description logic $\mathcal{EL}^{++}$ [10], with addition of (Horn) disjunction that does not add to the complexity [11].[7] Therefore, IkeWiki's native query language is more powerful but also computationally more complex than that of Semantic MediaWiki. Both wikis export their data in standard formats, so that existing tools can be used to query the data in further languages.

Besides the technical aspect of the employed query language, the use of queries in wikis strongly depends on the provided user interfaces. Both Semantic MediaWiki and IkeWiki enable editors to embed query results into wiki pages. The obvious advantage is that users that are not familiar with the query language can still view results of predefined queries. In Semantic MediaWiki, the query language is extended to allow advanced formatting of embedded results, e.g. for displaying times and dates within dynamic Timeline views (cf. Figure 1). In addition to embedded queries, it is also possible to directly evaluate queries and to browse the results.

Strong reasoning allows the query engine to answer more complex queries. But when designing the wiki query interface it must not be forgotten that we are still working on a wiki: queries should be easy to write, save, and share (like inline queries in *Semantic MediaWiki*), and answers should be traceable to the content of the wiki, which might require advanced explanation features to assist users in finding the source of a particular result.

4.3 Editing Support

Reasoning can not only be used to enhance the content presentation, but also to support editing the (textual and semantic) content. Typically, semantic annotation can be

---

[7] The query language extends $\mathcal{EL}^{++}$ by allowing concrete domains that are *non-convex*, but this does not increase expressivity in our case due to the absence of existential assertions on concrete roles.

Below is the complete ISWC workshop programme for 6th of November 2006. Please refer to the events' webpages for latest information on timing and registration.

	Title	deadline	start	end
SAAW2006	Semantic Authoring and Annotation Workshop	2006-08-10	2006-11-06 08:00:00	2006-11-06 12:00:00
Terra Cognita 2006	Terra Cognita 2006 - Directions to the Geospatial Semantic Web	2006-07-21	2006-11-06 08:00:00	2006-11-06 18:00:00
SWUI2006	The 3rd International Semantic Web User Interaction Workshop	2006-08-11	2006-11-06 08:30:00	2006-11-06 17:45:00
SEBIZ2006	First International workshop on Applications and Business Aspects of the Semantic Web	2006-08-05	2006-11-06 09:00:00	2006-11-06 12:30:00
SemanticDesktopWS2006	Semantic Desktop and Social Semantic Collaboration Workshop	2006-08-10	2006-11-06 09:00:00	2006-11-06 17:30:00
SSN2006	Semantic Sensor Networks Workshop	2006-07-10	2006-11-06 09:00:00	2006-11-06 12:30:00
SWESE2006	2nd International Workshop on Semantic Web Enabled Software Engineering	2006-08-10	2006-11-06 09:00:00	2006-11-06 18:00:00
WCMHLT2006	Web Content Mining with Human Language Technologies workshop 2006	2006-08-01	2006-11-06 13:00:00	2006-11-06 17:00:00

The same information in a timeline:

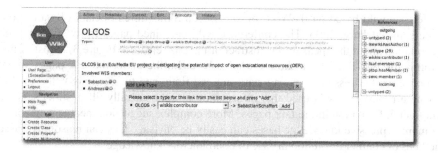

Fig. 1. Semantic MediaWiki can display the same query in different formats, such as the tabular view and timeline view shown above

Fig. 2. Annotations in IkeWiki are suggested based on the types associated with the two pages and the domain/range definitions of relations (in this case `wiskis:contributor`)

supported by exploiting ontological information: if a resource was classified to belong to a certain class, properties whose domain is a subclass of this class might be suggested for annotation. This is currently done in IkeWiki to simplify annotation by providing a list of suitable properties, see Figure 2. An AJAX-based interface allows to dynamically load and specialise such suggestions. Suggesting adequate annotations based on statistical and linguistic analysis will be subject to future research. Upcoming versions of Semantic MediaWiki will feature special annotations that can be used for marking deprecated properties. Explicatory messages will be displayed on any page on which deprecated properties are used, thus supporting convergence towards a unified knowledge model.

Reasoning can also be used to *avoid* inconsistent content in advance, by suggesting appropriate values for statements that are constrained by the existing knowledge base. In IkeWiki, templates that contain SPARQL queries can be used to dynamically compute suggested values. For example, we successfully used this technique to create a

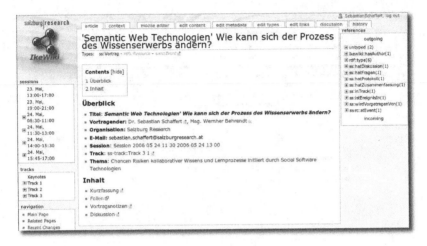

Fig. 3. Conference wiki of the "Social Skills durch Social Software" conference. Reasoning is used to automatically fill templates for talk, session, and track pages.

conference wiki based on IkeWiki for the "Social Skills durch Social Software" conference in Salzburg, 2006. The conference wiki contained pages for every talk with information about the speaker, the abstract of the talk, etc. (see Figure 3). Most of this information was filled from the knowledge base. Furthermore, the talk pages where associated with "sessions" having start and end time, and the sessions with "tracks" having a room. The wiki used this information to automatically fill in time, session, and track information in the talk pages. More complex suggestion mechanisms based on more expressive knowledge bases can easily be envisaged, as can reasoning-based methods of conflict resolution in case of contradictory knowledge.

4.4   Validating Formalised Knowledge

Background ontologies can constrain the statements within the wiki, and a reasoner can check if the knowledge does indeed adhere to these constraints. For example, it is possible to add axioms that state that each person may only have one father and one mother. A reasoner can then check if the knowledge is valid with regards to the background ontology.

Note that in order to do these tests, the system must enable average users to intuitively state the constraints they want to say. To this end, it is also useful if the chosen ontology language provides features such as (optional) constraint semantics [12], local closed world assumption [13,14], and default assumptions on uniqueness of names. Further possibilities to create unit tests, and the subtle semantic difficulties that can arise, are described in [15]. Most of the approaches can be applied in the setting of a semantic wiki.

Besides these logical constraints, the semantic wiki can use further resources from its ecosystem for more sophisticated checks. Often, it is possible to verify the content against the information in the knowledge base at the time it is entered. For instance, in

case of the conference wiki described in the previous section, the system could automatically verify whether the participants associated with an event are available during
this slot. Similar consistency verification can also be used for verifying the structure of
the human readable content. For example, meeting minutes of a project meeting might
be required to always conform to a certain schema.

5   Scenarios for Reasoning in Semantic Wikis

We illustrate our use cases with a number of concrete scenarios where reasoning in
semantic wikis is necessary and beneficial. Because semantic wiki engines currently
do not implement all of the conceived reasoning functions, some of the tasks in these
scenarios are currently not supported. To highlight these problems, we describe one
implemented scenario, one possible but not implemented scenario, and one currently
impossible scenario for reasoning in semantic wikis. One of the goals of this article is
to help the readers realise what advancements are needed in reasoning in order to be
able to address these issues.

5.1   Implemented: The Biology Taxonomy Scenario

In the Wikipedia, there is a huge collection of biological articles, ranging from *kingdoms*
over *families*, *genres*, to *species*. In the current, non-semantic Wikipedia, this collection
and the relationships (e.g. between a species and its genre) are maintained manually,
which leads to redundancies and inconsistencies. In a (currently hypothetic) Semantic
Wikipedia, reasoning can be used to address these issues.

Automatic inference of implicit taxonomy relations. Biology articles in Wikipedia
display a "taxonomy box" in the top right corner of the page, listing the relationships
between a species, its genre, its family, etc. An example of such a taxonomy box is
given on the right.

In today's Wikipedia, all this information is entered manually, for each biology article. Semantic wikis can improve
the situation in various ways:

- using a biology taxonomy as background ontology, a
  single relation from an article (e.g. a species) to the article describing its super-concept (e.g. a genre) would suffice to automatically infer all other relations (e.g. from
  the species to the family, order, class, kingdom),
- using appropriate inline queries, most of the taxonomy
  box can be computed, even without a sufficiently axiomatised background ontology,
- from the knowledge that the article describes a biological concept, semantic wikis can automatically infer
  that it a taxonomy box with relations to super-concepts
  should be displayed.

These applications exploit the methods described in the use cases *browsing and displaying*, and *querying* in Section 4.

Annotation support: offering only *relevant* relations as link types. In larger semantic wikis, there are often many different relations in the background model, most of which are irrelevant for a article. The wiki can use available information about a relations range and domain to suggest suitable annotations. In the biology taxonomy, for example, there might be a relation has Genre with domain Species and range Genre, and a relation has Family with domain Species ∪ Genre and range Family. For annotating a link from the page of the species *Bilberry* to the page of the genre *Vaccinium*, the IkeWiki's AJAX-based annotation editor (cf. Figure 2) can thus suggest the relation has Species. This is an example of the *editing support* use case of reasoning.

Query support: structured queries over the knowledge base. Reasoning based on the the biology taxonomy also allows to ask more complicated queries. For example, a user might ask for all species in the family *Ericaceae*, skipping the various genuses like *Vaccinium*. Such a query is not possible in a non-semantic wiki, and requires more extensive maintenance in a semantic wiki without reasoning support.

Challenges and Issues. The "biology taxonomy" scenario has been implemented successfully as a demonstrator in IkeWiki and will be shown in the tutorial.[8] Wikipedia's content, including all biological data, has also been imported into an installation of Semantic MediaWiki, augmented with automatically generated annotations. Nonetheless, there are a number of problems that we encountered:

- *Rule-based reasoning.* As IkeWiki and SMW rely on RDFS (or OWL DL) reasoning, there is no simple solution for axiomatising relations to biological super concepts, and IkeWiki currently implements the reasoning task in Java. Rule-based reasoning would be one solution for this problem. Axioms in many ontology languages can conveniently be represented as rules, but support for genuine rule languages is more problematic. If only restricted forms of rules are allowed, a suitable presentation to the user must be found to assist editing.
- *Representation of layout information.* There is currently no obvious way to infer a visual representation (such as "if the article is a biological concept, display a taxonomy box"). In IkeWiki, this functionality has been implemented in XSLT, but a proper integration into the knowledge base would be preferable. An existing approach for specifying layout in RDF is Fresnel[9], but from our experience expressing layout information in this format is rather hard and limited to RDF data (whereas the displaying of the taxonomy box affects the rendering of the page content).

5.2   Possible: Semantic Wikipedia

Augmenting a large-scale wiki such as English Wikipedia with semantic technologies would already be possible, but some challenges need to be addressed to make this extension successful. In contrast to the previous scenario, Wikipedia has a very broad scope,

---

[8] Online demo available at http://ikewiki.wastl.net:8080/
[9] http://www.w3.org/2005/04/fresnel-info/

Fig. 4. A simple example query on a semantically enhanced copy of Wikipedia, showing football players with their association

and no existing vocabulary or ontology is available to cover the whole domain. Moreover, Wikipedia is particularly large, both in terms of users and in terms of content. The possible uses of semantics in this scenario are also intractable, and we only give a few typical examples below.

Query answering. Being a general purpose encyclopaedia, Wikipedia gives rise to a number of interesting queries. Currently, those can only be answered by reading articles and manually building pages with the results of this research. This happens in practice, and has lead to the generation of many "list pages" such as the list of the largest cities in Spain. Of course, such list must be manually updated whenever some information changes, and inconsistencies are very likely. With semantic wikis, querying could be done dynamically by users through the wiki's query interfaces, or query results could be embedded into articles via *inline queries* to replace the current manually maintained lists (as shown in Fig. 4).

Quality control. Semantic data also provides a high-level view on article contents, enabling the automatic search for possibly wrong or incomplete information in large amounts of articles. This can be done by using domain-specific checks that are executed on parts of the semantic data. Such quality control also must involve the semantic annotations themselves: are relations used consistently? Which annotations are used too infrequently to be useful? Are there cases where multiple relations are used to model the same situation? Such tasks can be performed directly by the wiki, such that all editors can easily help to correct possible problems.

Analysing differences between wikis in different languages. Wikipedia is available in numerous languages, but each language differs in size and content. Comparing them is hardly possible, and usually only done by linking similar articles in different languages. Using semantic wikis, the content of different languages becomes machine-accessible and thereby comparable. Using known mappings between articles in different languages, the whole vocabulary of two wikis can be mapped. For instance, one could compare the population number of Paris as given in the French and Arab Wikipedia, without speaking either language. This can help to spot errors, as well as to understand cultural differences between the different language communities.

Challenges and Issues. The "Semantic Wikipedia" is not a reality yet, but semantically enhanced mirrors of Wikipedia are currently used for testing purposes. We think that the following challenges must be further addressed to enable this project:

– *Performance.* Computation times and memory usage are important for any large-scale web site, but these issues are especially problematic when offering reasoning-based services, such as semantic query answering, to a large audience. Semantic MediaWiki has always been considering performance as a critical success factor, but further improvements are needed to scale up to one of the of largest web sites on earth.
– *Usability.* It is desirable that semantic features are available to all users, even if they are not willing to learn the wiki's query language. This is partly realised by inline queries, but improved visual interfaces for constructing queries are an important next step. Similarly, annotation must be as easy as possible, and further simplification mechanisms might be needed. IkeWiki's current annotation support is a first step into this direction.
– *Interchange of data.* In order to compare data from different wikis, or to reuse such data within external applications, wikis need to export their semantic content in standardised formats. This is currently done for the simple data semantic wikis collect, but can become problematic when extending the ontological expressivity of each wiki. Indeed, especially rule languages currently hardly support information exchange via the Web (e.g. since they do not support URIs or standard datatypes).
– *Closed and open world.* The wiki itself can be perceived as a closed world for many applications of reasoning. Users are often interested in finding out which information was *not asserted* in the wiki, instead of what information was explicitly *asserted to be false*. For example, one might look for instances of (some subcategory of) the category *Marine mammal* that do not belong to the order *Carnivora*, to find vegetarian sea mammals. In Wikipedia, no species is explicitly classified as *not* belonging to a given order, but still most users would expect a closed-world behaviour in this case.
  On the other hand, any wiki is necessarily open and dynamic, and many kinds of conclusions should not be drawn from the absence of certain statements. For instance, from the fact that some person is not classified as female, one should certainly not conclude that this person is a man. In general, the data within the wiki should always be considered incomplete. A possible solution for dealing with this situation is to explicitly assume (certain) queries to have a closed-world semantics, even if this is not assumed for the knowledge base in general. Local closed world approaches provide a foundation for this [13,14].

5.3   Vision: Project Management Scenario

The "semantic wiki for project management" scenario is a vision of how semantic wikis with reasoning support might support complex social and collaborative tasks like project management. This vision requires significant development work and in some cases involves also reasoning problems that are yet to be solved.

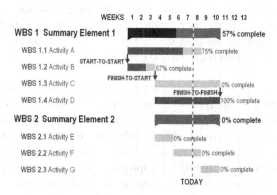

Fig. 5. Example of a Gantt diagram (source: Wikipedia); a semantic wiki for project management could provide such a diagram as a view on the data in the knowledge base for visualisation and interactive editing of project workplans

In recent years, wikis have increasingly be used as tools for project management. Major reasons for this are that wikis are easy to set up and use, allow everyone to edit, strongly connect knowledge via hyperlinks, and – most importantly – do not impose a rigid workflow by means of technical restrictions (instead, workflows are usually followed by social convention). Wikis thus provide the flexibility that is needed particularly in collaborative software development, where people and organisations with different cultures and backgrounds work together.

Unfortunately, existing wiki software is not particularly well suited for such tasks. On the one hand, current wiki systems are not really able to work with non-textual content such as spreadsheets, diagrams, or video material. On the other hand, they do not provide support for the semantically rich content that participates in processes like project management and software engineering.

A sufficiently developed semantic wiki system could support project management in a number of ways. Some of them are exemplarily given below.

Visualisation and editing of project data. Project management involves a lot of data about resources, dates, progress, meeting minutes, persons, etc. A lot of different visualisations have been developed to support these tasks, e.g. Gantt and Pert diagrams (see Figure 5), project progress reports, etc. Most of these visualisations are views on the same data. In a semantic wiki, such data could be represented formally in the knowledge base. The semantic wiki could then offer the user different visualisations of the data based on reasoning about the context. For instance, a page describing the workplan or project progress could automatically include a Gantt diagram, or a page describing a meeting could automatically show the project calendar and a list of persons that should attend the meeting. Both tasks involve querying and reasoning for retrieving the relevant knowledge from the knowledge base.

Likewise, interactive visualisations could allow to modify the project resources. A Gantt diagram about the project workplan could offer ways to e.g. add resources to a task, move task start and end via drag and drop, etc. Besides user interface issues, this kind of editing also involves reasoning. In this case, reasoning is in a sense "two way" (similar to view updates in relational databases), because on the one hand reasoning serves to transform the data in a suitable visualisation and on the other hand it transforms the visualisation back into the data.

Planning support. Project management also involves a lot of planning. A common planning task in project management is appointment scheduling. For example, a project manager might want to find a possible meeting date for all persons involved in a certain component of a software project when creating the description of the meeting in the project wiki. Obviously, this task requires different kinds of rather complex reasoning, like temporal reasoning for finding out appropriate dates and rule-based reasoning for determining whom to invite to the meeting. It would also be desirable for the system to fail gracefully in case a meeting date where all involved persons are free cannot be determined: in such cases the system should suggest a "good enough" solution.

Similarly, planning support in a semantic wiki can be useful in other project management areas, like resource planning (which requires constraint checking) or issue tracking.

Workflow support. A third area where reasoning in a semantic wiki for project management is important is workflow support. In a semantic wiki, project workflow models could be represented by some kind of ontology (not necessarily OWL DL, specific process modelling languages might be more appropriate). Reasoning would be used to guide the user along this workflow. For example, when taking meeting minutes, the system could automatically offer to enter action items into an action item list and provide a suitable editor for this task. For an action item, the semantic wiki could then offer to move along a defined workflow, e.g. from the state "open" to the state "closed". In the case of bug tracking, specific support for such workflows is already given by the system trac.[10] However, this support is specific to the case of bug tracking and does not follow an explicitly represented model.

Challenges and Issues. In order to realise a semantic wiki for project management, there are many challenges that need to be addressed in the area of reasoning. In the following, we mention a few of the most important ones (the challenges mentioned in the other scenarios are mostly relevant here as well):

- *Temporal reasoning.* Many tasks in project management require to reason over temporal data (e.g. appointment scheduling or task editing). However, current knowledge representation formats and reasoning languages do not offer much support in this area.
- *Constraint verification.* To ensure consistency of the data, a reasoning system needs to support the verification of constraints. Constraint verification, although not "generative", can also be considered a reasoning task, and has been studied much in the context of relational databases.
- *Active and reactive rules.* Many functionalities cannot be sufficiently covered by deductive systems. A system that closely interacts with users needs to support active

---

[10] http://trac.edgewall.org

or reactive behaviour. Active rules (or "Event Condition Action" rules) are a way to address this issue. In the context of the (Semantic) Web, such rules have e.g. been studied in the language *XChange* [16].

6   Related Work

Besides IkeWiki and SMW, a number of other semantic wiki implementations have been created, most of which remain research prototypes [17,18,19,20]. To the best of our knowledge, the most notable (and stable) system currently is *MaknaWiki* [21], which is similar to SMW and IkeWiki with respect to the supported kinds of easy-to-use inline wiki annotations, and various search and export functions. In contrast to SMW, IkeWiki and MaknaWiki introduce the concept of *ontologies* and (to some extent) *URIs* into the wiki, which emphasises use-cases of collaborative ontology editing that are not the main focus of SMW. MaknaWiki is tailored for closed-domain settings where a suitable schema for annotation can be anticipated. It supports the usage of expressive ontologies and integrates according inferencing features, but allows only administrators to change the ontological schema.

Besides text-centred semantic wikis, a number of collaborative database systems have appeared recently. Examples of such systems include *OntoWiki* [22], *Open Record*[11], *Metaweb*[12], and *OmegaWiki*[13], most of which are still preliminary or only very recent. Such systems typically use form-based editing, and are used to maintain data records instead of texts. OntoWiki draws from concepts of semantic technologies and provides a built-in faceted (RDF) browser. The other systems have their background in relational databases.

7   Perspectives and Conclusion

In this article, we discussed how reasoning can improve the use of semantic wikis in the areas of *browsing, querying, editing*, and *validation*, and which requirements and future challenges arise from these use-cases. We also highlighted first simple applications of reasoning within the semantic wiki systems *IkeWiki* and *Semantic MediaWiki*, which we currently develop, and described scenarios for further, more complex applications. Based on the above analysis, we plan to further improve reasoning support in a number of ways.

IkeWiki will be extended by a rule-based reasoning engine that allows to define more complex "views" on the RDF data in the knowledge base. Current experiments with connecting to SWI Prolog have been promising, but this system is not yet stable enough for inclusion in the main distribution. Second, we plan to extend IkeWiki by support for project management tasks, such as appointment scheduling and document management. To this end, we are currently investigating customised editing based on knowledge about the content of a wiki page as described in the third scenario.

---

[11] http://www.openrecord.org

[12] http://www.metaweb.com/

[13] The former *WikiData*, http://www.omegawiki.org

Semantic MediaWiki aims at providing a platform that can scale to the size of Wikipedia, and thus powerful reasoning is strongly constrained by performance requirements. The current stand-alone storage model based on MySQL will soon be augmented with optional bindings for (presumably faster) RDF stores. Bindings for reasoners as in [9] are also considered, but are hindered by the restricted query languages of many reasoners.[14] The main goal for extending expressivity are role hierarchies and role composition, as well as efficient DL constraints in the style of [12]. We do not intend to significantly increase the expressivity of the query language, since while sub-polynomial in complexity, queries are already very challenging in real-world scenarios.

We believe that experiences gathered in semantic wikis are highly relevant to many other applications of expressive semantics, since they provide typical situations for a number of problems that still need to be overcome by the Semantic Web community. As semantic wikis have many characteristics of "small semantic webs", many of these issues are equally relevant for the Semantic Web as a whole.

References

1. Brickley, D., Guha, R.V.: RDF Vocabulary Description Language 1.0: RDF Schema. W3C Recommendation (February 10, 2004) Available at `http://www.w3.org/TR/rdf-schema/`
2. McGuinness, D., Harmelen, v.F.: OWL Web Ontology Language Overview. W3C Recommendation (February 10, 2004) Available at `http://www.w3.org/TR/owl-features/`
3. Völkel, M., Schaffert, S., (eds.): 1st Workshop "From Wiki to Semantics" (SemWiki'06), Budva, Montenegro (2006)
4. Krötzsch, M., Vrandečić, D., Völkel, M.: Semantic MediaWiki. In: Proc. of the 5th Int. Semantic Web Conf. (ISWC'06), pp. 935–942 (2006)
5. Krötzsch, M., Vrandečić, D., Vötlkel, M.: Wikipedia and the Semantic Web – the missing links. In: Proc. of WikiMania2005 (2005)
6. Schaffert, S.: IkeWiki: A semantic wiki for collaborative knowledge management. In: 1st Int. Workshop on Semantic Technologies in Collaborative Applications (STICA'06), Manchester, UK (2006)
7. Schaffert, S., Westenthaler, R., Gruber, A.: IkeWiki: A user-friendly semantic wiki. In: Sure, Y., Domingue, J. (eds.) ESWC 2006. LNCS, vol. 4011, Springer, Heidelberg (2006)
8. Oren, E.: SemperWiki: a semantic personal wiki. In: 1st Workshop on The Semantic Desktop, Galway, Ireland (2005)
9. Vrandečić, D., Krötzsch, M.: Reusing ontological background knowledge in semantic wikis. In: Proc. of 1st Workshop "From Wiki to Semantics" (SemWiki'06) (2006)
10. Baader, F., Brandt, S., Lutz, C.: Pushing the EL envelope. In: Proc. 19th Int. Joint Conf. on Artificial Intelligence (IJCAI'05), Edinburgh, UK, Morgan-Kaufmann Publishers, San Francisco (2005)
11. Krötzsch, M., Rudolph, S., Hitzler, P.: omplexity boundaries for Horn description logics. In: Proc. 22nd AAAI Conference on Artficial Intelligence, Vancouver, British Columbia, Canada, AAAI Press, Stanford, California, USA (2007)
12. Motik, B., Horrocks, I., Sattler, U.: Integrating description logics and relational databases (December 6, 2006) Technical Report, University of Manchester, UK (2006)

---

[14] One problem is that the current SPARQL specification does not directly support OWL.

13. Rosati, R.: Autoepistemic description logics. AI Communications 11, 219–221 (1998)
14. Bonatti, P., Lutz, C., Wolter, F.: Expressive non-monotonic description logics based on circumscription. In: Doherty, P., Mylopoulos, J., Welty, C. (eds.) Proc. 10th Int. Conf. on Principles of Knowledge Representation and Reasoning (KR '06), pp. 400–410 (2006)
15. Vrandečić, D., Gangemi, A.: Unit tests for ontologies. In: Jarrar, M., Ostyn, C., Ceusters, W., Persidis, A. (eds.) Proceedings of the 1st International Workshop on Ontology content and evaluation in Enterprise, Montpellier, France. LNCS, Springer, Heidelberg (2006)
16. Bry, F., Eckert, M., Pătrânjan, P.L.: Reactivity on the web: Paradigms and applications of the language xchange. Journal of Web Engineering 5, 3–24 (2006)
17. Tazzoli, R., Castagna, P., Emilio, S.: Towards a semantic wiki wiki web. In: McIlraith, S.A., Plexousakis, D., van Harmelen, F. (eds.) ISWC 2004. LNCS, vol. 3298, Springer, Heidelberg (2004)
18. Souzis, A.: Rhizome position paper. In: Proc. of 1st Workshop on Friend of a Friend, Social Networking and the Semantic Web (2004)
19. Aumüler, D.: Semantic authoring and retrieval in a wiki (WikSAR). In: Gómez-Pérez, A., Euzenat, J. (eds.) ESWC 2005. LNCS, vol. 3532, Springer, Heidelberg (2005)
20. Kiesel, M.: Kaukolu – Hub of the semantic corporate intranet. In: Proc. of 1st Workshop "From Wiki to Semantics" (SemWiki'06) (2006)
21. Nixon, L.J.B., Simperl, E.P.B.: Makna and MultiMakna: towards semantic and multimedia capability in wikis for the emerging web. In: Proc. Semantics 2006 (2006)
22. Auer, S., Dietzold, S., Riechert, T.: OntoWiki – A tool for social, semantic collaboration. In: Gil, Y., Motta, E., Benjamins, V.R., Musen, M.A. (eds.) ISWC 2005. LNCS, vol. 3729, pp. 736–749. Springer, Heidelberg (2005)

Semantic Wiki Representations for Building an Enterprise Knowledge Base

Sören Auer[2], Berit Jungmann[1], and Frank Schönefeld[1]

[1] T-Systems Multimedia Solutions GmbH
Riesaer Str. 5, 01129 Dresden, Germany
{Berit.Jungmann,Frank.Schönefeld}@t-systems.com
[2] University of Leipzig
Abt. Betriebliche Informationssysteme, Johannisgasse 26, 04103 Leipzig, Germany
auer@informatik.uni-leipzig.de

Abstract. In the literature semantically enabled knowledge technologies are described as a new kind of web ([1], XI). In the science domain many ideas and interesting tool prototypes exist. In companies, however, there is less estimation for the effort and ways for using semantic web technologies. Special application scenarios for business purposes and experiences in real-life projects are necessary ([1], 303). This paper focuses on the need for semantic technologies from a business perspective and explains ideas of a scientific partner. Furthermore, the collaborative research project SoftWiki is introduced.

Keywords: Semantic Web, Wiki systems, Knowledge Engineering.

Currently, Wikis are used in T-Systems Multimedia Solutions for knowledge management, project management and requirements engineering. Limitations of current search technologies within Wiki systems are known in literature and named by different authors (e. g. [2], 141ff.) as followed:

- Query construction
- Lack of semantics
- Lack of context
- Presentation of results
- Managing heterogeneity

By using semantic representations or annotations the way of information representation can be improved ([1], 3ff). Finding useful pieces of knowledge within heterogeneous data with little human involvement (known as knowledge discovery) is the key for successful knowledge management ([3], 10).

Within the BmBF-project SoftWiki, which is jointly conducted with the Universities of Leipzig, Essen-Duisburg and other companies, T-Systems Multimedia Solutions gains experiences by using semantic web technologies and develops strategies for their applications within different projects. The aim of the cooperative research project SoftWiki is to support the collaboration of all stakeholders in software development processes particularly with regard to software requirements. User groups, which tend to be very large and · spatially distributed, shall be enabled to collect software requirements, to enrich them semantically and to classify and aggregate them.

G. Antoniou et al. (Eds.): Reasoning Web 2007, LNCS 4636, pp. 330–333, 2007.

The following project (from T-Systems' area of business) is a good example: An electronic shop software had to be developed for a large multi-national cooperation, where Requirements Engineering with a large and distributed user group plays a significant role. There is a special Requirements Engineering related task in the early phase of the extraction of requirements, which is still insufficiently supported by current tools. Involving a total of 63 stakeholders into the project caused a large amount of effort concerning coordination and documentation, which could not be handled properly by current tools.

The SoftWiki solution will be based on Semantic Web standards for terminological knowledge representation (such as RDF, RDF-Schema and OWL) and will be implemented with the help of generic means of semantic collaboration. This implementation will use next generation Web user interfaces (in the spirit of Social Software and the Web 2.0) fostering completely new means of Requirements Engineering with very large user groups.

Social Requirements Engineering has been identified as a special scenario of agile and distributed Knowledge Engineering. For this reason, the SoftWiki tool contains the following functionalities:

- a knowledge base visualized on the web as an information map, with different views on instance data
- intuitive wiki-like authoring of semantic content
- social collaboration
- semantic enhanced search strategies
- traceability of changes
- optional comments and discussions for every single part of the requirements engineering knowledge base
- Rating and Measurement of the popularity of content
- reward of the user activity

These techniques are used to accomplish the overall goal of lowering the entry barrier for collaboration based on semantic technologies. The SoftWiki tool is based on the generic knowledge engineering tool OntoWiki ([4]) as shown in the following figure:

The following base functionality is provided by OntoWiki: (1) to browse the contents of a knowledge base (KB) according to its class tree, (2) to search the KB for a keyword, (3) to select a different knowledge base, (4) to view a list of instances belonging to the selected KB and class, and to filter or to adopt the current view of the instances according to detected properties (and values).

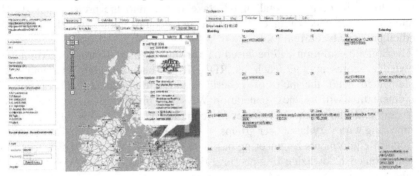

In addition to the presentation of all information attached to a certain instance in a textual representation, different views, e.g. the map or the calendar view (as shown above) allow to visualize the KB content in various ways.

Search

| Filter: | All classes | ▼ | All properties | ▼ | Submit Query |

		All properties	
Search returned 6 results.[c]		swrc:address (2)	
		swrc:booktitle (3)	

Relevance	Resource	swrc:name (1)	perty	Value
100%	AssistantProfessor: York Sure		name	York Sure
100%	InProceedings: Studies on the Dynamics of Ant Colony Optimization Algorithms		booktitle	Proceedings of the Genetic and Evolutionary Computation Conference (GECCO-2002), New York
100%	Proceedings: Business Process Management		address	Berlin, Heidelberg, New York
100%	InProceedings: REMINDIN': Semantic Query Routing in Peer-to-Peer Networks Based on Social Metaphors		address	New York, USA
100%	InProceedings: Developing and Managing Software Components in an Ontology-based Application Server		booktitle	Proceedings of the WWW2004 Workshop on Application Design, Development and Implementation Issues in the Semantic Web, New York, NY, USA, May 18, 2004
100%	InProceedings: Reuse Of Problem-Solving Methods In Knowledge Engineering (short paper)		booktitle	Proceedings of the 6th Annual Workshop on Software Reuse (WISR-6), Owego, New York, November 1-4, 1993

A semantic search engine enables the user to filter the results of an ordinary keyword search according to appropriate classes and properties. For example, a search for "York" can be restricted to the classes "Person" or "Address" (as shown above).

Based on this generic knowledge engineering functionality, the SoftWiki tool is able to create, enrich and manage requirements adhering to the requirements ontology [5], which was developed within the SoftWiki project and which is depicted in the figure below.

Main advantages of the SoftWiki tool compared to traditional Requirements Engineering tools are: (a) the web based accessibility resulting in ease of use (no software has to be deployed and people can be invited to collaborate by sharing a simple Web link), (b) the schema flexibility (the requirements ontology can be easily enhanced and extended in application and domain specific ways), (c) the increased interlinking possibilities (relevant information which is accessible on the Web or Intranet can be easily referenced and is just one click away).

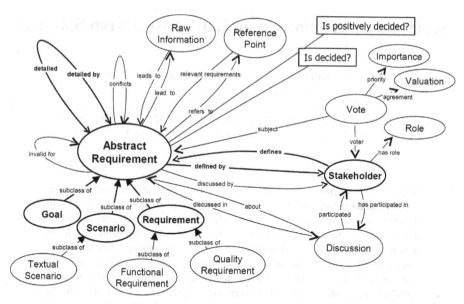

The implementation of the tool within production processes of T-Systems is still in progress. Hence, comprehensive evaluation results are still missing. The ultimate goal is to employ Requirements Engineering knowledge bases created by using the SoftWiki tool as crystallization points for enterprise wide information integration.

References

1. Davies, J., Studer, R., Warren, P.: Semantic Web Technologies – trends and research in ontology-based systems. John Wiley & Sons, Chichester (2006)
2. Bontcheva, K., Davies, J., Duke, A., Glover, T., Kings, N., Thurlow, I.: Semantic Information Access. In: Semantic Web Technologies – trends and research in ontology-based systems, pp. 139–169. John Wiley & Sons, Ltd. Chichester (2006)
3. Grobelnik, M., Mladenić, D.: Knowledge Discovery for Ontology Construction. In: Semantic Web Technologies – trends and research in ontology-based systems, pp. 9–27. John Wiley & Sons, Ltd. Chichester (2006)
4. Auer, S., Dietzold, S., Riechert, T.: OntoWiki – A Tool for Social, Semantic Collaboration. In: Cruz, I., Decker, S., Allemang, D., Preist, C., Schwabe, D., Mika, P., Uschold, M., Aroyo, L. (eds.) ISWC 2006. LNCS, vol. 4273, pp. 736–749. Springer, Heidelberg (2006)
5. Lehmann, J., Lauenroth, K., Riechert, T.: A Requirements Engineering Ontology. In: Franconi, E., Kifer, M., May, W. (eds.) ESWC 2007. LNCS vol. 4519. Springer, Heidelberg (2007)

Semantic Descriptions in an Enterprise Search Solution

Uwe Crenze, Stefan Köhler, Kristian Hermsdorf, Gunnar Brand,
and Sebastian Kluge

interface projects GmbH, Tolkewitzer Straße 49, 01277 Dresden, Germany
{uwe,stefan,kris,gunnar,basti}@interface-projects.de

Abstract. Today customers want to use powerful search engines for their huge
and increasing content repositories. Full-text-only products with simple result
lists are not enough to satisfy this community. Different content sources require
different analyzing and indexing strategies and a content-specific result set
presentation. There is a lot of research in the field of using semantic web technologies for information retrieval. A wide range of useful standard vocabularies
and powerful frameworks have been developed that can be used to gather,
transform and store metadata. However, in practise we see a gap between the
state of art of information retrieval and customer needs with a defined prise-
performance relation. It is a challenge to index a large file server with heterogeneous content annotated with metadata from different vocabularies, to provide
an ontology-based navigation, to produce semantic annotated search results, to
use faceted browsers as powerful filtering mechanism and do that with an out-
of-the-box solution, which is stable, has a good performance and provides a
simple way to configure it. With this viewpoint we present in this paper the
usage of RDF-based semantic descriptions in an enterprise search solution developed at interface:projects.This paper covers lessons learned from developing
a metadata-focused information retrieval system called *inter:gator*[1]. Especially
we discuss the challenges and possible solutions in an enterprise (-wide) search
scenario, and show the place where semantic descriptions matter in such a
solution.

1   What Is Enterprise Search?

First of all, enterprise search means federated search in different content sources. In
our context, content is unstructured text from documents, where a document can be a
text document, an email or a database record. On the other side we can interpret a
JPEG-picture combined with IPTC-metadata as a semi-structured document.

Enterprise search can be a stand-alone IT-solution or is embedded in a content
management system. In practice enterprise content management is more a vision as an
IT-solution. So an enterprise search solution has to integrate several content repositories. The research field of *Semantic Desktop* works on the other end of the software
stack – user interaction with content on the level of application clients, desktop and

---

[1] http://www.intergator.de/

G. Antoniou et al. (Eds.): Reasoning Web 2007, LNCS 4636, pp. 334–337, 2007.

search tools. But *Semantic Desktop* depends on a semantic backend. At this point all aspects come together: powerful enterprise search needs semantic context information from a metadata repository and *Semantic Desktop*, so for our work there are no differences between enterprise search and *Semantic Desktop*.

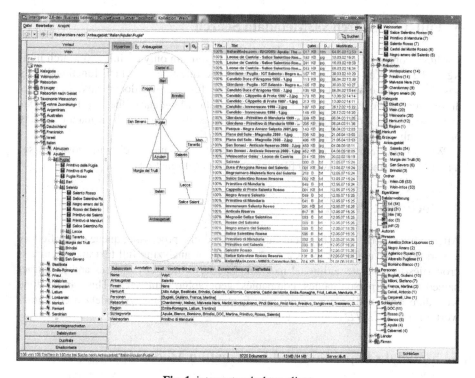

Fig. 1. inter:gator desktop client

2 Challenges for Search Solutions

The main challenge for indexing and search time is the amount of data. If we have 10.000 pages on a web server, we can do all analysis necessary for a rich search solution. But if we want to index a file server with >1.000.000 documents it is very strong to do more with it as full-text indexing (e.g. in such usage scenarios it is not reasonable to perform detailed linguistic and text structure analysis). Here are limitations for semantic notation of metadata also (see below).

Second challenge is the quality of data and text extraction tools. This is the ground of a universal search solution. No semantic analysis makes sense if the text and metadata extraction part is not a stable piece of software. It must run 7x24 hours without crashes and memory leaks (horrible content of many PDF-documents is one example for that).

Often different content sources require handling of different authentication schemas. Then security access for search results is the next challenge (think about different user management of databases and fileservers).

Last but not least – complexity of the processing infrastructure and semantic framework which consist of crawlers, modeling tools, analyzers, visualization components and semantic integration parts). Additionally there are limitations for linguistic components in mixed-language scenarios like dealing with IT-content.

3 Full-Text Search vs. Metadata Search

For huge content repositories (also the internet) you can only do full-text search until we will have Web 3.0 (the *Semantic Web*). The question is: which functionality is possible for an enterprise search solution with few million documents? Semantic-driven search technologies need lots of metadata. Metadata is the key for context-aware searching and the visualization of search results according the semantic aspects of the result set (see fig. 1).

What users helps is a combined full-text and metadata search with powerful semantic-aware (metadata-aware) filtering and proposal functions.

4 Document Processing

After extracting the text documents are processed in a processing queue controlled by a workflow. Several processors are responsible for analyzing full-text and document properties to generate additional metadata like keywords, key phrases and to extract named entities (person names, companies, geographic items etc.). This can be done with dictionary and/or rule-based classification mechanisms. A widely used framework for this is *GATE*[2].

5 Metadata Repository and Information Model

The base of semantic search is a semantic description of the metadata set. On top of this description we can use additional information models expressed in RDF(S) or OWL. But in our experience it is necessary to separate property descriptions from the property store. In our case the *Jena*[3] RDF-Store was the main bottle-neck to scale indexing and query performance. Possible solutions are a database-only (not RDF-based) property store or to store all properties in the full-text index also (as we do now with *lucene*[4]).

In the past, most of the knowledge management products use *topic maps* for semantic descriptions and visualize it as a semantic network. Now more and more solutions use a RDF(S) or OWL-based model, because of deep influences form the *Semantic Web* research. A lot of Java-based open source software (see footnotes) was developed based on the RDF technology.

OWL descriptions will be used by several components of an information retrieval system: system configuration, indexing engine and the search client graphical user

---

[2] http://gate.ac.uk/
[3] http://jena.sourceforge.net/
[4] http://lucene.apache.org/

interface (GUI). An important mission of an information model is to deliver a controlled vocabulary as dictionaries with expert terms or taxonomies or more complex domain ontologies.

6 Clustering and Classification

A main topic of this summer school is reasoning, so it is not necessary to talk about the benefit of model-based search query optimization by semantic reasoning, but there are other fields to use an information model also.

Clustering and classification are important techniques to make content accessible for users. Most of the established procedures have nothing to do with semantic descriptions. They are all about mathematical algorithms. But classification along Ontologies (or taxonomies) is an interesting aspect with many practical impacts.

7 Visualization and User Interaction

To present the search results better than a simple flat list is very important for satisfied search engine usage. The result set size and the number of different document properties determines the amount of data to be transferred from the search index to the client visualization components.

An innovative user interface is only usable if it has good performance und usability. In the most cases usability can be translated with "simple design". Very useful GUI elements for navigation and filtering are for example hierarchical facetted browsers.

For systematical investigations it is better to provide metadata catalogs as navigation elements and to present the user statistical views for significant associations between certain metadata. Analyzing user search terms and result sets allows to generate proposals for better search terms regarding the user input.

The search terms put in by the user are very important to discover the investigation context and to deliver proposals for result set grouping and search refinement. If we know the search context, it is possible to direct the user in his search process. But in an enterprise search solution out-of-the-box we have no hint about the search context. For this we would need a semantic description of the world. From the *Semantic Web* we know the effort of this.

Semantic Web Service Discovery and Selection in B2B Integration Scenarios

Andreas Friesen

SAP Research, CEC Karlsruhe
Vincenz-Prießnitz-Str.1, D-76131 Karlsruhe
andreas.friesen@sap.com

Abstract. There are various B2B scenarios where many candidate services with the same or similar capability (provided by the same or even different service providers) can be used for enterprise application integration. Hence, a requester driving a B2B integration scenario can choose among several candidate services offering a capability satisfying its requests. However, the optimal choice of the service to be invoked often depends on the parameters of the request at run-time and preferences of the requester. This article describes an approach for a dynamic (at run-time) web service selection based on semantic interpretation of offered service capabilities and the parameters specifying the run-time request. The proposed solution takes into account special conditions on service usage either contractually agreed between requester and provider or specified by the requester without the knowledge of the provider. In general, those conditions restrict the interpretation of the original service capabilities as offered by a service provider (and discovered by the service requester) and influence the choice of a service. The approach is illustrated on an example from the shipper-carrier domain.

1 Introduction

The advent of Service-oriented Architecture (SOA) and Web Services (WS) opened new possibilities for smooth Enterprise Application Integration (EAI) in intra- and inter-enterprise scenarios in a loosely-coupled manner. In principle, Web Services enabled enterprise applications can be used by anyone, from anywhere, at any time, and on any type of platform. The lack of formally represented semantic meaning in the WS technology stack causes the tasks of discovering, selecting, composing, and binding Web Services being considered as manual steps performed by a human. The recent advent of the Semantic Web and Semantic Web Services (SWS) promises new standardized means to formally capture the representation of the semantic meaning of data and interfaces. This enables the machines to automatically reason and to draw conclusions about the "intended meaning". The so-called Semantic Web Services promise a higher degree on automation concerning discovery, invocation, composition, and monitoring of Web Services.

The most general notion of the web service usage process consists of the following three phases: web service discovery, web service selection, and web service invocation. Thereby, the differentiation between the *abstract* and *concrete* service is

G. Antoniou et al. (Eds.): Reasoning Web 2007, LNCS 4636, pp. 338–343, 2007.

important. An abstract service is distinguished from a concrete service in that the former abstracts from the concrete service parameters which determine the latter. Thus, an *abstract service* describes a class of service parameter configurations that is associated with the web service capability. A *concrete service* describes a concrete service parameter configuration as it is delivered by the invocation of a web service. Hence, the web service capability description does not contain complete information about every possible concrete service that can be delivered by invoking the web service. Since the ultimate goal of a potential requester is to find and select a concrete service that optimally serves its needs. The selection and invocation steps inevitably overlap. Also the possible negotiation of service parameters between requester and provider leads to the inevitable invocations of the web service interface. Besides the obvious overlap of the conceptually seen different phases, successful service discovery does not necessarily lead to successful delivery of a service, since in the set of potential service candidates there might be no one that is finally able to define a concrete service on which both the requester and provider agree.

An *abstract goal* corresponding to *abstract service* can be used as a search criterion for Web Service discovery. Web Service discovery is based on comparing (in terms of relevance) the semantic description of an *abstract goal* (requested abstract service) against those of provided *abstract services* (web service capability descriptions). Web Service discovery is performed by matching the goal against available web service capabilities.

Service Selection starts from an already identified set of potential web service candidates which have been identified to be relevant for a discovery goal in the service discovery phase. It possibly involves negotiation of service parameters, and thus, invocation of the candidate Web Service. In general, figuring out which service to finally choose is beyond the information contained in the semantic descriptions of the discovery goal and web service capability descriptions. In this phase, the generalization to abstract services is given up and a concrete service with a concrete parameter configuration has to be defined, as it will be delivered later on.

2 Discovery and Selection in B2B Integration Scenarios

There are B2B integration scenarios that can be characterized by frequently occurring requests for a standardized service over a certain period of time. However, the number of requests (the total transaction value) usually justifies the efforts to negotiate about requester-specific conditions for service usage for a requester as well as for provider. The requester-specific conditions can be seen as constraints on the web service capability and must be consistently applied on the requester as well as provider side. These constraints cannot be part of the published web service capability since they are requester-specific, i.e., in general, for each requester different. Furthermore, there are also scenarios where the requester sets constraints on the service capability usage according to its own preferences. Hence, service requester does not negotiate with the provider on requester-specific conditions, i.e., it accepts the general terms of the provider. This type of constraints defines business rules of the requester.

The web service usage process for those kinds of scenarios can be characterized by a negotiation phase that results in a "service contract" or "service agreement" restricting the usage of the "static part" of the web service capability and potentially influencing its "dynamic part". "Static part" means here the declaratively described and published parameters of a WS capability. "Dynamic part" comprises the parameters of the WS capability that can only be accessed through the invocation of the WS interface. The contract can be used for an automatic pre-selection of suitable WS during subsequent concrete service requests. The pre-selection criteria apply to concrete service requests as long as the respective contract remains unchanged. A web service capability can be described as a set of service instances that can be potentially delivered by invoking the web service. A contract between a requester and provider can be seen as a subset of this set. A concrete request during the invocation of the web service can then be seen as an instance of the contract, the capability or some more general set.

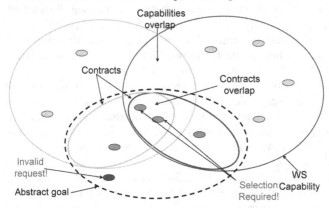

The result of the discovery phase based on the abstract goal describing the set of all potentially intended concrete requests is a list of web services that can completely or partially serve this goal. The web service capabilities may overlap. Subsequently, the result of the negotiation phase is a set of contracts that are subsets of the respective service capabilities at the one hand and subsets of the abstract goal at the other. Similarly to WS capabilities, the contracts may also overlap and eventually do not cover the abstract goal completely. Therefore, at runtime, WS selection is required if a concrete request is within the scope of overlapping contracts. It may also happen that some concrete requests can not be served at all, especially, if in the negotiation phase the abstract goal has not been completely covered by the set of available contracts. The introduced concepts are illustrated in the above figure. In principle, service selection can be implemented within the business logic of the requester's application, e.g., through some rule-based technology or even hard coded. In the following we introduce an elegant and compact solution that is completely configurable in declarative way. The introduced approach relies on Description Logics (DL) [1] and semantic techniques derived from the approach for semantic web service discovery introduced in [2].

In order to apply semantic discovery techniques introduced in [2] to the discovery and selection problem described above a domain-specific ontology is required. Based on that ontology an abstract service capability has to be build. The abstract service capability is provider-independent and covers all possible WS capabilities within the domain of discourse. For integration with some Semantic WS framework the abstract service capability must extend the WS description part, e.g., in OWL-S it's the "Service Profile". WS capabilities of the service providers and the abstract request of a service requester can be modeled as sub-concepts of the abstract WS capability.

The abstract request and WS capabilities are then used in the discovery phase in order to identify potential providers to negotiate with.

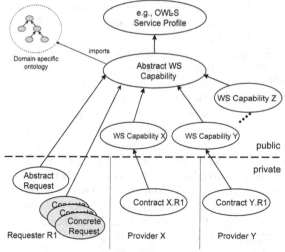

In the case of successful negotiations, the contract between a requester and service provider has to be modeled as a sub-concept of the WS capability. The concrete request is then described either as an instance or as a most specific sub-concept of the abstract WS capability according to the used ontology (see figure on the left for illustration). This means, a concrete request can be served by a Web Service if the subsumption test between the concrete request and the contract associated with a WS capability is successful. If several contracts match the concrete request a second selection step is required in order to choose between the remaining Web Services. This step usually requires invocation of the Web Services in order to get information necessary for the final selection according to the goals of the requester. The concrete selection goals are in general domain- and requester-specific making a generic solution complicated or even impossible.

3 Carrier Shipper Example

The application of the methodology described above is demonstrated now on a use case from the carrier/shipper domain. In this scenario, a shipper discovers potential carriers using an abstract shipment request and negotiates with them at the configuration time of the shipping system. The selection of a carrier for a concrete shipment request is performed (automatically) at run time.

Carriers, think for instance on some well known parcel carrier like UPS, offer a capability to ship some goods from one location to another (abstract shipment capability). To keep the example simple, we assume in the following that each carrier serves defined geographic locations (regions, countries, cities, zip code ranges, etc.) and accepts distinct types of items to be shipped (e.g., parcels, documents, containers, etc.), i.e., it provides a carrier-specific shipment service capability. We presume the existence of domain-specific (geographic locations and logistics) ontologies describing concepts and relationships used in the following examples. A shipper negotiates with a carrier on some shipper-specific conditions and may also have some internal preferences, i.e., in the case of successful negotiations a contract is established. Having the contract a shipper is prepared for automatic carrier selection at run time depending on the characteristics of the concrete shipment, internal preferences, and special conditions negotiated with carriers. Some information, e.g., the price for a concrete shipment or the duration of the delivery, can only be accessed by invoking a web service of a carrier. Therefore, possible final selection goals could look like "take the cheapest" or "take the fastest".

```
Shipment ⊑ (=1 shipFrom.Location)
        ⊓ (=1 shipTo.Location)
        ⊓ (>=1 shipItem.ShippingItem)
```

Now, a formally described "Abstract WS Capability" for the shipment domain has to be created. We call it "Shipment" and define as: *Ship one or more items of type ShippingItem from exactly one location of type Location to exactly one another location of type Location.*" (The formal description in (DL) is provided in the box on the left side).

```
CarrierA ⊑ ∃ shipFrom.(Europe ⊔ NorthAmerica)
         ⊓ ∃ shipTo.(NorthAmerica ⊔ Europe)
         ⊓ ∀ shipItem.(Parcel ⊔ Document)
         ⊓ Shipment
CarrierB ⊑ ∃ shipFrom.Germany
         ⊓ ∃ shipTo.Location
         ⊓ ∀shipItem.Document
         ⊓ Shipment
```

A carrier expresses the capabilities of its shipment services by inheriting and refining the ranges on the properties of the concept "Shipment". (Two examples in DL are provided in the box on the left side.) Similar to carriers, a shipper can express its shipping needs, i.e., its "Abstract Request" also by inheriting and refining the ranges on the properties of the concept "Shipment".

```
AbstractReqShipperX ⊑ ∃ shipFrom.Germany
⊓ ∃ shipTo.(Europe ⊔ NorthAmerica ⊔ AsiaPacific)
⊓ ∀ shipItem.(Document ⊔ Parcel ⊔ Container)
⊓ Shipment
```

If, for instance, the shipper has to ship any items of types "Parcel", "Document" and "Container" from Germany to any locations in "Europe", "NorthAmerica" and "AsiaPacific" then its abstract request can be defined in DL as illustrated in the box above. Since Abstract Request of a Shipper X has an intersection with the WS capabilities of the carriers A and B, the shipper can negotiate with the both carriers about the conditions on the usage of their shipping services.

```
ContractA.ShipperX ⊑ ∃ shipFrom.Germany
             ⊓ ∃ shipTo.(USA ⊔ Canada)
             ⊓ ∀shipItem.Parcel
             ⊓ CarrierA
ContractB.ShipperX ⊑ ∃ shipFrom.Germany
             ⊓ ∃ shipTo.AsiaPacific
             ⊓ ∀ shipItem.Document
             ⊓ CarrierB
```

The result of successful negotiations could then look like the contracts on the left. The contract with carrier A means: "Ship any items of type "Parcel" from "Germany" to any location in ("USA" or "Canada"). Accordingly, the contract with carrier B means: "Ship any items of type "Document" from "Germany" to any location in the region "AsiaPacific"".

```
RequestA ⊑ ∃ shipFrom.Frankfurt
         ⊓ ∃ shipTo.NewYork
         ⊓ ∀ shipItem.Parcel
         ⊓ Shipment
RequestB ⊑ ∃ shipFrom.Frankfurt
         ⊓ ∃ shipTo.Singapure
         ⊓ ∀ shipItem.Document
         ⊓ Shipment
```

Subsumption test	satisfiable wrt. KB
(RequestA ⊑ ContractAShipperX)	yes
(RequestA ⊑ ContractBShipperX)	no
(RequestB ⊑ ContractAShipperX)	no
(RequestB ⊑ ContractBShipperX)	yes

Now, let's assume that the following concrete shipment requests occur at run time (see the box on the left). In order to figure out all the carrier web services capable to perform a concrete shipment request, a subsumption test between each of the available contracts and the concrete shipment request has to be executed. The results of the subsumption tests between the two sample requests and the contracts with the carriers A and B are depicted in the box.

Obviously, according to the available contracts RequestA can be performed by carrier A but not by carrier B. Quite in contrary, the RequestB can be performed by carrier B but not by carrier A.

Since in the provided examples the contracts do not overlap, i.e., the intersection test (ContractA.ShipperX $\sqcap$ ContractB.ShipperX) is not satisfiable wrt. KB, there are no concrete shipment requests that can be potentially served by both carriers. However, this is of course possible, e.g., if the ContractA.ShipperX would be re-negotiated to ship not only parcels but also documents then a new concrete shipment RequestC: "Ship a Document from Frankfurt to NewYork" will be subsumed by both contracts. In the case of multiple carrier selection, the selected services must be ranked according to some selection goal. This usually requires the invocation of the carrier web service in order to retrieve information required for the final decision. The introduced solution has been implemented as a WSDL Web Service mediating between a shipper application and carrier web services. The prototype implementation enables the configuration of new carriers or update of the existing carriers in a completely declarative way.

While the most of the work in the area of Semantic Web Services focuses on the technical interoperability, i.e., the interoperability of the interfaces (inputs, outputs, ordering of the exchanged messages, etc.) the proposed approach focuses on the business compatibility, i.e., how to ensure the consistency of business requirements in B2B integration context under the assumption that systems are technically connected in an interoperable way.

References

[1] Baader, F., Calvanese, D., McGuinnes, D., Nardi, D., Patel-Schneider, P.: The Description Logic Handbook: Theory, Implementation and Applications. Cambridge University Press, Cambridge (2003)
[2] Li, L., Horrocks, I.: A Software Framework for Matchmaking Based on Semantic Web Technology. In: Proc. of the Twelfth World Wide Web Conference (2003)

Author Index

Lecture Notes in Computer Science

For information about Vols. 1–4231

please contact your bookseller or Springer

Vol. 4480: A. LaMarca, M. Langheinrich, K.N. Truong (Eds.), Pervasive Computing. XIII, 369 pages. 2007.

Vol. 4471: P. Cesar, K. Chorianopoulos, J.F. Jensen (Eds.), Interactive TV: A Shared Experience. XIII, 236 pages. 2007.

Vol. 4469: K.-c. Hui, Z. Pan, R.C.-k. Chung, C.C.L. Wang, X. Jin, S. Göbel, E.C.-L. Li (Eds.), Technologies for E-Learning and Digital Entertainment. XVIII, 974 pages. 2007.

Vol. 4443: R. Kotagiri, P.R. Krishna, M. Mohania, E. Nantajeewarawat (Eds.), Advances in Databases: Concepts, Systems and Applications. XXI, 1126 pages. 2007.

Vol. 4439: W. Abramowicz (Ed.), Business Information Systems. XV, 654 pages. 2007.

Vol. 4430: C.C. Yang, D. Zeng, M. Chau, K. Chang, Q. Yang, X. Cheng, J. Wang, F.-Y. Wang, H. Chen (Eds.), Intelligence and Security Informatics. XII, 330 pages. 2007.

Vol. 4425: G. Amati, C. Carpineto, G. Romano (Eds.), Advances in Information Retrieval. XIX, 759 pages. 2007.

Vol. 4412: F. Stajano, H.J. Kim, J.-S. Chae, S.-D. Kim (Eds.), Ubiquitous Convergence Technology. XI, 302 pages. 2007.

Vol. 4402: W. Shen, J. Luo, Z. Lin, J.-P.A. Barthès, Q. Hao (Eds.), Computer Supported Cooperative Work in Design III. XV, 763 pages. 2007.

Vol. 4398: S. Marchand-Maillet, E. Bruno, A. Nürnberger, M. Detyniecki (Eds.), Adaptive Multimedia Retrieval: User, Context, and Feedback. XI, 269 pages. 2007.

Vol. 4397: C. Stephanidis, M. Pieper (Eds.), Universal Access in Ambient Intelligence Environments. XV, 467 pages. 2007.

Vol. 4380: S. Spaccapietra, P. Atzeni, F. Fages, M.-S. Hacid, M. Kifer, J. Mylopoulos, B. Pernici, P. Shvaiko, J. Trujillo, I. Zaihrayeu (Eds.), Journal on Data Semantics VIII. XV, 219 pages. 2007.

Vol. 4365: C. Bussler, M. Castellanos, U. Dayal, S. Navathe (Eds.), Business Intelligence for the Real-Time Enterprises. IX, 157 pages. 2007.

Vol. 4353: T. Schwentick, D. Suciu (Eds.), Database Theory – ICDT 2007. XI, 419 pages. 2006.

Vol. 4352: T.-J. Cham, J. Cai, C. Dorai, D. Rajan, T.-S. Chua, L.-T. Chia (Eds.), Advances in Multimedia Modeling, Part II. XVIII, 743 pages. 2006.

Vol. 4351: T.-J. Cham, J. Cai, C. Dorai, D. Rajan, T.-S. Chua, L.-T. Chia (Eds.), Advances in Multimedia Modeling, Part I. XIX, 797 pages. 2006.

Vol. 4328: D. Penkler, M. Reitenspiess, F. Tam (Eds.), Service Availability. X, 289 pages. 2006.

Vol. 4321: P. Brusilovsky, A. Kobsa, W. Nejdl (Eds.), The Adaptive Web. XII, 763 pages. 2007.

Vol. 4317: S.K. Madria, K.T. Claypool, R. Kannan, P. Uppuluri, M.M. Gore (Eds.), Distributed Computing and Internet Technology. XIX, 466 pages. 2006.

Vol. 4312: S. Sugimoto, J. Hunter, A. Rauber, A. Morishima (Eds.), Digital Libraries: Achievements, Challenges and Opportunities. XVIII, 571 pages. 2006.

Vol. 4306: Y. Avrithis, Y. Kompatsiaris, S. Staab, N.E. O'Connor (Eds.), Semantic Multimedia. XII, 241 pages. 2006.

Vol. 4302: J. Domingo-Ferrer, L. Franconi (Eds.), Privacy in Statistical Databases. XI, 383 pages. 2006.

Vol. 4299: S. Renals, S. Bengio, J.G. Fiscus (Eds.), Machine Learning for Multimodal Interaction. XII, 470 pages. 2006.

Vol. 4295: J.D. Carswell, T. Tezuka (Eds.), Web and Wireless Geographical Information Systems. XI, 269 pages. 2006.

Vol. 4286: P.G. Spirakis, M. Mavronicolas, S.C. Kontogiannis (Eds.), Internet and Network Economics. XI, 401 pages. 2006.

Vol. 4282: Z. Pan, A. Cheok, M. Haller, R.W.H. Lau, H. Saito, R. Liang (Eds.), Advances in Artificial Reality and Tele-Existence. XXIII, 1347 pages. 2006.

Vol. 4278: R. Meersman, Z. Tari, P. Herrero (Eds.), On the Move to Meaningful Internet Systems 2006: OTM 2006 Workshops, Part II. XLV, 1004 pages. 2006.

Vol. 4277: R. Meersman, Z. Tari, P. Herrero (Eds.), On the Move to Meaningful Internet Systems 2006: OTM 2006 Workshops, Part I. XLV, 1009 pages. 2006.

Vol. 4276: R. Meersman, Z. Tari (Eds.), On the Move to Meaningful Internet Systems 2006: CoopIS, DOA, GADA, and ODBASE, Part II. XXXII, 752 pages. 2006.

Vol. 4275: R. Meersman, Z. Tari (Eds.), On the Move to Meaningful Internet Systems 2006: CoopIS, DOA, GADA, and ODBASE, Part I. XXXI, 1115 pages. 2006.

Vol. 4273: I. Cruz, S. Decker, D. Allemang, C. Preist, D. Schwabe, P. Mika, M. Uschold, L. Aroyo (Eds.), The Semantic Web - ISWC 2006. XXIV, 1001 pages. 2006.

Vol. 4270: H. Zha, Z. Pan, H. Thwaites, A.C. Addison, M. Forte (Eds.), Interactive Technologies and Sociotechnical Systems. XVI, 547 pages. 2006.

Vol. 4261: Y.-t. Zhuang, S.-Q. Yang, Y. Rui, Q. He (Eds.), Advances in Multimedia Information Processing - PCM 2006. XXII, 1040 pages. 2006.

Vol. 4256: L. Feng, G. Wang, C. Zeng, R. Huang (Eds.), Web Information Systems – WISE 2006 Workshops. XIV, 320 pages. 2006.

Vol. 4255: K. Aberer, Z. Peng, E.A. Rundensteiner, Y. Zhang, X. Li (Eds.), Web Information Systems – WISE 2006. XIV, 563 pages. 2006.

Vol. 4254: T. Grust, H. Höpfner, A. Illarramendi, S. Jablonski, M. Mesiti, S. Müller, P.-L. Patranjan, K.-U. Sattler, M. Spiliopoulou, J. Wijsen (Eds.), Current Trends in Database Technology – EDBT 2006. XXXI, 932 pages. 2006.

Vol. 4244: S. Spaccapietra (Ed.), Journal on Data Semantics VII. XI, 267 pages. 2006.

Vol. 4243: T. Yakhno, E.J. Neuhold (Eds.), Advances in Information Systems. XIII, 420 pages. 2006.

Vol. 4239: H.Y. Youn, M. Kim, H. Morikawa (Eds.), Ubiquitous Computing Systems. XVI, 548 pages. 2006.